Network Management Systems Essentials

Divakara K. Udupa

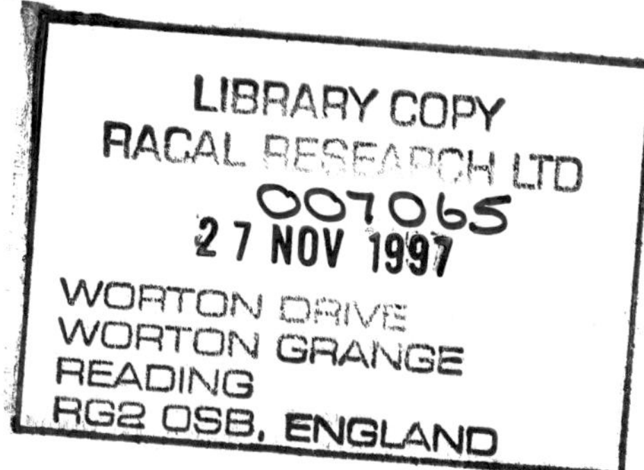

McGraw-Hill

New York San Francisco Washington, D.C. Auckland Bogotá
Caracas Lisbon London Madrid Mexico City Milan
Montreal New Delhi San Juan Singapore
Sydney Tokyo Toronto

Library of Congress Cataloging-in-Publication Data

Udupa, Divakara K.
Network management systems essentials / Divakara K. Udupa.
p. cm. — (McGraw-Hill series on computer communications)
Includes bibliographical references and index.
ISBN 0-07-065766-1
1. Computer networks—Management. I. Title. II. Series.
TK5105.5.U38 1996
004.6—dc20 95-22599
CIP

McGraw-Hill

A Division of The ***McGraw-Hill*** *Companies*

1 2 3 4 5 6 7 8 9 0 DOC/DOC 9 0 0 9 8 7 6 5

ISBN 0-07-065766-1

The sponsoring editor for this book was Marjorie Spencer, the editing supervisor was Jane Palmieri, and the production supervisor was Donald Schmidt. It was set in Century Schoolbook by Dina John of McGraw-Hill's Professional Book Group composition unit.

Printed and bound by R. R. Donnelley & Sons Company.

This book is printed on acid-free paper.

0-07-060362-6	McDysan/Spohn	*ATM: Theory and Applications*
0-07-042586-8	Minoli	*1st, 2nd, & Next Generation LANs*
0-07-042588-4	Minoli	*Imaging in Corporate Environments*
0-07-042724-0	Minoli	*Video Dialtone Technology: Digital Video over ADSL, HFC, FTTC, and ATM*
0-07-042591-4	Minoli/Vitella	*ATM & Cell Relay Service for Corporate Environments*
0-07-046461-8	Naugle	*Network Protocol Handbook*
0-07-911889-5	Nemzow	*Enterprise Network Performance Optimization*
0-07-046322-0	Nemzow	*FDDI Networking: Planning, Installation, and Management*
0-07-046321-2	Nemzow	*The Token-Ring Management Guide*
0-07-049309-X	Pelton	*Voice Processing*
0-07-707778-4	Perley	*Migrating to Open Systems: Taming the Tiger*
0-07-049663-3	Peterson	*TCP/IP Networking: A Guide to the IBM Environment*
0-07-051143-8	Ranade/Sackett	*Advanced SNA Networking: A Professional's Guide to VTAM/NCP*
0-07-051506-9	Ranade/Sackett	*Introduction to SNA Networking, 2/e*
0-07-054991-5	Russell	*Signaling System #7*
0-07-054418-2	Sackett	*IBM's Token-Ring Networking Handbook*
0-07-057442-1	Simonds	*McGraw-Hill LAN Communications Handbook*
0-07-060360-X	Spohn	*Data Network Design*
0-07-063263-4	Taylor	*The McGraw-Hill Internetworking Handbook*
0-07-063636-2	Terplan	*Effective Management of Local Area Networks: Functions, Instruments, and People*
0-07-067375-6	Vaughn	*Client/Server System Design and Implementation*

To order or to receive additional information on these or any other McGraw-Hill titles, please call 1-800-822-8158 in the United States. In other countries, contact your local McGraw-Hill representative. **BC15XXA**

To my mother, Varija; my wife, Rajalakshmi;
and my brother, Dr. Sudhakara

Contents

Preface

Network management is maturing into a separate, specialized field on its own merit and strength. The network management field is also constantly undergoing changes to meet new requirements. This book presents the latest material in this area, taking care to mention the issues involved in the design and implementations. As requirements vary to meet specific cases, the implementations will be slightly different.

Basically, this book covers important areas of network management. Network management faces its biggest challenges and opportunities in dealing with local area networks (LANs) in general and with the client-server area in particular. Therefore, I have emphasized the topic of network management for LANs where required. Internetworking of LANs and their management are becoming complex issues. Furthermore, LANs can be heterogeneous in nature and may use a variety of protocols. Network management is evolving into an important factor for the success of any LAN strategy.

In the network management arena, as in other areas of the computer industry, new alliances and consortiums to implement standards are formed. These alliances and consortiums issue their own standards, which, in some cases, have the potential to become de facto industry standards. Because of the constantly changing nature and focus of these bodies, overemphasizing the importance of any of them could cause the material in this book to become outdated quickly. The best way to avoid this is to briefly mention these groups and furnish their addresses, so that interested readers may contact them directly.

There is also a risk involved in writing a book based on product-specific details. Such a book can likewise become outdated very soon. New and better products are constantly introduced, and new features are added to existing products to meet customer requirements. Thus, to avoid this pitfall, I have deliberately kept away from specific product details.

The desire to remain as current as possible is one of the primary reasons for limiting this book to concepts, standards, and architectures. However, where I felt that it might be better to explain a principle with a specific implementation, I have done so to present a clear picture and better insight into the principles involved.

Objectives

Most books in the network management area are devoted to just one of the different parts that are covered in this book. You could find individual books on network management for OSI, TCP/IP, IEEE-based LANs, or SNA environment, but rarely will you find a book that covers all of these areas in one volume. This book fills that vacuum. All of these areas, including APPN and network management in the IBM peer-to-peer arena, have been covered.

Network management is an application-layer technology, but the lower layers are also important, so I have provided an introductory treatment of the layers below the application layer where it is helpful. This, in turn, necessitates treatment and coverage of computer networking material.

This book features Suggested Exercises (Appendix D). These exercises should help readers to appreciate the practical implications involved in implementing the theories presented in this book. In real-life situations, users need to closely examine and interrelate theories and applications, as well as make changes to meet specific implementation requirements. I have framed the questions in the Suggested Exercises to reflect this, and also to stimulate the creative problem-solving skills of the reader.

At the end of each chapter is an extensive list of references. For those who want to pursue further details, this may prove very handy. I have also provided a Further Reading section at the end of the book, in which are included those books that could not be appropriately placed at the end of a chapter. In some cases, the referenced material spans the subject matter of more than one chapter.

Intended Audience

Network management is a rapidly growing area; therefore, a wide audience will find this book useful.

- This book covers most of the popular network management protocols. Professionals in the computer industry who are interested in understanding different concepts, standards, and architectures in network management will find this book useful.

- Because different methodologies involved in network management are discussed in detail, this book is also useful for practitioners, including network customers, network consultants, network planners, network designers, and implementers in the network management area.
- A sufficient amount of material on network management in the LAN arena has been covered, so this will be a good reference book for professionals working with LANs.
- These days, network management approaches in the LAN and telecommunications areas are slowly converging. Some professionals in the telecommunications industry will find it useful for insight into network management in LANs.
- This book can also be used for both undergraduate and graduate courses. Some of the questions in the Suggested Exercises will be useful for term projects or independent study. Because network management is essential for the success of LAN-centric computing, there is a need for adding a companion course on network management to the present computer networking course. This book is suitable for such a new course.

How to Use This Book

Those who have a fairly good understanding of computer networking can skip Section 2.2, and Chapters 7, 11, and 13. And those who are interested in a particular protocol can go from Chapter 1 to the respective sections that deal with the topic of interest. For example, for readers interested in Internet Network Management only, Chapter 1 and Part 2 are a must. Also, they might find Chapter 19 interesting, because it concerns future trends in network management. Readers interested only in OSI may skip Parts 2 through 4.

Acknowledgments

When writing about standards, there is not much leeway. One can furnish only one's own interpretations. Because a major portion of this book is about standards, I have made use of IEEE/ANSI standards, OSI standards, ITU-T (previously CCITT) standards, and Request for Comments (RFC) from the Internet. I have also used material from many IBM manuals. From most of the organizations, except the IAB, I have been granted permission to use some of their materials, for which I am grateful.

I would like to thank the following organizations for granting permission to reproduce or adapt material from their copyrighted publications:

- The International Telecommunication Union (ITU) has granted permission to modify material for which they hold the copyright. The selection of the material is my sole responsibility and can in no way be attributed to the ITU.
  - Figure 2.6 is modified from Figure A-2, "(N)-layer management exchange," of ITU-T Recommendation X.700 (09/92), "Management framework for Open Systems Interconnections (OSI) for CCITT applications."
  - Figure 3.1 is modified from Figure 6, "Concept of management domains," of ITU-T Recommendation X.701 (01/92), "Information Technology - Open Systems Interconnections - System Management Overview."
  - Table 4.6 is modified from Table 4, "Correspondence between CMISE primitives and CMIP operation," of ITU-T Recommendation X.711 (03/91), "Common management information service definition for CCITT applications."
- The American National Standards Institute has granted the following permission as it relates to Table 5.3 and Figure 5.3 (Identifier Field only).

  This material is excerpted and reprinted from ISO/IEC 8824:1990 and ISO/IEC 8825:1990 with the permission of the American National Standards Institute (ANSI) under an exclusive licensing agreement with the International Organization for Standardization (ISO) and the U.S. National Committee of the International Electrotechnical Commission (IEC). No part of the aforemention standards may be reproduced in any form, electronic retrieval system or otherwise without the prior written consent of the American National Standards Institute, 11 West 42nd Street, New York, N.Y. 10036

- The Institute of Electrical and Electronics Engineers, Inc. (IEEE), has granted the following permission as it relates to Figures 11.6 (SNAP Header portion), 12.1, and 12.3.

  Various figures modified from IEEE Std 802-1990, *IEEE Standards for Local and Metropolitan Area Networks: Overview and Architecture,* and IEEE Std 802.1B-1992, *IEEE Standards for Local and Metropolitan Area Networks: LAN/MAN Management*, copyright © by the Institute of Electrical and Electronics Engineers, Inc. The IEEE takes no responsibility for and will assume no liability for damages resulting from the reader's misinterpretation of said information resulting from the placement and context in this publication. Information is reproduced with the permission of the IEEE.

- The Addison-Wesley Publishing Company has granted permission for the modification of material as follows:

- Figures 8.23 and 10.13 are adapted from Figure 6.3a-e and Figures 18.4, 18.5, and 18.6 are adapted from Figure 14.7.3a-c of *SNMP, SNMPv2, and CMIP: The Practical Guide to Network-Management Standards* by William Stallings, © 1993 by Addison-Wesley Publishing Company, Inc.

The addresses of the organizations from which standard documents can be obtained are furnished in Appendix C.

I would like to thank Jerry Crenshaw and others of IBM management for extending me help to write this book.

I am indebted to many reviewers, including some anonymous ones, who took great pains to review different chapters, and who provided me with excellent and thoughtful comments and valuable feedback. I am particularly indebted to Matthew Naugle, Sidnie Feit, Zerbaksh T. Bam, Bob Dey, Sudhir Nath, Paul P. Golick, John Q. Walker II, and Rick Rosinski for the thorough and meticulous review of the chapters I gave them. I am also grateful to other reviewers, including Raj V. Rajan, Kirk A. Preiss, Jeff F. Ferla, Michael L. Coy, Tim S. Huntley, and Jog S. Mahal. These reviewers have helped me to make the material as up-to-date and technically correct as possible. Of course, any errors are solely my responsibility.

I also would like to warmly acknowledge the help rendered at different stages of the book by my sponsoring editor at McGraw-Hill, Ms. Marjorie Spencer, with whom it has been a pleasure to work. I also would like to thank Jane Palmieri, my editing supervisor, and others at McGraw-Hill who helped me in the publication of this book. Additional thanks go to Ginny Carroll, the copy editor.

As mentioned earlier, I have presented the material in this book in a vendor-independent and consortium-independent manner. The opinions and conclusions expressed are solely mine. However, to improve the book, I welcome comments from readers. I will incorporate changes in future revisions. Please send comments to me at 7 Nutmeg Court, Durham, NC 27713.

Divakara K. Udupa

Chapter

1

Network Management: Introduction and Overview

1.1 Introduction

Network management has become a critical issue, especially in heterogeneous and multivendor computer networks. Also, for the success of client-server computing, effective and proper implementation of network management is essential. Client-servers with a large number of workstations need network management to manage and control the networks and the components of networks with their associated hardware and software. Like other areas of the computer industry, network management has been undergoing rapid technological advances to meet ever increasing challenges.

1.2 Challenges in Network Management

Before we examine what network management means, let us focus on its importance. In the early days of computing, computer networks were mostly *hostcentric* and homogeneous. In this scenario, a mainframe or host computer managed the networks. These networks were usually homogeneous, with a specific, tightly coupled protocol stack for internetworking and communicating among users. Users operate with personal computers, workstations, or terminals without much intelligence (known as "dumb terminals"), or a mixture of these. By and large, the protocol stacks were proprietary.

Within this discussion, it is worth mentioning that, these days, the *computer* has expanded to include desktop computers popularly known as personal computers, workstations, laptops, palm-held computers, and other computing devices, which have the intelligence to do computation and also to communicate with each other. With computer technology growing at an incredibly fast pace, it may not be proper to place limitations on what a "computer" can be.

Computers can connect to one another to form a *local area network* (LAN). In LANs, there are two important computer networking scenarios. The most popular scenario is known as *client-server* computing. In client-server computing, a client requests a service from a server and the server provides the service to the client. As an example, compiling a computer program in a client can be done by the compiler located in a server. On the other hand, in *peer-to-peer* computer networking, there are no fixed roles such as that of client or server, and any computer in the network can be a client or server. For our discussion purposes, we include both computer networking scenarios under LANs.

The evolution from hostcentric computer networks to heterogeneous LAN networks has been gradual. This transformation to LAN computing and networking is further complicated by existing applications and protocols from different standards bodies and vendors. However, the limitations of technology, protocols, and topology impose restrictions on the number of computers that can be connected to form LANs. Therefore, clusters of networks have become the trend. Once these islands of networks come into existence, the issue of connecting and managing networks becomes important.

To get a better appreciation of the problems involved in the present-day network management of LANs, let us look at some of the possible LAN environments. Some networks can be connected by *bridges* with similar LAN protocols. This scenario is shown in Figure 1.1. Here, networks A and B use similar protocols, and they are connected by bridges. Sometimes, network A and network B are known as *segments*. LANs may also be interconnected using Fiber Distributed Data Interface (FDDI) as a backbone, as shown in Figure 1.2. Here one network is using a token ring and the other network is using Ethernet. *Routers* are used to connect these networks to the backbone network.

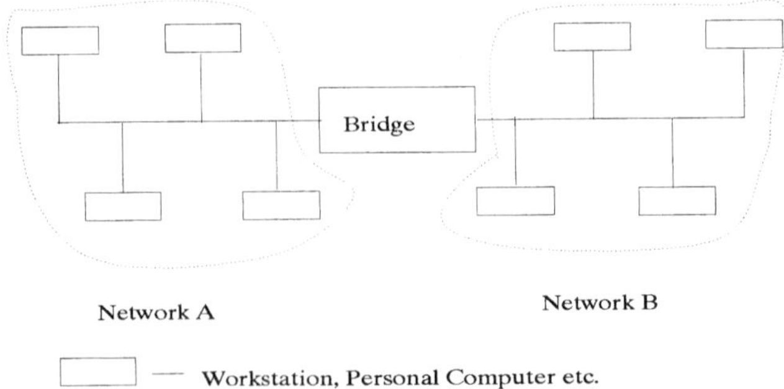

Figure 1.1 Networks with similar protocols.

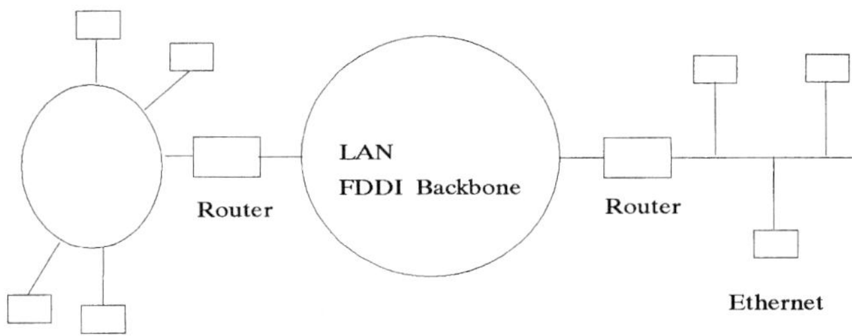

Figure 1.2 Networks connected by FDDI backbone.

Figure 1.3 Networks with mixed protocols.

There are also cases where dissimilar networks have to be interconnected. In this case, as shown in Figure 1.3, *gateways* are used for connecting the networks. Here one network may be using TCP/IP, and another one may be using Open Systems Interconnection (OSI) or System Network Architecture (SNA).

Also, these LANs may span buildings and cities to form a *metropolitan area network* (MAN). An extension of the MAN can be found in the *wide area network* (WAN), which covers a larger area than a MAN does. The topics of bridges, routers, gateways, LANs, MANs, and WANs will be discussed in detail in Chapter 11 on LANs.

After having discussed some of the LAN scenarios, let us take some simple examples of problems involved in managing different components of a network. Suppose we have to apply a software fix to all the computers in a network. How do we do it? We cannot take a diskette and apply the fix to all the computers, especially if there are thousands of them. Or what about isolating a fault in one computer? How can we say with certainty that a problem has occurred in X computer? And we need to be sure what caused the problem, and how it can be rectified.

These sets of problems assume serious proportions if computers are from different vendors. These computers may be using different software and hardware architectures. There are various ways of reporting the problems and different ways to rectify them. In some cases, these architectures may be such that the computers attached to different LANs may not communicate with each other. In some cases, it may be necessary to connect these networks to a centralized computer. How do we connect these LANs from different vendors and then manage them from a single, central point?

All of these factors make the network management of computer networks and their components, which may be widely dispersed with multivendor origins and multiprotocol operation, a highly challenging task. How we meet it is the topic of this book.

1.3 OSI Architectural Model

Because network management uses distinctions described by *open systems interconnection* (OSI) seven-layer architecture, it is imperative that we look into it right up front. The International Standards Organization (ISO) brought out the OSI architecture of seven layers for computer networking. The main idea behind partitioning computer networking functions into separate, independent subfunctions is to standardize each layer of activity more easily and expeditiously. Each layer is expected to carry out a set of functions and provide services to the layer above it.

As defined in OSI, a *system* includes computer hardware and peripherals, software, and applications, including those used for communications. *Open system* has different interpretations and connotations. We prefer the following definition: A system is said to be *open* if it supports a widely accepted and well-published set of standards. Openness is not concerned with the system technology, implementation, or how the systems are connected to one another.

The seven layers are as follows:

1. The *physical layer* deals with physical interfaces and details of the physical medium used to connect two open systems. It is concerned with mechanical, electrical, optical, functional, and procedural characteristics of the links used in data transfer.
2. The *data link layer* is responsible for reliable data transfer between two linked open systems. This may require flow control, error control and recovery, and synchronization.
3. The *network layer* provides a path for data transfer between end systems. In this layer, routing of data through a network of intermediate systems may be required. As a consequence, this layer is responsible for making connections when required, maintaining them, and terminating the connections when they are no longer needed.
4. The *transport layer* is concerned with data transfer from one end to another end. For this purpose, end-to-end error recovery and flow control may be required. Note that the network layer is con-

cerned with data transfer from one system to another, whereas, in the transport layer, we are talking about end-to-end data transfer.

5. The *session layer* is responsible for sessions between applications. This layer also provides services for establishing, maintaining, and terminating these sessions.
6. The *presentation layer* is primarily responsible for resolving differences in the way data is represented between two applications on either end. As an example, ASCII to EBCDIC translation, or vice versa, may be done in this layer. This layer also may provide services such as encryption and data compression.
7. The *application layer* provides services and functions required by user applications. In other words, this layer provides applications and services which are not provided by lower layers to support communication between the systems. In this layer, we may include *commitment, concurrency, and recovery* (CCR). Applications such as electronic mail and network management belong to this layer. Network management applications, which use network management, also form part of this layer.

From the preceding explanations, we notice that layers one through three are concerned with transferring data from point A to point B, whereas layers four through six deal with the data transfer from end A to end C. This is illustrated in Figure 1.4.

Having briefly characterized the OSI layers, let us define some terms used in network management.

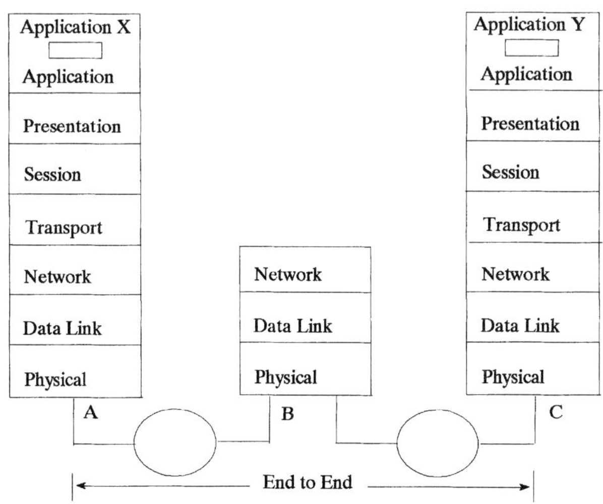

Figure 1.4 OSI seven-layer architectural model.

1.4 Network Management, Systems Management, and Enterprise Management

Network management, systems management, and *enterprise management* have been variously defined. This can lead to a lot of confusion and we will therefore clearly define what these terms will mean in this book. We define *management* as monitoring and controlling the resources in computers, the resources used in the connection and communication of computers, and the applications used in the computers.

There are, broadly, two models for *network management,* based on how the management activities are accomplished. This, in turn, is dependent on the computing environment. A LAN is a typical *distributed-computing environment.* Management of LAN environments can be done by peer-to-peer network management. Sometimes, this is also known as *distributed-network management.* Here managers, which undertake the network management activities, act more as peers, and there is no one central manager.

The other model is *hierarchical,* or *centralized, network management.* In this model, the network management is controlled from a single point, known as a *manager.* This manager may manage network resources from a centralized computing environment. This may cover the cases where one supermanager or one centralized controlling manager may manage devices via some intermediate managers. This supermanager is also known as the *manager of manager* (MOM). All these cases are grouped under *hostcentric network management.* Sometimes, this can also be termed *enterprise management.* Usually, hostcentric network management functions reside in the mainframe, as shown in Figure 1.5.

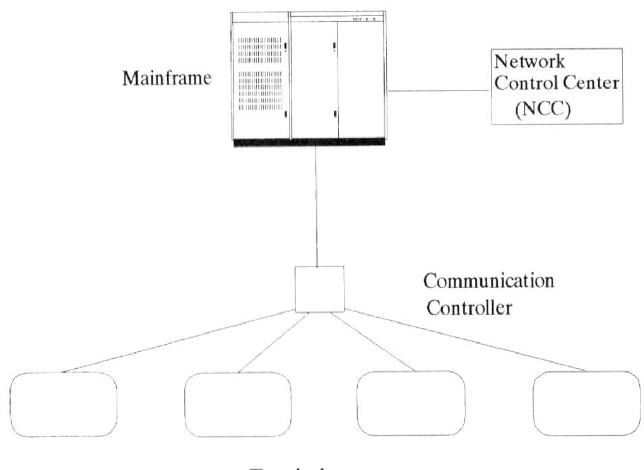

Figure 1.5 Hostcentric systems management.

Many definitions are in vogue for network management. We use the one provided by IEEE Standard 802.6-1990 [Reference 1.1, page 227]: "Network management provides mechanisms for the monitoring, control, and coordination of all managed objects within the Physical Layer and Data Link Layer of a node." The same document also defines systems management as follows: "Systems management provides mechanisms for the monitoring, control, and coordination of all managed objects within open systems. Systems management is effected through application layer protocol." Here we have to note that *skinny stacks* or trivial upper layers can also be used. From the definitions provided by the IEEE, it is apparent that network management is a subset of the activities in systems management.

In the preceding definitions, we have to be clear on the terms *monitoring, control,* and *coordination.* This is central to the concept of systems management. Let us examine the term *monitoring* first. Resources used in computer networks have to be continuously watched, and any untoward behavior leading to the deterioration of functioning of a resource, resources, or network has to be rectified. This is more a proactive action than a reactive one.

The resources have to be controlled. This means that we should be able to control how the resources behave so that they function properly. When resources have to be monitored and controlled, there is a necessary factor: coordination. If there is no coordination, the situation is a free-for-all, and chaos ensues. Not only do the activities of the managed resources have to be coordinated, but so do the facilities that monitor and control them.

1.5 Conventions Used in This Book

Unfortunately, *systems management* is a very generic term. Readers can confuse it with management of systems used in other disciplines. This confusion is compounded by the use of different terms in the computer industry. To focus on the topic of network management of computers, networking, and data communication equipment, we must zero in on the terms used; thus, we have used a consistent approach to terminology used in this book.

While treating the topics of OSI and SNA, especially in the peer-to-peer arena, *systems management* is the popularly used term; thus, it is better to use this term when dealing with these protocols. In Internet, *network management* is the prevalent term; hence, this term will be used when discussing this topic. While discussing IEEE-related management of resources and layer management, we will also use the term *network management.* In other places, where it is not specifically required to make distinctions between network management and systems management, the term *network management* has been used, as well.

1.6 Goals of Network Management

The goals of network management are:

- *Higher network availability:* This involves improving the operational efficiency, which means reducing system and network downtime and improving response times. Problems in a network should be responded to as quickly as possible. In many cases, it should be possible to rectify the problems unattended. But the access and transfer of management information will require processing power and involve network traffic. Therefore, performance must be considered in the design and installation of network management.
- *Reduce network operational cost:* Ultimately, cost reduction is one of the primary motives behind network management. Because the technology changes rapidly, management of heterogeneous systems and multiple protocols is desirable.
- *Reduce network bottlenecks:* In some cases, network administration can be performed from a central site. Under these circumstances, it may be preferable to centrally monitor and control the activity of a network. In other cases, this activity may be distributed.
- *Increase flexibility of operation and integration:* Networking technologies are changing at a fast rate to cater to changing requirements and needs. As new applications are used, protocols used in networking are also changing. It should be possible to absorb new technologies with the least cost. As an example, in LANs, data communication is common, but there may also be a need to integrate graphics, voice, and video capabilities as the application base expands. In addition, computer networks could be used to manage copiers and faxes.

  It should be possible to add new technology and equipment without much difficulty. Also, there should not be major problems in migrating from one release of network management software to another version. Network management applications should not be overly platform-dependent for their function.
- *Higher efficiency:* In some cases, some of the goals of network management overlap. If we reduce the network operational cost and improve the network availability, overall efficiency will increase. Here, factors such as utilization, operational cost, migration cost, and flexibility must also be considered.

- *Ease of use:* End-user interfaces are critical for the success of any product. The use of network management applications should not involve a major learning curve. User interfaces based on object-oriented principles and technology are helpful for network management applications.
- *Security:* Some network management functions may need security features. If some critical accounting data has to be secure, then there should be provisions for providing selective security. Here we are making the distinction between computer system and network and network management–related security. Our focus will be on the security of network management functions.

1.7 Network Management Systems Architecture

We can organize network management systems as shown in Figure 1.6. This division is based on different functions performed at different levels. To avoid confusion with OSI layers, we have used the term *level* instead of *layer.* It may be noted that this division of functions is made to explain the concepts of overall network management systems. At the lowest level, we have the *operating system and hardware.* The operating system may be DOS, Windows NT, OS/2 Warp, Windows 95, or a combination of these. Network operating systems, such as Novell NetWare or OS/2 LAN server, are also part of this level. The figure shows resources in a separate box, because the intention is to highlight network management of various resources. These resources may be on the same workstation as the operating system or they may be separate components, such as a bridge or a router. The resources that have to be managed are detailed in Section 1.8.

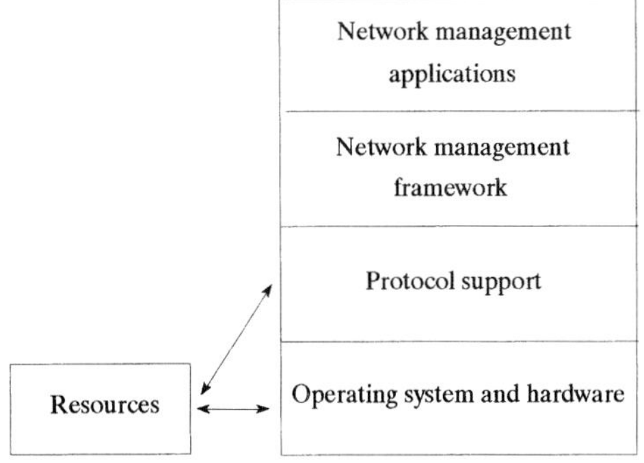

Figure 1.6 Network management systems levels.

Over the operating system and hardware, we need *protocol support.* Protocol support provides distinct services; hence, it must be treated as a separate level. Protocol support includes the following:

- Layers below the application layer in OSI, UDP/IP in Internet, or layers which have similar functionality.
- Management protocols such as SNMP, CMIP, or CMOL. (We will discuss these protocols in detail in later chapters.)
- Conversion of different protocols and multiprotocols which may also be needed for supporting heterogeneous and multivendor protocols.

The level above protocol support is the *network management framework,* which provides the base for various network management applications. In the computer industry, it is becoming a trend to enable and open up this level such that different vendors and alliance partners can write network management applications. The network management framework provides for the following:

- Manager and agent functions.
- Database support such as relational databases and object-oriented databases for storing data for many network management functions and applications support. We prefer to include database support in the network management framework, because network management applications sometimes need close access to the database for topology, status, inventory of resources, logs, and other data.
- View and user interface support, which are important for the success of software applications. The base for these functions is provided in this layer.
- Network management functions, such as configuration management and fault management.

The *network management applications* area is a growing market and has the potential to produce very innovative applications. Some examples include the following:

- The business management applications area is still largely untapped. With the growing client-server market, this area has challenges and potential, especially regarding the dispersal of computing equipment and environment.
- Easy-to-use view applications can ease the tasks of system administrators. The use of multimedia and artificial intelligence has wide possibilities in this area.

- Fault identification and fault diagnostic applications such as automation applications will be in greater demand to cater to the highly decentralized nature of networks.
- Performance-tuning applications are very important. Even though processor power is increasing at a rapid pace and constraints such as memory are becoming cheaper, demands on them are also increasing at a fast pace. Demands on processing power will increase as graphics, image, video, and audio applications become more prevalent.

In this book, the major emphasis is on the resources being managed, protocol support, and the network management framework. It is beyond the scope of this book to either discuss in much detail the operating system and hardware or examine in depth the network management applications area.

1.8 Resources to Be Managed

Management of computer networks involves monitoring and controlling the different hardware, microcode, and software components of networks. Some hardware components that need to be managed are:

- *Physical media and connections:* These include physical and data link layer–related equipment. Many LAN products are coming out for these layers. The protocols used vary from IEEE 802–related products, including FDDI, frame relay, B-Integrated Services Digital Networks (BISDN), asynchronous transfer mode (ATM), Synchronous Optical Network (SONET), and other emerging protocols. Also included are products such as adapters of different protocols, concentrators, and switches.
- *Computer components:* These include storage devices, processors, printers, and others. Though Ethernet, token-ring, and token-bus adapters are considered part of the computer components, they have not been included here. We prefer to lump them under the aforementioned physical media and connections category.
- *Connectivity and interconnection components:* This refers to hardware components such as repeaters, bridges, routers, gateways, hubs, and modems.
- *Telecommunication hardware:* These are modems, multiplexers, and switches, such as, for example, an ATM switch.

Typical software to be managed includes:

- *Operating system software:* This is the bare-bones system software provided on any computer. Some examples are DOS, Windows 95, and OS/2 Warp.

- *Application software and software tools:* The application software makes computers more popular and productive. With increasing integration of video, voice, text, and imaging, applications need to be managed. As the base of multimedia applications grows, multimedia applications need to be managed, too.
- *System software in client-server computing:* Some examples are NetWare servers and OS/2 LAN servers.
- *Interconnection software:* This includes software used in repeaters, bridges, routers, gateways, and hubs. In many applications, extra functionality is provided by adding software functions on the underlying hardware. These software applications are becoming complex, and are as important as the hardware.
- *Application software in client-server computing:* This includes the database server, file server, and print server.
- *Data communication and telecommunication software:* Management of software related to data communication and telecommunication protocols such as FDDI, ATM, and frame relay is necessary. We have specifically included this in the software section, because these protocols rely heavily on software.
- *Backbone telecommunication software:* This is increasingly used to connect different LANs. Though it is included in our earlier categories, we have added backbone telecommunication software here as well to account for the emerging backbone communication protocols.

The above mentioned wide variety of hardware and software to be managed is complicated by various protocols and differences among them. In addition, many proprietary protocols are popular and have a wide application base. Therefore, multiprotocol and multivendor products make connectivity and management daunting tasks. Broadly, the scope of network management is to manage both hardware and/or software products, which may be heterogeneous, multivendor, multiprotocol, and geographically dispersed, as well as managing the people who oversee these products.

Having introduced the topic of network management, we will examine different concepts and standards, including architectures, in the rest of the book. In some cases, to provide a better understanding and appreciation of the important concepts and methodologies involved in network management, lower-layer concepts are also briefly discussed.

1.9 Standards

As discussed earlier, there is a paradigm shift in the computing scenario. LANs and WANs are becoming increasingly popular. Also, with the introduction of fiber optics, telephone tariffs are coming down. At the same time, more applications, such as voice, video, text, graphics, and images, are being added to the computing environment. Simultaneously, these applications require bandwidth beyond what we have observed in the traditional transmission of voice or data.

This changing scenario is slowly bringing about the integration of data communication and telecommunications, which adds complexity to network management. The management of equipment must include switches and different components used in the telephone industry. In addition, computing and data transmission environments are becoming increasingly heterogeneous. The different types of equipment use a variety of protocols, from standards to the proprietary ones. This adds another dimension to the management of heterogeneous, as well as multiprotocol, environments.

As one guides through the maze of protocols, standards are being advanced by vendors belonging to the telephone industry, computer industry, and government agencies. There are basically two types of standards. *De facto industry standards* become established when a large segment of the user population accepts them or when a majority of vendors uses them. In some cases, such industry standards are the result of prominent players in an industry forming cooperative bodies and introducing products that conform to the guidelines developed by these bodies.

Formal standards are mostly brought out by international, regional, or national standards bodies. In many cases, there is close cooperation among these standards bodies. Governments and their agencies, by and large, prefer formal standards. The ISO is one such body, which, as the name suggests, is an important international standards organization primarily comprising governmental agencies. At the national level, most countries have their own standards organizations. Standardization is becoming important in facilitating the compatibility of hardware and software from different vendors. From this angle, concepts of *portability, connectivity,* and *interoperability* should be emphasized.

Let us examine what each term means. For portability, an application in one computer platform must be able to work with identical functions in another platform, or no modifications should be required to make an application work in different platforms. For portability purposes, application interfaces and functions provided to interact with lower-layer software should be similar.

By connectivity, we mean that a system from one vendor attaches to a similar system from a different vendor, and these systems must be able to work together. For example, two computers manufactured by different vendors must work together when connected as LANs.

Interoperability, which is closely related to connectivity, goes a step further. For interoperability, the protocols, formatting of data, and application environments must be similar, such that applications developed on two different platforms must work together. An application developed by one vendor must work with a similar application from another vendor. Let us look at an example. Electronic mail and electronic data exchange applications are quite common. For interoperability, two electronic mail systems must work together regardless of which vendors developed these systems.

Having examined some terms relevant to standardization, let us return to the topic of standards bodies. In the United States and elsewhere, computer networks connected to the Internet follow their own set of standards and have well-established procedures for bringing out standards. In addition, the Institute of Electrical and Electronics Engineers (IEEE) in the United States formulates standards for LANs and in other areas where there is a need for them. Usually, the IEEE concentrates on the standardization of lower layers such as the physical and data link layers. Most standards bodies work closely with one another and adopt each other's standards, where they are available, to avoid duplication of efforts and standards.

On similar lines, the U.S. government has issued its own set of standards, known as the Government OSI Profile (GOSIP) for procuring equipment. The details can be found in Reference 1.2.

As software applications become more sophisticated and are developed by many vendors, there is a trend toward open systems. For open systems, conformance testing to find out whether applications really conform to the standards is becoming a norm.

Many variations of standards are available; therefore, it is possible to have a set of implementations with different sets of standards at different layers. To facilitate smooth operation, some standard sets, known as *profiles,* have been developed by standards bodies. This reduces incompatibility and ensures that applications using the same profiles have interoperability.

Standards provide sufficient flexibility in implementation, which may create its own set of interoperability problems. To overcome this, many leading vendors are developing a set of profiles for network management. This effort is being pioneered by the Network Management Forum (NMF), which provides guidelines on how OSI standards must be implemented. In addition to the NMF, there are also vendor consortiums such as the Open Software Foundation (OSF), Unix International, and X/Open. Many applications are being brought out based on the work done by these groups. These consortiums also active in the network management area. Addresses for these organizations are provided in Appendix C.

A common pitfall of standards is that they take a long time to produce. Once a problem is identified, some standards bodies take years before they bring out widely accepted standards. This presents problems in some cases. People in the industry with problems needing immediate solutions cannot wait for many years for standards to resolve these problems. Still, standards are generally useful and good for everyone in the industry.

Another common complaint is that the OSI standards are too complex, and it is difficult to implement them. This may be one reason for the slow implementation of standards. Because standards bodies work on the basis of consensus, there are influences in different directions, leading to frequent changes. As a consequence, it is becoming a practice to wait for standards to stabilize and become international before implementing them.

1.10 Network Management Standard Functional Model

Different network management standards are prevalent. Some are closely related to one another and, in some cases, they extend earlier protocols, taking migration aspects into consideration. Extensibility is an important part of every standard. General standards must be applicable to specialized cases and applications. In network management standards, we are interested in the following key areas:

- *Management functional area:* This covers how network management functions are organized, how they interact with each other, and how they behave with the external components. The management functional area should also clearly delineate the scope of each network management function.
- *Informational area:* This deals with how resources are represented from the standpoint of management actions. This has to be done in a consistent manner to facilitate smooth and easy definition of new resources. Representation of resources should also cover the scope of the management operations that can be performed on these resources. We stress the scope, because it is very important to precisely define the boundaries of these resources from the management point of view and the interactions possible with external components. There should not be any room for ambiguity, because this leads to confusion during implementation and problems of interoperability.

- *Communications area:* This primarily covers management protocols. As we will notice, in network management, we use entirely different management protocols for communicating management information. The communications area should also include the communication stacks or profiles which are used to support the management protocols.
- *Conformance area:* This is a key area for interoperability. A set of guidelines should be clearly stated for checking whether an implementation has adhered to the standards outlined. During implementation, taking too much liberty may result in incompatible implementations. This can be checked only if there are precise and clear guidelines on how implementations are to be done.

1.11 Summary

In this chapter, we have looked into the challenges of network management. The OSI seven-layer architecture has been introduced. Terms such as network management, systems management, and enterprise management were explained, and the goals of network management and the resources that must be managed have been treated in some detail. An architecture for network management systems has been presented.

We also touched upon the subject of standards, discussing the need for them as well as their shortcomings. These discussions lay the groundwork for further examination of the topics of network management.

1.12 How the Book Is Organized

Network management is a rapidly changing field. When large and voluminous material is available, it is not possible to cover everything in a book of this nature. Consequently, the scope of the book is necessarily limited.

We mainly focus on the different network management system models. Though there are many standards bodies working in the network management area, we will examine the systems management model by the ISO. As mentioned earlier, the Internet is developing its own set of standards for network management. We will also look into the network management protocols developed by the Internet for the TCP/IP protocol suite. Readers may note that for the TCP/IP protocol suite, the preferred term is *Internet.* Because some may have become accustomed to the term *TCP/IP protocol suite,* sometimes it is referred to as such. Here it may be mentioned that there is not much difference between the terminology of network management used in Internet and that used in OSI systems management.

Also, the IEEE has developed its own set of standards for the protocols in the physical and data link layers. These are closely related and in many cases are complementary to the standards developed by the ISO and Internet. Besides, IEEE standards have relevance to the devices used for interconnecting LANs, MANs, and WANs. Because of this, IEEE network management standards have also been discussed in detail.

SNA protocols are popular and have a wide user base. With this in mind, we examine APPN, APPC, CPI-C, and Message and Queuing Interfaces (MQI). Systems Management in the SNA peer-to-peer environment and SystemView will also be discussed.

Chapter 1 has laid the foundation for this book. An introduction to network management systems was provided, and we have examined the challenges and goals of network management. We also briefly introduced the OSI seven layers. The remainder of this book is divided into five different parts, described as follows:

Part 1: OSI Systems Management

Part 1 covers the OSI lower layers and OSI systems management. OSI standards, developed by the ISO, have worldwide acceptability and, in some nations, conformance to these standards is mandatory. So, with the importance of open systems, Part 1 deals with the work done by different bodies of the ISO in computer networking and systems management.

Chapter 2 starts with a brief discussion of the lower layers of OSI. This chapter is basically devoted to an OSI systems management overview. In this chapter, we explain terms such as *manager* and *agent* and discuss systems management functional areas such as configuration management. (They are discussed in detail in Part 5.)

Chapter 3 details some of the important OSI systems management topics, such as management domains, management information hierarchies, filtering and scoping, synchronization, and allomorphism. Here, different state and relationship attribute details are discussed.

In Chapter 4, we discuss in detail topics such as ACSE, ROSE, and CMISE. Chapter 5 covers ASN.1 and BER in detail.

Chapter 6 discusses the OSI Structure of Management Information (SMI), especially different templates used in the definition of a managed object class. In this chapter, we primarily examine the Guidelines for the Definition of Managed Objects (GDMO) document.

Part 2: Internet Network Management

Part 2 discusses the TCP/IP protocol suite and Internet network management. The TCP/IP protocol suite, which includes network management, is very popular, which justifies including a separate part for the details of network management for this suite.

In Chapter 7, the lower layers of the TCP/IP protocol suite are discussed, including topics such as IP, ICMP, TCP, and UDP.

Chapter 8 is devoted to network management in the TCP/IP environment. Here we mainly focus on the details of SNMPv1, MIB-II, and the role of proxies.

Chapter 9 discusses Internet network management using RMON. In this chapter, RFC 1757 and RFC 1513 are examined in detail. Chapter 10 is centered around SNMPv2 protocols and changes to MIB in SNMPv2.

Part 3: IEEE LAN/MAN Management

Part 3 provides details on different components of LANS, layer management of LANs, and LAN/MAN network management. Without some basic idea of LANs and their concepts, network management in the LAN environment will not be meaningful and complete. The IEEE is a prominent player in this arena and has brought out many standards, which cover areas such as layer management, MANs, and WANs.

Chapter 11 is devoted to the physical layer, MAC, and the LLC layer of IEEE standards. Here we briefly discuss connectivity issues and topics such as bridges, routers, and gateways.

Chapter 12 covers the IEEE layer management. This chapter also includes a discussion of CMIP over LLC (CMOL). We also examine IEEE network management of LANs and MANs.

Part 4: Peer SNA and Systems Management

In this part, we discuss the emerging popular peer-to-peer protocols known as peer SNA, from IBM. Peer SNA protocols have an extra advantage of being compatible with the widely used SNA protocols. APPN and APPC facilitate the smooth migration to a peer-to-peer environment from a hostcentric environment.

Chapter 13 covers APPN, APPC, CPI-C, and MQI. In Chapter 14, we discuss systems management in the SNA peer-to-peer environment. SystemView is also discussed.

Part 5: Network Management and Issues

Part 5 offers a detailed discussion of network management functions and architectural models, a comparison of different management protocols, and future trends.

One problem in the area of network management is that there are no well-laid-out standards, except in OSI, on how to partition the network management functions. Some proprietary protocols such as SNA have a good division of network management functions. But it is not appropriate to slant the discussions with proprietary protocols or product-specific details while discussing specific network management functions. The discussion of network management functions should be generic and span wide-ranging areas. So we rely on OSI systems management functional areas. While using OSI as the basis, we branch out to a discussion of specific network management functions. The good news is that most of the products that are being introduced by and large follow the OSI systems management functional areas, in different flavors. Notice that when using OSI terminology, network management functions are referred to as *systems management functional areas.*

Chapter 15 provides details on configuration management, Chapter 16 covers fault management, and Chapter 17 deals with performance management.

Chapter 18 is devoted to the remaining systems management functional areas of accounting management and security management. Here we also cover the area of conformance testing and different international standards profiles.

Chapter 19 covers network management for the distributed environment. In this chapter, the impact of object-oriented technology on the network management arena is also dealt with. We will end the chapter with a discussion of the latest advances and future trends.

At the back of the book is a General References section. Because we have not covered certain areas, such as the Telecommunications Management Network (TMN), in this book, interested readers should consult the references provided. In addition, there are the following appendices:

Appendix A covers the ISO, ITU, and ISO Standardization Cycle.

Appendix B covers the IAB and Internet Standardization Process.

Appendix C provides addresses from which to procure network management–related publications.

Appendix D provides some specific exercises to ensure understanding of the book's content.

1.13 References

1.1 IEEE Standard 802.6-1990, Local and Metropolitan Area Networks, Distributed Queue Bus (DQDB) Subnetwork of a Metropolitan Area Network (MAN), New York, Institute of Electrical and Electronics Engineers, Inc., 1990.

1.2 Black, U., *Computer Networks, Protocols, Standards, and Interfaces,* 2d ed., Englewood Cliffs, N.J.: Prentice-Hall, 1993.

1.14 Further Reading

ISO DIS 7498-1 (X.200), Information Processing Systems, Open Systems Interconnection, Basic Reference Model, Part 1, 1992.

Stallings, W., *Networking Standards: A Guide to OSI, ISDN, LAN, and MAN Standards,* Reading, Mass.: Addison-Wesley, 1993.

Note: Most of the ISO documents are paired with IEC documents; therefore, we have omitted the corresponding IEC document from the References and Further Reading sections.

Part

1

OSI Systems Management

Chapter

2

OSI Systems Management Overview

2.1 Introduction

We start this chapter with a brief discussion of some of the important OSI concepts, followed by the topic of OSI systems management. It is appropriate to add a cautionary note here. We must be very careful when implementing OSI standards. The OSI furnishes broad guidelines for the definition of managed object classes and management operations, but it does not go into specific implementation details. While implementing standards, modifications may be made, and definitions and guidelines may be expanded to suit individual cases. Also, in some cases, the definitions are in place, but the details are still being worked out. In such cases, individual implementations need to be formulated.

Appendix A contains details on how OSI works and the way standards are formulated. Appendix A also has a brief overview of the International Telecommunication Union (ITU). ITU-T, a division of the ITU, brings out standards on its own and adopts some of the ISO/IEC standards. (ITU-T was previously known as CCITT.) Our main interest, from a network management point of view, is in the X Series standards of the ITU-T.

2.2 Important OSI Concepts

We will present a brief overview of OSI concepts; however, because it is beyond the scope of this book, we will not go into much detail on OSI layers below the application layer. For interested readers, there are many good books (for example, see Stallings in the Further Reading section) and OSI standard documents. Some commonly used OSI terms are:

- *Reference model:* This is the popular OSI seven-layer architecture and is used as the basis for the OSI standardization effort.
- *Service definition:* This is an abstract concept, and it includes a set of functions provided to the user of a layer. However, in the case of the application layer, the user is an application process. The service definition defines the capabilities that can be provided to a service user.
- *Protocol specification:* This furnishes a set of concrete rules which govern the interaction between two service providers and provides implementation guidelines. As conformance requirements and testing relate to the implementation of protocols, they apply to protocol specification only. Most of the OSI layers have service definition and protocol specification documents. The concepts of protocol specification are illustrated in Figure 2.1.

2.2.1 Concepts of the service access point (SAP)

In data communications, we often hear the term *entity.* Basically, an entity is an abstract concept (conceptual idea). An entity is that which provides services. These services can include error recovery, segmentation, and assembly. These entities provide the services of the *service access point* (SAP). The SAP is an addressing concept. It is a conceptual intersection between two layers and is referenced as the address by an upper layer that wants to access the services of lower layers. So an (*N*)-layer is accessed by the (*N*+1)-layer using the intersection point address as shown in Figure 2.1. In this figure, (*N*+1) address AddrB is important and is subject to OSI standardization. As far as AddrA is concerned, it is a local matter, and it is not within the purview of OSI standardization.

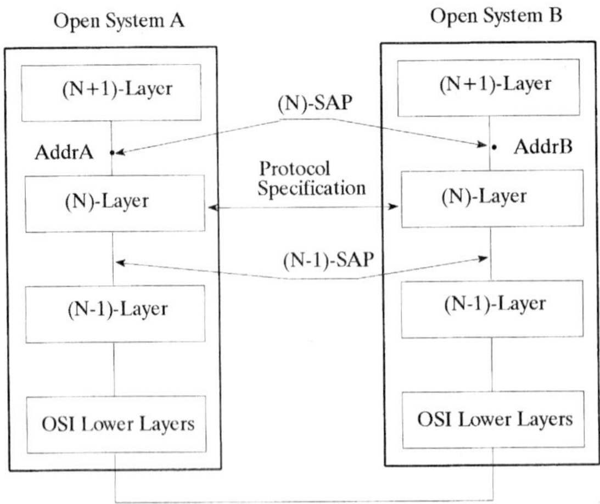

Figure 2.1 OSI layer concepts.

Primitives furnish further details on a state. There are four primitives: request, indication, response, and confirmation. When a request is sent, the sender may wait for a reply. In this case, the request is known as a *confirmed* request. In some cases, the sender may not bother for a reply to come from the responder. In such a case, the request is known as an *unconfirmed* request. These requests and responses sent between a manager and an agent have their own distinct names: request, indication, response, and confirmation. How they behave is shown in Figure 2.2. The commonly used generic terms *requestor* and *responder* are used in this figure.

When a requestor sends a message asking for a certain service to be performed by the responder, the requestor sends it in the form of a *request.* On the responder side, correspondingly, the responder receives a message asking the responder to perform a service. This becomes an *indication* on the side of the responder. When a responder has to send some message, it sends it in the form of a *response.* On the receiving side, the requestor sees the message as a *confirmation.*

In the preceding explanations, the broad term *message* is used to avoid the confusion that might arise if we referred to it with names such as event report, notification, command, or response. When specific terminology is required or clear distinctions are necessary, such terms will be well-defined and explained.

Each service will have an indication about the layer: for example, A, which refers to an application layer; a verb such as ASSOCIATE; and a primitive such as request. An example of a service is thus A-ASSOCIATE.request. Each service has parameters which convey information, including data and controls.

OSI and ITU-T protocols use a *finite state machine* (FSM) to explain functional aspects of the protocols. FSM is a mathematical modeling concept used to describe properties and behaviors of a system. A *state* is a distinct stage in a set of possible circumstances. In an FSM, there is an initial or starting state. A system begins its operation from the initial state. Some examples of states are *active, busy,*

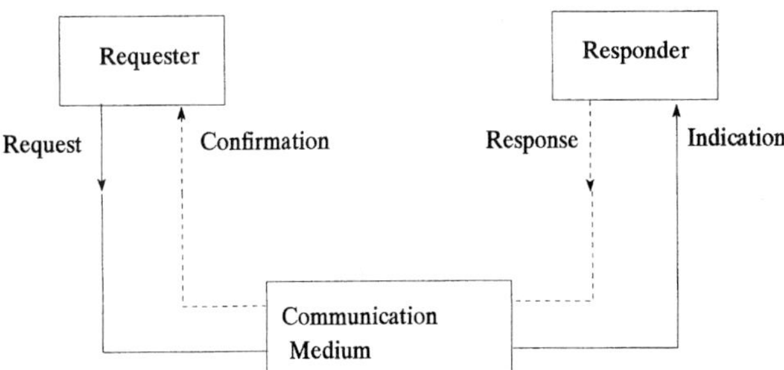

Figure 2.2 Requestor and responder messages.

and *idle.* Events occur because service primitives, such as A-ASSOCIATE.req, are received from a user. This event triggers an action or actions. An action causes a transition or change of state to happen. Figure 2.3 illustrates these concepts.

FSMs are represented graphically by a *state transition diagram* (Figure 2.3) and *state transition tables.* State transition tables use tabular structure, listing all the states in columns, and the events in rows. The intersections of rows and columns represent possible actions, which may also include transitions.

2.3 OSI Management Framework

The OSI management framework is defined in ISO 7498-4: Basic Reference Model, Part 4, Management Framework. In a systems management standardization effort, this document is a good starting point. It basically covers the following areas:

- Terms and general concepts
- Systems management model
- Informational model
- Systems management functional areas
- Systems management standardization framework

As we have seen earlier, OSI management was motivated by the need to control, coordinate, and monitor the resources of open systems. In Chapter 1, we discussed some of the resources that need management.

As shown in Figure 2.4, management information exchange using systems management communication protocols is done between *systems management application entities* (SMAEs). SMAEs are located in the application layer of our OSI seven-layer model. We will revisit SMAEs in Chapter 4.

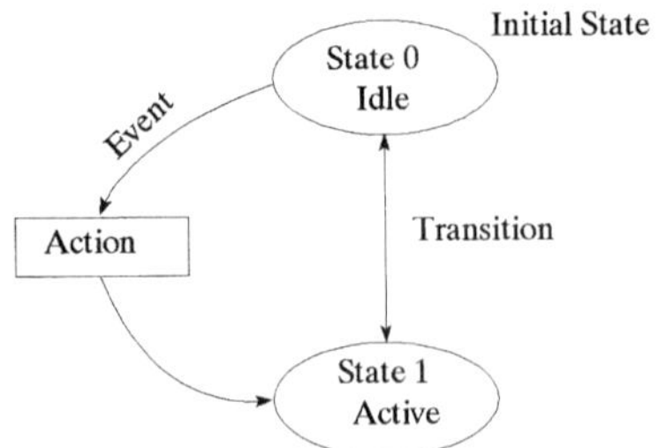

Figure 2.3 Concepts of a finite state machine.

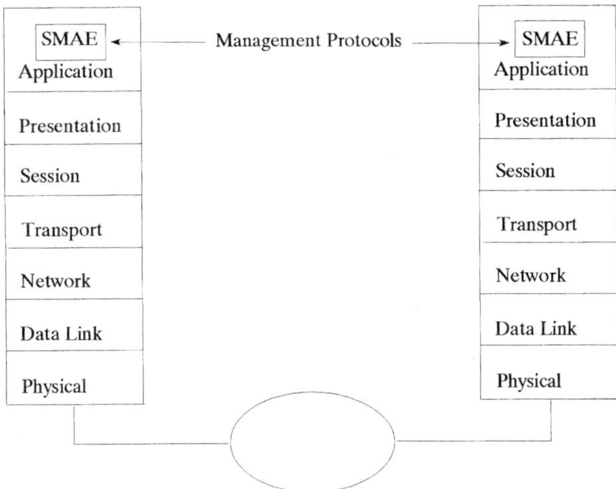

Figure 2.4 SMAE concepts.

2.4 Manager

A manager has the responsibilities for activities such as configuration management. To collect the data on configuration, a manager has to send commands or operations to collect it. In return, the manager receives replies to its commands. In between, if something goes wrong, the manager may get unsolicited information or notifications.

As an example, if component X has gone down, the manager would need to update its configuration database. For this, component X, which is represented as a managed object, may send a notification to an *agent*. Component X may be in the same system as the agent or may be in another system. The agent, in turn, will send a notification to the manager with the information that component X has gone down. Accordingly, the manager may update its configuration database.

Hence, a manager collects and collates the information received from the agents. A manager's responsibilities also include system administration functions. A manager may control the operation of remote agents. It may send commands and actions on the basis of information received from agents.

2.5 Agent

An agent can be on a workstation and must be present wherever accessing of resources is required. As shown in Figure 2.5, the agent has its own important role. It performs the following functions:

- An agent must manage its own environment, in which it must interact with managed objects. A workstation may have many

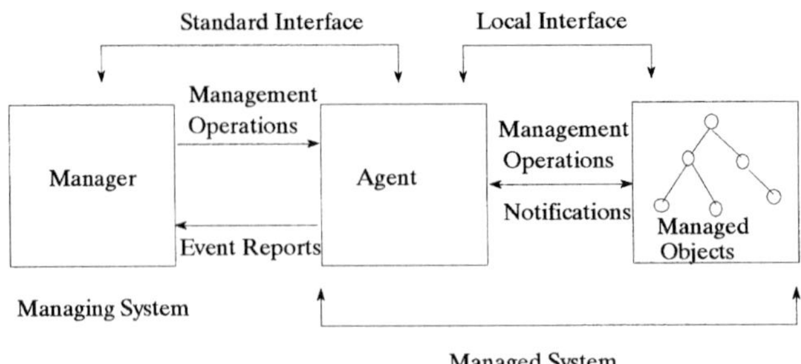

Figure 2.5 Manager/agent relationship.

objects defined, such as a printer, modem, mouse, and so on. The agent interacts with managed objects representing these resources and controls their operations. However, this interface is not standardized by the OSI.

- When an agent gets commands from a manager, it acts upon these commands and accordingly manages the managed objects. A manager may send a command to an agent to set the font in an object such as a printer. Here, *font* may be an attribute of the managed object *printer.*
- An agent may get some notifications from the managed objects. It forwards them to the manager. As an example, a printer attached to a workstation may be defined as a managed object. In turn, this managed object may send a notification or a message, which says that it has run out of paper. This must be forwarded by the agent to the manager.

However, in OSI standards, the roles of a manager or the boundaries between manager and agent roles are not strict. A SMAE that is a manager in one interaction may take up the role of an agent in another interaction. Similarly, a SMAE that was an agent may take up the role of a manager.

OSI standards do not cover how an agent deals with a managed object. OSI standards also do not state how an agent handles the managed objects that are outside the managed system boundary. As an example, an agent may ask for details on objects from another agent. In this case, the other agent forwards its data to the agent that asked for details. This is also not within the purview of standards.

For a manager and agents to communicate, each must know about the other; thus, the *application context* (AC) must be known. AC refers to the application service elements used between a manager and agents and the protocols used. Also there is a need to know which functions and functional units are supported by a manager and agents. (We will revisit some of these terms in Chapter 4.) Then, a knowledge of the managed object classes supported by agents and the relationships between functions and managed objects should be known. This is known as *shared management knowledge* between a manager and an agent.

This shared management knowledge is made known before an association is started and is stored in some file and restored every time an association is made between a manager and agent, or during the association establishment phase. While establishing an association, it must be possible to change the shared management knowledge.

2.6 Manager/Agent Starting

There are different terms associated with the starting of a manager and agent communication. Before system management operations, the manager and agents should know what to expect and how each one behaves. Each one will have to know the parameters, such as security features, that will be used. This is done differently in different protocols, and we will examine each one of them in respective chapters. The terms associated with the initial phase of manager and agent communication are:

- *Association:* Associated with CMIP
- *Affiliation:* Used in CMIP over LLC
- *Community:* Popular term for association in SNMP

2.7 Systems Management Model

OSI management comprises systems management, (*N*)-layer management, and (*N*)-layer operation. This threefold division should account for all possible situations that could arise in management, as we will see later.

Systems management covers managed objects in all seven OSI layers, including the application layer. It assumes reliable connection-oriented end-to-end transfer of management information. There is a caveat here: The OSI management framework does not preclude the use of connectionless services.

In layer management, the management of managed objects is limited to those in a particular layer, as shown in Figure 2.6. The management protocols make use of the communication protocols of lower layers. (*N*)-layer management is useful when it is not possible to go for all seven OSI layers. In such a case, we can use the layer management protocol, because this is strictly applicable to a particular layer. Layer management should not duplicate the systems management. An example of layer management is LAN/MAN management protocols which are limited to layers 1 and 2. These protocols have been developed by the IEEE, and are discussed in Chapter 12.

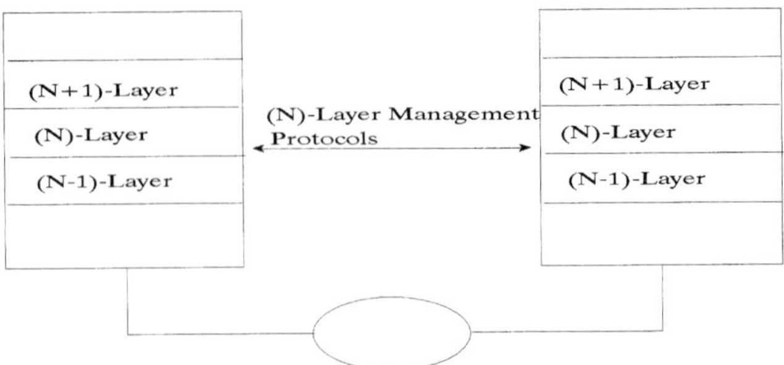

Figure 2.6 *(N)*-layer management.

Finally, *(N)*-layer operation is limited to monitoring and controlling a single instance of communication of management information within a layer. Layer operation is sometimes required, because some layer protocols may contain management information. An example of management information is the parameters that are exchanged in protocol data units while establishing connections. The standards within *(N)*-layer management and *(N)*-layer operation are beyond the scope of OSI systems management standards. However, the OSI management information model (Section 2.8) can be used by layer management.

The basic systems management model assumes management operations and notifications between peer systems. This model facilitates the distributed aspect of systems management. Sometimes, these peer systems are designated as managing systems and managed systems.

For systems management purposes, the roles of peer open systems are defined. One peer open system is assumed to take the role of a manager and the other peer open system is assumed to take the role of an agent for a given interaction. An agent may be distributed throughout the OSI environment.

2.8 Management Information Model

A managed object is an OSI way of viewing resources for management purposes. A resource can be described as a managed object. A managed object is an instance of a *managed object class.* A managed object class is a collection of packages, which can be mandatory or conditional. In packages, similar characteristics are grouped together. We will go into further detail on packages and managed object classes in Chapter 6. If we define *printer* as a managed object class, a Lexmark Laser Jet printer is an object instance; an HP Deskjet 560C would be another object instance. In Figure 2.8, managed object 1, managed object 2, and managed object *n* are instances of a managed object class. In object instances, the values of the characteristics are different. We come back to the topic of managed object class and how it is defined in Section 6.4.10.

For controlling the activities of resources, the manager and agents need to be aware of the details of the resources. The details of these managed objects, which are required for management purposes, are stored in a conceptual repository known as the *management information base* (MIB). The MIB is a conceptual model and it has no relation to how the data is physically or logically formatted and stored. Standards do not cover the storage aspect. Nevertheless, the syntax and semantics of how the information is exchanged are governed by the OSI protocols. However, these managed objects must be properly formatted for management purposes. The retrieval of data from the managed objects may involve the use of communication services provided by the layers below.

For OSI management, we have to take into consideration all the resources in the computer systems, including those related to data processing, data storage, and data communication. As an example, in fault management, we should consider the utilization of processors, hard disks, or CD-ROMs.

2.8.1 Managed object

The definition of a managed object must include properties. These properties with specific values that can be exchanged are known as *attributes.* The type of printer—e.g., dot matrix, laser jet, or laser printer—can be one of the properties. A managed object class definition must also include *operations* that can be performed on a managed object. Modifying or querying attribute values are examples of operations.

Managed objects can send *notifications* if a certain event occurs. A notification is an unsolicited message, which contains details of the message, including why a notification has occurred, where it occurred, and for whom the notification is intended. When the characteristics of a managed object, such as attributes, operations, and notifications, are defined, there must be a way to express their semantics and how they are related. This is done by *behavior.* These characteristics must be capable of manipulation by management operations.

There are two types of managed objects, as shown in Figure 2.7.

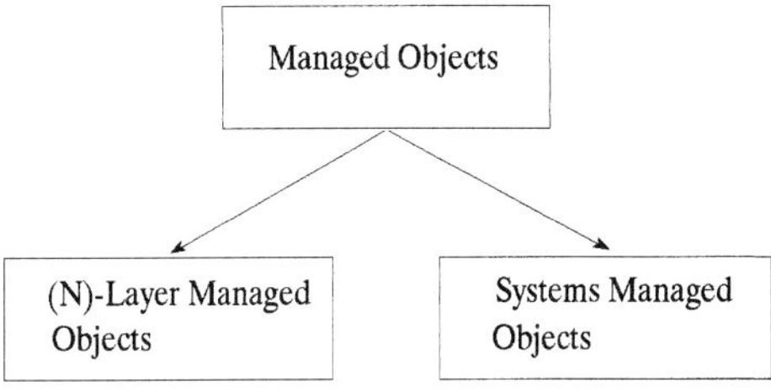

Figure 2.7 Managed objects classification.

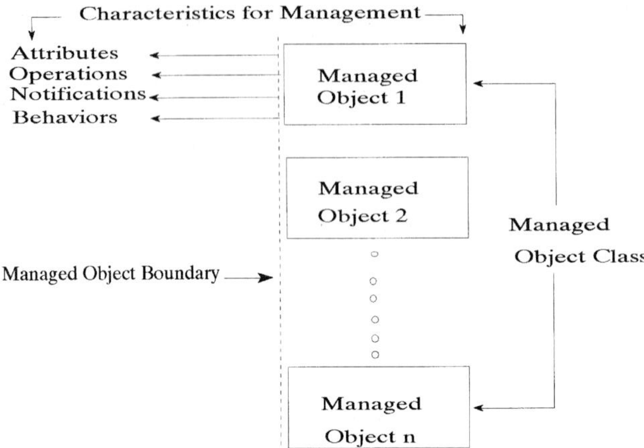

Figure 2.8 Managed object class concepts.

One type of object, known as an *(N)-layer managed object,* is relevant to one OSI layer. The other type of object is known as a *systems managed object.* Here, the systems managed object is used for systems management purposes and covers more than one layer.

For definition of managed objects, we perceive conceptually the managed objects as having a boundary, as shown in Figure 2.8. The characteristics of managed objects used for systems management are visible at and beyond the boundary. These characteristics include attributes, operations, notifications, and behavior. Hence, what is of interest are the properties at or beyond the conceptual boundaries. What is inside the managed object boundary is not needed for systems management purposes.

The process of creating a managed object as per rules is known as *instantiation.* For example, when a Create on a managed object class, tokenRing, is done, then a managed object created with, say, tokenRingID = 1594 is known as an *instance* of a managed object class tokenRing.

2.9 Management Knowledge Management Function

The management knowledge management function can be used by an application process for systems management purposes. ISO 10164-16.2 primarily provides the model for the management knowledge objects, defines the management knowledge managed object classes required, and maps management knowledge management function services to CMIS services. ISO 10164-16.2 ties up many loose ends and basically provides information on how a manager and agents can know about each other and how a manager can extract information on the managed objects managed by agents.

2.9.1 Management knowledge

Management knowledge refers to the management information required by an open system to associate and perform management operations on another peer open system. There are three types of management knowledge:

- *Repertoire knowledge:* This relates to the capabilities of a managed system, which pertain to the classes supported, the systems management functions supported, and the name bindings. (We will discuss name bindings in detail in Section 3.5.) Repertoire knowledge assists a manager in identifying the capabilities of managed systems without accessing them.
- *Definition knowledge:* This refers to the formal specifications of managed object classes, name bindings, test categories, relationship classes, and the management information definitions understood by a managed system.
- *Instance knowledge:* This provides the information on the managed objects in a managed system.

Management knowledge has further subdivisions for repertoire knowledge and instance knowledge. Repertoire knowledge subdivisions are:

- *Managed object class knowledge:* This provides details on the managed object classes supported by a managed system, such as initial values of the instances of objects, the packages supported, the allomorphs supported by each managed object class, and the constraints on each of the managed object classes. (We will examine allomorphism in Section 3.10.)
- *Naming schema knowledge:* This relates to the naming relationship between the managed objects made available by a managed system.
- *Relationship knowledge:* This refers to the relationship between managed object classes supported by a managed system and also the relationship of role bindings between managed object classes.
- *MIS-user knowledge:* This provides the titles, presentation address, application contexts, the functional units supported, and the management profiles of the SMAEs (manager and agents) supported.

Relationship knowledge and MIS-user knowledge have instance knowledge. Instance knowledge relates to the object instances associated with relationship managed object classes and instances of agents. Instance knowledge has the following subdivision:

- *Managed object instance knowledge:* This provides details on the instances of managed objects which are made visible by a managed system.

2.9.2 Management knowledge management function managed object classes

For realizing the management knowledge management function, ISO 10164-16.2 defines 15 managed object classes under *top* (see Figure 2.9) and two repertoire directory managed object classes. We will not discuss each of the managed object classes. Basically, the groups of managed object classes are:

- *Repertoire managed objects:* This refers to the information on the capabilities of a managed system, such as the managed objects supported and their name bindings.
- *Definition managed objects:* This provides details on management information supported by managed objects. These definition managed objects are useful while forming associations. Three types of definition managed objects are document objects, template objects, and ASN.1 module objects.
- *Discovery managed objects:* This group has details on the managed objects made visible by a managed system.

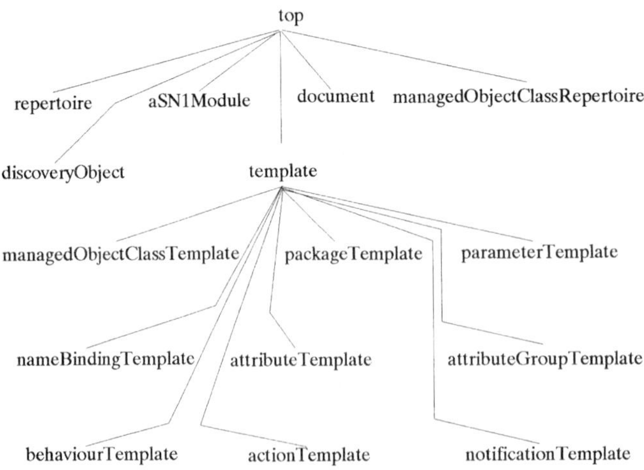

Figure 2.9 Management knowledge management function managed object classes.

- *Management knowledge directory objects:* These provide information on the capabilities and definition knowledge of the management systems. There are basically repertoire directory objects and definition directory objects under this category.

2.10 OSI Systems Management Functional Areas (SMFAs)

For the convenience of standardizing management, systems management activities are subdivided into different functional areas. Each functional area has specific responsibilities. The systems management functional areas are:

- Configuration management
- Fault management
- Performance management
- Accounting management
- Security management

2.10.1 Configuration management

Computer networks are expanding and becoming more complex. These networks need to be managed. The different components of networks cannot be managed without knowing where the various components are. Configuration management is used to locate the resources, including the failed ones, and also to keep track of the types of resources and their details.

One of the key objectives of systems management is to maintain continuous operation of a network. We have already seen that components of a network are modeled as managed objects. These managed objects will have addresses and names to distinguish them. These can be stored in directories, and these directories can be built using OSI directory services.

The data on managed objects, such as their state and how they are related to one another, is collected on a regular basis and, where there are changes, they can be collected in a manager, using unsolicited messages such as event reports. These changes must be reflected in the database on topology and status. These services may be used by other systems management functions such as fault management.

In addition, we may activate and deactivate managed objects. Sometimes, these may have to be done in a controlled manner. Also, we may want to change the configuration of the network. For example, a workstation may no longer be attached to network A; instead, it is now attached to network B. This change has to be known and accordingly reflected in the configuration. In addition, we may wish to change the parameters of systems. Most of these activities have been standardized by the configuration management functional area of systems management. We also need to manage day-to-day operations of the systems and resources. The configuration management function provides the support services to keep the systems and resources operational.

Software management. This function is within the configuration management functional area of OSI systems management. With the widespread use of computers, this is becoming an important function. When new computers are set up, software needs to be installed. It is not possible to hand-carry the diskettes for installing software; there should be a way to distribute the new software for installing new systems.

Once we have systems installed, they need to have the latest versions of software. In some cases, we need to apply fixes to software problems that have cropped up. The distribution of software fixes is a part of this function. Fixes usually should not be applied when a system is busy; this should be done at a particular time and requires a scheduling operation. We also need to keep track of the software installed, as well as fixes and versions. Sometimes this is referred to as *license management,* which is also a part of *change management.* Basically, change management involves all the activities that are required to keep track of changes in computer networks and the resources associated with them.

2.10.2 Fault management

Though some of the goals of fault management appear to be part of other areas of systems management, each area must perform its part of the function, and sometimes cooperative functioning and management are required. For example, after we analyze system performance, we need to identify problem areas and take corrective actions to overcome them. We may use log services or a cache to store the data.

We may also need the help of configuration management to identify precisely where a problem has occurred. Some form of automation routines may be required to apply fixes. For example, a token-ring lobe becomes nonfunctional. We may use automation to bypass the problem lobe and take some other corrective action to prevent a station from being disabled permanently.

Fault management is broadly concerned with the detection, isolation using analysis, and correction of unusual operational behaviors of systems in the OSI environment. These unusual operational behaviors include conditions such as deterioration of service and error situations. Effective fault management may require that errors be logged in a database.

This error log may be in an agent or manager, depending on the situation. In some cases, an agent may not have much memory. In such a case, the error log may be off-loaded to a manager. In some other cases, error logs may be in agents and a summary is maintained in the manager. Where to locate the error log depends on requirements and implementation decisions.

For detecting and isolating complex faults, it may be necessary to examine error logs and run diagnostic tests. Sometimes traces may be helpful. After the problems are isolated, they are corrected. One of the trends in systems management is to automate as much as possible fault management functions. By automation, we mean a set of procedures which are triggered to correct impending and actual problems without human intervention. This set of procedures may be accomplished by hardware, microcode, software, or a combination of them.

2.10.3 Performance management

When computers are working, we need to know how they are operating—for example, is the system getting overloaded? Is there enough workload? How is the performance during peak hours? How is the LAN behaving? Are there too many collisions while transmitting data? The answers to these questions fall within the realm of performance management.

To undertake capacity planning, we need to collect performance-related data. What are our response time targets? Are we achieving them? Can we improve the performance with better load balancing? Is any system becoming a bottleneck? How can we improve the performance by removing the bottleneck? Some of these questions require historic data to be answered. The historic data has to be stored in databases so that it can be analyzed, and correct answers can be arrived at.

Performance management is also concerned with the behavior and evaluation of the effectiveness of resources. For this, we may need to gather statistical data on the behavior of resources and store the data in databases. We can use the data to evaluate the performance of systems and networks and fine-tune them to maximize overall performance.

2.10.4 Accounting management

Here we must consider how much of the resources are being used and how much must be charged for using these resources. The accounting information can be from individual, department, section, and company levels, depending on the rate structure.

Accounting management includes informing relevant users and authorities about the usage of resources and the costs associated with their usage. In some cases, it may be enough to send monthly reports about computer facilities usage to managers instead of to individual users. In other cases, these reports may have to be sent to individual users and managers in the administrative chain. All these are included in accounting management.

In some cases, especially where computing resources are scarce, it may be necessary to set limits on the usage of resources. This is common practice in universities, where authorities do not want students to overload the centralized computing facilities. There are also cases where computing resources are out-sourced from some vendors and tight control on the usage of resources is desirable.

Furthermore, costs on resource usage may sometimes need to be combined and consolidated. As an example, some people work from home using modems. It may be necessary to consolidate the cost of telephone tariffs for this kind of work with other costs.

2.10.5 Security management

Security management must be very carefully and patiently implemented. It has become an important issue, especially in distributed computing environments with thousands of workstations. There are different levels of security to correspond to different levels of computing environments. There are threats of viruses creeping into networks. Without adequate precautions, important company information may be lost, or proprietary work that is being done may be stolen. Security management is a very important function for dealing with these threats.

Though systems management security is closely related to network security and computer system security, we will focus on security issues related to systems management functions, such as those dealing with accounting management and managed objects.

Some security management functions are:

- Reporting any security violations, using event reports to the manager, and maintaining logs. Unusual security violations must be brought to the attention of the network manager for prompt action.
- Creating, deleting, and maintaining security-related services like encryption, key management, and access control.
- Distributing passwords and secret keys as necessary when bringing up systems and at regular intervals afterwards.

2.10.6 Business management

The business management function is a collection of aspects from the configuration management, accounting management, and security management functional areas of the OSI systems management function. Business management is an important function with much potential, and it needs to be included in OSI systems management. First, all the hardware, software, and computing resources used are registered. Then, whenever there is a new user, this user is registered along with the details of the resources being used.

After collecting the details of all the computing resources, we use them to manage the cost. This is where financial administration enters the picture. The total cost of using the resources and how much is used by each individual user, department, or division needs to be computed.

Business management involves more long-range and strategic planning than does accounting management. A workload may increase or decrease, depending on the business climate. In such cases, short-term as well as long-term planning of data processing needs are appropriate. Once such plans are in place, they must be continuously monitored and updated.

Facilities planning is also a part of business management. How much of the resources will be located in a particular place? How best to place the resources? These concerns are very important where working space is at a premium. Some functions of business management will be discussed in this book as they are applicable to other functions.

2.11 OSI Systems Management Standards Overview

Systems management standards are pertinent to the application layer of the OSI. These standards can be broadly grouped into different areas, as shown in Figure 2.10. This classification indicates how these standards can be grouped to arrive at different systems management functional areas.

Basic and general systems management services relate to the general explanation of systems management functions. The documents under this category furnish general guidelines on systems management standards. Many OSI standards, such as OSI layer standards, systems management standards, and standards or domains, fall under this classification.

The next category relates to the management information model. Standards under this classification provide definitions of managed object classes and generic managed object classes that can be used for systems management. They all have a starting number of 10165 and are grouped under the *structure of management information* (SMI).

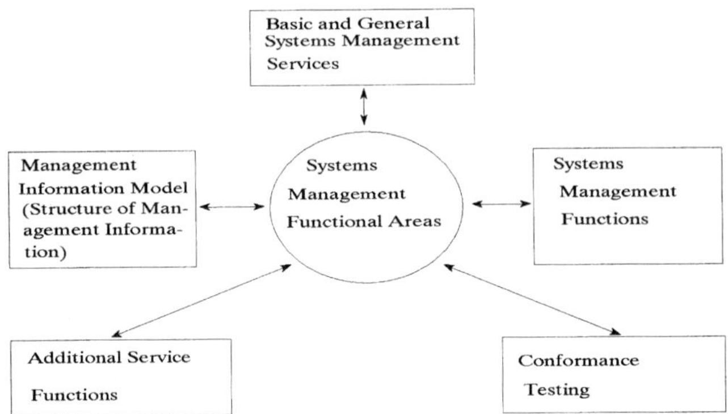

Figure 2.10 Relationship between systems management functional areas and standards.

Another group of standards relates to the specific systems management functions and includes object definitions required for them. They all start with 10164. Providing a systems management function such as performance management may require the help of more than one standard in the 10164 grouping. As an example, performance management may require 10164-11, which is the workload monitoring function, and 10164-13, which is the summarization function.

Other standards are needed to implement interoperable systems management functions, including standards for association and for the syntax of data being transferred, and the protocols used for communication between manager and agent. ACSE, ROSE, CMISE, and CMIP are categorized under additional service functions (discussed in Chapter 4). Security is a major consideration, especially when distributed computing receives wider acceptance. All of these issues are included under additional service functions.

These classifications are combined to make up the *systems management functional areas.* These SMFAs must be modular so that additional functionalities can be added more easily. For example, in the first release, all the bells and whistles required for security management may not be in place. These may be added in the second release or as the standards firm up. In some cases, depending on the needs and additional requirements, committees are set up to examine and formulate standards. This takes time, and must be considered when providing the systems management functions.

Once all the functions are provided, it is essential to ensure that for operations under different conditions and multivendor environments, they conform to the provided standards. There are also generic conformance standards which must be followed. These help to reduce incompatibilities.

2.12 Summary

In this chapter, the OSI concepts were briefly introduced, followed by a preview of OSI systems management standards; OSI management; some of the systems management terms, such as manager, agent, managed object, and managed object class; and systems management functions. This introduction to different terms used in systems management provides the basis for systems management architectures and implementations.

Systems management functions were discussed, as well as the overall organization of OSI systems management standards. We also presented the classification concepts of systems management standards.

2.13 Further Reading

ISO CD 10164-16.2, Information Technology, Open Systems Interconnection, Systems Management: Management Knowledge Management Function, 1994.

ISO CD 10164-19, Information Technology, Open Systems Interconnection, Systems Management, Part 19: Management Domain and Management Policy Management Function, 1994.

ISO DIS 7498-1 (X.200), Information Processing Systems, Open Systems Interconnection, Basic Reference Model, 1984.

ISO DIS 7498 AD1, Information Processing Systems, Open Systems Interconnection, Basic Reference Model, Addendum 1: Connectionless Mode Transmission, 1987.

ISO DIS 7498-3 (X.650), Information Processing Systems, Open Systems Interconnection, Basic Reference Model, Part 3: Naming and Addressing, 1984.

ISO DIS 7498-4 (X.700), Information Processing Systems, Open Systems Interconnection, Basic Reference Model, Part 4: Management Framework, 1989.

ISO DIS 10040 (X.701), Information Technology, Open Systems Interconnection, Systems Management Overview, 1991.

ISO DIS 10040 PDAM1, Information Technology, Open Systems Interconnection, Systems Management Overview—PDAM1: Management Knowledge Management Architecture, 1992.

Stallings, William (ed.), *Computer Communications, Architectures, Protocols, and Standards,* 3d ed., Los Alamitos, Calif.: IEEE Computer Society Press, 1992.

Stallings, William, *Data and Computer Communications,* 3d ed., New York: Macmillan, 1994.

Chapter

3

Systems Management Terms

3.1 Introduction

Before getting into the discussion on CMIS and systems management functional areas, familiarity with some of the concepts and terms used in systems management is appropriate. Though these terms will be used frequently in OSI systems management, network management in other protocols also uses many of the concepts enunciated in this chapter. For example, *polling* and *heartbeat* are frequently used terms in most of the network management protocols.

This chapter will examine some of the important systems management concepts, such as management domains; management information hierarchies; the registration, inheritance, and containment hierarchies; object naming; scoping and filtering; synchronization; polymorphism; and allomorphism. Scoping and filtering will be useful for fault management. Also, we will discuss the topics of management state and the attributes used for relationships, which pertain to connecting managed objects. Management state and relationships between objects are very important concepts for configuration management. Though we have already identified fault management and configuration management, these terms will be used in other systems management functional areas as well. In addition, some of the terms will be used in topics such as CMIP and managed object definitions.

A note of caution is needed here. We will discussing two important ISO Committee Draft (CD) documents: ISO CD 10164-19 on management domain and ISO CD 10164-17 on the changeover function. These documents cover some of the important concepts. Because these documents are in the CD stage, there is the possibility of changes. Before implementing these functions, make sure to get the most recent documents, which should be at least in the Draft International Standard (DIS) stage.

3.2 Communication Between Managed Objects and Agents

Exchanges of messages between managers and agents are done by *protocol data units* (PDUs). PDUs contain data from the layer above and control information of a layer. PDUs can take the form of a request or response. A manager can send a request to an agent, and the agent, in turn, sends a response. These requests and responses contain management information, which is contained in parameters. However, it is not cast in concrete that only a manager sends requests and an agent sends responses. In some cases, an agent may send unsolicited messages or notifications to the manager. The manager, in turn, may send responses to the notifications sent by the agent.

An agent must access managed objects frequently to know what is happening to them or how they are performing. One way is to do *polling,* in which the managed object is queried at constant time intervals. Polling is sort of like asking the managed objects "How are you doing?" Sometimes, polling is not that simple. For performance-oriented queries, managed objects may be required to send back large amounts of information. In polling, the time interval is an important factor. If it is done too often, there is increased network traffic. On the other hand, if polling is done at large intervals of time, up-to-date information on the state of the managed object may not be received. So the time interval used for polling is more of a design decision that reflects the goals to be achieved.

In OSI, however, in case of unusual conditions, notifications are sent by the objects to an agent. These notifications, in turn, are converted to *event reports* in agents and sent to managers. This is a better way of knowing the state of a managed object than polling. It avoids the unnecessary network traffic that results from polling. By and large, polling is unproductive and should be avoided.

Another way to access a managed object is to use another intermediary agent. This agent must be self-contained and is required to have intelligence to issue requests or responses, depending on the conditions observed in a managed object. Also, specific implementation-dependent methods can be used to access managed objects.

Sometimes a manager needs to know whether an agent is functional or "dead" due to some internal problems or a broken communication connection between a manager and an agent. In such a case, one uses *heartbeats,* whereby an agent sends to the manager at regular intervals a message saying "I am alive." Like polling, the heartbeat may also carry information on the state of an agent.

3.3 Management Domain

Management domain is an important concept that helps in distributing management functions. By carefully designing management domains, we are able to conveniently partition systems management into manageable portions. There may be some gateways, different computer systems belonging to different vendors, and different kinds of systems, from workstations to mainframes. How do we show these on the screen of a workstation? When we show topology, it must be of some use and make sense. One intuitive way is to break up the topology into easily manageable management domains. Imagine the case of a network that spans a large geographical area, connecting some continents. In this example, each nation could form one management domain.

A collection of managed objects for systems management purposes is known as a management domain. The division of management domains may be based on geography, functions, or technology, and it helps us to apply management policies to a group of managed objects. We show one example of the concept of management domain in Figure 3.1.

Management domains, to be useful, must have some unique names. They must include the managed objects that will be managed by that domain, and they must know how the managed objects and agents will communicate with one another. One managed object in a management domain may also belong to another management domain, as shown in Figure 3.1. From Figure 3.1, notice that management

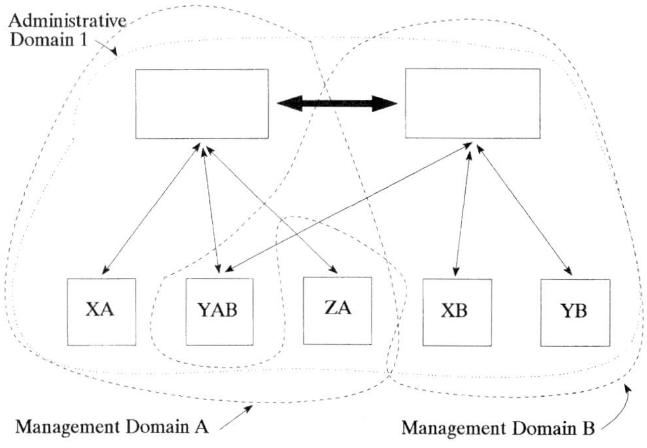

Figure 3.1 Management and administrative domains.

domain A has managed objects XA, YAB, and ZA as members. Similarly management domain B has managed objects YAB, XB, and YB as members. Thus, it is apparent that managed object YAB is a member of both management domains A and B.

After the whole network has been divided into management domains, what do we do? If there is no centralized control, there may be chaos. For this reason, we define another set of domains over this conceptual model. This is known as the management *administrative domain,* as shown in Figure 3.1. The functions of management administrative domains are as follows:

- They exercise control over managed objects and agents in the domain.
- They help us to change the boundaries of management domains if, for example, after some time, certain managed objects need to be under the control of another management domain.
- They can facilitate coordination when a managed object belongs to more than one management domain.

ISO 10164-19 provides information on managed object classes for management domains and management policies, models for the behavior of management domains and management policy, the services that can be performed, mapping of the services to CMIS services, and a model for retrieving information on the managed objects associated with management domains. Managed object classes defined for management domains are shown in Figure 3.2. The explanations of these managed object classes are as follows:

- *domainCoordinator:* This provides an interface to a management domain for management operations. domainCoordinator represents the functional aspects of a management domain, such as the members of the domain, relationship with a managementPolicy managed object, and the management policy as applied to members of a domain. A domainCoordinator can coordinate domains, superdomains, and subdomains. A domain within another management

Figure 3.2 Managed object classes for management domains.

domain is known as a subdomain. The parent management domain is known as the superdomain.

- *managementPolicy:* This is responsible for the management policies that can be applied to the members of a management domain. This managed object class has a list of the authorities allowed to access and modify the management policies.
- *conflictDetector:* This detects conflicts in management policies of managed objects in a management domain or management domains.

Some of the management operations that can be performed on a management domain are subdomainCreate, domainDelete, enrollMember, de-enrollMember, changeLocalName, listParents, listMembers, and listSubdomains. These management operations are used as action-type parameters in CMIS M-ACTION. (M-ACTION will be discussed in Section 4.7.) Similarly, the action types associated with management policies are policyCreate, policyDelete, policyScope, enrollRule, and de-enrollRule.

A management domain is created by a manager or an administration by creating an instance of a management relationship among management policy, a member of a domain, and a domain coordinator. In management domains, there are still some unresolved issues, including:

- Security issues involved in accessing other domains and managed objects in other domains.
- The strategy for backup when one domain fails. Do we allow one domain to be backup for another domain? The ISO 10164-19 document does not address this issue.
- ISO 10040 (Reference 3.1) mentions the administrative domains. For implementation purposes, administrative domains must be formally defined.

Standardization work is being done on some of the issues, but there are many disagreements, too. Standardization work in some areas of management domains is bogged down in committees. One of the sticking points is avoiding the discriminatory application of the domain concept, as occurred in message handling systems (X.400).

3.4 Management Information Hierarchies

Managed objects have relationships with one another. These relationships can be organized in a systematic manner by indicating how one managed object is related to another object. These relationships can be for different purposes. If managed objects are to be globally known to all, then they must have relationships indicating where they stand in a global naming structure. For this purpose, a *registration hierarchy* is used.

Because OSI management standards use object-oriented principles, it may be possible to use some characteristics already defined for other objects. This is done through *inheritance.* This relationship between managed object classes is provided by an *inheritance hierarchy.*

We may wish to have a relationship for naming a managed object. This relationship is shown by a *containment hierarchy,* also sometimes known as a *naming hierarchy.* These three hierarchies that are used for management purposes are shown in Figure 3.3. It should be noted that these hierarchies are independent of each other and are used for different purposes.

3.4.1 Registration hierarchy

A managed object class is identified by an ASN.1 object identifier. These object identifiers are formed by taking a sequence of integers in the registration tree. These numbers are registered, and the registration hierarchy tree is shown in Figure 3.4. Note that *ccitt* has not been changed to *itu-t* at the time of writing this book, although in the future, it is expected to be changed. The registration number for *Internet* is {1.3.6.1}. All systems management object identifiers, which are used in standard documents, are derived from {joint-iso-ccitt ms(9)}.

These numbers, from the root to the leaf of the registration hierarchy tree, are concatenated to form an *object identifier.* An object identifier is a series of integers used to uniquely identify a managed object class. We should note here that an attribute also has an object identifier to uniquely identify it.

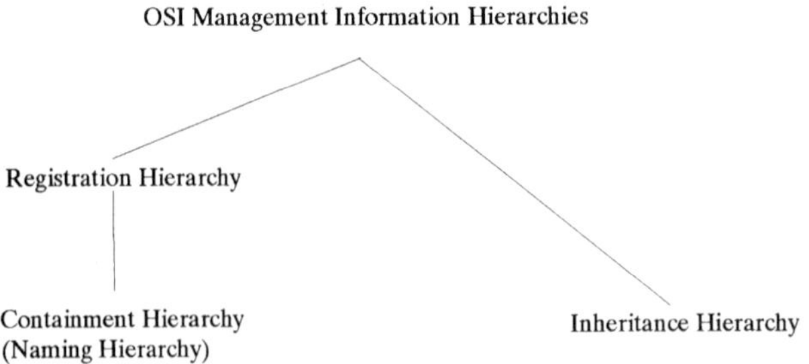

Figure 3.3 OSI management information hierarchies.

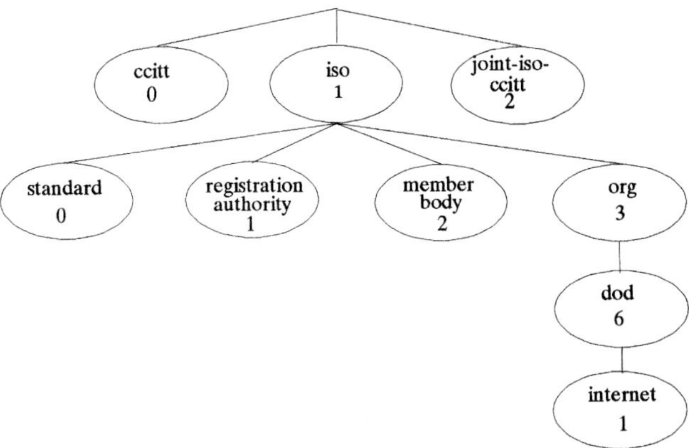

Figure 3.4 Registration hierarchy.

3.4.2 Inheritance hierarchy

It is important to know where a managed object class is positioned in the inheritance hierarchy tree. Property of inheritance is very useful, because we can derive characteristics from parents. In other words, it is not necessary to define the characteristics that parents already have. Parents, in turn, inherit properties from their parents; thus, a new managed object class definition reduces to properly positioning a managed object class in the inheritance hierarchy tree and adding some more characteristics.

Inheritance hierarchy is derived from the managed object class *top*. From *top,* various organizations and countries are derived. An example of an inheritance hierarchy tree is shown in Figure 3.5. Again, a

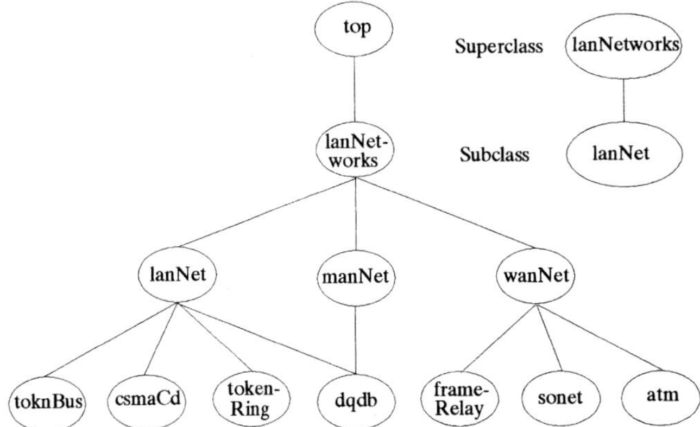

Figure 3.5 Inheritance hierarchy.

managed object class may be derived from one or more managed object classes, which facilitates inheriting characteristics from one or more managed object classes. We call this *multiple inheritance.* Figure 3.5 also illustrates multiple inheritance.

The managed object class *lanNetworks,* which is the parent of another managed object class *lanNet,* is known as a superclass with respect to the managed object class *lanNet.* Similarly, a managed object class *lanNet,* which is the child of managed object class *lanNetworks,* is known as a subclass.

3.4.3 Containment hierarchy

One managed object can represent a part of another managed object. This relationship is commonly known as *containment* and has inspired the structure used for constructing global names. This containment relationship is shown in Figure 3.6. Here, system *lansystems1* is known as a contained managed object in relation to *root.* And *root,* in turn, is known as a *containing object.*

The object instance of *lanNetwork* named *clientserver11* is a contained managed object with respect to the object instance of the system named *lansystems1.* Managed object *lansystems1* is the containing managed object.

The containment relationship is relevant to object instances. We must remember that it does not apply to managed object classes. Containment is a directed graph where arcs connect contained and containing objects. Containment relationships can refer to static and dynamic behaviors, which must be specified when defining containment relationships.

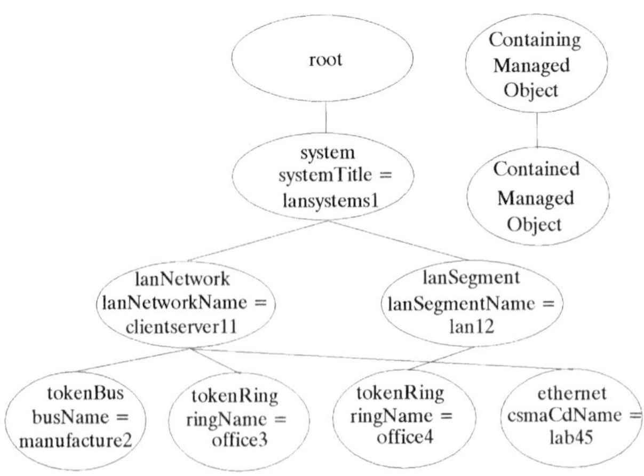

Figure 3.6 Containment hierarchy example.

3.5 Object Naming

Containment and naming are closely related to one another. A containment tree is used for naming a managed object. Every managed object must have a unique name. The containment hierarchy fans out from *root*. In the containment hierarchy, *root* is the starting point and represents a null object. Containment relationships can be described in the definitions of a managed object class, but are often late bound and described after classes are defined.

Referring again to Figure 3.6, some more terms used in defining a managed object class need to be explained. Here, the object instance of *lanNetwork* is a subordinate object in relation to the object instance of the managed object class *system*. The object instance of *system* is the superior object in relation to the object *lanNetwork*.

If we extend this relationship, *root* is the superior object class of *system*. This hierarchy of relationships forms a tree, known as the *naming tree*. It is important to mention how we name a managed object of a class that we are defining. The relationship of a subordinate object class to the superior object class is known as *name binding*. In our discussions, *naming tree* and *containment tree* are used interchangeably, because they mean the same thing.

Naming is important for uniquely identifying an object instance. In the containment tree, the distinguishing attribute, along with the name of an object instance, is known as the *relative distinguished name* (RDN). Referring to Figure 3.6, the RDN for *tokenRing* is {ringName=office3}. The RDN need not be unique at the same level; however, in relation to a superior managed object, the RDN must be unique.

The distinguishing attribute used for uniquely identifying a managed object is part of the mandatory package and, obviously, should have a fixed value throughout the life of the managed object. However, there need not be just one distinguishing attribute; there can be multiple attributes used for different name bindings.

In Figure 3.6, how do we distinguish between object instances of *tokenRing* with the RDNs *ringName=office3* and *ringName=office4* under the managed object classes *lanNetwork* and *lanSegment?* To uniquely identify the *tokenRing* object instances, we must move up the containment tree. For this, we need the help of the RDN of the parents. Starting from the beginning of the containment tree, if we concatenate the RDNs, we can derive the globally unique names. A globally unique name is known as a *distinguished name* (DN), and it is unique across the entire containment tree. The DN for *tokenRing* is {systemTitle=lansystems1, lanNetworkName=clientserver11, ringName=office3}. It is important to note that the containment tree and the physical containment of one resource by another need not be similar.

For naming a systems managed object, we use systemID or systemTitle. The ASN.1 for systemID can be a GraphicString, INTEGER, or NULL. NULL value is used when a system has not been configured or a systemID attribute is not used in naming. In systemTitle, the ASN.1 type can be a distinguished name, OBJECT IDENTIFIER, or NULL.

There are two forms of naming for systems management purposes: local or global. For global naming, we start from the root in the containment tree and proceed down the naming tree, concatenating the RDN until we arrive at the managed object desired. In contrast, for the local name of a managed object, we can start from any managed object in the naming tree. However, for OSI systems management, we take the systems managed object as a starting point for local names. The local name of a systems managed object is an empty sequence shown by {}. A local name may not be globally unique.

Let us examine this with the example shown in Figure 3.6. The global name for *tokenRing* is {systemTitle=lansystems1, lanNetworkName=clientserver11, ringName=office3}. In global naming, we use *root* as the reference point. Global names cannot be used for a system when the systemID and systemTitle are both NULL, because this would show that the system is unaware of its global name. In this case, the local name is {lanNetworkName=clientserver11, ringName=office3}. Because a systems managed object is represented by {}, {} is not included in the local name.

3.6 Scoping

When management operations are done on managed objects, *scoping* enters the picture. These management operations are provided by CMIS services. Scoping selects one or more managed objects for management operations such as Action, Delete, Get, and Set requests. The scoping is applied to a naming tree. The base object can be anywhere in a naming tree, but, to be successful, the request should be sent to the agent with the base object. The base object specified in the request is the reference point for scoping operations. Base object level is referred to as level zero, and, sometimes, the subtree below a base object is used in scoping.

There are different levels of scoping, explained as follows:

1. A base object alone is selected. This is the default action for scoping. In Figure 3.7, if the argument of a scoping operation is the base object only and the base object specified in a request is A, then the result is a selection of A. Note that the base object is A.

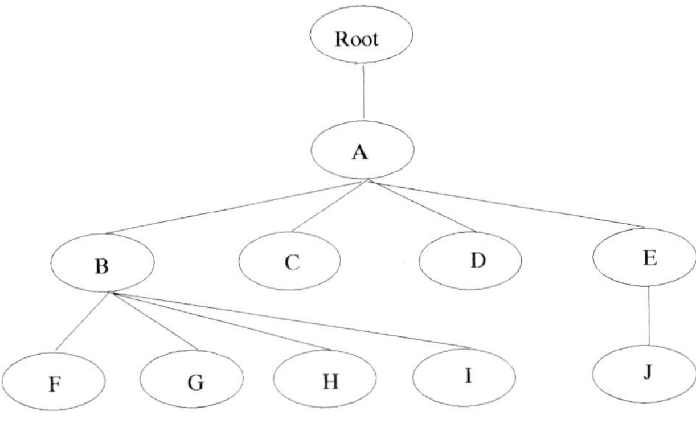

Figure 3.7 Scoping example.

2. The *n*th-level subordinates can be selected. For example, if *n* is the first level in Figure 3.7, the objects selected are B, C, D, and E.
3. Scoping can be applied to objects which include the base object and the subordinates up to the *n*th level. In Figure 3.7, take *n* as one; then managed object A will be selected in addition to B, C, D, and E.
4. Scoping can be extended to cover all objects in the subtree below the base object. If we take A as the base object, the selected objects from this scoped operation, are A, the objects in the first level (B, C, D, and E), and the objects in the second level (F, G, H, I, and J).

3.7 Filtering

Filtering is one more level of selection imposed on scoping. It can be used to choose a subset of managed objects that have been selected by the scoping operation. Those managed objects that have been chosen by scoping are further subjected to conditions furnished by filtering for the selection. If the managed objects pass the conditions, then they are selected; otherwise, they are left out. These conditions are formed by grouping logical operations such as *or, and,* and *not.*

When all conditions are true, the *and* condition is satisfied and becomes true. In the case of the *or* condition, if one or more conditions are true, then the whole condition set is true. In the case of *not,* the condition is true only if the nested filter (a combination of filters) is false.

For evaluating whether an attribute value matches a certain rule, there are matching rules. The first condition is that the attribute must be present. If the attribute is not present, then the comparing value is regarded as false. There are eight explicit matching rules:

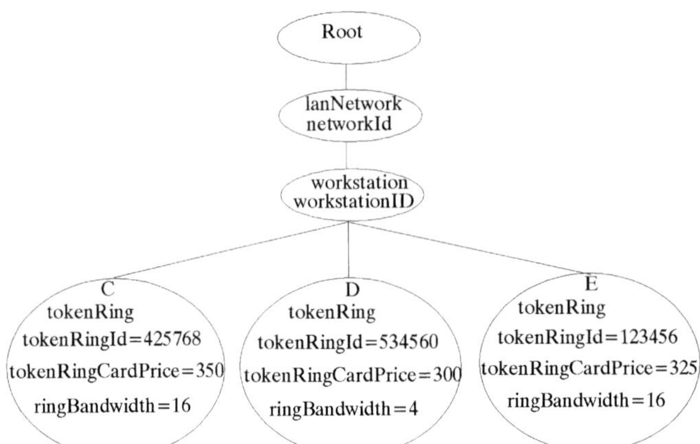

Figure 3.8 Filtering example.

1. *Equality:* We can test an attribute value to equality with an assigned value. As an example, in Figure 3.8, we can test whether *tokenRingCardPrice* has a value of 300. In this case, we get the object instance D. An attribute may have more than one value, in which case, we get a set of values. We can also use a set for comparison. This set also may have one or more members. For a matching rule to become true, members of the comparison set must be equal in value to all members of the attribute set. Otherwise, the matching rule evaluates as false.
2. *Greater than or equal to:* Here, the value supplied for comparison must be equal to or greater than the attribute value. For example, in Figure 3.8, if we take a comparison value of 350, we are looking for object instance values for the attribute *tokenRingCardPrice* of 350 and more. The object instance is C. For sets, the comparison set has only one member. For the matching rule to become true, the value of the member of the comparison set must be greater than or equal to one or more members of the attribute set, or else the matching rule evaluates as false.
3. *Less than or equal to:* In this test, the value used for comparison must be less than or equal to the attribute value. For comparison, let the value be 325. From Figure 3.8, for *tokenRingCardPrice,* the object instances with values less than or equal to 325 are D and E.
4. *Present:* This tests whether an attribute is present, and if so, then the comparison is evaluated as true. The attribute selected may be *collisionRate.* A cursory look at the *tokenRing* managed object class in Figure 3.8 reveals that there is no such attribute. In this case, there are no object instances which can be selected.

5. *Substring:* For this test, the attribute value substring must match the substring furnished for comparison. Let us check in Figure 3.8 for an object instance that has a *tokenRingId* of 123456. On comparing each element of the substring, the object instance of E is obtained.
6. *Subset of:* Here the set for comparison must be a subset of the attribute values. As an example, let the set of *tokenRingId* for comparison be {123456, 325}. On examination of the naming tree in Figure 3.8, only E matches. *Subset of* is applicable only to set-valued attributes.
7. *Superset of:* This test is applicable only to set-valued attributes, and all members must be present in the set presented for comparison. Referring to Figure 3.8 again, for *tokenRingId*, let the set for comparison be {123456, 325, 987234}. On comparison, there is no object instance matching this requirement.
8. *Non-null set intersection:* Again in Figure 3.8, let the set for comparison be {123456, 456789, 987234}. For this to be evaluated as true, there must be at least one *tokenRingId* with one of the above values. In our example, the object instance is again E.

We can combine these simple matching rules, and evaluate them as true or false. For example, let the combination of filters used be (*objectClass*=*tokenRing*) *and* (*tokenRingCardPrice* >= 350). The object instance is just C. For variation, let the combination of filters be (*tokenRingCardPrice*=300) *or* (*ringBandwidth*=16). The object instances are C, D, and E.

3.8 Synchronization

A manager may request from an agent information about how the agent performs operations on behalf of the manager. This is known as *synchronization.* Sometimes operations are performed on more than one managed object. Synchronization is part of a managed object behavior definition. We will examine what behavior means in relation to the definition of a managed object in Section 6.4.5.

Synchronization does not apply to a Create operation on an object. Here, intermediate operations are not visible. When operations on objects such as Get, Set, and Action include scoping, the issue of synchronization arises. The operations that can be performed on managed objects are explained in the next chapter. The synchronization operation can be of two types. The first is *atomic* synchronization, which is an all or nothing proposition. An initial check is made as to whether it is possible to satisfy the request for all objects. If it is not possible to retrieve all the objects, say for a Get, then an error is returned. Otherwise, all the objects are returned. The second type of synchronization is known as *best effort* synchronization. For example, for a Get operation, all retrievals are tried and whichever objects can be retrieved are returned. For those cases where retrieval fails, an error is returned.

3.9 Polymorphism

Polymorphism means having many forms and is primarily an object-ed-oriented concept. Managed object classes that respond to a common operation in a similar manner are said to exhibit the property of polymorphism. Referring to Figure 3.9, let us assume that we have many managed object classes in an undergraduate level based on a student's major. Thus, there are managed object classes such as *computerScienceStudent, computerEngineeringStudent,* and so on. Suppose we have an operation such as Grading for the managed object class *underGraduateStudent.* As a result of the property of inheritance, this operation of Grading will be inherited by *computerScienceStudent* and *computerEngineeringStudent,* and may need only slight modifications for the subclasses of *computerScienceStudent* and *electricalEngineeringStudent.* Here the managed object classes *computerScienceStudent* and *computerEngineeringStudent* are known as polymorphic.

3.10 Allomorphism

Allomorphism refers to the ability of one object instance to function as if it were part of more than one object class. To understand this concept, let us slightly modify our earlier example. Assume that a student, Joe Smith, is majoring in computer science. Further assume that we have managed object classes *xUniversityStudent, underGraduateStudent,* and *computerScienceStudent. Joe Smith* can

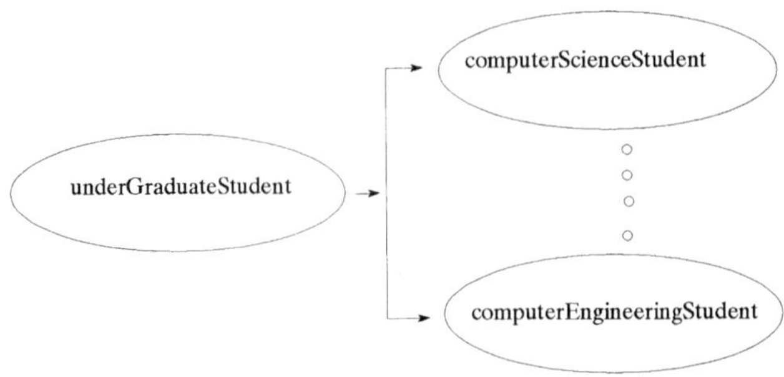

Figure 3.9 Polymorphism example.

be taken as an instance of the managed object class *computerScienceStudent.* However, the object instance *Joe Smith* can also be part of the managed object classes *underGraduateStudent* and *xUniversityStudent.* Here, *Joe Smith* has the characteristics of allomorphism. Allomorphism is used in OSI systems management to migrate to newer versions of the old or obsolete objects.

3.11 Management State

State describes operational and availability conditions of a managed object at a specific time. These conditions are included when appropriate in the definition of a managed object class as attributes. It is necessary to standardize the state for management purposes.

Management state attributes are broadly classified as *generic state* attributes and *status* attributes. The status attributes furnish further information on generic state attributes. The generic state attributes are operational, usage, and administrative, as shown in Figure 3.10. The status attributes used for management purposes are *alarm, procedural, availability, control, standby*, and *unknown*.

3.11.1 Generic state attributes

The *operational* state attribute indicates whether a resource is working. Management operation can only read the operational state of a managed object; hence, this state has only a read operation and is single-valued. There are two values for this attribute: *disabled* and *enabled.* When the operational state is not known, then the unknown status attribute with a value of true is used to reflect this condition.

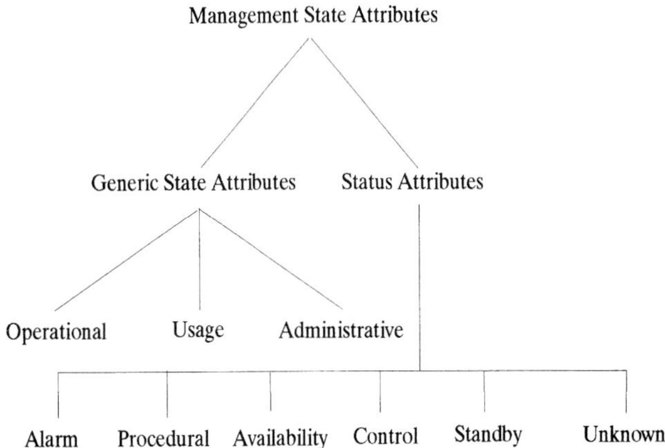

Figure 3.10 Management state attributes.

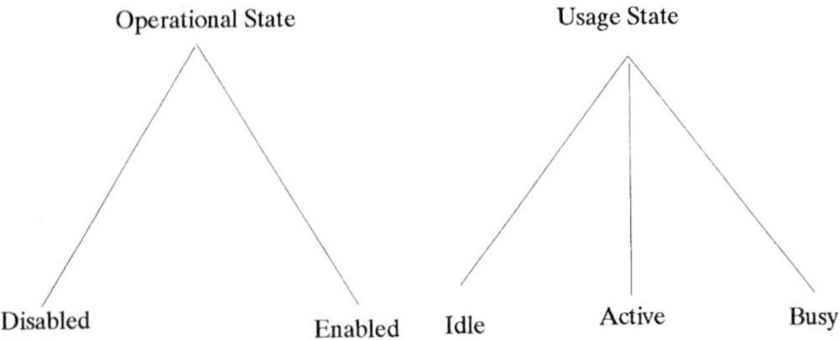

Figure 3.11 Operational and usage state values.

The *usage* state defines whether a resource is being actively used at a particular time. It mentions whether additional users can use this resource. There are three values: *idle, active,* and *busy.* The usage state attribute is also a read-only and single-valued attribute. When only one user is involved, the possible values are idle or busy. When a resource has an unlimited number of users, then the possible values are idle or active. As in the operational state, when resource state details cannot be furnished by the usage state, the unknown status attribute with a value of true is used. Operational and usage state values are shown in Figure 3.11.

The *administrative* state indicates how a resource is used under management operations. The possible values are *locked, unlocked,* or *shutting down,* as shown in Figure 3.12. Some managed object classes have only a subset of the three values. In some cases, there is no unlocked state. In some other cases, the shutting down value is absent, if there is no graceful shutdown characteristic. Administrative state values are stated while defining managed objects. Note also that the administrative state attribute is read-write and single-valued. That means that one can read the value of an attribute by using a Get operation and change the value by doing a Set operation.

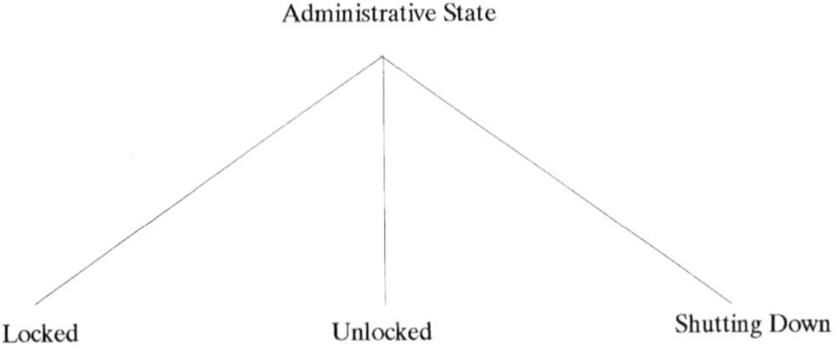

Figure 3.12 Administrative state values.

When defining a managed object class, it is possible to have one or more generic state attributes. However, when defining values, one must make sure that these values represent only a valid combination of possible values.

3.11.2 Status attributes

Status attributes furnish further details on the generic state attributes, such as *operational*, *usage*, or *administrative*. The status attributes defined are shown in Figure 3.10. Let us examine these status attributes individually.

The *alarm* status attribute indicates the status of alarms that have been generated. It can have a value of *under repair,* which states that the resource is being repaired. The values of *critical, major,* and *minor* indicate that one or more alarms have been detected and they have not been cleared. The possible alarm status values are shown in Figure 3.13. In all of these cases, including the under repair value, the operational state can be enabled or disabled. The last possible value, *alarm outstanding,* states that one or more alarms are outstanding against the resource and the condition due to these alarms may or may not have been disabled. It is not necessary that the alarm status attribute have values. Instead, this attribute may be an empty set, which indicates that none of the aforementioned values are present. The alarm status attribute is read-write, indicating that one can perform Get and Set operations.

The *procedural* status attribute is used when a resource has many phases of operations. If this value attribute is an empty set, then the managed object representing the resource is *ready.* This attribute has many possible values, as shown in Figure 3.14. One of them is *initialization required,* which indicates that this managed object has to be initialized before it can perform its normal role, and the operational state is disabled. On the contrary, a value of *not initialized* indicates that the managed object is capable of initializing itself and needs no

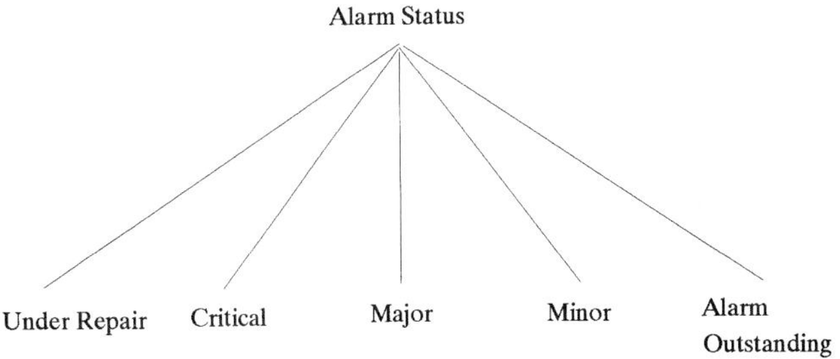

Figure 3.13 Alarm status values.

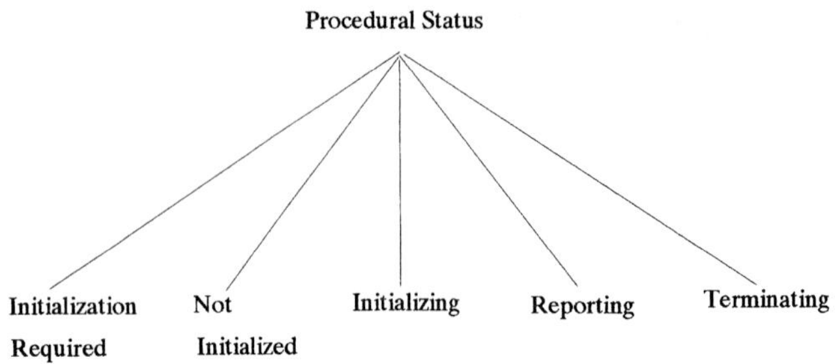

Figure 3.14 Procedural status values.

initialization to perform its normal functioning; however, initialization has not been started. The operational state here can be enabled or disabled. The value of *initializing* indicates that the initialization process is in progress, and the operational state may be disabled or enabled, depending on the definition of the managed object class. *Reporting* states that it is reporting the results of the operation that has been done, and the operational state is enabled. As the name suggests, the *terminating* value states that the resource is in a termination phase. Also, it is not necessary to have one of these values for an attribute; the value of an attribute can be an empty set.

The *availability* status attribute indicates whether a managed object is available. It has values of *in test, failed, power off, off line, off duty, dependency, degraded, not installed,* or *log full* (see Figure 3.15). Here, off line indicates that the operational state is disabled and needs some sort of intervention to make it available for use. Dependency states that some dependent resource is unavailable and the operational state is disabled. Other values are obvious, so the meanings are not discussed. Availability status is a read-only attribute. It is worth noting that the alarm, procedural, and availability status attributes add further meaning to the operational state attribute. As mentioned earlier in the case of other status attributes, this attribute can be an empty set, too.

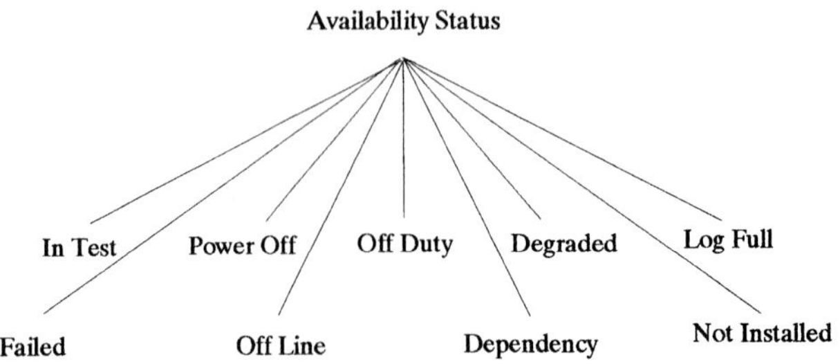

Figure 3.15 Availability status values.

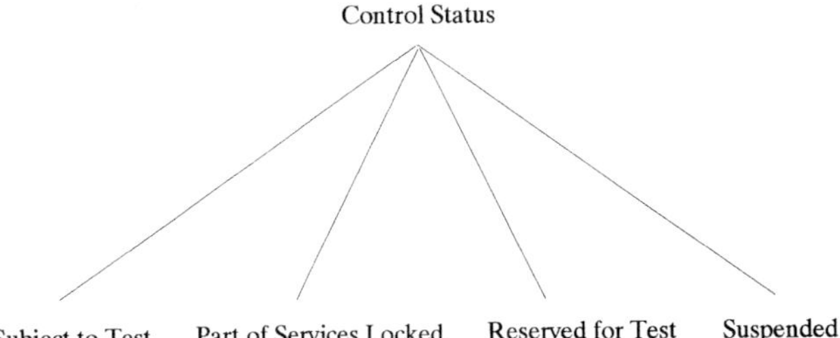

Figure 3.16 Control status values.

The *control* status attribute is read and write, and the values are (see Figure 3.16) *subject to test, part of services locked, reserved for test,* or *suspended.* The value of *subject to test* indicates that the resource may be subjected to tests during normal operation, and it may sometimes lead to abnormal behavior. *Part of services locked* means that some services of a resource may not be available for users. *Reserved for test* states that a resource is not available for normal users and is undergoing a test. *Suspended* indicates that a resource is not available for users.

The *standby* status attribute states the condition of a backup resource. This is a read-only attribute, and its possible values are shown in Figure 3.17. The value of *hot standby* means that the standby resource does not need initialization and contains all the information of the resource which the standby resource is backing up; thus, whenever a resource needs the backup to take over, the backup will be immediately available. However, in the case of *cold standby,* the backup resource needs some sort of initialization before it can take over from a resource. The value of *providing service* states that backup operation is already being done by the backup resource. *Unknown status* is used when the state of a resource is not known.

In addition to the state and status attributes used when defining a managed object class, there is also an attribute group of *state,* which represents a collection of all the state attributes. By using the state

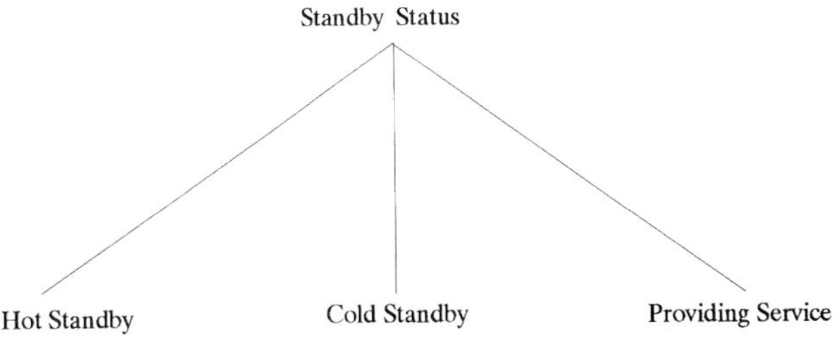

Figure 3.17 Standby status values.

attribute group, it is easier to perform management operations on the collection, because this avoids the need for the same management operation on each individual state attribute. In Section 6.4.3, we will examine in detail the meaning of attribute groups.

Whenever there are changes in the management state attributes of a managed object, an agent will send an M-EVENT-REPORT to the manager. This M-EVENT-REPORT can be a confirmed or nonconfirmed service. The parameters in M-EVENT-REPORT for reporting management state changes are *event type, event information,* and *event reply.* Here, we must be clear that the management state includes generic states and status.

Let us briefly look into the parameters and the values that go in these parameters when using M-EVENT-REPORT to report management state changes. Event type is used to report a change in the value of a state attribute. Event information furnishes details of the event due to a change in state and has a source indicator with three values: *resource operation, management operation,* and *unknown.* Event information also has an *attribute identifier list* and a *state change definition.* The state change definition has an *attribute identifier, old attribute value,* and *new attribute value.* There is no event reply parameter specified for the state change notification. In addition, the parameters used with M-EVENT-REPORT, such as notification identifier, correlated notification, additional text, and additional information, can also be used to furnish further details on state change. We will revisit M-EVENT-REPORT, along with the parameters used, in Section 4.7.1.

3.12 Attributes for Relationships

A system may consist of many managed objects. If so, how these objects are related or grouped becomes important. It is also important to know how relationships change when certain operations are done. For this, the relationship attribute *role* is used. The role attribute may have a single value or a set of values. A managed object class such as *printerUsed* may have another backup managed object class such as *printerBackup.* How these managed object classes are related and how the backup managed object class *printerBackup* behaves when the original managed object class *printerUsed* fails is important.

There are different kinds of relationships. Two managed objects have a *direct* relationship if one object explicitly states how it is connected to the other managed object. In Figure 3.18, the role attribute states that managed object X is connected to managed object Y.

The relationship becomes *indirect* if it is via one or more managed objects. Again referring to Figure 3.18, managed objects X and Y and

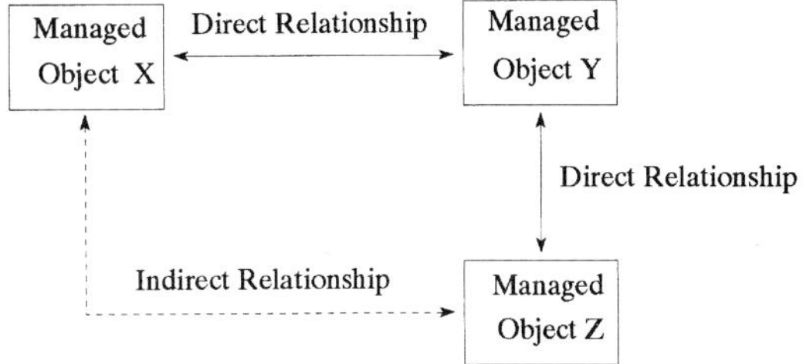

Figure 3.18 Direct and indirect relationships.

managed objects Y and Z have a direct relationship, whereas managed objects X and Z have an indirect relationship. The relationship between X and Z is necessarily derived from managed objects X, Y, and Z.

Two managed objects have a *symmetric* relationship (Figure 3.19) if both managed objects have the same role attribute and the rules of interaction are similar. As an example, two teachers may be teaching different sections of the same course. They may choose to grade and give similar tests to students. In another course, teachers teaching different sections may have their own independent styles of testing and grading. Here, the roles and rules governing the teacher and students are different. This is known as an *asymmetric* relationship (Figure 3.19).

When we define managed objects, we need specific definitions for the relationships. Without these, a relationship in different contexts may mean different things to different people. For example, two closely related companies may each have a CEO who is a member of the board of directors of the other company. Here the relationship roles are *reciprocal,* meaning that the relationships of both objects can be indicated by the definitions of the relationship of one of the managed objects to the other. This relationship need not necessarily be one-to-one. Instead, there can be more than one one-to-one relationship.

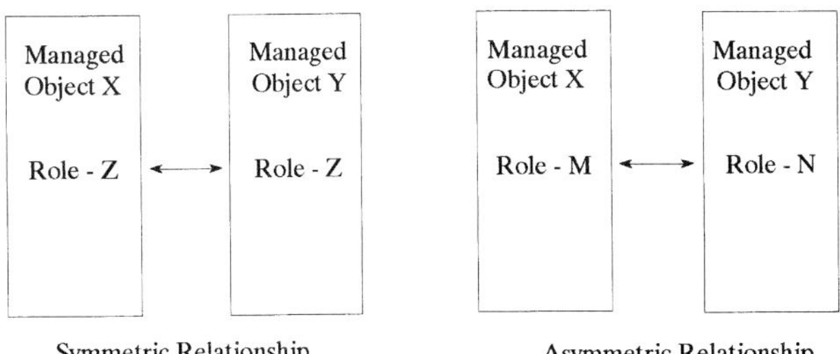

Figure 3.19 Symmetric and asymmetric relationships.

These reciprocal relationships can be changed by management operations such as Delete, Create, or Replace. When a relationship of one managed object is deleted, then the relationship of the other managed object is automatically deleted. When there is a change in relationship, then notification is emitted by the appropriate managed object. The information on a relationship can be obtained by doing a Get operation on the role attribute.

In a *one-way* relationship, one managed object is related to another managed object. In the previous example of the CEOs and boards of directors of two companies, assume that company A takes over company B. Here, only the CEO of company A sits on the board of company B; the CEO of company B does not sit on the board of company A. The relationship has been reduced to a one-way relationship. Management operations such as Delete, Create, or Replace can also be performed on a one-way relationship.

When two or more objects are related to one another, the type of role attribute specifies the nature of the relationship between managed objects. Refer to the two managed objects, X and Y, shown in Figure 3.19. The relationship between these two managed objects can be one-way or reciprocal, depending on how the attribute roles are defined in the two managed objects. If only managed object X's role attribute M has the relationship specified to managed object Y, then there is a one-way relationship. However, if the role attributes of both managed objects X and Y specify each other in the relationships, then there is a reciprocal relationship.

Various relationship types used for management purposes are shown in Figure 3.20. In a *service* relationship, priority must be used in the role attribute if there is more than one managed object forming a relationship. For example, assume that one provider object services more than one user-managed object. In such a situation, how the user-managed object makes use of the services of the provider object is governed by the priorities attached to the relationships in the user-

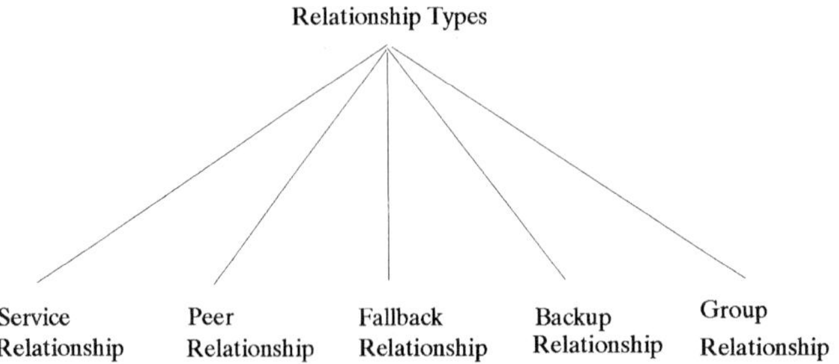

Figure 3.20 Relationship types.

managed object. A provider object acts in a service provider role, and a user object has a service user role.

When more than one provider-managed object is involved with a user-managed object, priorities in relationships are necessary. For example, a car (user object) may have to go to one service station for an oil change and another service station for brake repairs (providers).

Another type of relationship is that of *peers,* which is a symmetric relationship where similar managed objects communicate. For example, two professors teaching the same course in a school can be termed peers. One teacher may be senior faculty and the other may be a rookie. The senior teacher may not bother much about the rookie, but the rookie may consult the senior teacher on each and every issue. This is a one-way peer relationship.

Conversely, the senior teacher may wish to be a mentor to the rookie. Both may decide that they will closely follow one another and work as a team. This is a reciprocal peer relationship. As mentioned previously regarding reciprocal relationships, the role attributes of the managed objects refer to each other.

A *fallback* relationship is another popular type of relationship (see Figure 3.21). The fallback relationship is provided by indicating the role attribute of managed objects as primary or secondary. Managed objects Y and Z in Figure 3.21 have fallback relationship R_{YZ}. This relationship states that managed object Z is capable of providing backup service if managed object Y is incapable of providing service, but it does not indicate that Z is presently providing the backup service for Y.

The relationship between managed objects Y and Z is asymmetric. Here also, as seen earlier, there can be one-way or reciprocal relationships, depending on the definitions in the role attributes. When there is more than one backup object, the order in which fallback relationships are selected is determined by the priorities attached to the rela-

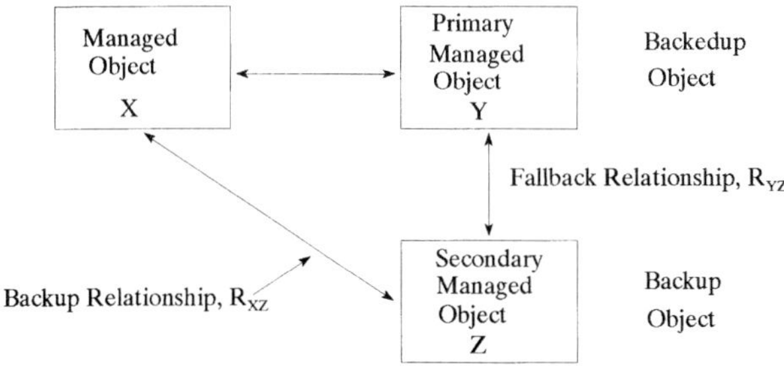

Figure 3.21 Fallback relationship.

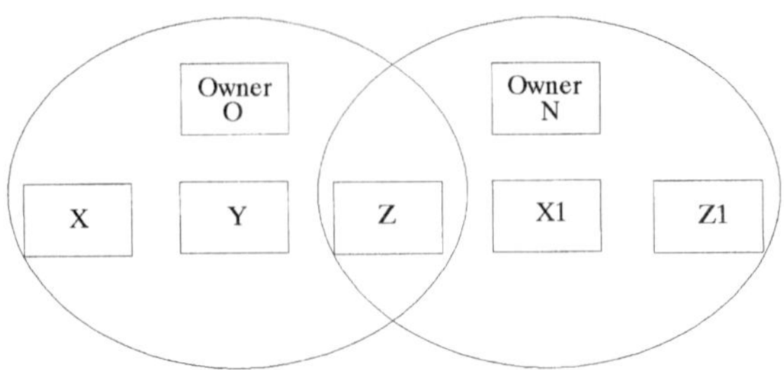

Figure 3.22 Group relationship.

tionships. The backup object in a fallback relationship must be in the unlocked administrative state.

When managed object Y fails and backup managed object Z provides the service, the relationship between the managed objects X and Z is denoted by the backup relationship R_{XZ}. This indicates that the backup managed object is providing the service. When the backed-up managed object Y resumes operation, the backup managed object Z will not be providing the service. A backup relationship may also have one-way and reciprocal relationships. Note that the creation or deletion of backup relationship R_{XZ} has no effect on the fallback relationship R_{YZ}.

A *group* relationship is illustrated in Figure 3.22. Grouping is an important concept used to combine managed objects based on functions, administrative reasons, or convenience for management purposes. As shown in the figure, managed object O is the owner, and managed objects X, Y, and Z are members in the group. Similarly, managed object N is the owner in the group, and managed objects Z, X1, and Z1 are members of this group. Notice that member object Z is common to both groups. In the group relationship, too, there can be one-way and reciprocal relationships. It should be noted that membership in a group can be changed and there are no restrictions that groups must be permanent once formed.

Attributes used for relationships are shown in Figure 3.23. In addition to these attributes, there is an attribute group for relationships.

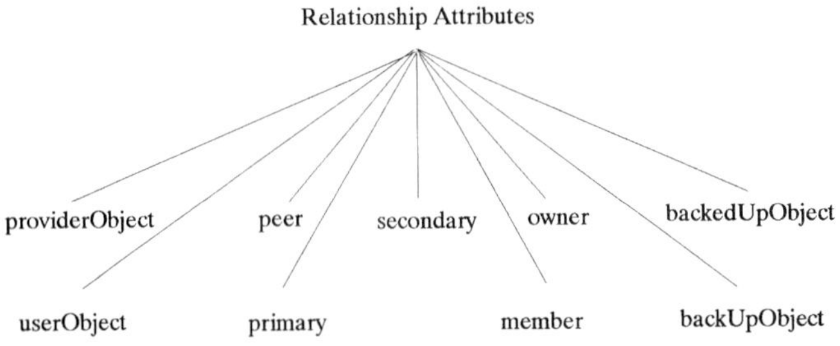

Figure 3.23 Management relationship attributes.

When a relationship changes, notification is emitted. This notification can be sent as an M-EVENT-REPORT. An agent sends M-EVENT-REPORTs to a manager. Parameters of an M-EVENT-REPORT are tailored to identify managed objects participating in a relationship and changes in the relationship. Details of the parameters of M-EVENT-REPORT for reporting relationship changes can be found in ISO 10164-3 (Reference 3.2).

3.13 General Relationship Model

ISO 10165-7, the General Relationship Model (Reference 3.3) primarily describes how to represent relationships between resources and the management operations that can be done on relationships. Managed objects can be tied to one another for management purposes by managed relationships, and the managed relationships which share the same definition can be grouped as a managed relationship class. A manager uses the managed relationships, and these managed relationships are useful for different systems management functions, especially for configuration management.

Management operations that can be performed on a managed relationship are BIND, ESTABLISH, NOTIFY, QUERY, TERMINATE, UNBIND, and USER DEFINED. The meanings of some of the management operations are obvious, so we will discuss only some of them. BIND refers to associating a managed object with a relationship. ESTABLISH stands for forming a managed relationship. NOTIFY is used to report on events associated with managed relationships. USER DEFINED, as the name suggests, can be used to carry a user-defined management operation. These management operations are mapped to systems management operations such as attribute-based and managed object–based management operations.

For relationships, *relationshipObjectSuperClass* under *top* is defined. This managed object class contains the relationship attribute group and the following attributes:

- *Relationship name:* Used for naming relationship objects
- *Relationship class:* Identifies the relationship class
- *Role binding:* Specifies how a managed relationship is represented

We have briefly discussed the General Relationship Model, but for further details, readers should consult ISO 10165-7 (Reference 3.3)

3.14 Changeover Function

ISO 10164-17, the Changeover Function document (Reference 3.4), discusses the functioning of backup service. Backup service relates to how a backup for a managed object is done and how it is terminated. We have already examined backup and fallback relationships in Figure 3.21. Changeover action causes a backup object to start backing up another backed-up object, and this operation is terminated by a changeback action.

A user can request backup services with a *changeOver* operation. Conversely, the backup services are terminated by a *changeBack* action. Both operations are in confirmed mode. Parameters used in changeOver and changeBack are furnished in ISO 10164-17 (Reference 3.4), and these operations are sent in the form M-ACTION from a manager to an agent.

3.15 Summary

In this chapter, we first introduced the concepts of management domain and management information hierarchies. We also examined how managed objects and agents communicate. While discussing management information hierarchies, we examined three different types of hierarchies: registration, inheritance, and containment.

The important concept of naming a managed object was examined in detail. Scoping and filtering were also discussed with examples, as were synchronization, polymorphism, allomorphism, management state attributes, and role attributes which govern the relationship between different managed objects.

3.16 References

3.1 ISO IS 10040 (X.701), Information Technology, Open Systems Interconnection, Systems Management Overview, 1992.
3.2 ISO 10164-3 (X.732), Information Technology, Open Systems Interconnection, Systems Management, Part 3: Attributes for Representing Relationships, 1992.
3.3 ISO 10165-7, Information Technology, Open Systems Interconnection, Structure of Management Information, Part 7: General Relationship Model, 1994.
3.4 ISO CD 10164-17, Information Technology, Open Systems Interconnection, Systems Management, Part 17: Change Over Function, 1994.

3.17 Further Reading

ISO 9834-1 (X.660), Information Technology, Open Systems Interconnection, Procedures for the Operation of OSI Registration Authorities, Part 1: General Procedures, 1993.
ISO 10164-2 (X.731), Information Technology, Open Systems Interconnection, Systems Management, Part 2: State Management Function, 1992.
ISO CD 10164-19, Information Technology, Open Systems Interconnection, Systems Management, Part 19: Management Domain and Management Policy Management Function, 1994.
ISO IS 10165-1 (X.720), Information Technology, Open Systems Interconnection, Structure of Management Information, Part 1: Management Information Model, 1992.

Chapter

4

Systems Management Support Functions

4.1 Introduction

In Chapter 2 (Sections 2.4 and 2.5), we discussed important concepts such as manager and agent. Management information must be communicated between a manager and agents. Without this, a manager cannot know what is happening in the objects under the control of agents. To build any useful system management functional applications, a manager needs to gather management information on objects and, sometimes, store it. For gathering this management information, there are rules governing the establishment and release of the connection between manager and agents.

Also, there are management protocols between manager and agents which must be explored. How frames are formed and carried between a manager and agents is examined in this chapter. We must note here that OSI standards furnish generic descriptions of services and protocols and rules for communications between peer systems. It is up to users to interpret these services and protocols and package them into meaningful profiles of management protocols between manager and agents. OSI standards also furnish generic definitions, such as those for service providers and service users. However, these terms have to be tailored to suit the system management requirements.

4.2 Application Layer Component Concepts

The topmost layer of the OSI reference model is the application layer. The application-layer functions and functions below the application layer are used by the *application process* (AP). Figure 4.1 illustrates

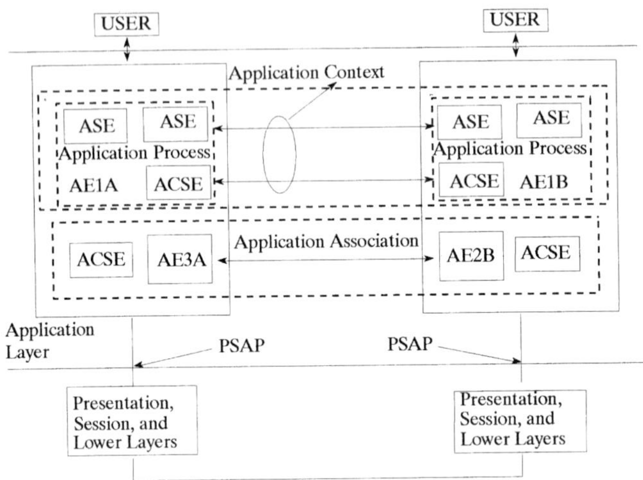

Figure 4.1 Concepts of application process, application entity, application context, and application association.

the concept of an AP. An AP combines all the information processing and communication aspects that are grouped together and given a single name for remote reference. An example of an AP is retrieval of information from a database. This database may be in another open system, so the retrieval will include different aspects such as establishment of an association and communication of the command, in turn consisting of query, receiving the response, and processing and presenting the response.

One AP may use one or more *application entities* (AEs) to represent its communications aspects. The application layer appears as a collection of AEs, each of which includes information for communicating with another peer AE. AEs use the immediate lower layer of presentation services to carry out the communication with each other. A cooperative logical connection between two AEs is known as an *application association* (AA). See Figure 4.1 for a depiction of an AA.

Functions of AEs required for cooperative processing are broken down further into *application service elements* (ASEs). These ASEs represent a collection of communication capabilities packaged into a module. One ASE may communicate with another ASE in the same application layer or with ASEs in other peer open systems using lower layers. They have their own service definitions and protocol specifications.

There are generic ASEs such as the *association control service element* (ACSE) and the *remote operations service element* (ROSE), as well as specialized ASEs such as the *common management information service element* (CMISE), the *systems management application service element* (SMASE), and *file transfer, access, and management*

(FTAM). The *reliable transfer service element* (RTSE) is used for bulk data transfers. Because the RTSE is not used in OSI management, we will not discuss it here.

There are advantages to classifying functions into generic ASEs. For example, if the establishment of an association for the transfer of messages such as in e-mail or a message handling system (MHS) is required, an ACSE can be used instead of "reinventing the wheel" to establish the connection. Then for any specific portion of the MHS, an MHS ASE can be used.

Let us return to the topic of the application context (AC), which was discussed in Section 2.5. For interoperability, ASEs and the rules for using them are grouped into identifiable ACs (see Figure 4.1). This application context is identified by an *application context name,* which is an ASN.1 object identifier. An application context assists in the cooperative working of AEs. This is one of the important parameters used during association or connection establishment. A run-time instance of an ASE is known as an *ASE invocation.* A collection of these invocations is known as a *control function* (CF).

4.3 Systems Management Service Elements

ASEs such as ACSE, ROSE, CMISE, and SMASE are used by a systems management application entity (SMAE), as shown in Figure 4.2. SMASE is used to form *management application protocol data units* (MAPDUs). These MAPDUs and pass-through CMIP APDUs carry management information from one SMAE to another SMAE. The communication of management information between SMAEs is car-

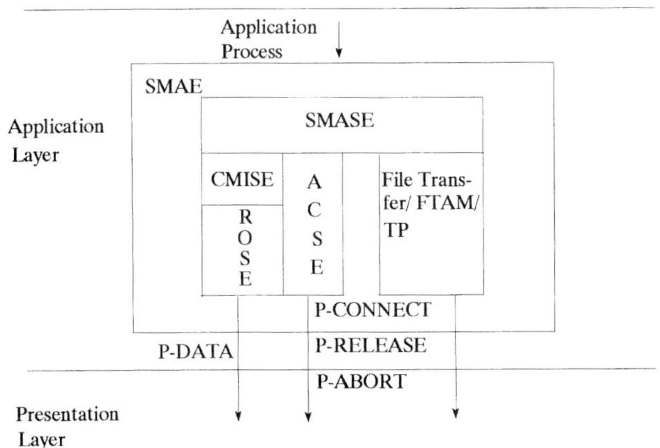

Figure 4.2 Relationship between systems management service elements.

ried out by the *common management information protocol* (CMIP), or possibly with other communication services provided by ASEs such as *file transfer* or *transaction processing* (TP).

In TP, the key concept is *transaction.* The properties of a transaction are atomicity, consistency, isolation, and durability. Atomicity means that either all operations of a unit of work are performed or none of the operations are performed. Consistency refers to the units of work being performed accurately, correctly, and with validity. By isolation, we mean that partial results of a unit of work are not available. And durability represents the characteristic whereby a failure or any other action does not affect the results of the unit of work performed.

SMASE uses CMIS services. This frame is formed in CMISE, then transformed into the CMIP protocol frame in the *common management information protocol machine* (CMIPM). Here CMIPM is a *finite state machine* (FSM). The CMIP APDU has the appropriate ROSE headers to form the frame suitable for transfer of management data via underlying presentation services to another SMAE.

However, initially, for the communication to take place between SMAEs, an association must be formed. This is a sufficiently complex operation. Two SMAEs involved in forming an association must support similar *functional units.* A functional unit is an abstract concept used for combining service options. These functional units assist in providing systems management services. It may be noted here that there are functional units for the presentation layer, as well as for the session layer. If functional units between two SMAEs are similar, there is not much of a problem. But there may be cases where functional units supported by SMAEs are not similar. For this reason, during association, the characteristics of the association need to be negotiated. This is done with the help of ACSE services. Successful interoperability is improved by the use of a standardized application context and standard profile which specifies common application-, presentation-, and session-layer options.

4.4 ACSE Services

For systems management purposes, management information needs to be transferred between a manager and agents. For data transfer between a manager and agents, a connection or association must be established initially. In addition, there should be the ability to release the connection when a manager and an agent do not want to communicate any longer. The ACSE services used for establishing an association and, subsequently, releasing the association formed are shown in Table 4.1. Release of an association means orderly closing and, in some cases, aborting the association. The prefix "A-" is added to ACSE services to distinguish them from other application-layer services.

TABLE 4.1 Application Control Service Element (ACSE)

Services	Type
A-ASSOCIATE	Confirmed
A-RELEASE	Confirmed
A-ABORT	Nonconfirmed
A-P-ABORT	Provider-initiated

ACSE services have the following two modes of operation:

- *Normal mode:* Used in OSI management. In normal mode, ACSE services use presentation and session services, and A-ASSOCIATE services furnish the parameters of both presentation and session services. In normal mode, session services–layer restrictions such as length must also be taken into consideration.
- *X.410-1984 mode:* Originally used with the MHS for ACSE. This mode uses a null presentation layer, and A-ASSOCIATE services do not provide presentation and session services parameters. There may be applications using this X.410-1984 mode, so for backward compatibility with the ACSE services of applications using the X.410-1984 mode, this mode has been provided. This mode is not used in OSI management.

ACSE services subsequently explained assume underlying connection-oriented services. ACSE services have also been defined for the connectionless mode of transmission. The major difference is that, in the connectionless mode of transmission, the presentation- and session-layer parameters must be specified in each service primitive. In connection-oriented transmission, once a connection is established, we need not provide all the presentation- and session-layer parameters all over again. We can reuse the knowledge of the connection already made. Also, in the connectionless mode of transmission, A-UNIT-DATA, used by the user of ACSE, gets converted to P-UNIT-DATA in the presentation layer.

4.4.1 ACSE application protocol data units (APDUs)

ACSE uses the following APDUs:

- *Application association request (AARQ):* A-ASSOCIATE.req gets mapped to AARQ by the ACSE service provider.
- *Application association response (AARE):* A-ASSOCIATE.rsp gets converted to AARE.

- *Release request* (*RLRQ*): A-RELEASE.req becomes RLRQ.
- *Release response* (*RLRE*): A-RELEASE.rsp gets converted to RLRE.
- *Abort* (*ABRT*): A-ABORT.req or A-P-ABORT.ind becomes ABRT.

4.4.2 A-ASSOCIATE

During the connection establishment phase, each side must agree on how they are going to exchange information. This phase is done by A-ASSOCIATE. It is during this phase that the application context and the rules for coordinating different ASEs are made. Here, negotiations on the functional units are also to be done. One of the functional units is the *negotiated release* functional unit. A-ASSOCIATE is a confirmed service, indicating that a reply is required.

A requestor sends its list of parameters and, on the other end, the acceptor may agree to the list furnished. Or else, the acceptor may send its own list of rules for communicating. If the requestor can use this list, then there is no problem. If the requestor cannot communicate with the list of the acceptor, it can send an ABORT.req.

In the following explanations, the terms *Calling, Called,* and *Responding* are used. Calling refers to the requestor of A-ASSOCIATE. Called corresponds to the intended acceptor of A-ASSOCIATE, while Responding is the actual receiver of A-ASSOCIATE. This distinction between Called and Responding is made because the actual receiver and intended acceptor of A-ASSOCIATE can be different in some cases. For example, there can be an alternate receiver of A-ASSOCIATE if the original A-ASSOCIATE fails for some reason or if the called address is a generic one. A-ASSOCIATE parameters for the X.410-1984 mode are as follows:

- *Mode:* This can be X.410-1984. Normal Mode is the default mode.
- *User Information:* This can be used by the requestor and acceptor to carry information to either end. One such example is forwarding passwords or keys to the other end. The AC may specify how this field is used and how the ASEs included are used in the AC.
- *Result:* The result of the association negotiation from the other (acceptor) side is provided in this field. It has three values: accepted, rejected (permanent), or rejected (transient). We have seen the action when an association and its terms are accepted. What happens when the other side is not able to accept the association and its associated terms? In this case, either *rejected* (*permanent*) or *rejected* (*transient*) is in the Result parameter, and the association is not established.

- *Result Source:* If an association is accepted by the acceptor, then this parameter has the value of the acceptor. On the other hand, if the association is rejected, then it will have the value of the service user, service provider, or presentation service provider.
- *Diagnostic:* This parameter can be used for providing diagnostic information, including specifically the reasons for rejecting an association.
- *Presentation Address (Calling, Called, and Responding):* These are respective presentation service access point (PSAP) addresses of the supporting presentation layer.
- *Quality of Service:* This indicates characteristics of services provided by the sessions layer, such as error rates, throughput, and others.
- *Session Requirements:* These provide for the negotiation of functional units.
- *Initial Synchronization Point Serial Number:* When we restart a session, it is resumed from this point.
- *Initial Assignment of Tokens:* This can be used for token assignments for purposes such as synchronization.
- *Session-Connection Identifier:* This is used to distinguish one connection from another.

In Normal Mode, A-ASSOCIATE has the following additional parameters:

- *Application Context Name:* This is a mandatory parameter and specifies the AC name chosen by the requestor. The acceptor on the other end may return the same AC name, indicating that it agrees with the AC that will be used. The acceptor may also suggest a different AC. If the requestor agrees, then there is no problem; otherwise, the requestor will issue an A-ABORT.req.
- *AP Title (Calling, Called, and Responding):* This field has a string associated with an AP.
- *AP Invocation-Identifier (Calling, Called, and Responding):* Each AP invocation is provided with a unique integer value to clearly identify one AP invocation from another AP invocation.
- *AE Qualifier (Calling, Called, and Responding):* This is a string provided to identify an AE with an AP.
- *AE Invocation-Identifier (Calling, Called, and Responding):* This is a unique integer value for an AE to identify an AE invocation.

- *Presentation Context Definition List:* This provides abstract syntaxes and their presentation context identifier (PCI) values.
- *Presentation Context Definition Result List:* This refers to the abstract syntaxes and PCI values of the responding presentation service provider from the acceptor.
- *Default Presentation Context Name:* The abstract syntax name is provided for default conditions.
- *Default Presentation Context Result:* This is, again, the abstract syntax name of the responding service provider.
- *Presentation Requirements:* Functional units which may be used by the user of presentation services such as an AE are indicated in this parameter.

In the preceding explanations, presentation parameters are governed by ISO-8822, the Connection-Oriented Presentation Service Definition. Similarly, the ISO-8326, Basic Connection-Oriented Service Definition, describes the session-layer parameters. Let us examine further how the associations between two AEs are formed. These AEs can be between a manager and an agent or two managers acting as peers. A user of an ACSE sends an A-ASSOCIATE.req to the ACSE. This A-ASSOCIATE.req gets converted to AARQ and is wrapped with the headers of P-CONNECT. AARQ becomes user data in P-CONNECT.req PPDU. This becomes user data for S-CONNECT.req SPDU in the session layer. In the transport layer, it becomes T-DATA.req. T-DATA.req is sent to the other end. In Figure 4.3, OSI lower layers refer to the layers below the session layer of the OSI seven-layer model. In other words, it includes layers such as the transport layer, network layer, data link layer, and physical layer. In Figure 4.3, for the X.410-1984 mode there is no presentation layer.

On the other end, another ACSE service user receives the frame as A-ASSOCIATE.ind. If the ACSE and AE are able to accept the terms of the association, the receiver of the ACSE forms A-ASSOCIATE.rsp, and the ACSE service provider converts to AARE and packages it with the header of P-CONNECT. Here we are making the assumption that we are in Normal Mode and are using presentation services. The AARE goes all the way down again picking the necessary headers and reaches the other end. The requesting ACSE service provider receives the AARE and converts it to A-ASSOCIATE.conf.

After having sent A-ASSOCIATE.req, an AE cannot send another service request, such as another A-ASSOCIATE.req, to the same recipient. It can send only A-ABORT.req to stop the association establishment procedures. A-ABORT.req is turned into A-ABORT.ind on the other end of ACSE, and the association is, naturally, not established.

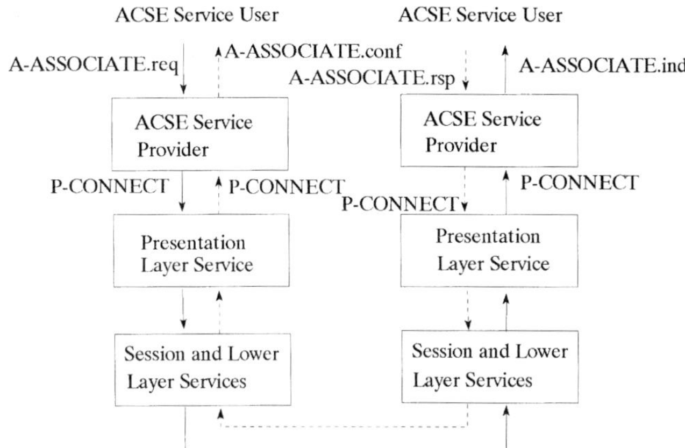

Figure 4.3 Functioning of A-ASSOCIATE (normal mode).

4.4.3 A-RELEASE

Once an association is established, obviously there is also a need to end the association when it is no longer needed. For this purpose, A-RELEASE is used. The key here is that no data or information in transit is lost. This is an orderly release. A-RELEASE can be sent from either the AE in a manager or the AE in an agent. This is a confirmed service indicating that a reply on this operation is required. However, if a negotiated functional unit has been agreed upon during association, then the session layer takes over the release of the connection.

A-RELEASE has the following parameters:

- *Reason:* In A-RELEASE.req, this indicates how an association must be terminated: as normal, urgent, or user-defined. In turn, the acceptor on the other end states in the Reason parameter of A-RELEASE.rsp one of the three values: normal, not finished, or user-defined. The acceptor may indicate that it has been accepted or that the data is remaining and there is flexibility on the part of an acceptor defining its own values for the user-defined values. This parameter is used in Normal Mode only.
- *User Information:* As is obvious from the name of the parameter, this consists of user data permitted within the rules set by the AC and the ASEs used. This parameter is used in Normal Mode only.
- *Result:* This is a mandatory parameter in response and confirm. Result is used by the acceptor to indicate whether or not the acceptor has accepted the request to release the association.

The A-RELEASE function is illustrated in Figure 4.4. The first thing to remember is that A-RELEASE.req can be sent from either AE. The functioning of A-RELEASE is similar to that of A-ASSOCI-

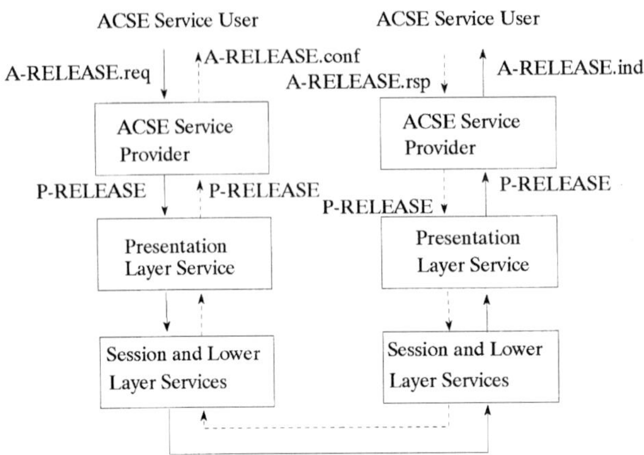

Figure 4.4 Functioning of A-RELEASE (normal mode).

ATE. One major difference is that we use the RLRQ APDU as user data for the P-RELEASE PPDU. The responder service provider provides the RLRE APDU to the presentation layer below it. When an association is released, then lower-level presentation and session services connections are also released. Here also, we assume Normal Mode operation.

4.4.4 A-ABORT

A-ABORT comes in handy when there have been errors, such as users no longer being able to communicate. A-ABORT can be compared to a fire alarm drill: Leave everything as it is and rush to the fire exit! A-ABORT is a nonconfirmed service, indicating that a reply is not expected. The important points to note are that it is an abnormal release and that data or information in transit may be lost. Receiving an A-ABORT will stop everything, including data transfer related to the association. A-ABORT.req is sent by an AE if there are problems. Also, an ASE can send A-ABORT.ind to an AE. A-ABORT can be sent by the AEs in a manager or an agent. A-ABORT has the following parameters:

- *Abort Source:* This indicates who initiated the A-ABORT. It can be a service user (AE) or a service provider (ACSE). Abort Source is used only in Normal Mode and is mandatory in A-ABORT.ind.
- *User Information:* This has the provision to include user information by the acceptor of an A-ABORT service. In the original version of session service standards, user information could be only nine octets in length. However, if we use the addendum to the original version, Unlimited User Data, this restriction is not there and we

can use any length to explain to the other end the reason for A-ABORT.

How the A-ABORT service functions is shown in Figure 4.5. The APDU used here is ABRT. The corresponding presentation service used here is P-U-ABORT. As we have seen, A-ABORT may be sent either by a user of an ACSE service, which is an AE, or by the ACSE service provider itself.

4.4.5 A-P-ABORT

A-P-ABORT.ind is sent by an ACSE service provider to an AE. The errors involved may be the result of internal errors in an ACSE or errors in layers such as the presentation layer and other layers below it. In such a case, a service provider uses A-P-ABORT to terminate the association. Like A-ABORT, there is also a possibility of loss of information in transit. Reason is the only parameter associated with A-P-ABORT. Reason Included is related to presentation-layer reasons. Because the functioning of A-P-ABORT is similar to that of other ACSE services, we have not repeated the steps involved in A-P-ABORT. In the presentation layer, we use P-P-ABORT instead of P-U-ABORT as used in A-ABORT. Here, too, the APDU used is ABRT as in A-U-ABORT.

4.5 Remote Operations Service Element (ROSE)

An illustration best explains remote operations. In Figure 4.6, an application entity AE1 requests an operation to be done on another

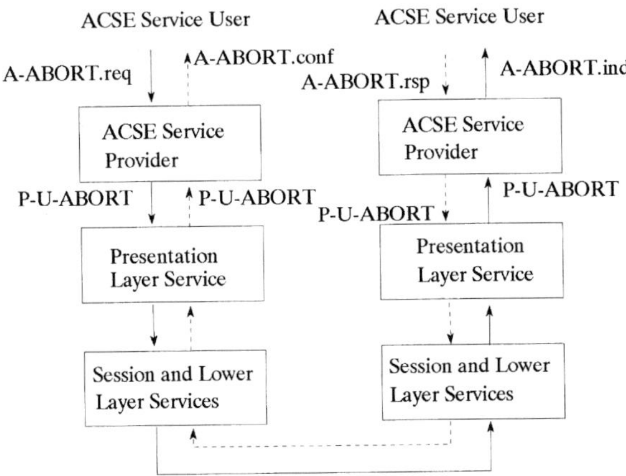

Figure 4.5 Functioning of A-ABORT (normal mode).

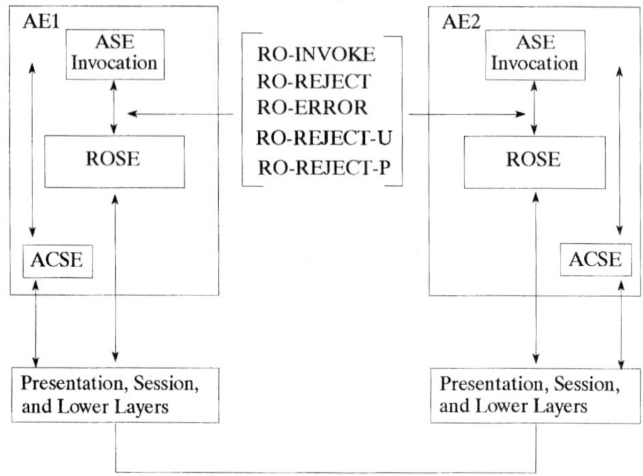

Figure 4.6 ROSE concepts.

TABLE 4.2 Remote Operation Service Element (ROSE)

Services	Type
RO-INVOKE	Nonconfirmed
RO-RESULT	Nonconfirmed
RO-ERROR	Nonconfirmed
RO-REJECT-U	Nonconfirmed
RO-REJECT-P	Provider-initiated

application entity AE2. The outcome of the operation is reported back. The operation done on AE2 is known as *remote operation*. Here AE1 is known as the *invoker* and AE2 is termed the *performer.* ROSE primitives are listed in Table 4.2. Except for RO-REJECT, all are nonconfirmed services. ROSE services are analogous to a *remote procedure call* (RPC). RPCs are similar to the subroutine calls found in programming languages, except that RPC calls are made to processes in another system.

At first, an association is formed between the invoking (AE1) and performing (AE2). AEs, using the association service, A-ASSOCIATE. After an association is formed for data transfer, ROSE interacts with the presentation service. These concepts are illustrated in Figure 4.6.

ROSE APDUs—ROIV, RORS, ROER, and RORJ—are formed in a *remote operation protocol machine* (ROPM), as shown in Figure 4.7. ROIV is used for invoking an operation on another system (performer). If there are no errors, then the results of the operation are

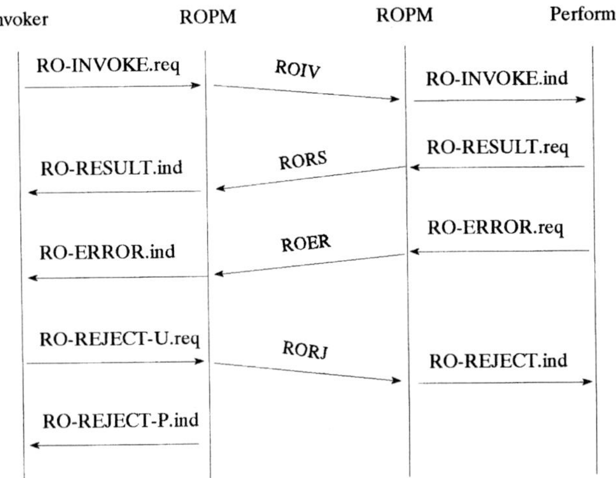

Figure 4.7 ROSE APDUs.

conveyed back to the invoker, using RORS. However, if there are errors, then the ROER APDU is used by the performer to report the errors to the invoker. If the invoker or performer cannot process an APDU, then the RORJ APDU is used. The correspondences between ROSE services and the APDU are provided in Table 4.3.

4.5.1 RO-INVOKE

The first service primitive of ROSE is *Invocation.* Here RO-INVOKE is used by AE1 to request that AE2 perform an operation. This operation may be a manager requesting an agent to create an object instance. The result of an operation by AE2 is transferred back to AE1 by RO-RESULT. RO-INVOKE has the following parameters:

- *Invoke-ID:* This is the identifier value of the RO-INVOKE.req and is a mandatory parameter.

TABLE 4.3 Mapping ROSE Services and APDUs

ROSE Services	APDU
RO-INVOKE.req/ind	ROIV
RO-RESULT.req/ind	RORS
RO-ERROR.req/ind	ROER
RO-REJECT-U.req/ind	RORJ
RO-REJECT-P.ind	RORJ

- *Linked-ID:* This is an identifier of the parent invocation. If the ROSE invocation is child of another invocation, then this value is used.
- *Operation Value:* This is a mandatory parameter, containing the operation number which is mutually agreed on between the invoker and the performer.
- *Argument:* This contains the argument for the operation stated in the Operation Value parameter.
- *Operation Class:* This can be synchronous or asynchronous operations. In synchronous operations, we wait for the reply to come before sending another operation, whereas in asynchronous operations, we are not bothered about receiving replies right away, and we can invoke other operations. ROSE has five class operations: Class 1 (synchronous with replies involving results and errors), Class 2 (asynchronous with results and errors), Class 3 (asynchronous with only errors), Class 4 (asynchronous with only results), and Class 5 (asynchronous with no results or errors).
- *Priority:* This states the priority of the invocation. Smaller numbers indicate a higher priority.

4.5.2 RO-RESULT

The result of a successful operation of a performer is included in the RO-RESULT.req parameter. Parameters used are Invoke-ID, Result, Operation Value, and Priority. Here Invoke-ID is the identifier of RO-RESULT.req and is the only mandatory parameter. If the Result parameter is present, then the Operation Value parameter is also present.

4.5.3 RO-ERROR

There is always the possibility of error while performing some processing. In the application entity AE2, if there is an error while performing an operation, RO-ERROR is used to report the errors. RO-ERROR's parameters are Invoke-ID, Error Value, Error, and Priority. Out of these four parameters, Invoke-ID and Error Value are mandatory parameters. Here, too, Invoke-ID is the invoke identifier of RO-INVOKE.req for which the error is being reported. Error data is placed in the Error parameter, and it is given a value which is placed in Error Value.

4.5.4 RO-REJECT

If there are problems in accepting an invocation as a result of error by the user of ROSE, such as AE1 or AE2, then RO-REJECT-U is used.

Here the user includes the Invoke-ID of the ROSE service from which the RO-REJECT-U has been generated. Invoke-ID is a mandatory parameter. Another parameter is Problem, which is mandatory, and can include Invoke Problem, Return Result Problem, or Return Error Problem parameters. Priority is an optional parameter.

RO-REJECT-P is used to inform a ROSE user if a problem is detected in the ROSE service provider. The Invoke-ID is that of the invocation which encounters the problem. This may be due to unrecognized fields, unacceptable structure, or badly structured PDUs. It may be noted that these problems can be in either the ROSE invoker or the ROSE performer.

4.6 Common Management Information Service Element (CMISE)

The common management information service element (CMISE) provides the management operations and notification used by CMIP and services defined by CMIS. The services provided by CMISE are shown in Table 4.4. Management information may be in the form of operations or notifications. Those processes which use these services are known as CMISE service users. The CMISE service provider provides the CMISE services.

From Table 4.4, we notice that M-GET, M-CREATE, M-CANCEL-GET, and M-DELETE are confirmed services. That means the responses have to be sent when these services are used. The remaining CMISE services such as M-EVENT-REPORT, M-SET, and M-ACTION can be either confirmed or nonconfirmed. The implication of nonconfirmed service is that no reply is sent. However, the confirmed responses can be linked together if required. As an example, if a scope request selects multiple managed objects, then the response consists

TABLE 4.4 Common Management Information Service Element (CMISE) Services

Service	Type
M-GET	Confirmed
M-SET	Confirmed/nonconfirmed
M-CREATE	Confirmed
M-DELETE	Confirmed
M-CANCEL-GET	Confirmed
M-EVENT-REPORT	Confirmed/nonconfirmed
M-ACTION	Confirmed/nonconfirmed

of responses from each of the managed objects selected. The Linked Identifier parameter is used to assemble the responses by the requestor of CMISE services. The prefix "M" used in CMISE services stands for management, and it indicates that these services are used for management-related operations and notifications.

For establishing associations prior to the use of CMISE services, A-ASSOCIATE is used. The parameters used with CMISE services are Functional Units, Access Control, and User Information. Here, additional functional units, which can be supported, are negotiated. If a Functional Unit parameter is not mentioned, then only the kernel functional unit is supported. The set of additional functional units, if agreed on by both the user and the provider, will be used for management operations and notifications.

Access Control establishes all the access control privileges for associations. However, if Access Control is mentioned as a parameter in a service request, it will be valid only for the invocation, and not for other management operations. Any user information that must be exchanged between a user and a provider can be included in the User Information parameter.

Finally, when connections are formed there should also be a means to break the connections. Usually, A-RELEASE is used for releasing the association between a user and a provider. However, when the situation is hopeless and nothing else works, then A-ABORT and A-P-ABORT can be used.

Some parameters are common to all the CMISE services (see Table 4.5). Some of these parameters are required, but the use of some of them is optional. Invoke-ID is one of the required parameters. Each CMIS operation is given a unique identifier to distinguish one CMIS operation from the other. Because many CMIS operations or the operation of just a particular kind can be performed, it is necessary to have this parameter. Whenever any management operation or notification is done, there is always a possibility of errors. So Errors is a conditional parameter used when sending a response or confirm.

Another CMISE parameter is Managed Object Class. It identifies the managed object class on which an operation is performed. Managed Object Instance refers to a specific object instance in a possible set of instances of a managed object class. These two parameters are not included in M-CANCEL-GET. Table 4.5 lists the parameters of the CMISE services.

4.6.1 M-EVENT-REPORT

When an object instance has something to report, such as a change of state or errors, then M-EVENT-REPORT is used. Naturally, the para-

TABLE 4.5 CMISE Services and Parameters

Services	Parameters
M-EVENT-REPORT.req/ind	Invoke-ID (M), Mode (M), Managed Object Class (M), Managed Object Instance (M), Event Type (M), Event Time, Event Information.
M-EVENT-REPORT.rsp/conf	Invoke-ID (M), Managed Object Class, Managed Object Instance, Event Type, Current Time, Event Reply, Errors.
M-GET.req/ind	Invoke-ID (M), Base Object Class (M), Base Object Instance (M), Scope, Filter, Access Control, Synchronization, Attribute Identifier List.
M-GET.rsp/conf	Invoke-ID (M), Linked-ID, Managed Object Class, Managed Object Instance, Current Time, Attribute List, Errors.
M-CANCEL-GET.req/ind	Invoke-ID (M), Get Invoke-ID (M)
M-CANCEL-GET.rsp/conf	Invoke-ID (M), Errors
M-SET.req/ind	Invoke-ID (M), Mode (M), Base Object Class (M), Base Object Instance (M), Scope, Filter, Access Control, Synchronization, Modification List
M-SET.rsp/conf	Invoke-ID (M), Linked-ID (M), Managed Object Class, Managed Object Instance, Attribute List, Current Time, Errors.
M-ACTION.req/ind	Invoke-ID (M), Mode (M), Base Object Class (M), Base Object Instance (M), Scope, Filter, Access Control, Synchronization, Action Type, Action Information.
M-ACTION.rsp/conf	Invoke-ID (M), Linked-ID, Managed Object Class, Managed Object Instance, Action Type, Current Time, Action Reply, Errors.
M-CREATE.req/ind	Invoke-ID (M), Managed Object Class (M), Managed Object Instance, Superior Object Instance, Access Control, Reference Object Instance, Attribute List.
M-CREATE.rsp/conf	Invoke-ID (M), Managed Object Class, Managed Object Instance, Attribute List, Current Time, Errors.
M-DELETE.req/ind	Invoke-ID (M), Base Object Class (M), Base Object Instance (M), Scope, Filter, Access Control, Synchronization.
M-DELETE.rsp/conf	Invoke-ID (M), Linked-ID, Managed Object Class, Managed Object Instance, Current Time, Errors.

NOTE: M stands for mandatory parameter.

meters must include various details, such as the type of information, when information was generated, when notification occurred, when response to a notification was generated, and details of the information.

M-EVENT-REPORT is important and is widely used for reporting notifications emitted by managed objects. Managed objects can emit notifications which the agents send as an M-EVENT-REPORT to managers.

When an M-EVENT-REPORT is sent, there is a possibility of errors, which are included in M-EVENT-REPORT.conf. These are included in the Errors service parameter. Figure 4.8 illustrates how M-EVENT-REPORT is used. In the figure, invoking and performing service users refer to the services, which may be a process in an agent or a manager. Because there is no response in the nonconfirmed mode, the figure is applicable only to the confirmed mode.

4.6.2 M-GET

It is possible to retrieve values from managed objects. For this purpose, the M-GET CMIS primitive is used. It is a confirmed service and can be canceled by an M-CANCEL-GET service. Here, too, the parameters supported must be able to retrieve the information from the object instances. There may be more than one object instance, so the parameters of scoping and filter are used to select a group of managed objects. In such a case, there is also the possibility of more than one reply. To handle this situation, the Linked-ID parameter is used. Figure 4.9 depicts M-GET without linked replies. Figure 4.10 illustrates the functioning of M-GET if linked replies are used. The synchronization parameter indicates how to retrieve the values. When an

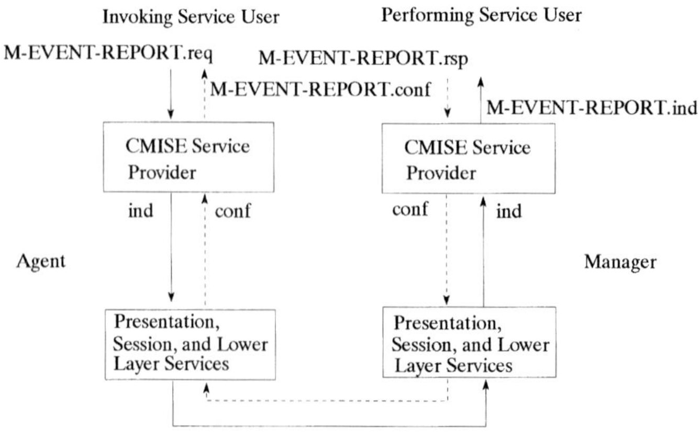

Figure 4.8 Working of M-EVENT-REPORT.

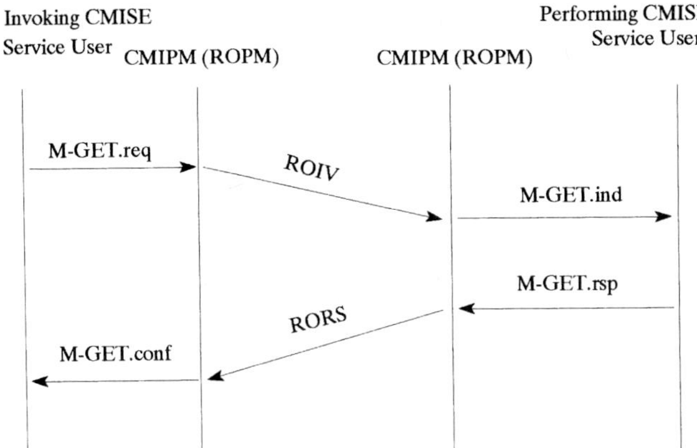

Figure 4.9 Functioning of M-GET without linked replies.

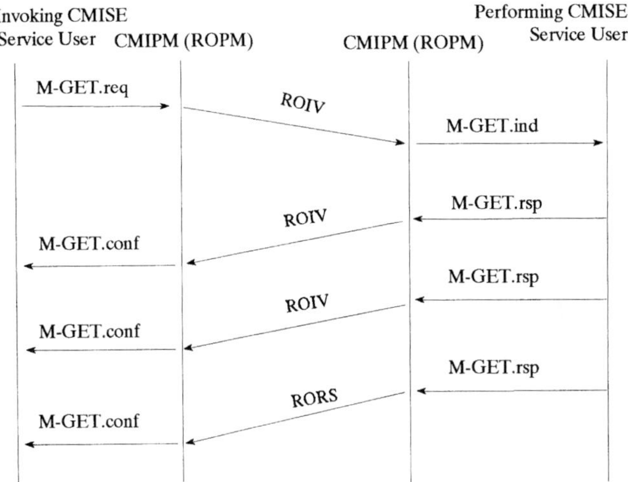

Figure 4.10 Functioning of M-GET with linked replies.

object instance value is retrieved, it may be important to limit the access to managed objects. For this purpose, the Access Control parameter is used. An example of how the M-GET functions is shown in Figure 4.11.

4.6.3 M-CANCEL-GET

As mentioned earlier, M-CANCEL-GET is used to abort any M-GET service that is pending. This service is useful when the amount of information being returned is unexpectedly large. The M-GET service

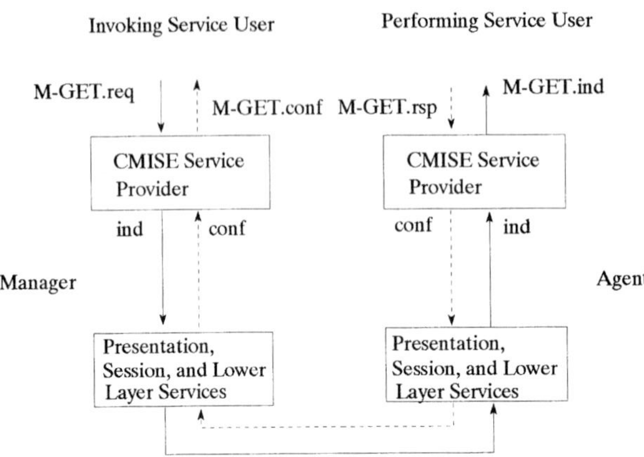

Figure 4.11 Functioning of M-GET.

may lead to long multiple replies. Besides, most of the information may be useless and, in some cases, it may be a duplicate of information already received. M-CANCEL-GET is very useful in such cases. Here, the Get Invoke-ID refers to the identifier of the M-GET operation to be canceled.

4.6.4 M-SET

The attribute values of managed objects may need to be changed to control the resource represented by a managed object. For this, the M-SET CMISE service is used. It has parameters such as Linked-ID, Scoping, Filter, Synchronization, and Access Control to control the operations done on an object instance or instances. The parameter list is similar to that of M-GET. While M-GET is used to retrieve the values of the object instances, M-SET is used to modify the values which have been assigned. M-SET can be a confirmed or nonconfirmed service.

4.6.5 M-ACTION

M-ACTION is used to perform management action on managed objects. This operation may be confusing. Why do we need it and where do we use it? Let us look at a special case in which some operation such as EXECUTE must be performed on an object instance or a set of object instances. In this case, EXECUTE can be packed in M-ACTION in Action Type and Action Information parameters. Except for M-ACTION, there is no other CMISE service that can be used to carry the operation EXECUTE. Hence, M-ACTION provides the escape mechanism to accommodate any operation that must be defined for a managed object class but that cannot be accurately modeled with a standardized attribute-oriented operation, M-CREATE or M-DELETE.

When defining managed objects, we must clearly spell out the operations that can be performed on them. M-ACTION, just as M-GET and M-SET, has parameters to identify a set of object instances and how they can be handled by Scoping, Filter, Synchronization, and Access Control parameters. They also have linked identifiers to receive multiple replies from more than one object instance. The definer of an M-ACTION can specify request/response syntaxes, the number of responses, and any other behavior that is required.

4.6.6 M-CREATE

When managed object classes are defined, instances of managed object classes must be created. For this purpose, the M-CREATE CMISE service is used. Managed objects that are created should subsequently be clearly identifiable. Thus, the reply should contain attribute values, the managed object class identifier which is the registered value, details on how to access the object instance, the superior object instance, and other details. The parameters of the superior object instance are optional, because the object instance's superior is obvious from that object's distinguished name.

4.6.7 M-DELETE

The reverse action of Create is Delete. For this purpose, the M-DELETE CMISE service is provided, and it is a confirmed service. M-DELETE has parameters to do the scoping and filtering to select a set of object instances. How these object instances are to be deleted is furnished by the Synchronization parameter. By using M-DELETE, the object instance or instances involved are deregistered. Some of the parameters, such as managed object classes and object class instances, are similar to those of the M-CREATE CMISE service.

4.7 Functional Units

For negotiating the CMISE services during association establishment, CMISE services are grouped into different functional units, which makes it easy to negotiate which services are to be included. Let us examine each one of the functional units.

4.7.1 Kernel functional unit

The kernel functional unit provides the basic CMISE services such as M-EVENT-REPORT, M-GET, M-SET, M-ACTION, M-CREATE, and

M-DELETE. However, it does not include specialized functions such as multiple replies, scoping, filtering, and synchronization capabilities. The parameters relevant to these services are included if functional units providing the specialized functions are included.

4.7.2 Multiple object selection functional unit

The multiple object selection functional unit is used for specifying the scoping and synchronization capabilities. These two capabilities are not applicable to M-EVENT-REPORT and M-CREATE. When this functional unit is specified, then the multiple reply functional unit is also required.

4.7.3 Multiple reply functional unit

The multiple reply functional unit makes use of the Linked-ID parameter in different CMISE services. This parameter is not used in M-EVENT-REPORT and M-CREATE. Combining multiple replies is a powerful concept and is very useful when a large amount of data in replies has to be sent. Some common scenarios for obtaining a large amount of data in replies are during operations involving multiple managed objects or due to M-ACTION, which can result in a large amount of data. These large continuous streams of replies may sometimes pose problems, in which case, one can use M-CANCEL-GET to stop further flow of data.

4.7.4 Filter functional unit

The filter functional unit makes use of the filter parameter. As we have seen earlier, the filter operation can be used along with scoping to select managed objects. The filter parameter is not available in M-EVENT-REPORT and M-CREATE.

4.7.5 Extended service functional unit

Availability of P-DATA is assumed for the CMISE services. To make use of the additional presentation-layer services, the extended service functional unit was anticipated. However, no one has attempted to standardize any use of this functional unit.

4.7.6 Cancel get functional unit

We have seen earlier that the kernel functional unit does not include M-CANCEL-GET CMISE service. So, to provide M-CANCEL-GET service, we must include this functional unit at the time of negotiating the establishment of the association.

4.8 Common Management Information Protocol (CMIP)

CMIS primitives (e.g., M-GET.req) are used by the CMISE users. These CMIS primitives are conceptually converted to CMIP PDUs in CMIPM, as shown in Figure 4.12. These PDUs are used to exchange management information between two peer open systems. CMIP operations, which are part of the CMIP PDUs, are listed in Table 4.6.

Basically, CMIPM converts a CMIS primitive to the equivalent CMIP PDU and uses one of the appropriate ROSE PDUs such as RO-INVOKE, RO-RESULT, and RO-ERROR to transfer the CMIP PDU to the lower presentation layer. As an example, CMIS M-GET.req maps to

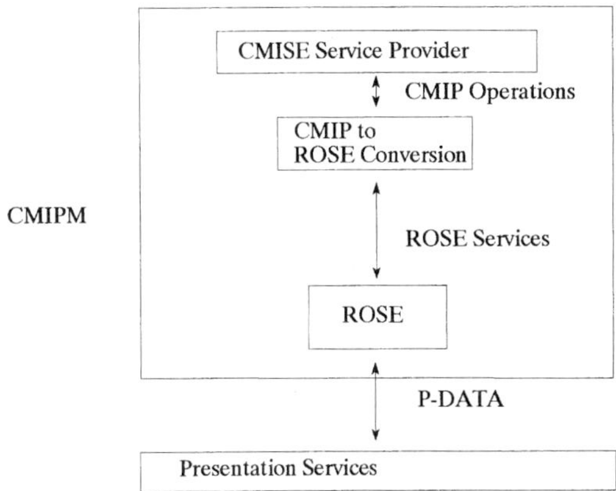

Figure 4.12 Relationship between CMIPM and presentation services.

TABLE 4.6 Mapping of CMISE Services and CMIP Operations

CMIS services	CMIP operation	Notes
M-EVENT-REPORT	m-EventReport	—
M-GET	m-Get	m-Linked-Reply for rsp/conf.
M-CANCEL-GET	m-Cancel-Get	—
M-SET	m-Set	m-Linked-Reply for rsp/conf.
M-ACTION	m-Action	m-Linked-Reply for rsp/conf.
M-CREATE	m-Create	—
M-DELETE	m-Delete	m-Linked-Reply for rsp/conf.

the CMIP m-Get operation, and this m-Get operation becomes a part of the RO-INVOKE PDU. It will be necessary to envelop this RO-INVOKE PDU with the parameters of P-DATA of presentation services.

On the other end, CMIPM also converts the PDU containing CMIP operation to a CMIS primitive and passes the CMIS primitive to the CMISE service user. One example of the conversion is that the CMIP m-EventReport operation gets mapped to the CMIS M-EVENT-REPORT.ind. Note that the terms CMIPM or ROPM can be misleading because of the "M." These are mainly FSMs, which can be software modules or microcode, and the term "machine" should be not interpreted beyond this in its scope.

4.9 Systems Management Operations on Objects and Attributes

There are two kinds of operations on managed objects. One is operations that can be done on attributes; the other is operations that can be done on managed objects of a managed object class. These operations are shown in Figure 4.13.

Get, Replace Attribute Value, Replace With Default Value, Add Member, and Remove Member operations can be done on attributes. These are used as explained in the following:

- For retrieving values of attributes of a managed object, a Get operation can be done.

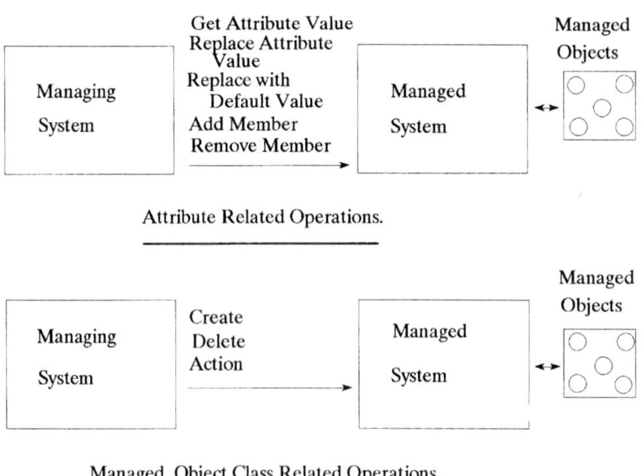

Figure 4.13 Managed object and attribute-related management operations.

- To set the values of one or more attributes of a managed object to specified values, a Replace Attribute Value operation is done.
- If the value or values of attributes are to be set to default values, a Replace With Default Value operation is used.
- For adding or removing members in the case of set-valued attributes, an Add or Remove Member operation can be used.

When defining a managed object class, it must include the operations that can be done by a managed system on managed objects and describe the semantics of each operation. Delete and Action are operations which can be performed on a managed object, as explained in the following:

- If an object instance can be created by a management operation, then a Create of an instance of the specified managed object class must be supported by the managed system for at least one name binding.
- If an object instance is to be deleted, then a Delete operation is done. However, it is not necessary that all managed objects support this. Here also, support for Delete is specified in the name binding.
- The Action operation is defined for use when none of the preceding operations can be done. If we want to do operations such as EXECUTE on a managed object class, Action can be used. These operations are packaged in the Action operation.

4.10 Pass-through Services

Pass-through services (see Figure 4.14) can be used by layer management, (*N*)-layer operation, or those cases which do not cover the OSI. Pass-through services can be mapped to management operations as shown in Table 4.7. Pass-through services provide the following:

- *Object-related operations:* Managed objects can be created and deleted, and actions can be performed on managed objects. They are done by using the primitives PT-CREATE, PT-DELETE, and PT-ACTION, respectively. Here, "PT" stands for pass-through services.
- *Attribute-related operations:* These include changing the value of one or more attributes to default values using PT-SET, reading the values of attributes via PT-GET, replacement of the value of one or more attributes with the help of PT-SET, and addition or removal of one or more members of sets using PT-SET.
- *Notifications:* These are sent for changes in attributes or managed objects. For this, PT-EVENT-REPORT is used.

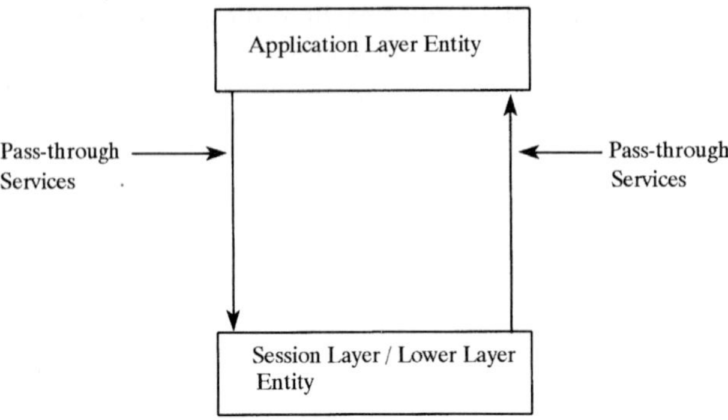

Figure 4.14 Pass-through services.

TABLE 4.7 Mapping of Pass-through Services and Management Operations

Pass-through services	Management operations
PT-CREATE	Create
PT-DELETE	Delete
PT-ACTION	Action
PT-SET	Replace, Add, Remove, and Replace-with-Default
PT-GET	Get
PT-EVENT-REPORT	Notification

4.11 Security

In this section, we will briefly review some of the security terms. We will not treat security in detail, because it is beyond the scope of the book.

One of the important security services is *authentication,* in which we check whether the participants are genuine by means of the exchange of secrets. For example, we might check whether user X is allowed to log in to a system and perform actions such as copying a file to his or her own system. For such verifications, Kerberos is one of the popular mechanisms. Kerberos was originally implemented in Project Athena at MIT.

Another security service is *data confidentiality.* There are different levels of data confidentiality possible, ranging from streams of messages to a specific field in a message. In data confidentiality, we guard against threats such as wiretapping and stealing of data. *Encryption* is the common mechanism used to provide data confidentiality. Encryption is done by using mathematical algorithms. *Access control* is commonly used to control the access to entities, and is achieved by means of access rights. As an example, one may have the access right to read a file but may not be allowed to write to a file. To ensure data integrity, we use a variety of mechanisms, such as *cyclic redundancy checks* (CRCs).

Nonrepudiation service is used to ensure that a sender or receiver does not deny a transmitted message. A *digital signature* is the popular mechanism to verify the signatures. As an example, X requests a bank to electronically withdraw a certain amount of money from his or her checking account, make a cashier's check, and send it to X by mail. In this case, the bank needs a certain amount of authorization, such as a signed electronic statement, as proof of the request. Once a signed electronic statement is sent, it must be verified that it really belongs to X. Digital signatures are used for such verifications, and there are different schemes for doing so.

Security management, which is one of the systems management functions, will be discussed in Section 18.3. Security is becoming an important issue in systems management. Only authorized administrators must be able to access certain data. Thus, the question of security involves the transfer of data between manager and agents. Access to the management information from managed objects may need to be restricted as well.

Another important consideration is how managers exchange data, especially in a distributed environment. Some information, such as accounting information, may need to be restricted and may not be forwarded to all the managers. This also involves many security issues.

Those interested in OSI security should refer to the extensive list of documents in Further Reading.

4.12 Summary

In this chapter, we discussed what ACSE, ROSE, CMIS, and CMIP mean. We examined these important OSI functions from the perspective of systems management and discussed how they can be grouped to support systems management functions. We also briefly discussed the topics of pass-through services and security.

4.13 Further Reading

ACSE

ISO 8649 (X.217), Information Processing Systems, Open Systems Interconnection, Service Definition of the Association Control Service Element, 1988.

ISO 8649 AM 1, Information Processing Systems, Open Systems Interconnection, Service Definition for the Association Control Service Element, Amendment 1: Authentication During Association Establishment, 1990.

ISO 8649 DAM 2, Information Processing Systems, Open Systems Interconnection, Service Definition for the Association Control Service Element, Draft Addendum 2 Covering Connectionless-mode ACSE Service, 1990.

ISO 8649 PDAM 3, Information Processing Systems, Open Systems Interconnection, Service Definition for the Association Control Service Element, Amendment 3: Application Context Negotiation During Association Establishment, 1992.

ISO 8650 (X.227), Information Processing Systems, Open Systems Interconnection, Protocol Specification for the Association Control Service Element, 1988.

ISO 8650 AM 1, Information Processing Systems, Open Systems Interconnection, Protocol Specification for the Association Control Service Element, Amendment 1: Authentication During Association Establishment, 1990.

ISO 8650 PDAM 2, Information Technology, Open Systems Interconnection, Protocol Specification for the Association Control Service Element, Amendment 2: Application Context Negotiation During Association Establishment, 1992.

ISO 8650-2, Information Technology, Open Systems Interconnection, Protocol Specification for the Association Control Service Element, Part 2: Protocol Implementation Conformance Statement Proforma (PICS), 1990.

DIS 10035 (X.237), Information Processing Systems, Open Systems Interconnection, Connectionless ACSE Protocol to Provide the Connectionless-Mode ACSE Service, 1990.

ISO 10169-1, Information Technology, Open Systems Interconnection, Conformance Test Suite for the ACSE Protocol, Part 1: Test Suite Structure and Test Purposes, 1991.

ROSE

ISO 9072-1 (X.219), Information Processing Systems, Text Communication, Remote Operations Part 1: Model, Notation, and Service Definition, 1989.

ISO 9072-2 (X.229), Information Processing Systems, Text Communication, Remote Operations, Part 2: Protocol Specification, 1989.

RTSE

ISO 9066-1 (X.218), Information Processing Systems, Text Communication, Reliable Transfer Part 1: Model and Service Definition, 1989.

ISO 9066-2 (X.228), Information Processing Systems, Text Communication, Reliable Transfer Part 2: Protocol Specification, 1989.

CMIS and CMIP

ISO 9595 (X.710), Information Technology, Open Systems Interconnection, Common Management Information Service Definition, 1991.

ISO 9595 AM 4, Information Technology, Open Systems Interconnection, Common Management Information Service Definition, Amendment 4: Access Control, 1992.

ISO 9595 PDAM X, Information Technology, Open Systems Interconnection, Common Management Information Service Definition, Amendment X: Allomorphism, 1990.

ISO 9596-1 (X.711), Information Technology, Open Systems Interconnection, Common Management Information Protocol Specification, 1991.

ISO 9596-2, Information Technology, Open Systems Interconnection, Common Management Information Protocol Specification, Part 2: Protocol Implementation Conformance Statement (PICS) Proforma, 1992.

ISO 9596 PDAM X, Information Technology, Open Systems Interconnection, Common Management Information Protocol Specification, Amendment X: Allomorphism, 1990.

OSI security

ISO 7498-2 (X.800), Information Processing Systems, Open Systems Interconnection, Basic Reference Model, Part 2: Security Architecture, 1988.

ISO 9160, Data Encipherment, Physical Layer Interoperability Requirements, 1988.

ISO DIS 9796, Security Techniques, Digital Signature Scheme Giving Message Recovery, 1990.

ISO 9797, Data Cryptographic Techniques, Data Integrity Mechanism Using a Cryptographic Check Function Employing a Block Cipher Algorithm, 1989.

ISO DIS 9798-2, Security Techniques, Entity Authentication Mechanisms, Part 2: Entity Authentication Using Symmetric Techniques, 1993.

ISO 9798-3, Security Techniques, Entity Authentication Mechanisms, Part 3: Entity Authentication Using Public Key Algorithms, 1993.

ISO CD 10181-1, Information Processing Systems, Security Frameworks in Open Systems, Part 1: Overview, 1991.

ISO DIS 10181-2.2, Information Processing Systems, Security Frameworks in Open Systems, Part 2: Authentication Framework, 1993.

ISO DIS 10181-3, Information Processing Systems, Security Frameworks in Open Systems, Part 3: Access Control, 1994.

ISO DIS 10181-4, Information Processing Systems, Security Frameworks in Open Systems, Part 4: Non-repudiation, 1994.

ISO CD 10181-7.2, Information Processing Systems, Security Frameworks in Open Systems, Security Audit Framework, 1991.

ISO 10736, Information Technology, Telecommunications and Information Exchange between Systems, Transport Layer Security Protocol, 1993.

ISO 10736 DAM 1, Information Technology, Telecommunications and Information Exchange between Systems, Transport Layer Security Protocol, Amendment 1: Security Association Establishment, 1993.

ISO DIS 10745, Information Technology, Open Systems Interconnection, OSI Upper Layers Security Model, 1992.

General

ISO CD 11587.2, Information Technology, Open Systems Interconnection, Application Context for Systems Management with Transaction Processing, 1994.

Chapter

5

Abstract Syntax and Transfer Syntax

5.1 Introduction

For two systems to communicate, it is necessary that each must understand the data sent from one system to the other. This can be done by using a language that has the same syntax and semantics.

In the application layer, we use *abstract syntax,* which states only how data is arranged and what meaning it has. One of the possible abstract syntaxes is *Abstract Syntax Notation One* (ASN.1). Between the application layer and the presentation layer, a local set of rules can be used to transform data; however, the syntax of the data transferred between presentation entities must be understood by each end. This is known as *transfer syntax.* Abstract syntax and transfer syntax are negotiated at the beginning, during association time.

One transfer syntax is *Basic Encoding Rules* (BER). BER state how data must be transformed before it is transferred to the other presentation entity. The local syntax can be purely dependent on the local protocols used. Figure 5.1 illustrates the concepts of abstract syntax and transfer syntax.

5.2 Abstract Syntax Notation One (ASN.1)

We will use a bottom-up approach to explain the concepts, starting with types and moving on to the definition of modules and macros. In ASN.1, the starting point is a *value.* An object instance can have a value. A collection of all these values is a *type.* These types are similar to the data types found in programming languages. We broadly classify the ASN.1 built-in types as follows:

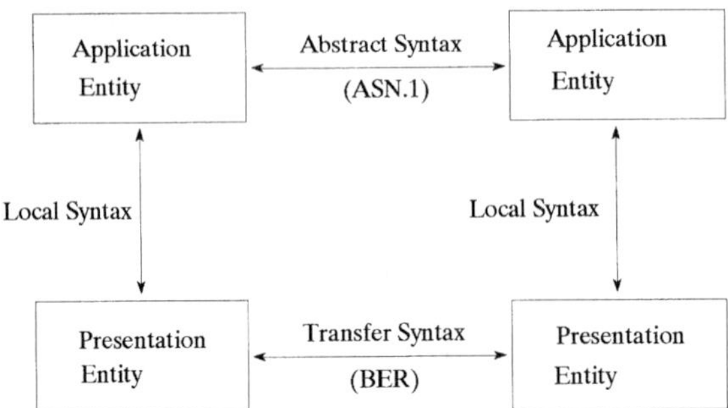

Figure 5.1 Abstract and transfer syntax concepts.

- Simple types
- Structured types
- Tagged types
- Subtypes

Like every formal programming language, ASN.1 has its own rules. Let us look into some of the important rules. They are explained as follows:

- *Keywords* appear in uppercase letters. An example of a keyword is:

  BOOLEAN

- A *type* and *module name* begin with an uppercase letter. A type consists of one or more letters, digits, and hyphens (-). Examples of types are:

  BOOLEAN (which is an ASN.1 built-in type)
  HouseNumber (described next)

- A new type can be formed using ASN.1 built-in types. This is done by *type assignment*. An example of a type assignment is:

  HouseNumber ::= INTEGER

  In the preceding definition, HouseNumber is a new type, "::= " means "defined as," and INTEGER is the ASN.1 built-in type. HouseNumber is also known as the *type reference.* We notice here that HouseNumber starts with the uppercase letter "H."

- An *identifier,* like a type, consists of one or more letters, digits, and/or hyphens. However, there is one difference between a type and an identifier: The first character of an identifier starts with a lowercase letter. An example of an identifier is:

newModule

- A type can have one or more values. We can assign a value to a type by *value assignment.* An example of a value assignment is:

houseNumber HouseNumber ::= 234

In the preceding example, houseNumber is a *value reference* (used for providing a value to a type), HouseNumber is the type for which the value is provided, "::= " stands for the assignment of a value, and 234 is the actual value. Note that the value reference houseNumber starts with a lowercase letter. The syntax for a value reference otherwise is the same as for a type reference.

- A comment starts with "--" and ends with either another "--" or a period. An example of a comment is:

-- this is a comment in ASN.1 --

ASN.1 built-in types are displayed in Table 5.1. Let us examine each one of them with examples.

5.2.1 Simple types

We can choose the BOOLEAN type for cases which have two states. As an example, the simple type Normal can be defined as follows:

Normal ::= BOOLEAN
-- the whole thing is a production --

TABLE 5.1 ASN.1 Built-in Types

BOOLEAN	SEQUENCE	Character String
INTEGER	SEQUENCE OF	EXTERNAL
BIT STRING	SET	OBJECT IDENTIFIER
OCTET STRING	SET OF	ObjectDescriptor
NULL	CHOICE	GeneralizedTime
ENUMERATED	ANY	UTCTime
REAL	Tagged	

In this example, Normal is a BOOLEAN type with two values, TRUE or FALSE. This case is an example of a *production.* A production has a name on the left, followed by "::=," and then a collection of sequences, which simply means a list of names. If there is more than one name, they are separated by "|," which stands for "or," as in many programming languages. Here, note that Normal starts with an uppercase letter because it is a type reference.

If we are not satisfied with just two states for a type, we can use an enumerated type to model the type. For example, assume that a type, EthernetAdapterStatus, has possible values of normal, degraded, offline, and failed.

EthernetAdapterStatus ::= ENUMERATED {normal (0), degraded (1), offline (2), failed (3)}

In this production, note that ENUMERATED is used for three or more states, and the first state (normal) has a value of zero. So the next state (degraded) has a value of one.

We want to have a counter which keeps track of the number of collisions in Ethernet over a fixed period of time. Let us call this counter "EthernetNumberCollisions." This can be defined in ASN.1 syntax as follows:

EthernetNumberCollisions ::= INTEGER

INTEGER can be used to model an integer variable. It can also be used to define cardinal variables. Here, *cardinal variable* means it has values as a set or sequence. Now let us assume that EthernetNumberCollisionsRange is a range of zero (no collisions) to 1000 collisions. Then *range* can be defined as follows:

EthernetNumberCollisionsRange ::= INTEGER {minimum(0), maximum(1000)}

Both BIT STRING and OCTET STRING can be used to define binary data. The main difference between them is that in BIT STRING, the number of bits used is not necessarily a multiple of eight bits, whereas in OCTET STRING, the length of the bits is in multiples of eight.

Let us go back to our example of EthernetAdapterStatus used in explaining the ENUMERATED data type. Using BIT STRING, it can be defined as follows:

EthernetAdapterStatus ::= BIT STRING {normal (0), degraded (1), offline (2), failed (3)}

In the preceding example, EthernetAdapterStatus will have a value of "1000" B or "8" H (hex string) for the normal.

Let us investigate the Character String type. Character String types are:

- NumericString
- PrintableString
- TeletexString
- VideotexString
- VisibleString
- IA5String
- GraphicString
- GeneralString

Out of these different Character String types, NumericString, PrintableString, and IA5String are important. NumericString consists of digits 0 through 9 and space. PrintableString consists of letters, which can be uppercase or lowercase, digits, punctuation marks (",", ".", ":", etc.), and space. IA5String stands for International Alphabet Number 5 and is the same as the ASCII character set. For details on TeletexString, refer to Reference 5.1 and on VideotexString, refer to Reference 5.2. The following are some examples of character strings.

```
AdapterCardType ::= PrintableString
   -- Here card type can be Ethernet, token ring, token bus.
AdapterCardType ::= NumericString
   -- Card type can be mapped as Ethernet to 0, token ring to 1, and so on.
```

Note that OCTET STRING may be used when an appropriate Character String type is not be available. As an example, we can define EthernetAdapterNumber as follows:

```
EthernetAdapterNumber ::= OCTET STRING
```

The NULL type is, by and large, used as a placeholder and is used if there is no element in a sequence.

The REAL type is used to model real numbers.

```
AdapterCardPrice ::= REAL
```

Because the adapter card price can be a specific number, for example $254.90, it is realistic to model it as REAL.

5.2.2 Structured types

Let us assume that, in some cases, an Ethernet adapter does not have a number to identify it. In that case, it can be modeled as follows:

```
EthernetAdapterNumber ::= CHOICE {NULL, OCTET STRING}
```

Here, the use of CHOICE states that the Ethernet card number can be either not there or an OCTET STRING. We will come back to the use of CHOICE later.

The SEQUENCE type is used to model a variable which has zero or more elements, in which the order of elements is important. In SEQUENCE type, we can have different types of elements, while the SEQUENCE OF type has only one type of elements.

```
EthernetCollisionsCounter ::= SEQUENCE
                              {highValue INTEGER,
                              lowValue INTEGER}
```

In this case, values in a collisions counter are expressed between the high and low values. Also, highValue and lowValue are just identifiers used for understandability; hence, lowercase letters as the initial characters are used. EthernetCollisionsCounter can also be expressed with the SEQUENCE OF type, because both the high and low values are mentioned with the same INTEGER type.

```
EthernetCollisionsCounter ::= SEQUENCE OF
                              {highValue INTEGER,
                              lowValue INTEGER}
```

Let us define one more counter for tokens lost in a token-ring network.

```
TokenRingTokensLost ::= SEQUENCE OF
                        {highValue INTEGER,
                        lowValue INTEGER}
```

These two counters, EthernetCollisionsCounter and TokenRing TokensLost, can be combined into a LAN counter. Because the types are different, they are combined into a SEQUENCE type variable.

```
LanSimpleCounterLimits ::= SEQUENCE
                           {ethernetCounter1 COMPONENTS OF
                           EthernetCollisionsCounter,
                           tokenRingCounter1 COMPONENTS OF
                           TokenRingTokensLost}
```

In the preceding definitions, COMPONENTS OF used with Ethernet-

CollisionsCounter and TokenRingTokensLost indicates that all elements of both sequences are included.

The use of SET and SET OF types is similar to that of SEQUENCE and SEQUENCE OF, except in one respect. In SEQUENCE and SEQUENCE OF, we noticed that the order of elements is important. If the order of elements is not important, then SET and SET OF can be used in place of SEQUENCE and SEQUENCE OF, respectively. While using SEQUENCE, SEQUENCE OF, SET, and SET OF, context-specific tagging helps to identify each variable. Context-specific tagging is explained under Section 5.2.3.

SET OF can also be used for variables in which the elements are of the same type and the order of data is not important.

```
LanWorkstationSerialNumbers ::=  OCTET STRING (SIZE (32))
LanSegment ::=  SET OF LanWorkstationSerialNumbers
```

In this example, LanSegment is modeled as a collection of workstations, and each workstation is identified by its serial number. The serial number has a length of 32 octets (8 bits each).

Next, let us examine the use of SET. A LAN network may have combinations of Ethernet and token-ring networks. The types used to model Ethernet and token-ring networks are deliberately kept different in the following example. We assume that the order of these is not important.

```
MacAddresses ::=  OCTET STRING (SIZE (6))
EthernetNetworks ::=  SET OF MacAddresses
TokenRingNetworks ::=  SET OF LanSegment
LanNetwork ::= SET
                    {etherNet   [0] IMPLICIT EthernetNetworks,
                     tokenNet   [1] IMPLICIT TokenRingNetworks}
```

In this example, MacAddresses has a length of six octets. LanNetwork is a set which has two elements: etherNet and tokenNet. In turn, etherNet is a collection of workstations, identified by MacAddresses. However, in the case of tokenNet, there are sets of LAN segments, each of which, in turn, is a set of serial numbers as elements. IMPLICIT will be explained in the next section.

Use of ANY requires that the specifications be furnished in another place before any data transfer can be done. It is mainly a placeholder for providing more details at a later time.

```
SoftwareVersion ::=  ANY
```

However, another version of ANY is ANY DEFINED BY. ANY

DEFINED BY supplements the ANY definition, providing actual specifications.

```
SoftwareVersion ::=  ANY DEFINED BY INTEGER
```

When only one of the alternative members of a collection has to be selected, then CHOICE is used. IMPLICIT tagging can be used if members belong to only a single data type.

```
ObjectName ::=  CHOICE
                {localUniqueName        GraphicString,
                 localUniqueIdentifier  NumericString OPTIONAL}
```

This states that ObjectName can be in one of these forms: localUniqueName or localUniqueIdentifier. Here, the keyword OPTIONAL states that localUniqueIdentifier may or may not be sent during data transfer to the other end, depending on circumstances.

Selection type makes use of the alternative types defined in CHOICE.

```
ObjectNameUsed ::=  SEQUENCE
                {easilyReadableName  localUniqueName <
                 ObjectName}
```

In this example, we have used one of the alternatives: localUniqueName, modeled by the ObjectName type.

5.2.3 Tagged types

A tagged type is used to model variables for removing ambiguities. In structured data types, which we have already seen, there are possibilities for confusion over such concerns as how the receiving end interprets data, when it receives data on ObjectName, and whether the data refers to localUniqueName or localUniqueIdentifier. Here, we need tagging to explicitly state that the data sent from the other end refers to localUniqueName or localUniqueIdentifier, removing the confusion.

A tag can be EXPLICIT or IMPLICIT. By using an IMPLICIT tag, there is no need to transfer the data type during data transfer to the other end, while in the case of an EXPLICIT tag, transfer of the data type is required. This is understandable. For example, a Character String that identifies a variable can mean a Numeric String or a Graphic String. To be clearly understood on the receiving end of the application entity, it is necessary to know exactly what is meant by a Character String.

If no IMPLICIT tag is specified, then it is assumed that an EXPLICIT tag is used. There is no mention of EXPLICIT in such cases. However, in module definitions, things are slightly different. If an IMPLICIT tag is used along with the module definition, then all the tags in the module are IMPLICIT. If a tag is left out or states that it is EXPLICIT, then it is assumed that the tagging used is EXPLICIT. Details on module definitions are provided in Section 5.2.4.

A user-defined tag has a class and a number within the square brackets []. The four user-defined tag classes are listed in Table 5.2. Let us examine each of them.

UNIVERSAL tag. The UNIVERSAL tag is used for data types as provided in ISO 8824 (X.208) (see Reference 5.3). The data types must be globally known and unique. Table 5.3 lists the different types of UNIVERSAL class tags. Let us look at an example of the UNIVERSAL class.

Assume that we are using an attribute, Counter, to keep track of beaconing in a token-ring card. At a particular time, Counter may have a value of 21. This may be represented as an INTEGER. Here, INTEGER is the type.

```
Counter ::= [UNIVERSAL 2] IMPLICIT INTEGER
```

In this production, definition of the UNIVERSAL class tag is used. The INTEGER type is UNIVERSAL 2, as per Table 5.3.

APPLICATION tag. The APPLICATION class is used to model the variables which are understood in the ASN.1 module being used. The presentation context understands the data type of the variable.

```
AnotherCounter ::= [APPLICATION 1] IMPLICIT INTEGER
```

In this example, [APPLICATION 1] is the tag. [APPLICATION 1] states that it is understood in the presentation context negotiated between the presentation entities. APPLICATION is the tag class and "1" is the number within the class. Here, IMPLICIT states that the

TABLE 5.2 ASN.1 User-Defined Tag Classes

UNIVERSAL
APPLICATION
PRIVATE
CONTEXT-SPECIFIC

TABLE 5.3 Different UNIVERSAL Class Tags

Tag	Type
UNIVERSAL 1	BOOLEAN
UNIVERSAL 2	INTEGER
UNIVERSAL 3	BIT STRING
UNIVERSAL 4	OCTET STRING
UNIVERSAL 5	NULL
UNIVERSAL 6	OBJECT IDENTIFIER
UNIVERSAL 7	ObjectDescriptor
UNIVERSAL 8	EXTERNAL
UNIVERSAL 9	REAL
UNIVERSAL 10	ENUMERATED
UNIVERSAL 11–15	Reserved for addenda to ISO 8824
UNIVERSAL 16	SEQUENCE and SEQUENCE OF
UNIVERSAL 17	SET and SET OF
UNIVERSAL 18	NumericString (Character string)
UNIVERSAL 19	PrintableString (Character string)
UNIVERSAL 20	TeletexString (Character string)
UNIVERSAL 21	VideotexString (Character string)
UNIVERSAL 22	IA5String (Character string)
UNIVERSAL 23–24	Time
UNIVERSAL 25	GraphicString (Character string)
UNIVERSAL 26	VisibleString (Character string)
UNIVERSAL 27	GeneralString (Character string)
UNIVERSAL 28–...	Reserved for addenda to ISO 8824

explicit stating of AnotherCounter as an INTEGER is not necessary during data transfer. In this example, AnotherCounter is understood to be INTEGER by the receiving presentation-layer entity.

CONTEXT-SPECIFIC tag. In structured types, there is the problem of distinguishing between different elements. There can be major confusion, especially when using CHOICE. Unless elements are specifically mentioned, it is hard for the receiver to understand which one was sent. To remove these ambiguities, we use context-specific tags. The number for these tags starts with zero. For example:

```
BeaconingCounter ::= SET
                     {counterName     [0] IMPLICIT VisibleString,
                      counterNumber   [1] IMPLICIT INTEGER }
```

In this production, BeaconingCounter is defined as a SET. By mentioning that it is a SET, order is not important. Here counterName has a context-specific tag of [0] and it states that it is the first element. Similarly, counterNumber has a context-specific tag of [1], and it is the second element.

PRIVATE tag. The PRIVATE tag may be used to identify data types which are used within an organization or a country.

```
BecCounter ::= [PRIVATE 3] IMPLICIT INTEGER
```

In this example, [PRIVATE 3] has been used to specify that this is a widely used type within an organization or country.

OBJECT IDENTIFIER and ObjectDescriptor. OBJECT IDENTIFIER is a set of names, numbers, or a mixture of the two associated with nodes from the root of the object identifier tree up to the object used, and it uniquely identifies an object. The object identifier tree is the same as the registration hierarchy tree (refer to Figure 3.4). The root of the object identifier tree has three nodes: ccitt, iso, and joint-iso-ccitt. The basic principles of assigning identifiers are that an organization is responsible for the assignment of identifiers below it and the organization must ensure that the identifiers it issues are unique. As an example, iso, with a node value of 1, is responsible for assigning object identifiers below it. It has four children, standard, registration-authority, member-body, and identified-organization, with identifier values of 0, 1, 2, and 3, respectively. Identified-organization issues its own set of unique identifiers to the nodes below it. These parent and children nodes are connected by arcs.

Each value or name in OBJECT IDENTIFIER represents the values or names of nodes in the object identifier tree. Let us form an arbitrary OBJECT IDENTIFIER for lanNetwork:

```
lanNetwork OBJECT IDENTIFIER ::=
                    {iso org dod internet private enterprises
                    Xenterprises 85}
```

Here, org has a value of 3 for the node below the iso, dod has a value of 6 assigned to the node from org, internet has 1 for the node from dod, private has a label of 4 for the node from internet, and enterprises has 1 assigned to the node below private. Let us assume that Xenterprises has 140 given to its node and in the Xenterprises, a value of 85 is assigned to lanNetwork. So for the OBJECT IDENTIFIER of lanNetwork, instead of using the textual form as previously given, we can also use the numeric form as follows:

```
lanNetwork OBJECT IDENTIFIER ::= {1 3 6 1 4 1 140 85}
```

Please note that OBJECT IDENTIFIER can also have a mixture of names and values, instead of just names or just values as we have shown in these examples. The OBJECT IDENTIFIER of lanNetwork, as indicated here, is difficult to understand. So ObjectDescriptor, which represents easily readable texts, must be sent along with OBJECT IDENTIFIER. Sometimes, ObjectDescriptor may not end up being unique, but the combination of ObjectDescriptor and OBJECT IDENTIFIER will become unique globally.

```
etherlanNetwork ObjectDescriptor ::= [UNIVERSAL 7] IMPLICIT
GraphicString(SIZE(8))
```

Here, etherlanNetwork is the name of the ObjectDescriptor used and is a GraphicString of eight octets.

EXTERNAL. The EXTERNAL type is useful for modeling variables by abstract syntax other than ASN.1. This can refer to the types defined outside a particular module, and there are no restrictions on the use of the type. The major difference between ANY and EXTERNAL is that EXTERNAL can be useful for defining data outside ASN.1. As can be seen from Table 5.3, the tag for EXTERNAL is UNIVERSAL 8.

```
DataTransferMode ::= EXTERNAL
```

Here, we are assuming that how we transfer the data is external to the module, which has DataTransferMode defined in it. We are assuming that for representation of data, we are using EBCDIC.

Date and Time. Nations use different ways of reporting date and time. Thus, when communicating between different users around the globe, it is better to standardize the representation of date and time. The data type used for this purpose is Time and the tags used are UNIVERSAL 23 for UTC (Coordinated Universal Time) and UNIVERSAL 24 for generalized time.

Three forms of generalized time are:

- *Calendar date:* 19940623235343.7. In this example, the first four digits represent the year (1994), the next two digits represent the month (06), the next two digits represent the day (23), the next two digits represent the hour (23), the next two digits indicate minutes (53), and the last digits indicate seconds (43.7). So, the date and time are June 23, 1994, at time 11 P.M., 53 minutes, and 43.7 seconds. This form represents local time.

- *Time of day:* 19940623235343.7Z. All digits represent the same terms as they do in the local time, but the addition of "Z" at the end indicates that the time refers to UTC time.
- *Time differential:* 19940623235343.7 + 1100. Here, local time is furnished as in the local time example. We can derive the UTC time from the time differential form of date and time representation. The UTC required is obtained by adding 11 hours to the local time.

Now let us examine universal time represented by UTC time. In this form, the date is represented by YYMMDD. Here, YY stands for the last two digits of a year, MM stands for the month, and DD represents the day of the month. The time can be of the form hhmm with four digits, or hhmmss with six digits. In this case, hh stands for hours (00 to 23), mm stands for minutes (00 to 59), and ss indicates seconds (00 to 59). This can be followed by either Z or a time differential which indicates the hours that must be added or subtracted to get the UTC time.

For example, 9406232235343Z is similar to the UTC listed under forms of generalized time. One difference is that 1994 becomes 94, and seconds are not carried to decimal places (43 seconds instead of 43.7 seconds). The other form, 9406232235343Z + 1100, means that to get the UTC, we must add 11 hours.

5.2.4 Module definitions

Module definitions are primarily used for grouping ASN.1 definitions. They also help in using type definitions defined in other places by making use of IMPORT and EXPORT mechanisms. Modules are analogous to functions in C language or subroutines in Pascal. There are module definitions in the definitions of managed object classes in standards and other documents. The following example illustrates this.

```
LanNetworkModule {iso org dod internet private enterprises Xenterprises
95}
        -- Above, LanNetworkModule is the module name, and {iso org dod
        -- internet private enterprises Xenterprises 95} is the assigned
        -- identifier.
DEFINITIONS EXPLICIT TAGS ::= BEGIN
        -- We have module body below.
IMPORTS
        RelativeDistinguishedName FROM InformationFramework
                                  {joint-iso-ccitt ds(5) modules(1)
                                  informationFramework(1)}
-- End of IMPORTS.
EXPORTS
```

```
        LanNetworkName ::= SEQUENCE of RelativeDistinguishedName
-- End of EXPORTS.
MacAddresses ::= OCTET STRING (SIZE (6))
LanWorkstationSerialNumbers ::= OCTET STRING (SIZE (32))
LanSegment ::= SET OF LanWorkstationSerialNumbers
EthernetNetworks ::= SET OF MacAddresses
TokenRingNetworks ::= SET OF LanSegment
LanNetwork ::= SET
        {etherNet  [0] IMPLICIT EthernetNetworks,
         tokenNet  [1] IMPLICIT TokenRingNetworks}
END
```

In the preceding definitions, IMPORTS states that RelativeDistinguishedName is defined in the InformationFramework and is used in this module. In the preceding module, LanNetworkName will be used in other module definitions. For this reason, it has to be mentioned in EXPORTS. Although it is not mandatory to have IMPORTS and EXPORTS, their use makes the definitions easier.

Notice that EXPLICIT TAGS immediately follows DEFINITIONS. We have deliberately introduced this to explain the idea behind using it. EXPLICIT TAGS is not necessary, because the default tag is "empty," which also means EXPLICIT TAGS. If we use IMPLICIT TAGS instead of EXPLICIT TAGS, then all of the tags we use in the module are IMPLICIT.

5.2.5 Subtypes

Subtypes, as the name suggests, make use of the existing types (see Figure 5.2). When subtypes are derived, they must have values. Subtypes are used in the following cases.

- When two are more types have common characteristics, subtyping makes the definition easier, if we include the common characteristics in a parent type. Subtypes include parent type and individual characteristics.

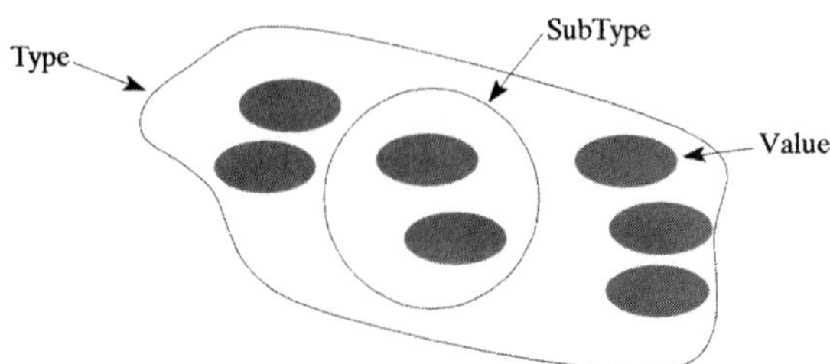

Figure 5.2 Types, values, and subtypes. (*Source: Reprinted with permission from* OSI Upper Layer Standards and Practices *by Baha Hebrawi, copyright 1993 by McGraw-Hill.*)

- If we want to limit the sizes or values of existing types, subtyping is helpful, making definitions of variables clear.
- If we wish to explain in more detail a subset with values, then subtyping is useful.

There are six subtypes. We will borrow some of the examples from previous sections to show how subtyping works.

Single value. Single-value subtyping permits only one value out of many possible values of a subtype.

```
TestResult ::= INTEGER (0 | 1 | 2)
```

In this case, we assign the values: pass is 0, fail is 1, and withdraw is 2. Thus, the results can be only one of these three states. "|" stands for "or."

Permitted alphabet. Assume that house numbers can be only numbers which range in size from 1 to 5 digits. In such a case, we can come up with the following permitted alphabet subtyping:

```
HouseNumber ::= IA5String (FROM ("0"|"1"|"2"|"3"|"4"|"5"|"6"|"7"
|"8"|"9") SIZE(1..5))
```

Contained. The contained subtype is helpful in forming a new subtype from the existing subtypes. In the example that follows, HouseAddress is a new subtype formed from subtype HouseNumber.

```
HouseAddress ::= INCLUDES HouseNumber
```

Value range. Value ranges are used for INTEGER, REAL, and types obtained by tagging. As an example, assume that employee serial numbers are derived from integer values from 1000 to 20,000. A value range can be defined as follows:

```
EmployeeSerialNumber ::= INTEGER (1000..20000)
```

Size constraint. Size constraint can be used for forming subtypes and includes the keyword SIZE. SIZE mentions the length of the subtype derived from a parent.

```
LanWorkstationSerialNumber ::= OCTET STRING (SIZE (32))
```

Here, too, LanWorkstationSerialNumber is a subtype of the parent type OCTET STRING and has a length of 32 octets. Let us modify this example and assume that the workstation serial numbers are OCTET STRING with varying size anywhere from 5 to 32 octets. The modification is as follows:

```
LanWorkstationSerialNumber ::= OCTET STRING (SIZE (5..32))
```

Inner subtyping. In the following example, we have made use of some of the inner subtyping keywords, such as WITH COMPONENTS, OPTIONAL, PRESENT, and ABSENT, to define subtypes of PureEtherLan and PureTokenLan. These two subtypes are derived from the parent, LanNetwork.

```
Bandwidth ::= INTEGER (1..4096)
-- Bandwidth can be from 1 to 4096 megabits per second
MacAddresses ::= OCTET STRING (SIZE (6))
LanSegment ::= SET OF LanWorkstationSerialNumbers
EthernetNetworks ::= SET OF MacAddresses
TokenRingNetworks ::= SET OF LanSegment
FDDIBackbonenetworks ::= SET OF MacAddresses
LanNetwork ::= SET
                    {networkID              GraphicString,
                     networkBandwidth       Bandwidth,
                     fDDIBackNet            FDDIBackbonenetworks,
                     etherNet               EthernetNetworks OPTIONAL,
                     tokenNet               TokenRingNetworks OPTIONAL}
PureEtherLan ::= LanNetwork (WITH COMPONENTS
                    {networkID              GraphicString,
                     networkBandwidth       Bandwidth,
                     fDDIBackNet            FDDIBackbonenetworks,
                     etherNet               PRESENT tokenNet ABSENT})
PureTokenLan ::= LanNetwork (WITH COMPONENTS
                    {networkID              GraphicString,
                     networkBandwidth       Bandwidth,
                     fDDIBackNet            FDDIBackbonenetworks,
                     etherNet               ABSENT tokenNet PRESENT})
```

5.2.6 MACRO

MACRO notation is used for defining locally the types and values of variables. It is used for extending ASN.1 grammar; however, it can make use of the ASN.1 type definitions. MACRO notation is used for specifying ASN.1 types and values for instances. TYPE NOTATION is used for defining local types, and VALUE NOTATION is used for local values.

However, use of MACROs presents its own set of problems. For ASN.1 data types, encoders are available, which convert them to BER. On the receiving end, BER is converted back to ASN.1 using a decoder. However, as MACRO extends the ASN.1 syntax, encoders and decoders should have the ability to parse extended grammar in MACROs. This requires modifications and further capability of encoders and decoders, which is an unnecessary strain on them.

```
SerialNumber ::=  OCTET STRING
With values of Val ::=  A3124BC0
WorkstationID MACRO ::=  BEGIN
-- workstationID is a MACRO name or identifier for the MACRO.
-- From BEGIN to END, we have MACRO body.
-- Begin type production.
TYPE NOTATION ::=
                "SerialNumber"
                " = "
                type
-- Begin value production
VALUE NOTATION ::=
                "("
                "Val"
                " = "
                A3124BC0
                ")"
     -- Supporting productions are not there or it is empty.
END
```

In this example, TYPE NOTATION furnishes the syntax of a new type and it is the VALUE NOTATION which furnishes the actual value.

5.3 Basic Encoding Rules (BER)

BER is used in the presentation layer, before the actual transfer of ASN.1 values, as shown in Figure 5.1. The data transfer is in the form of a stream of octets. The structure of BER can be of the form *identifier, length,* and *contents* (ILC), when the length of the contents is known. The identifier indicates the ASN.1 data type, the length supplies the length of the contents that follow the length field, and the contents contain the ASN.1 values to be transferred. This form is shown in Figure 5.3.

5.3.1 Identifier field

The structure of the identifier field is shown in Figure 5.3. Class consists of the eighth and seventh bits, and furnishes the tag used in data. Table 5.4 supplies the values of these bits for different classes. The sixth bit stands for either *primitive* or *constructed* (see Table 5.5), and bits 5 to 1 indicate the ASN.1 tag number. In Figure 5.3, bit 1 is the *least significant bit,* and bit 8 is the *most significant bit.* When data is transferred, bit 8 is transferred first and bit 1 is transferred last. Primitive refers to simple atomic tags, while constructed data elements are formed from other data elements.

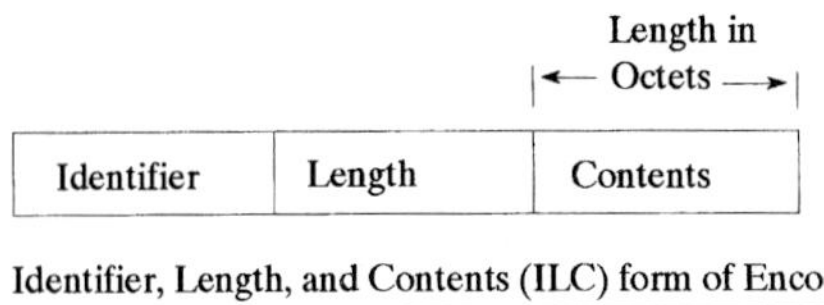

Identifier, Length, and Contents (ILC) form of Encoding

Identifier	Length	Contents	End of Contents

Identifier, Length, Contents, and End of Contents (ILCE) form of Encoding

Most Significant Bit → 8 7 6 5 4 3 2 1 ← Least Significant Bit

(← To Network)

Class	P/C	Tag Number

Identifier Field

Figure 5.3 ILC and ILCE types of encoding.

TABLE 5.4 Class Bits in the Identifier Field

Class	Bit 8	Bit 7
UNIVERSAL	0	0
APPLICATION	0	1
CONTEXT-SPECIFIC	1	0
PRIVATE	1	1

TABLE 5.5 P/C Values for Built-in ASN.1 Types

Built-in type	P, C, or P/C	Built-in type	P, C, or P/C
BOOLEAN	P	CHOICE	P/C
INTEGER	P	Selection	P/C
BIT STRING	P/C	Tagged	P/C
OCTET STRING	P/C	ANY	P/C
NULL	P	EXTERNAL	P/C
SEQUENCE	C	OBJECT IDENTIFIER	P
SEQUENCE-OF	C	Character String	P/C
SET	C	ENUMERATED	P
SET-OF	C	REAL	P

NOTE: P means primitive; C means constructed.

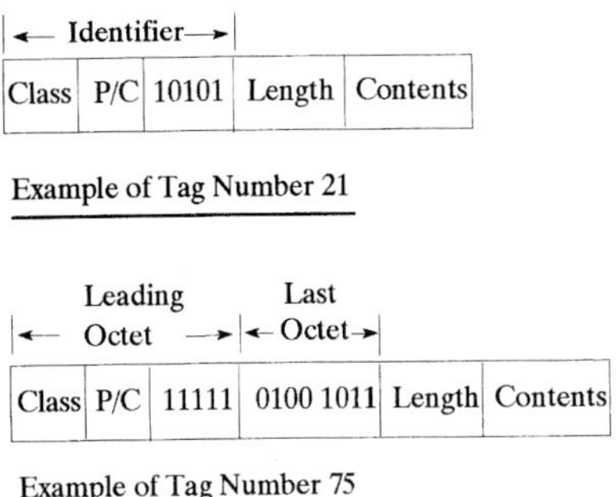

Figure 5.4 Example of tag numbers.

In tag numbers, bit 5 is the most significant bit and bit 1 is the least significant bit. Tags can be represented in two forms. If a tag number is 30 or less, then the short form with five bits is enough. In Figure 5.4, a tag number of 21 is shown.

However, when the tag number is 31 or more, then five bits are not enough to represent them. In that case, the five bits of the leading octet are set to 1, and the tag numbers are represented by the unsigned integers in the subsequent octets. The eighth bit in each of the following octets except the last one are set to 1. In the last octet, the eighth bit is set to 0 to indicate that this is the last octet to be used for calculating the tag number. In Figure 5.4, a high tag value (75) is shown.

5.3.2 Length field

Length forms can be one of two types, *definite* or *indefinite*. The definite form, in turn, can be either *short* or *long*. This concept is depicted in Figure 5.5. In the length field, the eighth bit determines what form is used. If it is 0, then it indicates a short form. The seven bits can hold up to a maximum of 127 octets. However, in the initial length octet, bits 7 through 1 cannot all be 1s, or “111 1111” B (127), because this is reserved for future extensions and compatibility with CCITT Recommendation X.409. Hence, only a maximum value of 126 can be used in the first octet that represents length. Figure 5.6 shows an example of 27 octets of data contents.

If more than 126 octets of length are to be indicated in the length field, then the long form is used. Here, the eighth bit is set to 1 in the first length octet. The subsequent bits from 7 to 1 furnish the number of length octets used.

As an example, the 375 length octets are shown in Figure 5.6. Here “000 0010” B indicates that there will be two additional octets that

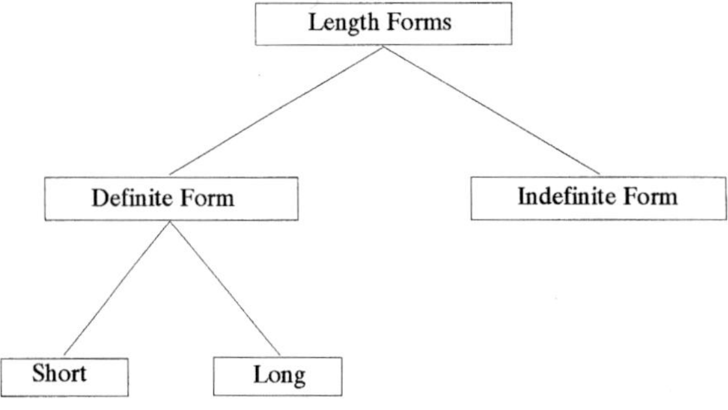

Figure 5.5 Different BER length forms.

|← 27 →|

0001 1011

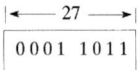

Length Short Form - 27 Octets of Data Contents Field

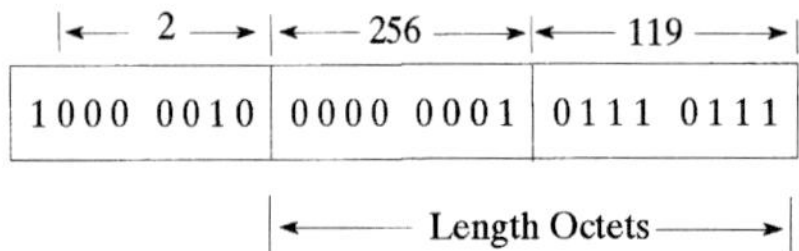

Length Long Form - 375 Octets of Data Contents Field

Figure 5.6 Example of short-form and long-form lengths.

will have to be used for computing the length of the data octets. The bits in the subsequent two length octets represent 375.

If the length of the data contents is not known, then the *indefinite* form of encoding is used, also known as the ILCE form. In the indefinite form, the eighth bit of the first octet of the length field is set to 1, and the rest of the bits from 7 to 1 are all set to 0. As usual, after the length field, we have data. After data, there are two octets of the end of contents field. The end of contents field is represented by "00 00" X, where X stands for a hexadecimal. We have to note here that because we have used "00 00" X for end of contents, we cannot have a value of "00 00" X in data.

5.3.3 Data contents field

Using examples, we will examine how built-in types are encoded.

BOOLEAN value. A BOOLEAN value can be either TRUE or FALSE. The encoding of a BOOLEAN value of TRUE is shown in Figure 5.7.

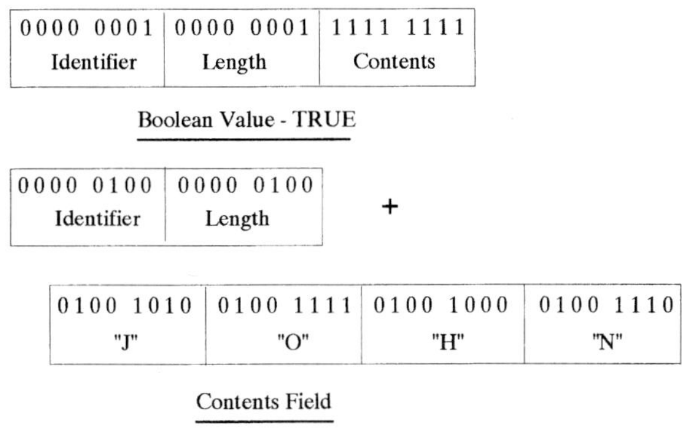

Figure 5.7 Encoding of BOOLEAN and OCTET STRING.

BOOLEAN belongs to the UNIVERSAL class, so bits 8 and 7 are both 0. Bit 6 is 0 because it is a primitive. The tag number for BOOLEAN from Table 5.3 is 1. Hence, the identifier field is represented as shown in Figure 5.7. The length of the data contents is one octet, so the length is shown as 1. The contents can be represented by "FF" X for the BOOLEAN value of TRUE. It may be noted that, instead of "FF" X, we can use any nonzero value in the first octet. For the BOOLEAN value of FALSE, the data contents octet is 0.

INTEGER value. For the INTEGER value, the data contents field has twos complement. The INTEGER value is derived by including all bits from all octets. When computing the twos complement, for a positive integer, the twos complement is the number itself. For a negative number, the ones complement is derived by reversing all the bits with 1 to 0 and bits with 0 to 1. Then the twos complement is obtained by adding 1 to the ones complement. Note that the operation is done on the binary representation of an INTEGER.

For the INTEGER value, too, we derive the identifier and length fields as described for the BOOLEAN value. For the data contents, 654 is represented as "028E" X and −654 is represented as "FD72" X, where X stands for hexadecimal representation.

REAL value. We use primitive encoding for REAL values. We use the tag nine of the UNIVERSAL class for encoding REAL values. If a REAL value is 0, then there is no contents field. A REAL value is given by:

$$\text{REAL value} = \text{Mantissa(M)}*\text{Base(B)}^{\text{Exponent(E)}}$$

Encoding of an AdapterCardPrice of $254.90 can be done as {25490 10 −2}. Here 25490 is the mantissa, 10 is the base, and −2 is the exponent. This is one of the six encoding schemes available for encoding REAL values [see ISO 8824 (X.208), Reference 5.3].

BIT STRING value. As can be seen from Table 5.5, BIT STRING can be encoded either as a primitive or constructed. When transferring data contents, if it is necessary to transfer a part of the data, then the constructed form can be used.

For primitive encoding, the BIT STRING identifier and length fields are derived in the same fashion as in BOOLEAN or INTEGER encoding. The data contents are broken as shown in Figure 5.8.

In Figure 5.8, in the data contents field, the first octet is known as the *initial octet.* There are other octets numbered from 1 to 5. The last octet is known as the *final octet.* The initial octet has the number of unused bits in the final octet. This number, represented by an unsigned binary integer, can be from 0 to 7. BIT STRING occupies one to five octets.

Let us show how a BIT STRING value can be represented, using some examples. First, a BIT STRING of “0B2FADE” X is taken. In the primitive form, it is as follows:

Identifier	Length	Data contents
03	05	050B2FADE0

In this example, because BIT STRING belongs to the UNIVERSAL class, bits 8 and 7 are each 0, the sixth bit is 0, and the other bits are set to a tag number of 3. The tag number is 3 for BIT STRING, from Table 5.3. Hence, the identifier has a value of 3. The length of the data contents is 5. In the data contents, “05” X indicates that unused bits in the final octet of “E0” X are 5. The initial octet of the data content field has “05” X.

Constructed forms. The same BIT STRING can be encoded in a constructed form as follows:

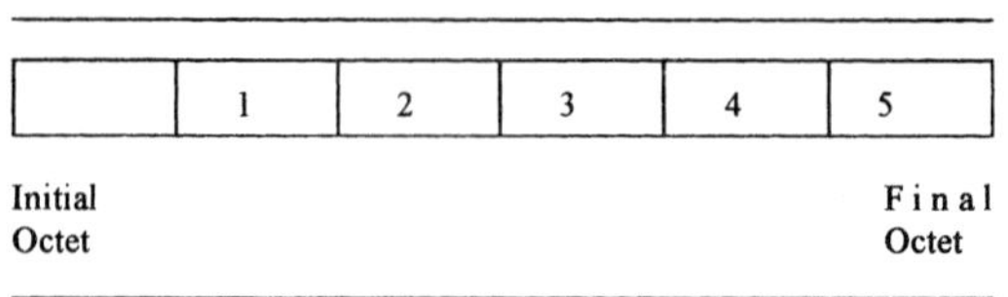

Figure 5.8 Data contents of BIT STRING values.

Identifier	Length	Data Contents		
23	0A			
	Identifier	Length	Data Contents	
	03	03	000B2F	
	03	03	05ADE0	

This constructed string has two primitive BIT STRINGs. Here "00" in the first BIT STRING indicates that all bits in the final octet are used. However, "05" X in the second primitive BIT STRING shows that five bits are unused in the last octet of the data contents field. Identifier "23" X stands for "0010 0011" B. Here, bit 6 is 1, because it is a constructed string. The tag number is again 3, because it is a BIT STRING. Each primitive BIT STRING has a length of five octets. So the total length of the constructed BIT STRING comes to "0A" X.

Indefinite form. We have modified the same example to show how the BIT STRING "0B2FADE" X can be converted to BER using the indefinite form.

Identifier	Length	Data Contents	EOC
23	80	050B2FADEO	0000

In the length field, "80" X stands for the indefinite form, and it is represented as "1000 0000" B, followed by length, data in the form BIT STRING, and end of contents.

NULL value. The NULL value is represented by a zero length octet, and the identifier field has "05" X.

OCTET STRING value. OCTET STRING can be encoded as a primitive or constructor. The constructor form is used when we transfer data values in parts. Here all the octets are used for values, unlike the encoding of BIT STRING values. Using OCTET STRING, "JOHN" will be encoded as shown in Figure 5.7. Here, we use the primitive form, and the UNIVERSAL class number for OCTET STRING is 4.

Constructed forms. As can be seen from Table 5.5, SEQUENCE, SEQUENCE OF, SET, and SET OF use constructed forms. Due to this, a P/C value of 1 is used for constructor. There are no firm rules on how different elements must be transmitted by a sender in the case of SET and SET OF. As we have seen earlier, in SET and SET OF definitions of ASN.1, no restrictions are placed on the order of elements. On the contrary, for SEQUENCE and SEQUENCE OF, the order of elements is important. So while forming transfer syntax, the order is preserved. The order of elements in ASN.1 is also preserved, if the values are sent for OPTIONAL or DEFAULT for all the cases. In this case, there is no distinction between SET, SET OF, SEQUENCE, and SEQUENCE OF.

OBJECT IDENTIFIER and ObjectDescriptor. In the case of OBJECT IDENTIFIER, we encode it after we make a conversion of the first two elements into one by using the first element × 40 plus next element. Each element uses bits from 7 to 1 of an octet. If an element cannot be represented by seven bits of an octet, more octets are used. Bit 8 of the first octet and each subsequent octet except the last one is set to 1. Bit 8 of the last octet is set to 0 indicating that it is the last octet used for calculating the value of an element. Let us return to our example of lanNetwork and see how an OBJECT IDENTIFIER is encoded.

lanNetwork OBJECT IDENTIFIER ::= {1 3 6 1 4 1 140 85}

The lanNetwork is encoded as shown in Figure 5.9. Because OBJECT IDENTIFIER falls under the UNIVERSAL class, bits 8 and 7 are both set to 0. Because it is primitive, bit 6 is 0. OBJECT IDENTIFIER has a value of 6 in the UNIVERSAL class, and so the tag number is 5. The first element of OBJECT IDENTIFIER for encoding is 1 × 40 + 3 or 43, so for encoding we use {43 6 1 4 1 140 85}. Each element is encoded using one or more octets. In Figure 5.9, we have used two octets to encode the value of 140. Note that, in the first octet, for representing 140, the eighth bit is set to 1 and in the second octet, the eighth bit is set to 0.

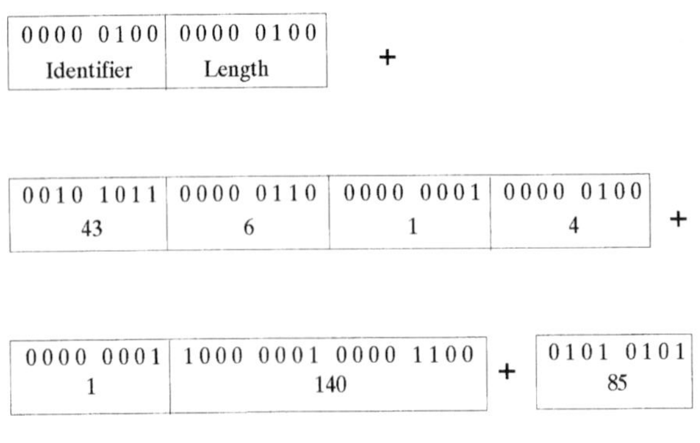

Figure 5.9 Example of encoding of OBJECT IDENTIFIER.

ObjectDescriptor is encoded as an OCTET STRING and the UNIVERSAL class value of 7 is used.

ANY and EXTERNAL. As we have seen earlier, ANY is used for defining a type later, but the type must be an ASN.1 type. ANY DEFINED BY further restricts the meaning of ANY, and it provides the location where the type is defined. So ANY and ANY DEFINED BY are encoded and decoded according to the rules used in the encoding and decoding of the ASN.1 types used.

EXTERNAL has relevance if it is defined, since data types other than ASN.1 may be used. There must be agreement on the encoding between the sending and receiving sides for the data to be useful.

5.4 Notes on the Use of ASN.1 and BER

MACROs are used for providing extensions to ASN.1 grammar and are expected to provide flexibility. But there is a price to pay for this flexibility. Compilers for MACROs are tough to design and implement. MACRO will be replaced by a new ASN.1 built-in type: CLASS. CLASS provides a template for defining MACROs.

In some cases, the encoding of ASN.1 types is not efficient. As an example, to encode a BOOLEAN value, three octets are required. Such lacunas can be overcome by using *Packed Encoding Rules* (PER). The PER compact encoding scheme enables us to represent the values by eliminating the use of identifier, length, or both, depending on the situation.

There are also many ways to encode some of the ASN.1 types. The encoding of a REAL value is one such example. These different forms of encoding add unnecessary complexity to the encoding and decoding of ASN.1 types. To overcome this pitfall, *Distinguished Encoding Rules* (DER) have been developed. DER enable us to zero in on one way to encode a particular ASN.1 type.

The use of ASN.1 and BER is not mandatory in applications for transferring data between application entities by OSI standards. It may or may not be used, depending on the applications.

One disadvantage of ASN.1 and BER is that they are difficult to understand. There are encoders which convert ASN.1 values to BER. The encoded data can be converted back to ASN.1 values using decoders. These encoders and decoders are commercially available. Note that encoder and decoder terms have become common in the industry and they are used for conversions from one format to another, but in this book, they specifically refer to the data conversions from ASN.1 to BER and from BER back to ASN.1. These encoders and decoders add complexity and extra processing and code. Extra processing has an effect on performance. It should be avoided as much as possible.

Encoders and decoders simplify the coding aspect, but they do not eliminate the extra steps involved in encoding and decoding. One might ask why we need these transformations if both the ends "speak" the same language. A partial answer is to use them only where they are needed. There may be cases in which the application entities span different languages and continents. In such cases, encoding and decoding may be useful.

Furthermore, a number of computer software vendors have joined together and formed groups known as the Desktop Management Task Force (DMTF) and Distributed Support Information Standards Group (DSISG). These groups are exploring the possibilities of managing desktop systems in multivendor, heterogeneous environments. Their focus is mainly on the workstation and personal computer arena. Their interfaces may eliminate the need for the use of ASN.1 and BER in desktops.

5.5 Summary

In this chapter, we have investigated ASN.1, used for communicating between application entities. ASN.1 concepts have been explained with examples. We also looked at the BER, used for transferring data between presentation layers. Finally, we discussed the practical aspects of using ASN.1 and BER.

5.6 References

5.1 T.61, CCITT Recommendations, Character Repertoire and Coded Character Sets for the International Teletex Service, 1992.
5.2 T.101, CCITT Recommendations, Data Syntax 1 for International Interactive Videotex Service, 1992.
5.3 ISO 8824 (X.208), Information Processing Systems, Open Systems Interconnection, Specification of Abstract Syntax Notation One (ASN.1), 1990.

5.7 Further Reading

Hebrawi, B., *OSI Upper Layer Standards and Practices,* New York: McGraw-Hill, Inc., 1993.

ISO 6093, Information Processing Systems, Representation of Numerical Values in Character Strings for Information Interchange Version, 1985.

ISO 8824-1, Information Technology, Abstract Syntax Notation One (ASN.1), Part 1: Specification of Basic Notation, Amendment 3: Rules for Extensibility, 1994.

ISO 8824-2, Information Technology, Open Systems Interconnection, Abstract Syntax Notation One (ASN.1), Part 2: Information Object Specification, 1992.

ISO 8824-3, Information Technology, Open Systems Interconnection, Abstract Syntax Notation One (ASN.1), Part 3: Constraint Specification, 1992.

ISO 8824-4, Information Technology, Open Systems Interconnection, Abstract Syntax Notation One (ASN.1), Part 4: Parameterization of ASN.1 Specification, 1992.

ISO 8825 (X.209), Information Technology, Open Systems Interconnection,

Specification of Basic Encoding Rules for Abstract Syntax Notation One (ASN.1), 1990.
ISO 8825-1, Information Technology, Open Systems Interconnection, Specification of ASN.1 Encoding Rules, Part 1: Basic Encoding Rules, 1992.
ISO 8825-2, Information Technology, Open Systems Interconnection, Specification of ASN.1 Encoding Rules, Part 2: Packed Encoding Rules (PER), 1994.
ISO 8825-3, Information Technology, Open Systems Interconnection, Specification of ASN.1 Encoding Rules, Part 3: Distinguished Canonical Encoding Rules, 1992.
Rose, M. T., *The Open Book, A Practical Perspective on OSI,* Englewood Cliffs, N.J.: Prentice Hall, 1990.

Chapter

6

Structure of Management Information

6.1 Introduction

We have seen in earlier chapters that to manage a resource, the resource must be represented as a managed object class. When representing a new resource, the inheritance hierarchy defined by the OSI is very useful. The new resource must be appropriately made a subclass of the managed object class, which closely resembles it. All the characteristics such as attributes, operations, notifications, and behaviors of the superclasses are inherited. Sometimes, inheritance property reduces the definition of a managed object class to a minor tweaking of characteristics.

It is also useful to understand how a managed object class is defined, which makes it essential that the concepts involved in the definitions of managed object classes be understood. We have investigated the meaning of a managed object class in Chapter 2 on OSI Systems Management Overview. This chapter will extend the concepts explained earlier by further examining how a managed object class is defined.

6.2 Overview of the Structure of Management Information Documents

The OSI Structure of Management Information documents start with 10165. The document 10165-1, Management Information Model, primarily furnishes basic building blocks for the definition of a managed object class. The 10165-1 document contains the following:

- Concepts of managed object classes and how they are defined
- Explanations of how managed object classes should be defined for compatibility and interoperability purposes
- Descriptions of management operations that can be done on attributes and managed objects
- Descriptions of filter operations that can be done on managed object classes, because filters are widely used in CMIP
- Descriptions of notifications that must be emitted by managed objects
- Discussion of the issues involved in the naming of managed objects, including the concept of containment, which are very important for consistency in implementation

Document 10165-2 defines the managed object classes required for systems management functions starting with 10164. The most important standard, 10165-4, specifies rules and provides templates for defining managed object classes. This document is popularly known as *Guidelines for the Definition of Managed Objects* (GDMO).

Document 10165-5 defines managed object classes which can be used in different layers. This document also provides definitions of resource-specific managed object classes such as ports. Document 10165-6 relates to the conformance testing of managed objects and systems management functions (this will be discussed in Chapter 18). To those involved in the systems management area, it is useful to know what is in each document; thus, we have furnished further details on these documents in Section 6.5. Since 10165-7, on the General Relationship Model, has already been examined in detail in Section 3.13, it is not covered here.

6.3 Managed Object Class

The definition of a managed object class needs the following:

- An *identifier* of the managed object class
- An *allomorph attribute* that identifies the managed object classes which are allomorphic to the managed object class defining the allomorph attribute
- A *name binding attribute* used to uniquely identify a managed object of the managed object class and stating the relationship of a managed object to its superior
- A *package attribute* which is a conditional attribute and contains a list of object identifiers of the packages used

6.4 Guidelines for the Definition of Managed Objects (GDMO) Templates

To avoid confusion in defining managed object classes, a formal ASN.1 format for definitions must be used. This standard format is known as a *template.* These templates are used for the definitions of components of managed object classes such as packages, parameters, attributes, attribute groups, behaviors, actions, or notifications. GDMO provide the following templates:

- *Managed object class:* In this template, inheritance relationships, which are central to the reuse of characteristics with other managed object classes, are defined. Managed object classes contain packages of behavior, attributes, attribute groups, actions, and notifications. Also, additional templates can be included or borrowed from other managed object classes. Figure 6.1 details the contents used in the definition of a managed object class.
- *Package:* Attributes, attribute groups, operations, notifications, behavior definitions, and parameters are collected to form an identifiable template. A package template can be inserted in managed object class templates.
- *Attribute:* This template is used for providing attribute syntax, and includes attribute syntax, rules to test the attribute values, behaviors, the attribute identifier, and parameters.
- *Attribute group:* When attributes are grouped for convenience, they form attribute groups. Attribute group templates indicate the

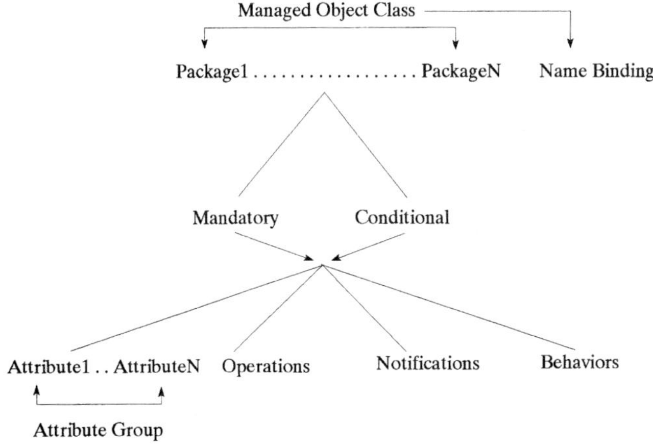

Figure 6.1 Managed object class definition.

set attributes, comprising the group and an identifier value to identify the attribute group.

- *Action:* This template is used to define the behavior and syntax of action types, which are carried in CMIS M-ACTION.
- *Behavior:* This template is used to extend the semantics of previously defined templates. It is helpful in further explaining managed object classes, name bindings, attributes, parameters and actions, and notifications which have been defined elsewhere.
- *Notification:* Notifications, which are carried in CMIS M-EVENT-REPORT, are defined in this template.
- *Parameter:* Parameters, used in defining attributes, operations, and notifications, are defined in this template. Specifications and parameter syntaxes along with the behaviors are also listed.
- *Name binding:* This template is used for uniquely naming a managed object. It specifies the naming attribute used for naming and identifies the superior object.

We have used a bottom-up approach in furnishing the details of these templates, starting with the explanation of attributes (Section 6.4.1) and proceeding to the managed object classes (Section 6.4.10) at the end. When using templates for defining managed object classes, certain conventions are used, and these are furnished in OSI document 10165-4. The important ones are:

- A semicolon (;) marks the end of each construct and the end of a template.
- All symbols and keywords are case sensitive. That means lower- and uppercase letters indicate different things. For example, "A" is different from "a."
- Comments start with "--" and end with "--" or the end of a line.
- Spaces, the end of a line, a blank line, or comments are valid delimiters.
- Whenever text is used in a template, one of the text-delimiter characters is used. These are: ! " # $ ^ & * ´ ` ~ ? @ \. However, the same text delimiter should be used at the start and end of the string representing the text. For example, if we use "!," then the text should also end with "!."
- The template label must be unique to a document. When defining templates, the syntax is <template-label> Template Name.

6.4.1 Attribute

A managed object class must have properties to be meaningful. These properties are known as *attributes*. An attribute must have a value. For example, the definition of a managed object class, tokenRing, can have an attribute such as tokenRingBandwidth. When defining this attribute, tokenRingBandwidth=16 indicates a token ring with a bandwidth of 16 Mbits.

Attribute values can be single-valued or set-valued. Single-valued attributes have only one value. *Set* is a mathematical concept. Set-valued means that there can be more than one value of the same type. In sets, ordering is not important, and there is no repetition of values.

An attribute may have more than one value. For example, assume that the managed object class, tokenRing, has an attribute, tokenRingBandwidth. We model bandwidth as an attribute, because bandwidths can vary. In tokenRingBandwidth=4,16,100, the attribute tokenRingBandwidth has different values, which are 4, 16, and 100 Mbits.

Attribute values are visible at the boundary of a managed object class. When we perform certain operations on a managed object class, these values can be retrieved or modified. For example, a Get on the attribute tokenRingBandwidth will retrieve the values of 4, 16, or 100. Similarly, when we do a Set on the attribute tokenRing Bandwidth, we can modify a value from 16 to 4.

For identifying an object, the managed object class must have at least one attribute used for naming, which is a mandatory attribute. This attribute identifier and value uniquely identify a managed object. The attribute is read-only. If this attribute can be deleted, then it is necessary to define an additional unique identification attribute.

6.4.2 Attribute template and definition

Let us define an attribute template for the managed object class tokenRing.

```
tokenRingBandwidth ::= INTEGER
tokenRingCardPrice ::= SET OF INTEGER
tokenRingID ::= tokenRingAddress
tokenRingAddress ::= OCTET STRING SIZE (4)
tokenRingBandwidth              ATTRIBUTE
        WITH ATTRIBUTE SYNTAX INTEGER;
REGISTERED AS                   {1 3 5 8 9 2};
tokenRingCardPrice              ATTRIBUTE
        WITH ATTRIBUTE SYNTAX SET OF INTEGER;
```

```
REGISTERED AS              {1 3 5 8 9 3};
tokenRingID                ATTRIBUTE
      WITH ATTRIBUTE SYNTAX tokenRingAddress;
REGISTERED AS              {1 3 5 8 9 4};
```

In the preceding definition of attributes for the managed object class tokenRing, observe the following interesting points:

- For defining the attributes, ASN.1 notations are used.
- tokenRingBandwidth is the template label, and ATTRIBUTE is the template name. The ATTRIBUTE template starts with tokenRingBandwidth and ends with ";" for REGISTERED AS.
- REGISTERED AS {1 3 5 8 9 2} is a *construct*; REGISTERED AS is the *construct name* and {1 3 5 8 9 2} is the *construct argument.*
- Formats for defining attributes follow a definite pattern, starting with the data type. This is followed by the definition of each attribute. Each attribute name has the keyword ATTRIBUTE. Then the data type of the attribute is defined by WITH ATTRIBUTE SYNTAX. The definition of the attribute ends with REGISTERED AS. These values are obtained either by internally defining the attributes or from standards bodies. However, the values must be unique and are indicated by the last numbers within the braces: 2, 3, or 4. Note that the registration numbers used are arbitrary; these are used just for explanation purposes.
- The attribute identifier values given by REGISTERED AS are used to identify the attribute, and they are in addition to the managed object class identifiers.
- Notice that tokenRingID is defined in terms of another data type, tokenRingAddress. We again define the data type of tokenRingAddress. Thus, the data type of tokenRingID is defined by the data type of tokenRingAddress.

An attribute template has some additional keywords, which will be explained next. Examine the attribute, counter1.

```
counter1                   ATTRIBUTE
      WITH ATTRIBUTE SYNTAX INTEGER;
      MATCHES FOR EQUALITY, ORDERING;;
REGISTERED AS              {1 3 5 8 9 5};
```

MATCHES FOR defines tests that can be performed on values of attributes for filter operation. If this is not indicated, then the tests on the values cannot be done, and they are not defined. Any specific attribute characteristics or indications of how attributes behave under matching rules are provided by MATCHES FOR or other behaviors. Behaviors that are specific to a managed object class are defined in the managed object class definition template.

The attribute counter1 is defined as an INTEGER which can take only a single value. MATCHES FOR is then defined; it means that we can test this counter for equality, i.e, whether the counter value has reached or is equal to 30. By having the qualifier ORDERING, we can also test whether the present counter value is greater than 30 or the value of 30 is greater. There are two semicolons because there are two qualifiers, EQUALITY and ORDERING.

```
tokenRingCounter            ATTRIBUTE
      DERIVED FROM counter1;
REGISTERED AS               {1 3 5 8 9 6};
```

In the preceding definition of the attribute tokenRingCounter, attribute characteristics are derived from another attribute, counter1. Here, counter1 is defined in a different place. Note that DERIVED FROM is absent if the WITH ATTRIBUTE SYNTAX is present. DERIVED FROM helps us to make use of attribute definitions already made. By defining new rules, we can further extend or restrict the definitions derived from another attribute.

Let us proceed in our definition of counter by adding a new keyword, BEHAVIOR.

```
counter2              ATTRIBUTE
      WITH ATTRIBUTE SYNTAX INTEGER;
      MATCHES FOR EQUALITY, ORDERING;;
      BEHAVIOR
            counterBehavior     BEHAVIOR
            DEFINED AS "Tests for equality and greater than values are
                        permitted.";
REGISTERED AS               {1 3 5 8 9 7};
```

DEFINED AS is used along with BEHAVIOR. DEFINED AS is followed by a string, and it supplies further meaning for the behavior of the managed object class, name bindings, parameters, attributes, actions, or notifications. Here, note that we have used quotes (" ") for text delimiters.

An attribute template uses the keyword PARAMETER. This is used for defining errors or processing failures. To define PARAMETER, we reference the label defined in a PARAMETER template (see Section 6.4.7).

```
counter3                         ATTRIBUTE
       WITH ATTRIBUTE SYNTAX INTEGER;
       MATCHES FOR EQUALITY, ORDERING;;
       BEHAVIOR
            counterBehavior              BEHAVIOR
            DEFINED AS  "Tests for equality and greater than values are
                         permitted.";
       PARAMETER counterThresholdDetails;
REGISTERED AS                             {1 3 5 8 9 8};
```

In the preceding definition of the counter3 attribute template, we have added counterThresholdDetails along with the keyword PARAMETER. PARAMETER counterThresholdDetails is defined outside the counter3 attribute, and it is defined in the parameter template.

An attribute can have a single value. For TokenRingBandwidth, it may be 4. It can also have values of 16 and 100. Here we need to use the data type SET OF. Types can also be SEQUENCE and SEQUENCE OF.

The attribute values can be a set of values of the same data type. These are restricted to a *permitted set.* The permitted value set mentions the values that an attribute can take. They may also be called *allowed values.* The value of an attribute cannot cross the limits of a permitted value set when modifying values. A permitted value set can be further restricted to a *required value* set. This set can be empty if no values are required; otherwise, it mentions the values an attribute is required to have.

When a managed object class has many attributes, it may be better to subdivide it into subordinate classes. This will improve the efficiency of operations that are performed on it.

6.4.3 Attribute group

A managed object class may have many attributes. For convenience and ease of operations, we can combine attributes into an attribute group. However, this restricts the operations we can perform on an attribute group. An attribute group has no value; hence, only those operations which do not require values can be performed on it.

Attribute groups are of two types: *fixed,* in which a collection of attributes is defined and more attributes cannot be added, and *extensible,* in which attributes can be added. Extensible attributes are defined in mandatory or conditional packages.

Attributes can be part of different attribute groups. In the following example, the attribute tokenRingID can be part of another attribute group in addition to the tokenRingGroup.

```
tokenRingGroup          ATTRIBUTE GROUP
GROUP ELEMENTS          tokenRingBandwidth, tokenRingCardPrice,
                        tokenRingID;
FIXED;
DESCRIPTION        "This includes tokenRingID of lanNet managed object
                   class.";
REGISTERED AS           {1 3 5 8 9 6};
```

In the preceding definition of the attribute group tokenRingGroup, the attributes tokenRingBandwidth, tokenRingCardPrice, and tokenRingID are grouped together. By adding the keyword FIXED, we have taken care that no more attributes can be added to the tokenRingGroup. If FIXED was not there, we could add one or more attributes, such as tokenRingBridge. Note that individual attributes such as tokenRingBandwidth, tokenRingCardPrice, and tokenRingID can be single-valued or set-valued attributes.

6.4.4 Action template

The action template is used in the definition of a managed object class. It maps to the action type parameter of CMIS M-ACTION service. For example, in a token ring, a ring station may have errors. When errors are hard errors or errors that must be rectified before a ring station becomes operational, there is no option but to bypass the ring station. When the errors are rectified, the ring station can be brought back into the token-ring network. To bypass the ring station, a new action, tokenRingBypass, is defined as follows:

```
tokenRingBypass                   ACTION
     BEHAVIOR                     ringStationBypass;
     MODE CONFIRMED;
     WITH INFORMATION SYNTAX CHARACTER STRING SIZE
     (128);
     WITH REPLY SYNTAX            CHARACTER STRING SIZE (128);
REGISTERED AS                     {1 3 5 8 9 6};
ringStationBypass                 BEHAVIOR
     DEFINED AS "When a ring station is to be bypassed on hard errors,
                this message is sent.";
```

The preceding definition of tokenRingBypass furnishes some interesting details. tokenRingBypass is the name of the action defined. For details of the behavior of this action, we must go to the behavior template labeled "ringStationBypass." By having the keyword MODE CONFIRMED, Action will have a confirmed message or reply after sending ACTION. If MODE CONFIRMED is not there, then Action is confirmed or unconfirmed as decided by the managing station.

WITH INFORMATION SYNTAX furnishes details of the information carried by Action. It is defined here as a string of messages which can be up to 128 octets. However, if this keyword is absent, then there is no information carried by Action.

The keyword WITH REPLY SYNTAX carries details of reply information that is sent as a result of Action. WITH REPLY SYNTAX is also defined as a string of messages with a maximum length of 128 octets. If this keyword is absent, then there is no reply associated with Action. Finally, REGISTERED AS is our usual identifier of the action template.

6.4.5 Behavior template

When a managed object is defined, it must be specified how attributes, operations on attributes, notifications, and name bindings behave. These details are explained in a behavior template. Behavior should be an extension of the earlier aspects of behaviors. It should not add new semantics or meanings to the previous ones.

```
tokenRingBridgeError            BEHAVIOR
        DEFINED AS "When a token ring bridge encounters errors, this
                    message is sent.";
```

6.4.6 Notification template

A managed object sends notifications when a certain internal or external event occurs. This is specific to a managed object. The notification must also contain information to be useful. The kind of notification and the information that it contains are defined when defining a managed object class. The notification type defined in the notification template is carried in the Event Information or Event Reply parameters of CMIS M-EVENT-REPORT.

For example, when a token-ring adapter is about to fail, it may provide an indication or emit a message saying that it is going to be "dead." This can be defined as follows:

```
tokenRingBeaconing              NOTIFICATION
REGISTERED AS                   {1 3 5 8 9 7};
```

Whether these notifications are logged internally or forwarded externally depends upon the *event forwarding discriminators* (EFDs). EFDs also determine whether these notifications generate confirmed or unconfirmed event reports. We will discuss EFDs in Chapter 16.

6.4.7 Parameter template

Parameters can be associated with attributes, operations, and notifications. They can be included in package, attribute, action, and notification templates. A parameter can define CMIS processing failures, notification requests and responses, or action requests and responses.

Referring to the example of counterThresholdDetails, a parameter template is defined as follows:

```
counterThresholdDetails          PARAMETER
        CONTEXT                  ACTION-REPLY;
        WITH SYNTAX              CHARACTER STRING (40);
REGISTERED AS                    {1 3 5 8 9 14};
```

After a threshold value of 30 is reached for soft errors in the network, this error message, Soft Errors Threshold, is exceeded by x number of errors, where x is any number from 0 to 29. However, when we reach the number 30 again, our counter wraps around. Soft errors are errors in ring stations in a token-ring network where one need not bypass the ring station.

In the preceding example, CONTEXT references conditions defined externally to this parameter template. As an example, CMIS parameters are defined in another place. The error message is carried in the CMIS M-ACTION Action Reply parameter. This parameter will be a Character String with a maximum of 40 octets.

6.4.8 Package template

The package template is used for grouping many characteristics of a managed object class. If we look from the top down of a managed object class template, the package template is one hierarchy below the managed object class template. In managed object class templates, package templates can be included using CHARACTERIZED BY or CONDITIONAL PACKAGES.

A managed object class consists of package templates. These package templates can be *mandatory* or *conditional.* Mandatory packages, as the name suggests, are required. However, the attributes in conditional packages will be present depending on the conditions spelled out in the definitions. For example, if a printer is the managed object class, the toner package will be present if it is a laser printer.

These packages, in turn, consist of attributes visible at our conceptual boundary, operations on a managed object, behavior of a managed object, and the notifications emitted by a managed object class.

In packages, we have to consider the following key points:

- The rules regarding the creation and deletion of managed objects must be spelled out. How managed object class instances relate to each other must be specified. If there is any relationship with other managed object class instances, these must be specified, too. Initial value managed object (IVMO) values are also outlined.
- The attributes and operations that can be done on these attributes should be indicated.
- Attributes have a property list which defines operations that can be done on them. The list can also supply details such as default values, initial values, permitted values, and required values. For example, the attribute tokenRingBandwidth can have a default value of 4 Mbits, if the network has 4 Mbits as the most common value. However, the permitted value can be anywhere from 0 to 100. The required values can be in the range of 1 to 16 Mbits. When there is a default value of 4 Mbits, in another token ring which has mostly adapters with values of 1 Mbit, we can set the initial values to 1 Mbit.
- The operations and notifications of managed object class instances are specified. As noted earlier, operations on attributes are Get, Replace Attribute Values, Replace With Default Value, Add Member, and Remove Member. However, the operations on a managed object class such as Create and Delete are part of the name binding template. Actions are defined in action templates.

Now, let us define a package by combining the concepts we introduced earlier.

```
tokenRingLan              PACKAGE
     BEHAVIOR             TokenRingLan
     ATTRIBUTES           tokenRingBandWidth      REPLACE-
                                                  WITH-
                                                  DEFAULT,
                          tokenRingCardPrice      GET,
                          tokenRingID             PERMITTED
                                                  VALUES
                                                  000000-
                                                  XXXXXXX,
                          tokenRingCounter        INITIAL
                                                  VALUE 0;
     ATTRIBUTE GROUPS     tokenRingGroup;
     ACTION               tokenRingBypass;
     NOTIFICATION         tokenRingBeaconing;
tokenRingLan              BEHAVIOR
     DEFINED AS           "This LAN segment connects token ring";
```

In the preceding template, we have left out REGISTERED AS. If CONDITIONAL PACKAGES is to be used, then REGISTERED AS is required.

6.4.9 Name binding template

We have already looked into the naming of a managed object in Chapter 3. We revisit some of the concepts as they relate to name binding. Each instance of a managed object class needs to have a unique name. This is formed by concatenating the relative distinguished names (RDNs) indicated in the naming tree. An RDN is unique with respect to it superiors. The RDN consists of the naming attribute used in the name binding template and the value associated with it.

Return to the example of tokenRing. In the naming tree, lanNetwork (Figure 3.6) is the superior managed object class, if we consider the tokenRing managed object class. To make up the name of a managed object instance, we concatenate RDNs. It is necessary for one attribute, known as a *distinguishing attribute,* to be unique in the managed object class tokenRing, and this is used to distinguish each instance.

Previously, we assumed that workstationIDs are uniquely assigned IDs for identification purposes in the tokenRing network. This enables the naming relationship of instances formed by using either networkAddress or workstationID.

```
tokenRingNaming                          NAME BINDING
     SUBORDINATE OBJECT CLASS            tokenRing AND SUB-
                                         CLASSES;
     SUPERIOR OBJECT CLASS               lanNetwork;
     WITH ATTRIBUTE                      workstationID;
     BEHAVIOR                            workstationIDnaming;
     CREATE                              WITH-AUTOMATIC-
                                         INSTANCE-NAMING;
     DELETE                              ONLY-IF-NO-CONTAINED-
                                         OBJECTS;
     REGISTERED AS                       {1 3 5 8 9 20};
workstationIDnaming                      BEHAVIOR
     DEFINED AS                          "This is unique identifier";
```

In the preceding name binding template, there are many interesting issues. The distinguishing attribute is workstationID. It is used for forming the RDN of lanNetwork. However, for forming a unique name or a distinguished name, name binding of the superior managed object class lanNetwork is used. SUBORDINATE OBJECT CLASS is actually the label of the managed object class template. AND SUBCLASSES here states that workstationID can be used for naming of subclasses of the managed object class tokenRing. BEHAVIOR should specify the choices that must be made if there is more than one name binding relationship.

When creating an object instance, one need not specify a name for the Create object operation. In Delete, by specifying ONLY-IF-NO-CONTAINED OBJECTS, the Delete operations are limited or restricted. A managed object which is being deleted may have zero or more objects contained in it, so before doing a Delete operation, the deletion of all the contained objects must be done first. Otherwise, there will be an error.

With another option, DELETES-CONTAINED-OBJECTS, it doesn't matter whether there are contained objects. They are deleted too.

6.4.10 Managed object class template

The definition of a managed object class is uniformly done in a standard template to avoid the confusion that might result from different people defining objects in different manners. This ensures that a managed object class defined in place A can be interpreted easily in place B. The good news is that we make use of templates we have previously defined. The managed object class template is at the top of the definitions hierarchy.

One of the important keywords is DERIVED FROM, which indicates that all the characteristics of the superclasses in the inheritance hierarchy will be inherited. The highest superclass is *top*. In other words, all managed objects are derived from the managed object class *top*. Also, all characteristics of superclasses are inherited, and none of them can be excluded. We can add more characteristics by including mandatory and conditional packages.

The presence of mandatory packages is indicated by the keyword CHARACTERIZED BY. As seen earlier, packages may have behavior, attributes, attribute groups, operations, and notifications. The presence of conditional packages is identified by the keyword CONDITIONAL PACKAGES.

Making use of earlier definitions, a managed object class, tokenRing, is defined.

```
tokenRing                          MANAGED OBJECT CLASS
      DERIVED FROM                 lanNet;
      CHARACTERIZED BY             tokenRingLan;
```

CONDITIONAL PACKAGE	tokenRingRouter PRESENT IF "connected to an FDDI backbone LAN";
REGISTERED AS	{1 3 5 8 9 2};

In the preceding definition of the tokenRing managed object class, the superclass is lanNet, which, in turn, may have its own superclasses. The mandatory package is tokenRingLan, which has already been explained. There is, however, one more conditional package of tokenRingRouter. It specifies that this conditional package will be present only if the token-ring network is connected to an FDDI backbone. In this case, definitions of tokenRingRouter will also be included. As mentioned earlier, REGISTERED AS gives the unique identifier for a managed object class.

Compilers are available for managed object class definitions. These compilers do the syntax checking on whether the managed objects defined follow the Guidelines for the Definition of Managed Objects (GDMO) format. These compilers furnish outputs in GDMO and ASN.1 formats. Some front-end editors take the user-friendly screen inputs for the definition of managed object classes in GDMO format. These editors do the syntax checking and provide definitions of managed object classes in GDMO format. This can be used as input to GDMO compilers.

6.5 Notes on the ISO 10165 Documents

The managed object classes defined in ISO document 10165-2 are furnished in Table 6.1. These are the core group of managed object classes, and they can be used for defining other managed object classes used in systems management. This document also defines attribute types, name bindings, packages, attributes, action types, parameter

TABLE 6.1 Managed Object Classes Defined in ISO 10165-2.

alarmRecord	objectCreationRecord
attributeValueChangeRecord	objectDeletionRecord
discriminator	relationshipChangeRecord
eventForwardingDiscriminator	securityAlarmReportRecord
eventLogRecord	stateChangeRecord
log	system
logRecord	top

types, and notification types. In addition, conventions for conformance and templates for compliance testing are specified in this document.

Packages defined in this document are presented in Table 6.2. This document, as mentioned, has attribute types such as counter, gauge, counter-Threshold, gauge-Threshold, and tideMark. These are useful for performance management. Twenty-five EVENT-REPORT–related attributes are also defined in this document and they are useful for different systems management functions. In addition, state and relationship attributes are defined in this document. Document 10165-2 is quite useful for defining our own managed object classes. It is, however, better to reuse definitions furnished in the document.

Document 10165-5 defines managed object classes which can be used as superclasses for defining the managed object classes of individual layers. These managed object classes, which are listed in Table 6.3, are known as generic managed object classes. Name bindings to be used are furnished in this document. These managed object classes can use inheritance and extend the definitions of managed object classes defined in document 10165-5. Some of the objectives are to reduce duplication of efforts and inconsistencies in the definition of managed object classes.

In addition, 28 attributes, which are used in the definition of managed object classes, have been defined in document 10165-5. One

TABLE 6.2 Packages Defined in ISO 10165-2

additionalInformationPackage	notificationIdentifierPackage
additionalTextPackage	dailyScheduling
attributeIdentifierListPackage	duration
attributeListPackage	externalScheduler
availabilityStatusPackage	sourceIndicatorPackage
correlatedNotificationsPackage	weeklyScheduling

TABLE 6.3 Generic Managed Object Class Definitions in ISO 10165-5

applicationProcess	port
communicationsEntity	sap1
communicationsInformationRecord	sap2
clProtocolMachine	singlePeerConnection
coProtocolMachine	subSystem
physicalMedia	

attribute group (Counters), three Actions (activate, deactivate, and deactivateWhenNoUsers), and one notification (communications-Information) have been defined. Note that clProtocolMachine can be used by an entity using a connectionless-mode communications function. Similarly, coProtocolMachine refers to a connection-oriented communication function.

6.6 Summary

In this chapter, we have discussed how a managed object class is defined using templates. This information is furnished in ISO document 10165-4, Guidelines for the Definition of Managed Objects (GDMO). Along with this, we examined the different templates, such as attribute, action, attribute group, notification, and behavior. An overview of ISO documents 10165-2 and 10165-5 was also presented.

6.7 Further Reading

ISO 10165-1 (X.720), Information Technology, Open Systems Interconnection, Structure of Management Information, Part 1: Management Information Model, 1991.

ISO 10165-2 (X.721), Information Technology, Open Systems Interconnection, Structure of Management Information, Part 2: Definition of Management Information, 1991.

ISO 10165-4 (X.722), Information Technology, Open Systems Interconnection, Structure of Management Information, Part 4: Guidelines for the Definition of Managed Objects, 1992.

ISO IS 10165-5 (X.723), Information Technology, Open Systems Interconnection, Structure of Management Information, Part 5: Generic Management Information, 1992.

Part

2

Internet Network Management

Chapter

7

TCP/IP Protocol Suite Overview

7.1 Introduction

In the Internet community, the TCP/IP protocol suite is used extensively for computer networking. TCP/IP is very popular because of the simplicity and openness of the protocols.

Note that there is a difference between "capital I" Internet and "small i" internet. The former is a global network formed by loosely organized and autonomous interconnected networks. It uses Internet Standards such as TCP/IP. Previously, it was called the National Science Foundation (NSF) backbone net. The TCP/IP protocol suite is also known as Internet. The scope of Internet Standards covers TCP/IP protocol suite and protocols, procedures, and conventions used in the Internet context. On the other hand, internet (lowercase) refers to a collection of networks not connected to the Internet, but using Internet Standards. TCP is a stream-oriented protocol and does not bother about record boundaries. It deals with bytes instead of records, as in some other protocols such as SNA. Also in TCP/IP, all computers are generically referred to as *hosts*. Notice that *host* in TCP/IP is a very generic term, which can mean a workstation, a personal computer, or even a mainframe. In the mainframe world, a mainframe is generally referred to as a host, unlike in the Internet arena. Devices which connect networks and forward Internet Protocol (IP) packets are known as *gateways,* which has here a broader meaning and scope than the gateways referred to in the LAN arena. TCP/IP gateways are similar to routers in the LAN arena. Currently, gateways may also be known as *IP routers.*

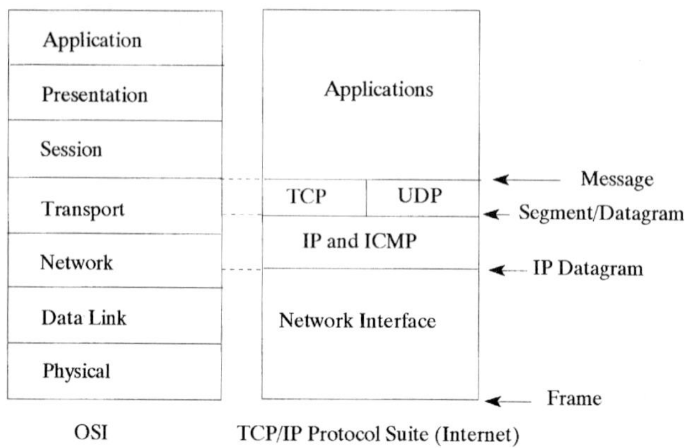

Figure 7.1 TCP/IP protocol stack.

The protocol stack of TCP/IP is shown in Figure 7.1. The first layer is the *network interface* (NI) layer. Internet does not have any standards defined for this layer. This layer can have Ethernet, X.25, or token rings. The NI layer corresponds to the physical and link layers of the OSI seven-layer architecture as shown in Figure 7.1. Access to the ports is achieved in the physical layer. In the link layer, one of the MAC layer protocols is used. The protocol can be Ethernet, CSMA/CD conforming to IEEE 802.3, or token ring conforming to IEEE 802.5.

The layer above the NI is the IP layer. This is a connectionless layer. Above this layer can be connection-oriented TCP or the connectionless *User Datagram Protocol* (UDP). On top of these layers are applications such as the *File Transfer Protocol* (FTP), *Simple Mail Transfer Protocol* (SMTP), *TELNET,* and *Simple Network Management Protocol* (SNMP).

As can be seen from Figure 7.1, a *message* or *stream of data* is transferred from the application layer to the TCP/UDP layer. When transferred to the lower IP layer along with the TCP/UDP header, this message is called a *packet.* This packet, in turn, is wrapped with proper IP headers and becomes an IP *datagram,* which is passed to the NI. In the NI layer, the IP datagram is again packaged with the appropriate NI headers; this is known as a *frame.* This frame is transmitted over the network.

Internet uses SNMP for network management. In the first version of SNMP, security was a weak link. To overcome some of the weaknesses of SNMP, it has been modified. The earlier SNMP is known now as SNMPv1 or SNMP version 1; the new modified protocol is known as SNMPv2 or SNMP version 2. Internet network management is covered in the next three chapters.

The main objective of this chapter is to introduce to readers the important lower-level protocols used in Internet network management, assuming SNMPs as the higher-layer application protocols. To understand SNMP, important concepts of the lower-layer protocols are required. Because this book deals with network management, only an overview of the lower-layer TCP/IP protocol suite is provided.

7.2 Internet Addressing

In IP, transmission of data and headers is done as shown in Figure 7.2. Octet 1 is transmitted first, then octet 2, and so on. An IP address has two parts: network number and host number. The IP layer recognizes the IP address only. IP address classes are Class A, Class B, Class C, Class D, and Class E (Figure 7.3). From Figure 7.2, notice that the main distinction among Class A, Class B, and Class C is in the division between network number and host number, also referred

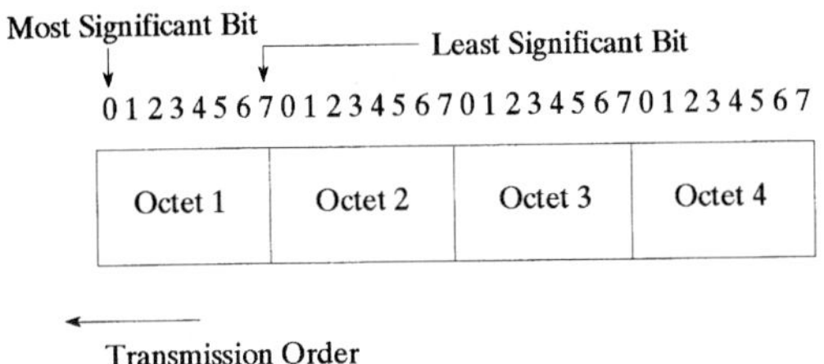

Figure 7.2 Internet header and data transmission order.

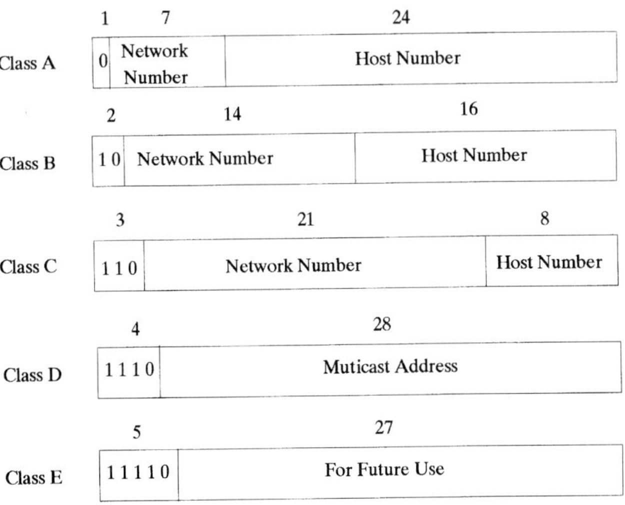

Figure 7.3 IP address classes.

to as the *rest field.* In Class D, the first four bits are 1110, and the remaining 28 bits are known as the *multicast address.* When IP packets have to be sent to a group of stations, this is known as multicasting. *Broadcasting* is an extension of multicasting, in which all the stations in a subnet receive the IP packet. In Class E, the first four bits are 1111. Class E addresses are reserved for future uses.

The main advantage of these classes is flexibility for arranging the networks. For example, a large number of workstations may need to be connected to form a network. In such a case, the Class A addressing scheme is convenient. If a relatively small number of workstations are to be connected to form a LAN, Class C may be appropriate.

The 32 bits of IP address are divided into four eight-bit fields. The IP addresses in *Dotted Decimal Notation* are formed by decimal numbers obtained from each of the eight-bit fields, and they are separated by periods (.). As an example, 183.127.2.35, a class B address, is shown in Figure 7.4. The network numbers are assigned by the Network Information Center (NIC). (The address of the NIC is furnished in Appendix C). At the time this manuscript was written, work on IP version 6 was ongoing. In IP version 6, an IP address will be 16 octets (128 bits). This will solve the present problem of a shortage of IP addresses.

A process in the application layer chooses the transport it requires. It decides whether it wants to use a connection-oriented service such as TCP or a connectionless service such as UDP. The next layer (TCP/UDP) wraps its own header to the data it received from the process in the application layer (see Figure 7.5). The action of wrapping a header on the data received from an upper layer is known as *encapsulation.* The internet layer, in turn, adds its own header and sends the data to the local NI. The local NI maps the IP address to the local network address.

If a packet is to be transmitted from one host in a network to a host in another network, then the local gateway address must be found and the packet must be transmitted to the right gateway. The gateway maps the IP address to the local network address and routes the packet to the destination host or another gateway in the path of the destination host. A packet may be delivered to a destination host by

1011 0111	0111 1111	0000 0010	0010 0011
183	127	2	35

Figure 7.4 Example of an IP address.

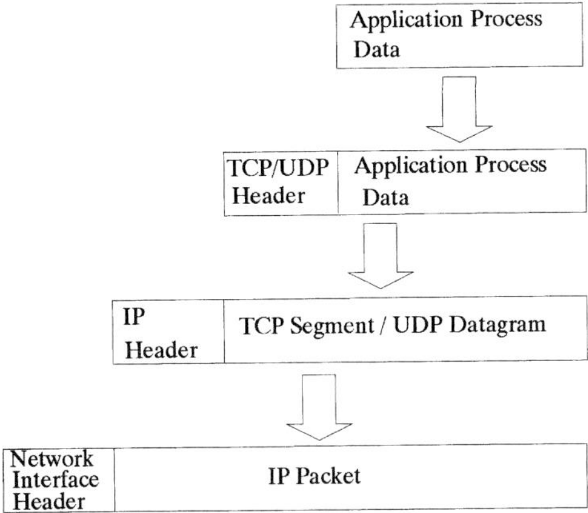

Figure 7.5 Encapsulation in TCP/IP.

more than one path. To avoid such a situation, the gateways have algorithms to calculate the right path.

7.3 Internet Protocol (IP)

The IP is a connectionless best-effort packet delivery service. In this protocol, there is no end-to-end guaranteed delivery, acknowledgment, flow control, retransmission, or error recovery. This protocol tries its best to deliver packets to the destination. The frames are discarded as a last resort. If connection-oriented support is required, then it must be provided by the upper layers. The IP layer deals with four-octet IP addresses.

The IP datagram is as shown in Figure 7.6, consisting of the IP header and the data portion. The first field in the IP header is the *version* of IP, which version is provided to furnish details of the IP software. Like any technology, changes do occur to account for advances. The present version is 4. The version field alerts the system to these changes and facilitates compatibility.

The IP header length is in multiples of 32 bits. The *length* field extends from the version field to the beginning of the data portion. Total length is inclusive of the IP header and data, and is measured in octets. Because the length field is 16 bits, it can accommodate up to 65,535 octets. However, there is also a restriction that hosts must be able to accept IP datagrams larger than 576 octets.

Though IP imposes an upper limit of 65,535, protocols used in the lower levels impose their own restrictions. For example, Ethernet has its minimum of 64 octets and maximum of 1518 octet frame length

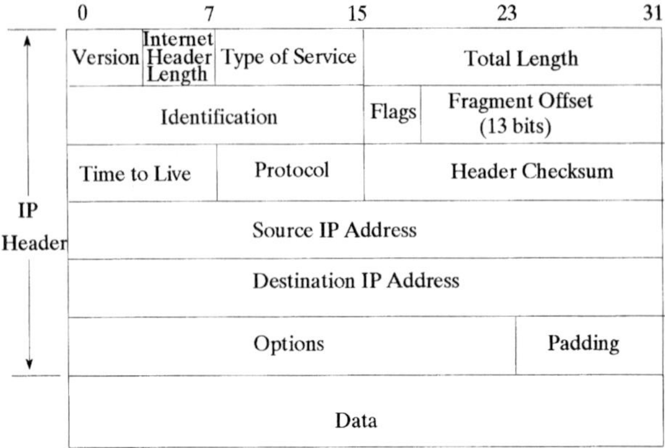

Figure 7.6 IP datagram.

limitations. So the length of datagrams sent in networks will be guided by limitations other than the ones imposed by the IP layer.

The *type of service* (TOS) field is one octet long. The first three bits indicate *precedence,* for which different levels are defined. High-precedence traffic is regarded as more important than low-precedence traffic. The TOS field is shown in Figure 7.7. The values that *delay throughput reliability* (DTR) bits can take are shown in Table 7.1.

Bits 6 and 7 of the TOS field are reserved for future use, and they are set to zero. However, RFC 1349 redefines the TOS field (Figure 7.7). Here the TOS field is taken as four bits; the last bit is labeled

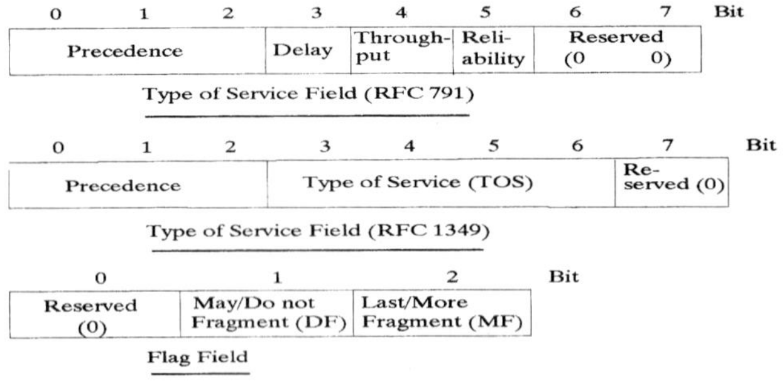

Figure 7.7 Type of service and identification fields.

TABLE 7.1 Significance of DTR Bits

Bit value	D (Delay)	T (Throughput)	R (Reliability)
0	Normal	Normal	Normal
1	Low	High	High

TABLE 7.2 TOS Field Values

Value	Meaning
1000	Minimize delay
0100	Maximize throughput
0010	Minimize reliability
0001	Minimize cost
0000	Default value or normal service

Must Be Zero (MBZ), and this bit is unused. TOS values mentioned in Table 7.2 are the values which will be tried. If the network cannot provide the TOS requested, then values used will be those of the network. Also, in Table 7.2, TOS values are interpreted as a set of integers and not as a set of bits as in Table 7.1.

When a datagram is larger than the size that can be handled by a network, then a gateway converts the datagram into smaller-size fragments which are multiples of eight. As an example, the IP datagram shown in Figure 7.8 can be converted to smaller datagrams as shown. This action of forming smaller datagrams out of a large one is known as *fragmentation,* also sometimes known as segmentation. However, these fragments are reassembled only in the destination host and not in the intermediate gateways.

The *identification* field is 16 bits in length (Figure 7.9). It has three bits of the *flag* field and 13 bits of *fragment offset.* In the flag field, the first bit (bit 0) is set to 0. Bit 1 has two options. If it is set to 0, then it indicates that the datagram may be fragmented. If it is set to 1, then the datagram cannot be fragmented. Bit 2 of flag again has two options. When fragmentation is done, this bit in the last fragment is set to 0. However, in other fragments, this bit is 1, indicating that there are more fragments of the datagram. The other IP field, *frag-*

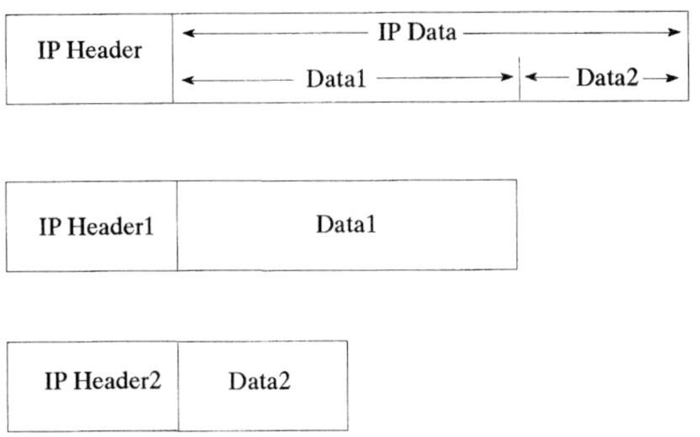

Figure 7.8 Example of IP datagram fragmentation.

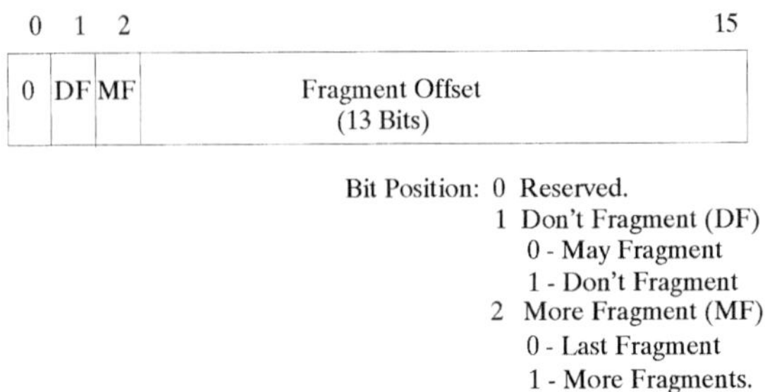

Figure 7.9 Identification field.

ment offset, furnishes the offset of the datagram, which is in units of eight octets. The first fragment has a fragment offset of 0.

The next IP header field, known as the *time to live* (TTL) field, is eight bits long and has time in seconds. TTL specifies how long a datagram remains in a system. Because a gateway is able to process a packet in less than a second, the TTL count is reduced by one. In such a case, the TTL counter becomes a maximum allowable count of hops for a packet to reach the destination host. When the TTL becomes zero, then a datagram destroys itself. This process is also known as *self-destruction* and prevents a datagram from making unnecessary cycles in the network.

The *protocol* field has the protocol number of the upper layer. For example, ICMP has a protocol number of 1, and the protocol number for TCP is 6. Assigned numbers of higher-layer protocols are furnished in Reference 7.1. The *header checksum* field provides the checksum of the IP header field only, and does not include the checksum of the data portion. It is obtained by adding the ones complement of different fields and then taking the ones complement of the sum. The source and destination IP addresses are the addresses of the sender and receiver. The destination IP address does not refer to the addresses of intermediate gateways.

The *options* field must be implemented in all hosts and gateways, but it is optional in datagrams. There are two types of options field, Case 1 and Case 2, as shown in Figure 7.10. In Case 1, the *option type* field is one octet long. Case 2 has a one-octet option type, one octet of *option length,* and the option data. The option length octet includes the length of the option data and two octets that include one octet of option type and one octet of option length fields. The option field (Figure 7.10, Case 1) has one bit of flag, two bits of option class (Table 7.3), and five bits of option number. Note that one octet of option type in Case 2 is the same as the option field of Case 1.

One bit of flag indicates whether the option field is copied into fragments on fragmentation. If it is zero, then the option field is not

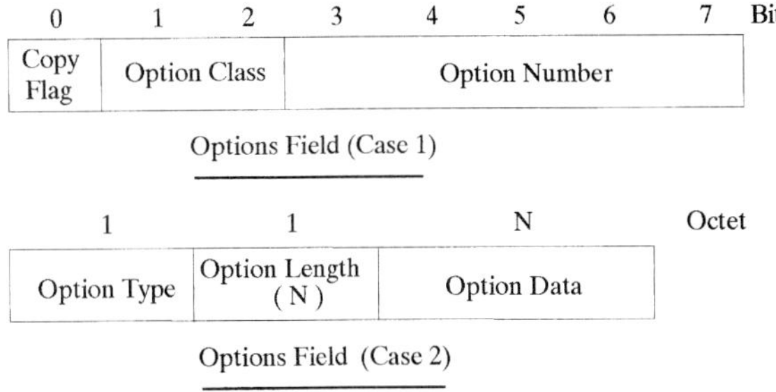

Figure 7.10 IP options field.

TABLE 7.3 Options Class Details

Class number	Meaning of class number
0	Datagram or control type
1	Reserved for future use
2	Used for debugging and measurement
3	Reserved for future use

copied and if it is set to one, then the option field is copied into all the fragments. The option field is quite useful for adding a variety of features, but options cannot be used unless they are accepted by the general Internet community.

The *padding* field is used to ensure that the IP header aligns on a 32-bit boundary.

7.4 Internet Control Message Protocol (ICMP)

ICMP is used for communicating error or control messages from one host to another host or from routers (gateways) to the host. ICMP is required in every IP layer. The ICMP message occupies the data portion of the IP. It has a header of its own and data. For an ICMP message, the protocol field in the IP header (Figure 7.6) is set to 1. The ICMP message is formed as shown in Figure 7.11. For ICMP, TOS is always set to 0000. The source address refers to the host address or router address which generated the ICMP message. The destination address is the address of the host or router to which the ICMP message must be sent.

The ICMP field always has an ICMP type field (Figure 7.11), which distinguishes different ICMP messages. There is also a code field, which gives more details about messages, and the checksum field, which furnishes the checksum for the ICMP message portion only.

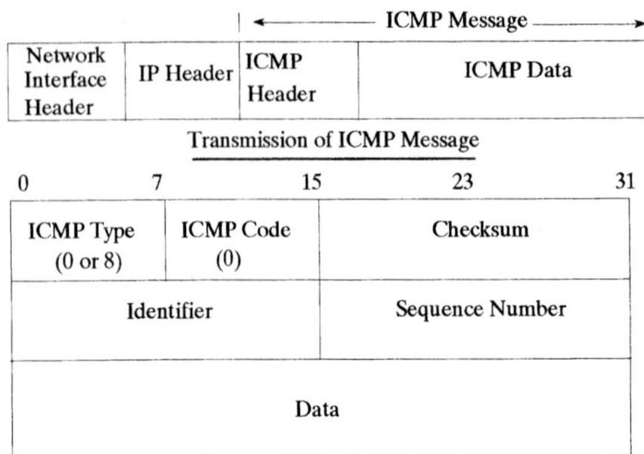

Figure 7.11 Transmission of ICMP message and echo reply and echo request ICMP messages.

This checksum is similar to the IP checksum.

The IP header and first 64 bits of the original datagram refer to the header and the data of the layer above ICMP. The layer above can be either TCP or UDP. The first 64 bits of data are used for matching processes which may use the ICMP message.

The ICMP messages are as follows:

Type	Description
3	Destination unreachable
4	Source quench
5	Redirect to change a route from the source
11	Time exceeded for IP datagram
12	Parameter problem

ICMP request messages:

Type	Description
8	Echo request
10	Router solicitation
13	Timestamp request
15	Information request (obsolete)
17	Address mask request

ICMP reply messages:

Type	Description
0	Echo reply
9	Router advertisement
14	Timestamp reply
16	Information reply (obsolete)
18	Address mask reply

The ICMP message is quite useful for discovering hosts and routers. The Packet InterNet Groper (PING) is used for checking the connectivity of a host with a remote host and getting the details of a host. It is also quite useful for network management. PING is an echo request and echo reply, and is useful for gathering data on hosts and routers. The ICMP message for an echo request and echo reply is shown in Figure 7.11. When an echo request is to be sent, the ICMP type is 8. The destination address is the address of the router or host IP which must send an echo of the message back to the sender. For the echo reply, which has same message sent in the echo request, the ICMP type is 0.

Identifier and sequence numbers are used for identifying and matching a message and its replies. If code is 0, then both identifier and sequence number may be 0. As we have seen earlier, echo request and echo reply can be used to gather data and statistics on the network and hosts and routers. They are also useful for debugging purposes.

7.5 Transmission Control Protocol (TCP)

TCP is a connection-oriented, reliable, packet-switching protocol used for communication between processes in host computers. These host computers are distinct and are part of a communication network. The data transfer is full-duplex, which means that the sender sends data in one direction and can simultaneously receive data from the opposite direction.

One of the strengths of the TCP protocol is its flexibility. It does not specifically mandate any protocol for the layer above it or the layer below. Usually, in Internet, the lower-layer protocol is IP. TCP is a stream-oriented protocol, and the combination of TCP layer data and headers is known as a *segment.*

An important concept in TCP is that of a connection. The concept of a connection is illustrated in Figure 7.12. TCP provides for a set of addresses or *ports* within each host. Many processes can be associated with a port. The IP address and port number identify a *socket.* A pair of sockets identify a *connection.* Before communication can take place, a connection must be established between processes. This connection is referred to as a *virtual circuit,* which is analogous to a telephone connection being formed before the start of a conversation.

In a network, segments of data may be damaged or corrupted, lost, duplicated, or delivered out of order. To account for this, there is provision for acknowledgment and retransmission. When data is sent by a sender, the sequence number of the first octet of data in the segment is also sent. At the same time, the sender starts a timer. The

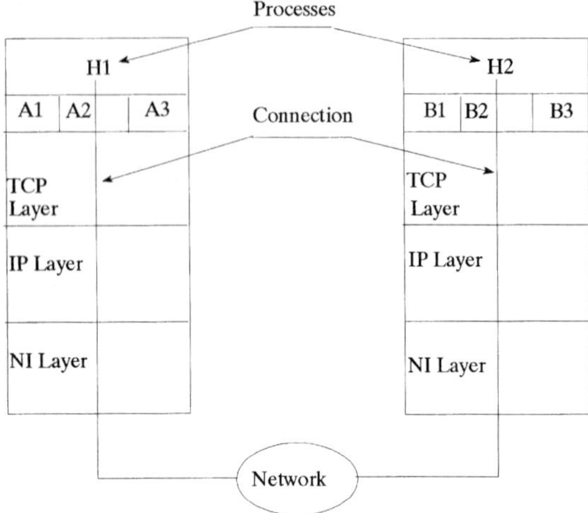

Figure 7.12 Concepts of a TCP connection.

receiving end sends an acknowledgment number. This acknowledgment refers to the sequence number of the next expected data octet to be sent by the sender. However, if the acknowledgment is not received before the timer runs out, then the sender retransmits the segment.

There is also provision for a checksum of the data to identify whether the data has been corrupted. We have seen earlier that IP does not provide a checksum of the data; it provides for a checksum of the IP header only. So TCP takes account of this fact to provide a reliable communication mechanism.

Flow control is achieved by means of a variable window that can be sent along with an acknowledgment by a receiver. If the receiver does not have much buffer space left, then it sends a smaller window. Conversely, where the receiver is willing to accept and process data at a faster rate, it adjusts the window to a larger number than the existing one.

Let us examine the important concepts of multiplexing and demultiplexing, depicted in Figure 7.13. The destination IP address identifies the destination host, and the source IP address identifies the source host address. In this figure, SA1 is the source host IP address, and DA1 is the destination host IP address. The applications A1, A2, and A3 are the source ports. It is assumed that they want to communicate with destination ports B1, B2, and B3, respectively. The process in Host 1, where applications are combined, is analogous to multiplexing, and the process in Host 2, where they are directed to the respective ports, is similar to demultiplexing seen in the data transmissions across a transmission medium.

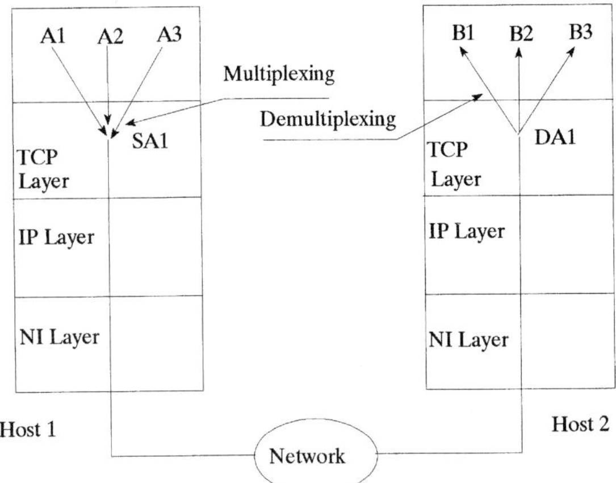

Figure 7.13 TCP multiplexing and demultiplexing.

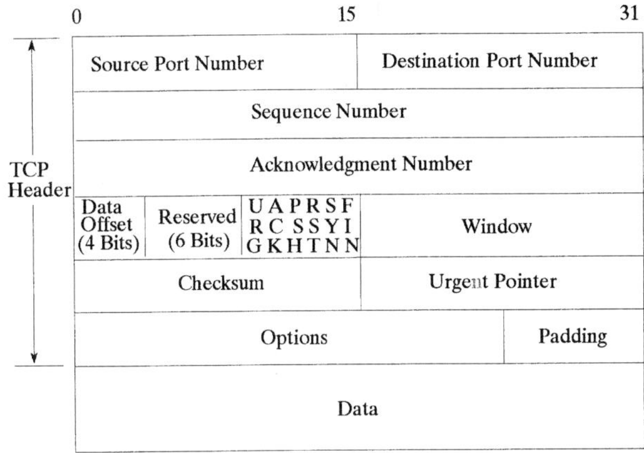

Figure 7.14 TCP segment.

A TCP segment is shown in Figure 7.14. It has a TCP header part and a data part. The TCP header has the following fields:

Source port number: A 16-bit field, containing a source port number.

Destination port number: Also a 16-bit field, with a destination port number where a data segment must be sent.

Sequence number: The sequence number of a data octet of a segment that is being sent from a sender. In the case of synchronization or when the SYN bit is set, it is the *initial sequence number* (ISN). The first octet of data starts from ISN + 1. Here note that the ISN need not always start with 0, or the first octet sequence number need not always start with 1. The sequence number is a 32-bit field.

Acknowledgment number: A 32-bit field, always sent once a connection has been established. This is the number of the first data octet which a receiver expects to receive next. For example, if a receiver has received data up to 100 octets, the receiver puts the acknowledgment number as 101. The receiver next expects a segment in which the data octet starts with 101.

Data offset: A four-bit field. A TCP header is a multiple of 32 bits. This field contains the length of the TCP header measured in terms of 32 bits. In a segment, data offset indicates where the data starts.

Reserved: Intended for future use and set to 0. It is six bits in length. It is a good idea to provide for a reserved field in any protocol. When technology changes or new technologies are incorporated, these reserved bits can be used.

The first six fields in the following list are all one-bit fields (see Figure 7.14).

URG: Urgent pointer significant field. TCP has provided for sending out-of-band urgent data. When this bit is set, the receiver is expected to process this segment first, interrupting all other activities. When the URG bit is set, the urgent pointer field has relevance.

ACK: Acknowledgment significant field. When this field is set, an acknowledgment number is sent.

PSH: Push function field. When this field is set, the sender is expected to send whatever data is available in the buffer instead of waiting for the send buffer to be filled up.

RST: Used for resetting a connection. When this bit is set, depending on the states of sender and receiver, actions are taken. For example, reset is sent when a segment for another connection is received.

SYN: For synchronizing sequence numbers. This is used in the beginning to establish a connection by means of a three-way handshake.

FIN: Used for closing a connection.

Window: A 16-bit field. Because the data in IP segments are in terms of octets, window states the number of octets which a receiver is willing to receive, starting from one.

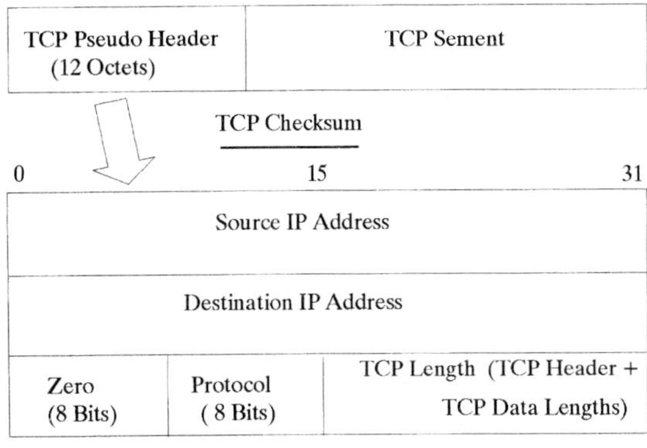

Figure 7.15 TCP checksum.

Checksum: A 16-bit field. The checksum is calculated as shown in Figure 7.15 and includes a TCP pseudo header and TCP segment. The TCP pseudo header has source and destination addresses, eight bits set to 0, the protocol (IP in most cases), and TCP length. The pseudo header is used for computing the checksum and is not transmitted while transmitting data. That is the reason for naming it a pseudo header. Here, TCP length is the sum of the TCP header and TCP data. This TCP length does not, however, include 12 octets of the TCP pseudo header. For checksum, header and text octets must be even. To make these even, sometimes the last octet is padded with 0. To form the checksum, the ones complement of the TCP header is taken, then the ones complement of the result is taken.

Urgent pointer: Provides positive offset from the sequence number in a segment. This points to data offset following urgent data. As mentioned earlier, this field is taken into consideration only if the URG bit is set. This is a 16-bit field.

Options: A variable-length field, with length in multiples of eight bits. Here, too, there are two options:

- Case 1: Has one octet of option.
- Case 2: Has one octet of option, one octet of option length, and variable-length options data. Here, as in the IP, length includes two octets due to the option and option length.

Options are defined as furnished in the following:

Options kind (in octal)	Options length (in octets)	Description
0	No length field	End of options list. There is one at the end of options list.
1	No length field	No operation. Used mainly for alignment on a word boundary.
2	4	Maximum segment size (MSS). Used to indicate maximum receive segment size. Used in segments when SYN control bit is set. When this is not mentioned, any segment size can be received.

Padding: A variable-length field used for padding such that data begin in a 32-bit boundary. Here also padding is done with zeros.

7.6 User Datagram Protocol (UDP)

SNMP, Internet Name Server, and Trivial File Transfer use the UDP protocol. This is a connectionless datagram service. UDP, in turn, depends upon the connectionless IP layer. As a result, there is no guarantee that data will be delivered; there may be duplicate frames sent, or data may be received in an order different from the order in which they were sent. Also, there is no acknowledgment that data has been delivered. However, if an application wishes to provide services that are available in a connection-oriented service, it is the responsibility of the application to incorporate them in upper-layer software.

In UDP, an application that wants to transmit data to another application uses a scheme similar to TCP. The data of the application are initially enveloped with a UDP header. Then, at the IP layer, the IP header is appended. In the NI layer, the network header is appended to the IP frame. This frame is transmitted over the Internet to the other end. On the receiving end, the NI layer removes the network layer header, and the IP layer strips off the IP header. The UDP layer, in turn, removes the UDP header and routes data to the appropriate application. If there is a mismatch or the proper frame is not received, the ICMP message can be sent to the original application with causes for the error.

The UDP datagram is as shown in Figure 7.16. It has 16 bits each of source port and destination numbers. The length field contains the number of octets of the UDP frame and includes the length of the

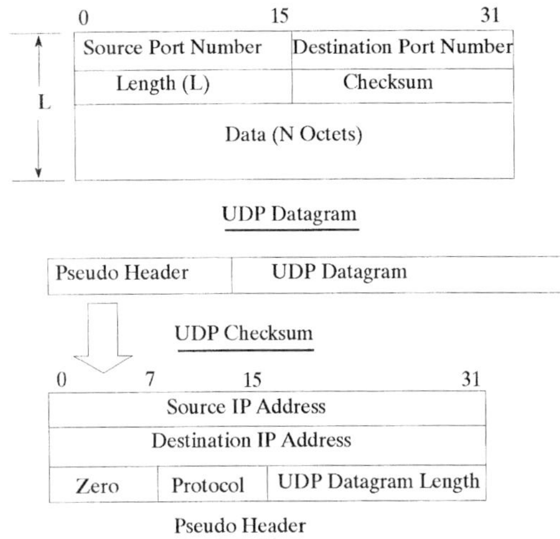

Figure 7.16 UDP datagram and UDP checksum.

UDP frame headers. The next field in the UDP header is the checksum field, which is an optional field. If it is not used, then this field has zeros; however, if the checksum field is used, it contains the ones complement of the checksum derived from a pseudo header.

The UDP pseudo header is similar to the TCP pseudo header. The UDP pseudo header has four octets each of source IP address and destination IP address, zero padding, protocol, and UDP length. One octet of zero padding is done to make the UDP frame a multiple of two. One octet protocol field is 17 for IP, and the two-byte UDP length field is the length of the UDP datagram in octets. However, the UDP length field does not include the length of the pseudo header. Thus, an application that wants to send data needs to know the IP addresses of source and destination beforehand in the UDP layer itself.

The use of checksum is mostly guided by the application. Note here that IP uses only the header checksum; it does not use the checksum over the IP data portion. Hence, if some validation of whether the UDP frame is the correct one is required, then the checksum in UDP is required.

In some cases, we may not want to have the overhead of computing the checksum, since the loss of some UDP frames may not matter much. One such case is that of monitoring the performance of a resource, where the loss of a UDP datagram may not mean much. Also, in some cases, a network may be very reliable, without the risk of losing frames. In other cases, the application may be critical and the loss of a frame may lead to problems. In such cases, it is better to use checksum. Also, when a network is unreliable, it is appropriate to use the checksum to make sure that the data delivered is correct.

7.7 Address Resolution Protocol (ARP)

We have seen that Internet knows only the IP address. Let us investigate how an IP packet is sent to the other end. An IP packet has a destination IP address. Then the local host looks at the ARP table and checks where the destination is. An ARP table is a sort of lookup table which has a mapping between an IP address and its corresponding physical address. Then the NI layer inserts the actual physical address of the destination host. The Ethernet or token-ring frame has this destination physical address.

On the destination side, this Ethernet frame is stripped of its physical address and routed to the right IP layer. When this happens, the destination is in the same network. However, it is possible that the destination could be another network, in which case, instead of the physical address of the destination host, the physical address of the IP router is appended in the Ethernet frame. In the IP router, a check is again made with a routing table to see where the destination IP address is. If there are many hops or steps required before a destination can be reached, then the physical addresses of the IP routers are successively inserted. In the last IP router, the destination host physical address is retrieved from the destination IP address to route the IP packet to the correct destination.

The next issue is how to build an ARP table. This is done by broadcasting an ARP request packet, which has a source IP address, source physical address, and destination IP address. When this packet is broadcast, each host examines the IP address and looks whether it matches its own IP address. If it matches, the host puts its IP address and physical address in the source. The earlier source IP and physical addresses are transferred to the destination IP address and the destination physical address, and the response is sent back.

In the original host that sent the ARP request packet, the ARP table now has the mapping of the destination IP address and physical address. It is possible that no host has a matching IP address when an ARP request packet is sent. In such a case, the IP address is not known.

The manner in which the IP packet handles cases in which mapping between the IP address and physical address is not known is implementation dependent. In some cases, when the mapping is not there, the IP packet is queued and an ARP request packet is sent. When the destination physical address becomes known, the ARP request packet is received. The IP packet is dequeued and sent to the destination. If the address is not known, the IP layer discards the packets. In some cases, these IP packets may not be queued. If the IP packets are not delivered, the upper layers are alerted by *timeouts*. For further details on ARP, refer to Reference 7.2.

7.8 Reverse Address Resolution Protocol (RARP)

RARP is the reverse process of ARP, in which mapping is from a physical address to the IP address. A station may have its physical address; it sends a RARP to a server giving its IP address, and the server maps the IP address and sends back the physical address. For details on RARP, refer to Reference 7.3.

7.9 Subnet Addressing

A network that uses a single access protocol under the control of a single administrative domain is known as a *subnetwork*. As a corollary to this definition, a subnetwork can be a collection of smaller networks. As we have seen earlier, the IP address consists of a network number part and a host number part (Figure 7.17). The network number part is used for routing from network to network. This provides the first level of routing. The technique of partitioning a network address to cover multiple networks is known as *subnet addressing*. Here, a host number is further divided into a subnet number part and a host number part, which enables one more level of partitioning of networks, and also helps in forming further routing levels.

In subnet addressing, to recover the network number part, a 32-bit subnet mask, which has all 1s in the network number and subnet number part, is used. The subnet mask has zeros in the rest of the mask. So when data is to be sent from station A, it goes to the appropriate router. The router uses the subnet number part to send it to

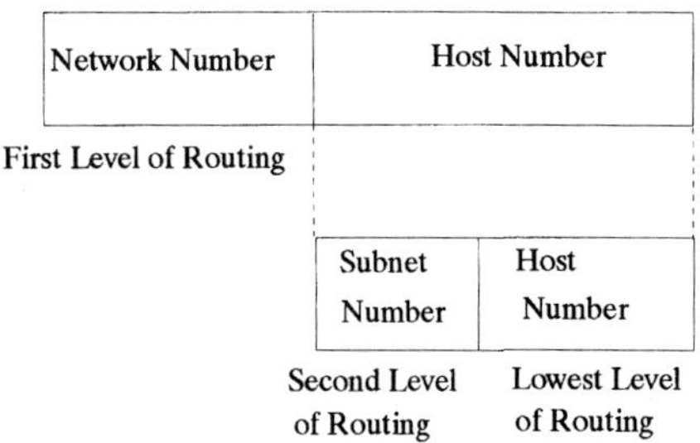

Figure 7.17 Subnet addressing.

the proper subnet or network; then the host number is used to deliver the data to the right destination host.

If all the networks are not using subnet addressing, routers use proxy ARP. According to this, for an ARP on a station address, the router answers by giving its hardware address for the address of a station. This is analogous to saying: I know station B's address; you can send frames meant for it to me. So when station A has to send the frame, it sends it to the correct router. The router, in turn, interprets the address and sends it to the right station.

7.10 Summary

Because network management belongs to the application layer, it is necessary to have some idea of the lower layers; therefore, we have examined the IP, ICMP, TCP, and UDP layers in this chapter. IP is important because it is the layer below TCP and UDP. TCP provides the connection-oriented transport in Internet, and the connectionless transport is provided by UDP. ICMP PING is used for the discovery process in network management, especially in configuration management. Some of the associated concepts such as ARP, RARP, and subnet addressing have also been dealt with here.

7.11 References

7.1 Reynolds, J., and J. Postel, *Assigned Numbers,* RFC 1700, 1994.
7.2 Plummer, D., *Ethernet Address Resolution Protocol: Or converting network protocol addresses to 48 bit Ethernet address for transmission of Ethernet hardware,* RFC 826, 1982.
7.3 Finlayson, R., *Bootstrap Loading using TFTP,* RFC 906, 1984. Finlayson, R., T. Mann, J. Mogul, and M. Theimer, *Reverse Address Resolution Protocol,* RFC 903, 1984.

7.12 Further Reading

Almquist, P., *Type of Service in Internet Protocol Suite,* RFC 1349, 1992.
Braden, R., D. Clark, S. Crocker, and C. Huitema, *Report of IAB Workshop on Security in the Internet Architecture,* RFC 1636, 1994.
Cerf, V., *The Internet Activities Board,* RFC 1160, 1990.
Cerf, V., *A View From the 21st Century,* RFC 1607, 1994.
Comer, D. E., *Internetworking with TCP/IP, Principles, Protocols, and Architecture,* vol. I, 2d ed., Englewood Cliffs, N.J.: Prentice Hall, 1991.
Deering, S., *ICMP Router Discovery Messages,* RFC 1256, 1991.
Huitema, C., *Charter of the Internet Architecture Board (IAB),* RFC 1601, 1994.
Kirkpatrick, S., M. Stahl, and M. Recker, *Internet Numbers,* RFC 1166, 1990.
Mogul, J., and J. Postel, *Internet Standard Subnetting Procedure,* RFC 950, 1985.
Parr, G., *More Fault Tolerant Approach to Address Resolution for a Multi-LAN System of Ethernets,* RFC 1029, 1988.

Postel, J., *Internet Control Message Protocol,* RFC 792, 1981. RFC 792 has been updated by RFC 950.

Postel, J., *Internet Protocol,* RFC 791, 1981. RFC 791 has been updated by RFC 1349.

Postel, J., *Transmission Control Protocol,* RFC 793, 1981.

Postel, J., *User Datagram Protocol,* RFC 768, 1980.

Socolofsky, T., and C. Kale, *A TCP/IP Tutorial,* RFC 1180, 1991.

Stallings, W., *Handbook of Computer-Communication Standards, Volume III, The TCP/IP Protocol Suite,* 2d ed., New York: Macmillan, 1990.

Chapter

8

Internet Network Management: SNMPv1 and MIB-II

8.1 Introduction

In Internet, the management of networks, devices, and hosts is referred to as network management, which is different from the terms used in OSI. To closely reflect the protocols and be consistent with the terms in the Internet community, we prefer to retain the term *network management* rather than *systems management.*

Originally in Internet, network management was done using the *Simple Gateway Monitoring Protocol* (SGMP). Then the *Simple Network Management Protocol* (SNMP) was defined for the management of networks and network devices. However, the syntax and semantics of SNMP are different from those of SGMP. The protocol stack of SNMP is shown in Figure 8.1.

The objects to be managed are defined in the *management information base* (MIB). These objects must follow a certain set of rules as mentioned in the *Structure of Management Information* (SMI) such that an object defined by the *X* group is compatible with the definition of the object by the *Y* group.

Note that objects in Internet and those in OSI are different. Internet objects are similar to attributes in OSI, and an Internet object group can best be described as analogous to an OSI managed object class. In Internet, an object is more like a variable found in programming languages; it has a syntax and semantics. Each object can have one or more object instances, each of which, in turn, has one or more values. In the following text, the terms *object* and *variable* are used interchangeably because of the closeness in the semantics of the two terms.

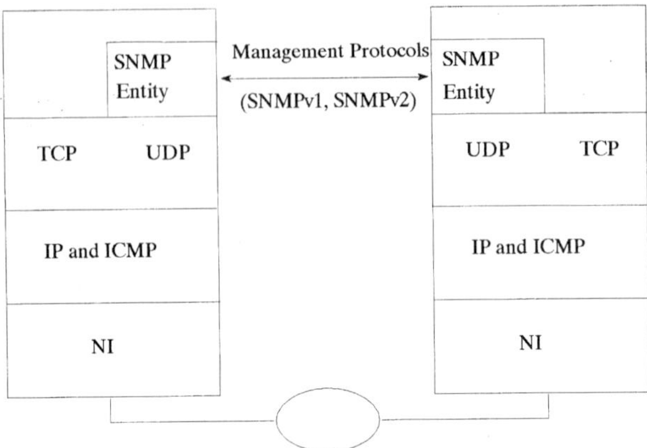

Figure 8.1 SNMP management protocols.

The network management system consists of one or more *network management stations* (NMSs) and one or more *network elements* (NEs) with network management functions, management information, and management protocols. The network management system is as shown in Figure 8.2 The concepts of manager and agent are relatively new in Internet network management. An NMS is analogous to a manager in concept, and the network management functions of NEs are rolled into agents. NMSs have the following primary functions:

- Retrieve values of objects in NEs using agents. This management operation is done by a Get.
- Change or alter the values of objects in NEs using agents. This can be done by a Set.

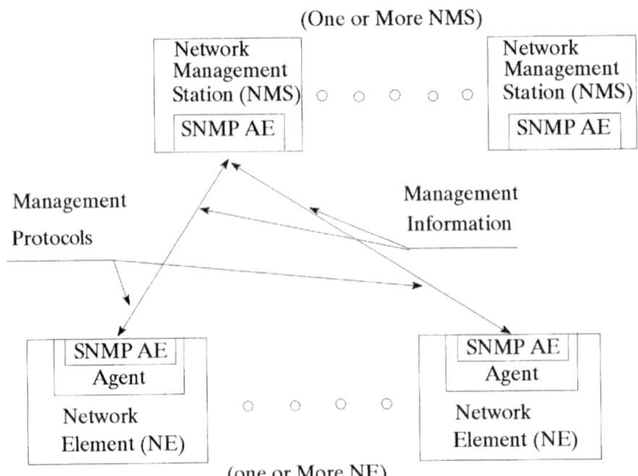

Figure 8.2 Internet network management.

Network management functions are responsible for monitoring and controlling the managed nodes. SNMP provides the management protocol for network management in the Internet world. The application entities, which can be manager or agent, exchange management information. These application entities are known as SNMP application entities. NMS sends requests and receives responses from the agents. They can also receive notifications known as *traps*. A trap is an unsolicited message sent from an agent. Agents reside in NEs, which are also sometimes known as *managed nodes*. These managed nodes are devices such as hosts, routers, LAN adapters, modems, multiplexers, hubs, and printers. Agents have the following important functions:

- They are instrumented to retrieve management information from the objects, which represent the resources.
- They alter the values of objects.
- They receive responses and traps and send them, in turn, to network management stations.

SNMP is used to communicate management information between a management station and the agents. The management applications are built on the top of network management stations. Some key philosophies involved in the design of SNMP are as follows:

- The management protocol should be as simple as possible and must be provided at least cost. The management protocols should have bare-minimum operations.
- Network management must be robust and able to provide the services, even when the state of the network is not quite reliable or when there are too many errors. SNMP must be able to handle the worst-case scenarios.
- The standard MIB will have core objects defined, and new objects to cover managed devices or managed nodes should be added to the MIB as needed. This extensibility should be easy.
- In the workload distribution between the NMS and the agents in the managed nodes, the major workload will be off-loaded to the NMS, such that it will be easy to add new managed nodes to the network. This will also help the easy extensibility of the managed nodes supported.
- The transport used for carrying management protocols is connectionless UDP. It is not necessary to have the facilities provided by a connection-oriented transport, because they add complexity to the transport.

- The initial objective was to have easy migration to the OSI network management. Now, due to the popularity of SNMP, this objective is in question. Some proponents of SNMP support abandoning the ultimate migration to OSI and, instead, favor the independent growth of Internet network management.

8.2 Internet Network Management Framework (SNMPv1)

The original network management framework consisted of RFC 1155, RFC 1157, and RFC 1212. This is known as SNMP Version 1 (SNMPv1) (see Figure 8.3). The syntax and semantics used for the definition of objects for network management are furnished in RFC 1155, and are known as the structure of management information (SMI). SMI primarily states how to define objects and how to access them. RFC 1157 furnishes the SNMP management protocol used for accessing the objects. This management protocol is used for monitoring and controlling objects. RFC 1212 furnishes guidelines for defining new MIB modules. RFC 1213 furnishes the definitions of a core set of objects known as MIB-II and which provide the base set for network management.

SNMP needs the support of the transport and network layers below it. The transport layer provides multiplexing and demultiplexing of services. This can result in the many-to-many relationships that are possible between SNMP entities. Also, transport protocols provide for the end-to-end checksum, thus improving the reliability of data transfer.

The network layer provides for the routing capabilities between networks. Also, this layer shields the SNMP entities from differences

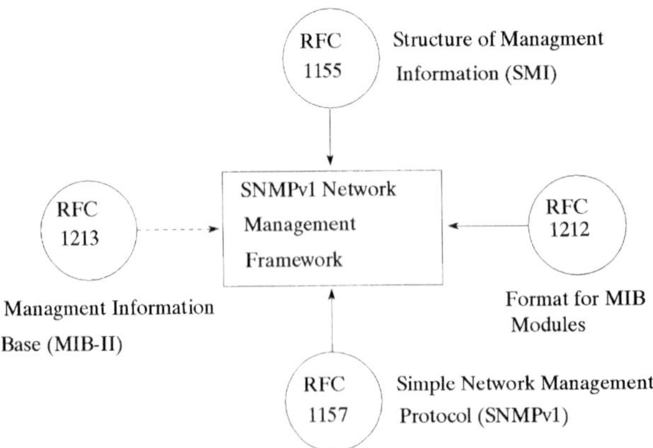

Figure 8.3 SNMPv1 network management framework.

in the media. In addition, the fragmentation and reassembly of packets of different sizes transmitted across the networks are provided by this layer. However, to reduce the possibility of fragments being lost, it is better to send small packets.

In some cases, it may not be necessary to use the transport and network layers. The network management functions may be provided directly over data link layers, as in the case of network management for point-to-point or out-of-band (OOB) management directly to the managed devices. In OOB, connections are sometimes made from management stations to the managed devices directly via dial-ups.

However, sometimes the network layer will be required. When management must be done over devices across networks, then it may be necessary to use the routing capabilities of the network layers. Skinny UDP/IP stacks may also be required in some cases. So, ultimately, these decisions must be made while designing management functions for networks.

Because much overhead is involved in maintaining one or more connections or establishing a connection and tearing it down for each SNMP entity operation on an object, a connectionless transport layer was preferred. This was one of the reasons for choosing UDP. As we have seen earlier, UDP provides unreliable datagram service as a tradeoff to keep the protocol simple. Every piece of management information is supposed to be carried in a single and independent transport datagram. With this, the complexity involved in assembling frames and the recovery for failures, such as frames not being received in order or lost frames being retransmitted, is avoided.

Internet network management operations are kept simple by limiting the operations to retrieve the value of a variable or set the value of a variable. Also, the traps sent from agents are very limited so as to reduce network traffic. Imperative commands, or commands which trigger some other action, are avoided. The Internet network management functions can be part of the network operations center (NOC). The NOC is usually a central location for monitoring the operation of a network and rectifying network problems.

The exchange of management information between an NMS and an NE is done by SNMPs. Each NE has a set of objects also known as the SNMP MIB view. We will discuss the SNMP MIB in detail in a later section. When an SNMP AE in an agent is associated with a set of SNMP AEs in one or more managers, this pairing is known as a *community* (Figure 8.4). Each community has an identifier known as the *community name.* The data type of the community name is OCTET STRING of a size from 0 to 255 octets. Only printable ASCII characters are allowed.

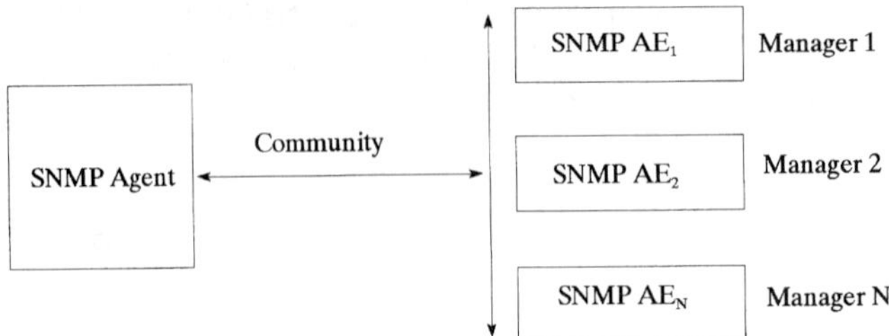

Figure 8.4 SNMPv1 community.

An SNMP message consists of a version identifier, an SNMP community name, and an SNMP PDU. The messages exchanged between an NMS and agents are independent of each other. Assume that we are keeping count of messages sent from an NMS to an agent. We have sent 15 messages, and message 16 is sent from the management station to the agent. Now, message 16 does not have any dependency on message 15. Also, in the SNMP implementation, it is recommended that message length not be more than 484 octets.

The SNMP community authentication scheme, defined by a set of rules, determines whether the messages sent between AEs are authentic ones. One example is that of an SNMP agent. It is possible that this agent would not send a trap to one particular manager, in which case, checking whether the agent is really allowed to send the trap must be done by the authentication scheme.

8.3 Internet Object

SNMP uses ASN.1 for defining objects and PDUs exchanged by the management protocol. However, all data types defined in OSI ASN.1 are not used. It was thought that by using a subset of data types, other data types could be constructed. ASN.1 data types used are INTEGER, OCTET STRING, OBJECT IDENTIFIER, NULL, SEQUENCE, and SEQUENCE OF. The data types not used in SNMP are BOOLEAN, OBJECT DESCRIPTOR, EXTERNAL, REAL, ENUMERATED, SET, and SET OF. Object types also must be encoded to be sent across a network. To keep the network management process simple, SNMP uses only a subset of the BER of OSI for transfer syntax. Definite length form and nonconstructor encodings are used. We discussed these terms in Chapter 5.

SMI permits two kinds of constructor types:

- *list* has the following syntax:

```
list ::= SEQUENCE { <type1>, ........<type>N}
```

"type1" stands for one of the ASN.1 primitive types defined in SMI. DEFAULT and OPTIONAL clauses are not allowed within the SEQUENCE of a list. We can imagine "list" as being analogous to a one-dimensional row or a column.

- *table* is defined as

table ::= sequence of <entry>

Here "entry" corresponds to the list constructor. "table" is two-dimensional and has one or more rows, with each row having one or more columns.

RFC 1155 states how the objects are to be defined. The syntax of an object is as follows:

- *Object name:* Should consist of the textual name along with the OBJECT IDENTIFIER. The textual name is known as OBJECT DESCRIPTOR. An example is sysLocation {system 6}. Here sysLocation is the OBJECT DESCRIPTOR, and {system 6} is the OBJECT IDENTIFIER. In Internet, the naming conventions for naming objects are similar to the ones used in OSI; however, the object name must be unique and easily identifiable, and it must be a printable string. {system 6} states that sysLocation is a child under "system" and is the sixth node in the object registration hierarchy. Note here that the object registration hierarchy in Internet is similar to that in OSI.
- *Syntax:* Refers to the syntax used by the object type and should map to one of the permitted ASN.1 data types. sysLocation object type syntax is DisplayString (SIZE (0..255)), for example, DURHAM2154.
- *Definition:* Contains an unambiguous description of the object type. This description is useful for instantiating object types.
- *Access:* States how the object can be accessed by management operations, and it is the minimum level of support for an object type. The values are read-only, read-write, write-only, and not-accessible. With read-only we cannot change the value by the SNMPv1 operation, SetRequest. The operations that can be performed for read-only are GetRequest and GetNextRequest. The access right of write-only enables the SetRequest operation to be done on an object. With read-write, one can perform GetRequest, GetNextRequest, and SetRequest operations. We will examine the SNMPv1 operations in detail in Section 8.7.
- *Status:* Refers to the implementation support to the object type. The values are mandatory, optional, or obsolete.

SMI standard RFC 1155 also defines the following object types:

- *Network address:* Presents options for stating addresses in different protocols. At present, only the Internet family of network addresses is allowed.
- *IP address:* Represents the 32-bit Internet address and is represented using OCTET STRING. For BER, only primitive encoding is allowed.
- *Counter:* A nonnegative integer value which increases from zero to the maximum value of 2^{32-1}. After reaching the maximum value, the counter becomes 0 and increases in value. This is also known as *wrapping around.*
- *Gauge:* A nonnegative integer, which can increase or decrease in value. The maximum value allowed for gauge is 2^{32-1}. One difference between a counter and a gauge is that in a gauge no wrapping around is allowed.
- *TimeTicks:* A nonnegative integer, which represents elapsed time, in hundredths of a second, since a particular action. The description of the object type must clearly state the particular action, such as the last update of an object.
- *Opaque:* Permits an object to transmit any data as an OCTET STRING. It is similar to the ASN.1 EXTERNAL type. Note here that an NMS and agents must have previous knowledge of the data type to parse the data.

8.4 SMI Definitions

SMI document RFC 1155 covers the object information model and a set of generic types used to describe management information. As we have seen earlier, MACROs extend the ASN.1 grammar, and the OBJECT-TYPE MACRO is included in SMI definitions. RFC 1155 defines SMI as follows:

```
RFC1155-SMI DEFINITIONS ::=  BEGIN
EXPORTS -- EVERYTHING
        Internet, directory, mgmt, experimental, private, enterprises,
        OBJECT-TYPE, ObjectName, ObjectSyntax, SimpleSyntax,
        ApplicationSyntax, NetworkAddress, IpAddress, Counter, Gauge,
        TimeTicks, Opaque;
-- the path to the root
Internet            OBJECT IDENTIFIER ::=  {iso org(3) dod(6) 1}
directory           OBJECT IDENTIFIER ::=  {Internet 1}
mgmt                OBJECT IDENTIFIER ::=  {Internet 2}
```

```
experimental        OBJECT IDENTIFIER ::= {Internet 3}
private             OBJECT IDENTIFIER ::= {Internet 4}
enterprises         OBJECT IDENTIFIER ::= {private 1}
-- definition of object types
OBJECT-TYPE MACRO ::=
      BEGIN
            TYPE NOTATION ::= "SYNTAX" type (TYPE ObjectSyntax)
                    "ACCESS" Access
                    "STATUS" Status
            VALUE NOTATION ::= value (VALUE ObjectName)
            Access ::= "read-only"
                        | "read-write"
                        | "write-only"
                        | "not-accessible"
            Status ::= "mandatory"
                        | "optional"
                        | "obsolete"
      END

-- names of objects in the MIB
      ObjectName ::= OBJECT IDENTIFIER
-- syntax of objects in the MIB
      ObjectSyntax ::=
              CHOICE {
                      simple SimpleSyntax,
-- note that simple SEQUENCEs are not directly mentioned here to keep
-- things simple (i.e., prevent misuse). However, application-wide types
-- which are IMPLICITly encoded simple SEQUENCEs may appear in the
-- following CHOICE.
                    application-wide ApplicationSyntax
}
   SimpleSyntax ::=
           CHOICE {
               number          INTEGER,
               string          OCTET STRING,
               object          OBJECT IDENTIFIER,
               empty           NULL
}
   ApplicationSyntax ::=
           CHOICE {
               address         NetworkAddress,
               counter         Counter,
               gauge           Gauge,
               ticks           TimeTicks,
               arbitrary       Opaque
               -- other application-wide types, as they are defined will be
               -- added here.
```

```
                }
                -- application-wide types
                        NetworkAddress ::=
                                CHOICE {
                                        Internet        IpAddress
                                }
                        IpAddress ::=  [APPLICATION 0] IMPLICIT
                                       OCTET STRING (SIZE (4))-- in
                        -- network-byte order.
                        Counter ::=  [APPLICATION 1] IMPLICIT INTE-
                                     GER (0..4294967295)
                        Gauge ::=  [APPLICATION 2] IMPLICIT INTE-
                                   GER (0..4294967295)
                        TimeTicks ::=  [APPLICATION 3] IMPLICIT INTE-
                                       GER (0..4294967295)
                        Opaque ::=  [APPLICATION 4] IMPLICIT OCTET
                                    STRING -- arbitrary ASN.1 value.
  END
```

Source: RFC 1155 (Structure and Identification of Management Information of TCP/IP-based internets, 1990).

8.4.1 ObjectSyntax

As we saw earlier, an object is defined using the OBJECT-TYPE macro. The data type of an object is ObjectSyntax. Though RFC 1155 does not have the simply constructed type (list and table), Marshall Rose (one of the original authors of RFC 1155), in *The Simple Book* (see Reference 8.1) also includes simply constructed in the ObjectSyntax.

SimpleSyntax is a CHOICE of one of the data types—INTEGER, OCTET STRING, OBJECT IDENTIFIER, or NULL. Application Syntax is again a CHOICE of the data types—NetworkAddress, Counter, Gauge, TimeTicks, or Opaque. We have already discussed the individual data types used in ApplicationSyntax.

8.4.2 OBJECT-TYPE MACRO extensions

The definition of OBJECT-TYPE MACRO has been further extended in RFC 1212 as follows:

```
IMPORTS
        ObjectName
                FROM RFC1155-SMI
```

```
        DisplayString
                FROM RFC1158-MIB;
OBJECT-TYPE MACRO ::=
        BEGIN
                TYPE NOTATION ::= "SYNTAX" type (TYPE
                ObjectSyntax)
-- must conform to RFC 1155's ObjectSyntax
                "ACCESS" Access
                "STATUS" Status
                DescrPart
                ReferPart
                IndexPart
                DefValPart
        VALUE NOTATION ::= value (VALUE ObjectName)
        Access ::= "read-only"
                | "read-write"
                | "write-only"
                | "not-accessible"
        Status ::= "mandatory"
                | "optional"
                | "obsolete"
                | "deprecated"
        DescrPart ::=
            "DESCRIPTION" value (description DisplayString)
                | empty
        ReferPart ::=
            "REFERENCE" value (reference DisplayString)
                | empty
        IndexPart ::=
            "INDEX" "{"IndexTypes"}"
                | empty
        IndexTypes ::=
            IndexType | IndexTypes "," IndexType
        IndexType ::=
                    -- if indexobject, use the SYNTAX value of the
                    -- correspondent OBJECT-TYPE invocation.
    value (indexobject ObjectName)
                    -- otherwise use named SMI type must conform to
                    -- IndexSyntax given below.
                | type (indextype)
        DefValPart ::=
            "DEFVAL" "{" value (defvalue ObjectSyntax) "}"
                | empty
END

IndexSyntax ::=
        CHOICE {
                number          INTEGER (0..MAX),
```

```
string          OCTET STRING,
object          OBJECT IDENTIFIER,
address         NetworkAddress,
ipAddress       IpAddress
}
```

Source: RFC 1212 (Concise MIB Definitions Status of this Memo, 1991).

DescrPart, ReferPart, IndexPart, DefValPart, and "deprecated" in Status have been added in RFC 1212. The DESCRIPTION clause indicates in detail the object type, furnishes details on implementation, and is an optional clause. REFERENCE, also an optional clause, provides a cross-reference to an object definition in some place or organization. The INDEX clause is used for object instance identification in a conceptual row. We may recall that an object corresponds to a row in a table. The INDEX clause is present only if the object type has a conceptual row. The clause DEFVAL can be used as the initial value when an instance of the object is created.

Let us take an arbitrary example of an object to illustrate the meanings of the different terms used.

```
tokenRingPrice OBJECT-TYPE
        SYNTAX INTEGER
        ACCESS read-write
        STATUS optional
        ::= {enterprises 100}
```

In the preceding object definition, tokenRingPrice is the OBJECT DESCRIPTOR, and the syntax of this object is INTEGER. {enterprises 100} is the OBJECT IDENTIFIER. ACCESS is read-write, stating that the values can be read or changed. STATUS optional states that this is an optional object which may be used.

8.5 Management Information Base (MIB-II)

In Internet, as with the OSI, the details of objects are stored in a database called the Management Information Base (MIB). MIB is an abstract concept applied to storing data. In the MIB, objects have the object type described by the OBJECT DESCRIPTOR along with OBJECT IDENTIFIER. MIBs are defined by different RFCs. The earlier MIB versions followed RFC 1065, Structure and Identification of Management Information for TCP/IP-based Internets, and RFC 1066, Management Information Base Network Management of TCP/IP-based Internets. RFC 1065 specified how the objects were to be defined and has been superseded by RFC 1155. RFC 1066 defined the objects, but was made obsolete by RFC 1156.

RFC 1155, Structure and Identification of Management Information for TCP/IP-based Internets, specified how the objects were to be defined. This RFC attempted to structure the definition of objects more like the OSI managed object class definitions. RFC 1156, known as MIB-I, contained the definition of objects. This became the Full Standard Protocol. Extensions were added to MIB-I in RFC 1158, and this version is known as MIB-II. This RFC added new objects to different groups and deprecated some objects. (*Deprecated* means that these objects will be removed in the next versions.) The idea behind these changes was to provide support for multiprotocol entities, as well as readability, clarity, and cleaning up.

RFC 1212, Concise MIB definitions, provided methods to clean up and remove the redundant object descriptions. RFC 1213, MIB-II for Network Management of TCP/IP-based Internets: MIB II, is yet another improvement over RFCs 1156 and 1158. It adds and refines objects defined in RFCs 1156 and 1158, and also makes use of RFC 1212.

However, readers should consult the latest IAB Official Protocol Standards, published often, for information about the current standardization maturity and requirement levels. Changes are frequently being made to accommodate new requirements and compatibility with OSI systems management.

8.5.1 Internet registration hierarchy

Objects must be uniquely identified for manipulation for management purposes, which is accomplished by using OBJECT IDENTIFIERs. OBJECT IDENTIFIERs are a series of identifiers derived by tagging the numbers attached to the nodes from the root in the registration hierarchy. These numbers are separated by periods.

In the registration tree shown in Figure 3.4, the registration tree at the starting point has three children with labels of ccitt(0), iso(1), and joint-iso-ccitt(2). Here, ccitt stands for the textual description of the International Telegraph and Telephone Consultative Committee, and "0" stands for the position within the root. Similarly, iso(1) stands for the ISO, and the joint-iso-ccitt(2) indicates joint administration by ISO and ITU-T.

The administrative control of each of the subtrees for assigning the numbers below them is the responsibility of the nodes. However, this may be delegated as we go down the tree. Under iso(1), org(3) is assigned to national standards organizations. The two nodes below org(3) have been assigned to the U.S. National Institute of Standards

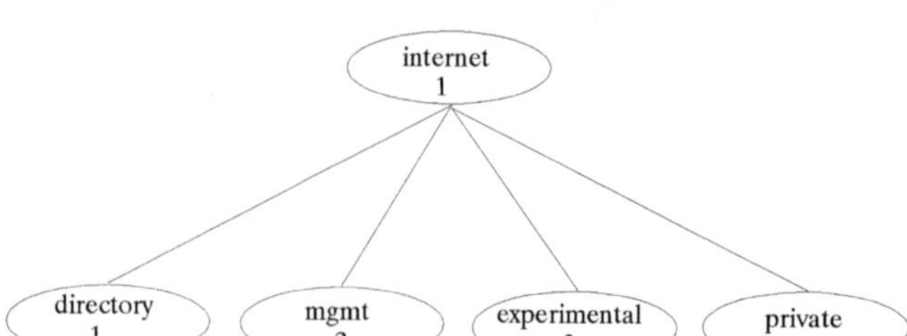

Figure 8.5 Internet registration hierarchy.

and Technology (NIST). Of the two, one node, dod(6), has been assigned to the Department of Defense (DOD), U.S. Here, internet(1) is the child under dod(6).

There are four children under internet(1), as shown in Figure 8.5: directory(1), mgmt(2), experimental(3), and private(4). The child directory(1) is reserved for the future use of OSI directory services. The Internet MIB-II is defined as a first child under mgmt(2). The IAB has delegated the authority to assign numbers in this subtree to the Internet Assigned Numbers Authority. So the object identifier would be 1.3.6.1.2.1. Here, 1 is from iso; 3 is from org; 6 is from dod, 1 is from internet; 2 is from mgmt; and the final 1 is from MIB-II.

The experimental(3) subtree is meant for objects used in Internet experiments. As an example, if an experimenter gets a number, 12, then the object identifier is 1.3.6.1.3.12. Here, except for the last two numbers, the registration numbers are the same. The next-to-last number, 3, is from the experimental node, and 12 is the number that has been assigned to the experimenter by the Internet Assigned Numbers Authority.

However, the private(4) subtree is used for numbering the objects registered by private bodies. For example, the ABCD Company may ask for a number for registering objects. If it receives a number of 100 from the Internet Assigned Numbers Authority, it will be under the private(4) subtree. The ABCD Company can define its own objects under this registration number of 100; for example, it may define an adapter for token ring as 25. Then the object identifier for token ring is 1.3.6.1.4.2.100.25. Here, the first four numbers are as explained earlier. The registration number of 4 indicates private, and 100 is the number for the ABCD Company. As already mentioned, the Internet Assigned Numbers Authority assigns these private numbers.

8.5.2 Object instance identification

To know the value of an instance of an object, it is necessary to identify the instance. This is done using the OBJECT IDENTIFIER. The following conventions apply for identifying object instances:

- *Scalar objects:* These have only one instance associated with an object. An example of a scalar object is snmpInBadValues. From Figure 8.21, the OBJECT IDENTIFIER for the snmp subtree is 1.3.6.1.2.1.11. By extending the snmp subtree, the snmpInBadValues OBJECT IDENTIFIER is 1.3.6.1.2.1.11.10 We have concatenated the subidentifier of 10 to the snmp subtree to get the OBJECT IDENTIFIER of snmpInBadValues. For each scalar object of snmpInBadValues, there is only one instance, and this instance is identified again by concatenating a value of 0 to the OBJECT IDENTIFIER of snmpInBadValues. So an instance identifier for the instance of snmpInBadValues is 1.3.6.1.2.1.11.10.0. The same procedure for deriving an instance identifier is shown as follows:

	OBJECT IDENTIFIER
snmp subtree	1.3.6.1.2.1.11
snmpInBadValues	1.3.6.1.2.1.11.10
An instance of snmpInBadValues	1.3.6.1.2.1.11.10.0

- *Columnar objects* (Figure 8.6): Only objects in a table, known as columnar objects, can be manipulated by SNMP. Tables in SNMP are two-dimensional. Instances of objects in tables are identified by the INDEX clause or the AUGMENTS clause. The INDEX clause refers to a row in a table. Note that the AUGMENTS clause is an addition in SNMPv2 (this will be discussed with SNMPv2 in Chapter 10). Let us take the example of ipAdEntIfIndex in ipAddrTable (Figure 8.12) and see how an instance identifier is formed. The OBJECT IDENTIFIER of the ip subtree (see Figure 8.11) is 1.3.6.1.2.1.4. The OBJECT IDENTIFIER of ipAddrEntry is obtained by concatenating subidentifiers 20.1 to the ip OBJECT IDENTIFIER. Hence, the OBJECT IDENTIFIER of ipAddrEntry is 1.3.6.1.2.1.4.20.1. The INDEX clause for ipAddrEntry has ipAdEntAddr (RFC 1213). The OBJECT IDENTIFIER of

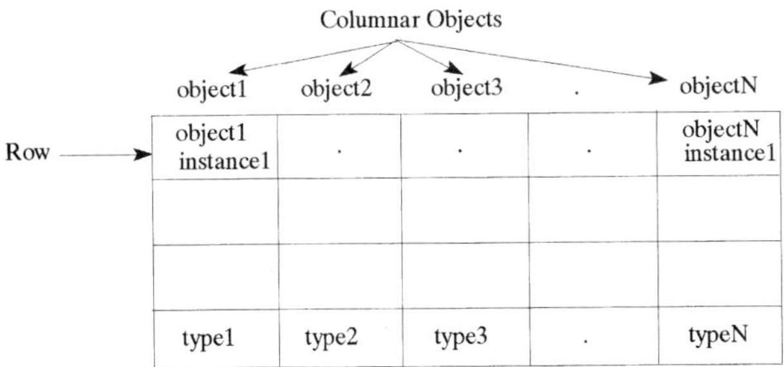

Figure 8.6 Concept of tables.

ipAdEntIfIndex is derived by concatenating the column number of 2 to the OBJECT IDENTIFIER of ipAddrEntry, which is 1.3.6.1.2.1.4.20.1.2. Now any row of ipAdEntIfIndex is indexed by the INDEX clause subidentifiers associated with ipAdEntAddr.

	OBJECT IDENTIFIER
ip subtree	1.3.6.1.2.1.4
ipAdEntIfIndex	1.3.6.1.2.1.4.20.1.2
Fifth instance of ipAdEntIfIndex	1.3.6.1.2.1.4.10.1.2.(fifth row value of ipAdEntAddr)

- *Conceptual rows and tables:* When the object types are just rows and tables, they are known as conceptual rows and conceptual tables. There are no instance identifiers associated with the conceptual rows and tables. They are not accessible by SNMP operations.
- *Lexicographic ordering: Webster's New Collegiate Dictionary* defines *lexical* as "of or relating to words or the vocabulary of a language as distinguished from its grammar or construction." OBJECT IDENTIFIERs are arranged in increasing value in SNMP MIBs. Referring to the previous example of the ip subtree, the OBJECT IDENTIFIER of ipAdEntIfIndex is lexicographically greater than the OBJECT IDENTIFIER of ip. This lexicographic ordering is useful for traversing a table without a management station actually knowing the OBJECT IDENTIFIER of an entry. For example, to retrieve the fifth instance of ipAdEntIfIndex, four GetNextRequest PDUs will be enough to obtain the value of the fifth instance.

The following rules are used for instance identification using the INDEX clause:

- *Integer-valued:* Has a single-value subidentifier to identify an object instance. These are nonnegative integers. The value of ifIndex, which can take any value ranging from 1 to the value of ifNumber, is an example of an integer-valued INDEX clause.
- *String-valued* (fixed-length strings): Has *n* octet length with *n* subidentifiers.
- *String-valued* (variable-length strings): Has *n*+1 octet length with *n* subidentifiers. The first octet has the value of *n,* which indicates the number of subidentifiers.
- *Object-identifier-valued:* Used with object identifiers. The first value is the number *n* of subidentifiers used along with the *n* subidentifiers.

- *IpAddress-valued:* Associated with four subidentifiers familiar in the IP address of the type a.b.c.d.
- *NsapAddress-valued:* Uses syntax similar to a fixed-length string with the length of the string as *n*.

8.5.3 Table manipulation

In MIB-II tables (Figure 8.6), each object is represented by a column; the value of each object instance is represented in a row. The way to retrieve values from a table is somewhat nonintuitive. The length of each column is traversed in its entirety, and then one moves on to the next column. To add the value of an object instance, the value is entered in a row with a set operation. To delete an entry, again using the set operation, the value is set to invalid.

Whether or not to remove the invalid entries is left as an implementation option. It is better to remove invalid entries when storage is a constraint; traversing the table will be faster with fewer entries. But this involves extra work—now and then, some sort of "cleaning" of the table to remove invalid entries must be done. If it is decided to do this cleaning, then it must also be determined how frequently to remove the invalid entries. Ultimately, these decisions involve tradeoffs that should be examined during the design stage.

8.6 MIB-II Details and Objects (RFC 1213)

It is necessary to follow rules when defining new MIBs. Old object types are not deleted, but they may be deprecated. The semantics of old object types should not be changed between versions. However, if it is necessary to change the semantics, then new object types must be formed. Some of these rules are formulated for the coexistence of multiple versions of MIBs.

In MIB, only the essential objects are defined. This has been done to make the implementations simple. However, there is enough flexibility to define the implementation of specific objects. The guidelines for defining new objects are provided by SMI. New objects can be added under the experimental subtree or under the enterprises subtree. Also, new versions of MIB can be released for the new standard objects, by which the definition of objects is sufficiently flexible in Internet.

MIB-II has added the data type, DisplayString. DisplayString is defined as OCTET STRING, and is a printable ASCII character string of size ranging from 0 to 255 octets. Another data type of PhyAddress is again an OCTET STRING used to represent media addresses. As an example, a token-ring address can be represented in binary in six octets.

Objects in Internet are classified into different groups. These groups are under {mgmt 2}, as shown in Figure 8.7, and the classification into groups assists in easily assigning object identifiers to the groups. Also, the objects under these groups must be implemented as a group. For example, if the TCP group is implemented, then all objects under the TCP group, such as tcpRtoAlgorithm, and tcpRtoMin, must be implemented.

Conventions used in the figures on MIB-II object groups (includes Figures 8.8 through 8.21) are:

- Each object group is shown in a separate figure. The object group name starts at the top.
- Some object groups have tables. Objects in these tables are shown in separate figures.
- The number after an object stands for the node within a group hierarchy. For example, sysDescr (1) stands for sysDescr {system 1}

In the explanations of the objects in MIB-II furnished subsequently, the syntax of the object type is supplied along with the object, in parentheses. For example, in sysDescr (DisplayString), sysDescr is the OBJECT IDENTIFIER, and DisplayString is the data type of the object. Also, in the following explanation, objects are mentioned. There are two types of objects: MIB-II objects and the object instance representing a resource, which is monitored by a network management system. This subtle difference between the two types of objects should be noted.

8.6.1 System group

The system group (Figure 8.8) is mandatory. The objects in this group broadly explain the names and versions of hardware and software,

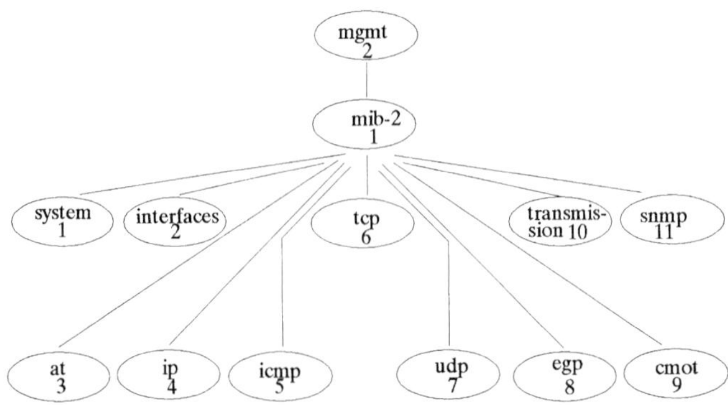

Figure 8.7 MIB-II objects group.

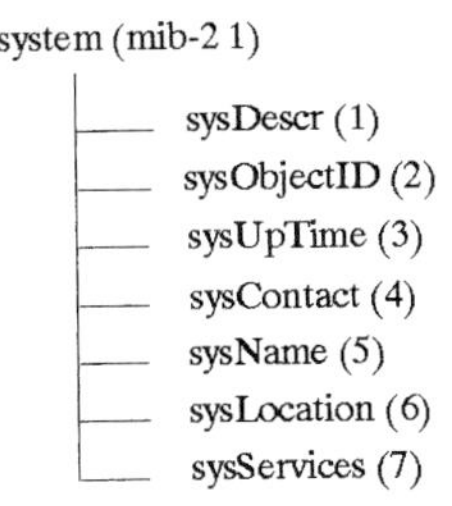

Figure 8.8 System group.

the vendor's subsystem, the length of time the network management system portion was up and running, the contact person for this node, the node's domain name, the physical location, and the sum of services the node provides. Concerning different objects in the system group, RFC 1213 states, "if an agent is not configured to have a value for any of these variables, a string length of 0 is returned." The return value of zero should be avoided for stating that an object is not supported. This can be ambiguous in some cases. It is hard to distinguish whether the value is actually zero or an object is not supported. For avoiding different interpretations during implementations, the unsupported cases should show theoretically impossible return codes instead of zero. This scenario is also well explained in implementations (Reference 8.2, p. 166).

Most of the objects in the system group are useful for configuration management. Some of the objects, such as sysDescr, sysObjectID, and sysContact, are also useful for fault management.

- *sysDescr* (*DisplayString*): Includes details of the system such as hardware name, hardware version, and software details on the operating system, networking, and communication.
- *sysObjectID* (*OBJECT IDENTIFIER*): Uniquely identifies the network management subsystem (agent) in the naming subtree. The naming tree for the subsystem is under the SMI enterprises subtree {1.3.6.4.1}. This helps identify an object representing the subsystem for network management.
- *sysUpTime* (*TimeTicks*): Refers to the elapsed time in hundredths of a second since an agent has been reinitialized or come up.
- *sysContact* (*DisplayString*): Supplies detailed information on the contact person for the managed node being monitored.
- *sysName* (*DisplayString*): Furnishes the contact name of the person who is administratively responsible for the managed node.

- *sysLocation* (*DisplayString*): Contains information on the actual physical location of the managed node.
- *sysServices* (*INTEGER*): Is calculated as the sum of the services provided by the managed node. Each layer has a value such as the following: physical—1, datalink/subnetwork—2, Internet—3, end-to-end—4, applications—7, OSI sessions—5, and OSI presentations—6. Then, for each layer a value of 2^{L-1} is calculated, where L stands for a layer value. For a managed node, the total of the services performed is calculated and reported in this object.

8.6.2 Interfaces group

The interfaces group (Figure 8.9) is mandatory. Here, *interface* refers to the interface associated with a subnetwork. This group consists of details such as the number of interfaces, the list of each interface, the objects at the subnetwork, details about the interface's manufacturer, interface details of the physical and link layer protocols, the size of the largest datagrams that can be sent or received, the interface's bandwidth, the physical addresses if available, the status of interfaces, and the details of the packets received or transmitted.

- *ifNumber* (*INTEGER*): The number allocated to the network interfaces of a managed node.

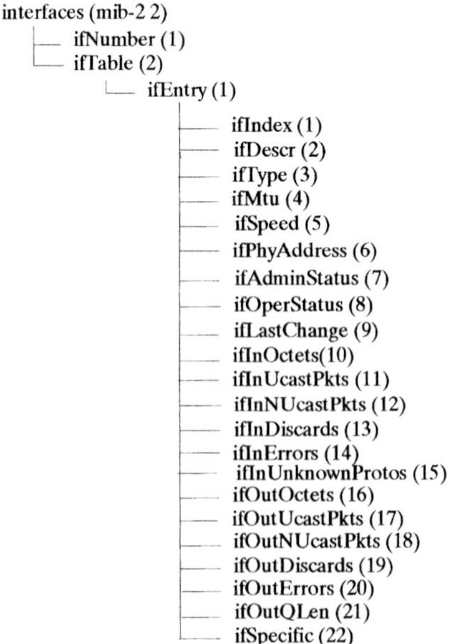

Figure 8.9 Interfaces group.

- *ifTable (SEQUENCE OF IfEntry)*: Furnishes a list of interface entries. The number of entries is equal to ifNumber.
- *ifEntry (SEQUENCE)*: Refers to the number of objects at and below the subnetwork layer.
- *ifIndex (INTEGER)*: A unique value for an interface, which ranges from 1 to the value of ifNumber.
- *ifDescr (DisplayString)*: Furnishes in textual string interface details such as the manufacturer's name, product name, and version of interface.
- *ifType (INTEGER)*: Provides the value of the protocol below the network layer. MIB-II has 32 values provided for different protocols. For example, Frame Relay has a value of 32.
- *ifMTU (INTEGER)*: Used for furnishing the largest datagram size in octets which can be handled by the interface.
- *ifSpeed (Gauge)*: Provides bandwidth (transmission rate) in bits per second.
- *ifPhysAddress (PhyAddress)*: Has interface's address below the network layer. For example, in the LAN interface, the MAC address is the physical address. If there is no physical address, then an OCTET STRING of zero length must be used.
- *ifAdminStatus (INTEGER)*: Describes the desired state of the interface. Values allowed are: up = 1, down = 2, and testing = 3.
- *ifOperStatus (INTEGER)*: Describes the current operational status of the interface with values of up = 1, down = 2, and testing = 3.
- *ifLastChange (TimeTicks)*: Refers to the elapsed time since the current operational state has been reached. However, if an object has attained current operational status before an agent is initialized, then the value is zero.
- *ifInOctets (Counter)*: Has the total number of octets received by the interface since last initialization.
- *ifInUcastPkts (Counter)*: Provides the packets delivered to the next layer. It excludes the broadcast and multicast packets. Note that this granularity of packets into different types is useful for performance management, where we may be required to analyze different types of packets for meaningful performance tuning. This granularity is also useful in fault management to identify problems.
- *ifInNUcastPkts (Counter)*: Takes account of the broadcast and multicast packets delivered to the next layer.
- *ifInDiscards (Counter)*: The total of packets received at an interface which have not been delivered to upper layers. These packets

were discarded even though there were no errors. One example furnished in RFC 1213 is the possibility of freeing up buffer space.

- *ifInErrors* (*Counter*): Provides the errors that have been noticed in the inbound packets. These packets have not been delivered to the upper layer. ifInErrors is useful for analyzing problems. If there are too many errors in the received packets, then reasons for the errors need to be identified. One drawback of SNMP is that there is no threshold data type. When a threshold value is reached, a trap should be sent indicating that action is required *now*.
- *ifInUnknownProtos* (*Counter*): Provides the number of PDUs received and discarded because the protocols are unsupported or unknown.

So far we have described objects used to analyze the PDUs that have been received. Data can be sent through an interface, too. Thus, some of the objects described as follows relate to the measurements on the PDUs transmitted.

- *ifOutOctets* (*Counter*): Used for counting the total number of PDUs transmitted out of an interface.
- *ifOutUcastPkts* (*Counter*): Furnishes the total number of nonbroadcast and nonmulticast PDUs, which were requested by the higher layers to transmit to an address. It includes those PDUs which have been discarded or not sent for different reasons.
- *ifOutNUcastPkts* (*Counter*): In ifOutUcastPkts, the broadcast and multicast PDUs transmitted were not counted. To compensate, in ifOutNUcastPkts, the PDUs requested by the upper layers to transmit via the interface to multicast and broadcast addresses are totaled. Here, too, we take into account those packets which were discarded or not sent.
- *ifOutDiscards* (*Counter*): Counts the PDUs that were discarded for reasons such as freeing up buffer space.
- *ifOutErrors* (*Counter*): Refers to the total number of PDUs which were discarded because of errors.
- *ifOutQLen* (*Gauge*): Refers to the length of the output queue. It is measured in terms of PDUs.
- *ifSpecific* (*OBJECT IDENTIFIER*): Refers to MIB definitions on media (Ethernet, token ring, and others) used at the interface. If this value is not present, then OBJECT IDENTIFIER {0 0} must be used.

```
at (mib-2 3)
  └─atTable (1)
       └─ atEntry (1)
             ├─ atIfIndex (1)
             ├─ atPhyAddress (2)
             └─ atNetAddress (3)
```

Figure 8.10 Address translation group.

8.6.3 Address translation group

The address translation group (Figure 8.10) has been provided for compatibility with MIB-I, and will be removed in MIB-III. This group is mandatory for all systems. The address translation group has one table, atTable, for mapping network addresses such as the IP address to the physical address such as the MAC address. However, reverse mapping is also required in some cases. Hence, each network protocol group will have its own address translation table.

- *atTable (SEQUENCE of AtEntry)*: This table has mapping of NetworkAddress such as an IP address to a physical address. If this table is empty, then it has zero entries.
- *atEntry (SEQUENCE)*: This refers to a single entry in the address translation table.
- *atIfIndex (INTEGER)*: This has the same value as that of ifIndex in the interfaces group.
- *atPhysAddress (PhysAddress)*: This refers to the physical address, such as a MAC address. A string of zero length invalidates an entry in the address translation table.
- *atNetAddress (NetworkAddress)*: This refers to a network address, such as an IP address.

8.6.4 IP group

The IP group (Figure 8.11) is also mandatory. This furnishes information on whether the IP gateway functions or the IP host functions are used. Here, only IP gateways forward datagrams, and IP hosts forward datagrams using source routing through the hosts. This group mainly furnishes the details on the datagrams, such as datagrams forwarded and datagrams discarded. Note that the gateways referred to are the "routers" in the industry. The IP group has the following three tables:

- *ipAddrTable (SEQUENCE OF IpAddrEntry)*: This has five columns and also has IP addresses. IpAddrEntry is a SEQUENCE

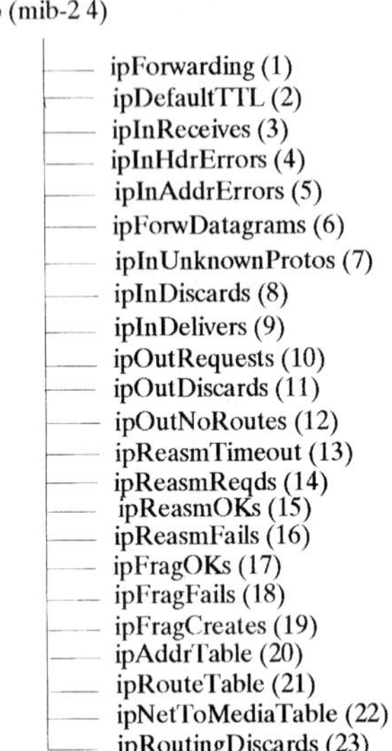

Figure 8.11 IP group.

of five entries, each representing a column in the ipAddrTable (Figure 8.12).

- *ipRouteTable* (*SEQUENCE OF IpRouteEntry*): This has 13 columns, and contains the routing information. Each row has one route to a particular destination. As seen in ipAddrTable, IpRouteEntry is a SEQUENCE of thirteen entries (Figure 8.13).
- *ipNetToMediaTable* (*IpNetToMediaEntry*): This has mapping of an IP address to a physical address. This address mapping is done by ARP and proxy ARP. This table has five columns. Here, too, IpNetToMediaEntry is a SEQUENCE of four entries (Figure 8.14).

Referring to Figure 8.11, the explanations of IP group entries are:

- *ipForwarding* (*INTEGER*): Has two values: forwarding = 1 and not-forwarding = 2. It primarily states whether or not a node acts as a gateway that forwards datagrams received.
- *ipDefaultTTL* (*INTEGER*): Contains default time-to-live value whenever this value is not supplied by the transport layer.
- *ipInReceives* (*Counter*): Refers to the total number of datagrams received by the IP layer from lower layers, including those with errors.
- *ipInHdrErrors* (*Counter*): Helps identify the PDUs received with errors in the header. These datagrams, as is the common practice, are discarded.

- *ipInAddrErrors* (*Counter*): Here, the datagrams that have invalid IP addresses are counted. These include invalid addresses, addresses not supported, and addresses which are not local addresses in hosts.
- *ipForwDatagrams* (*Counter*): Used for counting datagrams which have been forwarded. These datagrams can refer to datagrams forwarded in gateways or source routing datagrams.
- *ipInUnknownProtos* (*Counter*): Refers to the count of datagrams discarded due to unsupported or unknown protocols.
- *ipInDiscards* (*Counter*): Includes the datagrams discarded for reasons such as lack of buffer space. However, this count excludes datagrams which were discarded during reassembly.
- *ipInDelivers* (*Counter*): Refers to the number of datagrams which were successfully delivered by the IP layer to the immediate upper layer. It also includes the number of ICMP datagrams.
- *ipOutRequests* (*Counter*): The datagrams which are transmitted to the lower layer by the IP layer, including ICMP datagrams. Note that this counter excludes the count of datagrams in ipForwDatagrams. ipOutRequests can be regarded as a counter for datagrams flowing in the opposite direction to that of the ipInDelivers counter.
- *ipOutDiscards* (*Counter*): Used to count the outbound datagrams which have been discarded for reasons such as lack of buffer space, and also includes datagrams counted under ipForwDatgrams.
- *ipOutNoRoutes* (*Counter*): Refers to the data discarded because no routes to the destination were available, and includes datagrams counted in ipForwDatagrams. It also includes datagrams discarded due to failures of gateways.
- *ipReasmTimeout* (*INTEGER*): Furnishes the maximum amount of time in seconds that a fragment had to wait for the reassembly of fragments to a datagram.
- *ipReasmReqds* (*Counter*): Refers to the total number of fragments which were reassembled in the IP layer.
- *ipReasmOKs* (*Counter*): Used to count the number of IP datagrams which were successfully reassembled in this IP layer.
- *ipReasmFails* (*Counter*): A count of the number of failures in reassembly for reasons such as time out or errors. Note that this number is not the same as the number of IP fragments discarded.
- *ipFragOKs* (*Counter*): Refers to the number of successful IP fragments formed in this IP layer.

- *ipFragFails* (*Counter*): Some datagrams cannot be fragmented into smaller frames, if the don't-fragment bit is set. This counter takes care of these counts.
- *ipFragCreates* (*Counter*): Refers to the total number of fragments formed from IP datagrams for onward transmission to the lower layer.

As previously mentioned, ipAddrTable (Figure 8.12) has five columns:

- *ipAdEntAddr* (*IpAddress*): Has the IP address.
- *ipAdEntIfIndex* (*INTEGER*): Refers to the value for this interface and has the same value as that of ifIndex.
- *ipAdEntNetMask* (*IpAddress*): Has the subnet mask associated with an IP address. It has 1s in the network numbers, and 0s in the host numbers.
- *ipAdEntBcastAddr* (*INTEGER*): Refers to the least significant bit of the IP broadcast address.
- *ipAdEntReasmMaxSize* (*INTEGER*): Refers to the largest datagram size which can be formed by reassembling fragments. Values range from 0 to 65535.

The second table, ipRouteTable (Figure 8.13), has thirteen columns. Note that the information in this table refers to the routing information. The columns are interpreted as follows:

- *ipRouteDest* (*IpAddress*): Has the destination IP address.
- *ipRouteIfIndex* (*INTEGER*): The local interface number. Its value is the same as the value of ifIndex.
- *ipRouteMetric1* (*INTEGER*): Refers to the value used for the primary routing metric. The semantics are determined by the IPRouteProto value. The entry of IPRouteProto is explained after the next three entries. A value of −1 indicates that this entry is not used.

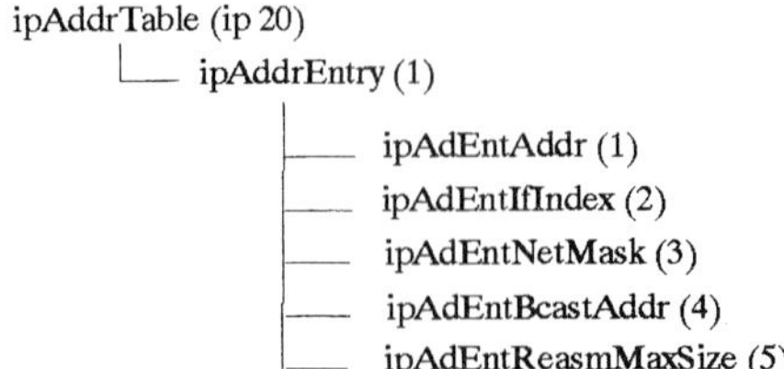

Figure 8.12 ipAddrTable.

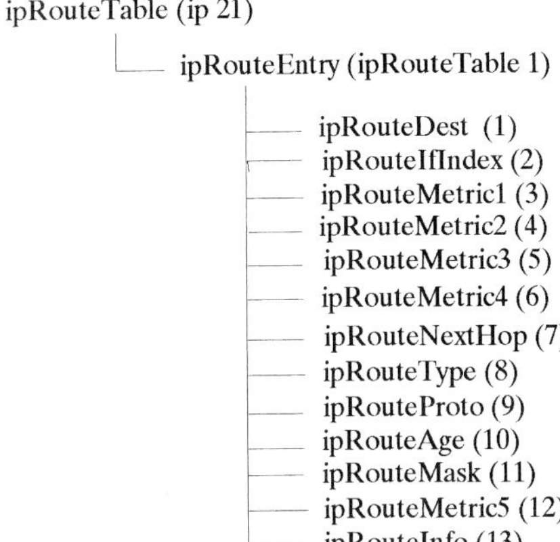

Figure 8.13 ipRouteTable.

- *ipRouteMetric(2-4) (INTEGER)*: Used to indicate the values of matrices of alternate routes.
- *ipRouteNextHop (IpAddress)*: Refers to the next hop IP address.
- *ipRouteType (INTEGER)*: Corresponds to the values associated with a route. The values are: other = 1, invalid = 2, direct = 3, and indirect = 4.
- *ipRouteProto (INTEGER)*: Corresponds to the routing protocols used for learning the routes. The values are: other = 1, local = 2, net-mgmt = 3, icmp = 4, egp = 5, ggp = 6, hello = 7, rip = 8, is-is = 9, es-is = 10, ciscoIgrp = 11, bbnSpfIgp = 12, ospf = 13, and bgp = 14. It is not necessary for the host to support these gateway protocols.
- *ipRouteAge (INTEGER)*: Refers to the value in seconds since the route was last updated.
- *ipRouteMask (IpAddress)*: Furnishes the subnet mask of a route.
- *ipRouteMetric5 (INTEGER)*: Also provides the alternate routing metric in addition to the ones already seen.
- *ipRouteInfo (OBJECT IDENTIFIER)*: Contains MIB definitions pertinent to a routing protocol. If this value is not there, then this value is set to OBJECT IDENTIFIER {0 0}.

As already mentioned, the third table used by the IP group is the IP address translation table identified as ipNetToMediaTable (Figure 8.14). It has the following four columns:

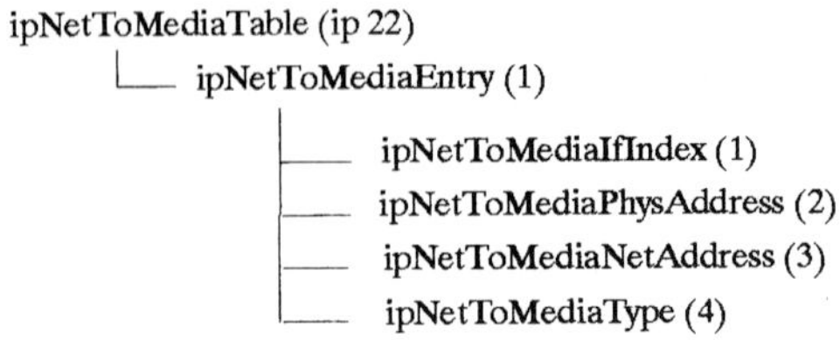

```
ipNetToMediaTable (ip 22)
  └── ipNetToMediaEntry (1)
        ├── ipNetToMediaIfIndex (1)
        ├── ipNetToMediaPhysAddress (2)
        ├── ipNetToMediaNetAddress (3)
        └── ipNetToMediaType (4)
```

Figure 8.14 ipNetToMediaTable.

- *ipNetToMediaIfIndex* (*INTEGER*): Contains the value associated with this interface and has the same value as the one used in ifIndex for this interface.
- *ipNetToMediaPhyAddress* (*PhysAddress*): Refers to the physical address, such as the MAC address of the interface.
- *ipNetToMediaNetAddress* (*IpAddress*): Has the IP address.
- *ipNetToMediaType* (*INTEGER*): Describes how the address translation is done. It has these values: other = 1, invalid = 2, dynamic = 3, and static = 4. A value of 2 invalidates an entry.
- *ipRoutingDiscards* (*Counter*): Contains the number of valid routing entries which have been discarded for reasons such as freeing buffer space. Note that ipRoutingDiscards is not part of the address translation table.

8.6.5 ICMP group

The ICMP group (Figure 8.15) implementation is mandatory. The ICMP group furnishes details on the ICMP messages, and basically has counters on different types and conditions of ICMP messages. These counters are useful for performance management. Objects used are:

- *icmpInMsgs* (*Counter*): Furnishes the total number of ICMP messages received, including those with errors.
- *icmpInErrors* (*Counter*): Refers to the ICMP messages which had errors for reasons such as bad checksum or bad length.

The following ICMP objects count the different types of ICMP messages received.

- *icmpInDestUnreachs* (*Counter*): Keeps count of the number of ICMP Destination Unreachable messages received.

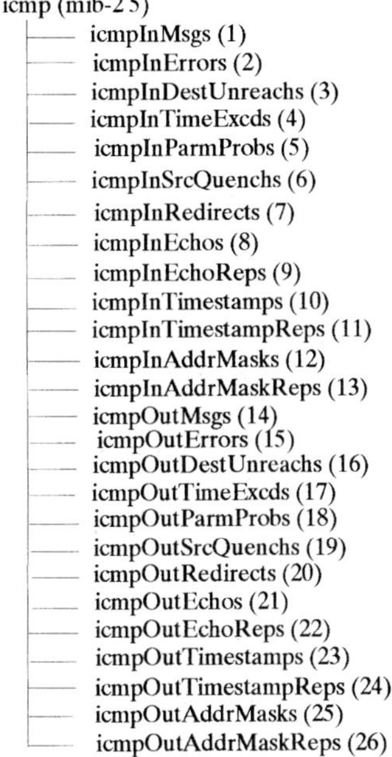

Figure 8.15 ICMP group.

- *icmpInTimeExcds* (*Counter*): Useful for keeping track of the number of ICMP Time Exceeded messages received.
- *icmpInParmProbs* (*Counter*): Refers to the total number of ICMP Parameter Problem messages received.
- *icmpInSrcQuenchs* (*Counter*): Keeps track of the ICMP Source Quench messages received.
- *icmpInRedirects* (*Counter*): Used for counting the total number of ICMP Redirect messages received.
- *icmpInEchos* (*Counter*): Refers to the number of ICMP Echo Request messages received.
- *icmpInEchoReps* (*Counter*): Used for totaling the number of ICMP Echo Reply messages received.
- *icmpInTimestamps* (*Counter*): Used for keeping track of ICMP Timestamp Request messages received.
- *icmpInTimestampReps* (*Counter*): Counts the total number of ICMP Timestamp Reply messages.

- *icmpInAddrMasks* (*Counter*): Furnishes the total number of ICMP Address Mask Request messages received.
- *icmpInAddrMaskReps* (*Counter*): Provides the total number of ICMP Address Mask Reply messages received.

In the ICMP group, "In" counters keep track of different ICMP messages received by a local IP entity. Similarly, there are corresponding "Out" counters, which furnish the counters of different ICMP messages sent from a local IP entity. There is no difference, except that one counter is for messages received, while the other one is for messages transmitted; hence, these "Out" counters and their explanations are not listed here.

8.6.6 TCP group

The TCP group (Figure 8.16) is mandatory if TCP is implemented. Here, instances refer to the TCP connections, and their values are valid only during a connection. This group provides details on the conditions of connections, relevant connection addresses, retransmission timeout values, and details on segments transmitted and received. Like other groups, this group has objects which will be useful for gathering information on a TCP layer. Objects defined for the TCP group are:

- *tcpRtoAlgorithm* (*INTEGER*): Furnishes the algorithm used for calculating the timeout value for unacknowledged segments. Values are: other = 1, which stands for none of the furnished algorithms; constant = 2; rsre = 3, which refers to MIL-STD-1778; and vanj = 4, which refers to Van Jacobson's algorithm.
- *tcpRtoMin* (*INTEGER*): Provides minimum permitted value for a retransmission timeout.

```
tcp (mib-2 6)
    |---- tcpRtoAlgorithm (1)
    |---- tcpRtoMin (2)
    |---- tcpRtoMax (3)
    |---- tcpMaxConn (4)
    |---- tcpActiveOpens (5)
    |---- tcpPassiveOpens (6)
    |---- tcpAttemptFails (7)
    |---- tcpEstabResets (8)
    |---- tcpCurrEstab (9)
    |---- tcpInSegs (10)
    |---- tcpOutSegs (11)
    |---- tcpRetransSegs (12)
    |---- tcpConnTable (13)
    |---- tcpInErrs (14)
    |---- tcpOutRsts(15)
```

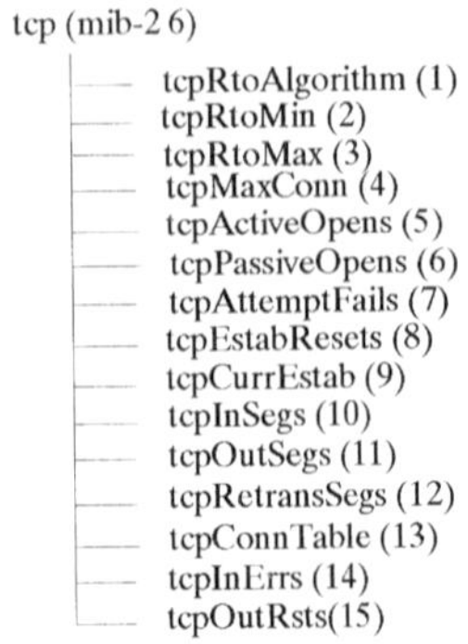

Figure 8.16 TCP group.

- *tcpRtoMax* (*INTEGER*): Refers to the maximum permitted value for a retransmission timeout.
- *tcpMaxConn* (*INTEGER*): Furnishes the maximum number of connections allowed in a TCP module. If the connections are dynamic, then a value of −1 is used.
- *tcpActiveOpens* (*Counter*): Provides the number of active open connections. The transitions from the CLOSED state to the SYN-SENT state are counted in the counter. Different TCP states are furnished in RFC 793 (Reference 8.3).
- *tcpPassiveOpens* (*Counter*): Refers to the number of passive opens. The transition from the LISTEN state to the SYN-RCVD state is considered for this counter.
- *tcpAttemptFails* (*Counter*): Keeps track of the total number of TCP connections which have made the transition from the SYN-SENT or SYN-RCVD state to the CLOSED state, and those TCP connections which have made the transition from the SYN-RCVD state to the LISTEN state.
- *tcpEstabResets* (*Counter*): Furnishes the total number of connections which have been reset. A reset is identified by a transition to a CLOSED state from either the ESTABLISHED state or the CLOSE-WAIT state.
- *tcpCurrEstab* (*Gauge*): Provides the total number of connections which are in the ESTABLISHED or CLOSE-WAIT states.
- *tcpInSegs* (*Counter*): Furnishes the total number of segments received on established connections by a TCP module. It also includes segments which are in error.
- *tcpOutSegs* (*Counter*): Provides the segments transmitted. However, this does not include segments which have been retransmitted.
- *tcpRetransSegs* (*Counter*): Keeps track of the segments that have been retransmitted from a TCP module. This is important data for performance analysis, because it indicates the state of the connections.

The TCP group contains tcpConnTable (Figure 8.17). This table has information pertinent to TCP connections, and has five columns:

- *tcpConnState* (*INTEGER*): Refers to the state of a TCP connection with these values: closed = 1, listen = 2, synSent = 3, synReceived = 4, established = 5, finWait1 = 6, finWait2 = 7, closeWait = 8, lastAck = 9, closing = 10, timeWait = 11, and

```
tcpConnTable (tcp 13)
    └── tcpConnEntry (1)
            ├── tcpConnState (1)
            ├── tcpConnLocalAddress (2)
            ├── tcpConnLocalPort (3)
            ├── tcpConnRemAddress (4)
            └── tcpConnRemPort (5)
```

Figure 8.17 tcpConnTable.

deleteTCB = 12. A management station (manager) may send only deleteTCB, which means the termination of a connection.

- *tcpConnLocalAddress* (*IpAddress*): Refers to the local IP address associated with a TCP connection.
- *tcpConnLocalPort* (*INTEGER*): Has the local port number associated with a TCP connection.
- *tcpConnRemAddress* (*IpAddress*): Contains the remote IP address of a TCP connection.
- *tcpConnRemPort* (*INTEGER*): Refers to the remote port number associated with a TCP connection.

The following additional TCP objects are also part of the TCP group:

- *tcpInErrors* (*Counter*): Refers to the total segments which have been received with errors. This data is useful for performance management. If errors exceed certain limits, it is worth the analysis. This may provide some useful information for rectifying the TCP connections and thus reduce the number of errors.
- *tcpOutRsts* (*Counter*): Contains the total number of TCP segments which were sent with the RST flag set.

8.6.7 UDP group

The UDP group (Figure 8.18) is similar to the TCP group, and the objects defined in this group are required if UDP is implemented. Here also, the UDP group furnishes details about UDP datagrams and UDP endpoints on which a local application is accepting datagrams. UDP has the following objects:

- *udpInDatagrams* (*Counter*): Contains the total number of UDP datagrams delivered to the user of a UDP module.

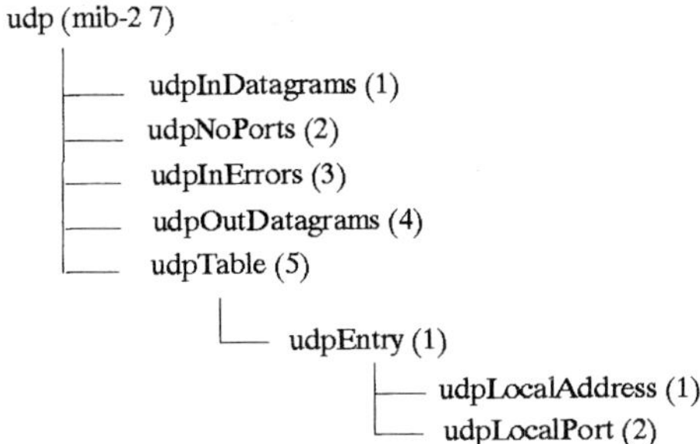

Figure 8.18 UDP group.

- *udpNoPorts* (*Counter*): Provides the number of UDP datagrams which could not be delivered because there was no application at the destination port.
- *udpInErrors* (*Counter*): Refers to the UDP datagrams which could not be delivered to the user. This excludes the number of UDP datagrams included in udpNoPorts.
- *udpOutDatagrams* (*Counter*): Pertains to the UDP datagrams sent from the user of a UDP module.

UDP has one table: udpTable with two columns. This table has information on the UDP local endpoints on which an application is receiving datagrams. The entries are:

- *udpLocalAddress* (*IpAddress*): Has a local IP address associated with a UDP.
- *udpLocalPort* (*INTEGER*): Contains the local port number associated with a UDP.

8.6.8 EGP group

The EGP group (Figure 8.19) objects must be implemented if EGP is used. EGP is the protocol used by routers and is explained in RFC 904. The EGP group provides details on EGP messages generated, messages not sent due to resource limitations in EGP, EGP messages received and their details, and conditions of EGP neighbors.

- *egpInMsgs* (*Counter*): Has the total number of EGP messages which have been received without errors.
- *egpInErrors* (*Counter*): When we exclude errors in egpInMsgs, it should be intuitively obvious that there should be a separate

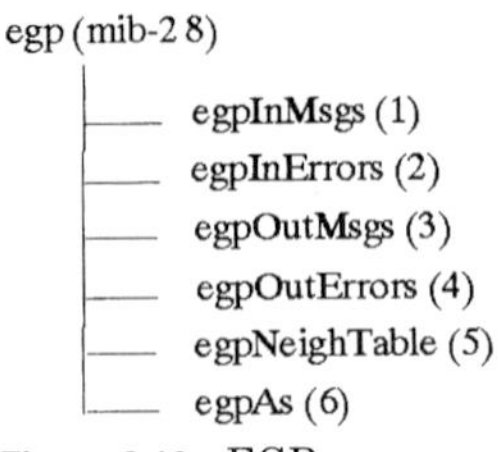

Figure 8.19 EGP group.

counter for the total number of EGP messages which have been received with errors. egpInErrors serves this purpose.

- *egpOutMsgs* (*Counter*): Contains the total number of EGP messages that have been generated by the EGP module. However, this does not cover messages which have errors.
- *egpOutErrors* (*Count*): Covers those EGP messages which have not been transmitted due to problems, such as resource limitations.

egpNeighTable (Figure 8.20) has information on the EGP neighbors and consists of the following 15 columns:

- *egpNeighState* (*INTEGER*): Has information on the state of the neighbor. The values used for describing the state are: idle = 1, acquisition = 2, down = 3, up = 4, and cease = 5.
- *egpNeighAddr* (*IpAddress*): Contains the IP address of the EGP neighbor.
- *egpNeighAs* (*INTEGER*): Refers to the autonomous system number of the remote EGP peer.

egpNeighTable (egp 5)
 egpNeighEntry (1)
  egpNeighState (1)
  egpNeighAddr (2)
  egpNeighAs (3)
  egpNeighInMsgs (4)
  egpNeighInErrs (5)
  egpNeighOutMsgs (6)
  egpNeighOutErrs (7)
  egpNeighInErrMsgs (8)
  egpNeighOutErrMsgs (9)
  egpNeighStateUps (10)
  egpNeighStateDowns (11)
  egpNeighIntervalHello (12)
  egpNeighIntervalPoll (13)
  egpNeighMode (14)
  egpNeighEventTrigger (15)

Figure 8.20 egpNeighTable.

- *egpNeighInMsgs* (*Counter*): Has the number of EGP messages received from the EGP neighbor that did not contain errors.
- *egpNeighInErrs* (*Counter*): Refers to the number of EGP messages from the EGP neighbor with errors.
- *egpNeighOutMsgs* (*Counter*): Has the number of EGP messages generated by the local EGP module to this neighbor.
- *egpNeighOutErrs* (*Counter*): Pertains to the number of EGP messages which were not transmitted by a local EGP node to the neighbor due to errors.
- *egpNeighInErrMsgs* (*Counter*): Refers to the number of EGP messages received from an EGP neighbor which were in error.
- *egpNeighOutErrMsgs* (*Counter*): Contains the number of EGP messages which were in error, but were sent to an EGP neighbor.
- *egpNeighStateUps* (*Counter*): Refers to the number of state transitions to the UP state from this EGP neighbor.
- *egpNeighStateDowns* (*Counter*): Provides the number of state transitions from the UP state to any other state for the EGP neighbor.
- *egpNeighIntervalHello* (*INTEGER*): Furnishes the time interval in hundredths of a second to send Hello messages.
- *egpNeighIntervalPoll* (*INTEGER*): Provides the time interval in hundredths of a second between poll messages.
- *egpNeighMode* (*INTEGER*): Furnishes the polling mode of the EGP neighbor. The value can be either passive or active.
- *egpNeighEventTrigger* (*INTEGER*): Used to provide the control variable to trigger Starts and Stops by operators.
- *egpAs* (*INTEGER*): Has the autonomous system number. Also note that this object is not part of egpNeighTable.

8.6.9 CMOT group

The objects required for CMOT are defined under {mib 9}. The subtree under cmot is labeled "oim." Because CMOT has been relegated to historical status, the chances of using these objects are remote.

8.6.10 Transmission group

The transmission group is meant for objects relating to the underlying transmission media. At first, they are included under the experimental category, but as they become mature, they are elevated to a new object identifier under the transmission group.

8.6.11 SNMP group

The SNMP group (Figure 8.21) defines the objects for one SNMP protocol entity. The implementation of the SNMP group is mandatory if SNMPs are supported. Depending on the implementation, a node can be either an agent or a management station. So, in some cases, the objects in the following list will be zero-valued. The SNMP group has a number of objects defined to reflect the different SNMP protocol entity messages that are received or delivered to the underlying transport protocol.

- *snmpInPkts* (*Counter*): Contains the total number of SNMP messages received by the SNMP module from the transport layer below the SNMP (i.e., UDP).
- *snmpOutPkts* (*Counter*): Refers to the total number of SNMP messages delivered to the layer below the SNMP.

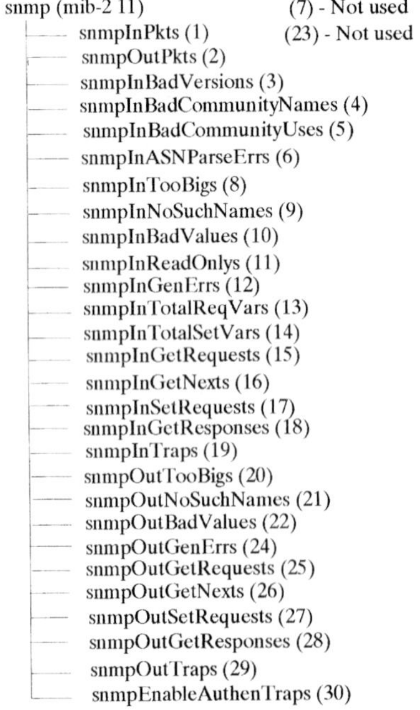

Figure 8.21 SNMP group.

- *snmpInBadVersions* (*Counter*): Provides the total number of SNMP messages which could not be processed due to unsupported versions.
- *snmpInBadCommunityNames* (*Counter*): Pertains to the SNMP messages received with bad community names.
- *snmpInBadCommunityUses* (*Counter*): Refers to the SNMP messages with bad community uses.
- *snmpInASNParseErrs* (*Counter*): Contains the total number of SNMP messages which had ASN.1 or BER errors.
- *snmpInTooBigs* (*Counter*): Refers to the SNMP messages received with tooBig in the error status field.
- *snmpInNoSuchNames* (*Counter*): The total number of SNMP messages received with noSuchName in the error status field.
- *snmpInBadValues* (*Counter*): Provides the total number of SNMP messages received with badValues in the error status field.
- *snmpInReadOnlys* (*Counter*): Can arise due to bad implementations of SNMP. This counter is similar to the earlier ones, and has the total number of SNMP messages received with readOnly in the error status field.
- *snmpInGenErrs* (*Counter*): Refers to the total number of SNMP messages which have genErr in the error status field.
- *snmpInTotalReqVars* (*Counter*): Contains the total number of MIB objects retrieved successfully due to SNMP GetRequest and GetNextRequest PDUs.
- *snmpInTotalSetVars* (*Counter*): Provides the total number of MIB objects which have been altered successfully due to SNMP Set-Request PDUs.

The following objects are used to keep track of different SNMP PDUs that have been received and processed:

- *snmpInGetRequests* (*Counter*)
- *snmpInGetNexts* (*Counter*)
- *snmpInSetRequests* (*Counter*)
- *snmpInGetResponses* (*Counter*)
- *snmpInTraps* (*Counter*)

The preceding lists indicated many objects which were used to count SNMP messages received with different values in the error status field. The following SNMP objects are used to keep track of messages sent out from an SNMP module. Those SNMP messages which contain "Out" are mirror images of those containing "In."

- *snmpOutTooBigs* (*Counter*)
- *snmpOutNoSuchNames* (*Counter*)
- *snmpOutBadValues* (*Counter*)
- *snmpOutGenErrs* (*Counter*)
- *snmpOutGetRequests* (*Counter*)
- *snmpOutGetNexts* (*Counter*)
- *snmpOutSetRequests* (*Counter*)
- *snmpOutGetResponses* (*Counter*)
- *snmpOutTraps* (*Counter*)
- *snmpEnableAuthenTraps* (*INTEGER*): Provides information about whether an SNMP agent is permitted to generate authentication failure taps. It has two values: enabled = 1 and disabled = 2.

Note that in the SNMP group, objects 7 and 23 are not used. Different SNMP PDUs will be discussed in the next section.

The MIB-II objects explained here can be classified and folded into different network management applications such as configuration management, fault management, performance management, accounting management, and security management. These applications can be made a part of the network management station. Leinwald and Fang (see Reference 8.4) provide a good breakdown of MIB-II into different network management functions.

8.7 How SNMPv1 Operates

SNMPv1 protocol definitions are provided in RFC 1157, and they are:

```
RFC1157-SNMP DEFINITIONS ::= BEGIN
IMPORTS
        ObjectName, ObjectSyntax, NetworkAddress, IpAddress,
        TimeTicks
        FROM RFC1155-SMI
-- top-level message
        Message ::=
                SEQUENCE {
                        version         INTEGER {Version-1(0) }, -- ver-
                                        --sion-1 of this RFC
                        community       OCTET STRING, -- community
                                        --name
                        data            ANY -- e.g., PDUs if trivial
                                        --authentication is being used.
```

```
-- protocol data units
        PDUs ::=
                CHOICE {
                        get-request                GetRequest-PDU,
                        get-next-request           GetNextRequest-PDU,
                        get-response               GetResponse-PDU,
                        set-request                SetRequest-PDU,
                        trap                       Trap-PDU
                }
-- PDUs
        GetRequest-PDU ::=
              [0]
                          IMPLICIT PDU
        GetNextRequest-PDU ::=
              [1]
                          IMPLICIT PDU
        GetResponse-PDU ::=
              [2]
                          IMPLICIT PDU
        SetRequest-PDU ::=
              [3]
                          IMPLICIT PDU
        PDU ::=
                SEQUENCE {
                        request-id                 INTEGER,
                        error-Status -- sometimes ignored
                                INTEGER {
                                    noError(0),
                                    tooBig(1),
                                    noSuchName(2),
                                    badValue(3),
                                    readOnly(4),
                                    genErr(5)
                                    },
                        error-index INTEGER, -- sometimes ignored
                -- variable bindings
                        variable-bindings VarBindList -- values are sometimes
                        --ignored
                        }
        -- trap PDU
        TrapPDU ::=
                [4]
                        IMPLICIT SEQUENCE {
                              enterprise OBJECT IDENTIFIER,
                                      -- type of object generating trap,
                                      -- see sysObjectID
                              agent-addr NetworkAddress,
                                      -- address of object generating
                                      -- trap
```

```
                              generic-trap -- generic trap type
                                      INTEGER {
                                              coldStart(0),
                                              warmStart(1),
                                              linkDown(2),
                                              linkUp(3),
                                              authenticationFailure(4),
                                              egpNeighborLoss(5),
                                              enterpriseSpecific(6)
                                              },
                              specific-trap   INTEGER, -- specific code,
                                      -- present even if generic-trap is
                                      -- not enterpriseSpecific.
                              time-stamp TimeTicks, -- time elapsed
                                      -- between the last (re)initialization
                                      -- of the network entity and the
                                      -- generation of the trap.
                              variable-bindings VarBindList
                                      -- interesting information.
                      }
        -- variable bindings
        VarBind ::=
                SEQUENCE {
                        name    ObjectName,
                        value   ObjectSyntax
                        }
        VarBindList ::=
                SEQUENCE OF VarBind
END
```

Source: RFC 1157 (A Simple Network Management Protocol, 1990).

SNMPv1 PDUs are furnished in Table 8.1. Note that these PDUs use the same data format. When one protocol entity sends a GetRequest, GetNextRequest, or SetRequest PDU, the response is a GetResponse PDU (Figure 8.22). When there are errors or special cases, then traps are sent from one protocol entity to another one. Traps are analogous to

TABLE 8.1 SNMPv1 Protocol Data Units

GetRequest
GetNextRequest
GetResponse
SetRequest
Trap

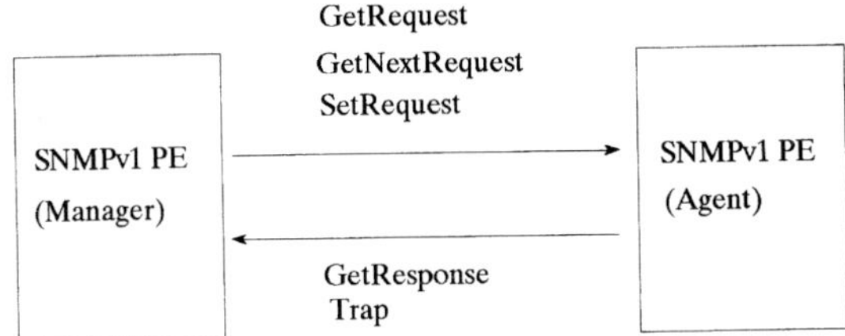

Figure 8.22 SNMPv1 management protocol PDUs.

notifications in OSI. Objects generate asynchronous notifications. In SNMPs, especially, GetNextRequest assumes that object values in the MIB are arranged in a tabular form.

The PDUs GetRequest, GetNextRequest, SetRequest, and GetResponse have request-id, error-status, error-index, and variable-bindings (Figure 8.23). In this figure, values for error-status and error-index for GetRequest, GetNextRequest, and SetRequest PDUs are always taken as zero. Request-id is used as an identifier for correlating the responses or for identifying duplicate responses. error-status indicates the kind of error. These are listed in Table 8.2. error-index gives the position of the variable which was responsible for the error. Variable refers to an instance of an object, and variable-binding

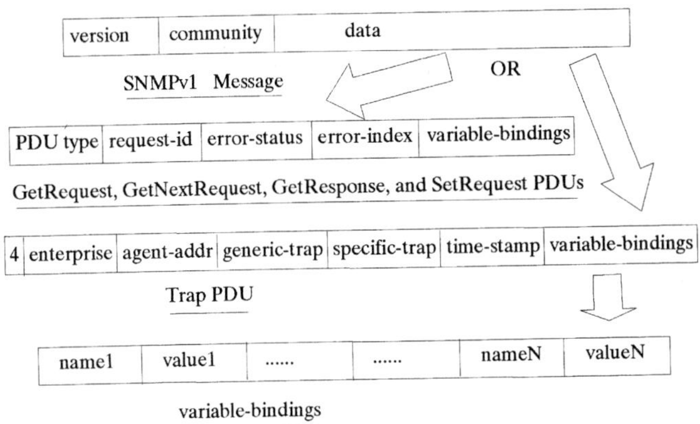

Figure 8.23 SNMPv1 PDUs.

TABLE 8.2 SNMPv1 Protocol Errors

noError
tooBig
noSuchName
badValue
readOnly
genErr

refers to the combination of a variable name and value. There can also be a list of variable names and values.

SNMP uses a combination of traps and polling for retrieving management information. Traps are expected to be sparingly used. When there is an error, then a trap is sent from an agent to NMS. Once this trap is received, the NMS must send a response. Subsequently, further management information is retrieved using polling.

8.7.1 Functioning of SNMPv1 PDUs

As mentioned earlier, SNMP is used for carrying messages from one *protocol entity* (PE) to another. A PDU is constructed in ASN.1 form and is then sent to an authenticator, along with the community name and source and transport addresses. The authenticator checks whether the sending and receiving protocol entities can really exchange messages. The result of the check, which can be an authentication failure or an ASN.1 object, is sent back to the PE. If the message has passed the authenticator check, it is formatted using BER and sent by the transport mechanism to the receiving PE. Generating an SNMPv1 message is shown in Figure 8.24.

On the receiving side, receiving a PE parses the data received and checks for version numbers. If the PDU fails during this action, then the datagram is discarded. After this operation, user data, community

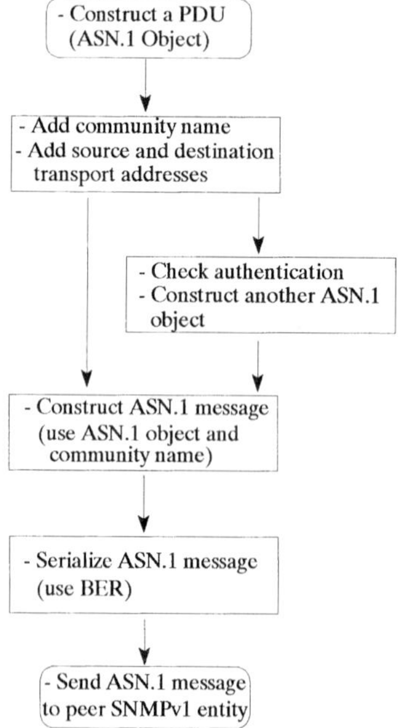

Figure 8.24 Generating an SNMPv1 message.

name, and source and destination addresses go to the authenticator. The authenticator checks whether the receiving PE can actually receive data from the sending PE. The result can be authentication failure. In such a case, a trap may be generated and sent to the sending PE. However, sometimes this trap is just logged and a record is maintained for any remedial action to be taken. On the other hand, if the authenticator passes the authentication process, the receiving PE processes the message and takes the appropriate action and sends the response back to the sending PE. The steps involved in the receiving end are shown in Figure 8.25.

Here we must note that some management applications may not need the security provided by authentication. In such implementations, the authentication steps may be skipped altogether for management applications. Also, in some cases, additional security steps may

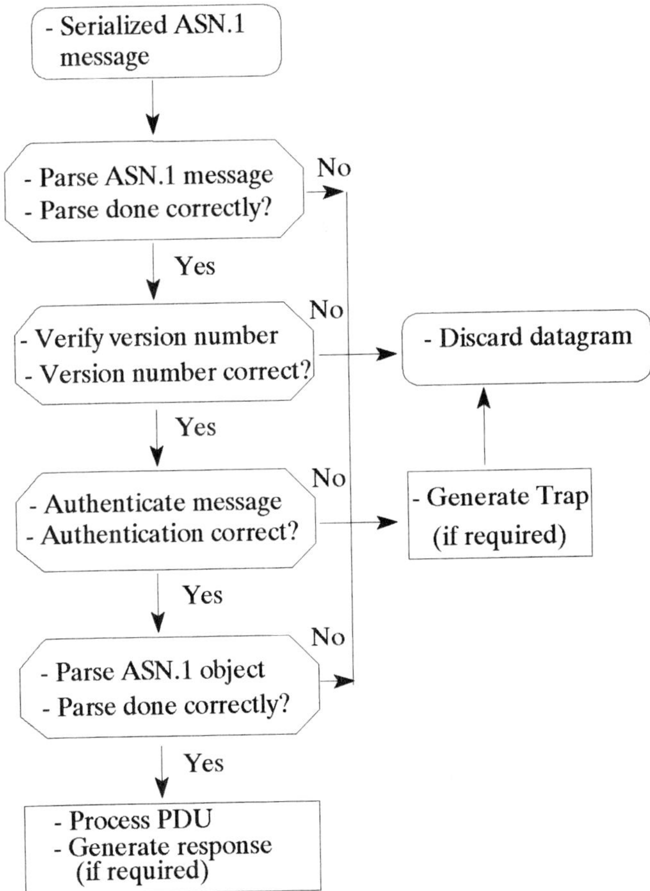

Figure 8.25 Receiving an SNMPv1 message.

be needed, such as extra access control functions. Thus, the level of authentication required is guided by implementation considerations.

When SNMPv1 protocols are used, errors such as those listed in Table 8.2 can be generated. The value of noError is 0 and they progressively increase in value by 1. Thus, badValue has a value of 3. Let us examine the individual SNMPv1 PDU function. When a GetRequest PDU is sent, the receiving PE checks whether the object name is correct. If the object name is not correct, then the error status is noSuchName. Afterwards, a check is made as to whether the object type is aggregate. Because SNMP does not allow aggregate object types, the error status of noSuchName is set for the aggregate object type cases.

A response for GetRequest must be within the capacity of the local PE. If it is not possible to generate responses, then the error status is set to tooBig. When processing a GetRequest, there may be errors. In such a case, the error status is set to genError. When there are no errors, the error status is set to noError. Responses in all cases are sent in the form of a GetResponse PDU.

GetNextRequest is similar to the GetRequest except that we retrieve the next value instead of the one furnished and the PDU type is different. Here the assumption is that MIB has object names arranged in a lexicographical order. However, if a lexicographical successor is not available, then error status is set to genErr.

In SetRequest, too, if a variable name is not available, then the error status is set to noSuchName. If the value of a variable whose value must be changed to the value furnished in SetRequest is not in conformity with ASN.1 language, type, length, or variable, the error status is set to badValue. The case of error status set to tooBig is similar to that explained earlier. If the value of a variable cannot be changed, then it is classified under genError. However, if the value of a variable is changed to the value mentioned in SetRequest, then the reply PDU of GetResponse has the error status set to noErr.

A trap is used to present problems or changes in Internet. A trap PDU consists of the object type generating the trap; the address of the object generating the trap, the generic trap type, the timestamp when the trap was generated, and any variable binding carrying relevant information. If the enterpriseSpecific trap is present, the specific trap field is present. Generic traps are listed in Table 8.3. In this table also, just as in Table 8.2, coldStart has a value of 0 and the values for other traps increase by 1. Hence, linkUp has a value of 3 associated with it.

Let us briefly review the meanings of different generic traps. The first trap is coldStart, which implies that an agent is reinitializing and the configuration and implementation details might have changed. Thus, the station receiving this trap will have to reset itself; whereas in the case of warmStart, there are no changes in the configuration and implementation details when reinitializing.

TABLE 8.3 SNMPv1 Traps Generated

coldStart
warmStart
linkDown
linkUp
authenticationFailure
egpNeighborLoss
enterpriseSpecific

The traps linkDown and linkUp are used when the communication links used are affected, and the affected link name and value are furnished in variable bindings. When a protocol message fails authentication, then the authenticationFailure trap is generated. egpNeighborLoss is generated when an EGP neighbor is no longer available. When traps cannot be specifically classified into any one of these above traps, then the enterpriseSpecific trap comes in handy. This trap can also be used to convey any specific trap that may be implementation specific. This is carried in the specific trap field.

8.8 Proxy

The proxy concept is very popular. It is possible that a management station is not able to manage a device such as a modem, bridge, or router because it responds to proprietary commands. In such a case, a proxy agent is used, as shown in the Figure 8.26. Between a management station and a proxy agent, standard protocols are used. However, between the proxy agent and the managed devices, proprietary protocols are used. The proxy assumes the role of an agent

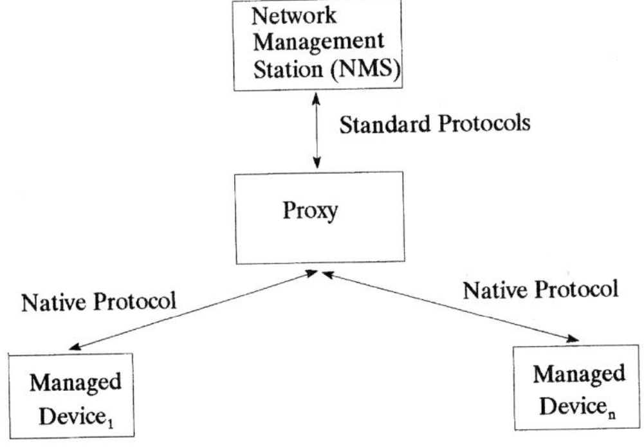

Figure 8.26 The proxy concept.

with respect to the manager and acts as a manager for managed devices.

One of the main functions of a proxy agent is protocol conversion. As an example, the standard command from the management station is converted or mapped to the semantically equivalent proprietary command and sent to the managed devices. As mentioned earlier, managed devices understand these proprietary commands. Similarly, responses to the commands sent to managed devices are mapped back to standard responses in the proxy agent.

The conversion from standard protocols to proprietary protocols can be done by two methods. One is the mapping or translation of each field of standard protocols to each field of proprietary protocols. However, in some cases, one-to-one mapping of fields may not be possible, because there may not be similar, functionally equivalent fields. In such cases, the best possible assumptions will have to be made.

Another method is by encapsulating the standard protocols within the data fields of the proprietary protocols. This information will have to be retrieved by the software or hardware in the managed devices, but the managed devices will have the added responsibility of interpreting standard protocol fields. In some cases, the information carried in standard protocols may prove to be redundant or may not be amenable for proper interpretation. In either case, it is possible that some information will be lost due to the inability to use one-to-one mapping or the inability to retrieve all the information. To overcome this, the proprietary protocols are normally continuously modified to keep abreast of the standards.

Furthermore, the introduction of a proxy agent adds complexity. The mapping of standard protocols to the proprietary protocol requires resources. Note that we are adding one more level to the communication between the management station and managed devices. Also, if the proxy is in a separate workstation, there are considerations such as additional backup in case of the failure of the backup. All these add to the complexity.

Also, a proxy agent provides the flexibility to enforce "under the cover" access policies. The SNMP MIBs do not have to bother about them. The access policy can be for managed devices represented as objects, and it will be between the proxy agent and the managed devices.

A proxy can also be used for selectively forwarding information to a management station. It may log the information it receives from managed devices. It may maintain details of aggregate objects. Aggregate objects are defined for combining the details on more than one object. The management system may ask the proxy to send the details on aggregate objects. The aggregate objects may also be defined for summary statistics, configuration details, etc.

8.9 SNMP over Different Protocols

SNMPs over different popular protocols have been defined. Some of them are:

- SNMP over IPX (RFC 1420)
- SNMP over Ethernet (RFC 1089)
- SNMP over AppleTalk (RFC 1419)
- SNMP over OSI (RFC 1418)

8.10 Summary

In this chapter, we have examined the basic philosophy of Internet network management and introduced the network management framework. With this as the basis, the Internet registration hierarchy was discussed. RFCs on MIB-II are the basic documents for Internet network management; thus, we examined the objects in the MIB-II. Different concepts of SNMPv1 were also dealt with in detail, as was the use of proxy agents, another important concept for handling multiprotocols.

8.11 References

8.1 Rose, M. T., *The Simple Book: An Introduction to Internet Management,* 2d ed., PTR Englewood Cliffs, N.J.: Prentice Hall, 1994. The first edition of the book was published in 1991.

8.2 Stallings, W., *SNMP, SNMPv2, and CMIP, The Practical Guide to Network Management Standards,* Reading, Mass.: Addison-Wesley, 1993. At press time, this book was being revised.

8.3 Postel, J., *Transmission Control Protocol,* RFC 793, 1981.

8.4. Leinwald, A., and K. Fang, *Network Management: A Practical Perspective,* Reading, Mass.: Addison-Wesley, 1993.

8.12 Further Reading

Case, J. D., M. Fedor, M. L. Schoffstall, and J. R. Davin, A Simple Network Management Protocol (SNMP), RFC 1157, 1990.

Cerf, V., IAB Recommendations for the Development of Internet Network Management Standards, RFC 1052, 1988.

Comer, D. E., *Internetworking with TCP/IP, Principles, Protocols, and Architecture,* vol. I, 2d ed., Englewood Cliffs, N.J.: Prentice Hall, 1991.

Davin, J. R., J. D. Case, M. Fedor, and M. L. Schoffstall, Simple Gateway Monitoring Protocol, RFC 1028, 1987.

Deering, S. E., ICMP Router Discovery Messages, RFC 1256, 1991.

Kastenholz, F., SNMP Communication Services, RFC 1270, 1991.

McCloghrie, K., and M. T. Rose, Management Information Base for Network Management of TCP/IP-based internets, RFC 1156, 1991.

McCloghrie, K., and M. T. Rose, Management Information Base for Network Management of TCP/IP-based internets: MIB-II, RFC 1213, 1991.

McCloghrie, K., and M. T. Rose, A Convention for Describing SNMP-based Agents, RFC 1303, 1992.

Mills, D., Exterior Gateway Protocol Formal Specification, RFC 904, 1984.

Rose, M. T., ISO Presentation Services on Top of TCP/IP-based internets, RFC 1085, 1988.

Rose, M. T., and K. McCloghrie, Structure and Identification of Management Information for TCP/IP-based internets, RFC 1155, 1990.

Rose, M. T., and K. McCloghrie, Concise MIB Definitions, RFC 1212, 1991.

Wijnen, B., G. Carpenter, K. Curran, A. Sehgal, and G. Walters, Simple Network Management Protocol Distributed Protocol Interface Version 2.0, RFC 1592, 1994.

Chapter

9

Remote Network Monitoring (RMON)

9.1 Introduction

Network monitors, also known as network analyzers or probes, are quite useful for network management. They basically collect and analyze the packets going through them. These data may be statistics, such as packet sizes, number of collisions, and number of packets per second. In relation to management stations, these network monitors are remote; hence, they are known as *remote network monitors* (RMON). These network monitors, by using the RMON MIB, can be extended to collect data for network management and to communicate with management stations. Note that the RMON MIB extends MIB-II. RFC 1271 defined MIB objects primarily for the Ethernet protocol. RFC 1513 is an extension of RFC 1271 and defines the MIB objects required for monitoring networks running on token-ring protocols. RFC 1757 makes RFC 1271 obsolete. RFC 1757 is basically the same as RFC 1271, except it corrects and clarifies some of the terms, such as channel and captureBuffer, used in RFC 1271.

9.2 Network Management with RMON

Management data collected by a network monitor is sent to management stations. This can be on an exception basis, that is, when changes happen. The location of the network monitors is implementation-dependent. One network monitor can be placed per segment, per subnetwork, or per token-ring network.

As an example, refer to Figure 9.1, in which there is one network monitor for each subnetwork. FDDI rings have management stations

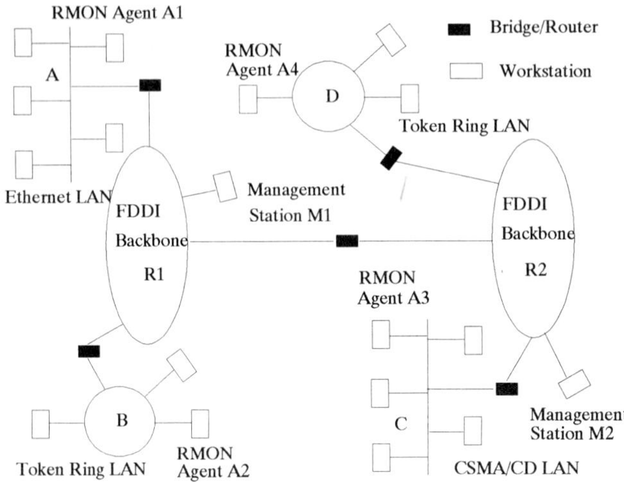

Figure 9.1 Network management using RMON. (*Source: Modified with permission from* Data Communications, *May 1992, copyright by McGraw-Hill, Inc., all rights reserved.*)

M1 and M2. Remote network monitors are placed in RMON agents A1, A2, A3, and A4, which provide functions such as protocol support for communication with management stations and error recovery for the remote network monitors. RMON agents act as intermediaries between remote network monitors and management stations. For transfer of data to management stations, these RMON agents can use SNMPv1 or SNMPv2 protocols. However, if RMON agents are to be implemented, SNMPv2 is preferable because SNMPv1 agents must ultimately migrate to SNMPv2 agents.

In Figure 9.2, we have made the assumption that RMON agents communicate with only one management station. It is not necessary to have this restriction; an RMON agent carrying a remote network monitor may send data to one or more management stations. Also,

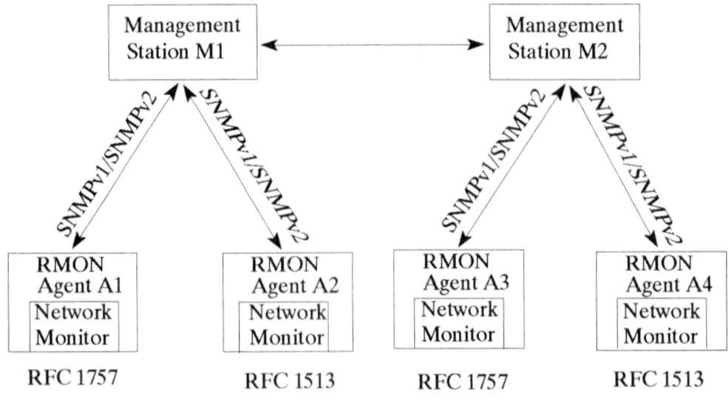

Figure 9.2 Management stations and RMON.

these RMON agents can be placed in hosts, routers, and bridges, and there are no set rules prescribed in RFC 1757 or RFC 1513 on the placement of remote network monitors.

This particular approach of having a network monitor exclusively for the purpose of network management has its own advantages. The network monitor can continuously collect data and selectively send it to the management stations. Also, when thresholds are crossed, events may be formed and alarms can be sent to the management stations. This action can help reduce network traffic, because the data collected is logged in agents with network monitors instead of transmitting every piece of data to the management stations. When the management stations need further details, they can access and collect the information required from the agents with remote network monitors.

9.3 Remote Network Monitoring Scenarios

RFC 1757 covers some of the scenarios where remote networking monitoring may be used. These include:

- *Offline operation:* Primarily relates to cases in which the network monitor operates as a stand-alone monitoring device. These cases can arise due to communication failure between the remote network monitor and a management station, or due to selective collection of data by a management station. Because a remote network monitor can operate independently of the management station, it can continue to perform its operation of continuously collecting and storing data. The management station, in turn, can retrieve these data stored whenever required.
- *Communication with management stations on an exception basis:* Because the remote network monitor can function independently of management stations, it can collect data on the network and log data for analysis at a later time. When problems are observed in the network due to crossing thresholds or failures, notifications can be sent to management stations. Management stations can retrieve the logged data for problem analysis and diagnostics.
- *Relevant data collection:* A monitor can also concentrate on the hosts in its portion of the network that have maximum traffic or errors and can log the data required for management stations. This will help in zeroing in on a portion of the network, as well as with the collection of data on the critical hosts in a network.
- *Multiple management stations:* Management stations may be organized on the basis of actions performed. Under these circumstances, it may be necessary to concurrently deal with more than one management station to which a network monitor is reporting.

Also, a breakdown by function, such as accounting, will help reduce the workload in management stations and makes it easy to focus on each of the functions. This can help to centralize the data required for certain network management functions such as configuration management. In many cases, configuration management activities need to be centralized in one management station. Similarly, under certain circumstances, it may be necessary to have centralized fault management, including monitoring, in another management station. So, a scenario where a remote network monitor may have to communicate with more than one management station becomes quite common, especially in large networks with thousands of workstations.

9.4 RMON for Ethernet (RFC 1757)

Objects defined in the remote network monitoring MIB are primarily for the Ethernet protocol. They can be expanded to cover token-ring and FDDI protocols. RMON objects are defined using the guidelines furnished in SMI (RFC 1155). However, in addition to the ASN.1 data types mentioned in SMI, RMON defines the following two data types:

- *OwnerString* (*DisplayString*): Contains information such as IP address, management station name, network manager's name, location, and phone number. This data type is used for identifying the owner of a resource, and helps in resolving conflicts when more than one management station is the owner of a resource. For example, if an instance of a resource is to be deleted by a management station, then there is the possibility that one management station may delete the instance created by another management station. But, by identifying the owner, a rule may be made that only the management station that created an object instance can delete that object instance. Thus, the data type OwnerString is useful when resources are shared by more than one management station.
- *EntryStatus* (*INTEGER*): Useful when a resource is shared by more than one owner. Suppose that an object instance is created by one owner. At the same time or later, another management station creates an object instance with conflicting values to the one that has been already created. In such a case, there can be major problems regarding the validity of values. The major question is which are the correct values? Under such circumstances, EntryStatus is quite useful because it helps to determine whether an object instance exists.

EntryStatus has these values: valid = 1, createRequest = 2, underCreation = 3, and invalid = 4. As we have seen previously, creating an object instance is equivalent to creating a row entry in a MIB table. So, when an object instance is created, we have the value createRequest. Creating an instance may lead to supplementary actions such as creation of more objects by an agent. During this operation, the value is set to underCreation. When this operation is completed, the value is set to valid, abort, or invalid, depending on the results of the object creation operation. Another management station that wants to create the same entry will get a result of error. Thus, it is prudent for a management station to check whether an object instance has already been created by checking EntryStatus.

After examining the new data types OwnerString and OwnerStatus, we can conclude that their primary objective is for facilitating resource sharing. This is due to the fact that network monitors can send monitored data to more than one management station, which is one of the salient points of RMON. These objects are transmitted across the wires using the BER, which was discussed in earlier chapters.

As shown in Figure 9.3, under the subtree {mib-2 16}, new groups for RMON are defined. Nine main groups are defined in RFC 1757. The tokenRing group, {rmon 10}, has been added in RFC 1513 specifically for monitoring networks working with the token-ring protocol. We will discuss each group individually.

9.4.1 Ethernet statistics group

Objects in the statistics group (Figure 9.4) are used to collect statistics on each of the monitored devices. The statistics group has one

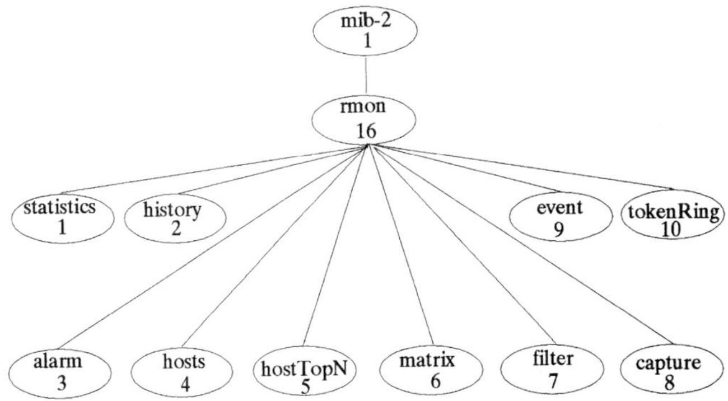

Figure 9.3 RMON objects (RFC 1271/1757).

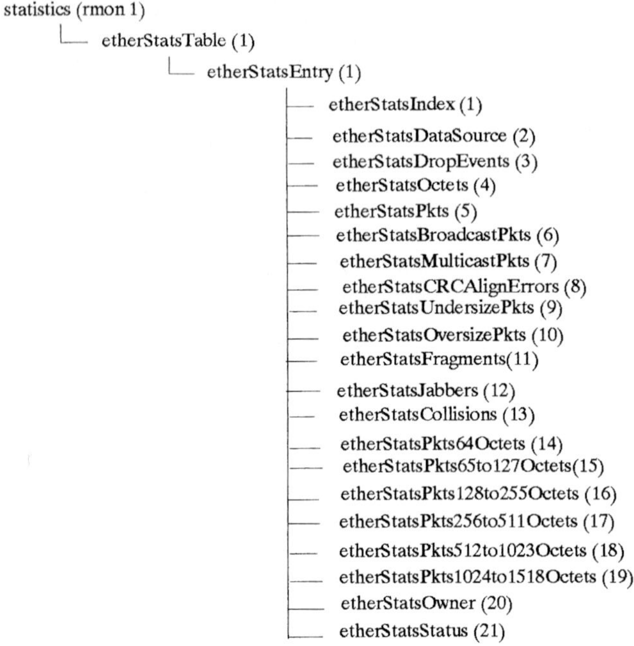

Figure 9.4 Statistics group.

etherStatsEntry1	etherStatsEntry2	......	etherStatsEntryN

etherStatsTable

etherStatsEntry1	etherStatsIndex1	etherStatsDataSource1	..	etherStatsStatus1
o	o	o		o
o	o	o		o
o	o	o		o
o	o	o		o
etherStatsEntryN	etherStatsIndexN	etherStatsDataSourceN	...	etherStatsStatusN

etherStatsTable

Figure 9.5 etherStatstable.

table, etherStatsTable, which is formed as shown in Figure 9.5. etherStatsTable will have a row for each Ethernet interface. Thus, there are etherStatsEntry1 to etherStatsEntryN in the etherStats-Table, and each etherStatsEntry has columns from etherStatsIndex and etherStatsDataSource up to etherStatsStatus. This procedure is followed in forming some of the tables in RMON and is similar to the ones used in MIB-II.

Data types for the statistics group are mainly counters, and they are created with a value of zero. In the statistics group, objects are:

- *etherStatsIndex (INTEGER)*: Provides the row position in the etherStatsTable.
- *etherStatsDataSource (OBJECT IDENTIFIER)*: Relates to the Ethernet interface from which a remote network monitor is receiving the data.
- *etherStatsDropEvents (Counter)*: Provides the number of times packets were dropped in network monitors for limitations of resources, such as lack of storage space.
- *etherStatsOctets (Counter)*: Provides the total number of octets received on the network monitor from an Ethernet interface. This includes the total number of data octets and FCS octets. However, these octets do not include the framing bits.
- *etherStatsPkts (Counter)*: Includes the total number of packets received, including those packets which had errors.
- *etherStatsBroadcastPkts (Counter)*: Furnishes the total number of good broadcast packets received in an Ethernet interface.
- *etherStatsMulticastPkts (Counter)*: While in etherStatsBroadcastPkts, the concern is good broadcast packets; in etherStatsMulticastPkts, a count of good multicast packets is kept.
- *etherStatsCRCAlignErrors (Counter)*: Provides the number of packets which were between length 64 and 1518 octets or had FCS errors. While counting the length, the FCS octets are included but the framing bits are excluded.
- *etherStatsUndersizePkts (Counter)*: Relates to the total number of good packets which had lengths less than 64 octets.
- *etherStatsOversizePkts (Counter)*: Refers to the well-formed packets which had lengths greater than 1518 octets.
- *etherStatsFragments (Counter)*: Provides data on packets which had bad lengths or FCS errors, and were of lengths less than 64 octets.
- *etherStatsJabbers (Counter)*: etherStatsFragments provides details on the bad packets which are of lengths less than 64 octets. We need to have data on bad packets which are over the Ethernet length limit of 1518 octets. etherStatsJabbers provides this data.
- *etherStatsCollisions (Counter)*: Provides the number of collisions in a subnetwork.

- *etherStatsPkts64Octets* through *etherStatsPkts1024to1518Octets:* Provide granularity for counters by breaking them into different counters for lengths of packets ranging from 64 to 1518 octets. Note that these packets also include the error packets.
- *etherStatsOwner* (*OwnerString*): Identifies the owner that created this row in the etherStatsTable. As we have seen earlier, OwnerString furnishes many details.
- *etherStatsStatus* (*EntryStatus*): Provides the status of the etherStats entry.

Objects in the statistics group are basically very useful for performance management, but some of them, such as etherStatsDropEvents, etherStatsCRCAlignErrors, and etherStatsUndersizePkts, will be useful for fault management, too. If corrective action is to be taken before a failure occurs, then it may be useful to have thresholds set for objects such as etherStatsDropEvents, etherStatsCRCAlignErrors, and etherStatsCollisions.

9.4.2 History group

In the history group, samples at fixed time intervals are collected and stored. This data can be used for analysis in fault and performance management. Objects in the history group are shown in Figure 9.6. As is apparent from the figure, there are two tables: historyControlTable and etherHistoryTable. historyControlTable provides information on how data are to be collected. Corresponding to a row in the historyControlTable (Figure 9.7), there are one or more rows of data in etherHistoryTable. etherHistoryTable has the actual data which is useful for analysis purposes. This pattern is followed by some tables in RMON MIB. RFC 1757 recommends that while collecting data, it is better to start data collection at the beginning of the next hour of the day. If data is collected for different stations in a network uniformly at the same time, data will be useful and meaningful for comparison purposes. Objects of the historyControlTable are:

- *historyControlIndex* (*INTEGER*): A unique identifier of an entry in the historyControlTable. Each entry defines a set of entries in the etherHistoryTable on an Ethernet interface.
- *historyControlDataSource* (*OBJECT IDENTIFIER*): Relates to the Ethernet interface on which a remote network monitor is collecting data.

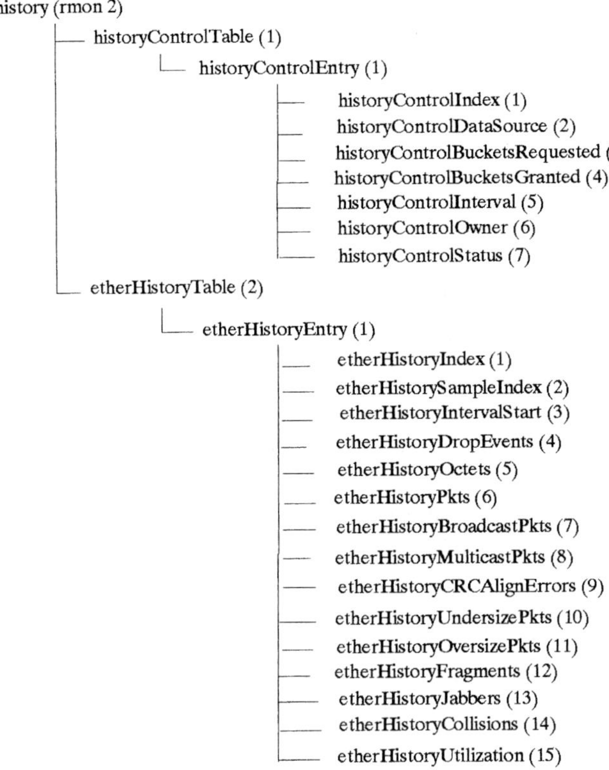

Figure 9.6 History group.

historyControlEntry1	historyControlEntry2	...	historyControlEntryN

historyControlTable

etherHistoryIndex1	etherHistorySampleIndex1	...	etherHistoryUtilization1
etherHistoryIndex2	etherHistorySampleIndex2	...	etherHistoryUtilization2
o	o	o	o
etherHistoryIndexN	etherHistorySampleIndexN	...	etherHistoryUtilizationN
o	o	o	o
etherHistoryIndex1	etherHistorySampleIndex1	...	etherHistoryUtilization1
etherHistoryIndex2	etherHistorySampleIndex2	...	etherHistoryUtilization2
o	o	o	o
etherHistoryIndexN	etherHistorySampleIndexN	...	etherHistoryUtilizationN

historyControlEntryN

etherHistoryTable

Figure 9.7 etherHistorytable.

- *historyControlBucketsRequested* (*INTEGER*): Provides the requested number of sampling intervals.
- *historyControlBucketsGranted* (*INTEGER*): In a network monitor there may be limitations on resources, so naturally, a network monitor cannot always provide the numbers of sampling intervals as requested in historyControlBucketsRequested. As a result, historyControlBucketsGranted furnishes the feasible number of sampling intervals, and, as is obvious, the historyControl BucketsGranted value is kept as close to the value requested by historyControlBucketsRequested.
- *historyControlInterval* (*INTEGER*): Refers to the sampling interval in seconds for each bucket. The value can be set from 1 to 3600 seconds.
- *historyControlOwner* (*OwnerString*): Identifies the owner which created this row in the historyControlTable. Because management stations will be using the data collected, historyControlOwner refers to a management station.
- *historyControlStatus* (*EntryStatus*): Provides the status of historyControlEntry.

etherHistoryTable has the data which have been collected over an Ethernet interface. Parameters for data collection are guided by historyControlEntry. The columns in etherHistoryTable starting from etherHistoryDropEvents up to etherHistoryCollisions are similar to those in the etherStatsTable, and mean almost the same thing, therefore, we will discuss those objects which are unique to the etherHistoryTable. These objects are:

- *etherHistoryIndex* (*INTEGER*): Has the same value as historyControlIndex. This entry links the historyControlTable and etherHistoryTable.
- *etherHistorySampleIndex* (*INTEGER*): Each etherHistoryIndex has one or more entries for etherHistorySampleIndex. This entry starts from 1, and each sample has a unique value increasing by 1.
- *etherHistoryIntervalStart* (*TimeTicks*): Refers to the sysUpTime when data collection was started.
- *etherHistoryUtilization* (*INTEGER*): Provides the best estimate of the mean physical layer network utilization in percentage over the time interval during which data collection was done. etherHistoryUtilization refers to the utilization over one Ethernet interface.

9.4.3 Alarm group

Implementation of the alarm group is optional. If it is implemented, then the event group must also be implemented because they are interrelated. In the alarm group (Figure 9.8), periodic samples are collected and then compared with the threshold values. If the value of a monitored variable crosses the threshold, then an event is generated. Objects in this group are useful for performance management. Events generated are useful for fault management. The alarm group uses an alarmTable which has entries stating how samples are to be taken and how the alarms are to be generated. The objects in the alarmTable are:

- *alarmIndex (INTEGER)*: A unique identifier which identifies a row in the alarmTable. alarmIndex refers to a sample for an object at a particular interval of time.
- *alarmInterval (INTEGER)*: States the time interval during which samples are taken from an object being observed.
- *alarmVariable (OBJECT IDENTIFIER)*: Refers to the identifier of the object being sampled. The object being sampled should have a data type of INTEGER, Counter, Gauge, or TimeTicks.
- *alarmSampleType (INTEGER)*: States how sample values are interpreted. It has two values: absoluteValue = 1 and deltaValue = 2. If the sample value is the absoluteValue, then it is compared against the threshold value for generating alarms. However, if it is a deltaValue, then the previous sample value is subtracted from the current value and this difference is compared with the threshold values.

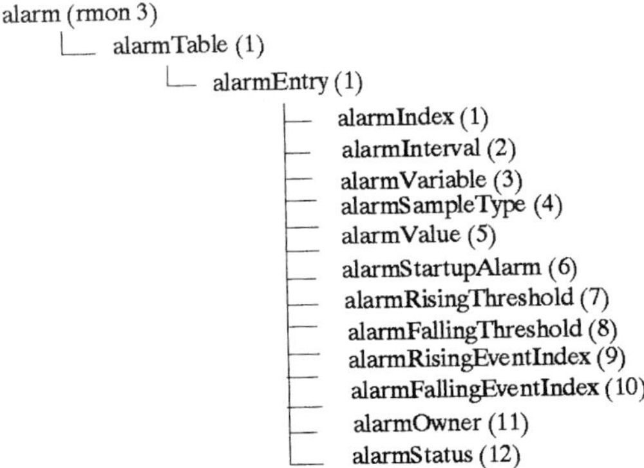

Figure 9.8 Alarm group.

- *alarmValue* (*INTEGER*): Provides the last valid sample value. A sample value is complete and available only at the end of a sampling period.
- *alarmStartupAlarm* (*INTEGER*): Has three values: risingAlarm = 1, fallingAlarm = 2, and risingOrFallingAlarm = 3. This states what type of alarm will be generated. When a sample value is greater than or equal to alarmRisingThreshold, and alarmStartupAlarm is equal to risingAlarm or risingOrFalling Alarm, then a single rising alarm will be generated. Similarly, when a sample value is less than or equal to alarmFallingThreshold and the alarmStartupAlarm is equal to fallingAlarm or risingOrFallingAlarm, then a falling alarm will be generated. These conditions can result in events being generated and sent to network monitors or management stations.
- *alarmRisingThreshold* (*INTEGER*): Represents a threshold value for a monitored object. A rising event can be generated when the sample value of a monitored object is greater than or equal to alarmRisingThreshold. The previous value should not have crossed the alarmRisingThreshold value. A rising event can also be generated if the first value of this entry is greater than or equal to the alarmRisingThreshold value and the associated alarmStartupAlarm is equal to risingAlarm or risingOrFallingAlarm.
- *alarmFallingThreshold* (*INTEGER*): Similar to the alarmRisingThreshold, but it represents a threshold value in the opposite direction. When a sampled value is less than or equal to this alarmFallingThreshold and when the value of the previous sampling interval was greater than the alarmFallingThreshold, a falling event is generated. A falling event is also generated if the value of the first entry is less than or equal to this threshold value and the associated alarmStartupAlarm is equal to fallingAlarm or risingOrFallingAlarm.
- *alarmRisingEventIndex* (*INTEGER*): Used to identify the event generated when a rising threshold is crossed. The value in this entry corresponds to the eventIndex in an eventTable. If there is no corresponding entry in eventIndex, then there is no relationship for this alarm entry with the event entry in eventTable. If this value is zero, then there is no valid entry in eventTable.
- *alarmFallingEventIndex* (*INTEGER*): While alarmRisingEventIndex is used when crossing rising thresholds, alarmFallingEventIndex is used when a falling threshold is crossed.

- *alarmOwner* (*OwnerString*): Refers to one or more management stations which configured this entry in alarmTable.
- *alarmStatus* (*EntryStatus*): Refers to the status of the entry in alarmTable.

9.4.4 Host group

The host group (Figure 9.9) contains statistics on each of the hosts discovered in the network. These are derived by noting good packets

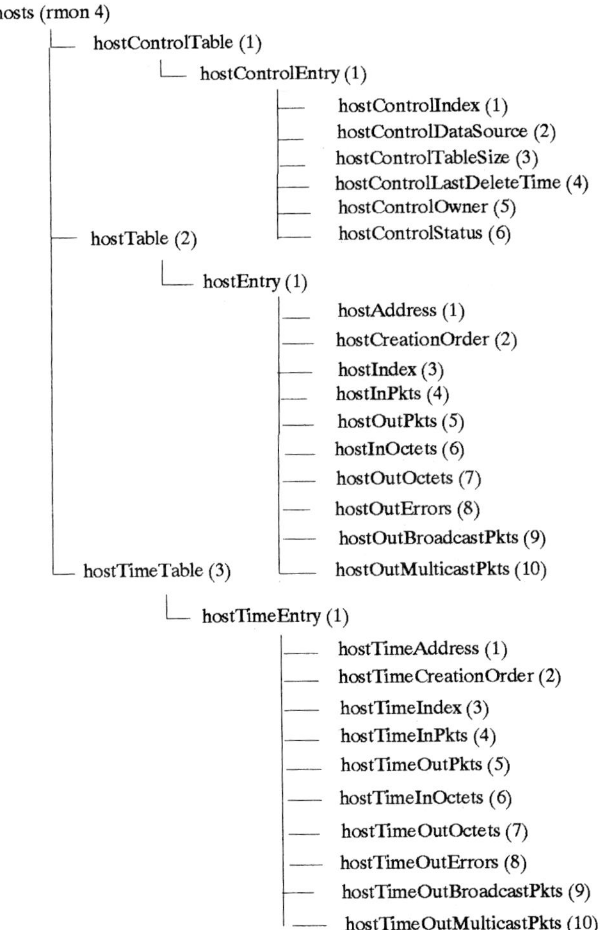

Figure 9.9 Host group.

received on the network. Each host is identified by the MAC address. The statistics on each host in the network are maintained in three tables:

- *hostControlTable:* The entries in this table determine how the statistics on hosts are to be maintained. Based on the parameters of this table, data is collected and entered in hostTable and hostTimeTable.
- *hostTable:* Has entries on each host based on the MAC addresses. These MAC addresses are used to index into hostTable.
- *hostTimeTable:* The rows in this table are arranged in order of hostTimeCreationOrder. The hostTimeCreationOrder column of the table starts from 1, and this is used for indexing into hostTimeTable. There is a subtle difference between hostTable and hostTimeTable. In hostTable, we index into the table using MAC addresses, while in hostTimeTable, we index into the table using hostTimeCreationOrder. The format of the data collected is the same for both tables. By indexing in the order in which the entries are created in hostTimeTable, it is easier to download these tables by means of management stations using SNMP. Also, it is easy to break the packets into manageable SNMP PDUs. The other advantage is that to get details of new hosts added after a download of data from hostTimeTable, entries must be downloaded after a particular value of *N* instead of downloading hostTimeTable all over again.

The entries in hostTable and hostTimeTable are useful for configuration, performance, and fault management. Knowing the addresses of hosts in a network by frequently downloading the entries in hostTimeTable helps in keeping track of the active hosts in the network. When entries are deleted from hostTimeTable, the configuration of the network on the hosts can be accordingly modified. The different objects of the host group are:

- *hostControlIndex* (*INTEGER*): Each discovered host in a network has an entry in hostControlTable. hostControlIndex is a unique identifier for a row and a host.
- *hostControlDataSource* (*OBJECT IDENTIFIER*): Identifies the source for data. This source can be any interface on a host and has a corresponding entry in ifIndex.
- *hostControlTableSize* (*INTEGER*): Corresponds to the number of entries in hostTable for a host. As the entries in hostTable and hostTimeTable have one-to-one correspondence, this number also refers to the number of entries in hostTimeTable.

- *hostControlLastDeleteTime (TimeTicks)*: Relates to the time when an entry was last deleted from hostTable. A zero value indicates that no deletions were made in hostTable.

hostControlOwner and *hostControlStatus* have the same significance as described earlier in other RMON MIB groups. In both hostTable and hostTimeTable, only the objects which need explanation will be examined, and we will avoid discussing those objects which are similar in meaning to the ones already explained. Some of the objects which need explanation are:

- *hostAddress (OCTET STRING)*: Refers to the MAC address of the host.
- *hostCreationOrder (INTEGER)*: A number from 1 to *N* and having a corresponding row in hostControlEntry. The numbers in hostCreationOrder are increased by one as a new entry is created.
- *hostIndex (INTEGER)*: The value in this column is the same as the value in hostControlIndex.
- *hostInPkts (Counter)*: Provides the number of good packets received through this host address, furnished by hostAddress, after adding this host to hostTable.
- *hostOutPkts (Counter)*: Identifies the total number of packets transmitted by the host, including the error packets.
- *hostInOctets (Counter)*: Contains the total number of octets received by this host after it was added to hostTable. hostInOctets does not include error octets and framing bits.
- *hostOutOctets (Counter)*: Furnishes the total number of octets transmitted by this host. It includes error octets, but does not include framing bits in the count of octets.
- *hostOutErrors (Counter)*: Relates to the number of error packets transmitted by a host after being added to the host table. This object is very useful for performance and fault management. hostOutErrors along with hostOutOctets can furnish solid information on how a host is behaving.
- *hostOutBroadcastPkts (Counter)*: A counter for the number of good broadcast packets transmitted by this host after this entry was added to hostTable.
- *hostOutMulticastPkts (Counter)*: Counter contains only the packets transmitted to multicast addresses after being added to the host table. Because the distinction has been made between multicast and broadcast, this counter naturally does not include the number of packets broadcast by this host.

The entries in hostTimeTable are:

- *hostTimeAddress (OCTET STRING)*: Pertains to the MAC address of the host.
- *hostTimeCreationOrder (INTEGER)*: The index used for hostTimeTable. The entries are arranged sequentially from one to *N*. This entry has the same value as hostControlTableSize of hostControlTable.
- *hostTimeIndex (INTEGER)*: Has the same value as hostControlIndex of hostControlTable.

In hostTimeTable, other entries, from *hostInPkts* up to and including *hostOutMulticastPkts,* have the same significance as described in hostTable.

9.4.5 HostTopN group

The HostTopN group (Figure 9.10) can be used to report the statistics on a group of hosts over a period of time. These statistics on selected hosts over a sampling interval is known as a *report* and is sent to one or more management stations. These statistics are derived from the host group. The interval for collecting data and start and stop times from the host group is determined by management stations. Once the data is collected in hostTopNTable, then it is available for management stations. The implementation of the HostTopN group is option-

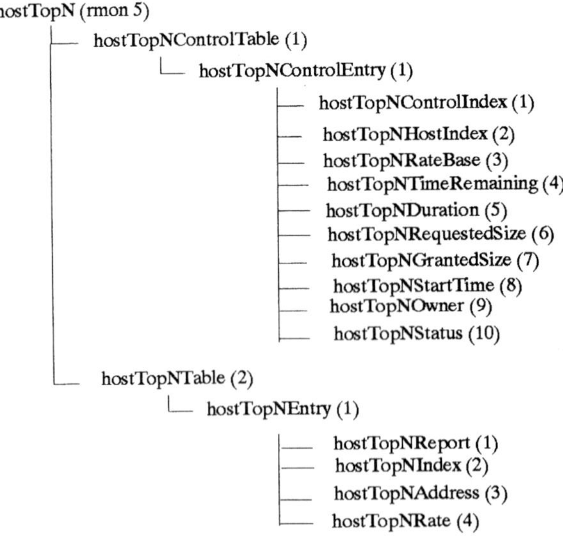

Figure 9.10 HostTopN group.

al. However, if this group is implemented, then the Host group must also be implemented. Data collected from the HostTopN group are useful for performance and fault management. The objects in the HostTopN group are:

- *hostTopNControlIndex (INTEGER)*: A unique entry which identifies a top *N* report for one interface.
- *hostTopNHostIndex (INTEGER)*: The value of this entry and the value of hostIndex in hostTable are the same.
- *hostTopNRateBase (INTEGER)*: Identifies an object in hostTable (Figure 9.9) on which data is collected. The values of the objects in hostTopNRateBase are: hostTopNInPkts = 1, hostTopNOutPkts = 2, hostTopNInOctets = 3, hostTopNOutOctets = 4, hostTopNOutErrors = 5, hostTopNOutBroadcastPkts = 6, and hostTopNOutMulticastPkts = 7. The significance of these variables is as explained in the host group.
- *hostTopNTimeRemaining (INTEGER)*: Provides the time remaining in the sampling interval to complete the data collection for hostTopNTable. Only when the value becomes zero will hostTopNEntry be available. If the value is nonzero, then host top *N* entries cannot be retrieved.
- *hostTopNDuration (INTEGER)*: Provides information on the sampling interval in seconds for the previous report, or, if the data is being collected, then this furnishes elapsed time since data collection started. The value of hostTopNDuration is set along with the value of hostTopNTimeRemaining.
- *hostTopNRequestedSize (INTEGER)*: Identifies the maximum number of hosts requested for hostTopNTable. Here, the default value is 10.
- *hostTopNGrantedSize (INTEGER)*: Furnishes the number of hosts on which data can be collected in hostTopNTable. Because there can be limitations on resources, sometimes this value cannot be equal to the value of hostTopNRequestedSize. This value should be set as close to hostTopNRequestedSize as possible.
- *hostTopNStartTime (TimeTicks)*: Provides sysUpTime at which hostTopNReport was started.

hostTopNOwner and *hostTopNStatus* have the same meaning as described previously for corresponding entries in other RMON groups.

HostTopN group also has hostTopNTable, which includes the following objects:

- *hostTopNReport* (*INTEGER*): Identifies a report. Its value is the same as the value of hostTopNControlIndex.
- *hostTopNIndex* (*INTEGER*): Identifies a row in the hostTopNTable. hostTopNIndex starts from 1 and increases by a value of 1.
- *hostTopNAddress* (*OCTET STRING*): Refers to the MAC address of a host.
- *hostTopNRate* (*INTEGER*): Provides the amount of change in the selected object, which is selected by hostTopNRateBase.

9.4.6 Matrix group

In the Matrix group (Figure 9.11), the statistics on conversations between two sets of MAC addresses are maintained in two tables:

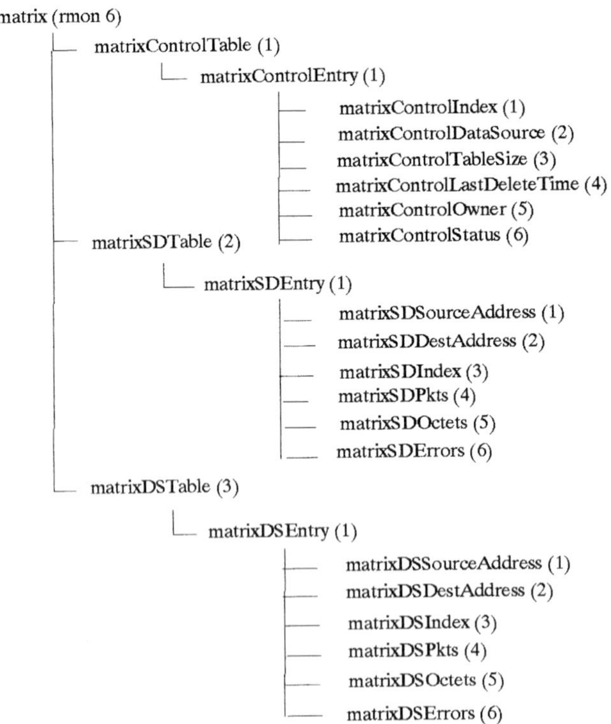

Figure 9.11 Matrix group.

matrixSDTable and matrixDSTable. Entries in these tables are controlled by the objects in matrixControlTable. In all these tables, when there are shortages of resources, the least recently used entries are deleted. Implementation of the matrix group is optional. matrixSDTable is primarily indexed on the basis of source and destination addresses. However, in matrixDSTable, the statistics on a conversation are indexed on the basis of destination and source addresses. So the major difference between these two tables is in the manner in which the tables are accessed for processing. These tables are useful for configuration, performance, and fault management. In configuration management, granularity may be depicted to the conversation levels, in which case, it is easy to collect data on active conversations from the matrix group. The explanations of objects in the matrix group are:

- *matrixControlIndex* (*INTEGER*): Uniquely identifies an entry in matrixControlTable. For each matrixControlIndex entry, statistics are stored in matrixSDTable and matrixDSTable.
- *matrixControlDataSource* (*OBJECT IDENTIFIER*): Represents the identifier of the source device on which conversation statistics are collected.

Other objects, from *matrixControlTableSize* through *matrixControl Status,* have the same meaning as corresponding objects in other groups.

- *matrixSDSourceAddress* (*OCTET STRING*): Refers to the source MAC address for the conversation on which statistics are being collected. Note that the MAC address identifies a host.
- *matrixSDDestAddress* (*OCTET STRING*): Refers to the destination MAC address.
- *matrixSDIndex* (*INTEGER*): Has the same value as matrixControlIndex in matrixControlEntry. This entry helps to associate matrixControlEntry with a row in matrixSDTable.
- *matrixSDPkts* (*Counter*): Provides the total number of packets transmitted from a source to the destination. It also includes error packets.
- *matrixSDOctets* (*Counter*): Refers to the total number of good octets transmitted from a source to the destination address. It does not include framing bits but does include error octets.
- *matrixSDErrors* (*Counter*): Includes error packets transmitted from a source to the destination address. By subtracting

matrixSDErrors from matrixSDPkts, statistics on the number of good packets can be recovered.

The objects of matrixDSTable have similar meaning to those in matrixSDTable.

9.4.7 Filter group

The filter group (Figure 9.12) helps in matching the conditions for capturing data or generating events. The concept of channels is used here. Input data is subjected to a set of filter rules stated in different variables in the filter group. Filter rules are applied to packet data and packet status. From the filter operation, a channel is obtained. The channel data can be stored with the aid of captureBufferTable. Note that *channel* is a technical concept and not a physical component. If the channel is enabled, then *events* are generated (see Figure

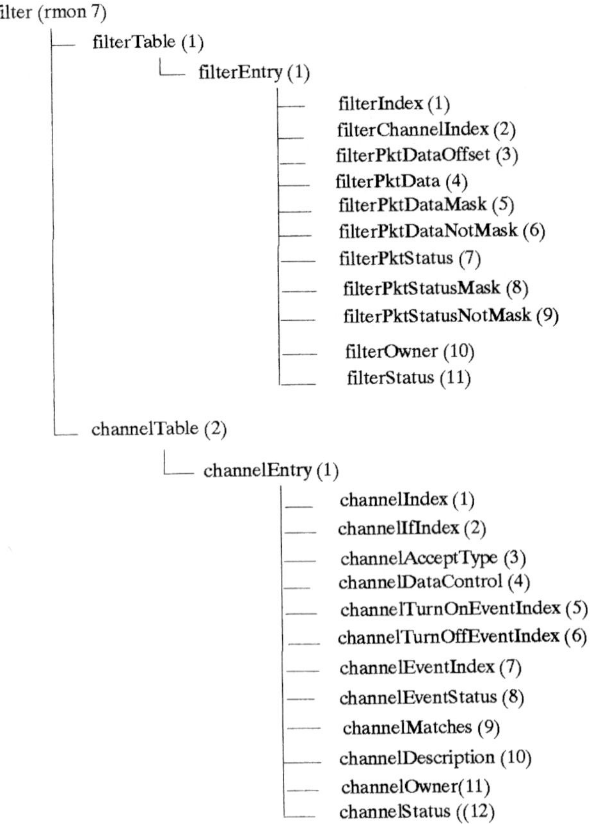

Figure 9.12 Filter group.

9.14). An event can also enable the channel on or off. From a channel, we can generate SNMP trap messages and log the events.

The filter group has two tables: filterTable and channelTable. The objects provided are:

- *filterIndex* (*INTEGER*): A unique index which identifies an entry in filterTable.
- *filterChannelIndex* (*INTEGER*): Identifies a channel and matches the channelIndex in channelTable.
- *filterPktDataOffset* (*INTEGER*): Points to the starting point in data after which a filter will be applied. The offset is measured after framing bits in a physical layer frame.
- *filterPktData* (*OCTET STRING*): Provides the data for filtering. It is used along with filterPktDataMask and filterPktDataNotMask.
- *filterPktDataMask* (*OCTET STRING*): Bits with 1s are relevant. filterPktDataMask is extended with 1s if it is shorter than filterPktData.
- *filterPktDataNotMask* (*OCTET STRING*): The inverse of the filterPktDataMask. If the filterPktDataNotMask is shorter than the filterPktData, then this mask is extended with 0s.
- *filterPktStatus* (*INTEGER*): Matched with the input packet, and the input bits relevant here are those corresponding to 1s in the filterPktStatusMask.
- *filterPktStatusMask* (*INTEGER*): Applied to the filterPktStatus, and only those bits which have 1s are relevant. Here, as with filterPktDataMask, if filterPktStatus is shorter than the filterPktStatusMask, then filterPktStatus is extended by adding 1s.
- *filterPktStatusNotMask* (*INTEGER*): Operates inversely to filterPktStatusMask.

filterOwner and *filterStatus* have the same meanings as described for corresponding objects in other groups.

The objects in the channelTable are:

- *channelIndex* (*INTEGER*): Identifies a unique entry in the channel table.
- *channelIfIndex* (*INTEGER*): Uniquely identifies an interface on the RMON device (just like IfIndex).
- *channelAcceptType* (*INTEGER*): Controls the actions of the filters associated with the channel. It has values of acceptMatched = 1 and acceptFailed = 2. In acceptMatched, packets will be accepted if

there is a match of packet data and packet status. In acceptFailed, for a packet to be accepted, the packet data match or packet status match must fail.

- *channelDataControl* (*INTEGER*): Controls the flow of data, status, and events through the channel. It has two values: on = 1 and off = 2. If the value is on, then data, status, and events can flow through the channel. If the status is off, then data, status, and events do not pass through the channel.
- *channelTurnOnEventIndex* (*INTEGER*): Controls the generation of events. If an event is generated, then this value has a corresponding value in the eventIndex entry in eventTable.
- *channelTurnOffEventIndex* (*INTEGER*): Will turn channelDataControl to off from on, after an event is generated. It also has an entry in the eventIndex entry in eventTable.
- *channelEventIndex* (*INTEGER*): Will identify the event to be generated when there is a packet match and channelDataControl is on.
- *channelEventStatus* (*INTEGER*): Used for controlling the flow of events. It has three values: eventReady = 1, eventFired = 2, and eventAlwaysReady = 3. When this object is set to eventReady, an event will be generated and the object will change to the eventFired state. The eventAlwaysReady state will disable flow control, and events will be generated freely.
- *channelMatches* (*Counter*): States the number of times there has been a packet match, including those cases where channelDataControl is off.
- *channelDescription* (*DisplayString*): Describes the channel.

channelOwner and *channelStatus* have the same significance as described for corresponding objects in other groups.

9.4.8 Packet capture group

On the basis of filters, packets are captured and stored in captureBufferTable of the packet capture group tables (Figure 9.13). As shown in Figure 9.14, a channel is associated with captureBufferTable. bufferControlTable determines how filtered data are stored in captureBufferTable. One row of captureBufferTable is used to store data on packets from a channel. The implementation of the packet capture group is optional. If the Filter group is implemented, then this group must be implemented. The objects in the packet capture group are:

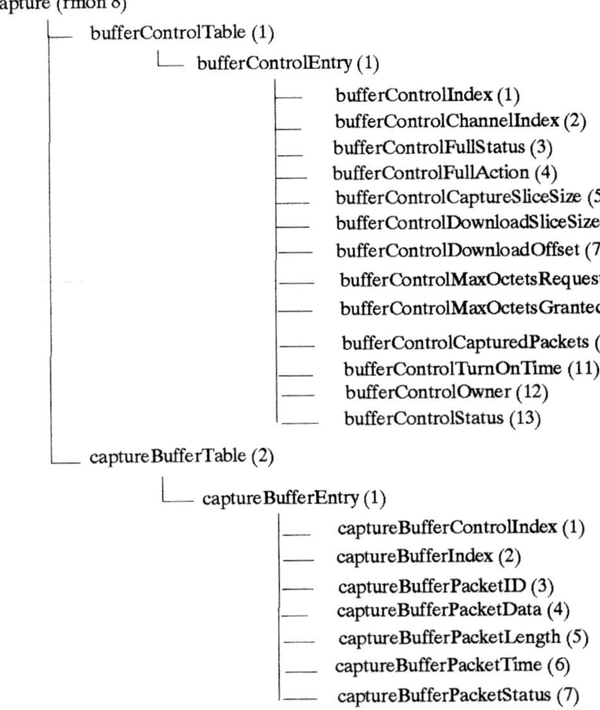

Figure 9.13 Packet capture group.

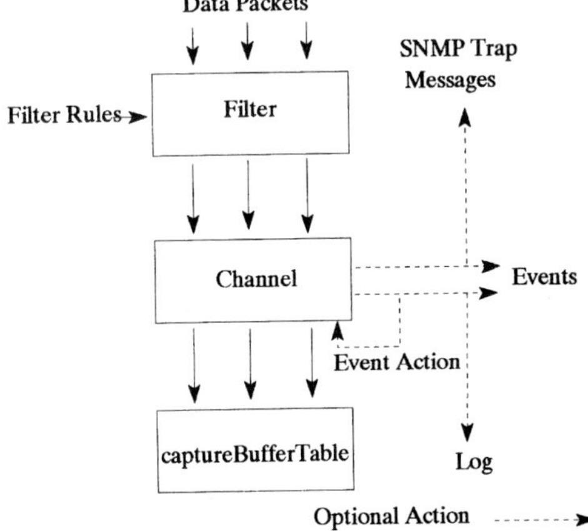

Figure 9.14 Concepts of filter, channel, capture, and events.

- *bufferControlIndex* (*INTEGER*): A unique index that identifies an entry in bufferControlTable.
- *bufferControlChannelIndex* (*INTEGER*): Identifies the channel. Its value is the same as the value in channelIndex.
- *bufferControlFullStatus* (*INTEGER*): Shows the status of the buffer which is used to store data received from filters. It has two values: spaceAvailable = 1 and full = 2.
- *bufferControlFullAction* (*INTEGER*): Will indicate the action to be taken when the buffer becomes full. It has two values: lockWhenFull = 1 and wrapWhenFull = 2.
- *bufferControlCaptureSliceSize* (*INTEGER*): Furnishes the maximum number of octets of each packet which will be stored in the capture buffer. If it is set to zero, then as many octets as possible will be saved in the capture buffer.
- *bufferControlDownloadSliceSize* (*INTEGER*): States the maximum number of octets that will be retrieved from a management station by an SNMP GetRequest or GetNextRequest PDUs. The default value is 100 octets.
- *bufferControlDownloadOffset* (*INTEGER*): States the offset after which data in the buffer will be retrieved by a management station with an SNMP GetRequest or GetNextRequest PDU. The default offset value is 0.
- *bufferControlMaxOctetsRequested* (*INTEGER*): Furnishes the maximum number of octets which a management station desires a capture buffer to save. A default value of −1 indicates that the request by the management station to the monitoring device is to save as many octets as possible.
- *bufferControlMaxOctetsGranted* (*INTEGER*): We have noted earlier that a monitoring device may have resource limitations. Under those circumstances, it is not possible to furnish the buffer space requested by a management station. bufferControlMaxOctetsGranted supplies the actual number of octets that can be saved, and if the default value is −1, then the capture buffer will save as many octets as possible.
- *bufferControlCapturedPackets* (*INTEGER*): Furnishes the number of packets actually stored at present in a capture buffer.
- *bufferControlTurnOnTime* (*INTEGER*): Provides sysUpTime when the capture buffer started functioning.

bufferControlOwner and *bufferControlStatus* have the same significance described for corresponding objects in other groups.

The captureBufferTable has the following entries:

- *captureBufferControlIndex* (*INTEGER*): Provides the index of an entry in captureBufferTable.
- *captureBufferIndex* (*INTEGER*): Increases in value by 1 from 1, and uniquely identifies an entry in captureBufferTable.
- *captureBufferPakcetID* (*INTEGER*): An index, in ascending order, describing the order of the packets received on an interface. These packets may be stored in one or more capture buffers, hence aiding in identifying the packets.
- *captureBufferPacketData* (*OCTET STRING*): Contains the captured data of a packet.
- *captureBufferPacketLength* (*INTEGER*): Furnishes the length of the captured packet and includes the FCS octets.
- *captureBufferPacketTime* (*INTEGER*): Furnishes the relative time in milliseconds when a packet was captured since the capture buffer was turned on.
- *captureBufferPacketStatus* (*INTEGER*): Provides the error status of a packet. The values defined are: packet length greater than 1518 octets = 0, packet length less than 64 octets = 1, packet had CRC or alignment error = 2, first packet in the capture buffer after an error was discovered = 3 and packet's order in buffer is only approximate = 4. The fourth bit definition is an addition in RFC 1757.

9.4.9 Event group

The event group (Figure 9.15) helps in the generation and notification of events. These events might have been generated due to conditions elsewhere in the MIB. It may be determined that when a certain threshold is reached an event is generated. Parameters of events are described in eventTable. When an event is generated, it may be necessary to log the event. Events are logged in logTable (see Figure 9.15). Here an SNMP trap may be generated and used to notify a managing station. The objects are:

- *eventIndex* (*INTEGER*): Identifies an entry in eventTable.
- *eventDescription* (*DisplayString*): Provides the description of the event.
- *eventType* (*INTEGER*): Describes the type of event. The values are: none = 1, log = 2, snmp-trap = 3, and log-and-trap = 4. If an event is logged, then a value of 3 is used and there is a correspond-

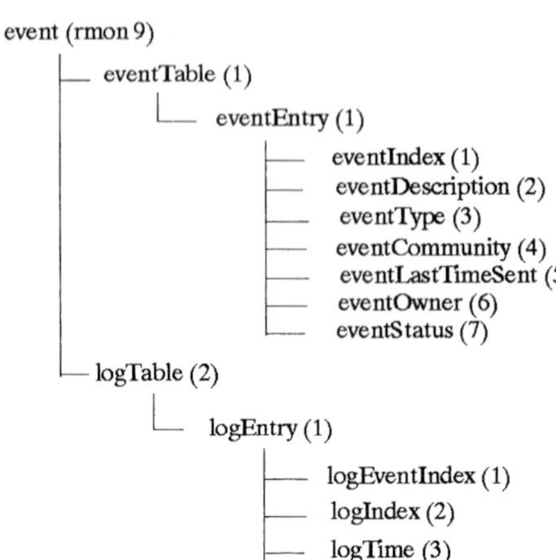

Figure 9.15 Event group.

ing entry in logTable. If an SNMP trap is sent to one or more management stations, then the value is 3. When the SNMP trap is logged the value is 4.

- *eventCommunity* (*OCTET STRING*): Names the SNMP community to which the SNMP trap must be sent.
- *eventLastTimeSent* (*TimeTicks*): Furnishes sysUpTime when an event was last generated. If it is set to 0, then no event was generated.

eventOwner and *eventStatus* have the same significance as described for corresponding entries in other groups.

- *logEventIndex* (*INTEGER*): Has the value of eventIndex for which a log was generated.
- *logIndex* (*INTEGER*): Identifies an entry in the log table.
- *logTime* (*TimeTicks*): Furnishes sysUpTime when an event that has been logged in logTable was created.
- *logDescription* (*DisplayString*): Presents the description of the event.

9.5 RMON for Token Ring (RFC 1513)

RFC 1513 extends the RMON MIB for the token-ring protocol by adding a new group for tokenRing under RMON (refer to Figure 9.3).

We discuss RFC 1513 separately, because it neatly describes extensions for the token-ring protocol. Because RFC 1271 is specifically tailored for collecting data on Ethernet protocols, new groups are exclusively added to statistics and history groups for the token-ring protocol. Error counters in a hostEntry for token ring will be incremented for isolating errors such as LineErrors, BurstErrors, ACErrors, InternalErrors, and AbortErrors. In token ring, matrix group error counters are not incremented. For bit mask interpretations for the filter group, refer to RFC 1513. The following new object groups have been added to the token-ring protocol:

- Token-ring station
- Token-ring station order
- Token-ring station configuration
- Source routing statistics

New data types in RFC 1513 are:

- *MacAddress* (*OCTET STRING* (*SIZE* (*6*)): Defines the MAC address used in IEEE Standard 802.1. When MacAddress is used, the source routing bit is stripped off. Details on the MAC address, source routing, and different LAN protocols are provided in Chapter 11.
- *TimeInterval* (*INTEGER*): Refers to a period of time, and is measured in intervals of 0.01 seconds.

Some of the concepts of token-ring protocols which may not be encountered in Chapter 11 are explained here.

9.5.1 Token-ring MAC-layer statistics group

The token-ring MAC-layer statistics group (Figure 9.16) consists of one table: tokenRingMLStatsTable. This table has statistics on the MAC layer for one token-ring interface, so the objects defined have significance to the MAC layer. We will discuss only those objects which are unique to this group and will not repeat the explanations of those objects which are similar to the ones we discussed with RFC 1757. As we have seen with RFC 1757, these statistics are useful for performance and fault management. In the following discussion, ML stands for MAC layer. The objects in the group are:

- *tokenRingMLStatsMacPkts* (*Counter*): Refers to the total number of octets in good MAC packets received. It does not include the packets which had errors. A good frame refers to a token-ring frame defined by IEEE 802.5 standards.

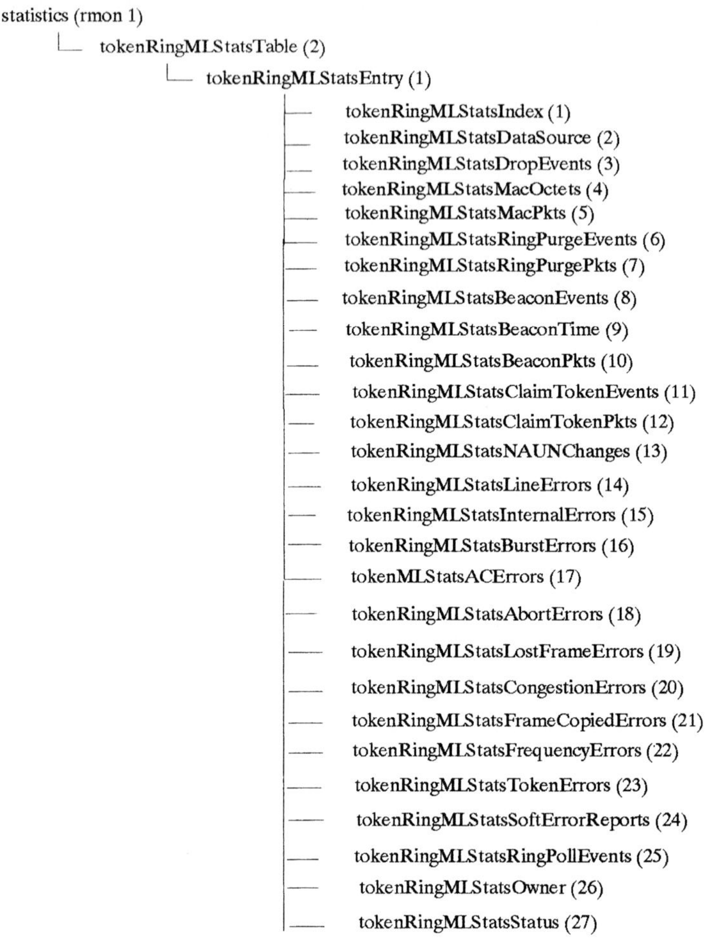

Figure 9.16 Token-ring statistics group.

- *tokenRingMLStatsRingPurgeEvents* (*Counter*): Specifies the number of times the ring purge state has been reached from a normal state. In token ring, data is received when a station is in a *normal repeat mode*. In this mode, a station will receive a frame and transmit it. A ring purge MAC frame must be sent before an active monitor originates a new token. When a ring purge frame is received, timers in stations are reset, and stations enter the normal repeat mode.
- *tokenRingMLStatsRingPurgePkts* (*Counter*): Refers to the total number of ring purge MAC packets.
- *tokenRingMLStatsBeaconEvents* (*Counter*): Refers to the number of times a beacon state has been entered. To understand this

counter, the concept of *beaconing* must be understood. In token ring, a ring can become nonoperational due to faults in stations, which are known as *hard errors*. A hard error in a station is usually detected by its immediate downstream neighbor. On receiving this frame, the downstream neighbor sends a *beacon frame,* which contains the address of its upstream neighbor and the information on the type of error. By knowing the address of the upstream neighbor, the ring station that has a failure can be pinpointed.

- *tokenRingMLStatsBeaconTime* (*TimeInterval*): Furnishes the duration of the beaconing state.
- *tokenRingMLStatsBeaconPkts* (*Counter*): Provides the total number of MAC beacon packets.
- *tokenRingMLStatsClaimTokenEvents* (*Counter*): Separates the entry to the claim token state into three states: from the normal ring state, from the ring purge state, and from the beacon state. In this counter, only the first two cases are taken, and the total number of times a token enters the claim token state is furnished. Note that the claim token process is done to elect a new active monitor.
- *tokenRingMLStatsClaimTokenPkts* (*Counter*): Refers to the total number of claim token MAC packets.
- *tokenRingMLStatsNAUNChanges* (*Counter*): Has the total number of *nearest active upstream neighbor* (NAUN) changes. Note that when an active monitor broadcasts an active monitor present MAC frame, the first ring station that receives this frame saves the source address of the active monitor present frame as the NAUN address. These NAUN addresses are useful for isolating errors in a segment.
- *tokenRingMLStatsLineErrors* (*Counter*): Provides the total number of line errors.
- *tokenRingMLStatsInternalErrors* (*Counter*): Refers to the total number of adapter internal errors.
- *tokenRingMLStatsBurstErrors* (*Counter*): Provides the total number of burst errors.
- *tokenRingMLStatsACErrors* (*Counter*): Refers to the total number of address copied errors.
- *tokenRingMLStatsAbortErrors* (*Counter*): A counter of the total number of abort delimiters in error-reporting packets.
- *tokenRingMLStatsLostFrameErrors* (*Counter*): Refers to the total number of lost frames.

- *tokenRingMLStatsCongestionErrors* (*Counter*): Provides the total number of receive congestion errors.
- *tokenRingMLStatsFrameCopiedErrors* (*Counter*): For counting frame copied errors.
- *tokenRingMLStatsFrequencyErrors* (*Counter*): Provides the total number of frequency errors.
- *tokenRingMLStatsTokenErrors* (*Counter*): For counting the total number of token errors.
- *tokenRingMLStatsSoftErrorReports* (*Counter*): Refers to the total number of *soft error* frames. Soft errors mean errors which temporarily make the rings nonoperational, although it is possible to recover from them. These soft errors can pose major problems if there are too many of them.
- *tokenRingMLStatsRingPollEvents* (*Counter*): Relates to the total number of ring polls initiated by an active monitor.

The other group in the token ring statistics group is the token ring promiscuous statistics group (Figure 9.17). According to *Webster's New Collegiate Dictionary*, one meaning of *promiscuous* is "composed of all sorts of persons or things." In the MAC layer statistics group, data was collected on just the MAC layer. It is necessary to know data

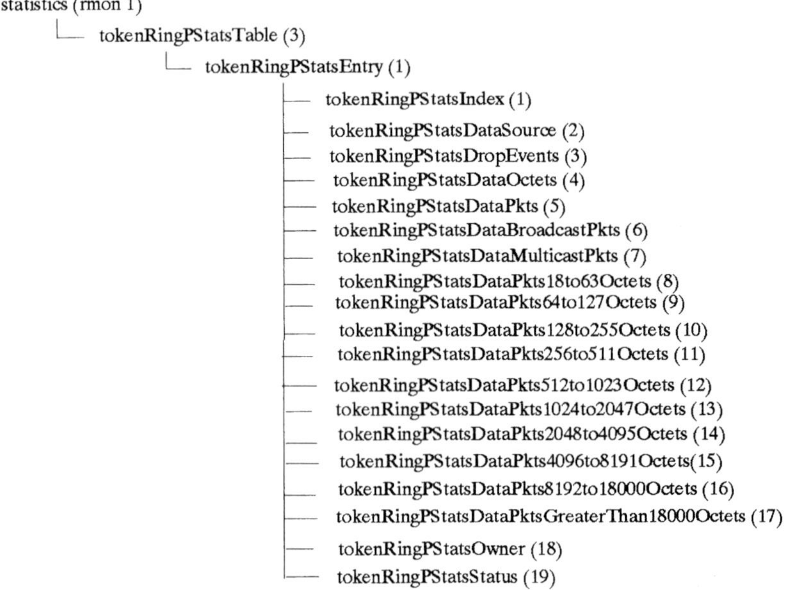

Figure 9.17 Token-ring promiscuous statistics group.

about the physical and link layers too. Hence, there is the token-ring promiscuous statistics group. Data on this group is also useful for performance and fault management. The objects in this group are similar to the data collected in etherStatsTable, thus, we will not discuss each of the objects in the group. Because there is no Ethernet restriction that the packets must be between 64 and 1518 octets, the range of packet length in token ring is greater.

9.5.2 Token-ring history group

Similar to the statistics group, the token-ring history group extends the history group described for RFC 1271. Here, too, history on a token-ring interface is collected and data are saved in tokenRingMLHistoryTable (Figure 9.18) for the MAC layer and in tokenRingPHistoryTable (Figure 9.19) for the non-MAC layer data. Data collected in these tables is useful for performance and fault man-

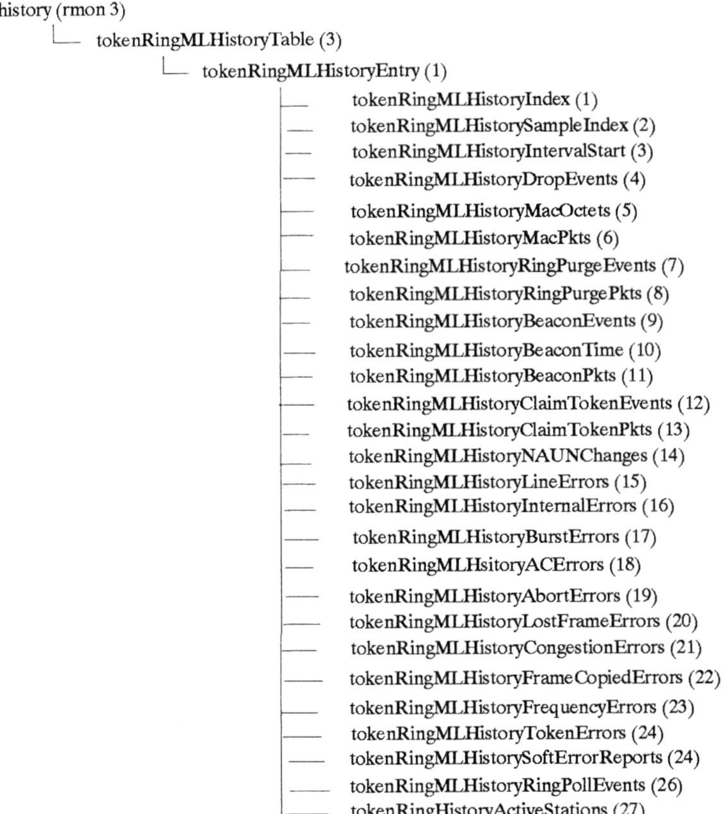

Figure 9.18 Token-ring MAC layer history group.

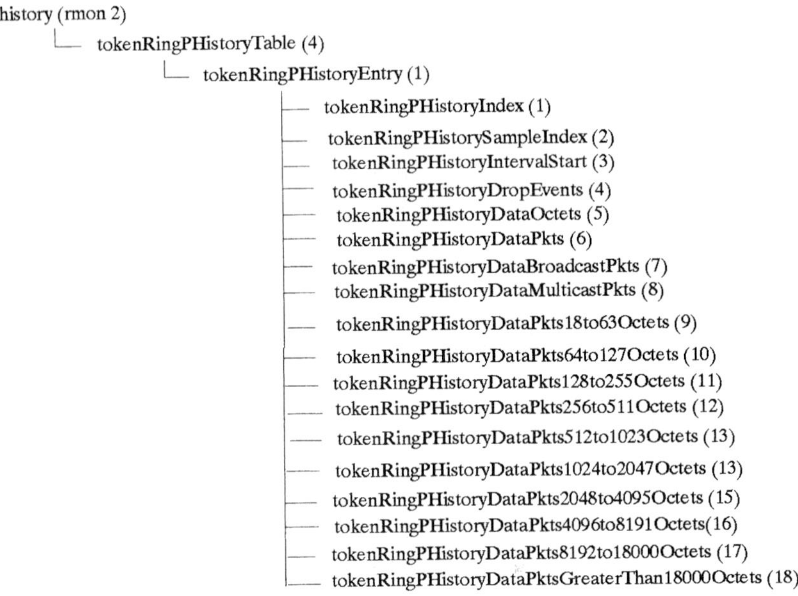

Figure 9.19 Token-ring promiscuous history group.

agement. The implementation of the token-ring history group is optional, but it requires the implementation of history groups mentioned in RFC 1757. The meanings of objects are similar to the corresponding ones in RFC 1757 and the token-ring statistics group, so we will not provide individual explanations.

9.5.3 Token-ring ring station group

The token-ring ring station group (Figure 9.20) contains the statistics and status of each station attached to a token-ring network. When there are resource limitations on the network monitor, the resources which have been inactive for the longest time must be freed. The implementation of this group is also optional. The data collected for this station are useful for configuration, performance, and fault management. RingStationControlEntry has parameters for collecting data on stations in the ring which have been discovered. ringStationEntry has the actual data on the stations. For this group, we will discuss those objects that have new meanings.

- *ringStationControlActiveStations* (*INTEGER*): Furnishes the number of active ringStationEntry in the ringStationTable.
- *ringStationControlRingState* (*INTEGER*): Presents the current status of the ring. The values are: normalOperation = 1,

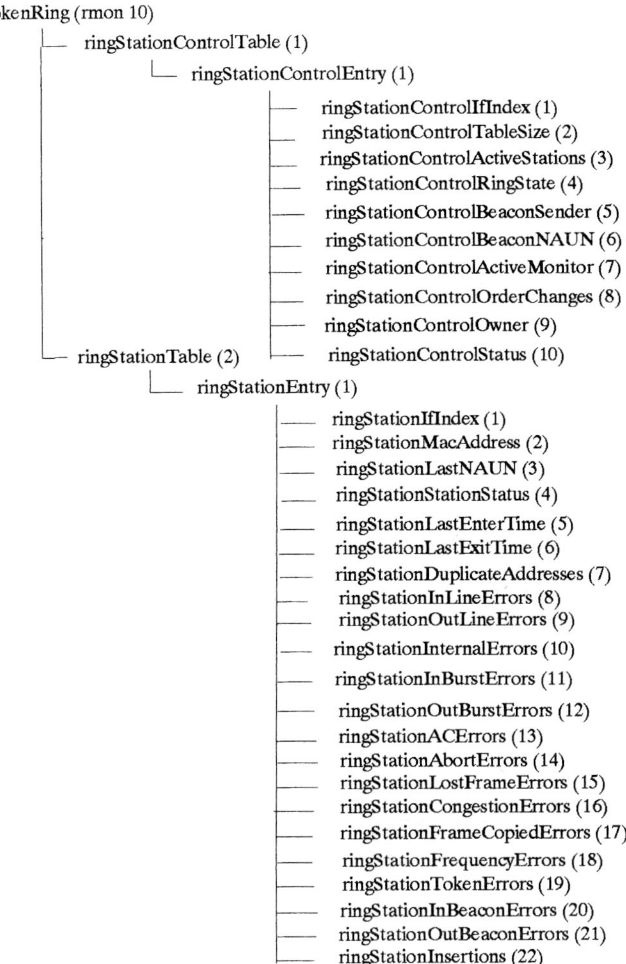

Figure 9.20 Token-ring ring station group.

ringPurgeState = 2, claimTokenState = 3, beaconFrameStreamingState = 4, beaconBitStreamingState = 5, beaconRingSignalLossState = 6, and beaconSetRecoveryModeState = 7. These status values can be useful for depicting status in appropriate colors, while showing the configuration and status of the token-ring network.

- *ringStationControlOrderChanges* (*Counter*): Contains the number of add and delete events in ringStationOrderTable (Figure 9.21).

ringStationControlBeaconSender, ringStationControlBeaconNAUN, and ringStationControlActiveMonitor refer to the address of the sender of the beacon frame, the address of the NAUN in the beacon frame, and the address of the active monitor, respectively.

ringStationTable furnishes statistics on a particular station in the ring. Here, ringStationStationStatus, which can have values of active = 1, inactive = 2, and forcedRemoval = 3, respectively, is very useful for depicting the status of a station in a ring in configuration management. These states of a station may be represented by different colors. In addition, ringStationLastEnterTime and ringStationLastExitTime indicate when a station entered and exited a ring and are also useful for configuration management. The value unknown, indicated by a value of 0 in these variables, can be shown by a specific color when depicting these stations in a ring.

9.5.4 Token-ring ring station order group

The token-ring ring station order group (see Figure 9.21) has ringStationOrderTable, in which stations are identified from the station on which the network monitor is placed. The order of a station relative to the station with the network monitor is furnished by ringStationOrderOrderIndex, and the address of the station is furnished by ringStationOrderMacAddress.

9.5.5 Token-ring ring station config group

The token-ring ring station config group (see Figure 9.21) manages token-ring nodes. Another popular term to describe managing token-ring nodes is the *configuration of nodes.* The following describes the nonobvious objects in ringStationConfigControlTable:

- *ringStationConfigControlRemove* (*INTEGER*): Has two values: stable = 1 and removing = 2. When RMON agents set the value of this variable to removing, it results in the remove station MAC frame. After this frame is processed, the RMON agent sets this variable to stable.
- *ringStationConfigControlUpdateStats* (*INTEGER*): Also has two values: stable = 1 and updating = 2. The behavior of this object is similar to the behavior of ringStationConfigControlRemove. When this object is set to updating, then the configuration information associated with this entry is updated. After this update is over, the RMON agent will set this object to stable.

ringStationConfigTable (see Figure 9.21) provides the configuration entries after a query by the ringStationConfigControlUpdateStats variable. These data are also useful for configuration management. Some of the associated variables needing explanations are:

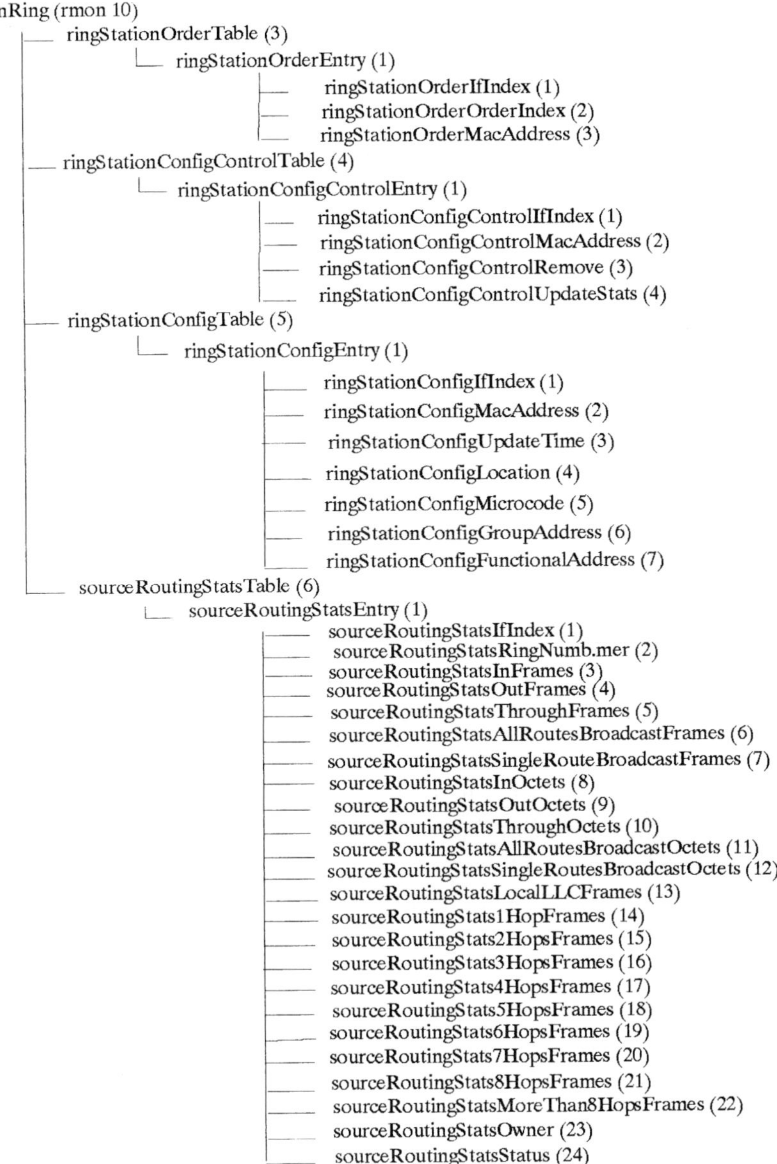

Figure 9.21 Token-ring ring station order, token-ring ring station config, and token-ring source routing groups.

- *ringStationConfigLocation* (*OCTET STRING*(*SIZE*(*4*)): Refers to the actual physical location of the station.
- *ringStationConfigMicrocode* (*OCTET STRING*(*SIZE*(*10*)): Indicates the microcode level of the station.
- *ringStationConfigGroupAddress* (*OCTET STRING*(*SIZE*(*4*)): Pertains to the low-order four octets of the group address recognized by the station.

9.5.6 Token-ring source routing group

The implementation of the token-ring source routing group (see Figure 9.21) is optional. Data in this group are collected in source routing bridges and are valid in source routing environments. In transparent bridging or mixed source and transparent bridge environments, the data are not accurate. sourceRoutingStatsTable provides a list of entries with statistics on source routing for token-ring interfaces. Source routing and transparent bridging will be discussed further in Chapter 11. Some of the variables in this group are:

- *sourceRoutingStatsRingNumber* (*INTEGER*): In an internetwork, there may be many rings, which are assigned numbers by management stations. It is this ring number that is entered here.
- *sourceRoutingStatsInFrames* (*Counter*): Provides the total number of frames sent to a token-ring station from another ring.
- *sourceRoutingStatsOutFrames* (*Counter*): Refers to the number of frames sent out from a ring.
- *sourceRoutingStatsThroughFrames* (*Counter*): Provides the total number of frames which went through a ring. Here, frames are received by a ring and they are transmitted to the next ring.
- *sourceRoutingStatsAllRoutesBroadcastFrames* (*Counter*): Refers to the total number of good all routes broadcast frames that were received.
- *sourceRoutingStatsSingleRouteBroadcastFrames* (*Counter*): Has the count of good frames received which had single route broadcast.

sourceRoutingStatsInOctets, sourceRoutingStatsOutOctets, sourceRoutingStatsThroughOctets, sourceRoutingStatsAllRoutes-BroadcastOctets, and *sourceRoutingSingleRoutesBroadcastOctets* have counts of octets instead of frames, which we saw earlier. The counts refer to good octets only.

- *sourceRoutingStatsLocalLLCFrames* (*Counter*): Provides the total number of frames received which had no RIF field. All route broadcast frames are not counted here.
- *sourceRoutingStats1HopFrames* through *sourceRoutingStatsMoreThan8HopsFrames* provide the frames for the hops mentioned. The all route broadcast frames are not counted. The source and destination stations are expected to be in the same ring.

9.6 Summary

This chapter has been devoted to remote network monitoring in general. RFC 1757 and RFC 1513, which deal with the cases of Ethernet and token ring, have been discussed in detail. The overall relationship with systems management functions, such as configuration, fault, and performance management, were also explained.

9.7 Further Reading

Miller, A. Mark, *Managing Internetworks with SNMP,* San Mateo, Calif.: M&T Books, 1993.

Stallings, W., *SNMP, SNMPv2, and CMIP, The Practical Guide to Network Management Standards,* Reading, Mass.: Addison-Wesley, 1993.

Waldbusser, S., Remote Network Monitoring Management Information Base, RFC 1271, 1991. (RFC 1757 makes RFC 1271 obsolete.)

Waldbusser, S., Remote Network Monitoring Management Information Base, RFC 1757, 1995.

Waldbusser, S., Token Ring Extensions to the Remote Network Monitoring MIB, RFC 1513, 1993 (RFC 1513 updates RFC 1271, which is replaced by RFC 1757).

Chapter

10

Internet Network Management: SNMPv2

10.1 Introduction

The original SNMPs did not have elaborate security arrangements. To overcome this major weakness, SNMP version 2, or SNMPv2, was released. Accordingly, the original SNMP is known as SNMP version 1, or SNMPv1. In SNMPv2, the following enhancements have been made to SNMPv1:

- In SNMPv1, security is a weak link. It is quite easy to learn the community name, which is as good as providing no security. To overcome this, the *digest authentication protocol* and *symmetric privacy protocol* have been added. Also, access control has been added.
- There have been major enhancements to the Structure of Management Information of SNMPv1. MIB-II has been extended to include managed objects for SNMPv2. The syntax and semantics of managed objects have been refined. Also, textual conventions have been enhanced to extend the semantics of the standard object types defined in SMI.
- More operational PDUs have been added. GetBulkRequest has been added to retrieve a large amount of management information. InformRequest has been added for communication between managers. InformRequest facilitates communication between managers in a distributed environment.
- Conformance statements have been added, and a strategy for the migration of SNMPv1 to SNMPv2 has been provided.

- The transport used for carrying SNMPv2 protocols has been made more flexible and defined for different environments.

The list of 12 RFCs, which constitute the SNMPv2 standards, is provided in Table 10.1.

10.2 SNMPv2 Architectural Framework

Any set of network management functions can be broadly broken up into different frameworks or models. Extending the concepts outlined in Section 1.10, SNMPv2 can be architecturally subdivided into different frameworks. However, we must note that there are certain interdependencies between these frameworks, and rigid partitions into different frameworks sometimes lack practical value. The frameworks are:

- *Administrative framework:* Relates to the concepts of party, context, and security.
- *Information framework:* Pertains to how the management information can be structured. This broadly includes SMI and textual conventions.
- *Operational framework:* Here the management protocols, the transport protocols, and the migrational aspects from SNMPv1 to SNMPv2 enter the picture.

TABLE 10.1 SNMPv2 Standard Documents

RFC numbers	Description of RFCs
1441	Introduction to SNMPv2
1442	Structure of Management Information (SMI)
1443	Textual conventions
1444	Conformance statements
1445	Administrative model
1446	Security protocols
1447	Party MIB
1448	Protocol operations
1449	Transport mapping
1450	Management Information Base (MIB)
1451	Manager-to-Manager MIB
1552	Coexistence between SNMPv1 and SNMPv2

- *Conformance framework:* States the minimum requirements to cater to the standards and the capabilities provided. Conformance is very important for interoperability.

Marshall T. Rose, one of the authors of the SNMPv1 and SNMPv2 standards, has included the conformance function in the informational portion, and refers to these frameworks as models in *The Simple Book* (see Reference 10.1). However, SNMPv2 RFCs describe the administrative framework, but do not refer to the other frameworks. So, in the following discussion, we refer to the administrative framework and have omitted the discussion on the basis of the classification of RFC documents in terms of the information, operational, and conformance frameworks.

10.3 Administrative Framework

We will first examine each term used in the administrative framework, then we will see how they are combined and function in Section 10.7.3.

10.3.1 SNMPv2 entity

Central to SNMPv2 is the concept of an SNMPv2 entity. In a generic sense, it is a process that performs network management operations. It generates SNMPv2 PDUs, such as GetRequest and GetNext-Request, and receives SNMPv2-Trap PDUs. It can concurrently communicate with many parties, as shown in Figure 10.1; thus, a process can have many threads at one time.

The SNMPv2 entity also interacts with a local database of access privileges of SNMPv2 parties, the list of all known SNMPv2 par-

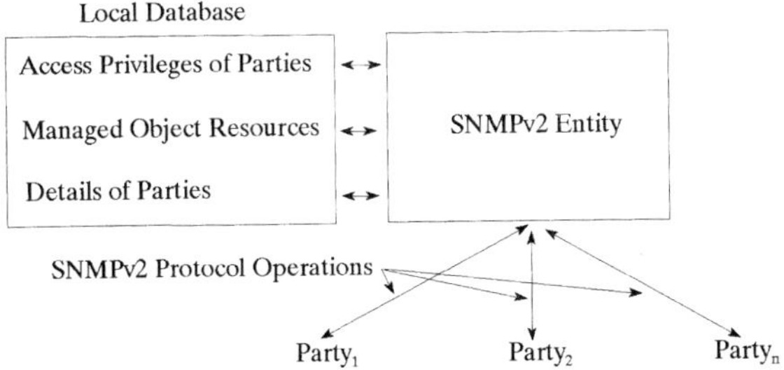

Figure 10.1 SNMPv2 entity concepts.

ties, and known resources. The SNMPv2 entity can take up the role of a manager, agent, or proxy, depending on the operations it performs. The role is dictated by the SNMPv2 protocol messages and traps.

If management operations are initiated by SNMPv2 protocol messages or the receiving of traps, then the entity is in a manager role. On the other hand, when these management operations are performed as a result of the receipt of protocol messages or sending a trap, then the role is that of an agent.

There is a provision for proxy SNMPv2 entities to account for the difference in protocols and the versions such as SNMPv1. Basically, the proxy agent role of the SNMPv2 entity makes it behave like an agent for a manager and act like a manager for another remote entity. Note that a remote entity need not be another SNMPv2 entity.

10.3.2 SNMPv2 party

An SNMPv2 party is a conceptual execution environment. A subset of protocol operations which an SNMPv2 entity can perform can be done on a party. An SNMPv2 party in ASN.1 is defined as follows:

```
SnmpParty :: = SEQUENCE {
        partyIdentity               OBJECT IDENTIFIER,
        partyTDomain                OBJECT IDENTIFIER,
        partyTAddress               OCTET STRING,
        partyMaxMessageSize         INTEGER,
        partyAuthProtocol           OBJECT IDENTIFIER,
        partyAuthClock              INTEGER,
        partyAuthPrivate            OCTET STRING,
        partyAuthPublic             OCTET STRING,
        partyAuthLifetime           INTEGER,
        partyPrivProtocol           OBJECT IDENTIFIER,
        partyPrivPrivate            OCTET STRING,
        partyPrivPublic             OCTET STRING
}
```

Let us briefly examine each term. Note that some of the terms will be explained in more detail later. The terms are:

- *partyIdentity:* An identifier to distinguish one party from another.
- *partyTDomain:* A transport domain which indicates the type of transport used. For SNMPv2, the default is UDP.
- *partyTAddress:* Furnishes the transport addressing information on which network management traffic is received. For

snmpUDPDomain, partyTAddress is formulated by concatenating the four-octet IP address and the two-octet port number. The default value is "0000 0000 0000" H.

- *partyMaxMessageSize:* Indicates the maximum size in octets of the messages that SNMPv2 is prepared to accept. As in earlier cases, this is tied to a party.
- *partyAuthProtocol:* Specifies the authentication protocol used. If authentication is used, there is verification of origin and integrity. At present, two authentication protocols used are v2md5-AuthProtocol and noAuth. If noAuth is used, then there is no authentication of origin and integrity.
- *partyAuthClock:* Represents the authentication clock, which is a notion of current time of a party.
- *partyAuthPrivate:* Has the private and secret key used for authentication. This value can be altered by a SetRequest operation, but the value cannot be retrieved by a management operation.
- *partyAuthPublic:* Used to carry a public key used in an authentication protocol.
- *partyAuthLifetime:* Indicates the maximum time allowed for message delays while using authentication.
- *partyPrivProtocol:* Specifies the privacy protocol used. Privacy protocols are used for data confidentiality. At present, the privacy protocols used are noPriv and desPrivProtocol. noPriv indicates that no privacy protocols are used.
- *partyPrivPrivate:* A party's private key used to support the privacy protocol. The value can be altered by a SetRequest management operation; however, it cannot be read by a management operation.
- *partyPrivPublic:* Refers to a party's public key used by the privacy protocol.

An SNMPv2 entity is termed nonsecure if the authentication protocol is noAuth and the privacy protocol is noPriv.

RFC 1447 defines partyMIB as well as some new data types, including:

- *Party* (*OBJECT IDENTIFIER*): Refers to the object identifier of an SNMPv2 party.
- *TAddress* (*OCTET STRING*): Denotes a transport service address.
- *Clock* (*UInteger32*): Refers to the nonnegative valued authentica-

tion clock. It is undefined for noAuth, and for v2md5AuthProtocol, it is incremented in value.

- *Context* (*OBJECT IDENTIFIER*): Indicates the object identifier of an SNMPv2 context.
- *StorageType* (*INTEGER*): Relates to the storage used for a conceptual row. It has the values: other = 1, volatile = 2, nonVolatile = 3, and permanent = 4. The volatile value states that the values are lost while rebooting; nonVolatile indicates that the values are in stable storage, and permanent states that the values cannot be changed or deleted.

Under the subtree partyAdmin (Figure 10.2), the following objects are defined:

- *noAuth:* States that the protocol does not have authentication.
- *noPriv:* Indicates that no privacy protocols are supported.
- *desPrivProtocol:* Stands for the DES privacy protocol support.

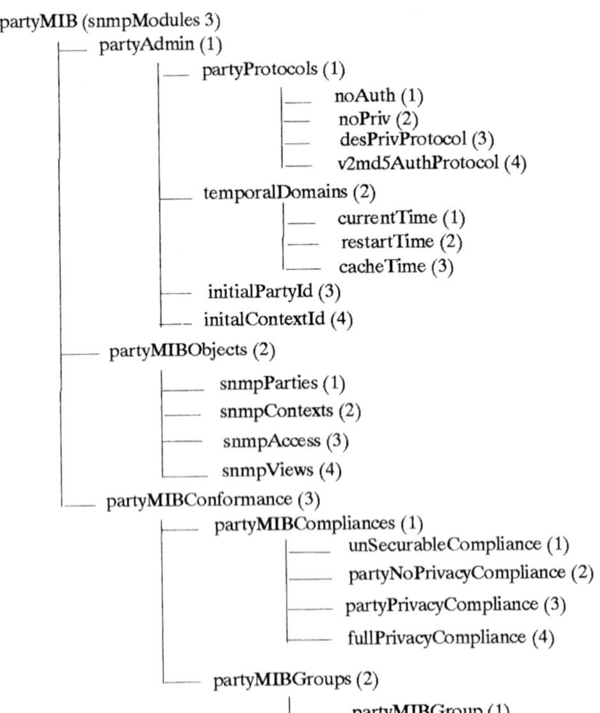

Figure 10.2 partyMIB objects.

- *v2md5AuthProtocol:* Indicates that the MD5 authentication protocol is supported.

Under the same subtree of partyAdmin (Figure 10.2), temporalDomains is defined. temporalDomains is related to time and has the following objects:

- *currentTime* (*OBJECT IDENTIFIER*): Refers to the management information at the current time.
- *restartTime* (*OBJECT IDENTIFIER*): Relates to the management information at the next reinitialization of a managed device.
- *cacheTime* (*OBJECT IDENTIFIER*): Indicates the management information that is cached in a managed device and is at most *N* seconds old.

In addition, partyAdmin has intialPartyId and initalContextId, which are primarily used for the initial configuration of devices with administrative policy information. RFC 1447 provides the initial party identifier, initial context identifiers, SNMPv2 context, access control policy, and MIB view information.

SNMPv2 party database group. The SNMPv2 party database group (Figure 10.3) has one partyTable. This partyTable has information on all the parties known to an SNMPv2 entity. partyTable has one or

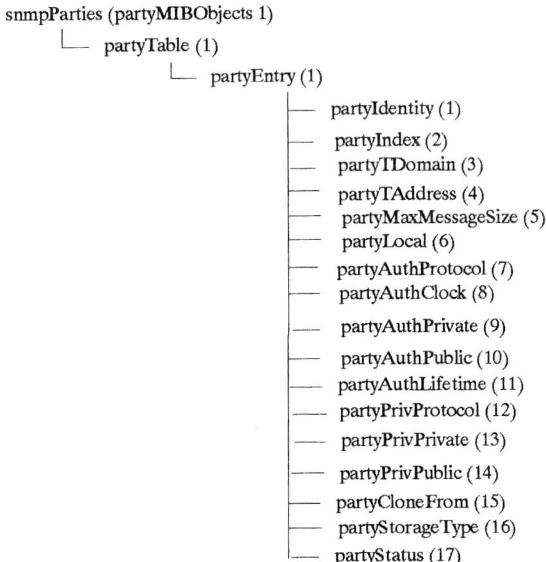

Figure 10.3 SNMPv2 party database group.

more partyEntrys. Because most of these terms have been discussed earlier, they will not be repeated. The new objects in partyEntry are:

- *partyLocal* (*TruthValue*): Refers to whether an SNMPv2 listens to SNMPv2 messages at partyTAddress. A value of true(1) indicates that SNMPv2 will listen to the SNMPv2 messages, while a value of false(2) signifies that SNMPv2 will not listen to the SNMPv2 messages.
- *partyCloneFrom* (*Party*): Indicates the identity of a party to clone authentication and privacy parameters.
- *partyStorageType* (*StorageType*): Refers to the storage type associated with this conceptual row in partyTable.
- *partyStatus* (*RowStatus*): Represents a row status of a conceptual row. The data type, RowStatus, will be discussed in Section 10.4.5.

10.3.3 SNMPv2 context

The SNMPv2 context concept is tied in with objects which an SNMPv2 entity can access. These objects can be local or remote. The differences are shown in Figure 10.4. If the context is local, the object resources represent the MIB view. In the case of a remote context, an SNMPv2 entity retrieves the management information from objects via a proxy.

SNMPv2 context database group. The SNMPv2 context database group (Figure 10.5) has information on the contexts known to an SNMPv2 entity. This group has one contextTable with one contextEntry for each instance of a context. The objects in this group are:

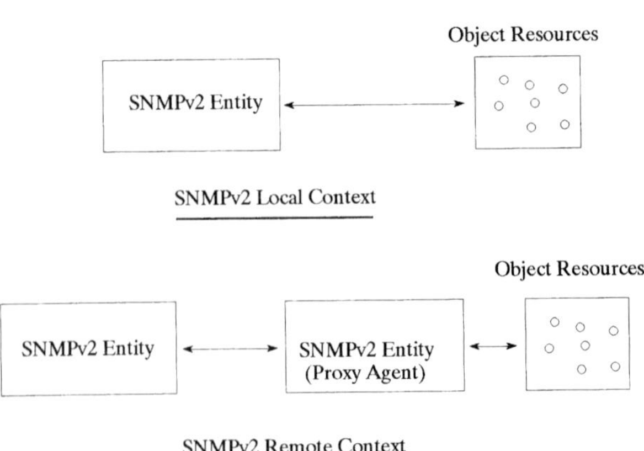

Figure 10.4 SNMPv2 context.

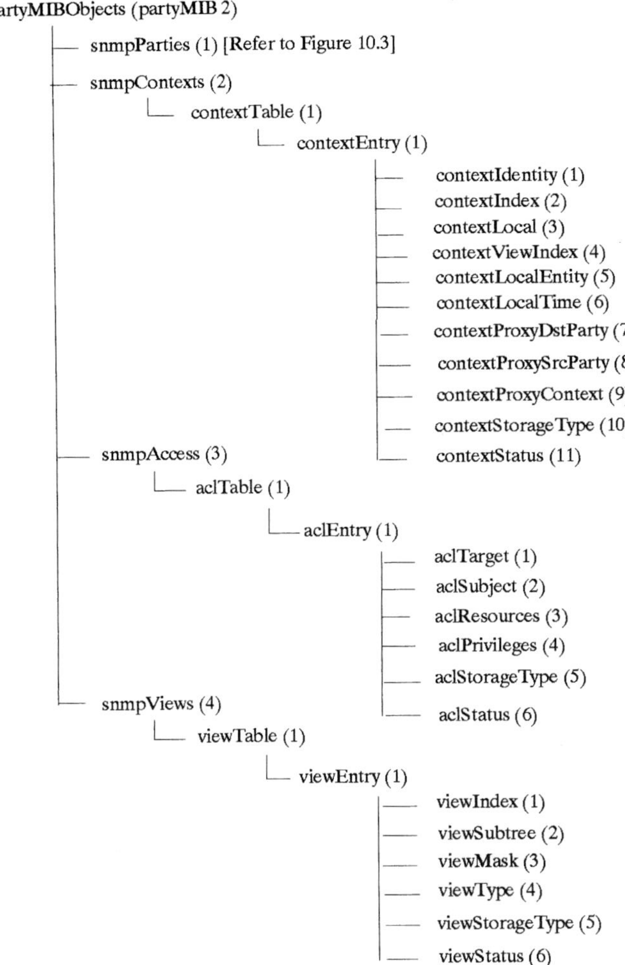

Figure 10.5 SNMPv2 contexts database, SNMPv2 access privileges database, and MIB view database groups.

- *contextIdentity* (*Context*): Identifies a context in an SNMPv2 entity.
- *contextIndex* (*INTEGER* (*1..65535*)): Has a unique value for each SNMPv2 context.
- *contextLocal* (*TruthValue*): Indicates whether this context is valid for this SNMPv2 entity.
- *contextViewIndex* (*INTEGER* (*0..65535*)): Indicates whether the context refers to a MIB view or a proxy relationship. If the value is zero, then it represents a proxy relationship.

- *contextLocalEntity* (*OCTET STRING*): Indicates a MIB view with local management information if it has a zero value, or a MIB view of some other local entity if it has a nonempty string.
- *contextLocalTime* (*OBJECT IDENTIFIER*): Represents the temporal context of the management information. This value is relevant only if contextViewIndex is greater than zero.
- *contextProxyDstParty* (*Party*): Has the value of the proxy SNMPv2 entity. This value is valid only if the value of contextViewIndex is zero; otherwise, contextProxyDstParty has a value of {0 0}.
- *contextProxySrcParty* (*Party*): Indicates the value of the source proxy in a proxy relationship. contextProxySrcParty behaves just like contextProxyDstParty.
- *contextProxyContext* (*OBJECT IDENTIFIER*): Represents the context of a proxy relationship. As we have seen earlier, this value is valid for contextViewIndex with a value of zero; otherwise, it has a value of {0 0}.
- *contextStorageType* (*StorageType*): Indicates the storage type used for storing the conceptual row in a contextTable. The default value is nonVolatile, which states that the data on context are not lost with rebooting.
- *contextStatus* (*RowStatus*): Has the status of the conceptual row.

MIB view database group. Each SNMPv2 party can access a certain portion of the MIB. The MIB view is a subset of all the objects associated with an entity. Objects included in a MIB view are defined in the MIB view database group (Figure 10.5). This group has one table: viewTable. MIB has subtrees which are included or excluded from an SNMPv2 party, depending on the viewMask provided. We will investigate the role of viewMask later. The objects in this group are:

- *viewIndex* (*INTEGER* (*1..65535*)): Has a unique value for each MIB view, which is the same as the contextViewIndex. (contextViewIndex was discussed with the context database group.)
- *viewSubtree* (*OBJECT IDENTIFIER*): Represents the object identifier associated with a MIB subtree.
- *viewMask* (*OCTET STRING* (*0..16*)): Determines whether or not a subtree is included in a MIB view. For example, refer to egpNeighAddr from Figure 8.20. The object identifier for the egp subtree (Figure 8.19) is 1.3.6.1.2.1.8. By extending this to

egpNeighAddr, the object identifier is 1.3.6.1.2.1.8.5.1.2. Using a viewMask of 101111, the obvious check of whether 1.3.6.1.2.1.8.5.1.2 is part of 1.3.6.1.2.1.8, is made as follows:

egp subtree object identifier	1.3.6.1.2.1.8
viewMask	1 0 1 1 1 1
Object identifier of egpNeighAddr	1.3.6.1.2.1.8.5.1.2
egp subtree object identifier	1.3.6.1.2.1.8
viewMask	1 0 1 1 1 1
Object identifier of udpLocalPort	1.3.6.1.2.1.7.5.1.2

In the preceding check, the second bit of 0 in viewMask is a wildcard match, and all the subidentifiers below it match. In viewMask, a bit value of 1 requires an exact match. In this example, notice that viewMask is shorter than the egp subtree identifier, so viewMask is extended with 1 1 1 1 to become 1 0 1 1 1 1 1 1 1 1. There is a match of egpNeighAddr; hence, egpNeighAddr is part of the egp subtree. However, in the second case of udpLocalPort, it is not included in the egp subtree, because there is a mismatch in the subidentifier place.

- *viewType* (*INTEGER*): Determines whether or not instances of viewSubtree and viewMask include a subtree of MIB view. Values are: included = 1 and excluded = 2. viewStorageType and viewStatus have the same significance as the corresponding entries previously defined.

10.3.4 SNMPv2 management communication

SNMPv2 management communication refers to the exchange of management information, such as SNMPv2 protocol messages between two parties, and is represented by an ASN.1 value as follows:

```
SnmpMgmtCom :: = [2] IMPLICIT SEQUENCE{
      dstParty            OBJECT IDENTIFIER,
      srcParty            OBJECT IDENTIFIER,
      context             OBJECT IDENTIFIER,
      pdu                 PDUs
}
```

An SNMPv2 context is tied to a party for accessing management information. The management information has the following fields: destination party identifier, source party identifier, context used for accessing the management information, and SNMPv2 protocol operation such as GetRequest.

10.3.5 SNMPv2 authenticated management communication

The syntax of authenticated management communication in ASN.1 is as follows:

```
SnmpAuthMsg ::= [1] IMPLICIT SEQUENCE {
        authInfo            ANY,        -- defined by authentication protocol
        authData            SnmpMgmtCom
}
```

10.3.6 SNMPv2 private management communication

Private management communication is used for protecting authenticated management communication from disclosure. The syntax in ASN.1 is as follows:

```
SnmpPrivMsg ::= [1] IMPLICIT SEQUENCE {
        privDst             OBJECT IDENTIFIER,
        privData            [1] IMPLICIT OCTET STRING
}
```

It has the destination party to which the message is sent and possibly encrypted data which must be guarded against disclosures such as eavesdropping. The format of SnmpPrivMsg is shown in Figure 10.9.

10.3.7 SNMPv2 access control policy

When a management operation is received, a check is made using aclTable as to whether the management operation can be done. aclTable has information on the source party, destination party, context, and the management operation allowed. The source party of an SNMPv2 party is known as a *subject,* and the destination party is known as a *target.* aclTable has identifiers to distinguish the subjects and targets, the resources which are to be accessed, and the access privileges associated with management operations. ASN.1 definitions for an SNMPv2 access control entry are:

```
AclEntry ::= SEQUENCE {
             aclTarget       OBJECT IDENTIFIER,
             aclSubject      OBJECT IDENTIFIER,
```

```
            aclResources    OBJECT IDENTIFIER,
            aclPrivileges   INTEGER
}
```

SNMPv2 access privileges database group. The SNMPv2 access privileges database group (Figure 10.5) is a database on the access privileges, which has one aclTable with one aclEntry for each subject of an SNMPv2 party and target SNMPv2 party for a particular context. The objects in this group are:

- *aclTarget (INTEGER (1..65535))*: Identifies the target SNMPv2 party and has the same value as the partyIndex object.
- *aclSubject (INTEGER (1..65535))*: Has a value for the source SNMPv2 party, and has the same value as the partyIndex object for the party.
- *aclResources (INTEGER (1..65535))*: Has the value of the SNMPv2 context and has the same value as the contextIndex object for the SNMPv2 context.
- *aclPrivileges (INTEGER (0..255))*: The sum of values associated with each management operation. The values for management operations are Get = 1, GetNext = 2, Response = 4, Set = 8, GetBulk = 32, Inform = 64, and SNMPv2-Trap = 128. For example, a value of 76 is obtained by adding the values of Response, Set, and Inform management operations. Note that the value of 16 is unused.

aclStorageType and *aclStatus* have the same significance as discussed earlier for corresponding objects in other groups.

10.3.8 SNMPv2 security

SNMPv2 has provided a secure environment by ensuring data integrity, data origin authentication, data confidentiality, and access control. Let us review what each term means.

Data integrity: Means that data has not been altered in any manner. The data can be corrupted or errors can creep in due to transmission errors or hardware or software errors. Data can also be maliciously tampered with by unauthorized users. Checksum helps to detect such errors.

Data origin authentication: Checks whether the originator of data is the one claimed in a message. In other words, this ensures that the originator is the one who is authorized to send the message.

Data confidentiality: Only the sender and receiver must know the details of the message, and any other user is expected not to know the contents of the message.

Data integrity and data origin authentication are provided by the digest authentication protocol, according to which a secret value known only to a sender and receiver is prefixed to the message and ensures data origin authentication.

For supporting data integrity, a 128-bit digest is calculated over the designated portion of the SNMPv2 message, which also includes a secret value. This message digest becomes part of the SNMPv2 message which is sent by the sender. For calculating this message digest refer to Rivest (see Reference 10.2). Source and destination timestamp values are also part of each message generated. The source timestamp value is the authentication clock value of a message's source, and the destination timestamp value is set to the authentication clock value of the message's intended receiver. The timestamp values help to make sure that the message is a recent one. However, for the digest authentication protocol, clocks must be synchronized between the originator and receiver. There are many ways to synchronize clocks; one method is presented in RFC 1446.

It is required that the digest authentication protocol be used by the originator and receiver only if both of them use it. If one of them does not use this protocol, it should not be used at all. Because it is preferable not to proliferate these algorithms in nonsecure environments, this requirement is sound and reasonable.

The symmetric privacy protocol is used for data confidentiality. Here messages are encrypted using keys known only to the originator and receiver of the messages. The Data Encryption Standard (DES) (see References 10.3 and 10.4) has been chosen. The mode of operation recommended is *cipher block chaining.* These standards have been published by the National Institute of Standards and Technology (NIST) and the American National Standards Institute (ANSI).

However, there is a caveat with RFC 1446. It does not specifically recommend which of the algorithms be used for message digest and encryption. Thus these algorithms are termed "acceptably secure" under present circumstances.

SNMPv2 security assumes that secret values must be shared between the parties. These have to be changed often so that security measures are not compromised. For clock synchronization and sharing of key values, there is a need for at least one management station to perform these tasks.

10.3.9 SNMPv2 partyMIB conformance

SNMPv2 conformance has objects as shown in Figure 10.2. These objects are used to check the compliance of the implementations. All the objects in this group are required to support snmpMIBGroup, noAuth, and noPriv protocols. The objects in the partyMIB Conformance group are:

- *unSecurableCompliance:* Provides the compliance statements for SNMPv2 entities which implement partyMIB. At this level of compliance, no support is provided for authentication and privacy protocols.
- *partyNoPrivacyCompliance:* Indicates the support for v2md5AuthProtocol for authentication and no support for privacy protocols.
- *partyPrivacyCompliance:* States that v2md5AuthProtocol is supported, but there is only partial support for privacy protocols, which indicates that the security parameter can access parameters such as creating and maintaining parties.
- *fullPrivacyCompliance:* Indicates the availability of v2md-5AuthProtocol and desPrivProtocol.

10.4 SNMPv2 Structure of Management Information (SMI)

Structure of Management Information for the SNMPv2 (RFC 1442) describes rules for defining modules, objects, and traps. Note that a module is a collection of related objects. SMI provides the following definitions:

- *Module definitions:* The ASN.1 macro, MODULE-IDENTITY, is used to provide the syntax and semantics when defining a module.
- *Object definitions:* The ASN.1 macro, OBJECT-TYPE, provides the syntax and semantics to define an object.
- *Notification definitions:* The ASN.1 macro, NOTIFICATION-TYPE, is used to describe a notification. Notification is unsolicited management information within either an SNMPv2-Trap-PDU or an InformRequest-PDU.

10.4.1 SMI definitions

SNMPv2 SMI definitions furnished in RFC 1442 are:

```
SNMPv2-SMI DEFINITIONS ::= BEGIN
-- path to the root
internet              OBJECT IDENTIFIER ::= {iso 3 6 1}
directory             OBJECT IDENTIFIER ::= {internet 1}
mgmt                  OBJECT IDENTIFIER ::= {internet 2}
experimental          OBJECT IDENTIFIER ::= {internet 3}
private               OBJECT IDENTIFIER ::= {internet 4}
enterprises           OBJECT IDENTIFIER ::= {private 1}
security              OBJECT IDENTIFIER ::= {internet 5}
snmpV2                OBJECT IDENTIFIER ::= {internet 6}
-- transport domains
snmpDomains           OBJECT IDENTIFIER ::= {snmpV2 1}
-- transport proxies
snmpProxys            OBJECT IDENTIFIER ::= {snmpV2 2}
-- module Identities
snmpModules           OBJECT IDENTIFIER ::= {snmpV2 3}
-- definitions for information modules
MODULE-IDENTITY MACRO ::=
BEGIN
      TYPE NOTATION ::=
                      "LAST-UPDATED" value(Update UTCTIME)
                      "ORGANIZATION" Text
                      "CONTACT-INFO" Text
                      "DESCRIPTION" Text
                      RevisionPart
      VALUE NOTATION ::=
                      Value(VALUE OBJECT IDENTIFIER)
      RevisionPart ::=
                      Revisions
                      | empty
      Revisions ::=
                      Revision
                      | Revisions Revision
      Revision ::=
                      "REVISION" value(Update UTCTime)
                      "DESCRIPTION" Text
      Text ::= """""" string """""" -- uses the NVT ASCII character set
END

OBJECT-IDENTITY MACRO ::=
BEGIN
      TYPE NOTATION ::=
                      "STATUS" Status
                      "DESCRIPTION" Text
```

```
                              ReferPart
      VALUE NOTATION ::=
                              value(VALUE OBJECT IDENTIFIER)
      Status :: =             "current"
                              | "obsolete"
      ReferPart :: =  "REFERENCE" Text
                              | empty
      Text :: =  """" string """"
END
-- name of objects
      ObjectName ::=          OBJECT IDENTIFIER
-- syntax of objects
      ObjectSyntax ::=
              CHOICE {
                              simple SimpleSyntax,
                              -- note that SEQUENCEs for conceptual tables
                              -- and rows are not mentioned here.
                              application-wide ApplicationSyntax
}
-- built-in ASN.1 types
      SimpleSyntax ::=
              CHOICE {
      integer-value           INTEGER (-2147483648..2147483647),
      string-value            OCTET STRING,
      object-IDvalue          OBJECT IDENTIFIER,
      bit-value               BIT STRING
}
-- indistinguishable from INTEGER, but never needs more than 32 bits for
-- a twos complement representation.
      Integer32 :: =  [UNIVERSAL 2] IMPLICIT INTEGER (-2147483648..
      2147483647)
-- application-wide types
      ApplicationSyntax ::=
              CHOICE {
      ipAddress-value         IpAddress,
      counter-value           Counter32,
      gauge-value             Gauge32,
      timeticks-value         TimeTicks,
      arbitrary-value         Opaque,
      nsapAddress-value       NsapAddress,
      big-counter-value       Counter64,
      unsigned-integer-value      UInteger32
}
-- in network-byte order (this is tagged type for historical reasons)
      IpAddress ::=  [APPLICATION 0] IMPLICIT OCTET STRING (SIZE
      (4))
-- this wraps
```

```
    Counter32 ::=   [APPLICATION 1] IMPLICIT INTEGER
    (0..4294967295)
-- this does not wrap
    Gauge32 ::=   [APPLICATION 2] IMPLICIT INTEGER
    (0..4294967295)
-- hundredths of seconds since an epoch
    TimeTicks ::=   [APPLICATION 3] IMPLICIT INTEGER
    (0..4294967295)
-- for backward compatibility only
    Opaque ::=   [APPLICATION 4] IMPLICIT OCTET STRING
-- for OSI NSAP addresses
-- (this is tagged type for historical reasons)
    NsapAddress ::=
    [APPLICATION 5]   IMPLICIT OCTET STRING (SIZE (1|4..21)
-- for counters that wrap in less than one hour with only 32 bits
    Counter64 ::=
         [APPLICATION 6] IMPLICIT INTEGER (0..1844674407370
         9551615)
-- an unsigned 32-bit quantity
         UInteger32 :: =   [APPLICATION 7] IMPLICIT INTEGER
         (0..4294967295)
-- definition for objects
OBJECT-TYPE MACRO ::=
BEGIN
    TYPE NOTATION ::=
                    "SYNTAX" type(Syntax)
                    UnitsPart
                    "MAX-ACCESS" Access
                    "STATUS" Status
                    "DESCRIPTION" Text
                    ReferPart
                    IndexPart
                    DefValPart
VALUE NOTATION ::=    value (VALUE ObjectName)
UnitsPart ::=         "UNITS" Text
                      | empty
Access ::=            "not-accessible"
                      | "read-only"
                      | "read-write"
                      | "read-create"
Status ::=            "current"
                      | "deprecated"
                      | "obsolete"
ReferPart ::=         "REFERENCE" Text
                      | empty
Indexpart ::=         "INDEX" "{" IndexTypes "}"
                      | "AUGMENTS" "{" Entry "}"
```

```
                              | empty
IndexTypes ::=                IndexType
                              | IndexTypes "," IndexType
IndexType ::=                 "IMPLIED" Index
                              | Index
-- use the SYNTAX value of the correspondent OBJECT-TYPE invocation.
     Index ::=                value(Indexobject ObjectName)
-- use the INDEX value of the correspondent OBJECT-TYPE invocation.
     Entry ::=                value(Entryobject ObjectName)
     DefValPart ::=           "DEFVAL" "{" value(Defval Syntax) "}"
                              | empty
     -- uses the NVT ASCII character set
     Text ::= """" string """"
END
-- definitions for notifications
NOTIFICATION-TYPE MACRO ::=
BEGIN
     TYPE NOTATION ::=
                          ObjectsPart
                          "STATUS" Status
                          "DESCRIPTION" Text
                          ReferPart
VALUE NOTATION ::= value(VALUE OBJECT IDENTIFIER)
ObjectsPart ::=         "OBJECTS" "{" Objects "}"
                        | empty
Objects ::=             Object
                        | Objects "," Object
Object ::=              value(Name ObjectName)
Status ::=              "current"
                        | "deprecated"
                        | "obsolete"
ReferPart ::=           "REFERENCE" Text
                        | empty
-- uses the NVT ASCII character set
Text ::= """" string """"
END
END
```

Source: RFC 1442 (Structure of Management Information for version 2 of the Simple Network Management Protocol [SNMPv2], 1993).

10.4.2 Information module

An information module is an ASN.1 module and provides information for network management. In SMI definitions, the term MODULE-IDENTITY was used. An information module is identified by a MOD-

ULE-IDENTITY macro. It provides the contact and revision history of the information module. There are three kinds of information modules:

- *MIB modules:* Contain information on related objects.
- *Compliance statements:* Provide compliance requirements for MIB modules:
- *Capability statements:* Have the capabilities of the agent implementations.

An information module need not have all three modules; instead, it can contain just one or more of them. Compliance and capability statements will be discussed in Section 10.6.

10.4.3 Explanation of new terms

Many terms have been used in SMI definitions for SNMPv1. Some of the new terms which need explanation are:

- *BIT STRING:* Used for enumerations, and starts from a value of zero.
- *NsapAddress:* A variable-length string used to represent the OSI address. The first octet provides the length of the OSI address and can be from three to twenty octets in length. A single octet with a value of 0 represents the default NSAP address.
- *Counter64:* A wraparound counter with a maximum value of $2^{64}-1$.
- *UNITS:* Has textual definition of the units of measurements, such as hours and minutes, associated with an object.
- *MAX-ACCESS:* Relates to the maximum level of access allowed for an object. Note the distinction between the access rights of read-write and read-create. read-write is the maximum level of access allowed. With the read-write access right, an object instance can be created in addition to the read-write permission.
- *INDEX:* Used for object instance identification in a conceptual row. A new keyword, IMPLIED, is used for objects with variable-length syntax.
- *AUGMENTS:* An alternative to an INDEX clause, it extends the conceptual row with reference to a base conceptual row provided by an INDEX clause. AUGMENTS is useful for extending the definitions of tables. As an example, if Table 2 is a logical extension of Table 1, then the AUGMENTS clause may be used to connect these two tables.

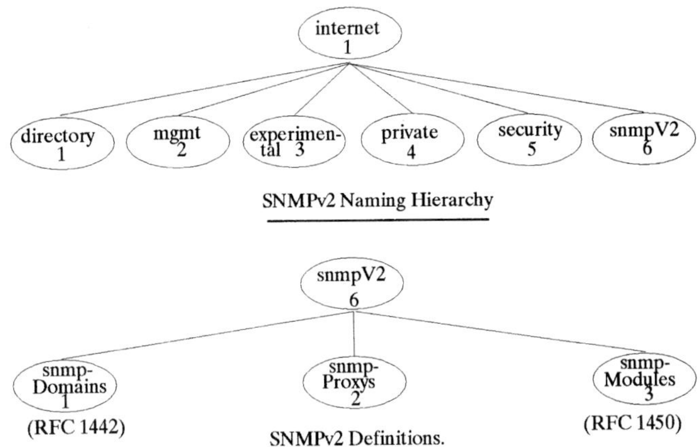

Figure 10.6 SNMPv2 naming hierarchy and object definitions.

10.4.4 Naming of objects

The naming hierarchy is shown in Figure 10.6. The snmpV2 object subtree is contained in the internet subtree. We have already discussed mgmt(2), experimental(3), and private(4) in Section 8.5.1.

Under the snmpV2 subtree are snmpDomains(1), snmpProxys(2), and snmpModules(3). snmpDomains is used for transport mapping, snmpProxys is for transport proxies, and snmpModules is for module identities.

10.4.5 SNMPv2 textual convention

The SNMPv2 textual convention is used for extending the semantics of standard data types in SMI. With this provision, SMI need not be modified often.

```
SNMPv2-TC DEFINITIONS ::=
BEGIN
IMPORTS
        ObjectSyntax, Integer32, TimeTicks FROM SNMPv2-SMI;
-- definition of textual conventions
TEXTUAL-CONVENTION MACRO ::=  BEGIN
        TYPE NOTATION ::=  DisplayPart
                           "STATUS" Status
                           "DESCRIPTION" Text
                           ReferPart
                           "SYNTAX" type(Syntax)
        VALUE NOTATION  ::=  value(VALUE Syntax)
        DisplayPart ::=    "DISPLAY-HINT" Text
                           | empty
```

```
        Status ::=          "current"
                            | "deprecated"
                            | "obsolete"
        ReferPart ::=       "REFERENCE" Text
                            | empty
        -- uses the NVT ASCII character set
        Text ::= """" string """"
    END
```

Source: RFC 1443 (Textual Conventions for version 2 of the Simple Network Management Protocol [SNMPv2], 1993).

RFC 1443 defines a base set of textual conventions which use the conventions of the TEXTUAL-CONVENTION ASN.1 macro, and they are:

- *DisplayString* (*OCTET STRING* (*SIZE*(*0..255*))): Represents the textual convention using the ASCII character set. It is used for easy readability. The length of DisplayString should not exceed 255 octets.
- *PhysAddress* (*OCTET STRING*): Used to indicate the media address.
- *MacAddress* (*OCTET STRING* (*SIZE*(*6*))): Represents the MAC address as defined by IEEE 802.1 with the least significant bit transmitted first.
- *TruthValue* (*INTEGER*): Provides a means to indicate a Boolean value, with *true* being 1 and *false* being 2.
- *TestAndIncr* (*INTEGER* (*0..2147483647*)): Tests first whether a value provided using a management protocol matches the value of the object instance. If the value matches, then the value of the object instance is increased by one. If the value of an object instance is the maximum value of 2147483647, then the object instance value wraps to zero. However, a mismatch between the value provided and the value of the object instance results in an *inconsistent value* error.
- *AutonomousType* (*OBJECT IDENTIFIER*): Can be used to extend objects with a distinct identifier. Here the key is "autonomous," and the extension must be easily distinguishable. This textual convention can be useful for defining additions to hardware and protocols.
- *InstancePointer* (*OBJECT IDENTIFIER*): Refers to the name of an instance of the first columnar object in a row. As explained earlier, *row* is an abstract concept used for manipulating tables.

- *RowStatus (INTEGER)*: Used to manipulate the creation and deletion of managed objects in conceptual rows. RowStatus has the values of active, notInService, notReady, createAndGo, createAndWait, and destroy.
- *TimeStamp (TimeTicks)*: The same as sysUpTime, which is the value in TimeTicks when an agent was last reinitialized.
- *TimeInterval (INTEGER (0..2147483647))*: Represents the interval in units of 0.01 s between two time periods.
- *DateAndTime (OCTET STRING (SIZE 8 | 11))*: Used to indicate the date and time. The length of DateAndTime can be 8 or 11 octets. The different fields have significance, as shown in Table 10.2. We have explained what UTC means, under Section 5.2.3. As can be observed from Table 10.2, we do not need octets 9, 10, and 11 for local time.

10.5 SNMPv2 MIB

There are some changes between SNMPv2 and SNMPv1 MIBs. The IMPORT statement refers to MIBs used in SNMPv2, and they are to be used. Under the snmpModules subtree (Figure 10.7), there are subtrees snmpMIB(1), snmpM2M(2), and partyMIB(3). snmpMIB has snmpMIBObjects and snmpMIBConformance subtrees. Again, below the snmpMIBObjects, there are snmpStats(1), snmpV1(2), snmpOR(3), snmpTrap(4), snmpTraps(5), and snmpSet(6).

TABLE 10.2 DateAndTime Representation

Field	Octets	Contents	Range
1	1–2	Year	0..65536
2	3	Month	1..12
3	4	Day	1..31
4	5	Hour	0..23
5	6	Minutes	0..59
6	7	Seconds (use 60 for leap second)	0..60
7	8	Deciseconds	0..9
8	9	Direction from UTC	'+' / '-'
9	10	Hours from UTC	0..11
10	11	Minutes from UTC	0..59

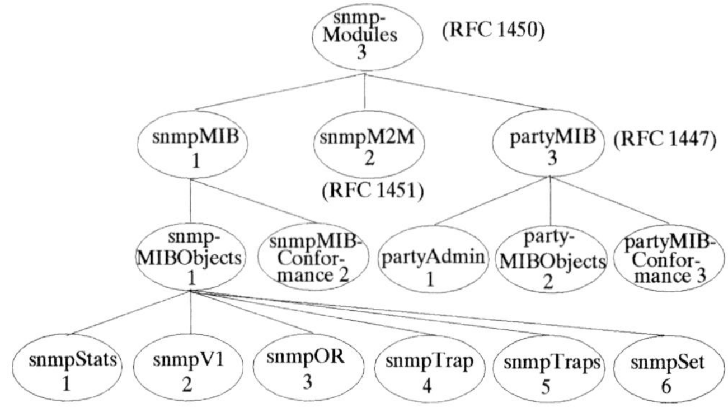

Figure 10.7 snmpModules.

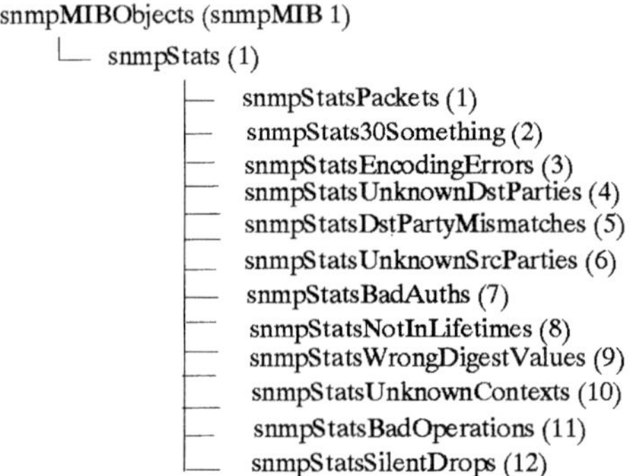

Figure 10.8 snmpStats group.

10.5.1 snmpStats group

The snmpStats group (Figure 10.8) objects are provided for collecting statistics of an SNMPv2 entity. It has objects such as snmpStatsPackets, which is used for counting the total number of packets received by an SNMPv2 entity from the underlying transport service. Most of the these objects can be used for performance and security management. The objects in this group are:

- *snmpStatsPackets* (*Counter32*): Refers to the total number of packets received from the transport service by the SNMPv2 entity.
- *snmpStats30Something* (*Counter32*): Contains the total number of packets with a hexadecimal value of 30 in the initial octet received by the SNMPv2 entity. These packets are misdirected SNMPv1 messages.

- *snmpStatsEncodingErrors* (*Counter32*): Refers to the total number of packets received by the SNMPv2 entity which had encoding errors.
- *snmpStatsUnknownDstParties* (*Counter32*): Has the total number of snmpPrivMsgs which had unrecognizable privDst field (Figure 10.9). This data can be used by the security management function.

The following statistics pertain to the total number of wrong SnmpPrivMsgs (Figure 10.9) that result from different fields being bad. The reasons for bad SnmpPrivMsgs are furnished along with the explanation of each object. These counters are useful for the security management function.

- *snmpStatsDstPartyMismatches* (*Counter32*): Has the number of SnmpPrivMsgs, for which there was a mismatch between the authData.dstParty and privDst fields.
- *snmpStatsUnknownSrcParties* (*Counter32*): Refers to the number of SnmpAuthMsgs which had unknown authData.srcParty.
- *snmpStatsBadAuths* (*Counter32*): Contains the number of privData.authInfo fields (Figure 10.9) incompatible with the source party authentication protocol.
- *snmpStatsNotInLifetimes* (*Counter32*): Used to count the messages when authInfo.authSrcTimestamp is less than the sum of the source party's clock and lifetime.
- *snmpStatsWrongDigestValues* (*Counter32*): Like its predecessors, it furnishes data on wrong SnmpAuthMsgs. Here a SnmpAuthMsg is treated as wrong when authInfo.authDigest field is not equal to the expected digest value.

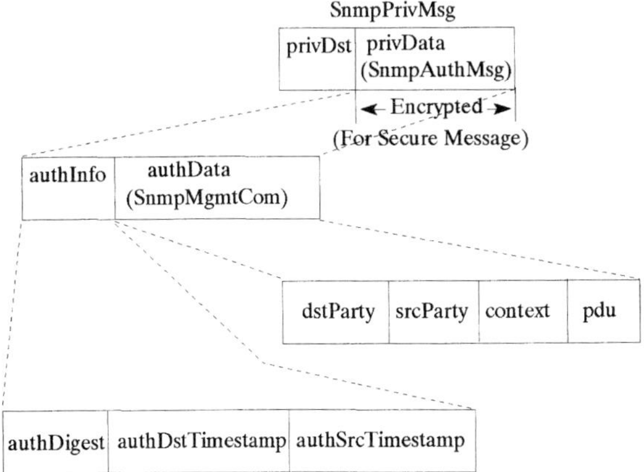

Figure 10.9 SNMPv2 message (snmpPrivMsg) format.

- *snmpStatsUnknownContexts* (*Counter32*): Refers to the total number of SnmpMgmtComs with unknown context fields.
- *snmpStatsBadOperations* (*Counter32*): Refers to the number of messages due to PDU types not being allowed in aclTable.
- *snmpStatsSilentDrops* (*Counter32*): Counts the management operational PDUs which have inappropriate sizes. The criterion for inappropriate size is that the size of the Response-PDU with an empty variable-bindings field for management operations such as GetRequest-PDU is greater than the limitations on the size of a message.

10.5.2 snmpV1 group

Some SNMPv2 entities may also implement SNMPv1. The objects in this subtree (Figure 10.10) are used to collect statistics of the

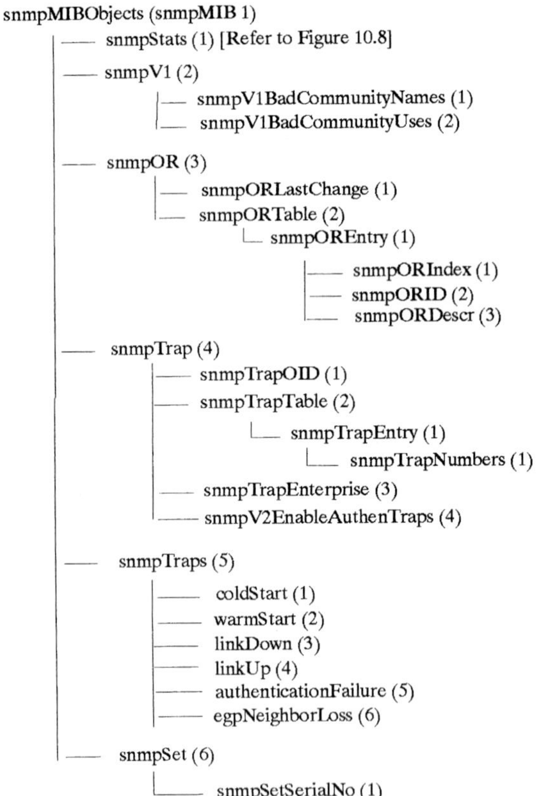

Figure 10.10 snmpMIBObjects.

SNMPv1 portion of the entity. This is mainly limited to the usage of community in the SNMPv1. These statistics are useful for security management. The objects in this group are:

- *snmpV1BadCommunityNames* (*Counter32*): Has the number of SNMPv1 messages which had community names unknown to an SNMPv2 entity.
- *snmpBadCommunityUses* (*Counter32*): Refers to the total number of SNMPv1 messages which had operation not allowed for the community specified in a message.

10.5.3 snmpOR group

Objects in the object resource group (Figure 10.10) are used by SNMPv2 entities which are acting in an agent role. These objects must be capable of being dynamically configurable, and are useful for configuration management. In this group there is one table: snmpORTable. In this table, each object has an instance identified by snmpOREntry with columns snmpORIndex, snmpORID, and snmpORDescr. Objects in the snmpOR group are:

- *snmpORLastChange* (*TimeStamp*): Has the most recent change, provided by sysUpTime, in snmpORID.
- *snmpORIndex* (*Integer32*): Is an identifier for identifying object instances in snmpORTable.
- *snmpORID* (*OBJECT IDENTIFIER*): Refers to the identifier used for identifying a resource in an SNMPv2 entity, and is similar to the sysObjectID object in MIB-II.
- *snmpORDescr* (*DisplayString*): Provides the description of the object resource in an SNMPv2 entity.

10.5.4 snmpTrap group

snmpTrap group objects (Figure 10.10) are used by SNMPv2 entities in the agent role to generate SNMPv2-Trap PDUs. Objects in this group are useful for fault management. In this group, there is one table, snmpTrapTable, which has one entry, snmpTrapNumbers. Objects in the snmpTrap group are:

- *snmpTrapOID* (*OBJECT IDENTIFIER*): Refers to the unique identifier of a trap.

- *snmpTrapNumbers* (*Counter32*): Has the total number of traps sent to an SNMPv2 entity. The benchmark for measurement is the most recent initialization or creation time of an SNMPv2 entity.
- *snmpTrapEnterprise* (*OBJECT IDENTIFIER*): Has the authoritative identification of the enterprise associated with a trap.
- *snmpV2EnableAuthenTraps* (*TruthValue*): Indicates whether an SNMPv2 entity can be disabled from generating an authenticationFailure trap. This object must be stored in non-volatile storage.

10.5.5 snmpTraps group

The snmpTraps group (Figure 10.10) refers to the well-known SNMPv2 traps. We have seen these traps in SNMPv1 (Section 8.7.1). These traps are useful for fault management.

10.5.6 snmpSet group

The snmpSet group (Figure 10.10) has one object and is used by SNMPv2 entities acting in a manager role to coordinate the use of an SNMPv2 set operation. This object can be used by performance management. One object in this group is:

- *snmpSetSerialNo* (*TestAndIncr*): Refers to the lock for coordinating the use of a set operation by a group of cooperating SNMPv2 entities.

10.5.7 snmpMIBConformance group

The snmpMIBConformance group (Figure 10.11) provides the compliance statements for SNMPv2 entities implementing SNMPv2 MIB. The compliance statements are provided by the snmpMIB-Compliance. snmpVIGroup is mandatory for SNMPv2 entities implementing SNMPv1. snmpMIBGroups refer to the compliance state-

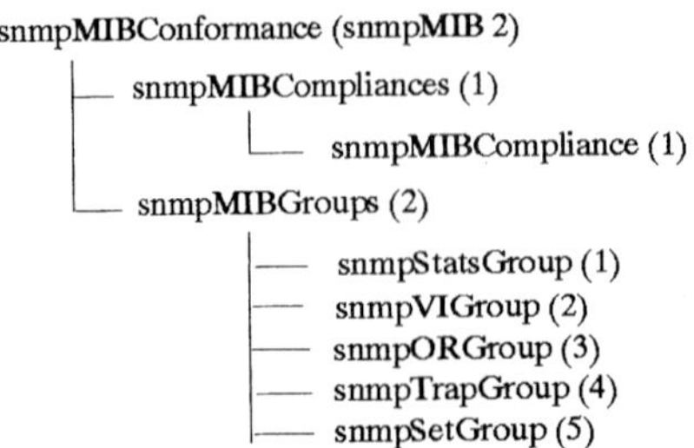

Figure 10.11 snmpMIBCOnformance group.

ments for the collection of objects for each of the SNMPv2 MIB groups we examined earlier.

10.6 Conformance Statements

Conformance statements define the acceptable level of implementation. An implementation can compare the actual functions provided with the benchmark provided in conformance statements to check whether the implementation satisfies the requirements. There are two types of notations used in SNMPv2, and they are defined in RFC 1447. The conformance notations are:

- *Compliance statements:* Refer to the requirements imposed on the objects in agents. This compliance is checked with the ASN.1 MODULE-COMPLIANCE macro.
- *Capability statements:* Capabilities provide the actual functions provided by objects in an agent and the ASN.1 AGENT-CAPABILITIES macro.

The objects used for conformance are combined to form a group, and the ASN.1 macro OBJECT-GROUP is used to provide the syntax and semantics for this group.

Let us examine each of the macros used in compliance and capabilities statements. SNMPv2 conformance macros are defined in RFC 1444, and they are:

```
SNMPv2-CONF DEFINITIONS ::=  BEGIN
-- definitions for conformance groups
OBJECT-GROUP MACRO ::=
BEGIN
        TYPE NOTATION ::=
                              ObjectsPart
                              "STATUS" Status
                              "DESCRIPTION" Text
                              ReferPart
        VALUE NOTATION ::=
                              value(VALUE OBJECT IDENTIFIER)
        ObjectsPart ::=       "OBJECTS" "{" Objects "}"
        Objects ::=           Object
                              | Objects "," Object
        Object ::=            value(Name ObjectName)
        Status ::=             "current"
                              | "obsolete"
        ReferPart ::=         "REFERENCE" Text
                              | empty
        -- uses the NVT ASCII character set
```

```
Text ::=  """" string """"
END
-- definitions for compliance statements
MODULE-COMPLIANCE MACRO ::=
BEGIN
      TYPE NOTATION ::=
                          "STATUS" Status
                          "DESCRIPTION" Text
                          ReferPart
                          ModulePart
      VALUE NOTATION ::=
                          Value(VALUE OBJECT IDENTIFIER)
     Status ::=           "current"
                          | "obsolete"
     ReferPart ::=        "REFERENCE" Text
                          | empty
     ModulePart ::=       Modules
                          | empty
     Modules ::=          Module
                          | Modules Module
     Module ::=           "MODULE" ModuleName -- name of module
                          MandatoryPart
                          CompliancePart
     ModuleName ::=       Modulereference ModuleIdentifier -- must not
                          --be empty unless contained in MIB Module.
                          | empty
     ModuleIdentifier ::= | value(ModuleID OBJECT IDENTIFIER)
                          | empty
     MandatoryPart ::=    "MANDATORY-GROUPS" "{" Groups "}"
                          | empty
     Groups ::=           Group
                          | Groups "," Group
     Group ::=            value(Group OBJECT IDENTIFIER)
     CompliancePart ::=   Compliances
                          | empty
     Compliances::=       Compliance
                          | Compliances Compliance
     Compliance ::=       ComplianceGroup
                          | Object
     ComplianceGroup ::=
                          "GROUP" value(Name OBJECT IDENTIFIER)
                          "DESCRIPTION" Text
     Object ::=           "OBJECT" value(Name ObjectName)
                          SyntaxPart
                          WriteSyntaxPart
                          AccessPart
                          "DESCRIPTION" Text
     -- must be a refinement for object's SYNTAX clause
```

```
    SyntaxPart ::=          "SYNTAX" type(SYNTAX)
                            | empty
    -- must be a refinement for object's SYNTAX clause
    WriteSyntaxPart ::=  "WRITE-SYNTAX" type(WriteSYNTAX)
                            | empty
    AccessPart ::=          "MIN-ACCESS" Access
                            | empty
    Access ::=              "not-accessible"
                            | "read-only"
                            | "read-write"
                            | "read-create"
    -- uses the NVT ASCII character set
    Text ::=  """" string """"
END
-- definitions for capabilities statements
AGENT-CAPABILITIES MACRO ::=
BEGIN
    TYPE NOTATION ::=
                            "PRODUCT-RELEASE" Text
                            "STATUS" Status
                            "DESCRIPTION" Text
                            ReferPart
                            ModulePart
    VALUE NOTATION ::=
                            Value (VALUE OBJECT IDENTIFIER) --
                            agents' sysObjectID [3] or snmpORID [4]
    Status ::=              "current"
                            | "obsolete"
    ReferPart ::=           "REFERENCE" Text
                            | empty
    ModulePart ::=          Modules
                            | empty
    Modules ::=             Module
                            | Modules Module
    Module ::=              "SUPPORTS" ModuleName -- name of module
                            "INCLUDES" "{" Groups "}"
                            VariationPart
    ModuleName ::=          identifier ModuleIdentifier
    ModuleIdentifier ::= value(ModuleID OBJECT IDENTIFIER)
                            | empty
    Groups ::=              Group
                            | Groups "," Group
    Group ::=               value(Name OBJECT IDENTIFIER)
    VariationPart ::=       Variations
                            | empty
    Variations ::=          Variation
                            | Variations Variation
    Variation ::=           "VARIATION" value(Name ObjectName)
```

```
                              SyntaxPart
                              WriteSyntaxPart
                              AccessPart
                              CreationPart
                              DefValPart
                              "DESCRIPTION" Text
    -- must be a refinement for object's SYNTAX clause
    SyntaxPart ::=            "SYNTAX" type(SYNTAX)
                              | empty
    -- must be a refinement for object's SYNTAX clause
    WriteSyntaxPart ::=       "WRITE-SYNTAX" type(WriteSYNTAX)
                              | empty
    AccessPart ::=            "ACCESS" Access
                              | empty
    Access ::=                "not-implemented"
                              | "read-only"
                              | "read-write"
                              | "read-create"
                              | write-only -- for backward compatibility.
    CreationPart ::=          "CREATION-REQUIRES" "{" Cells "}"
                              | empty
    Cells ::=                 Cell
                              | Cells "," Cell
    Cell ::=                  value(Cell ObjectName)
    DefValPart ::=            "DEFVAL" "{" value(Defval ObjectSyntax) "}"
                              | empty
    -- uses the NVT ASCII character set
    Text ::= """" string """"
END
END
```

Source: RFC 1444 (Conformance Statements for version 2 of the Simple Network Management Protocol [SNMPv2], 1993).

10.7 SNMPv2 PDUs

10.7.1 SNMPv2 PDU definitions

SNMPv2 PDUs are defined in RFC 1448.

```
SNMPv2-PDU DEFINITIONS ::=
BEGIN
IMPORTS
      ObjectName, ObjectSyntax, Integer32
            from SNMPv2-SMI
-- protocol data units
PDUs ::=
```

```
    CHOICE {
            get-request          GetRequest-PDU,
            get-next-request     GetNextRequest-PDU,
            get-bulk-request     GetBulkRequest-PDU,
            response             Response-PDU,
            set-request          SetRequest-PDU,
            inform-request       InformRequest-PDU,
            snmpV2-trap          SNMPv2-Trap-PDU
            }
-- PDUs
    GetRequest-PDU ::=                    [0] IMPLICIT PDU
    GetNextRequest-PDU ::=                [1] IMPLICIT PDU
    Response-PDU ::=                      [2] IMPLICIT PDU
    SetRequest-PDU ::=                    [3] IMPLICIT PDU
    -- [4] is obsolete
    GetBulkRequest-PDU ::=                [5] IMPLICIT PDU
    InformRequest-PDU ::=                 [6] IMPLICIT PDU
    SNMPv2-Trap-PDU ::=                   [7] IMPLICIT PDU
    max-bindings
     INTEGER ::=  2147483647
    PDU ::=
     SEQUENCE {
                         request-id     Integer32,
                         error-status   -- sometimes ignored
                             INTEGER{
                                  noError(0),
                                  tooBig(1),
                                  noSuchName(2), -- for proxy
                                  -- compatibility
                                  badValue(3), -- for proxy
                                  -- compatibility
                                  readOnly(4), -- for proxy
                                  -- compatibility
                                  genErr(5),
                                  noAccess(6),
                                  wrongType(7),
                                  wrongLength(8),
                                  wrongEncoding(9),
                                  wrongValue(10),
                                  noCreation(11),
                                  inconsistentValue(12),
                                  resourceUnavailable(13),
                                  commitFailed(14),
                                  undoFailed(15),
                                  authorizationError(16),
                                  notWritable(17),
                                  inconsistentName(18)
                             },
```

```
                                    error-index        INTEGER (0..max-
                                                       bindings), --
                                                       -- sometimes
                                                       -- ignored
                                    variable-bindings  VarBindList
                                                       -- values are
                                                       -- sometimes
                                                       -- ignored
                   }
              -- BulkPDU must be identical in structure to PDU
              BulkPDU :: =  -- must be identical in structure to PDU
                SEQUENCE {
                  request-id              Integer32,
                  non-repeaters           INTEGER (0..max-bindings),
                  max-repetitions         INTEGER (0..max-bindings),
                  variable-bindings       VarBindList -- values are ignored
                }
              -- variable binding
VarBind :: =
                SEQUENCE {
                  name                  ObjectName,
                  CHOICE {
                        value             ObjectSyntax,
                        unSpecified       NULL, -- in retrieval requests
                                          -- exceptions in responses
                        noSuchObject[0]       IMPLICIT NULL,
                        noSuchInstance[1]     IMPLICIT NULL,
                        endOfMibView[2]       IMPLICIT NULL
                }
          }
      -- variable-binding list
      VarBindList ::=
                 SEQUENCE (SIZE (0..max-bindings)) OF VarBind
END
```

Source: RFC 1448 (Protocol Operations for version 2 of the Simple Network Management Protocol [SNMPv2], 1993).

10.7.2 SNMPv2 protocol messages

SNMPv2 uses slightly different protocol messages (Figure 10.12) for communicating management information than does SNMPv1. The format of SNMPv2 PDUs, such as GetRequest, GetNextRequest, SetRequest, SNMPv2-Trap, Response, and InformRequest, are similar to those shown in Figure 8.23; however, there are some minor differences, as follows:

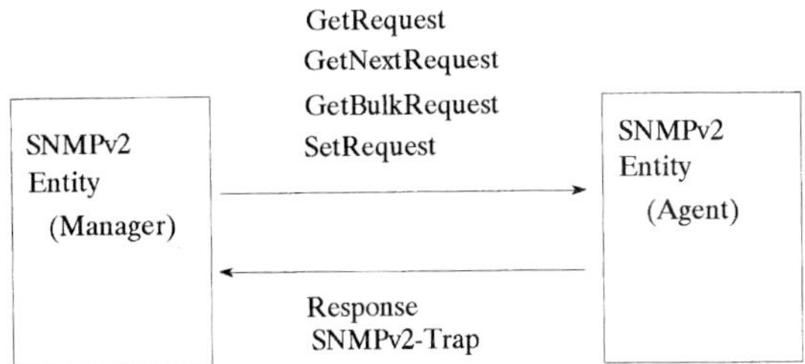

Figure 10.12 SNMPv2 protocol operations.

- A trap PDU of SNMPv1 is no longer there, and the PDU type of 4 used for the SNMPv1 trap is obsolete. The new value of the PDU type for SNMPv2-Trap is 7.
- The GetResponse of SNMPv1 is now known as the response PDU in SNMPv2.
- The GetBulkRequest PDU has been added, as shown in Figure 10.13. Note also that InformRequest is a new PDU.

A brief explanation of the SNMPv2 PDUs is as follows:

- *GetRequest:* When an application requests an SNMPv2 entity, this is generated by the entity and sent to an agent. This message is similar to the SNMPv1 GetRequest message. On the receiving end, this message is analyzed to check whether the request is a proper one. If it is a proper one, then the error status field is set to noError and the error index field is set to zero in the response and sent to the manager.
- *GetNextRequest:* This message is similar to the GetNextRequest in SNMPv1 messages and is based on the tabular concept of the SNMP MIB. If there are no errors, then the response has the next instance of a variable which has been sent in the request. If there are any errors, then the error status and error index fields correspond to the errors observed.
- *SetRequest:* This is a slightly trickier one. There are two steps involved: a validation phase and, if this succeeds, changes are

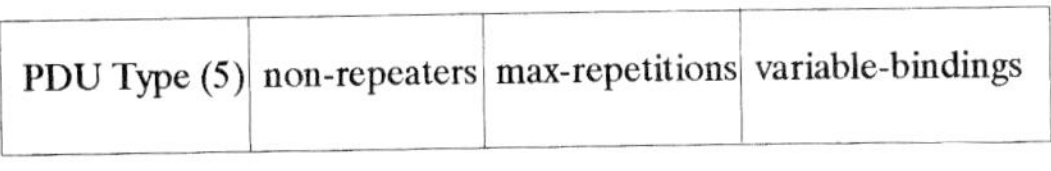

Figure 10.13 GetBulkRequest PDU.

made. During the validation step, a check is made of whether change on a variable can be made. If this is not possible, then the error status and error index fields are set accordingly in the response PDU. However, if the validation step is successful, then the value of the variable is set to the value mentioned in the SetRequest PDU. If the variable is not there, it is created and its value is set. In this case, in the response PDU, the error status field shows noError, and the error-index field is zero.

- *GetBulkRequest:* This is primarily used for retrieving a large amount of table data from the MIB, unlike GetRequest and GetNextRequest PDUs. Here also, if there are errors noticed in the receiving end, the error status and error index fields are set. If no errors are noticed, data is sent in the response PDU.
- *InformRequest:* This is a protocol message for conveying MIB information from one SNMPv2 entity to another SNMPv2 entity, both acting in the manager role. This is primarily meant for manager-to-manager communication. The receiving SNMPv2 checks to see if there are any errors. If errors are noticed while processing this PDU, the response PDU has the corresponding error status and error index fields set. If there are no errors, the MIB information is passed on to the application using the receiving SNMPv2 entity and generates a response to the sending SNMPv2.
- *Response:* This PDU is generated for GetRequest, GetNextRequest, SetRequest, and GetBulkRequest PDUs sent from a sender SNMPv2 entity. The sender SNMPv2 entity is the manager. The receiving SNMPv2 entity is the agent, and it prepares the response PDU and sends it back to the sending SNMPv2 entity. The sender SNMPv2 must be able to handle the errors generated and pass on the response PDU to the application using the sender SNMPv2 entity.
- *SNMPv2-Trap:* When an exceptional situation occurs in an SNMPv2 entity acting in an agent role, then a trap is generated and sent to the SNMPv2 entity consulting aclTable. The access privileges for SNMPv2 are maintained in the SNMPv2 access privileges database. The trap numbers in SNMPv2-Trap indicate the reasons why a trap has occurred. The SNMP traps as mentioned in SNMPv1 are used here, too.

10.7.3 Functioning of SNMPv2 protocols

The flow of how an SNMPv2 PDU is generated is shown in Figure 10.14. Basically, an originator SNMPv2 entity generates a management protocol PDU such as GetRequest. At first, an SNMPv2 man-

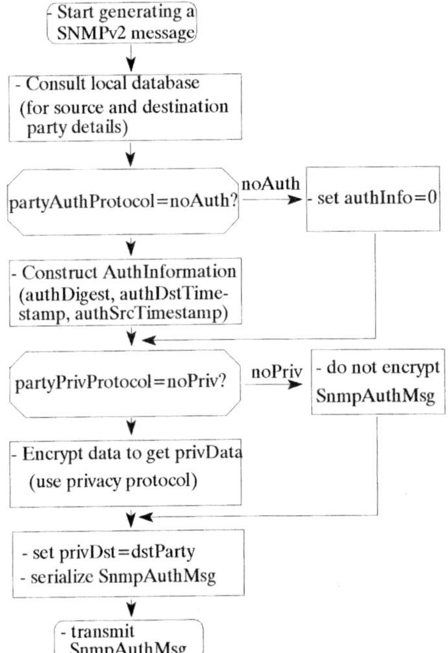

Figure 10.14 Generating an SNMPv2 protocol PDU.

agement communication (SnmpMgmtCom) is constructed. This has originator and receiver parties (Figure 10.9). This also has the context and SNMPv2 PDU fields. A local database is consulted for the context and the authentication protocol to be used.

From the SNMPv2 management communication (SnmpMgmtCo m), SNMPv2 authenticated management communication (Snmp AuthMsg) is constructed. This is derived by prefixing authentication information to the SNMPv2 management communication data. Here, if the authentication protocol is not used for a party, then the authentication protocol for the party is noAuth. In this case, the autholnfo field corresponds to an OCTET STRING value of zero length.

If partyAuthProtocol is 2md5AuthProtocol, then authentication protocol provides data origin identification and data integrity. snmpAuthMsg is supplied as an input to MD-5 message-digest algorithm (see Reference 10.2). The output from the message-digest algorithm is a 16-octet string known as digest. This digest goes in the authDigest field (Figure 10.9).

From SNMPv2 SnmpAuthMsg, SNMPv2 private management communication is (SnmpPrivMsg) constructed by prefixing the privacy destination field. Here, if the privacy protocol of the destination is noPriv, then the SnmpAuthMsg field is not encrypted. Otherwise, this field is encrypted, and it is formed using the privacy protocol.

The message to be sent to the destination party is SnmpPrivMsg. This has a privDst, which refers to the destination party. The intended message and private data are meant for the destination party. The private data field is possibly in the form of encrypted data. This private data is SNMPv2 authenticated management communication (SnmpAuthMsg). Then the SNMPv2 SnmpAuthMsg is converted to BER and sent to the destination party using the transport protocol and transport address of the receiving SNMPv2 party.

Figures 10.15*a* and 10.15*b* illustrate how an SNMPv2 PDU is treated on the receiving side. First, a check is made of whether the format of the message received is of the proper type. If the check is successful, then the destination is checked using the local database. From this, the ASN.1 string is recreated using decryption with the help of the privacy protocol. The authentication and context checking are also done on the receiving side, then access privileges are checked for management operations to be done. A check is also necessary to know whether the SNMPv2 context refers to the local object resources or remote object resources. In all this checking, the local database is consulted whenever required.

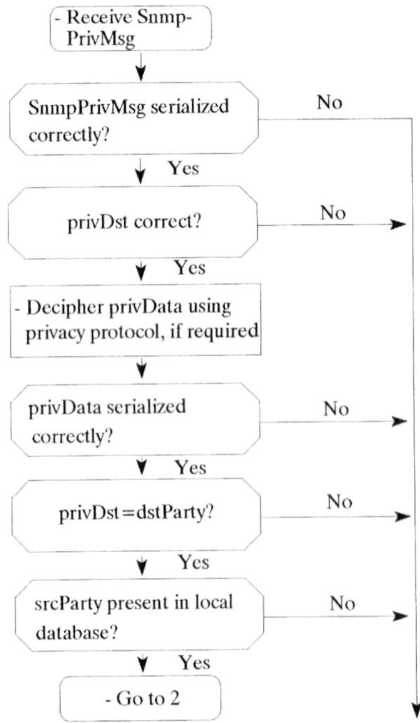

Figure 10.15*a* Receiving an SNMPv2 protocol message.

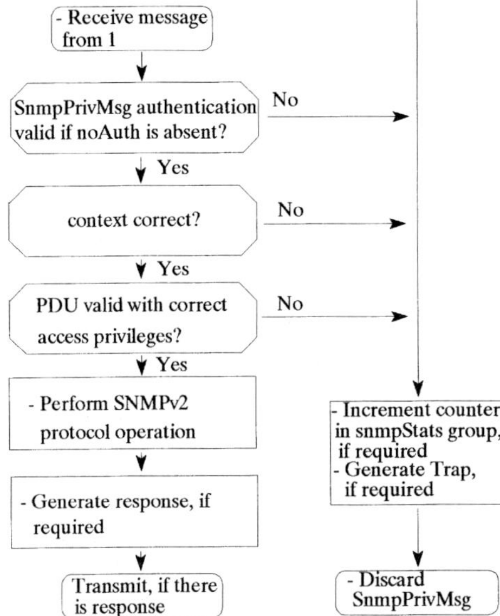

Figure 10.15*b* Receiving an SNMPv2 protocol message.

One of the key aspects of processing security protocols is that the originator is not sent any response indicating the reasons for the failure of the request. The primary reason for this action is that any unauthorized user need not be alerted that the request has been discarded. On the receiving side, the request is simply discarded.

10.7.4 Manager-to-manager communication

When there is a large network, it is difficult to centralize all network management activities in one place. The same is true of many networks internetworked to one another. In such situations, it is better to distribute the network management functions in different portions of the networks. This way each portion of the network can have a manager. For manager-to-manager communication, the InformRequest PDU and the manager-to-manager MIB have been created. These are explained in RFC 1451.

In Figure 10.16, manager-to-manager communication is illustrated. Manager A sends the InformRequest PDU and, in response, Manager B sends the Response PDU, which has the management information requested from B. However, to check whether the managers are functioning, polling is done frequently.

Some of the key concepts in manager-to-manager MIB, are:

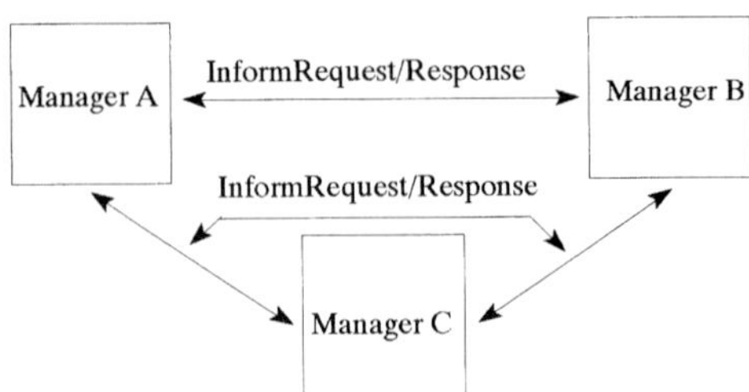

Figure 10.16 Manager-to-manager communication.

- *snmpAlarm:* This is a specific condition detected when a management variable falls outside a configured range. The checking for a configured range, such as crossing a threshold value, is done periodically by sampling. Only variables with the data type of INTEGER (Integer32, Counter32, Gauge32, TimeTicks, Counter64, and UInteger32) can be monitored for an alarm condition.
- *snmpEvent:* This triggers one or more notifications when an alarm condition is reached. These notifications are packaged in InformRequest PDUs.

Manager-to-manager MIB. The manager-to-manager MIB group (Figure 10.17) has the following three tables:

- *snmpAlarmTable* (Figure 10.18): Has the details on the variable to be monitored, such as sampling interval, threshold values, and the manner in which these threshold values are crossed. contextIdentity provides the context to be queried, and each context may have zero or more snmpAlarmEntrys associated with it.
- *snmpEventTable* (Figure 10.19): Furnishes details on the events generated by an SNMPv2 entity acting in a dual role of manager and agent. These events can be generated by alarm conditions associated with snmpAlarmTable or due to conditions defined in the NOTIFICATION-TYPE macro.
- *snmpEventNotifyTable* (Figure 10.20): Defines the destination and the type of notifications to be sent by an entity in a manager role on a event.

The objects in the snmpAlarm group (Figure 10.18) are:

- *snmpAlarmIndex (INTEGER (1..65535)):* Uniquely identifies an entry in the snmpAlarmTable.
- *snmpAlarmVariable (InstancePointer):* Refers to the object instance being sampled.

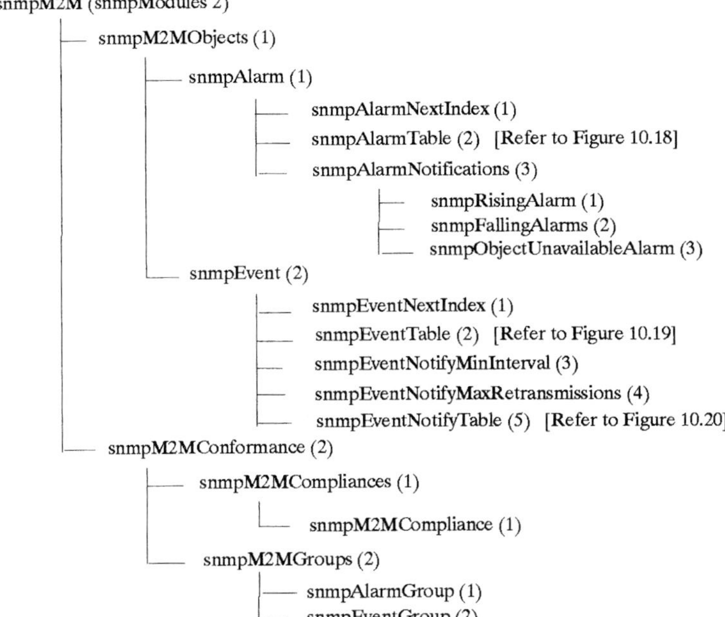

Figure 10.17 snmpM2M objects. (SNMPv2 manager-to-manager MIB Objects.)

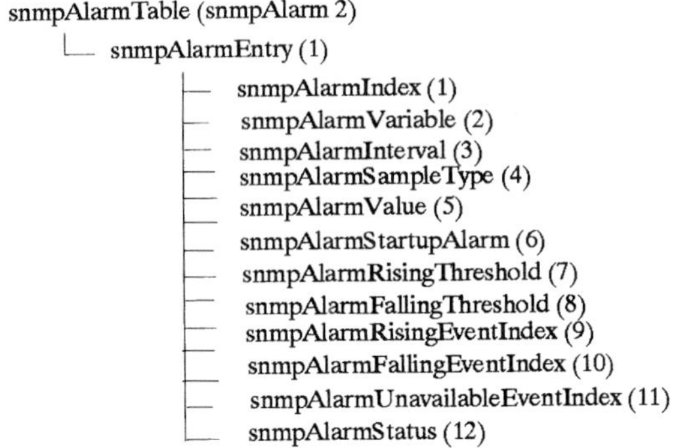

Figure 10.18 snmpAlarmTable objects.

- *snmpAlarmInterval* (*Integer32*): Indicates the time interval for sampling, in seconds.
- *snmpAlarmSampleType* (*INTEGER*): Specifies how sampling must be done. This object has two values: absoluteValue = 1 and deltaValue = 2. For absoluteValue, the sampled value of a variable at the end of the sampling interval is compared with the

snmpAlarmRisingThreshold and snmpAlarmFallingThreshold values. For deltaValue, the delta value is first derived by subtracting the value at the end of a sampling interval of the predecessor from the sampling value at the end of the sampling interval. This deltaValue is compared with the snmpAlarmRisingThreshold and snmpAlarmFallingThreshold values.

- *snmpAlarmValue* (*Integer32*): Refers to the last sampled value.
- *snmpAlarmStartupAlarm* (*INTEGER*): Indicates the alarm that may be sent when the first sample is compared with the threshold. This alarm has three values: risingAlarm = 1, fallingAlarm = 2, and risingOrFallingAlarm = 3.
- *snmpAlarmRisingThreshold* (*Integer32*): Furnishes the upper threshold limit.
- *snmpAlarmFallingThreshold* (*Integer32*): Indicates the lower threshold limit. Note that an event is generated when a sampled value crosses snmpAlarmRisingThreshold or snmpAlarmFallingThreshold.
- *snmpAlarmRisingEventIndex* (*INTEGER* (*0..65535*)): Indicates the entry in the snmpEventTable when the sampled value exceeds the value of snmpAlarmRisingThreshold.
- *snmpAlarmFallingEventIndex* (*INTEGER* (*0..65535*)): Associated with snmpAlarmFallingThreshold.
- *snmpAlarmUnavialableEventIndex* (*INTEGER* (*0..65535*)): Corresponds to a row in snmpEventTable. This row is used to generate an event when a variable being sampled is no longer available.

snmpRisingAlarm, snmpFallingAlarm, and *snmpObjectUnavilableAlarm,* defined by NOTIFICATION-TYPE macros, present the events generated when similar conditions to those seen in snmpEventTable are met.

An object in the snmpEvent (Figure 10.17) group is:

- *snmpEventNextIndex* (*INTEGER* (*0..65535*): Refers to the next available row for creating an instance of an event.

The following six objects are associated with snmpEventTable (Figure 10.19):

- *snmpEventIndex* (*INTEGER* (*0..65535*)): Identifies a conceptual row and is associated with notification to be sent for an invocation of a NOTIFICATION-TYPE macro.
- *snmpEventID* (*OBJECT IDENTIFIER*): Refers to the unique identifier of the event entry.

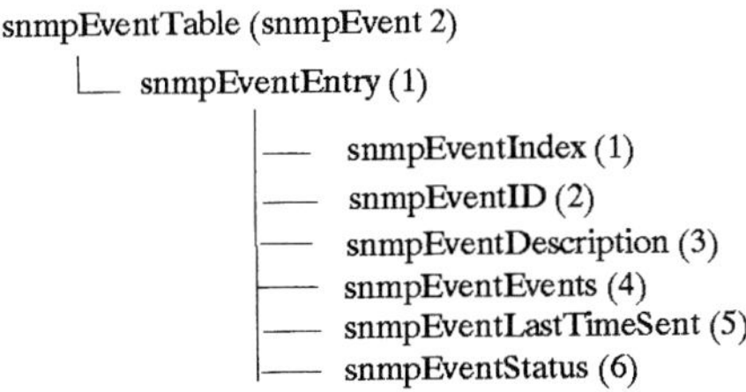

Figure 10.19 snmpEventTable objects.

- *snmpEventDescription* (*DisplayString* (*SIZE* (*0..127*))): Describes the event entry.
- *snmpEventEvents* (*Counter32*): Furnishes the number of events generated till now.
- *snmpEventLastTimeSent* (*TimeStamp*): Relates to sysUpTime, when an event was last generated. If this value is zero, then no event has been generated.
- *snmpEventStatus* (*RowStatus*): Provides the status of the snmpEvent entry.

We return to the explanation of the remaining objects in the snmpEvent (Figure 10.17) group.

- *snmpEventNotifyMinInterval* (*Integer32*): Provides the time interval for retransmitting InformRequest PDU.
- *snmpEventNotifyMaxRetransmissions* (*Integer32*): Represents the maximum number of InformRequest PDUs that will be sent.

snmpEventNotifyTable (Figure 10.20) has the following managed objects:

- *snmpEventNotifyIntervalRequested* (*Integer32*): Furnishes the time interval for retransmitting an InformRequest PDU.
- *snmpEventNotifyRetransmissionsRequested* (*Integer32*): Has the lesser value of the actual retransmissions of InformRequest or snmpEventNotifyMaxRetransmissions.

snmpEventNotifyTable (snmpEvent 5)
└─ snmpEventNotifyEntry (1)
  ├─ snmpEventNotifyIntervalRequested (1)
  ├─ snmpEventNotifyRetransmissionsRequested (2)
  ├─ snmpEventNotifyLifetime (3)
  └─ snmpEventNotifyStatus (4)

Figure 10.20 snmpEventNotifiyTable objects.

- *snmpEventNotifyLifetime* (*Integer32*): Represents the number of seconds the entry in snmpEventNotifyTable will remain active. After the expiry of the time, the snmpEventNotify status is set to "destroyed."
- *snmpEventNotifyStatus* (*RowStatus*): Used for representing the status of snmpEventNotifyEntry.

snmpM2MConformance objects present the description and configuration of the alarm and event group objects.

10.8 Transport Mapping for SNMPv2

SNMPv2 management protocols must be associated with a transport service for transferring the management information. However, there are different types of transport services that can be used for SNMPv2 (Figure 10.21). The term snmpDomains stands for the association of the SNMPv2 management protocols with a transport service. As we have seen, the SNMPv2 PDUs are serialized using BER. The following types of transport service for SNMPv2 have been defined:

- *snmpUDPDomain:* SNMPv2 over UDP is the preferred manner to transfer management information.
- *snmpCLNSDomain:* SNMPv2 over OSI's Connectionless-mode Transport Service (CLTS) is an alternative. Connectionless transport service works over the Connectionless Network Service.
- *snmpCONSDomain:* Here, SNMPv2 is transferred using the Connection-oriented Network Service (CONS). Here, connection-

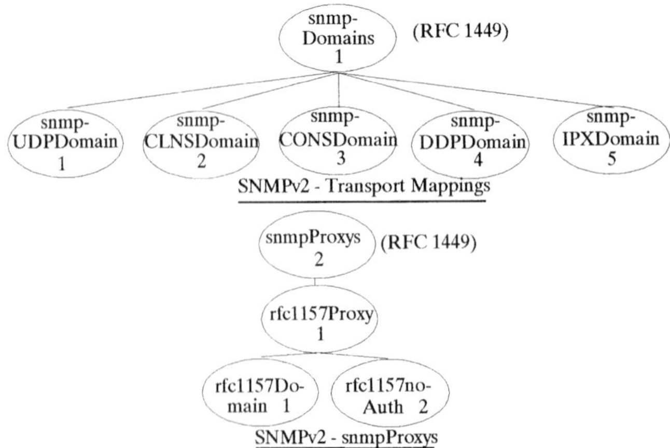

Figure 10.21 SNMPv2 transport mappings and snmpProxys.

less-mode transport service runs over the connection-oriented network service.

- *snmpDDPDomain:* SNMPv2 uses the AppleTalk® DDP for the transport service.
- *snmpIPXDomain:* SNMPv2 uses the NetWare® IPX for the transport service.

10.9 Migration from SNMPv1 to SNMPv2

For migration, proxy (see Figure 10.22) has been suggested. In a proxy approach, an SNMPv2 entity may be acting as a manager; the SNMPv1 entity can be in an agent role. However, in this case, the SNMPv2 proxy agent will have to convert the GetBulkRequest PDU to GetNextRequest PDU and set nonrepeaters and max-repetitions fields to zero. Traps will have to be modified in the proxy agent. In a bilingual approach, a manager functions as a proxy when dealing with an SNMPv1 agent. Here a manager maps SNMPv2 PDUs to SNMPv1 PDUs. Some of the strategies for migration are to:

- Upgrade management stations to SNMPv2. If this is done, it is easy to support SNMPv2 agents as they become available.
- Upgrade and acquire if required, new SNMPv2 agents. Once the management stations can handle SNMPv2, it is easy to add new SNMPv2 agents.

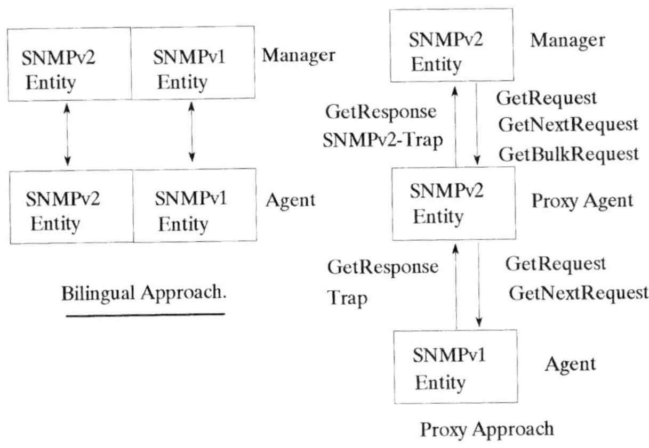

Figure 10.22 SNMPv1 and SNMPv2 coexistence.

- Handle the existing SNMPv1 agents, the proxy approach provides easy coexistence.

10.10 Device-Dependent Objects

In addition to the objects defined in MIB-II and other SNMPv1 and SNMPv2 documents, objects are defined for different media types. These are useful, and they can be incorporated in agents. Some of the device-specific objects defined in different RFCs are shown in Table 10.3. However, while implementing these objects, consult the latest *Internet Official Protocol Standards* on the requirement and maturity levels of these RFCs.

10.11 Advantages of SNMP

As mentioned in the beginning, SNMP is a simple protocol, and it is easy to add this protocol to the agents. Many applications using

TABLE 10.3 RFCs for Managed Objects for Devices

RFC number	Description of the RFC
1749	IEEE 802.5 Station Source Routing MIB Using SMIv2
1696	Modem Management Information Base (MIB) Using SMIv2
1695	Managed Objects for ATM Management Version 8.0 Using SMIv2
1694	Managed Objects for SMDS Interfaces Using SMIv2
1643	Managed Objects for the Ethernet-like Interface Types
1604	Managed Objects for Frame Relay Service
1595	Managed Objects for the SONET/SDH Interface Type
1525	Managed Objects for Source Routing Bridges
1516	Managed Objects for IEEE 802.3 Repeater Devices
1515	Managed Objects for IEEE 802.3 Medium Attachment Units (MAUs)
1512	An FDDI Management Information Base
1493	Managed Objects for Bridges
1407	Managed Objects for the DS/E3 Interface Type
1406	Managed Objects for the DS1 and E1 Interface Types
1317	Managed Objects for RS-232-like Hardware Devices
1315	Management Information Base for Frame Relay DTEs
1304	Managed Objects for the SIP Interface Type
1239	Reassignment of Experimental MIBs to Standard MIBs

SNMP protocols have been implemented. It is easy to get and modify SNMP code. Because Internet is quite popular, it has a large base, which itself is causing SNMP to be accepted as a de facto standard worldwide.

Also, it is easy to add objects required for specific implementations. This can done by adding object extension to the MIB. Continuous improvements and extensions are being added to the protocol with implementation experiences.

10.12 Limitations of SNMP

When SNMP was designed, the idea was to keep the management protocol simple. This has its own drawbacks. The network management has a whole range of functions in addition to the SNMP protocols defined. A framework for management functions such as OSI may be useful. Also, as distributed computing becomes popular, there are issues such as how different subnetwork managers behave, how the replication of management operational data collected by network management functions is done, and how the management operational data collected is archived. These aspects need to be standardized. Otherwise, there are possibilities of different vendors interpreting and implementing in different ways. This will also raise the problems of interoperability of network management systems.

As we move into a client-server environment with a large number of networks, management domains (see Section 3.3) and communications between them will assume a significant role. Management domains are also important for distributed network management. Incidentally, there is much work to be done in this arena in the Internet Network Management Framework.

A manager must enforce access control and authentication to ensure that important data are not compromised by intruders. This becomes critical when concepts of distributed systems are extended to Internet, and it still leaves a hole in SNMP security.

It is also necessary to define objects for the different network management functions, such as configuration management, fault management, security management, performance management, and accounting management. These may be borrowed from OSI. This is required as an interim measure, because the convergence of network management of OSI and Internet may take a while.

In configuration and fault management, relationships between different monitored objects are very important in tracing the origins of faults. Thus, relationships and attributes must be defined and standardized.

In configuration management, aggregation objects need to be defined. In some cases, the status of an object may be the aggregation of objects below a subtree. In such cases, the status will have to be combined by either simple or weighted aggregation. Also, the configuration may be a combination of objects; for example, a network may be a combination of an IP network, an OSI-based network, and an SNA network. To show the whole network, it is necessary to define aggregate objects. The health or status of a network may be represented by different colors.

The Internet group is focused on protocols used by the Internet community, and it expects a certain lower-layer stack. It also assumes certain physical-layer interfaces. So, the emphasis is on the TCP/IP protocol suite and on Ethernet LANs, while the other type of LANs based on token-ring protocols are also popular. As a result, the Internet stack gets priority while standardizing. This may be regarded as a strength as well as a weakness. It is a strength in that problems facing the Internet community get immediate attention, while others may have to wait longer for standardization.

Therefore objects may have to be specifically defined and extensions added to the MIB for many resources. This may result in defining the same resources in different manners, which can create problems for the interoperability of network management functions.

The definition of objects in OSI allows the use of inheritance and polymorphism. This makes possible the reuse of attributes; hence, the implementations becomes simpler with this approach. We have already explained polymorphism in Section 3.9. Polymorphism helps in the migration and coexistence of different versions of the same applications.

We have seen that in OSI, managed objects have attributes, operations, notifications, and behaviors. In SNMP, object definitions are less powerful and have only attributes and operations. As a result, they carry less information. The advantages of having notifications in the definitions of managed objects in OSI are flexibility and more power. To compensate for the absence of notifications in SNMP, traps and trap-directed polling are used. However, simplicity was one of the main considerations in the definition of SNMP, and lack of notification has not hindered many SNMP implementations.

As a final consideration, interoperability will be a problem if TCP/IP is not globally accepted. Otherwise, the integration of OSI protocols in some nations and Internet protocols in some other nations may lead to problems at a later date. Because the ultimate objective of Internet is to migrate to OSI standards, this may not be major obstacle in the long run.

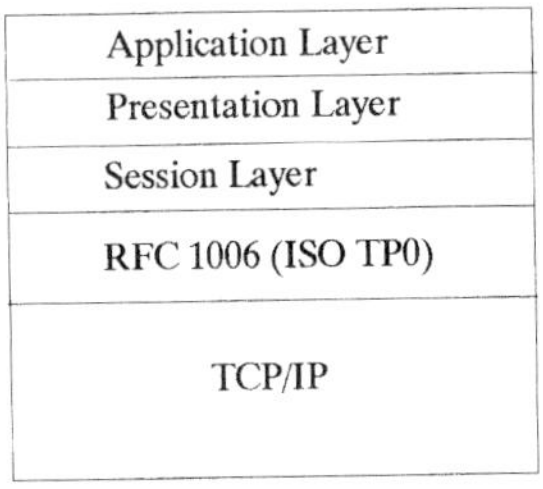

Application Layer
Presentation Layer
Session Layer
RFC 1006 (ISO TP0)
TCP/IP

Figure 10.23 Interoperability with OSI.

10.13 Interoperability with OSI

For interoperation between OSI and TCP/IP protocols, RFC 1006 (see Reference 10.5) is recommended. RFC 1006 mimics the transport layer on top of TCP (Figure 10.23). By this, layers such as the session, presentation, and application layers can run on top of TCP/IP protocols. This enables applications such as systems management and mail services to operate on TCP/IP. Some of the salient features of RFC 1006 are:

- *ISO transport Class 0 is supported.* Class 0 provides the most simple basic connection-oriented support during connection establishment and connection release phases. It does not provide a mechanism to detect protocol errors. Quality of service (QOS), which classifies transport services in terms of Class 0, Class 1, Class 2, Class 3, and Class 4, is not supported.
- *Some departures from Class 0 are made.* Initial data may be exchanged during the connection establishment phase; expedited data service is supported; and much larger Transport Protocol Data Unit (TPDU) size is supported. For performance reasons, a default TPDU size of 65531 is taken. However, smaller TPDU sizes are allowed, but they must be negotiated.
- *Network service is provided by the TCP.*
- *TPDU is encapsulated within each packet designed specifically for this RFC.* This packet consists of a packet header and the TPDU. The packet header has 8 bits for version, 8 bits of reserved field, and 16 bits of length field.

10.14 Notes on Systems Management Functions for TCP/IP

Having discussed SNMPv1, MIB, RMON, and SNMPv2, it is appropriate to peek into network management in Internet. In TCP/IP, there are no clear-cut rules regarding how to partition MIB-II objects into different systems management functional areas. Such classification has been discussed throughout Part 2. Unless there is standardization in this direction, the partitioning of MIB-II objects will not be uniform in implementations from different vendors.

These MIB-II objects will be in agents. The data on the MIB-II objects will be collected by the respective systems management functional areas (Figure 10.24). In addition, each of the device- and protocol-specific objects should be partitioned to different systems management functional areas. Agents send the management information on these objects to the respective systems management functions in managers, as illustrated in Figure 10.24. In this figure, note that it is not necessary to have MIB-II objects in all the agents. In some cases, such as that of a router, all MIB-II objects may not be supported; therefore, we should take the MIBs defined for a router. Similarly, an agent may not have device-specific objects. At the same time, we should remember that we may have to use proxy agents to incorporate the proprietary protocols and proprietary objects.

10.15 Notes on the Implementation of TCP/IP

TCP/IP protocol suite RFCs, including those of network management, change quite frequently to meet new requirements. Before implementing any RFC, one must ensure that it is the latest and is not superseded by a more recent RFC. To do so, the first document to consult is the *RFCINDEX,* which is an up-to-date index of the RFCs that have been released. The next document to consult during design and

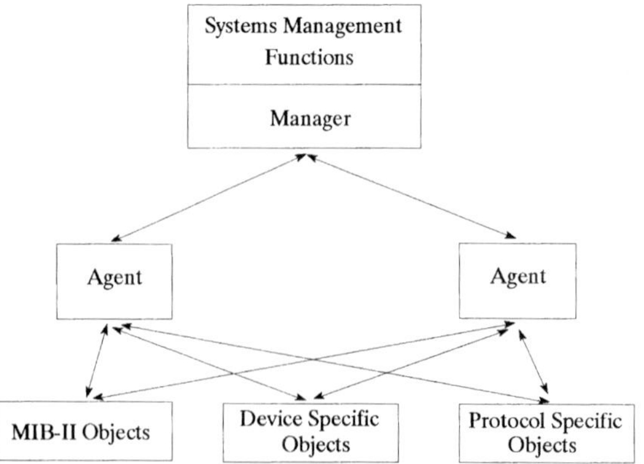

Figure 10.24 Systems management functions for TCP/IP.

implementation is the RFC on *IAB Official Protocol Standards,* which furnishes the requirement and maturity levels of RFCs. These two documents are regularly updated.

10.16 Summary

This chapter has been devoted mainly to SNMPv2 protocol details. SNMPv2 PDUs and extensions to MIB-II to support SNMPv2 were also discussed, as were important features in SNMPv2 such as security. Manager-to-manager communication was also examined. In the computer and telecommunication industry, some of the pertinent issues are whether to choose OSI or TCP/IP and how to make OSI and TCP/IP applications to interoperate. With these points in mind, we have discussed the merits and weaknesses of network management in Internet. From the interoperability point of view, a discussion on RFC 1006 was also warranted.

10.17 References

10.1 Rose, M. T., *The Simple Book: An Introduction to Internet Management,* 2d ed., PTR Englewood Cliffs, N.J., Prentice Hall, 1994.

10.2 Rivest, R., The MD5 Message-Digest Algorithm, RFC 1321, 1992.

10.3 Data Encryption Standard, National Institute of Standards and Technology, Federal Information Processing Standard (FIPS) Publication 46-1, 1988.

10.4 DES Modes of Operation, National Institute of Standards and Technology, Federal Information Processing Standard (FIPS) Publication 81, 1980.

10.5 Rose, M. T., and D. E. Cass, ISO Transport Service on Top of the TCP Version: 3, RFC 1006, 1987.

10.18 Further Reading

Case, J. D., K. McCloghrie, M. T. Rose, and S. Waldbusser, Coexistence between version 1 and version 2 of the Internet-standard Network Management Framework, RFC 1452, 1993.

Case, J. D., K. McCloghrie, M. T. Rose, and S. Waldbusser, Conformance Statements for version 2 of the Simple Network Management Protocol (SNMPv2), RFC 1444, 1993.

Case, J. D., K. McCloghrie, M. T. Rose, and S. Waldbusser, Introduction to version 2 of the Internet-standard Network Management Framework, RFC 1441, 1993.

Case, J. D., K. McCloghrie, M. T. Rose, and S. Waldbusser, Management Information Base for version 2 of the Simple Network Management Protocol (SNMPv2), RFC 1450, 1993.

Case, J. D., K. McCloghrie, M. T. Rose, and S. Waldbusser, Manager to Manager Management Information Base, RFC 1451, 1993.

Case, J. D., K. McCloghrie, M. T. Rose, and S. Waldbusser, Protocol Operations for version 2 of the Simple Network Management Protocol (SNMPv2), RFC 1448, 1993.

Case, J. D., K. McCloghrie, M. T. Rose, and S. Waldbusser, Structure of Management Information for version 2 of the Simple Network Management Protocol (SNMPv2), RFC 1442, 1993.

Case, J. D., K. McCloghrie, M. T. Rose, and S. Waldbusser, Textual Conventions for version 2 of the Simple Network Management Protocol (SNMPv2), RFC 1443, 1993.

Case, J. D., K. McCloghrie, M. T. Rose, and S. Waldbusser, Transport Mapping for version 2 of the Simple Network Management Protocol (SNMPv2), RFC 1449, 1993.

Data Encryption Algorithm, American National Standards Institute, ANSI X3.92-1981, 1980.

Data Encryption Algorithm, Modes of Operation, American National Standards Institute, ANSI X3.106-1983, 1983.

Galvin, J. M., and K. McCloghrie, Administrative Model for version 2 of the Simple Network Management Protocol (SNMPv2), RFC 1445, 1993.

Galvin, J. M., and K. McCloghrie, Security Protocols for version 2 of the Simple Network Management Protocol (SNMPv2), RFC 1446, 1993.

Kohl, J., and C. Neuman, The Kerberos Network Authentication Service (V5), RFC 1510, 1993.

McCloghrie, K., and J. M. Galvin, Party MIB for version 2 of the Simple Network Management Protocol (SNMPv2), RFC 1447, 1993.

McCloghrie, K., and M. T. Rose, Algorithms for Automating Administration in SNMPV2 Managers, RFC 1503, 1993.

Stallings, W., *SNMP, SNMPv2, and CMIP: The Practical Guide to Network Management Standards,* Reading, Mass.: Addison-Wesley, 1993.

Wijnen, B., G. C. Carpenter, K. Curran, A. Sehgal, and G. Waters, Simple Network Management Protocol Distributed Protocol Interface Version 2.0, RFC 1592, 1994.

Part

3

IEEE LAN/MAN Management

Chapter

11

LAN Overview

11.1 Introduction

In this chapter, we introduce the basic concepts of the internetworking of LANs. Treatment of these concepts is introductory in nature and is enough to cover the issues in network management, since it is beyond the scope of this book to go into further detail on LANs. For interested readers, an exhaustive list of useful books is provided in Further Reading at the end of the chapter.

In LAN networks, workstations or computers are connected to form a network. In a network, we are able to communicate from one workstation to any other workstation. There are limitations of distance and the number of workstations that can be connected to a network. These limitations are due to the protocols used in LANs. Ethernet, CSMA/CD, and token-ring are popular LAN protocols, which will be examined in later sections.

Networks need to be connected to other networks so that any workstation in one network can communicate with any other computer in another network. Such a connection is shown in Figure 11.1. Here, one network is based on token-ring protocols, and another network is based on Ethernet. These two networks are connected by bridges to the high-speed network based on Fiber Distributed Data Interface (FDDI) protocols. This high-speed network is sometimes known as a *backbone network.*

Some terms common in data communications are *circuit switching* and *packet switching.* Switching is referred to a connection, which may be temporary or permanent. Switching provides for the transfer of information between end points of systems or networks. In circuit switching, which is used in telephone exchanges, there is a permanent path between end users. Also, there is not much intelligence in

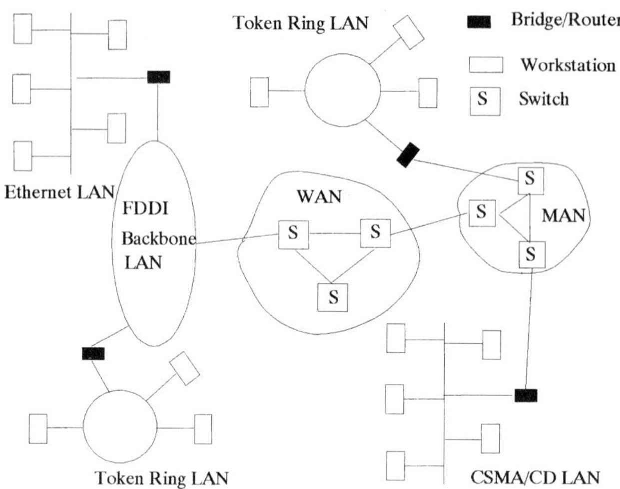

Figure 11.1 LAN, MAN, and WAN concepts.

circuit-switching networks to interpret the data during the life of connections.

In packet switching, the information to be transmitted is broken into packets by the sending station. These packets are assembled in the receiving station and do not have fixed routes and order. They may go through the intermediate systems using the best available route. Here, packets have network layer addresses, which are used for routing them. Also, there are error corrections and acknowledgments between intermediate systems. X.25 or SNA are examples of packet-switching protocols.

11.2 LANs, MANs, and WANs

The fundamental differences between LANs, MANs, and WANs are in the manner in which networks operate and the distances covered by networks. The technologies used in LANs, MANs, and WANs, are different. The overall view of these is shown in Figure 11.1. IEEE 802 (see Reference 11.1, p. 9) explanations of LAN and MAN are quite popular. With this as the basis, we will discuss each one.

LAN provides shared-medium peer-to-peer communication between stations in a network, and is expected to be controlled and used by a single organization. The geographical span of the network is very limited to a single office building or campus. There is no guarantee of security because of the broadcast nature of LAN protocols. This does not mean that security cannot be provided in LANs. It can be provided using Interoperable LAN/MAN Security (SILS) (see Reference 11.2).

FDDI rings can be used in a LAN. When the distance becomes larger, the help of telephone carriers may be necessary to connect networks. FDDI uses optical fiber for the transmitting medium and operates at 100 Mbits or more. Note that Mbits/s stands for megabits per second, and is used for data transfer rates. FDDI is quite popular as a backbone technology.

The data rates of MANs are higher and the scope is wider than for LANs. MANs can be controlled by a single organization but used by different organizations. In MANs, service in the cloud can be provided by carriers. They may also be used for the internetworking of LANs and may provide capabilities to carry integrated voice and data.

IEEE 802.6 (see Reference 11.3) provides the standards for the access protocol and is known as the Distributed Queue Dual Bus (DQDB). Data frames of 53 octet cells are used. In DQDB, data flows in two buses and data rates can be from 1.544 to 155 Mbits/s. For telephone carriers, Bellcore has published Switched Multi-megabit Data Service (SMDS) for MANs.

WAN's scope and use are on a wider scale than those of MANs. WANs may span different geographical locations and different controlling organizations. Also, public utilities such as telephone carriers may be involved in the transmission of data, which may include data, voice, video, image, and graphics. In WAN, the technology can be packet switching and may use frame relay and asynchronous transfer mode (ATM). ATM uses 53 octet cells for headers and data, and the data rates can be up to 2.4 Gbits/s. FDDI and ATM are popular LAN backbone protocols. WAN also has a provision for using circuit-switching technologies for carrying voice with data rates of multiples of 64 kbits/s.

11.3 LAN Topology

LAN topology describes how the workstations are connected. The Following LAN topologies are quite popular:

Mesh (Figure 11.2): Each workstation is connected to every other workstation in the network. This topology involves more wiring, but provides a good amount of redundancy such that if any station fails, the network can be still be up and running.

Star (Figure 11.3): A central station controls the network and the workstations are connected to a central station. Star topology is simple but places a greater burden on the central station.

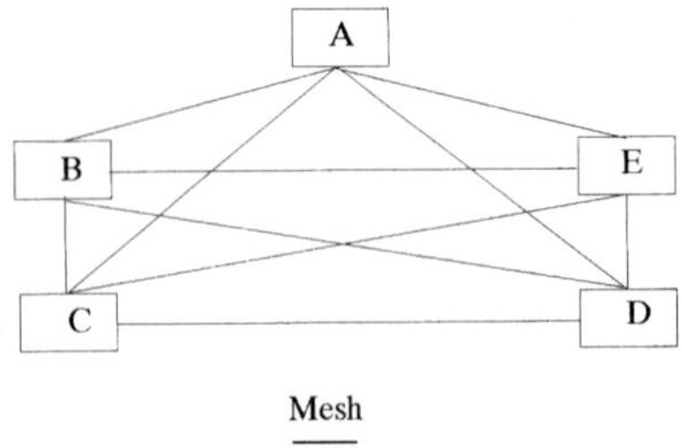

Figure 11.2 Mesh topology.

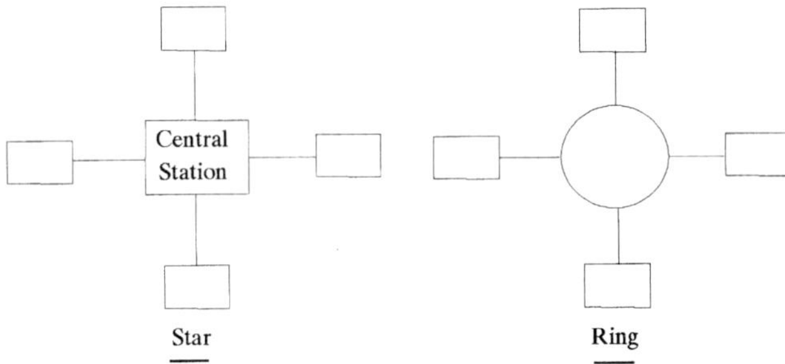

Figure 11.3 Star and ring topologies.

Ring (Figure 11.3): Data flow is in one direction, and the stations are connected to form a closed ring. This is popular in token rings and for backbone networks.

Bus (Figure 11.4): Workstations are connected to a common transmission medium. A transmission from one station is received by all the stations attached to the bus. This is quite popular in Ethernet.

Tree (Figure 11.4): This is an extension of the bus topology. The buses are connected to form a tree. This topology can be used for connecting workstations on different floors.

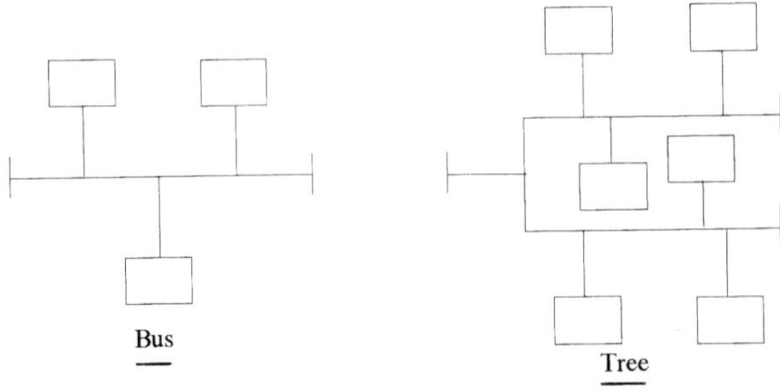

Figure 11.4 Bus and tree topologies.

11.4 LAN Layer Standards

In LANs, IEEE standards are widely accepted. Important IEEE LAN standards are:

- ANSI/IEEE 802.1B LANs: LAN/MAN Management
- ANSI/IEEE 802.1D: MAC Bridges (ISO 10038)
- ANSI/IEEE 802.2 Logical Link Control (ISO 8802.2)
- ANSI/IEEE 802.3 LANs: CSMA/CD Access Method (ISO 8802.3)
- ANSI/IEEE 802.4 LANs: Token-Passing Bus Access Method (ISO 8802.4)
- ANSI/IEEE 802.5 LANs: Token Ring Access Method (ISO 8802.5)
- IEEE 802.6 LANs: Distributed Queue Dual Bus Subnetwork (MANs)
- IEEE 802.9 Integrated Voice and Data (IVD)
- IEEE 802.10 LANs: SILS, Part B: Secure Data Exchange
- IEEE 802.11 Wireless LAN
- IEEE 802.12 100MB Voice Grade

In addition, IEEE technical advisory groups are working on the following standards:

- ANSI/IEEE 802.7 LANs: Broadband LAN
- IEEE 802.8 Fiber Optics

In LANs there are three layers:

- Physical layer
- Medium access control (MAC) layer
- Logical link control (LLC) layer

IEEE standards and mapping of these above LAN layers to the OSI layers is shown in Figure 11.5. The MAC layer performs some of the functions of the physical layer; the LLC layer provides some of the data link layer functions.

11.4.1 Physical layer

There are two popular transmission techniques: *baseband* and *broadband.* In baseband, the entire bandwidth is used for transmission of the information. If the medium is to be shared, then different time slices are allotted to different pieces of applications, which is known

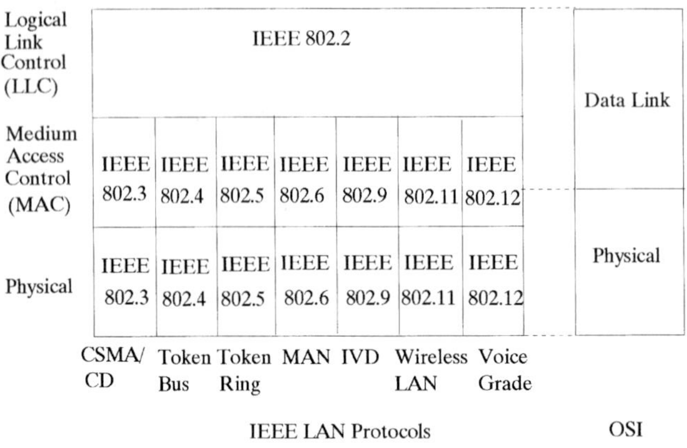

Figure 11.5 IEEE LAN standards.

as *time-division multiplexing* (TDM). In broadband, a physical medium is divided into logical channels, and in each channel the information of different applications is sent. This is known as *frequency-division multiplexing* (FDM). Television signals are transmitted using this method.

Different transmission mediums are used for connecting workstations to form LANs. Some of the popular transmission mediums are twisted pair, coaxial cable, and fiber optics. Twisted pair is used for telephone wiring in homes. Coaxial cables come with 75- and 50-ohm cable. 75-ohm cable is used in Community Antenna Television (CATV). The optical fiber is becoming popular for backbone networks.

These transmission mediums have different transmission characteristics and vary in cost. One of the important characteristics is the transmission distance. This is limited by the loss of signal strength due to physical and electrical characteristics. Data rate is another guiding factor, especially when voice and video data have to be mixed and transmitted.

11.4.2 MAC layer

Frames used in Ethernet and IEEE 802.3 are shown in Figure 11.12. Ethernet is the product of the original manufacturers of Ethernet cards led by Digital Equipment, Intel, and Xerox. This is slightly different from the IEEE 802.3 MAC frames. The Ethernet frame has an additional type field. The MAC layer provides for connectionless delivery of data.

IEEE 802.3 covers MAC- and physical-layer standards for CSMA/CD. IEEE 802.3 and its variations are used in Ethernet. IEEE

802.4 is used in token bus and IEEE 802.5 is used in token rings. The main concepts of each of the protocols will be discussed.

If a station sends information to more than one station, it is known as *multicasting*. If a station sends information to all the stations in a LAN, it is known as *broadcasting*.

11.4.3 LLC layer

The LLC layer adds further functions to the services provided by the MAC layer. The main purpose of the LLC layer is to provide error recovery and flow control. As the MAC layer is just concerned with connectionless data service, it expects the next-higher LLC layer to provide error recovery and flow control. As a result of the functions needed by the LLC layer, there are different frame formats to achieve these objectives. SAP addresses are provided in an LLC frame. However, IEEE 802.2 also has optional connectionless-oriented service. In this case, the LLC layer provides for the identification of SAPs.

Connection-oriented and connectionless-oriented services basically are concerned with how the packets or frames are sent. Common errors that occur when transmitting packets are listed in Table 11.1. Although these errors are interrelated, they have been categorized according to the reasons for them. The ways these errors are handled are different. Any corrupted data can be detected by a frame check sequence (FCS). The lost packets, duplicate packets, out-of-sequence packets, and undelivered packets can be detected by the LLC connection-oriented service.

LLC provides for the following three types of services to meet different requirements:

LLC Type 1 Connectionless Service: Also known as datagram service. Datagram service is sometimes compared to the postal service. When letters are posted, there is no guarantee how they reach the destination. Letters or packets do not necessarily follow a particular order or sequence. Letters may reach their destination out of sequence. Similarly, when a packet is sent, there is no guarantee

TABLE 11.1 Common errors when Transmitting Packets

Duplicate data
Lost data
Corrupted data
Out-of-sequence data
Undelivered data

that it will be delivered to the destination, and there is no order for delivery. The first packet sent in a network may be the third packet to reach the destination. Some packets may be lost, too.

Hence, there is no guarantee of delivery or the order of delivery, and no acknowledgment. If these functions are required, they must be provided by higher layers. LLC Type 1 service is used mainly for interactive traffic. Here no connections between SAPs are made before transferring data.

LLC Type 2 Connection-Oriented Service: A logical connection is required between two SAPs before any transfer of information takes place. This is sometimes compared to telephone connections. First, a connection must be made before data can be delivered. After data delivery, the connections are broken. Furthermore, the packets are sent in sequence. Packets that have not reached the destination need to be sent again. This service provides for sequencing of information transmitted, error recovery, and flow control. However, nothing comes free, and these services add their own complexity and extra steps. This service is used for applications which require a large amount of data transfer, such as in file transfer.

LLC Type 3 Acknowledged Connectionless Service: This includes some of the services found in LLC Type 1 and Type 2 services. Like LLC Type 1, there are no prior connections required before the transfer of data. However, when data is received, the sending station expects to receive acknowledgment from the receiving station. LLC Type 1 is used by TCP/IP, LLC Type 2 service is used by SNA, and LLC Type 3 is not used by any major protocols.

There is an unending debate as to whether connection-oriented or connectionless service should be used. Each service has its own advantages and disadvantages. In cases where data reliability is not important, data transmissions are of short duration, and simplicity is required, connectionless-oriented service is preferred. Connectionless service is also better when there is not sufficient justification for forming a connection before data transfer and bringing down the connection after data transfer. However, in those cases, where the data delivery and reliability are important and durations of data transmissions are long, connection-oriented service is preferred.

It is relevant to examine how the bits are organized and transmitted. IEEE and most of the standards bodies follow *canonical bit ordering,* in which bits are organized and data transmission is achieved as shown in Figure 11.6. For convenience in data transfer, the LLC frame has been modified to include the SNAP extension. The SNAP extension as shown in Figure 11.6 is five octets in length, and is known as the *protocol identifier.* This is subdivided into three octets of

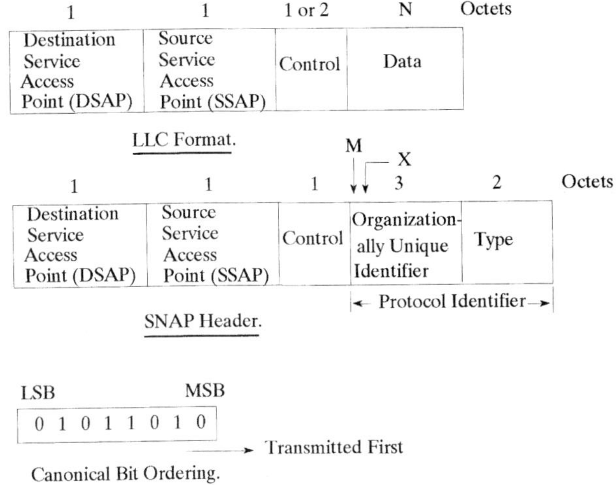

Figure 11.6 LLC frame and SNAP header.

the *organizationally unique identifier* (explained on page 321) and two octets of the locally administered type field. The M bit is always set to 0 and the X bit is set to 1 if the protocol identifier is assigned by IEEE. If the protocol identifier is assigned locally then the X bit is set to 1. We will discuss DSAP and SSAP (Figure 11.11) fields later.

When different types of services are required, naturally the frame formats have to be different. These are primarily provided by the control field which can be either one or two octets. Control fields for different frames, such as an unnumbered frame, a supervisory frame, or information, are similar to the HDLC control fields. The control fields used by different frames are shown in Figures 11.7, 11.8, and 11.9.

In the supervisory control frame shown in Figure 11.8, SS indicates the type of frame. These frames are mainly used for connection-oriented transmission. Frames for different values of SS are:

- B “00” — Receive ready (RR)
- B “01” — Receive not ready (RNR)
- B “10” — Reject (REJ)
- B “11” — Reserved

M (modifier) bits in an unnumbered frame (Figure 11.9) format give us different frames. They are interpreted as follows:

- B “000 00” — Unnumbered information (UI)
- B “101 11” — Exchange identification (XID)
- B “111 00” — Test (TEST)

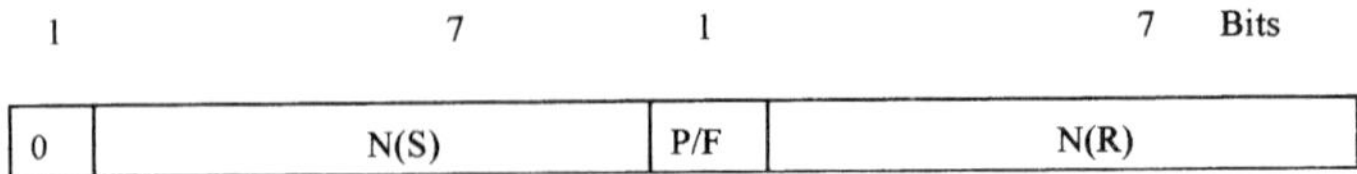

N(S) – Send Sequence Number
P/F – Poll/Final Bit
N(R) – Receive Sequence Number

Figure 11.7 Information frame.

1	1	1	1	1	1	1	1	1	7 Bits
1	0	S	S	X	X	X	X	P/F	N(R)

S - Supervisory Bits
X - Reserved Bits
P/F - Poll/Final Bit
N/R - Receive Sequence Number

Supervisory Frame

Figure 11.8 Supervisory frame.

1	1	1	1	1	1	1	1 Bits
1	1	M	M	P/F	M	M	M

M - Modifier Bit
P/F - Poll/Final Bit

Unnumbered Frame

Figure 11.9 Unnumbered frame.

The P/F bit is known as the poll and final bit. If it is P (set to 0), then it is an LLC command frame, and in the case of a final bit (set to 1), it becomes an LLC response frame.

In the MAC layer are the addresses of the stations, but this may not always be enough. Each station may have many processes or applications running at the same time. These applications must be uniquely identified if one application needs to send information to an application in another station. These applications are identified by an SAP, so while sending data from one application, the sender is identified by the *source service access point* (SSAP) and the destination application is identified by the *destination service access point* (DSAP).

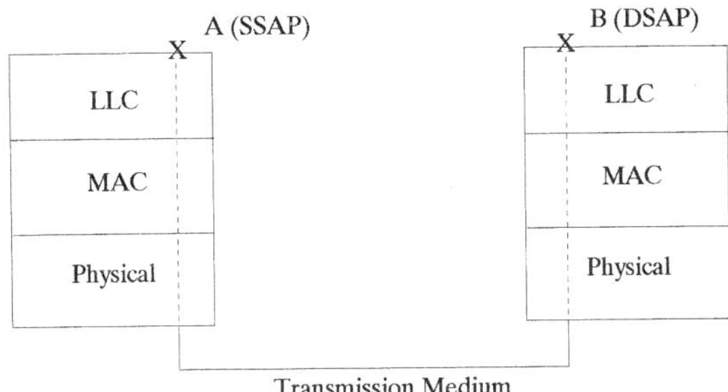

Figure 11.10 DSAP and SSAP concepts.

In Figure 11.10, application A wants to send some data to application B. Here, A is known as the SSAP and B is known as the DSAP. The data of application A is encapsulated with the LLC headers and passed on to the MAC layer. The MAC layer, in turn, encapsulates the LLC frame with its own headers. The MAC frame is transmitted via the transmission medium to the other end. On the receiving side, the MAC headers and LLC headers are removed before passing the data to application B.

The DSAP has one I/G bit field to identify whether it is an individual or group SAP (Figure 11.11). The U bit indicates whether it is a standard or user-defined SAP. Some SAPs have special significance; for example, B "1111 1111" indicates that the frame is for all SAPs. Also B "0000 0000," known as the null SAP address, is applicable to connectionless service.

The SSAP (Figure 11.11) also has a C/R bit which indicates whether it is a command or response. Note that the C/R bit is not part of the SSAP address. If it is set to zero, then it is a command. If the C/R bit is one, then it is a response. In both the DSAP and SSAP, the U bit indicates whether it is a user-defined SAP. If the U bit is set to one, it is an indication that it is an IEEE-defined SAP.

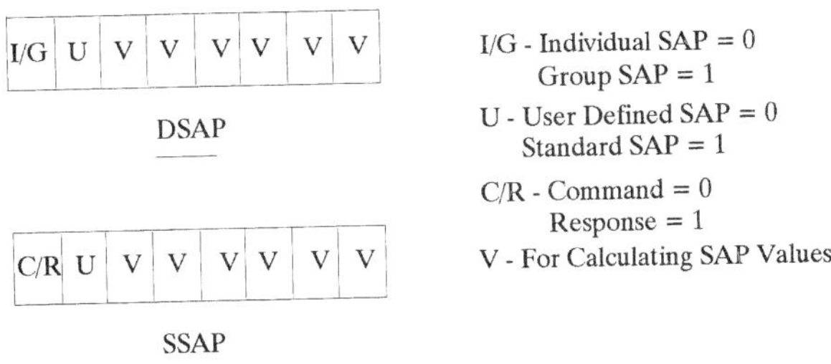

Figure 11.11 DSAP and SSAP fields.

11.5 LAN Protocols

11.5.1 CSMA/CD

The Carrier Sense Multiple Access/Collision Detection (CSMA/CD) protocol is furnished by IEEE 802.3 standards. CSMA/CD is also known as the listen-while-talk protocol, whereby a station with data to send listens to the transmitting medium. If no one is transmitting, then the sender sends the data. If there is a collision, indicated by a jamming signal, then the sender backs off for a random time and transmits again later.

The frame format of CSMA/CD is furnished in Figure 11.12. The LLC is enveloped by MAC fields. The MAC frame has the following fields:

Preamble: Used for synchronization by the receiving frame and is seven bytes long. The bits are alternately 1s and 0s.

Start frame delimiter (SFD): This is one byte long and indicates the start of a frame. It is B “1010 1011”.

Destination address (DA): There are two options here. The address can be two octets or six octets, as per standards. Earlier LANs used two octets, but the six-octet addressing format is typical these days. There is a restriction that all stations in a LAN must have either two- or six-octet addressing and not a mixture of them. The DA must be a unique physical address.

The two- and six-octet destination address formats are as shown in Figure 11.12. In the two-octet format, the first bit (I/G) indicates whether it is an individual address or a group address. If it is set

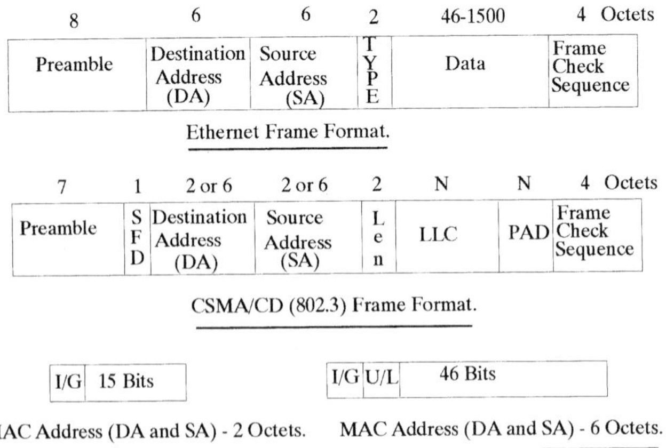

Figure 11.12 Ethernet and IEEE 802.3 CSMA/CD frame formats.

to zero, then it indicates an individual address; if the I/G bit is set to one, it indicates that it is a group address. Various group addresses are assigned to different destinations. For example, X "8001 4300 0000" identifies that the destination is a bridge. Similarly, X "FFFF FFFF FFFF" is used for broadcasting the data to all stations.

In six-octet addressing, the second bit (U/L) indicates whether the addressing is universally administered (B "0") or locally administered (B "1"). Universally administered addresses are also known as *burned-in addresses.* In the universally administered addresses, the U bit is always set to 0 and is divided into two parts of 24 bits each. The first part of 24 bits is known as *organizationally unique identifier* and is assigned by the IEEE to different manufacturers. The second part of 24 bits is assigned locally. These MAC addresses are built-in the adapter cards, which ensures a unique address. Similarly, the local administered addresses are furnished by the local network administrators, and they are assigned while an adapter is attached to a LAN.

Source address (SA): In this field, the address of the station which sent the frame is entered. It can also be either two octets or six octets. It must be of the same length as that of the destination address.

Length: Specifies the length in octets of the LLC field. In the LLC field, data is enveloped with the LLC headers and trailers.

LLC field: Has the LLC frame; data is part of the LLC frame.

PAD: An arbitrary-length field. PAD is added to make sure that the frame length satisfies the minimum frame-length requirement. The restriction of minimum frame length is imposed such that collision detection can be done effectively.

Frame check sequence (FCS): Has the results of the cyclic redundancy check algorithm. FCS includes all fields starting from the DA field. A sending station calculates the FCS and enters it in the FCS field. The receiving station again calculates the FCS for the received frame and compares it with the FCS in the FCS field. If they do not match, the frame is discarded.

11.5.2 Token bus

The token bus uses IEEE 802.4 standards. The Manufacturing Automation Protocol (MAP) uses a token-bus protocol. Here, for transmitting data, a station needs to possess the token, which is

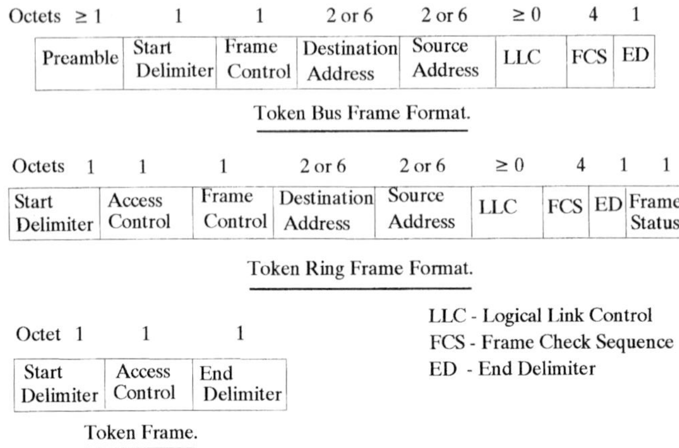

Figure 11.13 Token-bus and token-ring frame formats.

passed from one station to the next logical station. Here, the key is *logical.* A successor logical station need not necessarily be the next physical station. Also, there is a time limit beyond which a station cannot hold the token.

The frame format of IEEE 802.4 is shown in Figure 11.13. Most fields are similar to the ones in a CSMA/CD MAC frame. The frame control (FC) field is one octet long and it is of the form FFCC CCCC. Different values of FF have the following interpretations:

- B "00" — MAC control frame
- B "01" — LLC data frame
- B "10" — Station management frame
- B "11" — Reserved

CC CCCC represents frame types. As an example, B "00 0000" stands for claim token. For the LLC frames, it is of the form MM MPPP, where PPP stands for the LLC data priority and MMM refers to MAC action, such as Response. The ED field indicates the end of a frame.

11.5.3 Token ring

In token ring, a token, which is a three-octet frame of the form shown in Figure 11.13, rotates around a ring. Basically, the difference between token ring and token bus is that in token ring the configuration is physical rather than logical as in token bus. Here, a station wishing to transmit data must take the possession of a free token. If station has data and it does not have a free token, then it must wait till it receives a free token. To make sure that one station does not monopolize the data transmission, timers are usually set.

The IEEE 802.5 frame is slightly different from the 802.3 and 802.4 frames. Here, the SD field is one octet long. The Access control (AC) field is of the form PPPTMRRR and is also one octet long. This field is available in the token as well as in a MAC frame. PPP indicates the priority of a token. A station can use a token if the station's priority is less than or equal to the priority of the token.

In the AC field, T differentiates a token from a frame. If it is zero, then the frame is a token. If it is one, then it is a frame. The M bit, known as a monitor bit, is initially set to zero. When an active monitor, which is a station controlling the activity of the token, sees this bit, it is set to 1. If the active monitor sees this bit set to 1, then it assumes that the originating station has not been able to remove the frame or the priority token. It purges the token it receives and issues a new free token to circulate in the ring. This action of the monitor helps to eliminate tokens or frames that are continuously circulating in the ring.

RRR bits in the AC field are known as *reservation bits.* Any station that has a message with a high priority sets these bits to indicate that the next token should be issued with the requested priority. As shown in Figure 11.13, a token has an ED field, in addition to the SD and AC fields. It has intermediate (I) and error detection (E) bits. If the I bit is one, then it indicates that it is an intermediate frame while transmitting multiple frames. If it is zero, it indicates that there is only one frame or it is the final frame in multiframe transmission. Any station in the ring can set the error detection bit to 1 if an error such as an FCS error, an invalid frame format, or a code violation is observed.

In IEEE 802.5, FC indicates that it is a one-byte frame control field. It is of the form FFCC CCCC. FF bits are known as *frame type bits.* If FF bits are B "00", then it is a MAC frame. However, if these bits are B "01", it is an LLC frame. The CCCCCC bits are known as *control bits.*

The last field of the frame is known as the frame status (FS) field. Here, A stands for *address recognized bit* and C stands for *frame copied bit.* These bits are repeated, since they are not included in the FCS. When a destination station sees its own address, it sets the A bit to 1. Also, the destination station can copy the data, setting the C bit to 1. In this case, the originating station knows that the data meant for a destination station has actually been received by the destination station.

11.6 LAN Connectivity

Workstations need to be connected to one another so that users in these workstations can communicate with one another. They use different topologies such as star, ring, bus, tree, or a mixture of them. Along with these, they may use different architectures, standards, applications, and technologies, which place their own limitations on how these workstations are connected.

To overcome some of the limitations imposed, workstations can be connected to form segments and subnetworks. These segments and subnetworks can be connected using repeaters, bridges, routers, or gateways to form larger networks. Intelligent hubs also provide the connectivity to workstations, and they have the intelligence to overcome failures such as bypassing the defective lobes.

11.6.1 Repeaters

The LAN transmission medium, because of the attenuation or loss of signal strength due to physical and electrical characteristics, cannot be used to connect many workstations spread over a large distance. For example, assume that a 50-ohm coaxial cable can support a maximum segment length of only 500 m. If workstations are to be connected spanning a distance of more than 500 m, then repeaters can be used to connect segments (Figure 11.14). The workstations can be in different segments. Repeaters connect at the physical layer and they regenerate the signals, which carry the bits of zero and one. By this method, loss of signal strength is overcome.

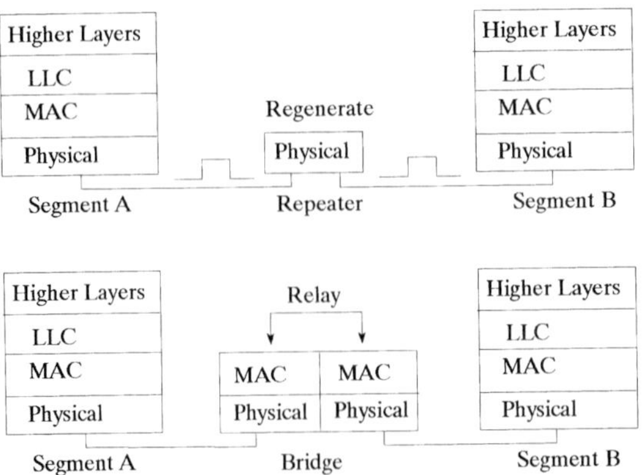

Figure 11.14 Repeaters and bridges.

11.6.2 Bridges

To increase the capacity of LANs, one of the usual practices is to add separate networks or segments, which can then be connected by bridges or routers. Bridges can be used when there is incompatibility in the hardware at the MAC layer or there is a need to increase the span of workstation connectivity (Figure 11.14). Bridges also help in isolation of faulty segments. If some workstation has undergone a major breakdown, such as a cable failure, then that segment can be isolated.

In bridges, the IEEE source and destination addresses are used to direct frames to workstations. Also, the MAC layer addresses must be unique. As a result, it is easy to identify any station on either side of a segment or subnetwork.

To connect to telephone carriers to transmit data across segments, sometimes remote or split bridges are used, in which bridge functions are divided into two bridges. There are two types of bridges: *transparent* and *source routing.*

Transparent bridge. Transparent bridges use IEEE 802.1D standards (see Reference 11.4). In transparent bridges, the sending station is not concerned about the route to a destination station. The destination address is searched in the address table maintained in the bridges. If the destination address is not found in the address table, the assumption is that the frame is meant for a station on the other side of the LAN, so it is forwarded. A frame is discarded if it is observed that the destination address is found on the port on which it is received.

In transparent bridges, address tables are constructed by a learning process. When a data frame is received, the source address is recorded. In bridges, the process of forwarding some frames and discarding some frames is known as *filtering.* In addition to using destination addresses for filtering, additional criteria can be used for controlling the network traffic.

Topology data between bridges are exchanged with the help of bridge protocol data units (BPDUs). These BPDUs are encapsulated within LLC frames, as shown in Figure 11.15. To identify the frames carrying BPDUs, the following addresses are used:

- Source and destination address fields have a group address of X "01-80-C2-00-00-10".
- SSAP and DSAP have values of B "0100 0011".

Source routing bridge. IBM LAN products use source routing. It is described in ISO 10038 Amendment 2 (DAM 2). In source routing, all bridges and rings are numbered. The sender enters the routing path in a frame while transmitting the frame. Routing information is car-

Octets	8	1	6	6	2	1	1	2	N	4
	Preamble	SFD	DA	SA	LEN	DSAP	SSAP	LLC	BPDU	FCS

LLC Frame for BPDU (802.1D)

Octets	1	1	1	2 or 6	2 or 6	2-30	N	4	1	1
	Start Delimiter	Access Control	Frame Control	Destination Address	Source Address	RI	DATA	FCS	ED	Frame Status

Source Routing Information Frame

SFD - Start Frame Delimiter
DA - Destination Address
SA - Source Address
LEN - Length
DSAP - Destination Service Access Point
SSAP - Source Service Access Point
LLC - Logical Link Control
FCS - Frame Check Sequence
BPDU - Bridge Protocol Data Unit
RI - Routing Information
ED - End Delimiter

Figure 11.15 Bridge frames.

ried in the routing information (RI) field. The information field comprises the RI field and DATA field, as shown in Figure 11.15. Route discovery for transmitting frames involves two stages. In the first stage, a source station sends a TEST or an IEEE 802.2 XID command with the destination address and no routing information. If the destination is within a ring, then the destination sends a response. However, if the response is not received within a specified time, then it is assumed that the destination station is in another ring. To discover the routing for stations outside a ring, all-routes broadcast or single-route broadcast is used.

In all-routes broadcast, in each bridge, frames are broadcast by all possible routes. As a result, a destination may have one or more routes from a source. The destination station, in turn, sends frames back on all possible routes. The source station selects the best route for transmitting data to a destination station.

To reduce the traffic involved in the route discovery process, single-route broadcast is used. Here, a source sends a frame in a particular designated route and the destination station sends data via all the routes possible. The sending station, depending upon the routing policy, will decide the best route.

Transparent and source routing bridges have their own advantages. In source routing, bridges have limited functions and the sending station must figure out the route to the destination. It has the advantage of allowing parallel and alternate paths. However, the route discovery process is more complex because of the broadcast involved. In transparent bridges, to avoid loops, alternate and parallel paths are not allowed. The routes can be dynamically learned, adding flexibility to the routing.

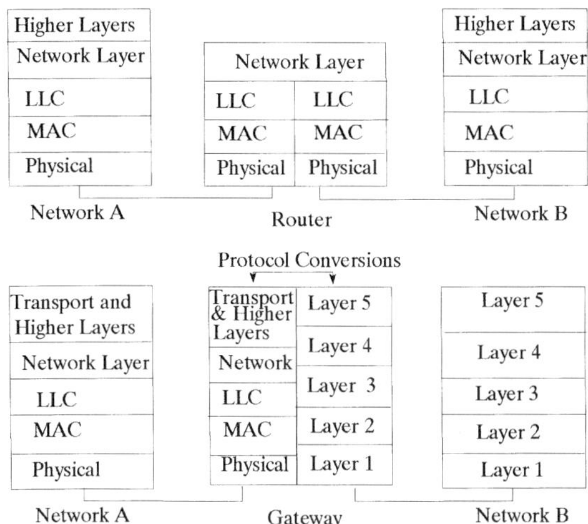

Figure 11.16 Routers and gateways.

11.6.3 Routers

The network layer has the routing information. When different protocols are used or MAC layer addresses are not uniform, then routers can be used to connect different segments or networks (Figure 11.16). In a router, protocol conversion is made and the network address and network control are retained.

Network protocols and routing protocols are used by routers to recognize the addresses. In network protocols, intermediate systems and end stations use these addresses for routing. Whereas in routing protocols, intermediate systems and, occasionally, end stations use these addresses to gather routing information.

Some of the popular network protocols are:

Internet Protocols (IP): A connectionless datagram service, discussed in detail in Chapter 7.

Internet Packet Exchange (IPX): A connectionless datagram service used in Novell and similar to Xerox Network Systems (XNS).

ISO 8473 Protocol: Supports connectionless network service. In some cases, it may be necessary to provide connection-oriented data service in higher layers.

Some of the popular routing protocols are:

Routing Information Protocol (RIP): Developed as a part of XNS. Here, routers broadcast routing information at regular intervals to the connected neighbors, and the end stations listen to the broadcasts. The routing information is regularly updated by the end stations and routers, based on these broadcasts. RIP is also used in Internet and it is furnished by RFC 1058 (see Reference 11.5). Note that RFC 1723 updates RFC 1058.

ISO 10589: Used to exchange routing information between routers.

ISO 9542: For exchanging routing information between intermediate systems and end stations.

Open Shortest Path First (*OSPF*): Promoted as a routing protocol by the Internet community. Its details are furnished in RFC 1583 (see Reference 11.6). The routing can be done using a hierarchical structure, which is useful for large networks. Also, to reduce network traffic, routing updates are sent only when there are changes. The routing table updates are sent in intervals of 30 minutes.

In routers, we have the additional responsibility of understanding network layers. A router must recognize network layer addresses. It translates network layer addresses to the proper addresses of networks and required workstations. Routers must also understand the protocols used in different segments. Some router implementations support subnet addressing and proxy ARP. These terms were explained in detail in Chapter 7.

11.6.4 Gateways

In bridges and routers, it is assumed that the layers above the data link or network layers are compatible. However, there can be cases where there is a incompatibility in different layers up to the application layers. In such cases, for complete protocol conversions, gateways are used (see Figure 11.16). Here, protocols on one side of a network are converted to protocols on the other side of the network. The protocols on either side are normally dissimilar. Though the bridges and routers have various standards, standards have not been developed for gateways.

11.7 Summary

In this chapter, we briefly examined different aspects of LANs. Starting with LAN topology, we discussed the different layers of LANs. LAN protocols such as CSMA/CD, token bus, and token ring are very important for a discussion on network management, so we examined these. Because connectivity is an important topic in the LAN area, repeaters, bridges, routers, and gateways were discussed.

This chapter will form the basis for our discussion on layer management for LANs in the next chapter.

11.8 References

11.1 ANSI/IEEE Standard 802-1990, Standard for Local and Metropolitan Area Networks: Overview and Architecture, Institute of Electrical and Electronic Engineers, Inc., 1990.

11.2 IEEE Standard 802.10-1992, Standard for Local and Metropolitan Area Networks: Interoperable LAN/MAN Security (SILS), Institute of Electrical and Electronic Engineers, Inc., 1992.

11.3 IEEE 802.6, LANs: Distributed Queue Dual Bus Subnetwork (MANs), Institute of Electrical and Electronic Engineers, Inc., 1990.

11.4 ANSI/IEEE Standard 802.1D-1993 (ISO 10038-1993), Standard for Local and Metropolitan Area Networks: MAC Bridges, Institute of Electrical and Electronic Engineers, Inc., 1993.

11.5 Hedrick, C., Routing Information Protocol (RIP), RFC 1058, 1988. RFC 1058 has been updated by RFC 1388 and obsoleted by RFC 1723, Malkin, G., RIP Version 2 Carrying Additional Information, 1994.

11.6 Moy, J., OSPF version 2, RFC 1583, 1994.

11.9 Further Reading

ANSI/IEEE 802.2 (ISO 8802.2), LANs: Logical Link Control, Institute of Electrical and Electronic Engineers, Inc., 1989.

ANSI/IEEE 802.3 (ISO 8802.3), LANs: CSMA/CD Access Method, Institute of Electrical and Electronic Engineers, Inc., 1993.

ANSI/IEEE 802.4 (ISO 8802.4), LANs: Token-Passing Bus Access Method, Institute of Electrical and Electronic Engineers, Inc., 1990.

ANSI/IEEE 802.5 (ISO 8802.5), LANs: Token Ring Access Method (ISO/IEC 8802.5), Institute of Electrical and Electronic Engineers, Inc., 1992.

ANSI/IEEE 802.7, LANs: Broadband LAN, Institute of Electrical and Electronic Engineers, Inc., 1990.

Held, G., *Token-Ring Networks, Characteristics, Operation, Construction and Management,* New York: John Wiley, 1994.

ISO 8473, Information Processing Systems, Data Communications, Protocol for Providing the Connectionless-mode Network Service, 1988.

ISO DIS 9542, Information Technology, End System to Intermediate System Routing Information Exchange Protocol for Use in Conjunction with the Protocol for Providing the Connectionless-mode Network Service, 1994.

ISO 10038 DAM 2, Information Processing Systems, Local Area Networks, MAC Sublayer Interconnection, Amendment 2, MAC Bridging, Source Routing Supplement, 1992.

ISO 10589, Information Technology, Telecommunications and Information Exchange Between Systems Intermediate System (IS) to IS Intra-Domain Routing Information Exchange Protocol for Use in Conjunction with the Protocol for Providing the Connectionless-mode Network Service (ISO 8473), 1992.

Kessler, G., and D. Train, *Metropolitan Area Networks: Concepts, Standards, and Services,* New York, McGraw-Hill, 1992.

Muller, Nathan J., *Intelligent Hubs,* Norwood, Mass.: Artech House, 1993.

Perlman, R., *Interconnections, Bridges and Routers,* Reading, Mass.: Addison-Wesley, 1992.

Romkey, J., Nonstandard for Transmission of IP Datagrams over Serial Lines: SLIP, RFC 1055, 1988.

Simpson, W., The Point-to-Point Protocol (PPP), RFC 1548, 1993. RFC 1548 has been obsoleted by RFC 1661, Simpson, W. (edited), The Point-to-Point Protocol, 1994.

Stallings, W., *Advances in Local and Metropolitan Area Technology,* Los Alamitos, Calif.: IEEE Computer Society Press, 1993.

Stallings, W., *Handbook of Computer-Communication Standards: Volume II, Local Area Network Standards,* New York: Macmillan, 1990.

Stallings, W., *Local and Metropolitan Area Networks,* 4th ed., New York: Macmillan, 1993.

Chapter

12

IEEE Network Management of LANs and MANs

12.1 Introduction

In this chapter, the different IEEE network management protocols used in LANs and MANs will be discussed. IEEE standards are complementary to the standards developed by the ISO, and some of the IEEE 802 standards have been adopted by the ISO, as we have seen in the previous chapter. The IEEE 802.1 committee is assigned the responsibility of network management standards for the LLC, MAC, and physical layers (Figure 12.1). For each layer, the IEEE has developed standards for layer management; work on some of them is ongoing. Note that revision to the management portion of IEEE Standard 802-1990 is in process at press time. In addition, separate sections are devoted to management in each of the IEEE 802 standards, such as CSMA/CD and DQDB provided in IEEE 802.6.

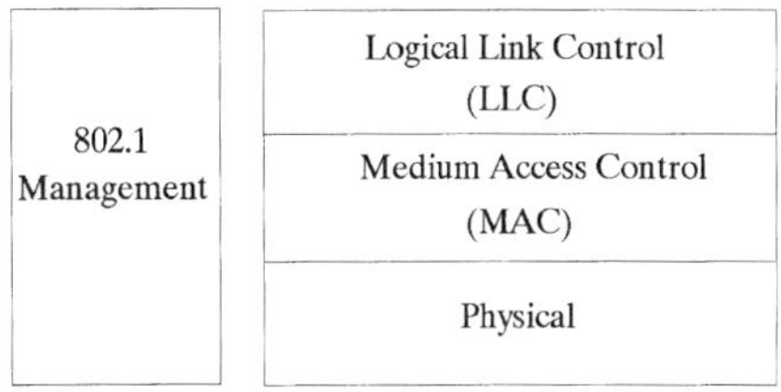

Figure 12.1 Scope of IEEE network management.

12.2 IEEE Layer Management

Chapter 2 of this book indicated that ISO standardization work does not cover layer management, which is provided to manage the objects in each layer. Layer management of one layer is independent of that provided by other layers, and in each layer it is performed by a layer management *managed object.* In earlier IEEE standard documents, this layer management managed object was known as the *layer management entity* (LME). The layer management managed object has the following responsibilities:

- It manages objects within a layer, and provides controlling and monitoring functions within a layer. For example, if a systems management function such as performance management wants to gather statistics on the number of collisions in CSMA/CD, performance management does the collection of statistics via the layer management managed object.
- A *network management process* (NMP), which can be a manager or an agent, interfaces with a layer management managed object using the interface provided by the *managed object boundary.* In earlier IEEE documents, this managed object boundary interface (see Figure 12.2) was known as the *layer management interface* (LMI). The NMP exercises control over a layer using the management managed object. Again using the example of performance management, if there is a need to reset the number of collisions counter, it is done with the aid of a management managed object.

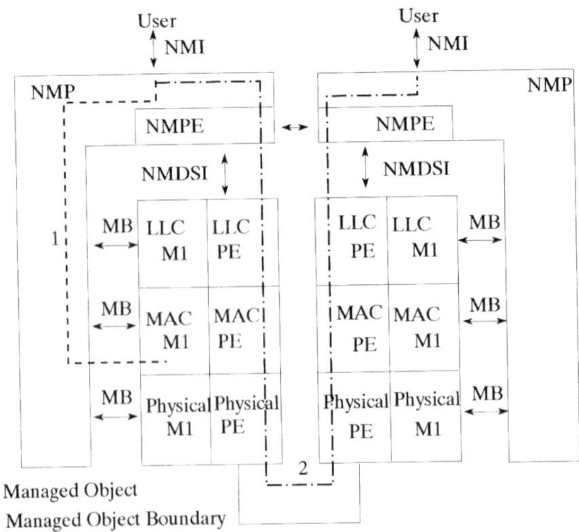

Figure 12.2 IEEE layer management. (*Source: Modified with permission from* Network Management Standards *by Uyless Black, copyright © 1992, published by McGraw-Hill.)*

The changes in terminology (*LME* becomes *managed object* and *LMI* becomes *managed object boundary*) are intended to make the definitions more generic, making it easier to relate IEEE protocols to TCP/IP as well as to OSI.

In addition to the layer management managed object, each layer has a *protocol entity* (PE), which provides the needed functions of a layer. Different functions of a layer are standardized by the IEEE. Basically, there are three aspects of network management as it relates to the components connected with LANs, MANs, and WANs:

- *Local management within a node:* This is not standardized by the OSI. The IEEE has provided standards for this function. For example, a user of network management functions interfaces to the NMP using the network management interface (NMI). Within an NMP, it is decided which managed object for a layer can provide the management functions, and NMP routes the user request to the appropriate managed object, with the help of the managed object boundary, as shown by flow 1 in Figure 12.2.
- *Remote management:* For a network management user wishing to manage a layer management managed object in a remote node, the NMP uses the NMI interface as in the case of local management within a node. Here, the NMP determines that this management operation request is intended for a remote layer management managed object. The NMP uses the help of the *network management protocol entity* (NMPE), which transforms the request to a *network management data service interface* (NMDSI) NMDS-DATA.request. This PDU goes all the way down the LLC, MAC, and physical PEs. On the receiving side, it traverses all the way up to the NMPE residing in the NMP at the remote node. Here also, it is the NMP which routes the PDU to the appropriate layer management managed object using the managed object boundary. This flow (2) is shown in Figure 12.2.
- *Network management:* Overall network management is provided using cooperative arrangements between manager and agents, and they are governed by OSI standards, TCP/IP, or any other appropriate protocols.

12.3 Layer Management Service Definitions

12.3.1 Primitive types

The IEEE has furnished service definitions for the NMI, managed object boundary, and NMDSI interfaces. The NMI and managed object boundary use primitive types, which are slightly different from the OSI primitive types discussed in Section 2.2.1. The primitive types are:

- *Invoke:* Used to request that a certain service be performed on behalf of the invoker of a service. This is analogous to a request. The Invoke primitive is used by the user of an NMP to request a service from the NMP or by *an* NMP to request a service from a layer management managed object.
- *Reply:* Furnishes the results of a service request. A layer management managed object or an NMP furnishes the Reply to an Invoke from an NMP or a user of an NMP, respectively.
- *Notify:* Identical to a Notification in OSI and the result of an event in a management managed object or an NMP. It is forwarded from a layer management managed object to an NMP or from an NMP to the user of an NMP.

12.3.2 Service primitives

The management operations of a layer are similar to those of CMISE services in OSI. They are:

- *GET:* Used to retrieve the value of a given attribute of an object.
- *SET:* Can be used to set the value of an attribute to the one furnished along with the SET.
- *ACTION:* Used to force the state of an object to a particular state or to initiate a sequence of operations on an object.
- *COMPARE-AND-SET:* A new management operation not seen in OSI. As the name suggests, this operation facilitates comparing the value of an attribute to the furnished value. If it matches, then the value of the attribute is set to a new value which is furnished as a parameter of COMPARE-AND-SET.
- *EVENT:* Similar to a Notification in OSI. It is triggered when something unusual happens. EVENT is sent by a layer management managed object either to an NMP or by an NMP to the user of an NMP.
- *TRACE:* Used primarily to report the activities of a remote station. When an NMP in a remote station receives a TRACE Invoke, the remote NMP sends a response in the form of a TRACE Reply. This TRACE Reply contains information about the NMP and the activities performed by it. If a remote NMP has problems, this is the best way to get information on the problems.

NMI service primitives are meant to access and manipulate objects in a layer. They vary according to the interface used. NMI service primitives are:

- NM-SET-VALUE Invoke
- NM-SET-VALUE Reply
- NM-COMPARE-AND-SET-VALUE Invoke
- NM-COMPARE-AND-SET-VALUE Reply
- NM-GET-VALUE Invoke
- NM-GET-VALUE Reply
- NM-ACTION Invoke
- NM-ACTION Reply
- NM-EVENT Notify
- NM-TRACE Invoke
- NM-TRACE Reply

12.3.3 Parameters of NMI service primitives

Parameters used by NMI service primitives are:

- Exchange-Identifier
- Resource-Identifier
- Resource-Required-Flag
- Source-Address
- Destination-Address
- Access-Control-Information
- Actual-Quality-of-Service
- Parameter-List
- Action-List
- Action-Result-List
- Event-Identifier
- Event-Values
- Report-Address
- Trace-Operator-List
- Trace-Report

- Operation-Status

12.3.4 LAN managed object boundary service primitives

The IEEE service primitives used by managed object boundary services are the same as the ones used by the NMI except that the prefix "LM" is used instead of "NM," and NM-TRACE.invoke and NM-TRACE.reply are absent. TRACE is not noticed in the managed object boundary, because the interface is between a managed object and an NMP in the same node.

Parameters of managed object boundary service primitives are:

- Parameter-Identifier
- Parameter-Value
- Test-Parameter-Identifier
- Test-Parameter-Value
- Access-Classes
- Status

12.3.5 NMDSI service primitives

The NMDSI interface is quite simple and uses only NMDS-DATA.request and NMDS-DATA.indication as service primitives.

Parameters of the NMDSI service primitives are:

- Source-Address
- Destination-Address
- Priority-Field

In addition to these service primitives, there is a Load management operation. This is particularly useful to transfer machine code from a server to a LAN station. The LOAD operation is governed by the IEEE System Load Protocol (see IEEE 802.1E, Reference 12.1).

12.3.6 Management PDUs

Management PDUs are used for the exchange of management information between NMPs. Here, the roles of the NMPs can be those of a manager and an agent or a manager and another manager. The exchange of management information can take the following forms:

- *Load:* Used for transferring machine code from one station to another station in a network.

- *Request and Response:* Exchanges take place between a manager and agents.
- *Event:* An unsolicited notification from an agent to a manager.
- *Trace:* Useful when there are problems in one of the agents. Trace can be requested by a manager to identify the problems in one or more agents or managers.
- *Private:* Not defined in standards, and can be used for specific proprietary protocols.

PDUs used for the exchange of information between a manager and agents are:

- LoadPDU
- RequestPDU
- ResponsePDU
- EventPDU
- EventACKPDU
- TraceRQPDU
- TraceRSPDU
- PrivatePDU

12.4 IEEE LAN and MAN Management

The first question that comes to mind is: Why do we need separate management protocols for LANs and MANS, when we already have OSI systems management protocols such as CMIP? The OSI systems management is an application-layer function. This assumes that there are six other layers of OSI below the application layer to support systems management. However, sometimes in a LAN environment, it is not possible to support the other six OSI layers. There may be memory constraints or other constraints. For this reason, the IEEE 802.1 B LAN/MAN management standards have been developed to provide "skinny" network management functions for LAN and MAN environments. IEEE LAN/MAN management has the following limitations:

- It does not have the capability to undertake segmentation and reassembly of management PDUs.
- It has no network support for routing; hence, LAN/MAN management is limited to a subnetwork.

LAN/MAN management can be used to manage devices in the physical and data link layers of the OSI. In addition, where it is not possible to have all six layers, such as at the time of initialization, IEEE 802.1 standards can be used. The protocol whereby CMIP is carried over logical link control is known as *CMIP over LLC* (CMOL). Peer protocols are used, meaning that either a manager or an agent can initiate these services.

12.4.1 IEEE LAN/MAN management architecture

LAN/MAN management service (LMMS) defines the services that are available to a *LAN/MAN management user* (LMMU). LMMS makes use of the service primitives defined for CMIS (Section 4.6). A protocol entity is needed to provide the LMMS services and the *LAN/MAN management protocol entity* (LMMPE) fills this gap. The management protocol exchanged between two peer LMMPEs is known as the *LAN/MAN management protocol* (LMMP), and the PDU used by the LMMPEs for the exchange of management information is referred to as LMM_PDU. A comparison of the OSI data link and physical layers with the LMMP is shown in Figure 12.3. A key point is that the LMMP does not use the P-DATA services of the presentation layer and other lower layers.

A manager is the user of an LMMPE. The LMMPE converts the commands from a manager to the CMIP protocol data units (CPDUs) with suitable packaging and header information. A manager, also referred to as a *managing process,* provides commands to manipulate the managed objects and sometimes receives the Event Reports emitted by managed objects. A manager may be in a remote workstation and may wish to know the management information from the managed objects (Figure 12.4). LAN/MAN resources are represented as managed object classes. Managed objects contain the information required for management and these data may be stored in an optional MIB.

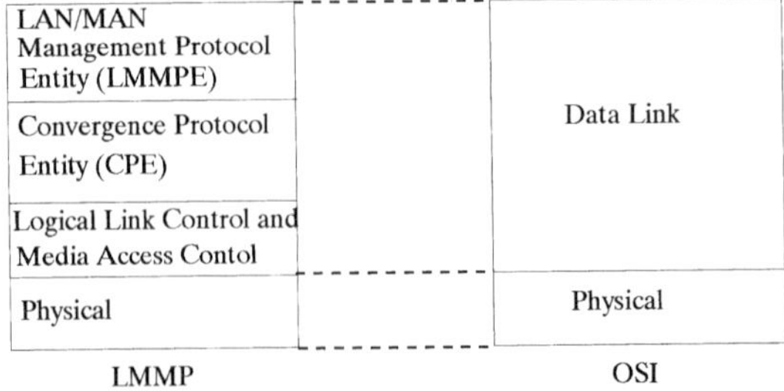

Figure 12.3 LAN/MAN management protocol layers.

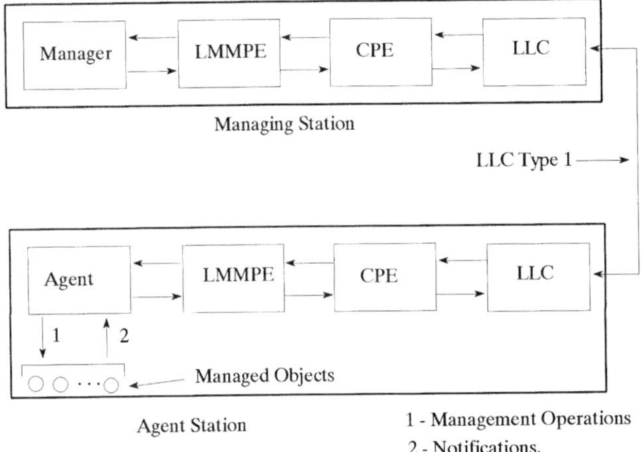

Figure 12.4 LAN/MAN management information exchanges.

There is a key difference between LMMS services and CMIS services. LMMS uses connectionless-mode services. As a result, explicit associations are not formed before the transfer of management information or release of associations. Hence, ACSE services are not required.

12.4.2 CPE functions

The convergence protocol entity (CPE) layer is responsible for providing reliability and maintaining logical association between LMMUs. The CPE layer is provided over the LLC type 1 and is concerned with the management aspects of a LAN/MAN workstation. As data is being transferred over the connectionless LLC type 1 service, the CPE may use the reliability provided by the LLC type 1 procedures. This is known as *basic* reliability.

On the other hand, a CPE may provide its own timeouts and retries. For example, when a command is sent from the CPE, it may be better to start a timer. If the timer expires, then it indicates that the data transferred might not have been received by the agent or that the underlying communication mechanism has broken down. In this case, it is necessary to know the retries that must be done. These services may be provided by the CPE. This is known as *enhanced* reliability.

The CPE may provide services to handle data being received or commands being sent, because of the possibility of data being received out of sequence, the ordering of data according to time (temporal ordering), or the loss of information.

However, when a large frame is received from an LMMPE, it is not broken into smaller frames (segmentation is not done). If a segmentation facility is provided, it is necessary to assemble the frames to recover the original frame. This inverse operation is known as *reassembly*. Because segmentation is not provided, naturally, reassembly is not provided. Besides, since the objective is to have as small a subset of functions as possible, it is logical that segmentation and reassembly are not provided in our "skinny" CPE.

From this, it is evident that the CPE provides many functions needed for the reliable exchange of management information between a manager and agents. In a way, it is a substitute for the many upper layers of the OSI.

12.4.3 CPE services

Two CPE instances can communicate only when they have enough knowledge or *awareness* of each other. Such a relationship between two CPE instances is known as *affiliation,* and the minimum requirement is that each CPE know the instance identifier of the other. These CPE instances are known as *affiliates.* For example, if A and B are two communicating CPE instances, then B is known as an affiliate of A. There are three possible types of affiliates. If a new relationship is established by A with C, then C is a *new affiliate* and B is now known as the *old affiliate.* Suppose A and B were communicating, and an entirely new CPE instance D has been created. In this case, D becomes the *changed affiliate.* Because affiliation provides awareness of the peer CPE, ACSE services are not required.

When sending data from one LMMPE, an LMMPE uses the CPE-Data.request primitive. After sending the CPE-Data.request to a peer CPE, the reply is received in the form of a CPE-Data.indication. The parameters of CPE-Data are:

- *Destination Address:* The address of the CPE which must receive the CPE User Information.
- *Source Address:* The originating CPE's address, provided by the requesting peer.
- *Quality of Service* (*QOS*): Parameters of Priority and Reliability refer to how User Information must be handled. Priority indicates the priority for sending User Information. There are basic and enhanced reliability services provided by the CPE. Basic reliability means the use of LLC type 1 procedures without retries and timeouts; whereas, with enhanced reliability, retries and timeouts are used for recovery purposes.

- *Status:* Refers to the status of the CPE from which CPE-Data.request was sent. The three values for Status are new affiliate, old affiliate, and changed affiliate.
- *User Information:* Contains the LMM_PDU which must be sent to the other end.

The LMMPE is the service user of the CPE (Figure 12.4), which, in turn, tries to package data according to its convention and pass the data to the LLC below. A failure in the lower layers or in communication services is possible. It is equally likely that the receiving side or the agent, as used in our example, is not able to comply with the CPE-Data.request. In this case, CPE-Abort.indication is used to inform the user above that the LMMPE is not able to comply with its request to pass the information to its peer LMMPE.

The parameters of CPE-Abort.indication are:

- *Reason:* States whether a failure was due to the timeout of the timer set in the CPE, resource limitation, or failure of the underlying services.
- *User Information:* When there is a failure, this provides the details of the information of the requesting CPE user.

One CPE communicates with another CPE through a *CPE identifier.* This is necessary to identify the remote CPE with which one CPE communicates, because there are many possible CPEs in a network. However, over time, the two CPEs may change their affiliations or the addresses which were used for communicating. For reporting the change of address of an affiliate, CPE-Status.indication is used to inform the LMMPE above about the changed address.

Parameters of CPE-Status.indication are:

- *CPE Identifier:* When an affiliation changes, the reporting CPE enters its identifier in this parameter. For example, affiliate C was the earlier CPE instance identifier, and it is now changed to D. If C is reporting the change of status via CPE-Status.indication, the CPE Identifier parameter indicates D.
- *Status:* Has the value that it is a changed affiliate.

12.4.4 LMMS services

As seen in Section 4.9, management operations can be performed on the attributes of managed objects or on the managed objects themselves. Attribute-related operations are Get Attribute Value, Replace

Attribute Value, Replace Default Value, Add a Member, and Remove a Member. Managed objects–related management operations are Create an Object Instance, Delete an Object Instance, and Action. A Notification emitted by a managed object can be related either to an attribute or a managed object.

LMMS services can be used by a manager to perform management operations or by an agent to send a Notification on a managed object. Note that there is a one-to-one correspondence between CMIS and LMMS services. However, LMMS may use the ROSE Operation Class 2, which is asynchronous. Recall that in asynchronous operations there is no need to wait for replies, and one can continue transmitting commands. LMMS may also use the ROSE Operation Class 1 services. This is a synchronous operation which states that before the next command is sent, the reply for the first command must be received. Synchronous operation is a more orderly process than asynchronous operation.

As mentioned earlier, LMMS does not use the association services; instead, the association is performed by having awareness in both the provider and the user. The CPE instance identifier is unique across the system and can be syntactically defined as:

CPE instance identifier ::= {<CPE address>,<CPE instance number>}

The CPE address refers to the LSAP address. The CPE instance number is unique across a CPE address and is an arbitrary integer determined when instantiating a CPE. This may be done when rebooting the system or during initialization.

12.4.5 Functioning of the CPE

The CPE receives a CPDU from the user, which is then mapped to the LLC type 1 data units DL-UNITDATA.request to be sent across the wires. Usually in these primitives, the header information is found with the addresses of sources and the destination CPEs. Because there can be different kinds of data that may be sent in DL-UNITDATA, the management information must be identified, so the address type bit of the DSAP address is set to 0 and the DSAP and SSAP are both set to the bit patterns 1000000.

The data parameter of DL-UNITDATA contains the CPDU received from the user of the CPE. There is a priority parameter to indicate the priority with which the DL-UNITDATA must be sent. LLC type 1 restrictions, such as the maximum CPDU, must be taken into consideration when implementing this management function; then this DL-UNITDATA is sent across the wires. All of these functions can be packaged in one workstation. The data being sent is usually in a remote workstation, where the agents and the managed objects reside. Note that the manager and agent are not set roles; an agent can also act as a manager under some circumstances. In some cases, the agent itself may act as a manager of remote stations.

On the other end, a workstation may have LLC type 1, CPE, LMMPE, and agent services (see Figure 12.4). Data received across the wires undergo the reverse operation on the other end, and the command is received as an indication by the agent, which then sends these requests to the concerned managed object or objects. The results are then sent all the way back to the manager.

12.5 Managed Object Classes for LAN/MAN Management

Managed object classes for LAN/MAN management are defined in IEEE 802.1B (Reference 12.2) and IEEE 802.1F (see Reference 12.3). In 802.1B, the managed object classes defined are specifically for use with the LMMP and CPE. In addition to these, some common managed object classes that can be used along with the 802 standards have been defined in 802.1F. Managed object classes in IEEE 802.1B and 802.1F follow the guidelines provided in ISO 10165 SMI standards (see References 12.4–12.7).

12.5.1 Managed object classes defined in 802.1B

Managed object classes (Figure 12.5) have been defined for LAN/MAN management and are subordinate classes of the managed object class *top*. It is interesting to note that the two managed object classes, oNotificationTypeTableEntry and oEventReport DestinationTableEntry, are used for Event Reports. Details of the managed object classes are as follows:

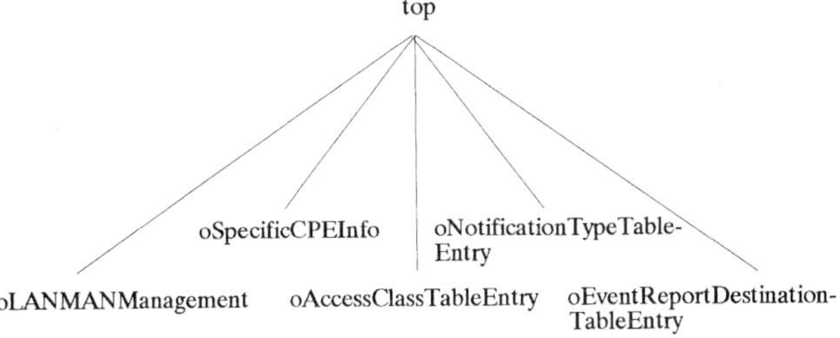

Figure 12.5 LAN/MAN management managed object classes (IEEE 802.1B).

- *oLANMANManagement (mandatory)*: A managed object class carries information on the CPE timer and retry limit. oLANMANManagement has two attributes: aLMMName and aDefault CPEInfo. aLMMName carries a fixed identifier with a value of LMM and has the name of the LAN/MAN managed object instance within the systems managed object. Though the RDN of LMM is fixed as "LMM," the DN will provide a unique name because the name of the systems managed object is not unique. aDefault-CPEInfo has the default values for CPE timeout and retry.
- *oResourceTypeId (mandatory)*: This managed object class is explained in Section 12.5.2.
- *oSpecificCPEInfo (optional)*: This has the default CPE timeout and retry values in the oLANMANManagement managed object class. These values can be overridden using the oSpecificCPEInfo managed object class. There can be zero or more instances of oSpecificCPEInfo within an instance of the oLANMANManagement managed object class. This object has two attributes: aCPEAddress and aDefaultCPEInfo. aCPEAddress refers to the LSAP address of a remote CPE. aDefaultCPEInfo will indicate the timeout and retry values which will override the values provided in the aDefaultCPEInfo attribute of the oLANMANManagement managed object class instance.
- *oAccessClassTableEntry (optional)*: An instance of an AccessClassTableEntry managed object class is an entry in the access class table (ACT). In the access class table, oAccessClassTableEntry represents a row. Five attributes of oAccessClassTableEntry are aAccessClassTableEntryName, aManagedObjectClasses, aPassword, aLocalAccessClasses, and aRemoteAccessClasses. The ACT has a list of managed object classes and has access rights to them by local and remote managers. The ACT is discussed in detail in Section 12.10.
- *oNotificationTypeTableEntry (optional)*: An instance of oNotificationTypeTableEntry has a list of notification types, the managed object classes, and the destinations to which the event reports must be sent. Again, each instance represents an entry in the notification type table. Attributes of the oNotificationTypeTableEntry managed object class are aNotificationTypeTableEntryName, aNotificationTypes, and aEventReportDestinations. Each attribute represents a column in the notification type table.

  The notification type table has the following columns:

  1. *Notification type table entry name:* Has the object identifiers of the managed object classes in the first entry.

2. *Notification types:* Identifies the notification types which are emitted by the managed objects. An example of a notification type is a notification sent when a counter threshold for collisions reaches a certain limit.
3. *Pointer to event report destination table:* Has a pointer to one or more entries in the event report destination table. Also, if the field is empty, then corresponding managed object class instances do not send Event Reports, because there is no pointer to the event report destination table.

- *oEventReportDestinationTableEntry (optional)*: One instance of this managed object class represents an entry of the event report destination table. Attributes of this managed object class are aEventReportDestinationTableEntryName and aEventReport-DestinationAddress. A conditional package of PQOSPackage may be optionally included in this managed object class.

Entries in the event report destination table are:

1. *Destination Index:* Corresponds to the entry number of the event report destination table. Entries in the pointer to event report destination table column of the notification type table and destination index match.
2. *Destination Address:* Identifies the CPE address to which Event Reports must be sent. If the CPE address is NULL, then the destination is the local manager.
3. *Quality of Service:* Refers to the QOS value on how the Event Reports are to be delivered. As seen earlier, QOS can be either basic or enhanced. This entry is part of the conditional package of PQOSPackage.

When a managed object emits a Notification to an agent, then the agent looks at the notification type table. From there it goes to the corresponding entry in the event report destination table and retrieves the CPE address(es), if available, of the manager(s) to whom Event Reports are sent. Event Reports are sent using the QOS furnished in the QOS column of the event report destination table.

12.5.2 Managed object classes defined in 802.1F

The 802.1F standard, known as Common Definitions and Procedures for IEEE 802 Management Information, defines managed object classes (Figure 12.6) which can be used for defining managed objects in LAN/MAN management. Recall that new managed object classes can be defined using the properties of inheritance and polymorphism.

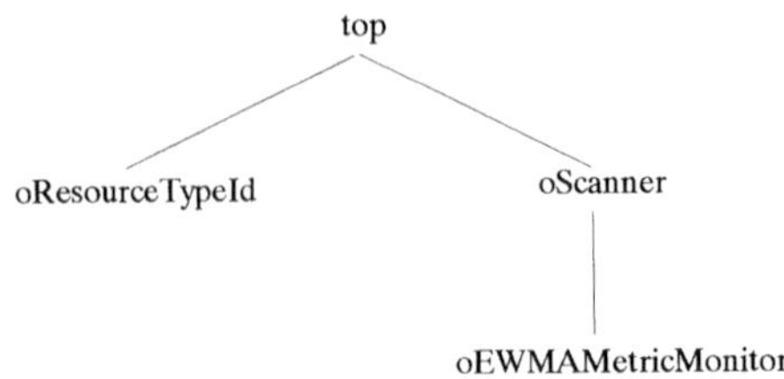

Figure 12.6 IEEE 802.1F managed object classes.

These topics were discussed in Chapter 3. Managed object classes defined in 802.1F are the following.

- *oResourceTypeId*: An instance of this managed object class can be used to contain information on a managed system resource in the LAN/MAN system. Such information may include resource name, manufacturer's name, organizational identifier, version, and any other product information. For inheritance purposes, this is derived from the superclass of top. This managed object class for naming is a subordinate class of system, and, as a result of being defined as such, system, an instance of this managed object class can be contained in any other managed object class representing a resource. oResourceTypeId is quite useful for network management functions such as configuration management, performance management, and fault management. Attributes of oResourceTypeId are read-only, and they include:

  1. *aResourceTypeIdName*: Has "RTID" as the unique name.
  2. *aResourceInfo:* Contains details on product information, which can include ManufacturerOUI, ManufacturerName, ManufacturerProductName, and ManufacturerProductVersion. ManufacturerOUI, represents an organizationally unique identifier.

- *oScanner*: The purpose of using the oScanner managed object class is to derive the oEWMAMetricMonitor managed object. In 802.1F, oScanner has a limited role and is a subset of the Scanner managed object class defined in 10164-13. Scheduling is not supported and there will be a single gauge or a derived gauge in one managed object. Note that the derived-gauge value is obtained by subtracting the successive counter values.

  Also, there is only one conditional package, pConfigurationEventsReporting. This package, as the name suggests, provides the Notifications to be issued for configuration changes such as state changes, changes in attribute values, creating objects, and deleting objects. These Notifications are particularly useful for dynamically updating configurations. We will further examine the Scanner managed object class in Chapter 17.

- *oEWMAMetricMonitor*: EWMA stands for *exponentially weighted moving average*. An oEWMAMetricMonitor managed object monitors the value of an attribute at fixed intervals of time. It may be noted that EWMA gives greater weight to the recent values than to the old values. Monitored value may be a counter or a gauge. If there is a counter difference package, then the monitored value represents a gauge; otherwise, it is a counter. If more than one observation for an attribute must be made, then a separate monitor object is used, and a Notification that a new monitor managed object has been created is sent to the manager. When the counter or gauge value crosses a threshold value, a QOS alarm is sent to the manager.

  The attributes of oEWMAMetricMonitor are:

  1. *aObservedManagedObjectInstance:* Identifies the instance of a managed object containing the attribute being monitored.
  2. *aObservedAttributeIdentifier:* While aObservedManaged ObjectInstance referred to the instance of the managed object, aObservedAttributeIdentifier is for the attribute being monitored.
  3. *aDerivedGauge:* If the counter difference package is present, then the aDerivedGauge value indicates the difference in counter values. Otherwise, this has the latest gauge value of the monitored object.
  4. *aEstimateOfMean:* Contains the estimate of the EWMA mean value.
  5. *aSeverityIndicatingGaugeThreshold:* Provides the threshold value. When the EWMA mean value exceeds the threshold value provided by this attribute, then Notifications are sent to one or more managers.
  6. *aMovingTimePeriod:* Provides the time periods during which an attribute must be monitored.

12.6 LAN and MAN Station Discovery

In a LAN network, stations may come up for reasons such as being installed and powered on or as the result of a change in configuration. Similarly, stations may be powered off because of changing physical locations or failures. In such cases, the network must be able to detect these changes.

Agents manage a set of managed objects. From the management point of view, a manager should know when an agent has come up or gone down or if there is a change in the list of objects managed by the agent. For these purposes, the IEEE has defined a peer protocol, which is known as the *discovery* protocol and is furnished in 802.1k (see Reference 12.8).

Discovery may be initiated by an agent or a manager, depending on the circumstances. There are exchanges between manager and agents when there is a change in configuration or during initialization periods. These exchanges furnish configuration details, which may be stored in databases used for topology.

Discovery services include *Agent Present* and *Manager Present* services. The Agent Present service is used when an agent station comes up; there are changes in the list of managed objects of an agent, or in reply to the Manager Present services. Agent Present can be sent to one or more managers with whom an agent wishes to communicate.

Agent Present has two parameters:

- *Solicited:* Indicates whether an agent is sending the Agent Present on its own or is sending it in response to the Manager Present. When an agent sends an Agent Present on its own, it is known as *unsolicited* and the value is false. When an agent sends the Agent Present in response to a Manager Present, it is known as a *solicited* response and the value is true.
- *Class-Instance List:* Has an unordered list of managed object classes supported by the agent. Each managed object class may have its own unordered list of managed object class instances. However, if Class-Instance List is empty, then it shows only the presence of the agent.

As can be concluded from the name, Manager Present is sent by a managing station to inform one or more managed stations (agents) that the managing station is active and it can manage the managed object classes. Manager Present can be used for checking the configuration of the managed object classes now and then. The list of managed object classes can be changed using this operation. It is an unconfirmed service.

The parameters of Manager Present are:

- *Respond If:* Indicates under what conditions the Agent Present request must be sent by the agent. These conditions are determined by Event Reporting. The Event Reporting service will be discussed in Section 12.7. Agent Present will be sent if Event

Reporting is enabled for one or more managed object classes or instances. Agent Present can also be sent when Event Reporting is disabled for one or more managed object classes. The last alternative is to send the Agent Present request irrespective of the enabling or disabling of Event Reporting.

- *Class-Instance List:* Provides the unordered list of managed object classes. Each managed object class, in turn, may have its own list of unordered managed object class instances. If Class-Instance List is empty, it states that the manager is interested in all the managed object classes and instances of the managed object classes.

Let us examine how Agent Present and Manager Present work. In Figure 12.7, the agent station has its own agent, managed object classes, and object class instances, and the manager is located in the manager station. When a manager wants to inform the agent that it is operational or wants to change the configuration, it sends a Manager Present. This may be sent to one or more agent stations in which a manger is interested (1).

After receiving the Manager Present, one or more agents send the response of Agent Present. As seen earlier, Agent Present can also have its list of managed object classes and instances. Here, the Agent Present is solicited and is sent in response to Manager Present (2). Then if a manager wants to receive Event Reports from managed object classes or instances in the agent station, the manager sends the Event Report Enable to the agent (3). After receiving the Event Report Enable req, the agent sends back the Event Report Enable conf to the managing station (5). This is analogous to informing a manager, “Yes, I have made the necessary arrangements to send Event Reports, if there are any changes to managed object classes or any instances mentioned in the Event Report Enable req.”

Another case of an agent initiating Agent Present is shown in Figure 12.8. Here, one agent wants to send the Agent Present due to

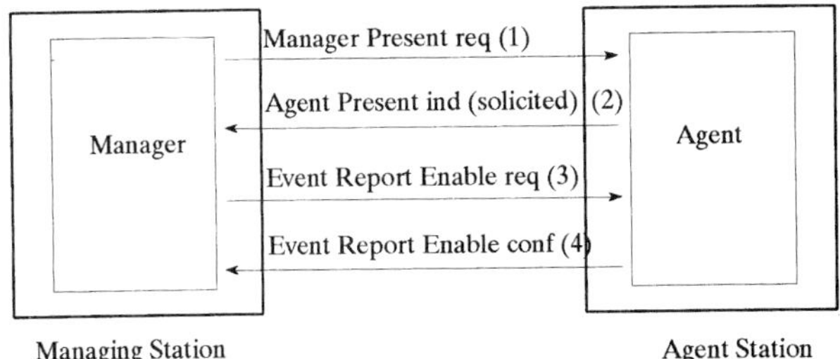

Figure 12.7 LAN/MAN discovery—manager initiated.

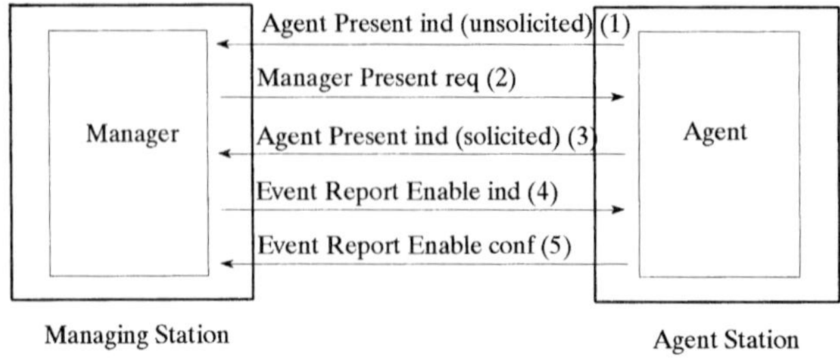

Figure 12.8 LAN/MAN discovery—agent initiated.

changes in the list of managed object classes and instances, so the agent sends the Agent Present to one or more interested managers (1). This is an unsolicited response. In reply, the manager can send a Manager Present to one or more agents (2). The agent or agents, in turn, send the solicited Agent Present ind to the manager (3). In response, one or more managers send the Event Report Enable, which furnishes the list of managed object classes or instances from which a manager is interested in receiving Event Reports (4). As we have seen in the previous case, the agent sends an Event Report Enable conf to the manager (5).

This discovery process may be used to dynamically discover the workstations in a LAN network. By periodically using the discovery process, the topology of a LAN network can be accurately and dynamically determined and stored in a topology database.

12.7 Event Forwarding Enable Service

The Event Forwarding Enable service identifies to the agent managed objects on which Notifications are sent to a manager. As shown in Figure 12.9, a manager sends an Event Forwarding Enable req to the Discovery and Event Forwarding Enable/Disable (DEFED) protocol entity. The DEFED PE converts the Event Forwarding Enable req to M-ACTION.req. The rest of the flow of M-ACTION.req to the agent and then backwards from the agent to the manager is illustrated in Figure 12.9.

Event Forwarding Enable is a confirmed service. This can be used initially when Agent Present is sent from an agent or when a manager wants to change the Event Reports that are reported to it. The basic function of this primitive is to create the entries in the notification type table and event report destination table. These two tables are optional in an agent station. Parameters of an Event Forwarding Enable service request are:

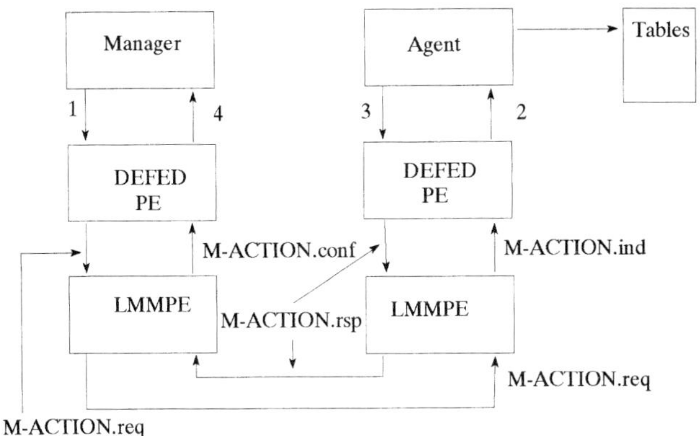

Figure 12.9 Event Forwarding Enable.

- *CPE Retry Timeout:* A QOS parameter. If the CPE Retry Timeout value is furnished, it is to be used in exchanges between a manager and an agent. This applies to Event Reports sent by an agent. If the CPE Retry Timeout value is not furnished, then the value used will be that of LLC type 1.
- *CPE Retry Counter:* Furnished if the CPE Retry Timeout is supplied. If the CPE Retry Counter value is not furnished, then the basic QOS is used.
- *Class-Instance List:* Can have the list of managed object classes, each of which has its own list of object class instances. In this case, Event Reports are sent to one or more managers in this list. If this list is empty, then Event Reports on all the managed objects that report to an agent are sent to a manager. If the instance list is empty, then the Event Reports on all the instances of the list of a managed object class are sent to the manager.

The response to the Event Forwarding Enable service from the agent will have the following parameters:

- *Character Set:* Has the characters that are supported by the agent.
- *Enable Response:* Has two forms. The first is known as the system Enable Response code. It can be Enabled, indicating that all the managed object classes and instances that have been mentioned in the Class-Instance List of the Event Report Enable have been enabled. Another value of a system enable response code can

be Reenabled, indicating that the managed object classes and instances were already enabled for sending Event Reports to the manager. Then it is possible that Access Denied can be used when managed objects cannot be accessed by a manager. If there are too many managers to which Event Reports must be sent, then Enable Response—Too Many Managers can be sent. The other form of Enable Response has a Class-Instance Status List containing instances of a list of managed object classes. Each managed object can have a class Enable Response code, or it can have another Class-Instance List of its own. The class Enable Response code can take similar values such as Enabled, Reenabled, Access Denied, and Too Many Managers. In addition, it has Class Not Supported to indicate which managed object class has not been supported. The forms of the instance Enable Response code are the same as those of the class Enable Response code, except that instead of class, there is an object class instance.

12.8 Event Forwarding Disable Service

The Event Forwarding Disable service can be sent by a manager or an agent. When some managed objects are deleted or are no longer valid, then an agent sends this to inform a manager about the list of managed objects which might have been changed. This is an unconfirmed service; thus, no reply is expected. In Figure 12.10, note that flows 1, 2, 3, and 4 refer to the agent-initiated Event Forwarding Disable, whereas flows 5, 6, 7, and 8 are the result of a manager-initi-

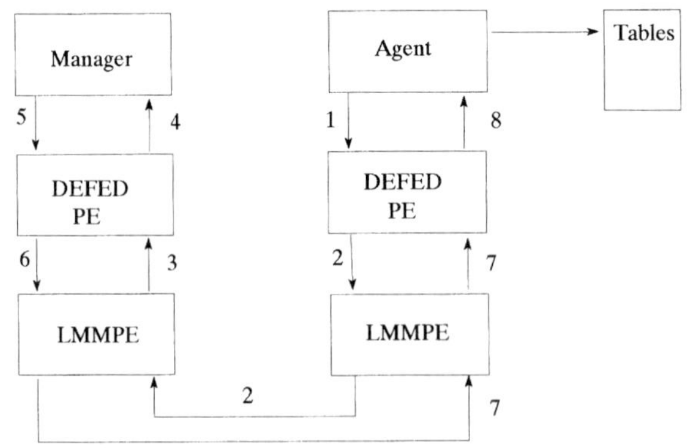

Figure 12.10 Event Forwarding Disable.

ated Event Forwarding Disable. The Event Forwarding Disable service has the following parameters:

- *Originator:* Has the CPE address of the manager or agent which originated the Event Forwarding Disable.
- *Class-Instance List:* Takes a form similar to the ones discussed with the Event Forwarding Enable service.

The effect of Event Forwarding Disable (Figure 12.10) is to change the notification type table and event report destination table entries. As a result of Event Forwarding Disable, the managed object classes and their instance list entries are deleted from these two tables.

12.9 Discovery Event Forwarding Enable/Disable (DEFED) Protocol Machine

DEFED supplements the LMMS services. The protocol used is known as the DEFED protocol and is a peer protocol exchanged between managers and agents. As previously seen, when notification type table and event report destination table entries are changed due to the deletion of managed objects or additions to the table entries, then a manager must be informed of the changes. DEFED services are used to do this. In managers, DEFED is used for manipulating the managed objects, and information on managed objects is carried to the agents via an Event Forwarding Enable request.

For DEFED services, a new managed object class, oDEFED, is defined in the 802.1k standard (see Reference 12.8). When an Agent Present request is submitted to the DEFED protocol entry, it is converted to an M-EVENT-REPORT request by LMMS services (Figure 12.10). When this is received in the manager, the DEFED protocol machine converts it to an Agent Present indication primitive, and an Agent Present indication is issued to the manager.

In a manager, Manager Present and Event Forwarding Enable are provided by the LMMS M-ACTION. LMMS M-ACTION is converted to an M-ACTION request by the DEFED protocol machine on the manager side. On the agent side, these are converted to the Manager Present or Event Forwarding Enable indication. If the mode is confirmed, then the DEFED protocol machine issues an M-ACTION response to the manager side.

12.10 Access Control

Access control provides only for password checking of whether a manager is allowed to access a managed object class or the attributes of the managed object class. In addition to password checking, there can be other security features such as authentication, confidentiality, and integrity of management data. Whenever a managed object class, instance, or attribute must be accessed, then the *access control function* (ACF) is used. It checks the requested services on the managed object class, instance, or attributes for access rights. If permission is granted, then only the requested service is allowed; otherwise, the requested service is rejected.

The ACF has an *access class table* (ACT). Table 12.1 is an example of an ACT. Its first column is the access class table entry name. The ACT entry name contains the instance of the managed object class, AccessClassTableEntry. It is taken as the entry number in the ACT. The next column is the value of the managed object class to which access control information is applicable. If this set has no entries, then the password and the other entries are applicable to all managed objects.

The password column contains the password, which is an OCTET STRING. The set of access classes for a local manager and a remote manager is a series of bit strings which indicate whether, when the password matches, access is to be granted or not. As per the example, managed object class *X* can be accessed by both the local and remote managers if the password matches. However, the managed object *Y* can be accessed by only the local manager; it cannot be accessed by the remote manager because the second bit of B '100000' is zero. Access control information is received using the access control field of the LMMS primitive.

For accessing local objects, access control is implementation-dependent, and standards have not defined it. If no password is supplied, the access is denied and it is treated like a case of an unmatched password. In all cases in which passwords do not match, permission to perform a requested operation is denied.

TABLE 12.1 Example of an Access Class Table

Access class table entry name	Managed object class	Password	Local access classes	Remote access classes
0	*X, Y*	A596B	110100	100000
1	*W*	B7865	100001	110000

12.11 FDDI Network Management

Network management standards for FDDI, Station Management Standard ISO 9314-4, are still in the draft stage, so we will review only their salient points. The station management (SMT) of FDDI has the following functions:

- *Connection management:* Provides services for management of media attachment to a network.
- *Ring management:* Aids in the management of the FDDI ring and keeping the ring operational.
- *SMT peer-to-peer services:* Used for acquiring information about other peer stations.
- *Local node management:* Used for the management of entities associated with different FDDI layers in the same node.

Network management application functions for FDDI can be built on the basis of these station management functions. Managed object classes defined for station management are SMT, MAC, PATH, and PORT. These managed object classes operate under the control of agents. SMT transmits operations, and the managed objects respond and can emit Notifications.

Discovery in FDDI determines the stations in the FDDI ring and is achieved by the neighbor Notification process. At regular time intervals, a station sends the neighbor Notification information frames to its upstream and downstream neighbors, and the neighbors transmit responses back.

12.12 Bridge and Router Management

Note that the discussion in this section is not part of any standards. We have attempted to briefly crystallize some thoughts on this topic. Bridges and routers must be defined as managed object classes. The attributes that must be monitored must also be included in the definition of these managed object classes. Some of the attributes for bridges are:

- Details of the bridge manufacturers, such as versions, addresses, model numbers, and price
- Details of LAN protocols supported, whether they are Ethernet, CSMA/CD, token ring, OSI, or IP
- Bandwidth of networks supported

- Bridging strategies used, such as whether bridges support transparent bridge or source routing
- Status of the bridge, such as whether it is up, down, or in a testing mode
- Number of in frames, that is, the number frames received over a period of time
- Number of frames transmitted, that is, the number of frames that have been delivered to the neighbor
- Number of frames that have been received with errors
- Number of frames that have been discarded by bridges
- Any unknown protocols
- Details of security features provided
- Number of collisions

For routers, more attributes, in addition to the bridges, are required, because they need to be involved in conversions in the network layer. Additional attributes required for routers can include:

- Forwarding of the frames
- Support for fragmentation
- Routing table details and mapping of addresses
- Any unknown protocols

Network management functions for routers and bridges can be done by servers in the client-server model. However, these servers need to be managed in one centralized place.

12.13 Issues in LAN/MAN Network Management

The network management function is for the overall network and must be integrated with the station management functions provided by the FDDI. For example, in Figure 12.11, network A uses Ethernet protocols, networks B and D use token-ring protocols, and network C uses CSMA/CD protocols. In order to be of some meaning and utility, the network management functions of networks A, B, C, and D and rings R1 and R2 must be integrated.

The network management function provided in a manager must have applications such as configuration management, accounting management, performance management, security management, and

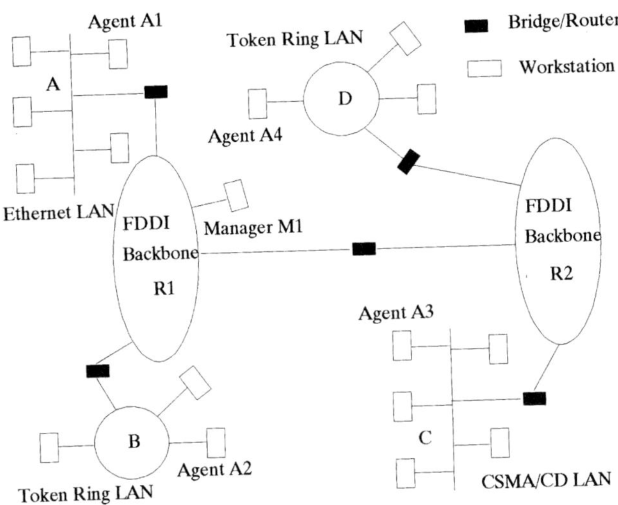

Figure 12.11 LAN/MAN management example—model 1.

fault management. These functions can be offered in stages or in releases.

One of the major problems with such networks is the mix of protocols used. Here, heterogeneous network management is required. In Figure 12.11, networks A, B, C, and D and rings R1 and R2 have different protocols. Some of them may be using different protocols for transport such as TCP/IP, SNA, and IPX/SPX. In addition, it is likely that they may be from different vendors.

Another important consideration is where to place the manager. Should there be managers for each of the networks or one overall manager? If a manager is placed in each network, how do the managers interact with one another? What protocols are used?

The requirements of the networks are very important concerns in the design of the network management functions. Restrictions, such as the speed of networks and the storage capabilities, must be taken into consideration. Some functions, such as configuration management and fault management, may require logging of data that need large storage capacities. Also, network traffic must be considered, since the management functions themselves can generate a considerable amount. In all designs, there should be a certain amount of flexibility to enable future expansions.

The token-ring and Ethernet networks may have to be managed by the manager. Here the management protocol may be CMIP over LLC (CMOL), in which case, there can be agents in all the stations. These agents may communicate with one agent, or this agent can be a proxy agent.

Because OSI SMT standards are in the draft stage, other protocols, such as CMIP or SNMP, can be used for IP-related networks. An alternative is to use SNMP protocols across the FDDI ring and use SNMP through the token-ring and Ethernet stations.

In a similar manner, CMIP may be used in the ring and CMOL may be used in token ring and Ethernet. However, if it is necessary to mix and match network management protocols, then proxy agents will have to be used.

Two models for network management have been provided. In model 1 (Figure 12.11), there is one manager M1 and agents are spread throughout networks A, B, C, and D and rings R1 and R2. Manager M1 is located in ring R1. In this case, proxy agents are used to connect to network A and network B. Proxy agents translate the local protocols to the protocol in ring R1. However, for connecting to ring R2, a router is used. If we use a client-server model, the manager can be in the same workstation as the server, or it may be in an entirely different workstation.

There are certain advantages to this scheme. We can get a total view of the configuration and it will be easier to carry out network management functions, but, network traffic will be higher. If the network is very large, the workload on the workstation that has the manager will be very heavy.

In model 2 (Figure 12.12), networks A, B, C, and D and rings R1 and R2 each have a manager. A skinny CPE can be used for management purposes in networks A, B, C, and D. The protocols followed can be those of the respective networks. But there is one problem with this arrangement: It is tough to get an integrated view of the networks.

To integrate the networks, the managers can become proxy agents, which will translate the data and forward it to one central manager. Another concept has been used in some cases: *manager of managers,* in which one manager becomes a central manager and manages the other managers.

Another question is: When do we collect data from the managers in networks A, B, C, and D? Do we do it periodically or only when there are certain questions relating to the other managers? Answers to these questions change our requirements and designs, which are also dependent on the goals of the network management system.

12.14 Summary

This chapter first examined IEEE layer management, providing details such as the services available and the PDUs supported. IEEE

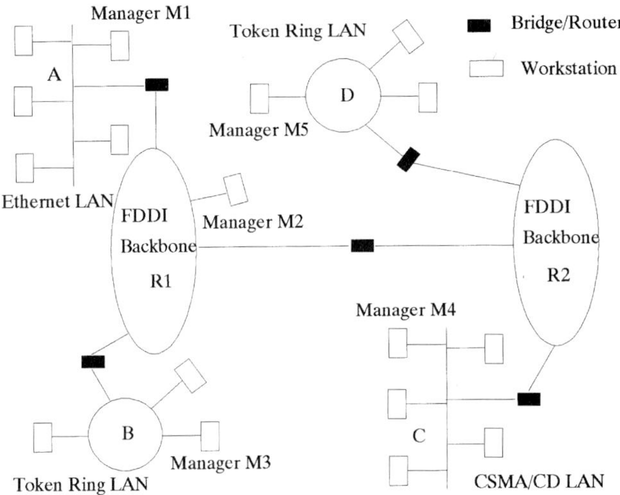

Figure 12.12 LAN/MAN management example—model 2.

LAN/MAN management standards, including LMMP protocols, Event Forwarding Enable, Event Forwarding Disable, the discovery mechanism used in LANs, and Access Control were also discussed. We investigated the different managed object classes defined for LAN/MAN management and peeked into FDDI station management and network management of bridges and routers.

12.15 References

12.1 IEEE 802.1E, LANs: System Load Protocol, Los Alamitos, Calif.: IEEE Computer Society Press, 1990.

12.2 IEEE 802.1B, LANs: LAN/MAN Management, Los Alamitos, Calif.: IEEE Computer Society Press, 1992.

12.3 IEEE 802.1F, LANs: Common Definitions and Procedures for IEEE 802, Los Alamitos, Calif.: IEEE Computer Society Press, 1993.

12.4 ISO 10165-1 (X.720), Information Technology, Open Systems Interconnection, Structure of Management Information, Part 1: Management Information Model, 1991.

12.5 ISO 10165-2 (X.721), Information Technology, Open Systems Interconnection, Structure of Management Information, Part 2: Definition of Management Information, 1991.

12.6 ISO 10165-4 (X.722), Information Technology, Open Systems Interconnection. Structure of Management Information, Part 4: Guidelines for the Definition of Managed Objects, 1992.

12.7 ISO IS 10165-5 (X.723), Information Technology, Open Systems Interconnection, Structure of Management Information, Part 5: Generic Management Information, 1992.

12.8 IEEE 802.1k, Supplement to 802.1B: Dynamic Control of Event Forwarding, Los Alamitos, Calif.: IEEE Computer Society Press, 1993.

12.16 Further Reading

Black, U., *Network Management Standards: The OSI, SNMP, and CMOL Protocols,* McGraw-Hill, New York, 1992.

IEEE 802.3p and q, Supplement to CSMA/CD: GDMO and Layer Management, Los Alamitos, Calif.: IEEE Computer Society Press, 1993.

Stallings, W., Local And Metropolitan Area Networks, 4th ed., New York: Macmillan, 1993.

Stallings, W., Advances in Local and Metropolitan Area Technology, Los Alamitos, Calif.: IEEE Computer Society Press, 1993.

Terplan, K., *Effective Management of Local Area Networks: Functions, Instruments, and People,* New York: McGraw-Hill, 1992.

Part

4

Peer SNA and Systems Management

Chapter

13

Overview of Peer SNA

13.1 Introduction

IBM data communication architectures and products cover a wide spectrum and have been evolving for over 20 years. To limit the treatment of the vast area of *System Network Architecture* (SNA), our focus in this chapter will be on its basic principles and the latest IBM peer-to-peer communication. For more details, readers should consult the materials cited in the Reference and Further Reading at the end of the chapter.

13.2 SNA Basic Concepts

13.2.1 Architecture

SNA was announced in 1974, and has become a popular architecture with many implementations around the world. In its early days, SNA was hierarchical in nature with the host controlling the whole network. This was a hostcentric view, as shown in Figure 1.5.

SNA architecture has been continually improving to meet the changes and trends in the computing industry. Present SNA architecture has seven layers, as shown in Figure 13.1. The functions of each layer are:

- *Transaction services:* Primarily responsible for providing distributed computing and services. This layer has been added to provide peer-to-peer communication.
- *Presentation services:* Facilitates the formatting of data when required, and is useful for program-to-program communication. Presentation services also supports conversations.

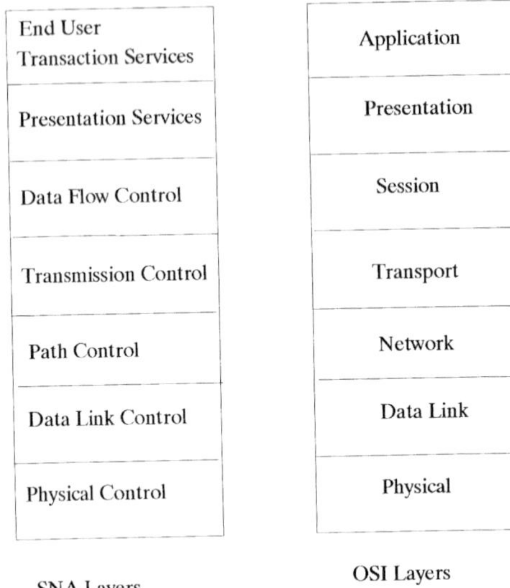

Figure 13.1 SNA layers. (*Source: Modified by permission from* Systems Network Architecture, Technical Overview, *GC 30-3073-2, September 1986, copyright by International Business Machines Corporation.*)

- *Data flow control:* Has the responsibility for flow control for LU-LU (pronounced "LU to LU") sessions, and for assembling frames into larger frames.
- *Transmission control:* Used to provide security functions, and for supporting flow control of data at the session level.
- *Path control (PC):* Has routing capabilities, and provides for the segmentation and reassembly of frames known as message units.
- *Data link control (DLC):* Refers to protocols required to ensure reliable transfer of data between stations. DLC functions include link level error recovery, sequencing of packets, acknowledgment of packets, and synchronization of data transfer between stations. Some of the popular protocols supported by SNA are SDLC, X.25, token ring, Ethernet, frame relay, and ATM.
- *Physical control:* Refers to the electrical, mechanical, and physical characteristics of the transmission medium, and is also responsible for providing support to establish, maintain, and terminate connections.

13.2.2 Network addressable unit (NAU)

It is essential to understand the concept behind the term *node* before discussing *network addressable units* (NAUs). System Network

Architecture's Technical Overview (see Reference 13.1, pp. 1–7) defines an SNA node as "the portion of a hardware component that, along with its associated software components, implements the functions of the seven architectural layers." NAUs allow users to gain access to a network, manage and control it, and manage the resources in nodes. SNA has the following NAUs:

- *Logical unit* (*LU*): Provides for the end-user access to a network, and manages the exchange of data between end users.
- *Physical unit* (*PU*): Manages the links. The PU has hardware and software to support this function.
- *Control point* (*CP*): Responsible for managing a T2.1 node and its resources (discussed in Section 13.4.1).

13.3 Networking Blueprint

The IBM Networking Blueprint (Figure 13.2) was announced in 1992. It is geared towards providing networking and systems management functions and solutions in heterogeneous and multivendor environments. It also tries to merge a wide range of existing and future protocols and technologies. Approaching the blueprint from the bottom up, the lowest layer is the *physical layer,* which consists of devices such as adapters, ports, and wiring between computers. These days, it is not always necessary that computers be connected to one another by means of traditional wiring; wireless communication between computers is also becoming popular. The Networking Blueprint can accommodate these extensions.

Above the physical layer is the *subnetworking layer,* comprising LANs, MANs, and WANs, and emerging technologies. LANs may have

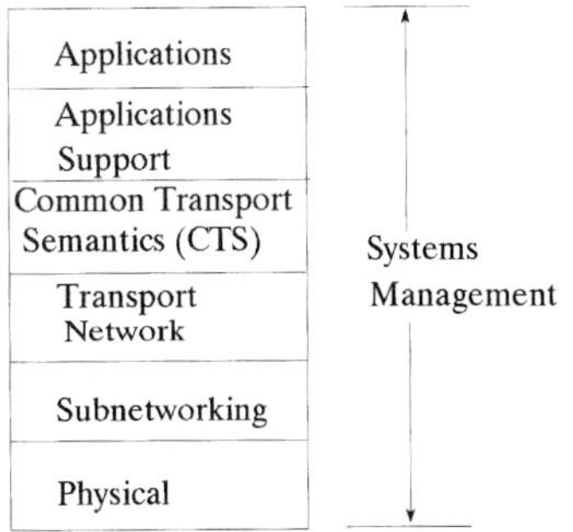

Figure 13.2 IBM Networking Blueprint layers. (*Source: Modified by permission from an IBM SE's* Introduction to Messaging and Queuing with MQI, *ZZ81-0328-00, First Edition, December 1992, copyright by International Business Machines Corporation.*)

protocols such as CSMA/CD, token ring, or token bus. Recall from Chapter 11 that LANs may be connected to form WANs and MANs.

Above the subnetworking layer is the *transport networking layer,* which caters to a wide range of transport protocols such as SNA/APPN, OSI, TCP/IP, NetBIOS, or IPX/SPX. In this layer, the transport mechanism for data transmission from one computer to another computer is provided. Routing capability may be needed in this layer, too.

The next layer up is known as the *multivendor application support layer.* Between the transport networking and the multivendor application support, *common transport semantics* (CTS) is necessary for the application support layer to access the transport layer below it. CTS does not provide the transport mechanism itself; it provides the interface to the underlying transport mechanism. In the multivendor application support layer, there are functions to support the applications above it. There may be APPC, OSF DCE, Message Queuing, applications such as FTAM, X.400, TELNET, FTP, or distributed services.

Above the application support layer are *common programming interface-communication* (CPI-C), *Remote Procedure Call* (RPC), and *Message and Queuing Interface* (MQI). Also in this layer are systems management applications which manage the layers below.

Communication models between two communicating entities can be classified as:

- *Conversational model:* Used by most of the transaction programs. Here there is a synchronous exchange of information between two peers. This model is appropriate for distributed peer-to-peer transaction processing.
- *Call model:* Similar to an RPC call, where one peer asks for information from another peer by making a call. Here, the initiator waits for the reply to come from the responder, which constitutes a synchronous call. The RPC call model is popular in a client-server environment, where sequential calls are sometimes appropriate.
- *Messaging model:* Uses the queuing mechanism to exchange information between two entities. The concept of messaging is analogous to electronic mail. Here, one system delivers a message in the receiver's queue or a common queue. The receiver retrieves the message and performs the required processing. If a response is needed, the receiver places the response in another queue or common queue, and the sender retrieves the message from this queue. The messaging model is useful for parallel processing because work splitting and simultaneous transactions can be performed. Messaging will be covered in more detail in Section 13.7.

The IBM Networking Blueprint provides application interfaces to each one of the three communication models. Also, it can be noted from Figure 13.2 that systems management applications form the topmost layer; however, these applications provide systems management functions to all the layers below them. In other words, the scope of systems management applications involves both the hardware and software and spans all the layers of the Networking Blueprint. Note that *systems management* is the IBM term for network management.

Because this book is devoted primarily to network management systems and their essential characteristics, we will not examine the different components of the Networking Blueprint. However, we will examine some of the popular components commonly associated with the peer SNA of the Networking Blueprint.

13.4 APPN

In *Advanced Peer-to-Peer Networking* (APPN), the primary focus is on providing easy solutions to the dynamic configuration of networks. Topology changes are dynamically recognized and the routing and flow control functions have been simplified. The requirement on SNA to work in environments other than the host was also an important consideration in the development of APPN. APPN can work in purely LAN networks connected to one another and in client-server environments. APPN is an implementation of the Type 2.1 (T2.1) node architecture.

13.4.1 Structure of the T2.1 node

The components of a T2.1 node are shown in Figure 13.3. The T2.1 node includes the *node operator facility* (NOF), *control point* (CP), LU 6.2, PC, and DLC. While we defer the discussion of LU 6.2 to Section 13.5, let us examine the different components of a T2.1 node. The NOF has the following functions:

- *Operator interface:* Inputs data to a T2.1 node configuration and session parameters. This operator interface can be via human operator, a command file, or a transaction program (TP).
- *Operational control:* Can be actions such as activating and deactivating link stations, defining and deleting LUs, and querying CPs.

In a T2.1 node, the CP is the key element. It creates, manages, and destroys the PC and DLC instances. The CP also manages the LU 6.2 sessions, and helps in link activation and deactivation.

The *transaction program* (TP) interfaces with LUs and provides user-defined functions. PC and DLC, which provide the traditional

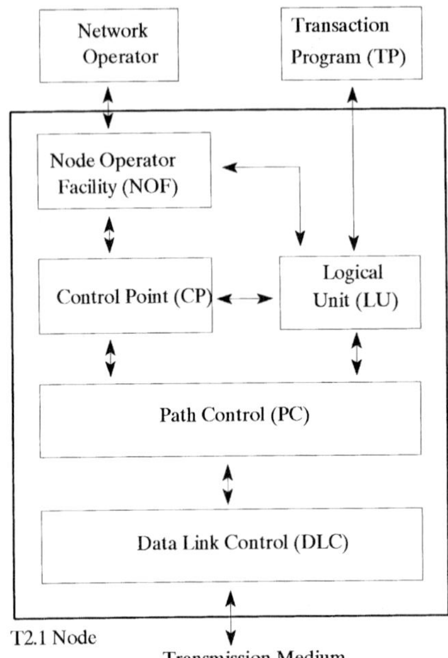

Figure 13.3 Components of a T2.1 node. (*Source: Modified by permission from IBM International Technical Support Centers*, APPN Architecture and Product Implementations, *Tutorial GG24-3669-01, Second Edition, June 1992, copyright by International Business Machines Corporation.*)

SNA functions, are included in APPN. Note that each DLC process is an instance with one DLC manager, and a DLC process manages one or more ports. In addition to the components we have discussed, APPN networks use the following components:

- *Port:* The actual hardware attached to a link. This may also be referred to as an *adapter.* Port characteristics are defined by the NOF.
- *Link:* In APPN, there is a logical connection between two T2.1 nodes. The Role of a link, which connects two nodes, can be designated as *primary, secondary,* or *negotiable.* The Role is largely associated with who sends the BIND. The primary sends the BIND. In the initial stages itself, it is possible to define which node is primary and which is secondary. If the Role is negotiable, then the role of primary or secondary will be determined during the link activation stage.
- *Link station:* Represents the hardware and software needed to manage a link. The characteristics of link stations, such as link station name and link station role, can be predefined by the NOF or negotiated during link activation time.

- *Transmission group (TG)*: Refers to a logical connection between two nodes and is represented by an integer from 0 to 255. There can be many connections between nodes, in which case they are known as *parallel TGs.* When a node has connections with more than one node, the TGs are termed *multiple TGs.* TG numbers are assigned during link activation times.

Link activation involves the optional steps of connect, *exchange identification* (XID) exchange, and contact. For switched connections, the connect step is required. For XID exchange, a null XID can be sent to determine if the partner link station is active or XID3 (a format of XID) to identify the partner. The partner link station is identified by the CP name. Also during the contact step, XID3s are exchanged. XID exchange will determine the roles and exchange the information such as TG number and link details.

Data between link stations will be exchanged in the *basic transmission units* (BTUs). The manner in which this data exchange is done must be negotiated during link activation time. For example, if a partner link station does not support reassembly of segments, then the data will have to be sent in a form suited to the partner link station in a single BTU. However, if a partner link station supports the reassembly of packets, then PC segments the data into a *basic information unit* (BIU), as shown in Figure 13.4. In the adjacent CP, the data is reassembled by PC.

For the sake of simplicity, APPN resources such as CP and LU are identified by resource names. These resource names are internally converted to addresses in the network. CPs and LUs are also known as network accessible units (NAUs). Notice that, in the context of

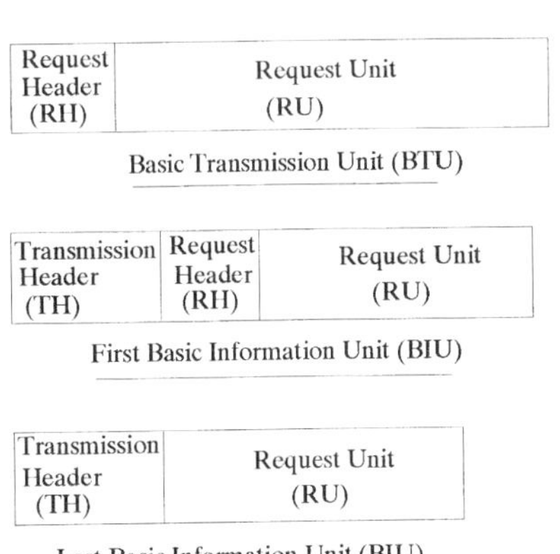

Figure 13.4 Path control segmentation. (*Source: Modified by permission from IBM International Technical Support Centers*, APPN Architecture and Product Implementations, *Tutorial GG24-3669-01, Second Edition, June 1992, copyright by International Business Machines Corporation.*)

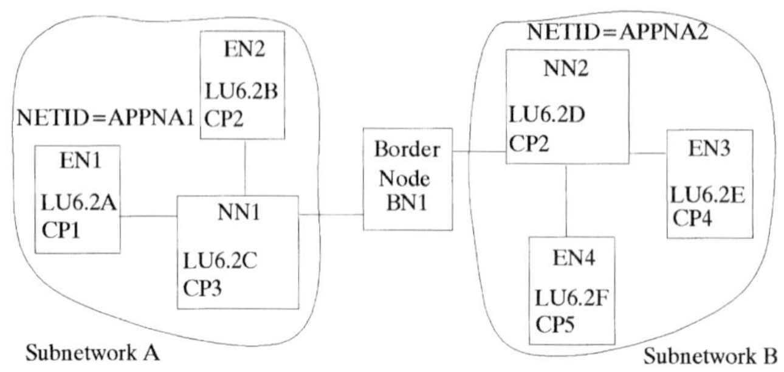

Figure 13.5 Network qualified names in APPN networks.

APPN, "network addressable unit" has changed to "network accessible unit," which reflects the change in the naming convention. In APPN, unique resource names are used to identify the resources, unlike the addresses used in traditional SNA.

Figure 13.5 is an example of an APPN network, which is partitioned into subnetworks A and B. Each subnetwork must have an identifier, known as the *network identification* (NETID). Subnetwork A has one NETID, APPNA1, and subnetwork B has a different NETID, APPNA2. These NETIDs can be from one to eight bytes long. Again, within a network, resources such as CPs and LUs must have unique names known as *network names,* which are provided using the NOF.

The NETID and network name are concatenated to obtain the network qualified names. For example, the network qualified name for LU6.2B is APPNA1.LU6.2B. Notice in Figure 13.5 that the network name CP2 for resources such as EN2 (subnetwork A) and NN2 (subnetwork B) can be the same.

13.4.2 Types of APPN nodes

For peer-to-peer communication, different APPN nodes (Figure 13.6) have been defined. These nodes have various functions included in them. APPN nodes range from the simplest, without much functionality, to the most complicated, with functions such as *directory services* (DS) and *topology and routing services* (TRS). DS will be discussed later. TRS is basically a database on Class of Service (COS) and different nodes and their connections. Some APPN nodes have been defined for migration from hostcentric to peer-to-peer communications. The following APPN nodes have been defined.

- *Low entry networking end node* (*LEN EN*): This is the base T2.1 node. An LEN EN does not have many of the APPN functions. It just provides connection to other LEN nodes, APPN end nodes, or

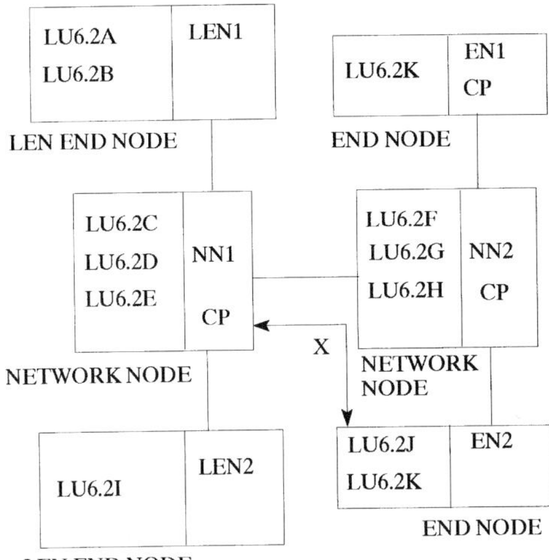

Figure 13.6 Different types of APPN nodes.

APPN *network nodes* (NNs), establishes a session between the LU 6.2s, and transports data between the adjacent LEN ENs or adjacent APPN NNs. An LEN EN cannot establish a CP-CP session. The help of an adjacent APPN NN is required for locating the resources of nonadjacent nodes.

Because the LEN EN does not have much capability and intelligence, it requires data such as local LUs, adjacent LUs, local CP name, and adjacent CP name to be defined either manually or through some application programs.

- *End node* (*EN*): This provides support for CP-CP sessions, and also permits the resources such as LUs and CP name to be registered in the adjacent APPN NN. So, when it is necessary to locate a resource such as LU 6.2, the broadcast, a directed search, is received by an NN. The NN has knowledge of the resources of the ENs that have been registered. As a result, the NN knows the location of the resources. However, to make sure that the connection is still working with the EN, the NN sends verification to the EN. DS support is available, and Class of Service (COS) database support is optional in EN.

  There are two types of EN nodes: authorized and unauthorized. Authorized ENs can register the resources with the NNs; in the case of unauthorized ENs, the resources must be defined in the NNs.

- *Network node* (*NN*): This provides directory services and routing functions, and supports CP-CP sessions. In a purely APPN network, the NN node performs most of the functions, including routing. Also, in an APPN network, NNs are able to locate a resource within a network and the best route from a source LU to a destination LU for a CP-CP session.

When an NN notices a change in a network, such as establishing a connection to a network, the topology information is broadcast to the adjacent active NN. This is done by each NN; thus, the latest topology information is propagated throughout the APPN network. By these actions, the topology information of a network is continuously updated.

A resource may have alternate paths to a node. The best route to be taken between the LUs is determined by weighting the COS information, node properties, and the transmission group. The optimal route with the least weight is selected. For COS information, a COS database is maintained in the NN.

There are also facilities for registering the directory of each NN in a centralized directory. As a result, if the location of a resource is required, then the central directory is searched first. This saves considerable effort because the alternative is the costly broadcast search.

Directory services (DS) is the key element for locating resources in APPN networks. DS is a table with the CP names and the resource names used by the CPs. EN nodes have their local directories and they include the TG number, CP name, and LU names. These must be defined by the NOF or other application programs.

Each NN has a *cache directory* and a *local directory.* The directory has the origin and destination CP names, and the LU names. It also has details of resources within the local NN and the ENs and LENs which this directory serves. The cache directory contains the results of the latest search of resource details. It is maintained in both the origin and destination NNs. When this cache directory becomes full, the least recently used entry is purged. The directory entry also contains the best route to a resource. When an EN or LEN asks for a search of a resource, then the cache directory is searched. If the search is successful, in the case of a nonverify option, the result of the search is forwarded to the requesting EN that asked for its location with a Locate.

The following APPN nodes have been provided for the purpose of migration and connectivity to the subareas.

- *Boundary and peripheral node:* In the traditional SNA, the *system services control point* (SSCP) controlled the resources within its domain. The SSCP resides in a subarea node. A subarea node used for APPN connectivity is known as a *boundary node.* In this environment, which is hierarchical in nature, the SSCP always starts a session with the peripheral node. These peripheral nodes can be either a T2.0 or T2.1. Because a T2.0 node does not have many functions, an SSCP must start a session and control it.

- *Composite node:* There are two types of composite nodes, depending on the functions they provide. These are the *composite LEN EN* and the *composite network node* (CNN). With the introduction of these, a subarea can be represented as a composite node and can be part of an APPN network. Inside the composite nodes, subarea protocols are used. As a result, any LU, including those in the composite nodes, can have a session with another LU.

  However, there is a need for protocol conversions in the composite nodes. Here, APPN protocols must be converted to the subarea protocols when APPN communication must take place from one LU in an APPN network to the LU in the subarea. Similarly, protocol conversion must be done when an LU in a subarea domain wants to communicate with an LU in an APPN network.

- *Virtual routing node (VRN):* This can also be defined for the APPN LAN networks (see Figure 13.7). For example, the end nodes EN2, EN4, and EN5 can be grouped into one combination and defined as a VRN. This reduces the resource definitions and the routing required. The NOF must define the VRN. The VRN is not an actual APPN node; it is the capability to lump a number of nodes together for the ease of transportation of data. The VRN is also known as the *connection network.*

- *Border node:* For CP-CP sessions, NETIDs must be the same, and the topology information transfer can occur only within the APPN

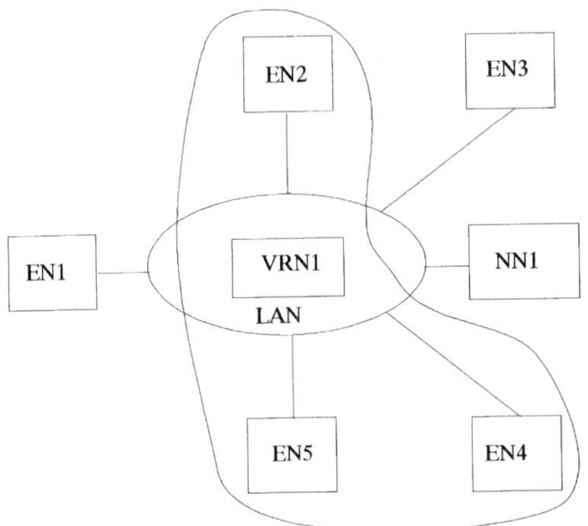

Figure 13.7 VRN in an APPN LAN network.

network with the same NETIDs. Thus, to establish a session between CPs in different networks with different NETIDs, border nodes are used (Figure 13.5). However, the topology information does not cross the subnetwork boundaries.

Let us return to the example of the APPN network in Figure 13.6. Here, two LEN ENs, LEN1 and LEN2, are connected to the APPN NN, NN1. Because LEN1 and LEN2 do not have APPN DS, for the resources LU6.2A, LU6.2B, and LU6.2I to be known, they must be defined in NN1. Then, only they will be known in the network.

Two APPN NNs, NN1 and NN2, are connected to each other. They provide the directory and routing services for the resources in the network, including those of the LEN EN and APPN ENs. APPN ENs, EN1 and EN2, are connected to the APPN NN, NN2. Here, note that EN2 can have two paths to NN1. One can be direct, as denoted by X in Figure 13.6, and another indirect via NN2. Here, only one CP-CP session between EN2 and NN1 can be active. The other path can be used as a backup path in case of failure in one route.

Similarly, in the APPN LAN network of Figure 13.7, workstations can have APPN EN functions, and at least one workstation must be an APPN NN. This is required because directory and routing facilities are provided by the APPN NN. This NN acts as a directory and routing server for the APPN NN network. Even though the figure shows the APPN LAN network as a token-ring network, there is no restriction that it can be only a token-ring network; instead, it could be an FDDI backbone or an Ethernet protocol–based network.

13.5 APPC

Advanced Program-to-Program Communication (APPC) is an implementation of the LU 6.2 architecture. As we have seen, LUs are end-user interfaces which are available to users. LU 6.2 provides many services and includes a set of functions between path control and the transaction programs (TP). TPs usually require a communication connection for a short period of time.

The LUs have logical connections known as *sessions* (Figure 13.8). TPs use these sessions for communication between them. The temporary use of sessions by TPs is known as a *conversation*. Note that sessions are between LUs and conversations are between TPs. Three types of TPs are:

- *Application transaction program (ATP)*: Usually written by users.
- *Service transaction program (STP)*: Supplied by IBM, this is part of the application layer of SNA.

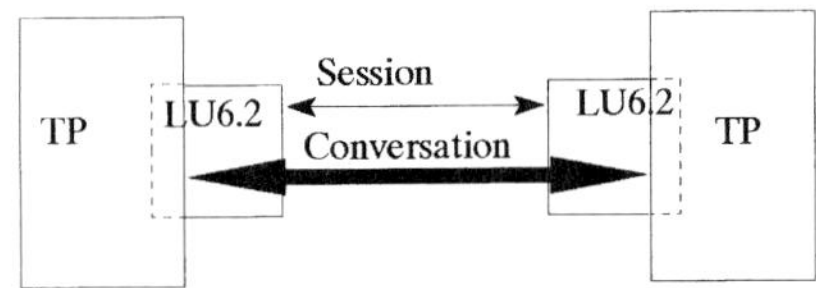

Figure 13.8 Concepts of session and conversation.

- *Control operator transaction program* (*CTP*): Primarily used to define the LU and its resources and control the session characteristics, such as when the sessions will be activated and deactivated, the number of sessions, or the partner LU. CTP provides an operator interface to carry out these functions.

LU 6.2 needs some facilities for managing sessions. First of all, each session must be started and terminated when it is no longer needed. When there are a number of these sessions, they need to be managed. The data must be transmitted through a session in a particular format. When data is transmitted a confirmation may be needed, and it may be necessary to recover from failures. All these services for managing sessions in LUs are provided.

A session between LUs will have a set of characteristics known as Class of Service (COS). APPC uses only a subset of SNA COS. COS for a session which is negotiated and agreed on between local and remote LUs is known as *mode*. Some of the mode parameters are Request Unit (RU) sizes, security level such as cryptography, link characteristics, and window sizes.

LU 6.2 provides half-duplex function in each session. It needs two sessions, known as half-sessions, to function in a full-duplex form. LUs can have multiple and parallel sessions between LUs. For example, take the four LUs shown in Figure 13.9 marked Chicago, New

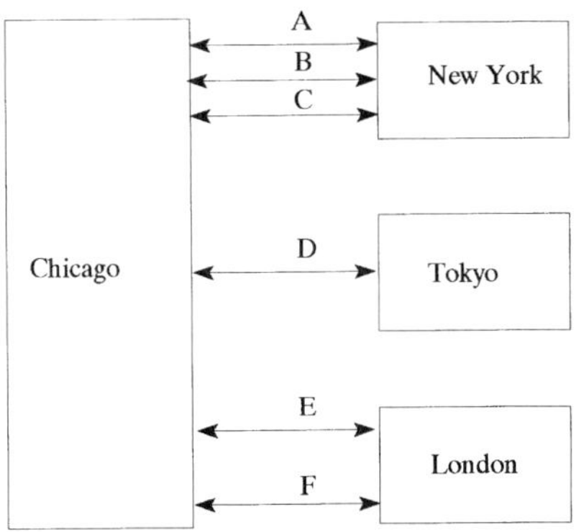

Figure 13.9 LU 6.2 session concepts.

York, Tokyo, and London. There can be three parallel sessions between Chicago and New York, and at the same time, Chicago can have multiple sessions with New York, Tokyo, and London.

The components of an LU 6.2 are as shown in Figure 13.10. It has a *resource manager* (RM) and a *session manager* (SM). The RM controls the interface to the upper layers of the SNA such as transaction services and presentation services. It creates the instances of the transaction services and the presentation services, and controls the communication of these with the instances of lower services such as data flow control and transmission control. It destroys these instances when they are no longer needed. The key is that the instances of the upper layers of SNA are created for each half-session of the LU 6.2. If more sessions are required, there will be corresponding instances. Note also that the ATP, CTP, and STP interface with the presentation services.

The SM is responsible for managing the lower half-sessions of the LU 6.2. These sessions communicate with the half-sessions of the partner LU for transfer of data. The SM, like the RM, is responsible for the creation, maintenance, and termination of the lower half-sessions. In Figure 13.10, A represents one instance of a half-session. For each session, there will be instances similar to A. The SM is also responsible for communicating with the CPs in a PU.

The NOF is the key operator interface, and is required for the initial configuration of the LUs. This can be used to define the session

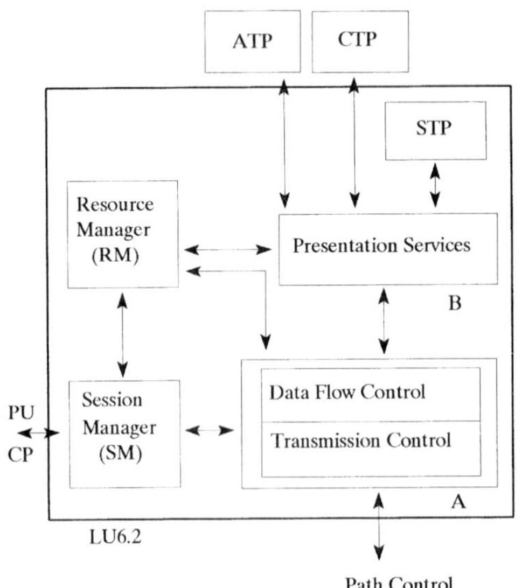

Figure 13.10 Structure of an LU 6.2. (*Source: Modified by permission from IBM International Technical Support Centers,* APPC and CPI-C, *GG24-3520-01, July 1991, copyright by International Business Machines Corporation.*)

characteristics or modes of a session, the number of sessions with a partner, and for activating the local LU.

Activating an LU creates the data flow control and transmission control instances. By using the START_TP command, the presentation layer and the transaction layer instances are created by the RM. The START_TP command can be used by the NOF, by CP, or by application programs. These steps are required to activate the sessions on the local LU. Similar steps are required on the partner LU side.

Session characteristics, such as the highest synchronization level, are usually negotiated by the BIND command, which is normally sent by the primary. The LU which sends the BIND command is known as the *primary logical unit* (PLU), and the LU which receives the BIND command is known as the *secondary logical unit* (SLU). The NOF in a T2.1 node determines whether an LU is a PLU or SLU.

There are two types of LU 6.2s: independent and dependent. In independent LU 6.2, any LU can be a primary or secondary, and between LUs there can be multiple and parallel sessions. Usually, in the host environment, the SSCP is the primary and the LU in the peripheral node is the secondary. The LU involved in a session with the SSCP is distinguished by being named as dependent LU. Independent LUs are an extension to the dependent LUs to account for peer-to-peer communication.

The communication between TPs uses the *general data stream* (GDS), which consists of a length, a GDS_ID, and the data, as shown in the Figure 13.11. For LU 6.2, only a subset of GDS_IDs is used. The length is inclusive of the four bytes due to the length field and GDS_ID field (each two bytes) plus the length of the data carried in the conversation. The data stream allows the nesting of one or more GDS data streams within the data field. For example, the data field can have one more sets of GDS data stream with its own length, GDS_ID, and data, as shown in the figure.

The partition of the interface between the LU 6.2 and the TPs is known as the *protocol boundary*. The LU 6.2 protocol boundary defines a set of verbs, which are a set of commands and responses

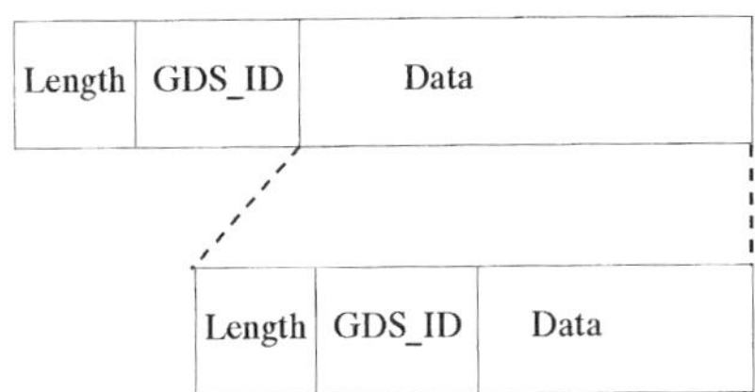

Figure 13.11 GDS data format and nesting of GDS data.

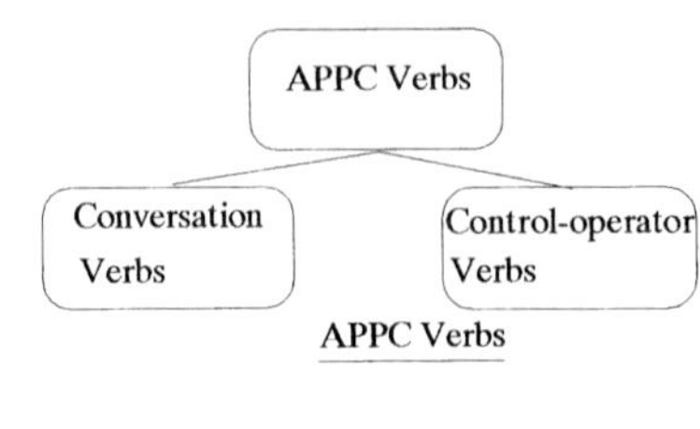

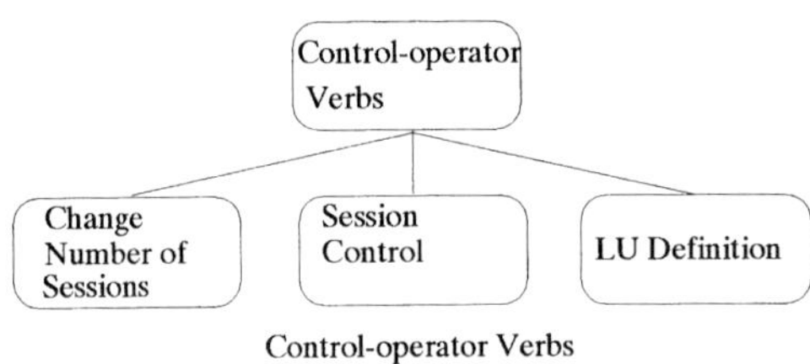

Figure 13.12 Classification of APPC verbs.

used to build applications and do communication between TPs. The verbs can be basically subdivided into *conversation verbs* and *control operator verbs,* as shown in Figure 13.12. The main purpose of a conversation verb is to provide functions for the program-to-program communication, while control operator verbs are used by network operators to control the functioning of the LUs and sessions. The conversation verb can be divided into the following categories:

- Basic conversation verbs
- Mapped conversation verbs
- Type-independent conversation verbs

13.5.1 Basic conversation verbs

Basic conversation verbs have the following primitives:

- *ALLOCATE:* Used for obtaining a session for a conversation from a pool of sessions on the local and remote LUs. As we have already seen, TPs use sessions for a conversation. In ALLOCATE, a session is identified and it has a unique identifier known as the *conversation identifier.*
- *DEALLOCATE:* The reverse of ALLOCATE. Here, a session is returned to the pool of sessions, which facilitates the reuse of sessions for conversations. Also, because the sessions are already

available, the steps associated with creating and destroying pools are reduced. ALLOCATE and DEALLOCATE verbs help in dynamically creating conversations.

- *SEND_DATA:* Used by a TP for sending data to the remote TP.
- *SEND_ERROR:* When a TP detects an error in the data received or confirmation request, it can use this verb to inform the remote TP of the error. After the completion of SEND_ERROR, the local TP is in the send state and the remote TP is in the receive state.
- RECEIVE_AND_WAIT: Used for receiving data. If the data is already available, it receives the data. If the data is not available, the local TP waits for it to arrive from the remote TP; then the local TP processes it.
- *REQUEST_TO_SEND:* Used to change the state from the receive to the send condition. Alternately, REQUEST_TO_SEND can also be used to inform the remote TP that the local TP wants to send data. The remote TP, after receiving the REQUEST_TO_SEND, sends the SEND indication to inform the local TP that it can send data.
- *CONFIRM:* A confirmation request asking the remote TP to confirm whether the data has actually been received. After sending the CONFIRM, the local TP waits for a reply from the remote TP.
- *CONFIRMED:* The response sent from a remote TP for a CONFIRM request.
- *GET_ATTRIBUTES:* Helpful for retrieving details of a conversation such as the mode name, the name of the remote LU, and synchronization levels.

When implementing APPC, certain verbs must be implemented. These are known as the BASE set. In basic conversation verbs, all the verbs in the preceding list are in the basic set. Some verbs can be implemented depending upon the implementation. These are known as the OPTION set. These profiles, like the profiles in OSI, are developed for easy implementation.

While the preceding verbs belong to the BASE set, the following verbs belong to the OPTION set:

- *FLUSH:* Used for the transmission of data when the send buffer is not full.
- *PREPARE_TO_RECEIVE:* When a remote TP is sending data, it can receive PREPARE_TO_RECEIVE. When it receives this verb, it indicates that the local TP wants to send data to the remote TP. This is an implicit command to change the direction of data flow.

- *RECEIVE_IMMEDIATE:* Indicates to the remote TP that it must receive the data right away.
- *POST_ON_RECEIPT:* Useful for sending a signal. When an event occurs, a Notification (signal) is sent to the sender.
- *TEST:* Used to check whether data has been received.
- *PREPARE_FOR_SYNCPT:* Indicates that the synchronization will be done and to prepare for synchronization. The concept of SYNCPT is discussed in Section 13.5.3.

13.5.2 Mapped conversation verbs

Mapped conversation verbs are similar to the basic conversation verbs but they are easier to use. They add a prefix of "MC_" to the basic conversation verbs. The MC_GET_ATTRIBUTES does not belong to the BASIC set, so the OPTION set has, in addition to those of the basic conversation verbs, MC_GET_ATTRIBUTES.

13.5.3 Type-independent conversation verbs

Type-independent conversation verbs are used for both the basic conversation verbs and the mapped conversation verbs, and furnish details which cannot be obtained from either of them.

- *GET_TP_PROPERTIES:* Returns the attributes that are common to all the conversations between two TPs. This verb belongs to the BASE set.
- *SYNCPT:* (Figure 13.13): Used to establish synchronization points.
- *SET_SYNCPT_OPTIONS:* Can be used to change the synchronization options.
- *BACKOUT:* (Figure 13.13): Used to back up the data to the last synchronization point.

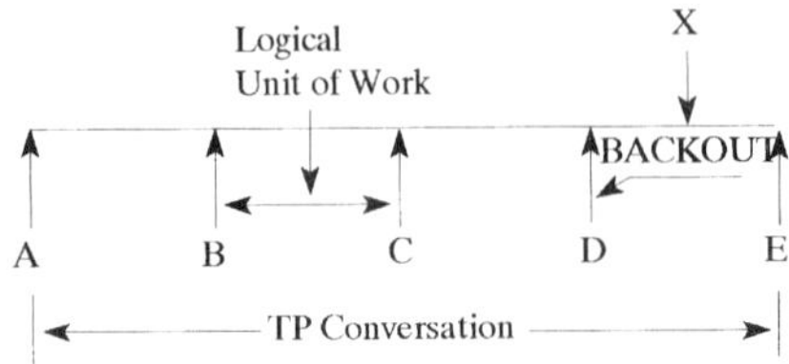

Figure 13.13 Concepts of SYNCPT and BACKOUT.

- *GET_TYPE:* Helps in determining if a TP supports the basic conversation verb or the mapped conversation verb.
- *WAIT:* Ensures that a POST signal or notify is done when data is received. However, a separate issue of RECEIVE is required to retrieve the data.

In the above set of verbs, except for GET_TP_PROPERTIES all the other verbs belong to the OPTION set.

When two TPs communicate, there may be failures, in which case, different actions can be taken depending on the synchronization level opted for. The options to be taken are mentioned in the SYNC_LEVEL parameter. In some cases, the data transferred is not critical. Then there is the option of having SYNC_LEVEL set to NONE, and no synchronization will be done. This alleviates the many steps that must be taken to perform synchronization. In other cases, a simple confirmation that the data has been received is enough. This is accomplished by having SYNC_LEVEL set to CONFIRM.

In those applications where the data transfer is important and there is a need to maintain consistency of data, the parameter SYNC_LEVEL must be set to SYNCPT. In this case, two-phase commit is used. These conversations that use SYNCPT are known as *protected conversations*. A conversation can be broken into different synchronization points, as shown in Figure 13.13. When there is a failure at point X, BACKOUT will ensure that the data is brought to the state at synchronization point D.

13.5.4 Control operator verbs

Control operator verbs are used by an operator to configure and change the initial details required by APPC, such as the definition of the local and remote LUs to define the Quality of Service. They also help to control the sessions. The following control operator verbs belong to the BASE set:

- *CHANGE_SESSION_LIMIT:* Used for changing the mode from one value to another value
- *INITIALIZE_SESSION_LIMIT:* Changes the mode value from zero to a some positive number
- *PROCESS_SESSION_LIMIT:* Processes the CNOS (change number of sessions), and sends it to the remote LU
- *RESET_SESSION_LIMIT:* Reverses the operation done by the verb INITIALIZE_SESSION_LIMIT, and the mode is changed to zero from a nonzero positive integer

The semantics of the control operator verbs are similar to those of the verbs already described, so explanations of each of the following verbs have not been repeated. The following control operator verbs belong to the OPTION set:

- *ACTIVATE_SESSION*
- *DEACTIVATE_SESSION*
- *DEFINE_LOCAL_LU*
- *DEFINE_MODE*
- *DEFINE_REMOTE_LU*
- *DEFINE_TP*
- *DELETE*
- *DISPLAY_LOCAL_LU*
- *DISPLAY_MODE*
- *DISPLAY_REMOTE_LU*
- *DISPLAY_TP*

In addition to these verbs, there are implementation verbs. Even though these are used primarily for compatibility purposes for the applications already developed, they can also be used to implement new applications. These implementation-dependent verbs need to map and document their relationship with the APPC verbs.

13.6 CPI-C

A system-dependent and consistent application programming interface to services and languages is provided by CPI-C. This interface is also known as the SAA resource recovery interface. While APPC provides a generic interface to applications, CPI-C provides a portable interface requiring the use of specific function calls and parameters. CPI-C makes the use of APPC by applications easier. CPI-C implements all the conversation verbs provided by APPC.

A CPI-C program is the same as a TP in APPC. Two CPI-C programs, called *partners,* communicate using conversations. CPI-C uses two types of conversations for the exchange of control information and data:

- *Mapped conversation:* Has a flexible data format for conversation between partners. This data format naturally must be known and agreed on by both partners.
- *Basic conversation:* Makes use of a standard data format for conversation between partners, and does not need much negotiation

between partners because the data format used is already known to the partners. A two-byte length field is used, followed by the data.

Because most of the function calls have semantics similar to those of the APPC verbs, we will not deal with each of them individually. Figure 13.14 shows how data exchange can be done using different CPI-C function calls.

13.7 MQI

As we have seen earlier, MQI is an important architected interface to applications in the IBM Networking Blueprint. MQI is useful for applications with high traffic and has the following components:

- *Message:* A collection of data which provide some meaning to application programs.
- *Message queue:* A storage area for holding messages, it is owned by a queue manager. A message queue has a queue name for identification, message priority, and queue creation rules associated with it.
- *Queue manager:* A system program and the key element in MQI. It creates, deletes, and manages a queue, and normally resides in each node requiring MQI functions, as shown in Figure 13.15. It provides the application programming interface to applications. A queue manager can own one or more message queues.

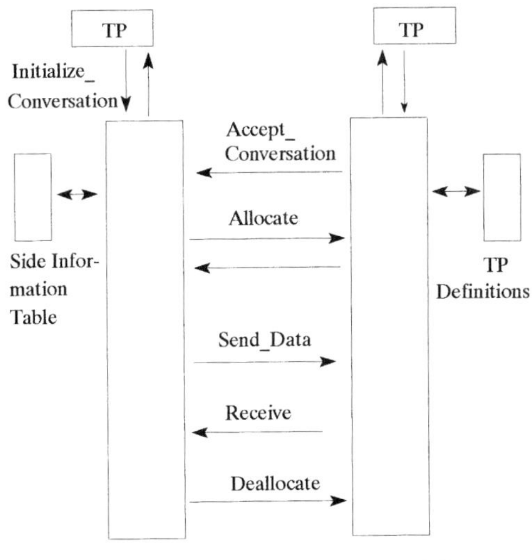

Figure 13.14 Example of CPI-C flows.

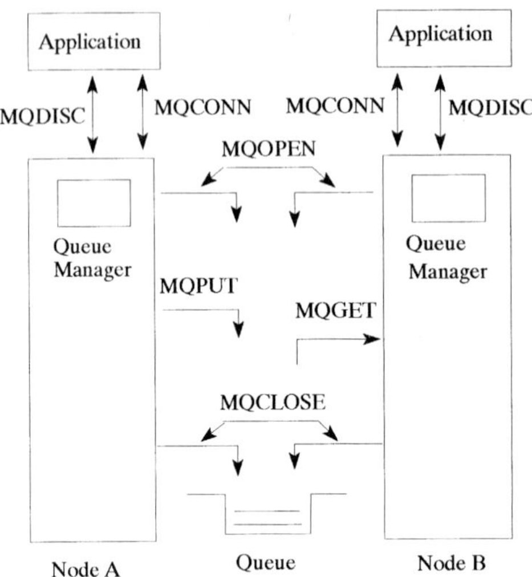

Figure 13.15 Example of Message Queuing Interface (MQI) flows.

13.7.1 MQI verbs

- *MQCONN:* Used for establishing a connection with a queue manager. This is the first step before initiating any communication.
- *MQOPEN:* Useful for creating a queue if one is not there; if a queue is already there, that queue is opened. In both cases, a check is made as to whether the initiator has the authority to create or open a queue.
- *MQPUT:* Transfers data to a queue.
- *MQGET:* Retrieves data already placed in a queue. Here, there are different options to retrieve messages from a queue.
- *MQINQ:* Can be used to query the attributes of a queue, such as the number of messages which need to be processed.
- *MQSET:* Facilitates setting the attributes of a queue. This function makes a queue operationally flexible.
- *MQCLOSE:* A reverse operation of MQOPEN. When a connection to a queue is opened, then it must be closed, too. In addition to closing an open connection to a queue, MQCLOSE can also be used to delete a queue.
- *MQPUT1:* Combines the functions associated with MQOPEN, MQPUT, and MQCLOSE. The MQPUT1 verb enables the data transfer to a queue with one operation. In some cases, it may be enough to transfer just one message to a peer. Under such circumstances, this is a very useful function.

- *MQDISC:* Used for terminating the connection with a queue manager.

Figure 13.15 shows how different verbs can be used to transfer data between two peers.

13.8 Summary

This chapter is devoted primarily to an introduction to peer SNA. We started with the Networking Blueprint, which is an IBM architecture for interoperability in heterogeneous and multivendor computing environments. APPN, APPC, CPI-C, and MQI were also discussed.

13.9 Reference

13.1 IBM Corporation, GC30-3073, System Network Architecture, Technical Overview.

13.10 Further Reading

IBM Corporation, GC20-1868, SNA Sessions Between Logical Units.

IBM Corporation, GC24-3520, SNA APPC and CPI-C Product Implementations.

IBM Corporation, GC30-3072, SNA Concepts and Products.

IBM Corporation, GC30-3084, SNA Transaction Programmer's Reference Manual for LU Type 6.2.

IBM Corporation, GG24-3364, SNA APPN/Subarea Networking Design and Interconnection Considerations.

IBM Corporation, GG24-3428, Program-To-Program Communications in SAA Environments.

IBM Corporation, GG24-3669, SNA APPN Product Implementations.

IBM Corporation, SC26-4399, SAA Common Programming Interface Communications Reference.

IBM Corporation, SC30-3269, SNA Format and Protocol Reference Manual: Architecture Logic for LU Type 6.2.

IBM Corporation, SC30-3422, SNA Architecture Logic for Type 2.1 Nodes.

IBM Corporation, SC31-6808, SNA LU 6.2 Reference: Peer Protocols.

IBM Corporation, LY43-0081, SNA Network Product Formats.

Peterson, David, M., *Enterprise Network Management: A Guide to IBM's NetView,* New York: McGraw-Hill, 1993.

Ranade, Jay, and George Sackett, *Introduction to SNA Networking: A Professional's Guide to VTAM/NCP,* 2d ed., New York: McGraw-Hill, 1994.

Walker II, John Q., and Peter J. Schwaller, *CPI-C Programming in C: An Application Developer's Guide to APPC,* New York: McGraw-Hill, 1995.

Note: The year of publication for IBM manuals has not been provided. The order number (e.g., SC30-3422) for the publications is sufficient to procure the latest IBM publications.

Chapter

14

SNA Systems Management and SystemView

14.1 Introduction

This chapter focuses on systems management in the IBM environment. NetView, introduced in 1986, was one of first network management products of IBM. It was a collection of products, and since then it has undergone major changes to cater to the network management in a heterogeneous and multivendor environment. NetView has also been expanded to cater to object-oriented technology with the introduction of the object data cache, Resource Object Data Manager (RODM). The approach in this book has been to avoid discussion of specific products; so, although the author has been associated with NetView, we will continue this practice and not explore the details. However, for those interested in NetView, there are many good books and a vast amount of material on NetView products.

After a brief overview of SNA/Management Services (MS), we will focus primarily on the latest systems management architecture of IBM: SystemView. SystemView is again an effort by IBM to cater to network management of existing and future products and to meet the challenges in multivendor and multiprotocol environments. SystemView also takes into account the standards such as OSI and Internet. Notice that the present term for network management in SNA is *systems management*. This change has been made to reflect the changes in network management since its introduction and to keep the semantics of systems management similar to that of OSI.

14.2 SNA Management Services (SNA/MS)

SNA/MS was geared toward providing network management in SNA and non-SNA environments. As part of SNA/MS, the following new terms were defined.

14.2.1 Focal point

The focal point provides centralized network management functions for one or more entry points. This concept has been extended to cover peer-to-peer networks such as the APPN network. In one network there can be more than one focal point performing different network management–related operations. There are two possible scenarios. In one case, different focal points may handle different network management functions. In the other case, different focal points may handle different portions of a network (see Figure 14.1). In addition, a focal point can be nested within another focal point. Nesting of focal points enables there to be a hierarchy of focal points with different levels of network management support and permits the distribution of focal points in different places. For example, a nested focal point in an APPN network may be placed in an NN node which is very close to the network, and the nesting focal point may be located near a console (Figure 14.1) from which human intervention is possible. Focal points also include the concepts of primary and backup, which are provided to improve reliability. If the primary focal point fails, then the backup is kicked off, thus maintaining smooth operation.

14.2.2 Entry point

An entry point is responsible for sending network management data about the resources in the domain of the entry point and about the entry point itself to a focal point for managing and controlling the

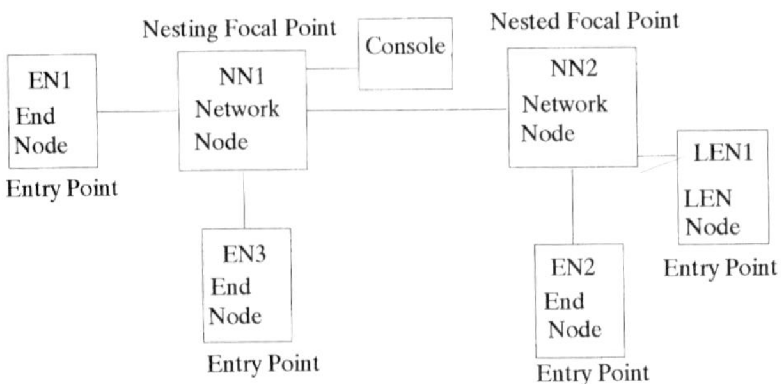

Figure 14.1 Multiple focal points and nesting of focal points.

network. An entry point responds to commands by a focal point and acts on the resources it controls.

14.2.3 Service point

A service point is used to communicate with non-SNA resources. Non-SNA resources interact with a focal point via a service point. The service point converts the non-SNA protocols to the SNA format and transmits the network management data to the focal point. In a similar manner, the SNA format data from the focal point are converted to the relevant non-SNA format in the service point.

It is necessary to investigate the different types of nodes to get a better feel for SNA/MS. Nodes were discussed in Section 13.2.2. There are basically three types of nodes: subarea, peripheral, and APPN T2.1 nodes. Recall that a group of resources are combined in a node. These nodes vary in complexity and function. Subarea node type 5 manages and controls a network; subarea node type 4 routes and controls the flow of data in network. Peripheral nodes do not have as much intelligence as subarea nodes, and they require the support of subarea nodes, which is provided by the *boundary function* (BF) in a subarea.

There are two types of data transfer: *nonbulk* and *bulk*. Nonbulk data has relatively smaller frame sizes and must be delivered to the destination without much delay. *Network Management Vector Transport* (NMVT) and *Multiple Domain Support* (MDS)–*Message Unit* (MU) are used for the nonbulk data transfer. On the other hand, bulk data transfer requires large message sizes or transfer of files. These data files are, by and large, not of immediate operational significance, as can often be noticed in static configuration. These bulk data can be transferred over LU 6.2 sessions using SNA/Distribution Services (DS) or SNA/File Services (FS).

Enterprise management is a term often heard in the SNA environment. Enterprise management refers to managing and controlling the networks, the systems attached to the network, and user applications. Enterprise management has a broad scope, covering all aspects of management including strategic, tactical, and operational levels, and is described in Information Systems Management Architecture (ISMA) (see IBM publications GE20-0662, GE20-0749, GE20-0750, and GE20-0751, References 14.1–14.4).

14.2.4 SNA/MS node elements

Network management requirements are met primarily by special node elements incorporated into SNA/MS. SNA/MS uses three management flows: unsolicited, request with reply, and request without reply. SNA/MS node elements are:

- *Local management services (LMS)*: Provides partial network management function in the context of overall network management support. The different flavors of LMS are:

  Physical resources LMS generates unsolicited notifications on problems in a physical resource such as hardware, software, or microcode and sends them to either CPMS or PUMS (see next item).

  Logical unit LMS is a part of each LU and provides unsolicited notifications on problems in the LU, enabling response time data to be measured.

  Program supervisor LMS is useful for altering the hardware and software configurations of a node when required.

- *Physical unit management services (PUMS)*: A component within a PU, providing network management functions to the LUs within a PU's domain. PUMS (Figure 14.2) communicates with SSCP via an SSCP-PU session, and with other peripheral nodes using CP-MSU. Upon request, a PU supplies information such as the number of active sessions managed by the PU, the number of active LUs, and the configuration of the PU. The PU gets the information on the problems in a link via a data link control (DLC) manager. We have already discussed the different types of LMS which communicate with PUMS.

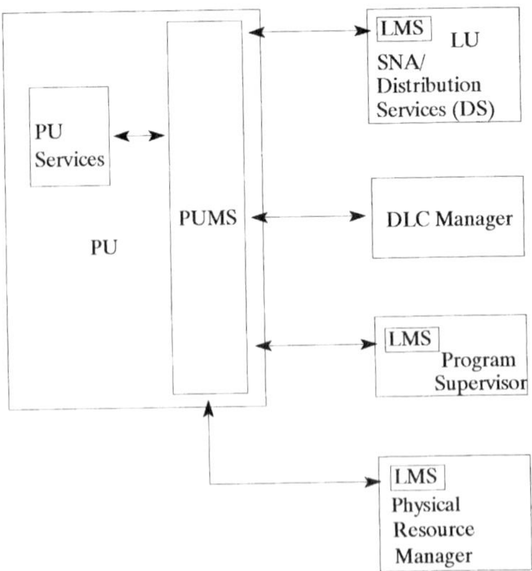

Figure 14.2 Physical unit management services (PUMS) structure. (*Source: Modified by permission from* Class Notes–Open Distributed Management RTD 3097C, Skill Dynamics, An IBM Company, Version 93-1, *copyright 1993 by International Business Machines Corporation.*)

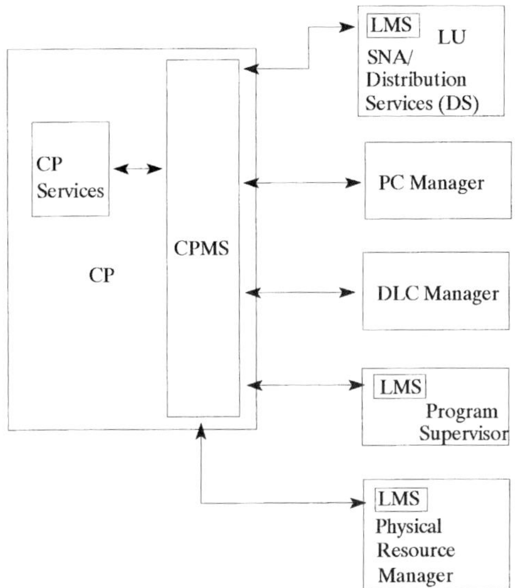

Figure 14.3 Control point management services (CPMS) structure. (*Source: Modified by permission from* Class Notes–Open Distributed Management RTD 3097C, Skill Dynamics, An IBM Company, Version 93-1, *copyright 1993 by International Business Machines Corporation.*)

- *Control point management services* (*CPMS*): A key element in the management of APPN nodes. CPMS (Figure 14.3) are part of an APPN node and provide the network management support to the APPN node. CPMS report the problems noticed within a CP, using unsolicited notifications to other CPMS. The path control (PC) manager and DLC managers send unsolicited notifications to CPMS if they encounter problems. We have already discussed the roles of LMS which interact with CPMS. Notice that APPN networks are peer-to-peer networks, and that is why CPMS communicate with one another to provide overall network management.

14.2.5 Function sets

A function set provides a set of MS services for a node. There are two types of subsets for a function set: base and optional. In every function set, the base subset must be implemented, but the optional subset, obviously, need not. SNA/MS uses a collection of function sets to provide the network management functions. For example, an APPN EN includes the function sets MDS, EP_ALERT, and MS_CAPS.

Some of the important function sets are:

- *MULTIPLE_DOMAIN_SUPPORT* (*MDS*): Used to transport nonbulk MS data between APPN nodes via CP-CP sessions or LU-LU sessions using LU 6.2 protocols.

- *MS_Capabilities* (*MS_CAPS*): Permits the nodes to form relationships between focal point and entry point, and track and maintain them.
- *SEND_DATA_SSCP_PU:* Allows a peripheral node to send MS information to a host SSCP.
- *RECEIVE_REQUEST_SSCP_PU:* Permits a peripheral node to process requests from an SSCP.
- *EP_ALERT:* Required for sending alerts to a focal point. This is required for the peripheral node and APPN nodes.

For details on other function sets, readers should refer to IBM SC-3346 (see Reference 14.5).

14.2.6 Management service unit (MSU)

MSU is the formatted data structure used to convey MS data. Which message must be used depends upon the nodes and the usage. There are three formatted data structures for conveying MS data:

- *NMVT:* Used for transferring network management data over an SSCP-PU session to support the peripheral nodes. NMVT has a header, procedure-related identifier (PRID), flags, and MS major vector. The NMVT has the architecture shown in Figure 14.4 and consists of length, key, and one or more subvectors. A subvector can also have length, key, and data, while another type of subvector can have one or more subfields. A subfield, in turn, can have length, key, and data. *Alert* is a key feature of the network management that is sent for abnormal behavior. It has a unique header identified by X "41038D".
- *Control point MSU* (*CP-MSU*): Can be sent over a CP-CP or LU-LU session. It has the LU 6.2 GDS data format (Figure 13.11) described in Chapter 13. Alerts and other MS major vectors are enveloped with GDS headers and length fields.
- *Multiple domain support message unit* (*MDS-MU*): Uses the GDS format and is used for SNA/MS communication between APPN nodes.

SNA/MS has the following network management functions:

- Problem management
- Performance and accounting management
- Configuration management

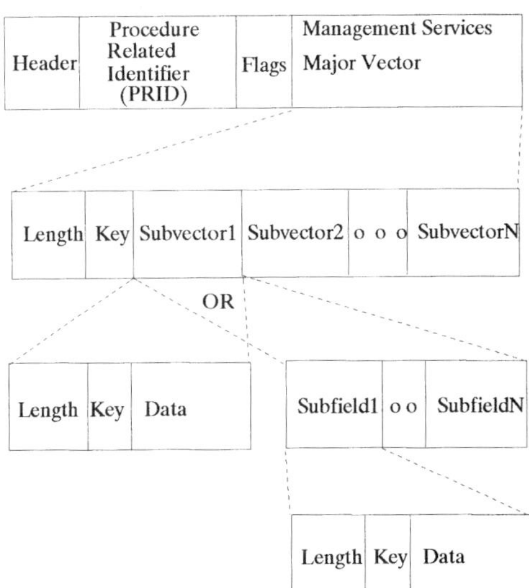

Figure 14.4 Network management vector transport (NMVT) frame format. (*Source: Modified by permission from* Systems Network Architecture, Technical Overview, *GC 30-3073-2, September 1986, copyright by International Business Machines Corporation.*)

- Change management
- Operations management

We will not discuss these network management functions because they have been superseded by the SystemView disciplines.

14.3 SystemView Goals and Objectives

SystemView is a major effort to integrate a wide variety of products covering different standards, protocols, and vendors spread across the globe. Some of the major goals of SystemView are the following:

- *Consistent systems management:* IBM has many popular systems management products. One of the tasks is to provide an easy and consistent systems management platform. Also, systems management solutions must cover a wide range of products and architectures from different vendors.
- *Smooth integration with standards:* Many standards, such as OSI, Internet, and IEEE network management standards, are quite popular. In addition, there are many bodies which are releas-

ing standards. SystemView must contend with these various standards, with openness being a key requirement.

- *Easy migration path:* There are many legacy products which IBM has all over the world on different platforms ranging from PC to mainframes. SystemView needs to consider support and easy migration to the existing products and existing architectures such as SNA.
- *Ability to handle future technologies:* SystemView also must consider emerging technologies such as object-oriented technologies, including the object-oriented databases. At the same time, SystemView needs to contend with distributed processing, parallel processing, and multiprocessing.
- *Integration of different technologies:* Data communication and telecommunications are slowly merging. Also, client-server environments are becoming popular. These aspects must be taken into consideration in SystemView.
- *Automation capabilities:* These days, many systems management functions are labor-intensive, involving high cost. These manual operations must be automated as much as possible by providing functions which solve the problems with the least human intervention possible.

In SystemView, a set of technical objectives has been developed. Some of the important ones are:

- *Enterprisewide scope:* The scope of SystemView is vast, covering the whole enterprise, which includes LANs, client-server environments, computing center, networks, vendor products, and partial configurations. The enterprise can be of any size or complexity, and the management tasks can range from abstract functions to the management of different types of resources.
- *Interoperability and portability:* Some of the requirements for interoperability of the functional elements of a system are consistency in syntax and semantics of characteristics such as naming, security, transport protocols, management protocols, data definitions, data formatting, and functions. So, a common management platform which can function under different conditions and different underlying systems transparently is one of the key SystemView objectives. This will enable easy portability, integration, and functioning under different multivendor, heterogeneous systems.
- *Protocol transparency:* There are many popular networking protocols such as OSI, TCP/IP, and SNA. Most of the management protocols use tightly coupled protocol stacks underneath them; for exam-

ple, TCP/IP uses SNMP, OSI has CMIP, and SNA makes use of SNA/MS. As a result, management applications using different management protocols and protocol stacks cannot interoperate. To enable them to work together, a common transport and protocol conversions will be required. Though there are many solutions, such as providing proxies, it is not always as easy as conceived, which sometimes leads to loss of information and performance problems. To overcome some of these drawbacks, SystemView intends to provide management applications transparent to transport protocols, with the management protocols making use of industry standards as much as possible.

- *Shared resources:* Resources, data, and functions are common factors in computing. The manner of accessing and processing them can be different for different enterprises and vendors. The resources, data, and functions can be represented as objects using industrywide applicable syntax and semantics. With this approach, commonality among resources, data, and functions is easier to achieve, and also enables easier sharing of objects across the industry. So SystemView has stressed industry-accepted data modeling techniques such that the objects can be easily and consistently accessed, processed, and shared.
- *Easy-to-use and consistent end-user interface:* The end-user interface is one area where there are lot of inconsistencies in the industry, and it greatly depends on the implementation below the end-user interface. As result of this dependency, the end-user interface must change if there are changes in the implementations. Thus, a primary objective is to make end-user interfaces as independent and seamless as possible. Also, provision must be made for technological developments in the end-user interfaces.
- *Evolutionary growth:* Formulating systems management solutions across the industry is a daunting task, so SystemView has adopted an evolutionary approach to achieving the objectives with the participation and cooperation of other vendors. This also protects existing investments and ensures that changes are made as smoothly as possible.

The *SystemView framework* encompasses a systems management structure known as SystemView, products, and solutions to the systems management issues of information systems. Information systems cover a wide range of computing resources such as hardware, software, processes (including functions), and services. The framework is flexible enough to include one or more networks, which can be hierarchical or distributed in nature. It is transparent to implementation details, such as whether the resources are from one vendor or many vendors or the protocols associated with them. The framework provides a consistent easy-to-use user interface, the ability to share data, and a base for improved automation capabilities.

The SystemView framework consists of the following:

- *Levels:* Levels of activity such as administration, planning, operation, and execution must be covered in the systems management solution. While managing applications is represented by administration and coordination levels, agents are related to execution levels.
- *Dimensions:* These must cover the integration of systems management from different perspectives, such as the user interface, shared management functions, and shared data.
- *Disciplines:* These must provide solutions to the whole range of systems management activities.
- *SystemView infrastructure:* This is an interface between managing applications, and includes the common management interface (CMI), common communication services, and interenterprise services.

One of the strong points of SystemView is that the emphasis is on modeling the data as objects, which helps in focusing on the commonalities of the resources. While most of the objects are modeled using the Management Information Model (ISO 10165-2) and Guidelines for the Definition of Managed Objects (ISO 10165-4), the end-user interface objects are an exception. They use OSF/Motif and Common User Access Architecture (CUA). These points must be noted as we examine the SystemView Data Model and SystemView Object Model. We will examine each of the components of the SystemView framework.

14.4 SystemView Levels

SystemView refers to a set of characteristics as levels and breaks down SystemView management functions and agents to these levels. These levels have a broad scope, from the conceptual to the actual implementation. They have no concrete relationship to the actual physical systems, people, or locations. The three levels (Figure 14.5) are explained in the following sections.

14.4.1 Administration level

The administration level is related to enterprisewide planning and administration. Some of the administration-level activities are:

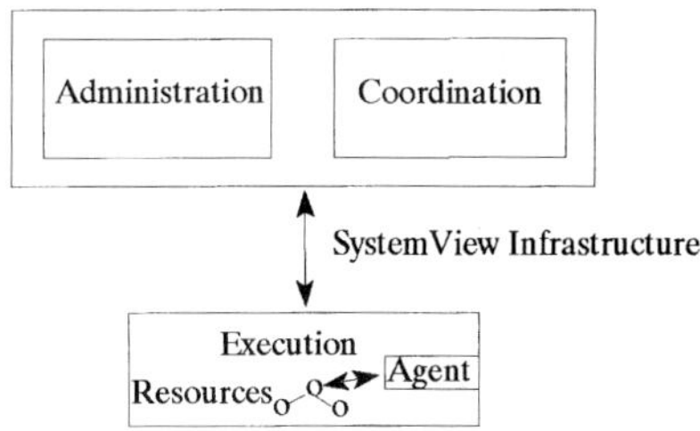

Figure 14.5 SystemView levels.

- *Policy formulations, goal setting, and validation:* These are key issues in the enterprisewide planning of information systems. These tasks must define the interfaces, functions, administrative data, resource configurations, and user interfaces; then policies on how these tasks will be implemented must be laid out; and validation and conformance criteria must be established.
- *Workload distribution:* Workload distribution of the activities defined by the preceding step must be done, which may involve different organizations, networks, and systems with different data storage media. These activities, like others, are related to the time span, and this key factor must be considered when doing the workload distribution. SystemView supports the distributed nature of networks, organizations, and data access and storage.
- *User interaction:* User interaction in different forms and different organizations is needed in managing information systems. This activity can be diverse in nature, with many variables involved.

14.4.2 Coordination level

The coordination level deals with the interaction between manager and agents to meet the goals set by the administration level. Manager and agent concepts are related to roles of applications. One or more SystemView applications can assume a manager's role. A manager sends commands to agents and receives responses and notifications from agents. A manager controls one or more agents. One strong point of SystemView is that there are no set rules on how managers are organized. They may communicate between each other either directly or by information passing through management databases. Between managers, there can be either a hierarchical or a peer-to-peer relationship. Also, these managers are distributable in that they can be decomposed into easily distinguishable functions and distributed among different processors.

A manager controls the agents within a domain, which may be mapped to territories, business areas, and organizations. It is better to have easily and distinctly partitioned domains.

14.4.3 Execution level

The execution level is concerned primarily with how agents operate, how agents operate in conjunction with managers, and how the resources represented by managed objects are handled by the agents. One of the primary requirements is that an agent must be able to interpret and manipulate a subset of the SystemView data model. There is no restriction on the implementation of agents—they can be on the hardware, software, or microcode, or a combination of them. Also, there is no restriction on the location of an agent. An agent function can be on one system or distributed over different systems. Agents need the following capabilities:

- *Data and information passing:* This is an important requirement for an agent. When a manager requests data using commands, then the data must be sent to a manager in the form of a response, and notifications may also be sent to managers from an agent. Data may also be sent to a manager on crossing thresholds.
- *Self-sufficiency:* An agent may experience a failure in the communication link between a manager and the agent. In such an event, the agent must be able to function independently, storing data, and when a manager comes up, the manager must be able to retrieve data from the agent. In addition, an agent must have the ability to update data on configuration and status on its own.
- *Resource sharing:* An agent may report to one or more managers. This is very useful to distribute the management functions over a wide set of managers, thus facilitating the distribution of the data on management resources.
- *Remote operation:* An agent needs to be remotely manipulated, and it must be able to easily configure the resources it controls. In the future, many commands to agents which, in turn, control the resources, will be unattended.

14.5 SystemView Dimensions

SystemView dimensions are an implementation view of systems management functions, and they are classified as shown in Figure 14.6.

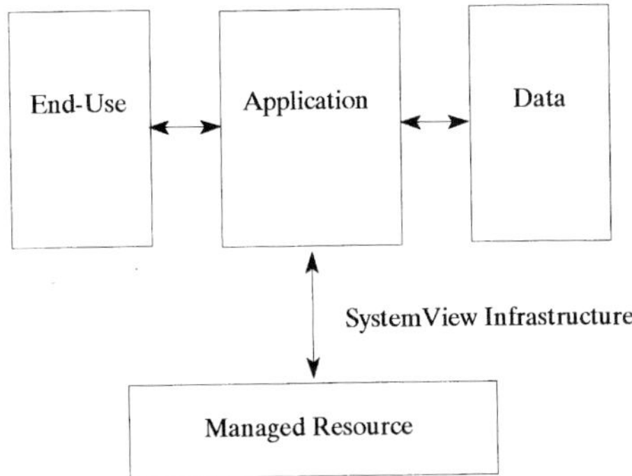

Figure 14.6 SystemView dimensions. (*Source: Modified by permission from* SystemView Structure, *SC31-7038-00, March 1993, copyright by International Business Machines Corporation.*)

14.5.1 End-use dimension

The end-use dimension is concerned with the user interface styles, facilities, and services of SystemView applications. These end-user interfaces present an easy-to-use consistent view of the applications, hiding the complexity of the implementations, providing for multitasking of them, and providing location transparency. The overall objective is to minimize the difficulties of users from a wide range of products. The end-use dimension provides help facilities, object-oriented–based user interfaces, and command interfaces to experienced users. Also, for flexibility, the presentation and business functions have been separated (Figure 14.7). Note that the business function interfaces with other dimensions.

14.5.2 Application dimension

The application dimension is responsible for a suite of consistent and integrated management applications with a well-defined interface to the agents. These applications can be from IBM or products from other vendors, and they include different disciplines and levels. The application dimension interfaces with the consistent end-use dimension, and also interfaces, as can be seen from Figure 14.6, with the managed resource dimension having an agent. An agent, in turn, must interface with managed objects. Access to the data dimension uses a consistent interface to data. The application dimension, which has a set of distinguishable functions, provides flexibility to integrate and package products. There is also emphasis on the automation aspects of the systems management with data being stored in one place.

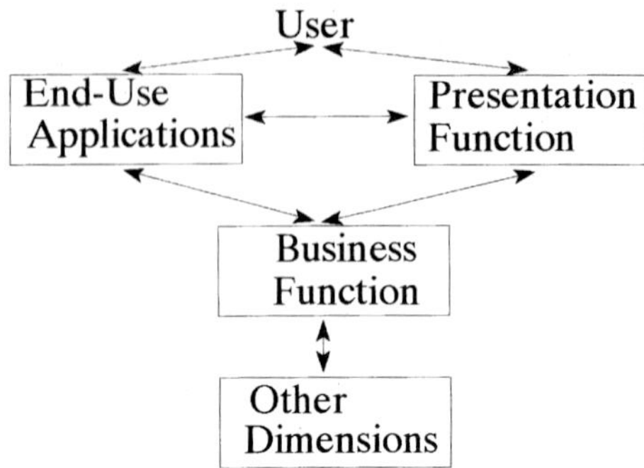

Figure 14.7 Relationships in the end-use dimension.

14.5.3 Data dimension

The data dimension is concerned with the storing, accessing, and sharing of management data. The application dimension accesses and manages the data dimension. In the data dimension, there are two logical databases: the Enterprise Information Base (EIB) and the Control Information Base (CIB). The administrative data can be stored in the EIB and operational data in the CIB. These logical databases interface with managing applications (Figure 14.8). One of the problems with the management data is that though management data is available, it is dispersed all around. To complicate the problem further, storing of data depends on the storage technology, and data is inconsistently stored. SystemView tries to overcome these shortcomings by having a consistent interface and data representation using consistent data models.

14.5.4 Managed resource dimension

The managed resource dimension is responsible for providing a consistent management view of resources in a system. This is accomplished by representing the resources as managed objects. The

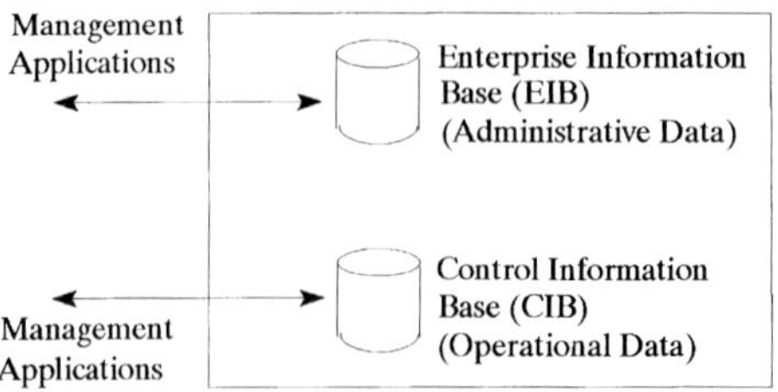

Figure 14.8 Data dimension.

agents, which interface with the management applications, control and manipulate the managed objects. Management applications operate on the top of the SystemView infrastructure; however, management applications interact with agents using a common management interface (CMI). Hence, management applications are transparent to the individual quirks of the managed objects. As a result, it is easy to add new resources, and the agents may not need many modifications. This provides for the characteristic of easy extensibility.

14.6 SystemView Infrastructure

The SystemView infrastructure consists of a CMI, common communication services, and interenterprise services. The CMI between the manager and agent facilitates easy migration of systems management applications, and is the base for writing management applications by different vendors. Common communication services are responsible for supporting different transport protocols of OSI, SNA, and TCP/IP. With the communication services, it is easier for applications to be transport-independent. Interenterprise services are useful for providing services between enterprises for activities such as help desk–type support; providing services to hardware, software, and microcode; consulting services; and coordination of different versions of software.

14.7 SystemView Disciplines

SystemView breaks up systems management functions into a well-defined and orderly classification of disciplines for convenience in the development of architecture and applications. At the same time, these disciplines are interrelated and sometimes they must be integrated to provide applications, which perform specific systems management functions. These disciplines are analogous to the OSI systems management functions. Note that there is no one-to-one mapping between SystemView disciplines and OSI systems management functions.

SystemView defines a *SystemView process* as a combination of well-defined steps and the execution of these steps to achieve a specific systems management task or tasks. These processes and systems management tasks are grouped into a *discipline*. A total combination of these disciplines provides overall systems management functions. SystemView disciplines and their mapping to OSI systems management functions are shown in Figure 14.9. Let us examine each of the SystemView disciplines more closely.

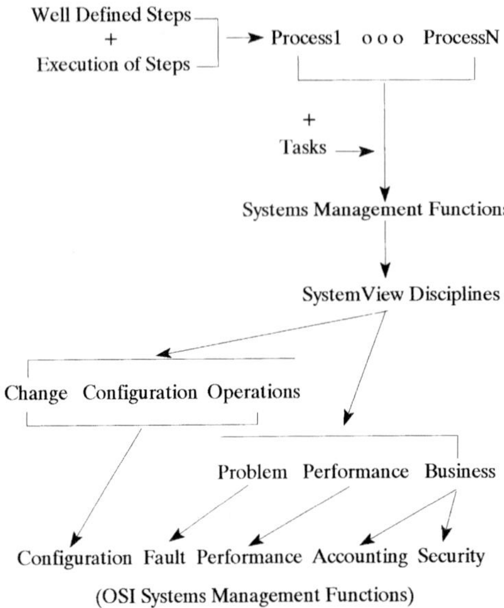

Figure 14.9 SystemView disciplines and mapping to OSI systems management functions. (*Source: Modified by permission from* SystemView Concepts, *SC23-0578-01, December 1993, copyright by International Business Machines Corporation.*)

14.7.1 Problem management

Problem management in SystemView is similar in semantics to OSI fault management. These problems can be in hardware, software, microcode, or medium, and they may be in workstations or computer networks. Problem management encompasses the following areas:

- *Problem identification:* Relates to the detection of a problem or problems out of a variety of possible problems which have resulted in deterioration in the functioning or failure of a component or components of an information system. This may require steps such as the correlation of the problems encountered, referral to the past problem history data, and analysis of the problems.
- *Problem reporting:* Refers to the reporting mechanism used for problems. It includes the generation of problem reports in different formats, and tracking the problems throughout their life cycles.
- *Problem solution:* Includes steps such as the assignment of a problem to the right person or application (may be an automation routine), escalation of problems in the correct manner to the contacts, appropriate solution selection, solution of the problems, verification that the problems have been correctly rectified, and closure of the problems. This step may also include recovery from faults.

For example, if a token-ring lobe has problems, it must be bypassed until it is rectified. Problem solution also includes automation. As we enter a client-server environment, the automation of most of the steps in the problem solution arena becomes a matter of paramount importance and necessity.

- *Problem policy formulations:* Include general guidelines on how problems are to be solved, how the data on problems are to be stored, and how these problems are to be tracked. The primary objective of policy formulations should be reducing the cycle time for rectifying the problems and minimizing the impact of problems with the overall objective of cost reduction.

14.7.2 Performance management

Performance management deals with performance issues such as tuning a network, analyzing the performance, optimizing the performance, and providing solutions to performance-related concerns. Broadly, the performance management discipline involves the following functions:

- *Performance policies:* Refer to the determination of overall performance goals for an information system. Policies must identify the performance standards, how these standards are tracked and reported, how they can be improved on a continual basis, and how the data on performance are stored and retrieved for future use.
- *Performance measurement:* Relates to the actual measurement of performance of systems and components in an information system. It must also deal with such aspects as performance tuning, performance tracking, and reporting.
- *Performance control:* Deals with how the performance measurements and improvements relating to the performance policies are laid out. This function should provide good feedback on the performance.
- *Performance capacity planning:* Must cater to future needs and how the systems are to be utilized to meet future objectives and requirements.

14.7.3 Operations management

The operations management discipline is related purely to the operational aspects of computing resources, which in turn relate to the specific area of workload on computer systems. As is evident from Figure

14.9, operations management is part of the OSI configuration management. Operations management deals with the following issues:

- *Workload policy formulations:* Encompasses areas such as the assessment of present workload and anticipated workload over time, and analyzes these to meet the information system needs of an enterprise, including both short- and long-term planning.
- *Workload planning:* Lays out the operational procedures for the whole enterprise. These functions require a lot of attention in enterprises with large information systems. Workload planning also involves how the operational data are collected, stored, and retrieved.

14.7.4 Configuration management

Configuration management deals with the relationship between resources. This discipline becomes a major issue, especially with the proliferation of client-server environments, in heterogeneous multiprotocol, and multivendor environments. Configuration management involves the following steps:

- *Configuration planning:* Deals with the particular configuration of hardware and software required in different systems associated with the information system of an enterprise. It also considers future configuration requirements such that the migration from present to future is smooth. Here, the key is the total information system.
- *Configuration design:* Covers the detailed working of how different configurations are managed and integrated into well-tuned systems. These have many challenges, especially in the integration of different systems.
- *Configuration manipulation:* Must implement solutions for storing, updating, and retrieving configuration data. In large enterprises, this can be a daunting task, especially if the computing systems operate in a decentralized fashion. These configuration data may be about different versions of a wide variety of software, model details of hardware, and the network configurations. These network configurations can be physical or logical and can be static or dynamic.

14.7.5 Change management

SystemView has a separate discipline for change management, and the functions included in the change management are elaborate. With the dispersal of workstations in different locations, it becomes very difficult to manage and keep track of software and hardware. It poses a bigger challenge to apply software fixes, software updates, and new software to different workstations. In such circumstances, it is better to automate them as much as possible, because the management of software becomes a difficult task, especially if the information systems are spread out across the globe. Some of the functions involved in change management are:

- *Policy formulations and planning:* Deals with formulating companywide uniform policies such as types, scheduling changes, distribution, and installation of new or updated software and hardware. This also involves planning functions such as costing, evaluation of different alternatives, and setting policies for changes.
- *Change scheduling:* An important function, in which the time when changes are to be applied must be considered. These changes should cause the least possible disruption of work activities. In some cases, changes are made during off-shift hours or weekends.
- *Distribution and installation:* Involve the actual application of changes and their verifications. The change may be to a new software or hardware, or it may simply be applying updates to existing software or hardware. This step must include installation and synchronization of updates across the board to different systems. These changes may not be uniform; i.e., all the workstations may need one set of changes, while another set of minicomputers may individually require different types of updates. After the changes are made, it is necessary to make sure that the changes have been correctly applied. It may also be necessary to back up to the original state when the changes do not meet the requirements.
- *License management:* Involves keeping track of software used, maintaining licenses, and continuously updating and monitoring different resources in the information systems. New licenses may need to be acquired or updates may simply need to be procured. Software update is also important because it concerns the number of licenses that have been covered and the time when the software update is done.
- *Tracking and analysis:* Required for change management to be useful. If the data on the resources are not kept up-to-date, then there can be problems. Also, the available data must be examined and analyzed to derive the maximum advantage from a change management perspective.

14.7.6 Business management

Business management is unique in SystemView. Some of the areas of business management are often overlooked in other network management protocols. Even though business management is mapped to the combination of functions in OSI systems management, the business management of SystemView is quite extensive and covers a broad spectrum of activities of information systems.

- *Inventory management:* Involves keeping track of resources, including their locations, pricing information, and conditions throughout their life cycles. These data must be optimized to reduce the expenses on inventory.
- *Security management:* Concerns how the resources are accessed and handled, and may involve different security levels for different classifications of employees. Here, broad guidelines on the security aspects are required.
- *Financial and accounting management:* Involves the cost aspect of resources in information systems. Though inventory management and financial and accounting functions are closely related, the overall function of cost reduction must be worked out by these personnel in coordination with the personnel in inventory management. It also involves budgeting activities and tracking costs.
- *Planning:* Covers a wide range of activities involving information systems and resources. It requires close attention to future needs, scheduling the acquisition resources to meet the requirements, and awareness of the associated costs. It also concerns the requirements placed on user communities to deliver the anticipated operations and performance. It may also require capacity planning related to the location of resources.

14.8 SystemView Object Model

SystemView relies heavily on object-oriented technology. Some of the major advantages of using object-oriented technology are:

- *Management of resources* is easier and simpler. Resources are modeled as managed objects and the characteristics are defined using standard templates. Only management-related and relevant characteristics are selected in the definition of objects. With this type of definition, commonality among resources is the key point and makes the sharing of resources between applications much simpler. Also, managing applications is not tied to the resources being managed.

- *Changes and the addition of resources* are more manageable than in the traditional environments. By making use of inheritance, new objects can be attached to the object models; thus, the addition of new resources will require inheriting many of the existing characteristics, as well as adding a few. Even the adjustments needed to accommodate changes in resources may be reduced to tweaking a few attributes.
- *Hiding of data* is a major gain. One of the fundamental principles in objects is the hiding of data and making it accessible only to the methods. With this hiding of data from the outside world, objects are more structured and easier to manage.

To improve the interoperability between objects, they have been defined using Guidelines for the Definition of Managed Objects (ISO 10165-4). We discussed GDMO concepts in Chapter 6. For distributed applications, object-oriented standards of the Object Management Group (OMG) are adopted. By using the industry standards, the SystemView Object Model (Figure 14.10) has improved the compatibility among the different resources used in management. The different dimensions of SystemView are represented as objects and form part of the SystemView Object Model, which comprises the following:

- End-use objects
- Managed-resource objects
- Management application objects
- Data objects

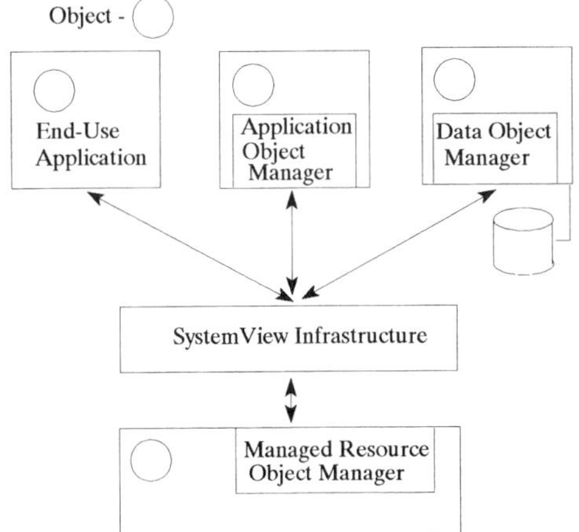

Figure 14.10 SystemView object model. (*Source: Modified by permission from* SystemView Structure, *SC31-7038-00, March 1993, copyright by International Business Machines Corporation.*)

The concept of object managers is used in manipulating objects. An object manager hides the implementation details. Requests for actions on objects are routed to the object managers. The requests to object managers trigger methods to interface with the infrastructure. There is no restriction on how the object managers must be implemented.

14.9 SystemView Data Model

A major problem encountered in systems management is the incompatibility in data representation in the computer industry. Different vendors represent data in different forms. To integrate these data on different resources is a major challenge. To overcome this problem, IBM has produced the data model for SystemView. The SystemView data model closely follows the standards to represent data in a consistent and uniform manner such that it is easy to integrate applications of other vendors following similar standards. A key goal of the SystemView data model is to represent data definitions in a consistent manner so that systems management functions conforming to the data model avoid the problem of interoperability.

The data model is an abstract concept for representing data so that it is useful for systems management purposes. It provides an object-oriented interface to data objects and hides the implementation details of objects. Object definitions are part of the data dimension.

Primary areas of the SystemView data model are administration, controls, and resources. As can be seen from Figure 14.11, these areas are further subdivided into collections, which, in turn, are divided into classes.

Over time, many applications will migrate to SystemView, which necessitates guidelines for implementation and how the implementations conform to the architecture. Thus, conformance requirements have been defined. At present, they are focused more toward the end-use dimension. Level 1 product must conform to CUA 89 or higher, and Level 2 product must conform to CUA 91 guidelines.

At the time of writing this book, a SystemView-based implementation known as *Karat* has been announced. Karat consists of systems management services, on which systems management applications can be built, and systems management applications, which provide end-to-end systems management capabilities across the enterprise.

14.10 Summary

This chapter is devoted primarily to SNA systems management, which has evolved over the years from being hostcentric to accommodate peer-to-peer LAN environments, as well as the smooth integra-

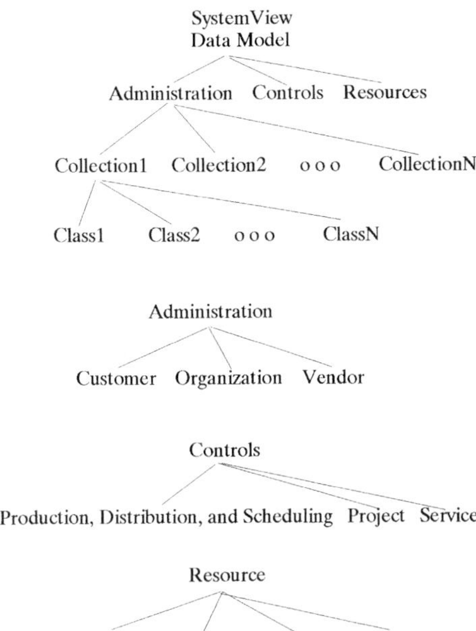

Figure 14.11 SystemView data model.

tion of these two environments. To cater to the challenges of network management in multivendor and multiprotocol environments and from hostcentric to distributed computing environments, IBM introduced the SystemView architecture. This architecture, which has matured over time, is based on object-oriented technology. The consistent data modeling of resources provides for interoperability with different environments.

14.11 References

14.1 IBM Corporation, GE20-0662, A Management System for the Information Business Volume I, Management Overview.

14.2 IBM Corporation, GE20-0749, A Management System for the Information Business Volume II, The Information Systems Service Mission.

14.3 IBM Corporation, GE20-0750, A Management System for the Information Business Volume III, Information Systems Development Mission.

14.4 IBM Corporation, GE20-0751, A Management System for the Information Business Volume IV, Managing Information System Resources.

14.5 IBM Corporation, SC30-3346, SNA Management Services Reference.

14.12 Further Reading

Allen, M. O., and S. L. Benedict, "SNA Management Services Architecture for APPN Networks," *IBM System Journal,* vol. 31, no. 2, 1992.

IBM Corporation, SC23-0578, SystemView Concepts.
IBM Corporation, SC31-7038, SystemView Structure.
IBM Corporation, G326-0126, IBM Enterprise Network Management NetView Family Guide.
IBM Corporation, GC30-3073, System Network Architecture, Technical Overview.
IBM Corporation, GC34-4354, Systems Application Architecture, SystemView Data Model, Concepts and Planning.
IBM Corporation, GC34-4481, SystemView Data Model, Overview.
IBM Corporation, GG24-3999, Systems and Network Management in Distributed Environments.
Irlbeck, B. W., "Network and System Automation and Remote System Operation," *IBM Systems Journal,* vol. 31, no. 2, 1992.
Peterson, David M., *Enterprise Network Management: A Guide to IBM's NetView,* New York: McGraw-Hill, 1993.
Szabat, M. M., and G. E. Meyer, "IBM Network Management Strategy," *IBM Systems Journal,* vol. 31, no. 2, 1992.
Trindell, L. D., *NetView: A Professional's Guide to SNA Network Management,* New York: McGraw-Hill, 1993.
Warner, Jr., W. E., *IBM Systems Management Strategy and Direction,* IBM Corporation, 1994.
Williams, Raymond, Enterprise Management, Introduction to Management Protocols, 1st ed., 1993. (IBM Document No. RCW1001-01.) A revised version of this appears as Chapter 17 of *LAN Times: A Guide to Interoperability,* by Tom Sheldon (McGraw-Hill, New York, 1994).

Note: The year of publication for IBM manuals has not been provided. The order number (e.g. GC30-3073) for the publications is sufficient to procure the latest IBM publications.

Part

5

Network Management and Issues

Chapter

15

Configuration Management

15.1 Introduction

We briefly discussed configuration management in Chapter 2. In this chapter, we'll examine the details. Here, the discussion of configuration management covers the functions defined in OSI. Different OSI documents must be combined to form a meaningful configuration management function. Because our focus is on the design and implementation of configuration management, we will also discuss issues not covered by OSI protocols. For full implementation of configuration management (Figure 15.1), the following primary functions are necessary:

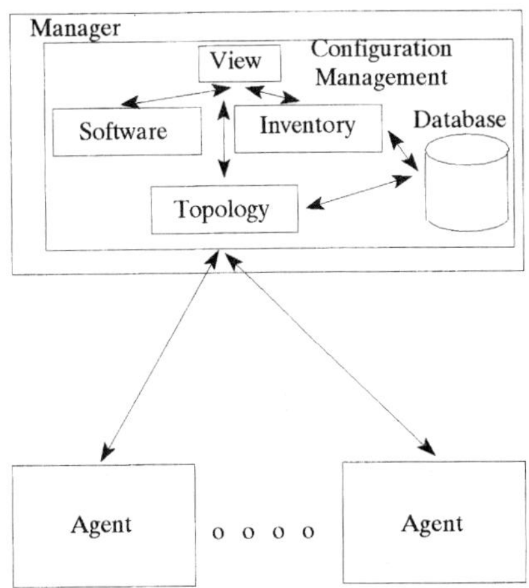

Figure 15.1 Configuration management overview.

- *View management:* Related to user interface issues, especially the graphic user interface (GUI). Though view management is required by other systems management functions, we prefer to discuss it in this chapter; it is more closely related to configuration management than to any other systems management function.
- *Topology management:* Refers to the issues related to forming and dynamically maintaining topology and status, including database, discovery mechanisms, and directories. A directory can be used for name resolutions. Note that a topology database is also required by other systems management functions.
- *Software management:* Concerned with software distribution and scheduling. This is also referred to as *change management.* Software management includes license management, although license management can also be included under inventory management.
- *Inventory management:* Deals with keeping track of computing resources, and may also include capacity planning. Inventory management is sometimes known as *asset management.*

We have used these terms and classifications for convenience in designing and implementing configuration management. Many different terminologies are used in the industry. In general, these classifications are functionally close to the different terms used.

15.2 View Management

The end-user interface should be easy to use and meaningful. View management may be based on different operating systems such as Windows 95, OS2 Warp, Unix, and others. End users can interact in different ways with the systems management functions. If an end user uses the command-line interface, the user should be able to send commands and get the results. While using command-line interface, different approaches may be used.

Figure 15.2 illustrates the concepts of synchronous and asynchronous modes, when using commands and replies. In synchronous mode, a command is sent and the user waits for a reply. The next command can be sent only after a reply is received. However, in asynchronous mode, the user need not wait for replies to come back; instead, he or she can continue sending commands and the replies are received in their own time.

In sophisticated view management systems, the user has the capability to define the rules on how commands are handled—in other words, the ability to customize the command-line interface. Then,

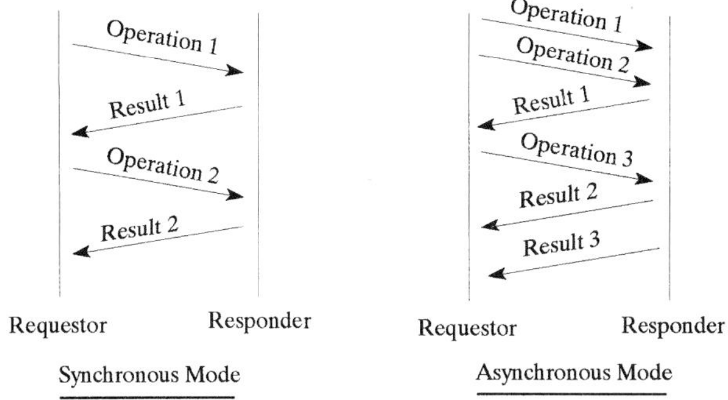

Figure 15.2 Commands and replies: synchronous and asynchronous modes.

based on these rules, the commands must be interpreted and routed to different command processors. Not only is it necessary to be able to view the results obtained, but they need to be stored so that they can be viewed later or customized reports can be generated later. It must be possible to print these reports. In each case, the ability to customize how and when the end user views and then generates, formats, and schedules the reports is important.

Panels have more requirements than the command-line interface. One should be able to navigate easily from one panel to another, as well as to skip levels. It must be possible to customize panels—for example, to open up many windows in a panel, to customize the size of windows, and to select the colors of the panels and sizes and fonts of texts. Also, there should be defaults for average users. Some users have strong viewpoints on how their panels should look and this factor must be taken into account when designing this component.

Panel design is quite complex, and it involves human factors, too. To avoid some of the pitfalls in products, it is often better to enlist the help of potential users up front to make sure they like the design. That way, changes can be incorporated from the start. Potential customers can provide useful feedback.

Some of the design issues that might have been overlooked may be noticed at this stage. View management is closely related to other components such as topology, configuration, fault, and performance management. From a user panel, one should be able to manipulate different systems management functions. For ease of use, there must be integrated or partitioned views.

Views need zooming ability. Users may want to zoom into a problem or have a broader picture. It should be easy to switch from one set of views to another. Also, when viewing, there should be provision to include, exclude, and refresh the views.

Another important aspect of panel design is the help facilities. The effectiveness of help facilities is dependent on the information contained in them and how it is presented to users. If the help facilities are to be used in different nations, relevant factors are language and differences in its use due to variations in cultures, religions, traditions, and accepted practices and norms.

But the key in all these operations is the ability to easily customize to individual requirements. Sophisticated users, especially, will have particular requirements that the design should be able to accommodate. If a user wants to write an individual application, it must be possible to do so. Thus, flexibility is another key factor.

15.2.2 View management architecture model

Initial views can be set up in different ways. The way initial views are depicted may be dependent on the sizes of the networks and the resources involved. Based on the requirements, there are different options for arranging these views, one of which is to divide and conquer. Network views (Figure 15.3) can be partitioned in the following manner:

- *Subnetworks:* A network view can be partitioned on the basis of LAN segments, LANs, backbone LAN, WANs, the carrier portion, and so on. This approach is most appropriate for the client-server environment.
- *Management domains:* For some systems management functions, a management domain can be a good way to partition a large network.
- *Geography:* If a network is large, spanning different states and nations, partitioning of views based on geography may be a useful way to zoom into the problems. The whole network can be broken down into countries, countries into convenient geographic locations such as states or cities, and geographical locations into buildings, floors, and individual offices.

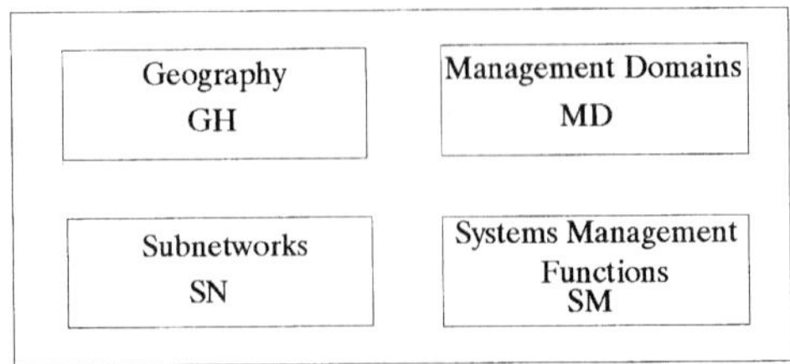

Figure 15.3 Starting point of views.

Once we partition the network views, we must be able to integrate them, too. This is important because sometimes the disjoint views may not present the details we need. When different partitioned views are provided, it must be possible to switch from one set of views to another. For example, someone viewing the configuration of a network in the United States may want to switch to a view of the United Kingdom, or to an integrated view of the network all over the world.

We should not limit ourselves to showing the state of the network statically, which just shows how the components are connected. To be of some use in problem determination, we should be able to dynamically view the state of the network. For example, we should be able to depict the state of a workstation which has failed typically by turning the icon for the workstation red on a topology map, and then we can investigate the component responsible for the failure of the workstation.

Depending on the circumstances, it may be desirable to see a physical or logical network view. The connection between a server and requestors may have both logical and physical views. However, another problem arises: How do we connect these logical and physical views? For example, if an adapter has a problem, the system administrator may want to know which adapter has failed. The logical view many not provide sufficient detail, so there is a need to correlate the physical and logical resources, which makes it easy to locate the physical resources. Once these physical resources are located, corrective actions can be taken with the use of fault management, or human intervention may be necessary.

It may be possible when sophisticated automation hardware and software become available that the fault management will kick off an automation routine which will resolve the problem. For example, if a software fix is required, this can be downloaded by a system administrator to the specific resource in the network requiring the fix. This resource may be a workstation, bridge, router, hub, or connector.

Key to all of these design questions is the definition of resources as managed objects. All the resources in the physical and logical views are represented as managed objects, which have the ability to be managed by agents. These objects need to be correlated to one another for problem isolation and diagnosis. Note that just the definitions of these objects by themselves are not enough; the data on these objects must be stored in a database for later use.

Resources can be physical entities such as a monitor at a workstation, an operating system like DOS or Windows 95, or logical entities such as files, sessions, or requestors. These resources can be combined to make a system. A workstation is a system. In this fashion, hierarchies can be built that can conveniently represent the entire network.

As an example, a network view can be partitioned into different subnetworks (Figure 15.4). Clicking on the subnetworks shows the next hierarchical view of the subnetworks connected by bridges, routers, or gateways. In the subnetworks, the line (A) indicates that there are extensions to the network. If there is no line (B), it is the end of a view. When a user further clicks on the subnetworks, the next level of view, composed of intelligent hubs, workstations, and so on, is displayed. Each view can be generically termed a system.

Going down one level displays the views of the software and hardware resources, such as monitors and operating systems. Along with the views, the details are usually displayed, and further details are usually provided by the option to go to another panel offering texts and figures.

As mentioned earlier, one of the techniques adopted is to break up the total network into convenient management domains (Figure 15.5). If a view is too big, it can be accommodated in different pieces, which then must be combined to get an integrated picture. Clicking on management domains gets the next level, which has the management domains named. These management domains are further partitioned into the hierarchy of managers, and the agents reporting to the manager are supplied.

As an example (refer to Figure 15.5), in management domain MD2, agent A1 reports only to manager 1 and agent A3 reports to both

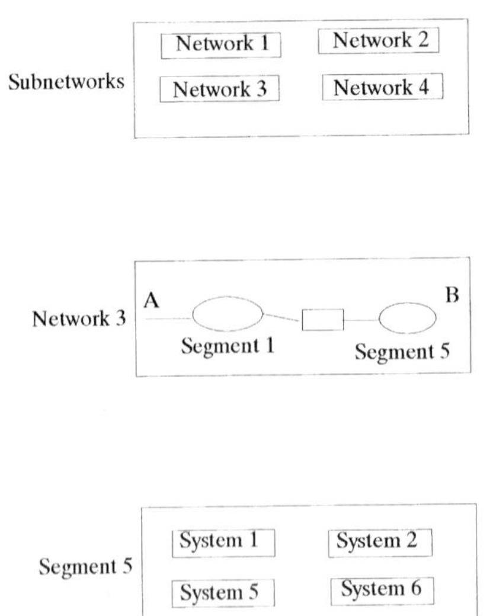

Figure 15.4 Subnetwork views.

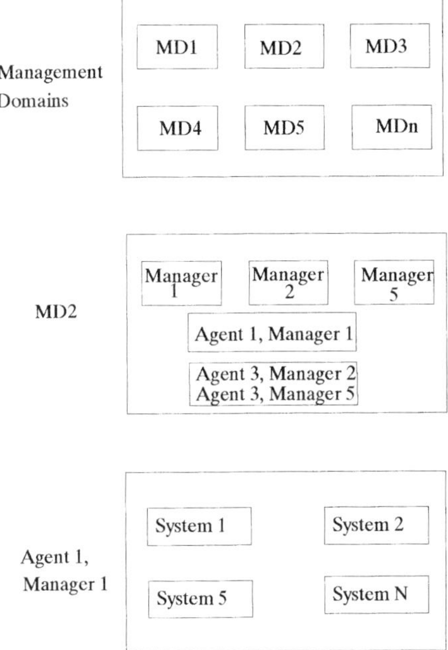

Figure 15.5 Management domain views.

manager 2 and manager 5. Clicking further on the views in the management domain shows the next level, which has systems associated. The system can be further subdivided into the resources. Note that Figure 15.5 does not follow through up to the resources level.

Figure 15.6 depicts another view, which is by geography. Here, there can be a hierarchy of views such as nations, states, places, buildings, floors, rooms, systems, and resources. The last view in the figure can be arranged in the order of the system management functions. These views again need the capability to be tailored, and there must be options to activate and deactivate them. In some cases, it may be better to select and deselect the views.

There can be no hard and fast rules on the hierarchy of views. If a network is located in only one nation or state, then there is no need to put up a world map as a starting view every time. There should also be ways to bypass the hierarchy of different levels. It should not be necessary to navigate through the levels of countries, states, and places each time to get to buildings; it should be possible to go directly to buildings.

Another very important point to note is that these views should be well integrated and consistent. A physical system WS1 in the management domain view must mean the same thing as a physical sys-

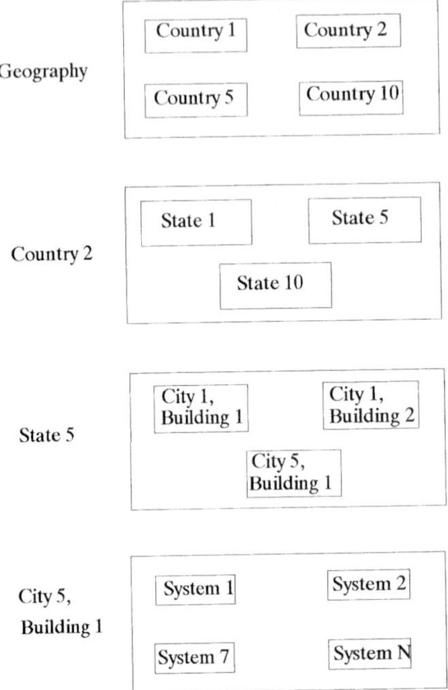

Figure 15.6 Views by geography.

tem WS1 in the view by geography. When a user looks at WS1 in the management domain, the user must be able to switch over to the fault management function view without navigating too many steps downward or upward. It should also be possible to send commands from the command line while in the middle of view functions. When forming views, there are different ways data can be shown in a panel. They may contain fewer details at the first pass. A user who is more interested in the details may have to go the next level or the next menu in the panel.

It may be desirable to view data in a sorted fashion. Especially in systems management functions such as accounting management and performance management, bar graphs and pie charts are useful. As mentioned earlier, there must be facilities to format and print the data, especially if there is a large amount of it.

When there is a call from a user to the help desk, a system administrator may wish to see where the actual problem is. By starting with the network, the administrator may quickly track the problem being reported, but it must be possible to narrow it down with the least amount of navigation. This is an important consideration during the design phase. In some systems, a fast track to pinpoint failure is provided whereby one can zero in on the problem directly.

In addition, color schemes need to be well designed to depict the different states of the resources of a network. For example, red may indicate that a resource has failed, green that a resource is working, and blue that the resource has crossed the threshold value. However, it should be possible to customize the colors based on the user's preference, and further details should be available on each state, if desired.

15.3 Topology Management

Topology management keeps track of the status of the resources and how they are connected in a network. Both topology management and inventory management are required for resolving problems in the network. Topology management is tricky. There may be thousands of workstations, bridges, and routers connected to form LANs and WANs. They are interconnected to form an integrated network. This problem becomes more complex if these resources are from different vendors "speaking" different protocols and the resources span different geographical locations. In such a situation, the issue is how to depict the network in an integrated fashion and, when required, how to zero in on a portion of the network. If possible, the problem should be rectified without human intervention.

Networks can have planned configurations, which means that this view shows how the configurations were originally intended. This is required for comparison with actual configurations to reveal deviations from the planned ones. It is interesting to analyze the reasons for departing from the planned configurations.

When a workstation has a failure, there may be many sources of the problem, such as a software failure, which, in turn, may be due to a bug in the program or incompatibility, and may need a fix. Hardware failure may stem from many sources, such as the adapters, the hubs, or parts of the workstation itself. There may be a failure in the connections to the network or in the bridges and routers.

With so many possibilities for failures, a user at a workstation may call the help desk to assist with the problems. The help desk personnel must be able to view the network and the workstation, and must have the up-to-the-minute details to zero in on and address the problems. For this, the dynamic or latest state of the network must be known at the help desk. When failures occur, it should be possible to isolate the adapter that has broken down and activate a backup. If this operation cannot be done, it may be possible to bypass altogether the failed workstation, in which case a service representative may be dispatched to repair the workstation.

Also, there are occasions when traffic in a portion of a network becomes too heavy, resulting in traffic that is too slow across the network; in an Ethernet segment, there may have been many collisions. In these situations, it should be possible for the system administrator to be proactive and take corrective actions such as switching some of the workstations to a less-utilized LAN segment.

Topology data can be of a dynamic or static nature. When there are changes to resources or they are created or deleted, there is dynamic topology data. One of the major problems is how the topology is first formed and how the data is stored. For this, one must know how to identify each component of the network. Here, also, there are different ways that connections can be presented to the end users. One is the physical connections, which may be made differently than logical connections. A topology database must have at least the following information:

- State of the resources
- Status of the resources
- Relationship among the resources
- Physical details of the resources

This storing of topology data may create its own problems. If massive amounts of data are stored, the system administrator's (manager) workstation will need a lot of storage, too. So a balance must be struck between how much data is required and how the objects are stored. If the status of the components must be made dynamic, then we have to consider the time interval in which the data on the network and its components is collected. If the interval is too short, then massive data must be handled by the network. This in itself may create heavy traffic in the network. On the other hand, if one uses too large an interval, the data may be stale. The workstation might have had its failure some time back, but the system administrator does not yet have knowledge of the failure. In addition, storage considerations must be taken into account. Again a balance is necessary between the requirements and the constraints of the total system.

If there is enough main memory, a cache can be maintained, and this will improve the performance. Because it is necessary to maintain data dynamically on topology and status changes, and these changes must be reflected on the workstation views without much time elapsing since the data was received, a cache can be of considerable help.

When a network is large, there is potential that a large number of objects and their instances will need to be stored. This may become a limitation on some workstations that do not have much processing power and storage capacity. In these situations, the placement of managers and agents must be done carefully.

For example, in a token-ring network, an agent can collect and store all the data required in its MIB for its portion of the network. Similarly, the agent in another Ethernet network segment can collect the information for its segment. Here, only workstations with agents need to have processing power and storage capacities. The other workstations need not have much storage and processing capacity, but, for backup purposes, it is better to have additional workstations with sufficient processing and storage capabilities. These additional workstations may have backup agents.

However, in this scenario, there will be some time delay involved. The responses for the commands from the manager will take some time, because the agents will have to collect data and then send the responses back to the manager. Another alternative is for the agents to periodically poll and collect data from the workstations and store the data in the MIB. In this case, when a command is received from a manager, the response can be sent immediately. But even here, depending on the period during which data is collected by the agent, some time delay is involved.

Instead of this, another technique can be used in which the workstations can send any changes at regular intervals. However, there is one problem with this approach. If a workstation has failed for some reason, then an agent may not know about it at all; it may assume that the workstation did not have any major change. To overcome such contingencies, timers are usually set, and it is assumed that if an agent has not heard from a workstation for a certain amount of time, the workstation is no longer operational. When the timer expires, the agent may poll the workstation to check whether it is working or there was no change from the previous reporting period.

As we have seen earlier, the collection of data places a burden on network traffic and storage capacities. Also, redundant data may sometimes obscure problems where actual attention is required. To resolve some of the problems, it is necessary to have a complete picture of the network dynamically, and to be of some use, this dynamic picture of the network must be further integrated with components such as performance management and fault management. So providing the flexibility to choose the resources and the periods when they are to be monitored is very important.

The main point of the preceding discussion is that, to be useful, the activities of different sets of system management need to be coordinated. The user must be able to make intelligent decisions or at least alert concerned people in system administration. As networks become more sophisticated, rules may have to be formulated and concepts of artificial intelligence incorporated into the front end of view management and topology management.

15.3.1 Discovery

To locate the individual resources of a network, each resource needs to have a piece of software or hardware which identifies it. Data on the resources must be collected by the agents and transmitted to the managers. This identification process is known as *discovery,* and it is an important function. Unfortunately, there are different ways for hardware or software resources to identify themselves, varying from standard to proprietary methods depending on the vendors. Some of the important discovery techniques are:

- *OSI notifications:* Emitted when objects are created, deleted, or changed, and also when there are changes in states and status. These notifications, which are delivered as EVENT-REPORTs to managers, must be continuously monitored to form the initial topology and to dynamically update the topology later on.
- *TCP/IP PING and traceroute:* Packet InterNet Gopher (PING) can be used to acquire information about the connectivity. In PING, the ICMP echo reply is received for an ICMP request. Also, the traceroute function can be used for information about the route from a source device to a destination device. In traceroute, UDP packets are sent to an IP address and wait for ICMP replies.
- *IEEE Manager Present and Agent Present:* These have already been discussed in detail in Chapter 12.

In addition to these methods, there are discovery mechanisms specific to proprietary protocols. To form the topology in a multiprotocol environment, different discovery mechanisms must be used.

Different strategies can be used when building a topology database. One of these is to build this database right at the beginning and then continuously update it based on the regular information on the network components. This is known as *dynamic topology updating.* However, it takes a lot of time to build the topology database up front, and this may become an irritation to some users.

The topology database can also be built as one goes, which means that the system management portion would come up quickly, or the initialization time, including the discovery and the process for building the network, takes comparatively less time. Then, in the background, the network components are gradually discovered as needed. This method requires some time for the topology database to stabilize.

Those devices that are not discovered will not be found in the topology database, and thus cannot be shown in the views. Here, static configuration may be useful. The comparison of views obtained by static configuration and the views obtained by discovery are useful in identifying the reasons why some components were not discovered. Note that static configuration may be the same as planned configuration or may have a different configuration.

15.3.2 Data collected in database

The data collected in the topology database constitutes a major portion of systems management–related data. All data pertaining to systems management, such as topology, fault, performance, accounting, and security data, can be centralized in this database, which will be simpler to implement. However, there are problems associated with collecting data in a central place. The database may become huge. An alternative is to collect data for different systems management functions in different databases than in the topology database, but this brings up the problem of coordinating different databases.

Some of the data that may be stored in the database are:

- *Product specification data:* This includes details on the resources, such as the following:

  Hardware details, which can be manufacturers' details, processor details, communication card details, details of workstation such as model number and serial number, main memory details, hard disk details, multimedia attachment details, cost details, and so on.

  Software details, which pertain to the operating system software and include versions, sources, and prices; word processor details; networking operating system details; and connectivity, communication, and system management software details.

  Accessory details, which can cover data related to the printers, plotters, networks, etc.

- *Security data:* Refers to the authorization, authentication, and access rule details of users, system administrators, and others.
- *Fault and performance management data:* Contains data on problems logged and threshold details.
- *Accounting data:* Refers to the data on usage and the hardware and software costs.
- *Performance data:* Contains data on counters and threshold levels.

15.3.4 Object directories and X.500 directory

Data on object instances can be stored in the databases of their respective agents. To manipulate and manage the managed objects, it is necessary to know where each agent is located, which can be in a directory. Each agent may support different protocols, so the information on these protocols is also required. This protocol-related information may be stored in the same directory. Though there are many popular directory implementations, we limit our discussions to the popular X.500 directory of OSI.

Our interest in X.500 directories is from the point of view of name management. ISO 9594-1 (X.500), page 8, states: "The Directory is a collection of open systems which cooperate to hold a logical database of information about a set of objects in the real world." Directory services is concerned with storing information, the organizational structure of the information, and the operations that can be done on the information stored. It is a sort of database for OSI applications. A directory is analogous to a telephone directory, which contains information such as name, address, and telephone numbers, and, like a telephone directory, can be organized in a particular order for easy retrieval of information.

A process that accesses a directory on behalf of another process or user and performs operations such as requests for information or modify in a directory is known as a *directory user agent* (DUA). A DUA (Figure 15.7) is an application process, and it interacts with a *directory system agent* (DSA), which is the access point for a directory.

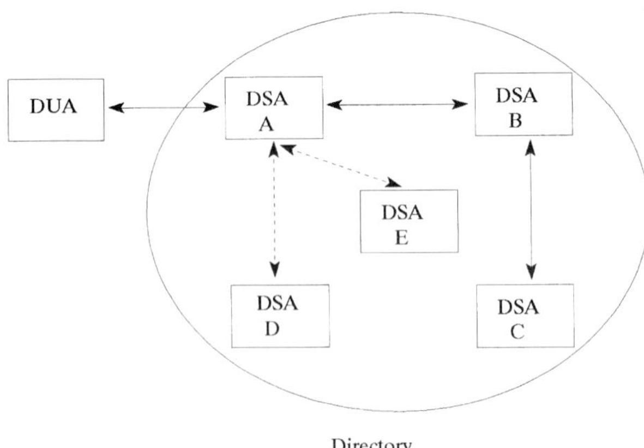

Figure 15.7 Directory functional model.

Directory models. For convenience, directory models are classified into different functional areas, such as the information model, functional model, organizational model, and security model.

Information model. The information model describes how the managed object entries are organized and what they mean. There are basically two concepts here: the *directory information base* (DIB) and the *directory information tree* (DIT). The DIB is a logical database of managed objects. Each managed object in the DIB has an entry, which consists of one or more attributes. An attribute has a type and one or more values. If an attribute has more than one value, then one of them is called the *distinguished value.* This is analogous to a primary key in a database. The concepts of entry and attribute are illustrated in Figure 15.8.

These managed objects are related to each other in a hierarchical fashion, and they can make use of inheritance characteristics. This organization is known as the DIT. To uniquely identify a managed object in the DIT, we use a *distinguished name* (DN). We have already seen how DNs are formed out of relative distinguished names (RDNs) in Section 3.5. However, the DIT uses the concept of *alias* whereby managed objects in the leaves of a DIT can have alias entries. An alias is just a pointer to another managed object and provides alternate naming for the managed objects.

Functional model. The functional model furnishes details on how operations can be performed on a directory. A user who wants information establishes an association with a DUA and a DSA, using an operation called a directory *bind.* An association is released by using a directory *unbind.* DUA queries are in the form of requests and responses. A DUA asks for information from a DSA, resulting in one of the following cases:

- The answer is available in and returned by the DSA.

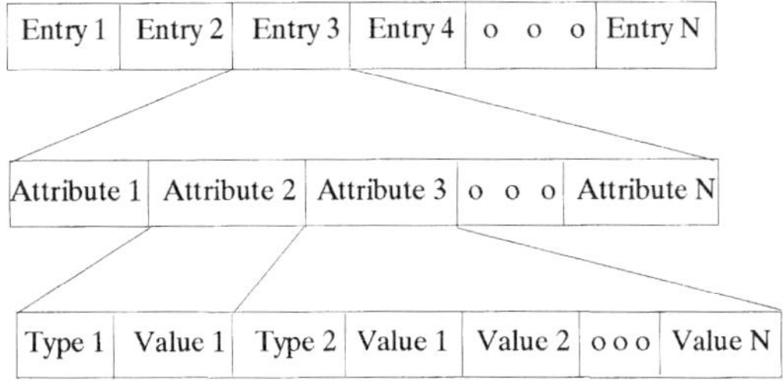

Figure 15.8 Directory information base (DIB) entry.

- If the DSA does not have an answer, it refers in its response to another DSA, which may have the answer. Then the concerned DUA queries the appropriate DSA. This is known as the *referral* mode.
- DSA A queries DSA B for the results and this operation continues to DSA C until the actual response is returned. This mode is known as the *chaining* mode.
- The request is sent concurrently to two or more DSAs, so any DSA that has the answer replies to the DSA that sent the request. This DSA, in turn, sends its reply to the DUA which sent the request in the first place. This is know as the *multicasting* mode, and is similar to the multicasting found in LANs. In Figure 15.7, multicasting requests and responses are shown by dotted lines.

Organizational model. From the organizational point of view, a directory is divided into *directory management domains* (DMD) for the sake of administrative and operational convenience. A DMD is a subtree of a DIT, and it consists of DUAs and one or more DSAs. DMDs are further classified as *administration DMD* (ADDMD), with powers to charge tariffs, and *private DMDs* (PRDMDs), which, obviously, cannot charge tariffs.

Security model. It is essential that the data stored in the form of managed objects are properly secure and that they do not fall into the wrong hands. This becomes all the more important when we disperse these managed objects in many places. Thus, a security model has been defined by OSI for directory services.

The security model consists of the authentication framework and access control. The authentication framework uses *simple authentication* and *strong authentication.* In simple authentication, passwords are used to check whether one is a genuine user. Strong authentication uses public key cryptographic systems (PKCS). To make sure that the data has been originated by a genuine user, a digital signature can also be used. In addition, access control is used to check the rights of a user to access certain managed objects.

Operations on a directory. The operations that can be performed on a directory are analogous to operations on a database or on files. There are primarily two types of operations: *interrogation* and *modify.* In all the operations, there will be errors if there are security violations, operations cannot be performed or chained by a DSA, wrong names and attributes are supplied, or we abandon the operation in progress by aborting it.

Interrogation consists of the following operations:

- *Read:* In a read operation, the DUA supplies the DN of a managed object and information on whether attribute types only or both attribute types and values are required. If the operation is successful, then values of the requested operation are returned; otherwise, information on the reasons for errors are returned.
- *Compare:* This operation can be used to check whether an attribute has a particular value; for example, checking whether password is correct. The compare mechanism allows for the hiding of data. In compare, we supply the object name and attribute value, and in return we get the result of the comparison in the form of true, false, or errors.
- *List:* This operation returns a list of the RDNs of the subordinates of a node, when we supply the name of a managed object. The list can also have arguments. An error can also be returned for a list operation.
- *Search:* This is useful for searching portions of a directory. Here, we supply the name of a managed object, scoping parameter, and filtering parameter, and the search operation returns information from the selected entries or errors. For example, we supply a last name and get the telephone numbers of the users matching this last name.
- *Abandon:* This is a cancel operation to abort the previously mentioned operations. Here, we supply the identifier of the operation to be canceled.

Flexibility is required for the use of directories. The interrogation operations permit us to query the directory data. But we need to add entries, remove entries, and modify entries once they are in a directory. In all the modify operations, NULL is returned for the success of an operation or an error is returned for the failure of an operation. Modifications are made using the following operations:

- *Add Entry:* This allows the addition of an entry to the leaf of a DIT. The DUA supplies the DN, attribute, and its values, if any.
- *Remove Entry:* This is the reverse of Add Entry. The DUA supplies the DN of an entry to be deleted. Note here that we can remove only a leaf entry.
- *Modify Entry:* This allows attributes and their values to be changed. Modify can also be used for changing alias entries. The changes can be addition, removal, or replace. They are atomic in the sense that all the changes of a particular operation are carried out or none of them are performed.

- *Modify RDN:* This can be used to modify the RDN of an entry. The DUA supplies a DN and new RDN of the entry to which the RDN must be modified.

Directory protocols. Directory protocols govern the interactions between DUA and DSA, DSA and DSA, and replication and the administrative services used in replication. There are two forms of replicated information: cache copies and shadowing information. The four directory protocols are:

- *Directory access protocol* (*DAP*): This explains how a DUA accesses a DSA.
- *Directory system protocol* (*DSP*): This governs the interactions between DSAs in a directory. There are provisions for chained operations such as chained read, modify, and search.
- *Directory information shadowing protocol* (*DISP*): This states how replications, which are used for easy searches and for reliability of DSAs, are to be done.
- *Directory operational binding management protocol* (*DOP*): This indicates how DSAs can alter the administrative characteristics.

Note that we have briefly looked at directories from the angle of network management. For further details, refer to Directory Services in the Further Reading.

Notes on directories and databases. ISO directories are becoming popular and some implementations are available. From the network management point of view, they are quite useful, and it is better to have standard directories for storing managed objects because this improves interoperability. In addition to ISO, there are many bodies working on standardized object directories.

The location of directories and how they are managed are important considerations. Also, one must consider what data objects are placed in a directory. There can be different strategies for how the directory and the MIB of an agent can be arranged. A directory can be placed in one manager. The agents can have the database of object definitions and object instances. The magnitude of the data or the size of data that can be stored in an MIB of the agent are primary concerns.

A frequent question is: Do we place all the object data, including the configuration, in each respective agent, or do we have an agent which, in turn, can act as manager to many other agents? This intermediate manager can forward the commands to the appropriate agents, acting as a sort of proxy agent. It may also forward the events it received from the agents to the manager.

An agent workstation may not have much hard disk memory and processing power. The network data rate is also an important consideration. We can distribute the database of the objects in an agent to different agents. Another alternative is to put the topology database in a server and let different agents get data as a client. This reduces the demands placed on an agent. While designing and implementing the databases, it is important to consider the effective breakup of databases to do some load balancing. The topology database, which can be a massive one, complicates the issue of how the database is positioned. At the same time, we must consider the constraints that may limit the efficiency of the way these databases are managed and manipulated.

15.4 Software Management

Software management is an important part of configuration management, because it determines the rules for applying software changes to the systems in the network and executes software distribution. However, here too, the requirements may vary. Software management is done to customize the installation and distribution of software. This does not mean that hardware setups and installations cannot be done. As technology improves, this aspect will require attention by configuration management. Whatever products will be installed, they must be capable of flexible installation from a remote location.

In a client-server environment, there are can be a large number of clients connected to a server or set of servers. Each client may require its own configuration. For example, one client might want simple word processor software, but another client may require additional graphics software. So, the software requirements may vary from client to client, and it must be possible to distribute and install customized software for each client.

Even when doing software configuration, there are two possibilities. One is the case of a new user being connected to the system, which can involve different requirements and setups ranging from simple to the most complicated. Also, new users may have to be configured to have their software installed at different times. Alternatively, the configuration may be a simple matter of applying software updates to a workstation.

This installation includes the distribution of the software from a central location. It should also be possible to do installations and, if required, modify the installations from the client. For example, a user in a client may want a specific type of software update. It should be possible for the user to download the required software update from servers. The distribution of software involves the transfer of data across the network. Usually for software distribution, file transfer mechanisms are used.

Errors are possible when doing the installation, in which case, there should be facilities for reinstalls. The installation errors may be logged in clients and transferred to the servers. To cater to the wide requirements of users, policies or rules are necessary for setting up or updating the workstations. A set of policies must be formed in the remote site, which can be a server, too. These policies must have the ability to be tailored to meet specific installation or update requirements, and the installation must be done under the guidance of these policies.

It is also necessary to schedule the downloading of the software. It may not be desirable to do such massive transfers during peak hours and they may have to be done when network traffic is light or during off hours, thus requiring scheduling. Also, it must be done according to the instructions set up by the software management function. When software is transferred, it is necessary to keep track of the details of the software, including:

- *License management:* May be on the basis of workstations or users. It may be better to keep track of these details by workstation, because users may frequently change workstations. Some software may be licensed from one or more vendors, who may charge on the basis of software licenses used or on the basis of usage of the software. It is necessary to keep track of the licenses.
- *Resource profile:* Involves user profile details such as name, location, phone number, privileges if any, and other details. These may vary slightly from installation to installation.
- *Pricing details:* May include the price and release year of the software.
- *Version details:* Includes the version of the software.
- *Sources:* Should include the details of the source of the software, such as the address of the source and support information, especially any help telephone numbers.
- *Activity:* Includes details such as whether it is a new install, update, or fix.

Having discussed some of the issues in software management, let us examine ISO software management. ISO software management–related documents consist of the Software Management Function (ISO 10164-18) and Scheduling Function (ISO 10164-15), to which work items on command sequencing must be added.

We will briefly discuss the software management function first. The following software management functions have been defined:

- *Backup:* May be used to perform backup of a software item.
- *Delete:* Can be used to delete software from a managed system.
- *Deliver:* Used to deliver one or more software items.
- *Execute:* For executing executable software.
- *Get:* Can be performed to obtain information about software.
- *Install:* Concerns software installation procedures; also includes customizing the software installation and updating.
- *Restore:* Used to restore the software already backed up.
- *Revert:* Relevant when we want to go back to the original software; can be applied to newly installed software or patches.
- *Set Administrative State:* For making software available for use. It is intended to control the usage of the installed software. Installed software can be made unavailable for use by setting the Set Administrative State to locked.
- *Validation:* Used to check the functionality of the software. It can also be used to check whether the previously delivered software is usable.
- *Terminate Validation:* Can be used to terminate the validation being done.

For the purposes of software management, the following managed object classes have been defined:

- *softwareUnit:* This refers to the resource which accepts delivery of the software. After the delivery of the software, it must be customized before installing. After installation, it is made available or unavailable by setting Set Administrative State to the unlocked or locked state using PT-SET.
- *executableSoftware:* This is a subclass of the softwareUnit managed object class; thus, it inherits the characteristics of that class. In addition, the executableSoftware managed object class has an Execute Program operation and mandatory usage state attribute. Values of Usage State are: idle, active, and busy.
- *softwareDistribution:* This is useful for distributing software to a target managed system, which is done by performing a delivery operation from a managing system to the softwareDistribution managed object (Figure 15.9). The softwareDistribution managed object class is a subclass of the software managed object class defined in CCITT Recommendation M.3100, Generic Network Information Model.

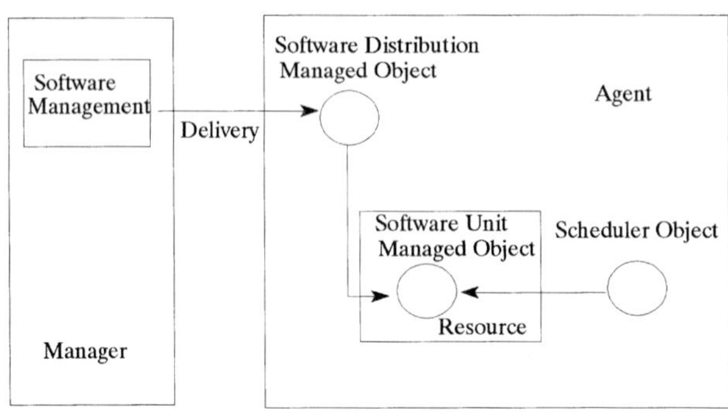

Figure 15.9 Software distribution model.

Though the scheduling function is required by other systems management functions such as performance management and fault management, we prefer to discuss its basic features with software management because the two are closely related. The scheduling function provides a model for a scheduling object, service primitives and their parameters, the managed objects for scheduling, and conformance requirements. The scheduled managed object refers to the managed object whose activities are to be scheduled. There are two types of scheduling: *internal* and *external*. Internal scheduling is used for a managed object as a whole, and external scheduling must be used when the activities of more than one managed object must be scheduled or activities on multiple managed objects are to be scheduled.

Let us briefly examine the inheritance hierarchy of scheduler managed object class. The scheduler managed object class is derived from OSI top. The subclasses of scheduler managed object classes are: dailyScheduler, weeklyScheduler, monthlyScheduler, and periodicScheduler.

The managed object classes defined in the scheduling function are:

- *scheduler:* This is the superclass of all the scheduler objects and provides the scheduler identifier, activities to be scheduled, and the duration of the schedule.
- *dailyScheduler:* This refers to the daily intervals available of a scheduled managed object class. dailyOperationScheduler managed object class is a subclass of dailyScheduler.
- *weeklyScheduler:* This is useful for scheduling activities on a weekly basis. The granularity of intervals per day and days of a week are provided by the multipleWeeklyScheduling package.

Here, weeklyOperationScheduler managed object class is a subclass of weeklyScheduler.

- *monthlyScheduler:* This is useful for scheduling activity for a month, and it uses the multipleMonthlyScheduling package. monthlyOperationScheduler managed object class is a subclass of monthlyScheduler.
- *periodicScheduler:* This can be used for scheduling activity on a regular basis, and has the periodicSchedulingPackage. It can also have the periodicSynchronizationPackage. periodicOperationScheduler managed object class is a subclass of periodicScheduler.

The operation scheduler managed objects are used to schedule Get, Set, and Action operations on the scheduled managed objects on a daily, weekly, monthly, or periodic basis.

For scheduling functions, schedulerObjectPackage and duration are defined in ISO 10165-2. In addition to these packages, the following new scheduling packages have been defined in ISO 10165-15:

- *mulipleDailyScheduling:* This provides the sequence of time intervals for a day when scheduled activities will occur.
- *multipleWeeklyScheduling:* This extends the activities provided by mulipleDailyScheduling to a week.
- *mulitpleMonthlyScheduling:* This extends the activities when a scheduled managed object will be available during time specified for a month.
- *operationsSchedulingPackage:* This identifies the operations to be scheduled in a scheduled managed object.
- *periodicSchedulingPackage:* This provides the time periods for triggering an activity.
- *scheduledActivitiesPackage:* This identifies the scheduled managed objects using the scheduler object.
- *resynchronizationModePackage:* This indicates the way a time period is defined or redefined when the operation of a period in a scheduler managed object is activated.
- *scheduledManagedObjectsPackage:* This has a list of the scheduled managed objects being served by a scheduler managed object.
- *schedulerObjectPackage:* This provides the naming attribute for the scheduler managed object; hence, it can be used to suspend or resume functioning of the scheduler managed object.
- *operationNotificationPackage:* This contains the results of the operations on a scheduled managed object.

15.5 Inventory Management

Inventory management keeps track of all the computing resources in an organization. The manner in which inventory management can be structured depends upon the organizational setups. In small organizations, the inventory may consist of all the computing resources which may be limited to one building. In large organizations, it may be composed of resources in different divisions and nations. Inventory management is closely related to fault management and topology management. Inventory management is sometimes known as *asset management*. Inventory details are very important for the following reasons:

- *Costing:* There is an associated cost in carrying inventory. In addition, it is necessary to calculate the expenditures for computing resources. In some cases, inventory cost can form the basis for decisions on procuring capital equipment such as hardware and software. Inventory costs contribute a large amount to the cost structure of a company. Having accurate details of inventory is useful for calculations such as quantities to reorder. It also helps to determine how much inventory should be carried.
- *Planning:* These inventory details provide an idea of future needs, and are required for short- and long-range planning. Inventory details may also be required when undertaking organizational expansions or reduction of resources.
- *Capacity planning:* In some nations such as Japan, space is at a premium. There is a cost associated with the placement of resources which are being used, and also with the storage of unused resources. Additionally, there is the need to store and dispose of computing resources as changes occur. Thus, the inventory details should be accurate for capacity planning.
- *Repair and replacement:* In a client-server environment and with the proliferation of workstations, it is necessary to have accurate and up-to-date knowledge of where the computing resources are located. Without this, it is difficult to send repair personnel or to replace a resource.

Some of the inventory details are:

- *Hardware:* This should include details of source, date and price of procurement, location, and models, with their respective capacities. Resources can span a wide range of products, from workstations to communication cards. Inventory details must also include when hardware problems occurred and how they were rectified. Such information may be maintained on-site or a reference can be made to a trouble-ticket database. Also required are the details of user profiles, which are helpful in determining the levels of hardware and software used. The required levels vary depending on the functions performed; for example, a software developer has a different requirement than people involved in personnel functions.

- *Software:* Details are similar to those of hardware.
- *User profiles:* These can be part of the details of the hardware or software, and can be maintained separately with a linkage to different hardware and software.
- *Networks:* These can include details such as networks used, their cost, source, and personnel to be called for repairs and problems.
- *Support personnel:* This should include details of the personnel involved in supporting computing and data processing.

15.6 Summary

Configuration management has a wide range of responsibilities and is closely tied to some of the other systems management functions; therefore, it was discussed in detail in this chapter. From the implementation point of view, it is necessary to break up configuration management into subdisciplines such as view, topology, software, and inventory, which were examined closely. In this chapter, the OSI as well as non-OSI issues of configuration management were covered.

15.7 Further Reading

ISO 10164-1, Information Technology, Open Systems Interconnection, Part 1: Object Management Function, 1993.

ISO 10164-2, Information Technology, Open Systems Interconnection, Part 2: State Management Function, 1993.

ISO 10164-3, Information Technology, Open Systems Interconnection, Part 3: Relationship Management Function, 1993.

Directory services

Hebrawi, Baha, *OSI Upper Layer Standards and Practices,* New York: McGraw-Hill, 1993.

ISO 9594-1 (X.500), Information Technology, Open Systems Interconnection, The Directory, Part 1: Overview of Concepts, Models, and Services, 1990.

ISO 9594-2 (X.501), Information Technology, Open Systems Interconnection, The Directory, Part 2: Models, 1990.

ISO 9594-3 (X.511), Information Technology, Open Systems Interconnection, The Directory, Part 3: Abstract Service Definition, 1990.

ISO 9594-4 (X.518), Information Technology, Open Systems Interconnection, The Directory, Part 4: Procedures for Distributed Operations, 1990.

ISO 9594-5 (X.519), Information Technology, Open Systems Interconnection, The Directory, Part 5: Protocol Specifications, 1990.

ISO 9594-6 (X.520), Information Technology, Open Systems Interconnection, The Directory, Part 6: Selected Attribute Types, 1990.

ISO 9594-7 (X.521), Information Technology, Open Systems Interconnection, The Directory, Part 7: Selected Object Classes, 1990.

ISO 9594-8 (X.509), Information Technology, Open Systems Interconnection, The Directory, Part 8: Authentication Framework, 1990.

DIS 9594-9 (X.525), Information Technology, Open Systems Interconnection, Replication, 1993.

Note: Revisions and amendments to the preceding directory documents have been made since the original publication.

Marshall, Rose T., *The Open Book: A Practical Perspective on OSI,* Englewood Cliffs, N.J.: Prentice Hall, 1990.

Software management

Edel, Tom, 1993. "CID: Remote OS/2 Configuration, Installation, and Distribution of PC Software," *IBM Personal Systems,* January 1993, pp. 42–46. (G325-5020-00)

Emami, Khalil, and Theodore Shrader, "Putting the Configuration into CID," *IBM Personal Systems,* 1993, pp. 47–53. (G325-5020-00)

ISO 10164-15, Information Technology, Open Systems Interconnection, Systems Management, Part 15: Scheduling Function, 1994.

ISO CD 10164-18, Information Technology, Open Systems Interconnection, Systems Management, Part 18: Software Management Function, 1994.

Chapter

16

Fault Management

16.1 Introduction

In this chapter, we will discuss in detail fault management and the related issues. OSI has done extensive work in this area and is used as the basis for many products. It may be observed that the OSI documents, Alarm Reporting Function (ISO 10164-4), Event Report Management Function (ISO 10164-5), and Log Control Function (ISO 10164-6), need to be folded into the fault management function. We also discuss the associated topics of trouble tickets and automation. Trouble ticket is mainly a problem-tracking mechanism. Automation is related to fault isolation and diagnosis without manual intervention.

Fault management consists primarily of the following components:

- *Problem reporting and detection:* This includes reporting of problems using alarms and events; it also includes logging of faults and errors. Correlation and filtering of alarms and events are also important functions, as is anticipating future problems.
- *Problem diagnosis:* This relates to diagnostic and testing procedures for problem detection.
- *Problem correction:* This involves manual and automated methods of solving problems. Automation overlaps with problem reporting and detection.
- *Problem tracking:* This is used to track a problem through its life cycle. Trouble ticket is usually used for problem tracking.

Note that this classification of components is not an OSI definition, but is useful for understanding fault management concepts in an orderly fashion. A fault involves an abnormal condition or conditions requiring management action, and results in the failure to operate in a specified manner. Errors, on the other hand, may occur normally and they may not result in the abnormal operation of a resource. An example of an error is FCS errors, which are handled at the respective layers. A fault is also sometimes called a problem. So, we have used the terms "problem" and "fault" interchangeably here.

In large networks where there are tens of thousands of workstations and different components, it becomes very difficult to isolate problems. When a problem occurs, it is important to know the cause right away to rectify it. Details are required for the analysis of the problems, and, in some cases, the dumps must be examined. So when a problem occurs, there must be a log of problems and details for analysis.

However, a log of the problems by itself is not enough. Details on the probable causes and the recommended diagnostic actions are needed, and these must be immediately available in displays or views in managers. Problems may be the result of various causes, and it is also possible that one problem may be responsible for different alarms being generated. So, it is necessary to correlate these problems into a single cause if there is a chance of multiple messages being generated.

One of the ways fault management can be arranged is as shown in Figure 16.1. Here, agents send alarms for problems to a manager, where these alarms need to be correlated and filtering may be used to log the data in a database. These data must be available to the user of fault management. To reduce network traffic, agents also need to filter the notifications they send to managers. Note that the technique

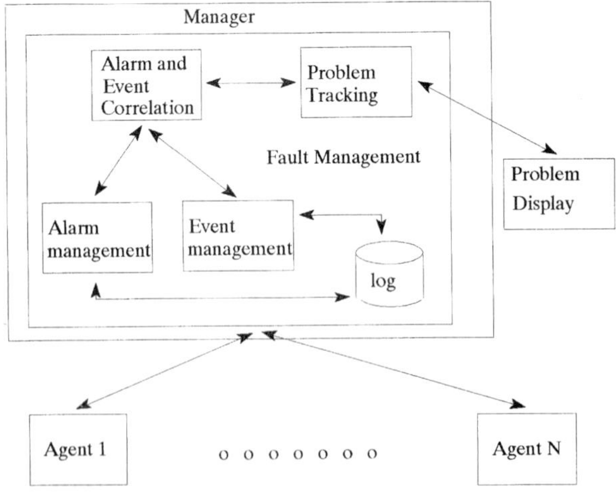

Figure 16.1 Fault management overview.

explained here is one of many possible alternatives available for folding in these OSI definitions. When implementing, constraints such as memory size, storage capacities, speeds of processors, and performance-related issues of workstations used in agents and managers must be considered.

16.2 Alarm Reporting Function

As discussed earlier, notifications are messages emitted by managed objects. Alarms constitute a subset of notifications and are generated when unusual conditions occur. These may be generated due to detected abnormal conditions, as for example, when there is a degradation of service beyond a certain threshold value. A paper jam occurring beyond a specified value in a printer may be the time to generate an alarm.

Alarms may be generated for more than one reason, so to isolate the sources, the alarms must be correlated. From these correlated alarms, the reason or source for the alarm condition must be identified. These alarms are reported in a standardized manner, and must carry enough information to identify the nature and source of the problems and how they can be remedied. If such problems occur frequently, further information may be required to analyze and study the trends.

The Alarm Reporting Function (ISO 10165-4) deals with user requirements, services provided, the protocol necessary to provide the service, the parameters used in alarms, and conformance issues. Alarms are carried in M-EVENT-REPORTs from agents to managers. These alarms are packaged in the alarm reporting service, which is present both in the managed system, which is the agent, and the managing system, which is the manager.

Alarms are very important for problem determination. Data in alarms carry not only help in determining the source of problems, but some of them may indicate the diagnostic steps that can be initiated. From this angle, each parameter is discussed. The alarm reporting service includes parameters in the M-EVENT-REPORT, which is sent to a manager (Figure 16.2). In the following explanation of parameters, M refers to mandatory, U stands for user option, C is associated with conditional, and P relates to parameters which are directly mapped to CMISE service primitive parameters. The parameters of the alarm reporting service are:

- *Invoke Identifier (P)*: This is a unique identifier, which distinguishes one alarm from another.

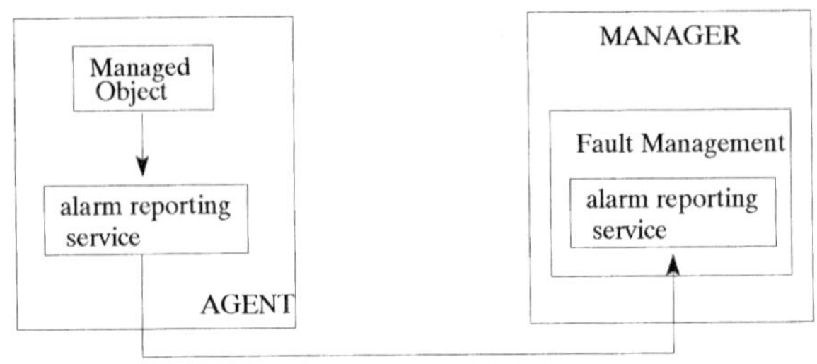

Figure 16.2 Alarm reporting service.

- *Mode* (*P*): This indicates whether the EVENT-REPORT that is being sent from the alarm reporting service is a confirmed one. For a confirmed message, we need a reply as to whether the message has been received. For a nonconfirmed message, we just send the message and do not bother for a reply.
- *Managed Object Class* (*P*): This refers to the managed object class for which the alarm has been generated, and may be registered values. A workstation may be a managed object class.
- *Managed Object Instance* (*P*): This indicates the managed object instance; for example, in the workstation managed object class, an object instance can be IBMPS/2/224567.
- *Event Type* (*M*): This indicates the type of alarm. Five alarm types are:

  Communications, which is used for carrying information from one point to another point

  Quality of Service, which relates to the service that is being offered

  Processing Error, which is used for software or processing faults

  Equipment, which is associated with a fault in equipment

  Environmental, which is concerned with the surroundings of the equipment

- *Event Information:* This provides information on the events. Event information is standardized such that this does not cause confusion or result in different interpretations. Event information contains the following parameters:

  Probable Cause (*M*) is required in each EVENT-REPORT. ISO 10164-4 defines probable causes used by the alarm reporting service. These probable causes are mapped to the values furnished in CCITT X.721/ISO 10165-2, Definition of Management Information.

The resulting probable cause values are carried in the Probable Cause parameter. In addition to the probable causes defined in ISO 10164-4, probable causes can also be defined and registered for specific purposes. Probable cause information is very important in problem detection, and supplies an indication of the problems.

Specific Problems (*U*) is used for furnishing further information on the probable cause. Here, only managed object class identifiers are used. One can add one's own list to suit specific conditions; for example, if Probable Cause indicates a LAN error, the Specific Problems parameter may be used to specify the list of workstations and the adapter where the error has occurred.

Perceived Severity (*M*) has six severity levels, in order of decreasing severity: critical, major, minor, warning, indeterminate (severity level cannot be determined), and cleared. In the example under Specific Problems, the severity level might indicate critical. Due to an error in the adapter, the workstation in the network is not operational, and when that adapter is fixed, then the cleared severity level can be used.

Backed-up Status (*U*) indicates whether the managed object emitting the alarm has a backup. The information supplied in the severity field enables us to determine whether we need to use the backup provision. A value of *true* indicates that a managed object emitting the alarm has been backed up, while a value of *false* indicates that it has not.

Back-up Object (*C*) is present only if the Backed-up Status parameter value is *true,* and specifies the object instance which is providing the backup support.

Trend Indication (*U*) is present when more than one alarm on a managed object has already been sent, and they have not been cleared. This parameter has three possible values: more severe, to indicate that the present alarm is of a severity higher than any outstanding alarms already reported; no change, to indicate that the severity of this alarm is the same as the highest severity of alarms already sent; and less severe, to indicate that there is at least one alarm among the outstanding alarms which has a higher severity than the severity of the alarm being sent. The LAN adapter, used in our earlier example, might have sent some alarms before failing. The Trend Indication parameter assists in predicting how the LAN adapter has behaved and when it may fail, and it will be absent if there are no outstanding alarms.

Threshold Information (*C*) is present when an alarm is sent due to the crossing of a threshold value. For example, in an Ethernet network, X is the limit for the packets retransmitted due to collisions of packets over a period of time Y. When X is exceeded due to heavy traffic, an alarm indicating the state of the network can be sent. Threshold Information has details such as packets retransmitted, or the identifier of the threshold attribute, the threshold value of X, the actual value of the counter, and the time when the counter was last reset. For this, the Threshold Information parameter has four subparameters: triggered threshold, threshold level, observed value, and alarm time.

Notification Identifier (*U*) points to the identifier which may be used for future notifications. If more alarms are sent, this identifier will be in the Correlated Notifications parameter. For example, a LAN adapter card may have many ports, one of which has problems. It is also possible that other ports will experience similar problems. In this case, when reporting the problems of other ports, we can use this identifier in the Correlated Notification to indicate that a particular type of problem with a LAN adapter card is related to the different ports.

Correlated Notifications (*U*) has Notification Identifiers along with object instances, if required, of all the notifications which are related to the present notification. The object instances' names are carried if the present notification is not from the same object instance. For example, an alarm may be sent due to problems in port 1. If there have been problems with ports 3, 5, and 6, we include the Notification Identifier of each port. These are very important if we have to analyze the problems in the LAN adapter card. If there are standby ports available, then we can use one of them. However, if a majority of ports experience the same problems, then it may be better to make use of the backup LAN adapter card. So, the correlation of the notifications is very important for problem detection. If the notifications are not properly correlated, it is possible that indicators may be pointing in different directions, when only one direction really needs to be indicated.

State Change Definitions (*U*) can be used to specify the state transition associated with this alarm.

Monitored Attributes (*U*) identifies one or more attributes, and their values, of the managed object sending alarms.

Proposed Repair Actions (*U*) contains registered managed object identifiers. If the repair action is known to the managed system, then it is indicated. The repair action may be something such as a retry, switch to a standby, or bypassing a connection. It is important to note here that we can define and register automation routines as managed objects for correcting problems. We can specify one or more managed object identifiers of such a routine for problem correction.

Additional Text (*U*) has the provision to include free text. This parameter may be used to explain the alarm. When mapping proprietary alarms to the standard alarms or vice versa, there may be some fields which cannot be mapped one to one. The Additional Text parameter can be used for mapping purposes.

Additional Information (*U*) contains a set of registered managed object identifiers, a significance indicator, which indicates whether the problem information must be parsed to fully understand the problem information, and problem information on the event, which must be parsed. This field can also be used for mapping proprietary alarm schemes to standard alarms, when there is no one-to-one mapping of parameters.

- *Current Time:* This states the time when the response was generated and is included in the response and confirm.
- *Errors:* This is used only in response and confirm, if there is any failure in the form of an M-EVENT-REPORT.

16.3 Event Report Management Function

Notifications emitted by managed objects must be selectively manipulated by choosing some of them before sending them to one or more managing systems. Also the frequency of sending the notifications to managing systems must be flexible. We may need to send these notifications to different destinations, such as forwarding notifications to the backup systems. To manipulate the manner in which notifications are reported, two managed objects, *discriminator* and *eventForwardingDiscriminator*, have been defined in the Definition of Management Information (ISO 10165-2), and the event report management function is described in ISO 10164-5.

The main idea behind the provision of managed object classes, such as discriminator and eventForwardingDiscriminator, is to add flexibility and control the way notifications are converted to event reports and the reporting of the event reports to the managing systems. From Figure 16.3, notice that the discriminator managed object class is a subclass of top, and the managed object class, eventForwarding-Discriminator, is a subclass of discriminator. The managed object class, discriminator, acts as a sort of filter which determines which notifications are to be forwarded and the intervals at which they must be sent. The attributes of discriminator are:

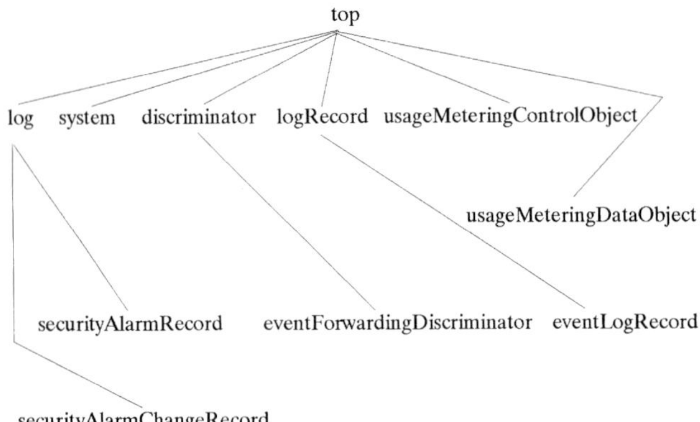

Figure 16.3 Inheritance hierarchy of the discriminator managed object class.

- *Discriminator id:* A unique identifier of an object instance of the discriminator managed object class.
- *Discriminator construct:* This has the tests such as the equality and inequality condition of attributes, presence of attributes, and negation of any of these conditions. These tests are done on the parameters of a management operation or notification.
- *Administrative state:* This refers to the administrative state of the discriminator. The administrative state has the values locked and unlocked. The managing system controls the administrative state of a discriminator. If the discriminator is locked, then information processing by it is not allowed. In the unlocked state, obviously, information processing by the discriminator is permitted.
- *Operational state:* This relates to the operational state of an object instance of the discriminator managed object class, which can be enabled or disabled. In the enabled state, the object instance of discriminator is available for use, while in the disabled state, it is not.

The Managed object class, discriminator, has mandatory notifications such as state change, attribute value change, object creation, and object deletion. If required, further notifications can be defined. Notifications from managed objects, after processing, get converted to potential event reports. A potential event report has information from the notification emitted by a managed object and information derived from the local processing that was done.

The scheduling of the event reports is controlled by the optional scheduling packages. The scheduling packages defined for the discriminator managed object class are:

- *Availability status package:* This will be present if any of the other scheduling packages are available. It has only one attribute: availability status.
- *Duration package:* This controls the starting and stopping of a managed object through the use of start time and stop time attributes.
- *Daily scheduling package:* This provides the list of start and end intervals, during which time the discriminator will be available. The default is 24 hours.
- *Weekly scheduling package:* This provides the days of the week and list of time intervals during which the discriminator will be available.
- *External scheduler scheduling package:* This has the name of the external scheduler which will control the scheduling of the discriminator.

The operation of the eventForwardingDiscriminator managed object class is shown in Figure 16.4, in which the potential event report becomes the input to the *event forwarding discriminator* (EFD). The EFD determines where the event reports are to be sent. It sends the event reports to the destination mentioned in the destination attribute of eventForwardingDiscriminator.

The managed object class, eventForwardingDiscriminator, has the attributes destination, optional backup destination package, and the optional confirmed or nonconfirmed mode package. Note that the eventForwardingDiscriminator managed object class inherits the attributes, notifications, and behaviors of the discriminator managed

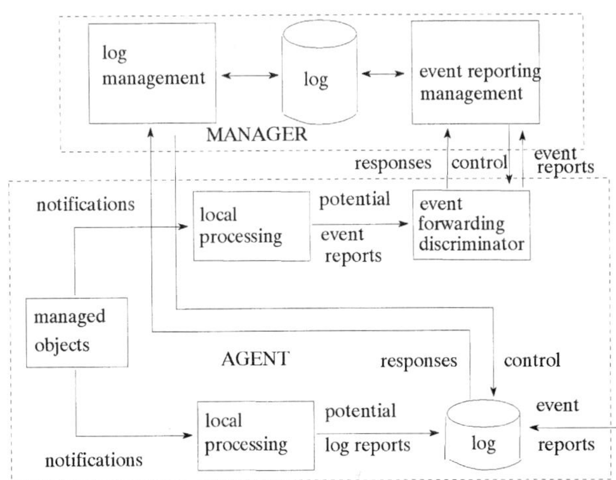

Figure 16.4 Event and log management.

object class. If required, the event reports are sent to the backup destination or destinations. Event reports can be sent in a confirmed or nonconfirmed mode.

The managed object classes, discriminator and eventForwardingDiscriminator, emit their own notifications. Like operations on any managed object class, the managed objects of discriminator and eventForwardingDiscriminator can be created, deleted, read, modified, suspended, and resumed by manipulating administrative states. PT-CREATE is used to create an event forwarding discriminator managed object. PT-DELETE is used to delete an event forwarding discriminator managed object. PT-SET is used for modifying, suspending, and resuming operations associated with the event forwarding discriminator managed object. PT-GET is used to read the attributes. In Figure 16.4, control refers to the management operations such as PT-CREATE, PT-DELETE, PT-SET, and PT-GET, and the responses are from these management operations.

The event reporting function, as can be noticed from Figure 16.4, has the event forwarding discriminator (EFD). The management operations that can be done on the EFD are initiation, termination, suspension, resumption, modification, and retrieval. These functions are similar to those of the managed object class, discriminator. Management operations are controlled by the event reporting management function of fault management.

Because our objective is to use the event report management function for overall fault management, event reporting management needs to be integrated with the fault management function of the manager. The event report management function can determine whether it needs to log the event reports in a database. The database and the way that logging of event reports is done depends on the database chosen. Usually, it is better to use the same database application used by other management functions instead of metaphorically reinventing the wheel. For example, if one uses an SQL database for configuration management, use SQL for logging, too.

16.4 Log Control Function

The Log Control Function (ISO 10164-6) document primarily covers user requirements, services provided, and the protocol required to provide the services, and it defines the relationship with other systems management functions and conformance requirements. Events and notifications that are received may need to be stored for later use and sometimes for problem analysis. This repository is known as a *log*. Log records, which have a particular form and units of information, are stored in the log. In the inheritance hierarchy, both managed object classes, log and logRecord, are subclasses of the managed object class top, as shown in Figure 16.3.

However, there needs to be flexibility in how the logs are managed, how the storing of data is scheduled, and how the data are stored. These managed objects need to be manipulated in a proper fashion to be of use in fault management.

The managed objects that emit notifications may go through some processing to generate potential log records (Figure 16.4). A potential log record consists of information required for a log record. The potential log records are sent to one or more logs in the local system, and are sent through filters or discriminators before actually being stored in the log. We have already discussed discriminators in the previous section. These discriminators or filters have a set of rules which determine how the log records are stored. These represent the local notifications.

A log may also store the event reports received from other systems. These event reports are also processed just like potential log records before actually being logged. A log is a repository of log records. The managed object class, log, has mandatory and conditional packages. The mandatory package used in the log managed object class has the following attributes:

- *Log id:* This is a unique identifier used to identify the instance of a log. For example, log12 and log13 are different instances of logs.
- *Discriminator Construct:* This is the filter discussed earlier. It may be used to manage the parameters of the information being logged.
- *Administrative State:* This has two states: unlocked and locked. The administrative state determines whether one will be able to do any logging. In the locked state, no new log records can be created, whereas in the unlocked state, new log records can be created.
- *Operational State:* This also has two states: enabled and disabled. In the enabled state, the log is available for use, and in the disabled state, it is not.
- *Log Full Action:* This determines what to do when the log becomes full. When log records are stored, there may be a stage when further logging can no longer be done. The Log Full Action attribute indicates what to do in such cases. In case of wrap, the new log records replace the oldest log record, which means the oldest log record will no longer will be available. In case of halt, no more logging will be done.
- *Availability Status:* This has two states: log not full and log full. When the state is log full, no new records can be added, but whatever records are logged can be retrieved.

To make logging of data flexible, there are additional conditional packages which may be used in defining the log managed object class. The conditional packages are:

- *Finite log size package:* This conditional package is used if the log size is finite. This package has attributes which provide the size of the log, the current size, and the number of log records.
- *Log alarm package:* This has the capacity threshold alarm attribute. This package is present when the log size is finite, and also when log full status is reached and logging is halted. It is defined as a percentage of maximum log size.
- *Scheduling packages:* These determine how the logging activity is to be scheduled. These scheduling packages are similar to the ones discussed in the previous section.

In addition to the managed object class, log, there is the managed object class, logRecord. Instances of logRecord are used in storing information in logs, and they may be retrieved or deleted, but the attributes cannot be modified. logRecord has the following attributes:

- *Log Record Identifier:* This is a unique identifier within a log to distinguish each log record. This is a number, which is increased sequentially in ascending order.
- *Logging Time:* This is the time when the log record is entered in the log repository.

A manager should be able to manipulate logs. To do this, the manager has the capability to create a log using PT-CREATE and to delete a log using PT-DELETE, to suspend and resume the log activity using PT-SET, to modify the log attributes by PT-SET, to delete log records by PT-DELETE, and to retrieve log records by PT-GET. Here, scoping and filtering may be used to delete and retrieve multiple log records with one request.

Recall from the previous section that event reporting management also controls how the event logs are made. In a similar fashion, log management functions control the operations of logs and log records in the agents. The log management function also interacts with the event log.

16.5 Confidence and Diagnostic Testing and Test Management

ISO 10164-12 on Test Management and ISO 10164-14 on Confidence and Diagnostic Testing are closely related. The former defines how the confidence and diagnostic testing are to be conducted and specifies the managed object class required for the testing. The managed object class, testObject, is defined in 10164-12 and the other confidence and diagnostic testing related managed object classes are defined in ISO 10164-14. Let us briefly investigate the ISO 10164-14 standard document. It specifies the following:

- Requirements for confidence and diagnostic testing
- Confidence and test categories that relate to the requirements
- Relevant managed object classes
- Compliance requirements

The following classification of confidence and diagnostic tests have been defined:

- *Connection test:* Provides the ability to test a real or virtual connection between two resources to support a desired function.
- *Connectivity test:* Used to check whether a connection can be established between two resources.
- *Data integrity test:* Can be used to verify whether data can be exchanged between two resources without being corrupted, and also measures the time taken for data exchange.
- *End connection test:* Used to test the operability of a connection between a managed resource and a second resource.
- *Loopback test:* Can be useful to check whether data can be sent and received over a connection path within a specified time and at an acceptable rate.
- *Protocol integrity test:* Tests whether a managed object, which is being tested for functionality, can undertake protocol interaction with an associated managed object.
- *Resource boundary test:* Used for verification of the correctness of the resources within a system. The test is conducted by observing interaction between a resource and its environment.
- *Resource self-test:* Concerned with the testing of the ability of a resource to perform its allotted function at a given time.
- *Test infrastructure test:* May be performed on a managed open system regarding its ability to initiate tests, return result reports, and respond to monitoring and control actions.

A manager has a test conductor, which is an application process, and it issues one of the preceding test requests to an application process known as a test performer, which resides in an agent. This may result in immediate test results or, alternatively, test results in the form of an event report at a later time sent from the test performer to the test conductor. These tests are useful for problem diagnosis.

16.6 Trouble Ticket

Trouble ticket is basically a front-end application to fault management, whereby problems are monitored. A problem is given a unique number and it is tracked from its inception to its resolution. This is also known as *tracking throughout the life cycle.* There can also be a finer granularity of problems, such as incidents. A ticket number can be assigned to these incidents instead of to problems.

The general architecture of trouble ticket is shown in Figure 16.5. Users, including system administrators, can manually log a problem. Alarms can also report problems to trouble ticket. This is classified under "problem input" in the figure. Once a problem is registered with trouble ticket, trouble ticket interacts with its database, which contains a history of problems, persons responsible for resolving the problems, and an inventory of computing resources including spares. Trouble ticket can use its own database or it can make use of the inventory and topology database. This database should also maintain a history of past problems, which may be required for future analysis and tracking problems based on different criteria.

The problem-resolving mechanism shown in Figure 16.5 is responsible for actions to be taken on the problems encountered. There is also a problem-reporting and display mechanism, which is responsible for generating reports and summaries of problems. There can be interaction between the problem input and problem-reporting and display components, so that outputs of the problems are available, depicted in consoles or hard copies. These also may take different forms, for example, a user may want a report of the problem outputs of a segment of a network. This reporting mechanism should incorporate the flexibility to generate customized reports.

At least the following items must be included in trouble ticket:

- Date and time when a problem occurred.
- Description of the originator of the problem.
- Brief description of the problem, including the source and probable causes of the problem.
- Priority for problem resolution, i.e., whether it must be solved immediately, or can be delayed.
- Current status of the problem.

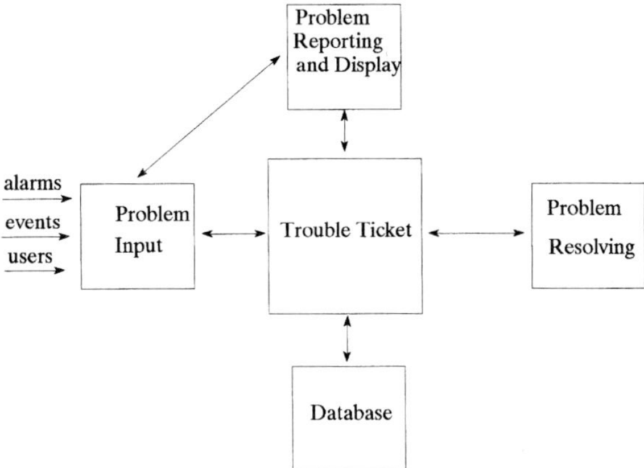

Figure 16.5 Architecture for trouble ticket.

- Details of the location and the device which had the problems.
- Who would verify the problem after it is resolved.
- Description of the contact to whom to report after resolving the problem.
- Description of the person responsible for resolving the problem.
- Whom to contact if there is any difficulty in resolving the problem.
- Date and time when the problem was resolved.
- Details on who resolved the problem and how.

Trouble ticket must be flexible. There may be instances when a problem which had a particular priority becomes a critical problem, thus necessitating that the priority be reassigned during the problem resolution stage. Under such circumstances, it must be possible to easily reassign the priority and take quicker problem resolution actions. In a similar manner, one must be able to assign different routes and personnel to problem resolution.

16.7 Trouble Ticket and Automation

When a network becomes too large, it is better to automate as many fault management functions as possible. Trouble ticket and automation can be intelligently brought together to resolve the problems, as shown in Figure 16.6. As soon as a problem is registered in trouble ticket, it must be decided whether the problem resolution requires manual intervention. If so, then it must be determined who will handle the problem, and whether it is a hardware, software, or network

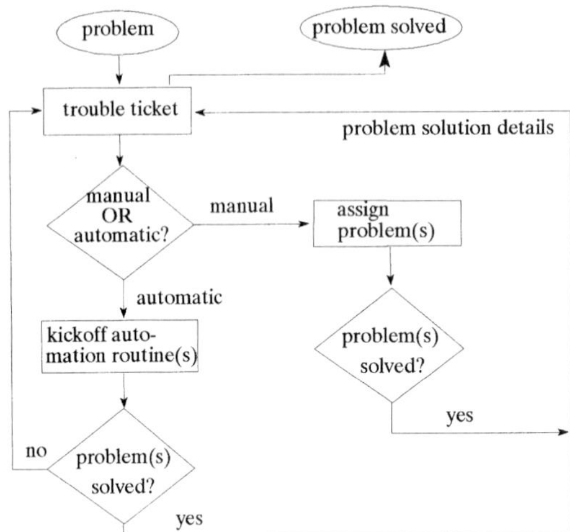

Figure 16.6 Relationship between trouble ticket and automation.

problem. Accordingly, the appropriate person is sent to resolve it. If it cannot be resolved by this person, another person with more appropriate expertise is sent; for example, when a hardware analyst checks the problem, he or she may find out that it is a software problem and another sort of technician is required.

While a problem is being attended to, trouble ticket must be continuously informed of the progress and the people involved in the resolution of the problem. Once a problem is resolved, the details of the problem resolution must be conveyed for recording purposes and future reference.

However, if automation can be used, the problem is sent to an automation routine, which may be simple or complicated, depending on the intelligence put into these routines. From here, an appropriate routine is kicked off, which may perform actions such as resetting a computer, initializing a computer, or bypassing a failed workstation.

It is possible that an automatic routine will not be able to resolve the problems, in which case, it may be necessary to return to the decision cycle to determine whether to use manual routines. After a problem is resolved, the details on how it was resolved are sent to the trouble ticket system. In each case, times and problem-handling procedures must be recorded in trouble ticket. This will help in future problem resolutions.

16.8 Notes on Fault Management

When there are failures or threshold values are reached, a problem is reported to fault management using alarms. Thresholds enable us to identify impending problems before they occur. As mentioned earlier, the fault management function must, in turn, be integrated with the view management, topology management, and configuration and change management functions for diagnostic purposes. The details about alarms, such as probable causes and recommended actions, are useful for identifying the sources of problems. In some cases, it may be necessary to correlate one or more sources of problems and make them available in view management.

Problems can be displayed in the console of the network administrator, who tries to zero in on a problem with the help of topology management. A problem is rectified by sending somebody to do the repairs, or if there are automation facilities, some corrective software routines are downloaded to the proper workstation. The problems may include critical failures or may involve degradation of service, which may need immediate attention. If these problems are attended to in a proactive manner, it is possible to avoid some of the critical failures.

The amount of intelligence put into fault management determines how quickly problems can be remedied and how much they should be automated. For some problems, the least possible human intervention is optimum.

For software errors, we should be able to apply fixes from the network administrator's console, and the help of topology management and the software management components of configuration management may be necessary. The application of artificial intelligence in problem identification and diagnostics is appropriate here. With the expanding size of networks, manual intervention for many problems becomes cost prohibitive and, in some cases, humanly impossible. These fault management functions also must include automation applications and provide diagnostic steps. When there is a problem, a user must be able to activate one of the possible solution routines remotely from the managers.

As stressed earlier, all data must be amenable to being formatted and printed. Also, problem details must be available for analysis at a later time if required. Users must be able to review these problem data. The problem data in logs depends upon how much detail is needed for later analysis. When considering the storing of problem data, we need to take into account constraints such as the capacities of logs and workstations.

16.9 Summary

We have discussed different fault management components such as alarm reporting, event reporting, and the log control function, in this chapter, as well as confidence and diagnostic testing and test management functions. As we have stressed in many places, automation is an important and badly needed function with a lot of potential. Integrated trouble ticket and automation will go a long way to solving some of the limitations of the present fault management function.

16.10 Further Reading

ISO 10164-4 (X.733), Information Technology, Open Systems Interconnection, Systems Management, Part 4: Alarm Reporting Function, 1992.

ISO DAM1 10164-4, Information Technology, Open Systems Interconnection, Systems Management, Part 4: Alarm Reporting Function, Amendment 1: ICS Proforma, 1993.

ISO 10164-5 (X.734), Information Technology, Open Systems Interconnection, Systems Management, Part 5: Event Report Management Function, 1993.

ISO DAM1 10164-5, Information Technology, Open Systems Interconnection, Systems Management, Part 5: Event Report Management Function, Amendment 1: ICS Proforma, 1993.

ISO 10164-6 (X.735), Information Technology, Open Systems Interconnection, Systems Management, Part 6: Log Control Function, 1993.

ISO DAM1 10164-6, Information Technology, Open Systems Interconnection, Systems Management, Part 6: Log Control Function, Amendment 1: ICS Proforma, 1993.

DIS 10164-12, Information Technology, Open Systems Interconnection, Systems Management, Part 12: Test Management Function, 1992.

DIS 10164-14 (X.737), Information Technology, Open Systems Interconnection, Systems Management, Part 14: Confidence and Diagnostic Test Categories, 1994.

Johnson D., NOC Internal Integrated Trouble Ticket System Functional Specification Wishlist, RFC 1297, 1992.

Olson, L., and A. Blackwell, "Understanding Network Management with OOA," W. Stallings (ed.), *Network Management,* IEEE Computer Society Press, Los Alamitos, Calif., 1993, pp. 147–152. This paper is reprinted from *IEEE Network Magazine,* July 1990.

Chapter

17

Performance Management

17.1 Introduction

We briefly touched upon the performance management function in Chapter 2. In this chapter, we will revisit it in detail. The results of performance management can be used for tuning the performance of a network and its resources. If a network has many collisions or too many packets are being retransmitted, it's a good idea to investigate the causes. Performance management helps isolate the causes of bottlenecks, and corrective actions help improve the performance.

The performance management function, like other systems management functions, is primarily used by systems administrators. The main functions of performance management are:

- *Performance data collection:* This must be done on resources being monitored, and the data are stored in a database. This database may be in agents or managers, depending on the resources available in them. If the database becomes too big, then only the statistical summary and trend analysis results can be stored there.
- *Data analysis:* This is required to extract important information from the performance-related data. Trend analysis and statistical significance testing are useful. The analysis of the performance-related data may itself consume much of the resources, so this analysis can be done during off-peak hours.
- *Problem reporting:* This function uses alarms based on threshold and is required to make use of the performance-related data. When thresholds are crossed for errors, alarms are sent.
- *Display and formatting:* This is very important for presenting the performance data. These data can be from multiple agents, and the

data collected may have to be formatted on an agent basis, on a set of agents, and as summary data. The display of the data requires graphical user interfaces, and printing it requires formatting flexibility. In addition to the history of problems, the ability to have a snapshot of problems at any instant is necessary.

Figure 17.1 shows how the performance management function can be placed in a manager. Though display and formatting is part of the function required in performance management, it can be part of other systems management functions as well, which is the primary reason for placing this function outside performance management.

The performance management function must be tailored to meet specific requirements, such as whether the systems involved operate in a hostcentric or a client-server environment. Also, the protocols used for networking different computers or workstations may vary; thus, the requirements will be different. Factors such as individual cases, computing environments, and protocols used must be considered when designing performance management functions. In addition to other standard documents, performance management uses primarily Workload Monitoring Function (ISO 10164-11) and Summarization Function (ISO 10164-13).

17.2 Issues in Data Collection

Data collection is an important activity in performance management. Basically, there are two types of data. The first is static or unchanging data, and the second is dynamic data, meaning data that are continu-

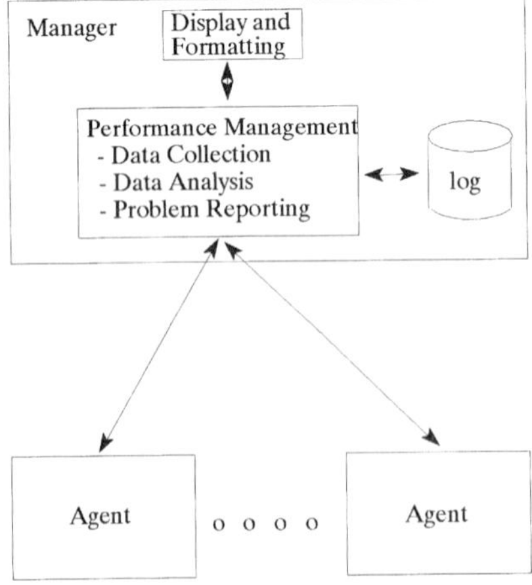

Figure 17.1 Performance management overview.

ously updated. Data collection is also of two types: one-time data collection and continuous data collection using event reports and polling. Some of the important issues involved in data collection are as follows.

- Starting and stopping of data collection must be flexible.
- Data collection may involve one managed object, a subset of managed objects, or all managed objects.
- Data collection sometimes needs to be remotely controlled.
- A time stamp is required on data collected. If the data is collected over a large geographical area, then time synchronization is required.
- After data collection, the data needs to be stored and displayed. Provision must be made for what to do if logs and databases become full.
- Data is usually collected in agents and then transferred to managers. How this data is transferred impacts on the performance.
- Access to data on performance, accounting, and security management may have to be limited to important people such as systems administrators.

17.3 Counter, Gauge, and Threshold

There are certain attributes which are commonly used in managed objects for performance management purposes. These attributes are *counter, gauge, threshold,* and *tidemark,* and they are defined in ISO 10165-2, Definition of Management Information.

17.3.1 Counter

A counter is an abstraction for a counting process. For example, there can be a counter for the packets transmitted. There are two types of counters, as shown in Figure 17.2. One is nonsettable, which means it is possible only to read the values of these counters; they cannot be changed by a management operation such as Set. In a settable counter,

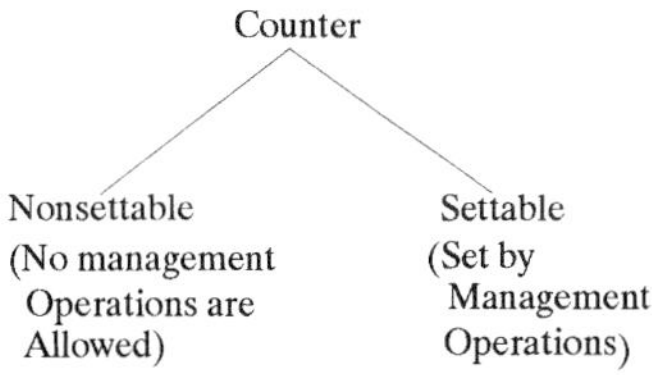

Figure 17.2 Counter classifications.

the values can be changed by a management operation, and these counters can be read. Counters have various characteristics:

- The initial value is zero.
- The value can only go up, incremented by one.
- The value wraps around when it reaches the maximum.

17.3.2 Gauge

Gauge is a dynamic variable. It can be the number of users logged in to a server in a client-server environment, and its value can be an integer or real. The value of a gauge can change in either direction, which means that the value can increment or decrement. It is a read-only attribute; therefore, to retrieve the gauge value, a Get operation can be done. When counter values are provided, a gauge value can be derived, as shown in Figure 17.3, by subtracting the Counter1 value from the Counter2 value.

17.3.3 Threshold

A threshold is analogous to a benchmark and is used in counters and gauges. A counter threshold can have a simple single comparison value or it can have multiple comparison values, in which case, notifications can be sent when each comparison value is reached. When a maximum value is reached, there is wraparound of the counter.

Gauge thresholds are slightly different from counter thresholds. With gauge thresholds, there are notifyLow and notifyHigh values. When these values are crossed, notifications are generated. The notifyHigh value must be greater than or equal to notifyLow.

17.3.4 Tidemark

When a gauge is operating, it can reach the lowest and highest values, which are recorded by the tidemark attribute. There are three

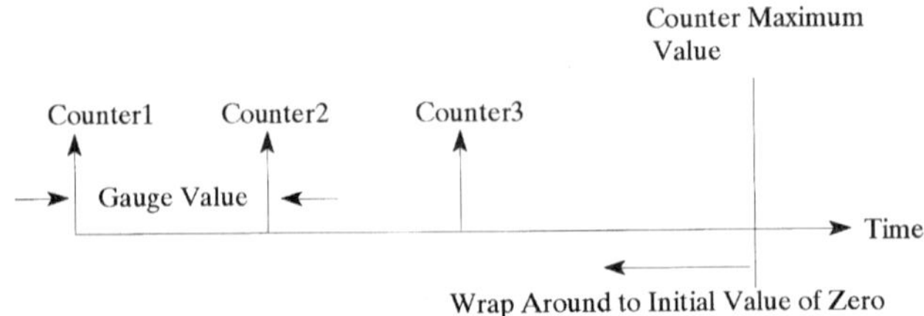

Figure 17.3 Counter and gauge concepts.

values for the tidemark attribute: current value, value before the last reset, and last reset time. A Get operation can be performed to retrieve the values associated with a tidemark. A Set can be done to reset the former value to the current value and the last reset time to the current time.

Whenever certain performance-related thresholds are reached, alarms are sent to a systems administrator, which alerts the systems administrator that some action is required. For example, in an Ethernet network, when frame collisions reach certain predetermined threshold values, then an alarm can be sent to a system administrator. The performance data are stored in a database. The time frame for which the data are logged is important: How many days' data do we store in the database? The volume of performance data may become too large and the database may grow too big, so that storage becomes a constraint. The performance data are usually stored in logs in managers, but if storage is a constraint, one alternative is to store only a summary of the data, saving the actual data in logs stored on CD-ROMs or tapes. If problems occur and it becomes necessary to retrieve these saved data, then they can be transferred to the database associated with performance management.

17.4 Workload Monitoring Function

If a user wants information about one or more attributes of a managed object or is interested in the attributes' behavior over a period of time, such monitoring can be done by defining metric objects. Metric objects have one or more attributes, which use the data derived from one or more attributes of an observed managed object. However, this does not prevent us from including additional attributes in observed managed objects for performance measurement or monitoring a resource. The Workload Monitoring Function (ISO 10164-11) covers primarily the following items.

- It specifies user requirements for the function.
- It Defines the generic metric and workload monitoring managed object classes.
- It specifies how management requirements are met by the metric and workload monitoring managed object classes.
- It provides conformance requirements.

17.4.1 Metric objects

Metric refers to a value calculated from observed attribute values. Metric objects provide objects for the statistical measurement of variables represented by attributes in the definition of observed managed objects. These metric objects have the details to undertake performance measurements, including an identifier to distinguish metric objects, an identifier to single out the managed objects and the attributes being monitored, algorithms used in the statistical measurements, information about the manner in which attributes are monitored, and the threshold values used for reporting alarms.

Whenever these metric object instances are created or deleted by managed systems, notifications, which are converted to alarms, are sent to the managing systems. Also, there is a correspondence between the metric object and managed object attributes. There is a relationship between the attributes of a metric object and the managed object which is being observed or monitored, and this relationship is formed while a metric object is created. A metric object may be contained in the managed object being observed or it may have a separate containment hierarchy. Note that one metric object is used for capturing data of a single attribute of a managed object which we are monitoring.

17.4.2 Monitoring process

The first step in the monitoring process is to collect or capture the data of observed managed objects. These observed managed objects must be relevant to performance measurements, and the data must be collected at regular intervals known as sampling intervals. The sampling interval should not be too small, in which case there will be a large amount of data and communication overhead. However, if this interval is too large, the data collected may not be of much use.

If the metric object definition has the conditional package of conversion, then conversion must be performed. This conversion involves transforming the counter values to those of gauges. This is best explained with an example: If ten minutes before, the number of reads by a file server was 15, but the number of reads is now 20, then the gauge value is + 5.

The data also must be converted by smoothing techniques to smooth out the noises. Here, the main objective is to find the trends. These calculated gauge values are then compared with thresholds to generate notifications when the thresholds are crossed. Depending upon the implementation, the data conversion and data enhancement may or may not be required. The metric object can be adjusted by changing different attributes. In particular, it must be possible to change the sampling periods.

17.4.3 Workload monitoring models

Broadly, OSI provides three models for the monitoring of workload. Note that these are only models. For implementation purposes, one may need to combine them to monitor a resource. The models are:

- *Resource utilization model:* This is used primarily for measuring how a resource is being used. This may be an instantaneous measurement, such as server utilization in a client-server environment, or it can be measured over a period of time to obtain the mean server utilization.
- *Rejection rate model:* This is useful when a resource can no longer service a request for use because of capacity limitations. For example, connections from a requestor to a server may be rejected because the server has already used up all the connection numbers available. However, this must be over a period of time to be useful.
- *Resource request rate:* The number of requests for a service is important during some occasions. It also must be measured over a period of time to make comparisons. An example can be monitoring the logon connections to a file server or a database server.

17.4.4 Metric managed object classes

For monitoring a managed object's attributes, metric managed object classes, such as monitorMetric, gaugeMonitor, meanMonitor, movingAverageMeanMonitor, ewmaMeanVarianceMonitor, and ewmaMeanPercentileMonitor, have been defined. Here monitorMetric managed object class is derived from the managed object class of scanner. gaugeMonitor and meanMonitor, in turn, are subclasses of monitorMetric. And scanner is a subclass of the managed object, top. We will look into the scanner managed object class in Section 17.5. Brief descriptions of the metric managed object classes are:

- *monitorMetric:* Monitors the derived gauge values of an attribute of a managed object at specific intervals of time known as *granularity periods* (GPs). If a counter difference package is present, then we use two successive counter difference values to get the value of the derived gauge. However, if the counter difference package is absent, then the attribute value is a gauge value. When a monitorMetric object is created, the scanner id, observed object instance, observed attribute id, granularity period, presence of counter difference package, and one of the scheduling packages we discussed in the log control function (Section 16.4) must be specified.

- *gaugeMonitor:* A subclass of the monitorMetric managed object class, used for generating alarm notification when a threshold value is crossed. For this purpose, the severityIndicatingGaugeThreshold attribute has been defined. The gaugeMonitor managed object also has a conditional specificProblemIndication package to specify the type of monitoring being done. Note that the gaugeMonitor managed object monitors a gauge or a counter type of a managed object.
- *meanMonitor:* Also a subclass of the monitorMetric managed object class. Here, we apply the criterion that the mean of the gauge value crosses a specific threshold to generate an alarm notification. The attribute being monitored can be a gauge or a counter type. For calculating the mean, the timeConstant attribute provides the time period over which the mean must be calculated. This managed object has the attribute, severityIndicatingGaugeThreshold, which also provides the threshold level to be applied to the mean. The meanMonitor metric object has the scanner id for naming the managed object. The estimate of the mean attribute has the mean value calculated over a period of time.

The following managed object classes are derived from meanMonitor:

- *movingAverageMeanMonitor:* Has two conditional packages, *exponentially weighted moving average* (EWMA) and *uniformly weighted moving average* (UWMA), or ewmaGaugeMean and uwmaGaugeMean. Depending on the conditional packages used, the derived gauge value is calculated using one of the algorithms. In both cases, initial values and incrementing time constants are required. EWMA and UWMA algorithms are provided in the annexure of ISO 10164-11.
- *ewmaMeanVarianceMonitor:* A subclass of the mean metric managed object class. The mean and variance of a gauge or derived gauge for counters are calculated using the EWMA algorithm. For calculating mean and variance, the time constant value for the mean, the time constant value for the variance, the EWMA gauge mean, and EWMA gauge variance packages must be included. In addition, initial mean and variance values must be provided. For generating alarms, the threshold is applied to the estimated mean.
- *ewmaMeanPercentileMonitor:* More generic than the ewmaMeanVarianceMonitor metric object, it has the estimates of mean, median, *n*th percentile, 100-*n*th percentile, and largest and smallest gauge values or derived gauge values for counter types.

This managed object class has the attributes pctTimeConstant, estimOfLargest, estimOfSmallest, estimOfMedian, estimOf100-PCTPctile, timeConstant2, estimOfPCTPctile, numberOf-Replications, and timeBetweenReplications. Here, PCTPctile stands for the percentile value. Number of replications refers to the number of samples used for the calculations. The time constant and percent time constant for the EWMA algorithm and the initial values of each abovementioned attribute must be provided when an ewmaMeanPercentileMonitor metric object is created.

Metric managed objects generate notifications under the following conditions:

- When resource utilization crosses a threshold value
- When the request or rejection rate crosses a threshold value

Metric managed objects use the alarm reporting service for reporting alarms generated due to notifications (refer to Chapter 16). Parameters used by the alarm reporting service for metric objects are:

- *Alarm Type:* The value of Quality of Service is used.
- *Probable Cause:* This has Threshold Crossed as the cause for alarms.
- *Specific Problem:* This has one of the values Resource Utilization, Rejection Rate, or Resource Request Rate.
- *Perceived Severity:* This can have one of the values severe, early warning, or cleared.
- *Threshold Information:* This is used to provide the gauge threshold for the gauge monitor managed object or for the mean threshold of the mean monitor managed object.
- *Monitored Attributes:* This has attribute identifiers and values of the observed object instances and attributes.
- *State Change:* This optional parameter indicates a state transition associated with an alarm.

Metric objects must follow certain well-defined steps to make meaningful use of the data collected from the attributes of the managed objects being observed. While details of the OSI managed object classes used for performance management have been furnished, note that they are only broad guidelines. When implementing them, their definitions must be tailored to suit the local conditions. The requirements must also be examined and matched against the managed object class definitions.

17.5 Summarization Function

The Summarization Function (ISO 10164-13) has the following details:

- Scope and requirements of the document
- Managed object classes for summarizing attribute values of the managed objects at a specified time for performance measurement purposes
- Details on how to observe and report instantaneous statistics on the attributes of the managed objects being monitored
- Model for the behavior of summarization objects
- Conformance requirements

The data collected over different managed objects are summarized such that summary reports can be formulated. The managed object classes used for summarization are defined in the summarization function (ISO 10164-13), and we briefly look into what these summarization managed object classes mean in the next section.

Summarization managed object classes help to identify one or more attributes of one or more managed objects and report the summary values of these or the individual values, using event reports, to the managing systems. There can also be a subset of the attributes and managed objects. Statistical measurements can be derived from the values of the attributes collected. Note that, for clarity, we prefer to use the term *observed managed object* instead of *monitored managed object.*

There should also be the flexibility to report values of monitored managed objects and their attributes at one point of time, over a period of time, or periodically over fixed intervals of time. When a large quantity of data is collected, the attributes and the managed objects whose data are being collected should be known. These summary data on managed objects can be collected by managing systems by issuing an M-ACTION request to the summarization object or by event reports from the summarization object (Figure 17.4). Summarization managed objects can also be used to collect data on managed objects, including those defined for management purposes such as fault management and support managed objects such as the metric objects and the log record objects.

17.5.1 Summarization managed object classes

The managed object class, scanner, is inherited from top and provides the ability to summarize the data of managed objects including those

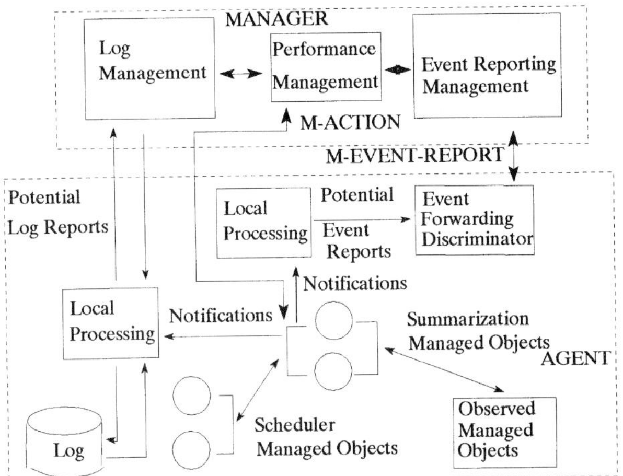

Figure 17.4 Relationship between summarization managed objects and performance management.

of the metric objects. The term *scan* means the sampling process used for monitoring attributes of managed objects at a specific period of time. When this scan is repeated at regular intervals (granularity periods), it provides a set of data. However, it should be possible to control the intervals for observations to make the summarization process flexible. The interval for observation is provided by the granularity period attribute in the scanner.

For the summarization of data, the following attributes are necessary:

- The identities of the managed objects and the attributes of the managed objects being observed
- The contents of the summary reports
- The granularity period (GP), if required, reporting period (RP), and the frequency of observation of the attributes of the managed objects

Basically, there are two types of scanners, as shown in Figure 17.5. In nonbuffered scanners, notifications are emitted at the end of each GP. In buffered scanners, these data are collected across different scan times and are combined to form a single notification at the end of each RP. In Figure 17.5, note that each RP is made up of two GPs for a buffered scanner.

Different flavors of scanner objects are defined by the OSI for summarization purposes. They provide flexibility on how the data can be collected, and the attributes and the managed objects on which data is collected and summarized. Depending on specific implementations,

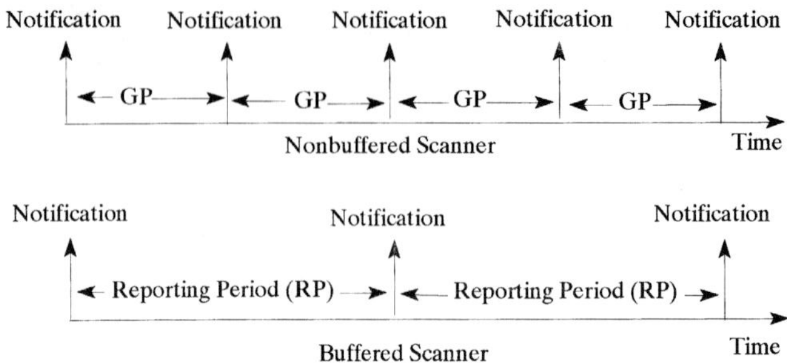

Figure 17.5 Buffered and nonbuffered scanners.

these scanner objects can be chosen. The managed objects for scans are selected either explicitly by using their names or by using a scoping and filtering mechanism. The following managed object classes have been defined for summarization:

- *simpleScanner:* Observes the same set of attributes across a set of managed objects and generates a report at the end of each granularity period. It sends summary results in an M-ACTION response.
- *dynamicScanner:* Has the ability to dynamically select the attributes on the basis of selection criteria mentioned in M-ACTION.
- *dynamicSimpleScanner:* A subclass of dynamicScanner. It observes the same attributes of selected managed objects and reports the observed values.
- *ensembleStatisticScanner:* Provides the statistics calculated for attributes of selected managed objects and included in the summary report.
- *heterogeneousScanner:* Used for scanning different attributes of a set of managed objects and reports results at the end of each granularity period.
- *bufferedScanner:* Reports results at the end of reporting periods instead of granularity periods. The results of the scan at each granularity period are stored in buffers. Also, bufferedScanner scans the attributes for inclusion in the result being reported.
- *homogeneousScanner:* Uses the set of attributes of selected managed objects, and collects data and reports them.
- *meanScanner:* Reports at the end of the granularity period the mean of observed attributes of one or more managed objects. In the reply for each attribute type, the number of samples and the mean is reported. An ACTION reply may also have summary results along with the mean.

- *meanVarianceScanner:* Provides the number of samples, sample mean, and sample variance for each attribute type.
- *minMaxScanner:* Collects observations on the same set of attributes of a group of object instances. Each attribute type of minMaxScanner has an array, as shown in the Figure 17.6.
- *percentileScanner:* Similar to minMaxScanner, but with more data in each array for an attribute type; it is shown in Figure 17.6.

The following managed object classes are inherited from eventLogRecord.

- *scanReportRecord:* Represents logged information from scan report notifications or event reports.
- *statisticalReportRecord:* Similar to scanReportRecord, except that this is used to represent logged information of statistical reports.
- *bufferedScanReport Record:* Refers to the logged information from the buffered scan notification or event reports.

17.5.2 Service definitions

Summarization managed objects are created, deleted, or modified by PT-CREATE, PT-DELETE, and PT-SET, respectively. PT-GET can be used to retrieve information from summarization managed objects. The following event types are defined:

- *Scan Report:* Refers to the summary report of a single scan of observed attributes of one or more managed objects.
- *Buffered Scan Report:* Provides the summary report on observed attribute values of one or more managed objects over an RP, which

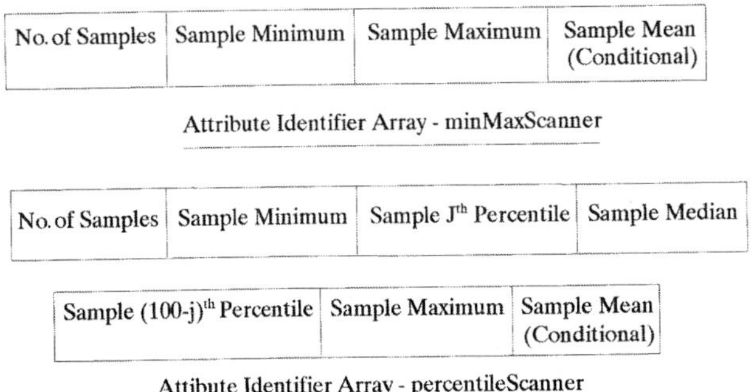

Figure 17.6 Attribute identifier array.

covers one or more GPs. The data of each GP is stored in buffers and, at the end of the RPs, the summary report is sent in an M-EVENT-REPORT.

- *Statistical Report:* Consists of summary results of a single scan of observed attribute value of one or more managed objects, and also includes derived statistical results from the same set of attributes.

These scanned data are included in the notifications, which, after processing, get converted to an M-EVENT-REPORT. These M-EVENT-REPORTs formed in the managing systems are sent to the managed systems (Figure 17.4). Each one of these event types has different parameters. Readers should consult ISO 10614-13 for details.

The following actions can be performed on summarization objects:

- *Activate Dynamic Simple Scan Report:* Responsible for activating summary results by a summarization object on the observed attributes of one or more managed objects. The identification of the attributes and the managed objects and the selection criteria are contained in the M-ACTION arguments. The M-ACTION response has the summary results needed.
- *Activate Scan Report:* As the name suggests, this activates summary results from a single scan by the summarization object. The M-ACTION response contains the needed summary result.
- *Report Buffer:* Results in the reporting of the scan result held in a buffer. Alternatively, it may result in a fresh scan of the observed attributes of one or more managed objects. The results are sent in response.
- *Activate Statistical Report:* Supplies summary results and the derived statistics from the same attributes from a single scan.

In these above cases, M-ACTION is sent from a manager to a summarization object in the agent. The results of the scan are sent back in the M-ACTION response. M-ACTION also has the facility to subset the managed object classes and the attributes by using scoping and filtering. As in the case of M-EVENT-REPORT due to notifications, readers need to consult ISO 10164-13 for details on parameters.

17.6 Notes on Performance Management

A major consideration of performance management is how the data are displayed and presented. Presentation of the data and the summary report must be easy to interpret and the reasons for any abnormal behaviors must be readily apparent. Pie charts, bar charts, trend analysis, and other graphical forms of display should be available for use.

Because some of the performance data are very important, it may be better to provide for backup facilities if there are failures in the managers. It is possible to designate an alternate manager which starts collecting the performance data if there is a failure of an active manager. Once the failed manager comes up or has been restored, it can again start collecting the performance data, and the data collected by the backup manager may be transferred to the original manager.

How the performance data is processed is also important. Because sometimes the volume of performance data can be too large, the processing may be done during off-peak times, such as nights, holidays, or weekends, to reduce the load on the manager's processors. Performance-related data collected can include the following:

- *Utilization:* Can be data such as server utilization, CPU, disk, database, memory, printer, and cache. These data must be collected to facilitate easy display. When presenting utilization, it should be possible to get an idea of the resources used and resources available. For example, when presenting hard disk utilization, how much memory is available, how much memory is used, and what the utilization is should be apparent.
- *CPU details:* Must provide information on CPU busy time, interrupt rate, and processes running.
- *Memory details:* Contain such information as page in and page out rates, number of pages swapped in and out of disks, and total number of page faults.
- *Cache details:* Provide such information as percentage of cache hit, total number of hits and misses, and cache read and write lists. Total number of cache read hits and misses can also be provided.
- *Printer details:* Can have details such as printer id, printer fonts, throughput rate, total number of print requests, total number of pages printed, and average time per print request.
- *Communication ports:* Will have details such as port id, throughput rate, total number of read and write requests, and average time per request.
- *Reads and writes:* Related to files, disks, and communication ports. Some of the data are disk access rate, read access rate, write access rate, average read time, average write time, and average number of bytes for read and write operations.
- *Packets received and transmitted:* Can refer to the packets received, packets transmitted, bytes received, bytes transmitted, packets retransmitted, and bytes retransmitted. We can further classify the packets into good and error packets.

- *Creates and deletes:* Primarily related to files. It is also possible to include file opens and file closes.

The key idea to note here is that of identifying the managed objects about which we want to collect data. These should be primarily critical resources, where savings and improvements can be done. There is no point in including trivial resources or resources which do not lead to substantial savings. "Substantial savings" is a relative term, and it depends on the specific requirements of an organization, so, when implementing, the resources for performance measurement should be chosen very carefully. Performance data collection and analysis involve the use of resources in a network and the storage and computing power of workstations.

In all of these situations, there can be high and low values such that when certain threshold levels are reached, notifications are sent. This may also be the time to analyze the reasons for high or low values.

To be effective, performance management must work in close cooperation with fault management. If a major performance problem is noticed or some impending problems are observed, then fault management enters the picture. If a resource is causing a major performance bottleneck, it is a good idea to investigate reasons. If required, in such cases, we may isolate the resource. Configuration management is useful for displaying the resources that are causing serious performance problems.

17.7 Summary

In this chapter, we investigated the OSI performance management–related documents: Workload Monitoring and Summarization Function. The guidelines provided in these two documents must be incorporated to form performance management. We also discussed the design and implementation issues involved in performance management.

17.8 Further Reading

ISO DIS 10164-11 (X.739), Information Technology, Open System Interconnection, Systems Management, Part 11: Workload Monitoring Function, 1992.

ISO 10164-13 (X.738), Information Technology, Open Systems Interconnection, Systems Management, Part 13: Summarization Function, 1994.

ISO 10165-2 (X.721), Information Technology, Open Systems Interconnection, Structure of Management Information, Part 2: Definition of Management Information, 1991.

Chapter

18

Systems Management Functions and Conformance

18.1 Introduction

We have already looked into configuration management, fault management, and performance management in previous chapters. In this chapter, we will examine the other two OSI systems management functions: accounting management and security management. Because *conformance* is an important issue in standardization, we will also examine the conformance issues with particular reference to systems management. Conformance and profiles are closely related topics, so we will discuss International Standard Profiles (ISP).

Finally, we will discuss the issues involved in integrating systems management functions into a cohesive network management framework (refer to Section 1.7). Sometimes these network management frameworks are referred to as *platforms*. The respective systems management functions are closely related to one another and, in some cases, it is difficult to rigidly partition them. Also, OSI standards are still being developed for some of the functional areas. Much work still must be done to integrate them into a cohesive systems management framework. This may not be done because OSI does not cover specific implementation details. Integrating these functions into systems management involves converting standards to implementations; hence, we will discuss the various design and implementation issues that arise.

18.2 Accounting Management

When resources such as workstations are used in a network, it is necessary to maintain a record of their usage. This is required for accounting purposes, for performance purposes, and for control of the usage of resources, especially to prevent misuse of important resources. The issue of how to charge for usage is implementation-dependent. It is sometimes necessary to charge on a departmental basis for costing purposes.

The accounting management function in OSI standards is classified under the Usage Metering Function, ISO 10164-10.2. Let us look at some of the terms generally used in OSI accounting management. The process of monitoring the utilization of resources for accounting and controlling purposes is known as *usage metering,* which is an abstract concept. The data on utilization of a resource for a specific period of time by a specific user is stored in a *usage record.*

18.2.1 Requirements of accounting management

We can summarize the requirements of accounting management as follows:

- *Usage of resources:* To get an accurate picture of the utilization of resources, measurement and collection of data are required. These methods must be flexible to adjust the collection of data to a broad variety of resources. Also, the data needs to be collected and stored in usage records in a standardized manner. Usage records should be self-contained and should not require the help of some other system to interpret the data.
- *Controlled collection of data:* There must be suitable means to control the collection of data, requiring actions such as starting, suspending, and resuming data collection.
- *Ability to generate bills:* There should be facilities to generate bills based on usage, which may require details such as duration of the usage, along with the times, geographical location of the resource, type of service being offered by the resource, and the type of tariff. There must be an ability to access the accounting data and generate bills instantaneously or in real time.

18.2.2 Accounting process

The accounting process has been divided into the following subprocesses:

- *Usage metering:* Responsible for the creation of accounting records. Several accountable events can create an accounting record. At the same time, one service process may result in one or more accounting records. The OSI accounting management standard refers to a service process as *service calls.* We use the term *service process* to make it more generic and to avoid confusion with the term service call term as used in the telecommunication industry.
- *Charging process:* Combines accounting records of a service process into *service transaction records,* which contain tariff information. The charging process is also responsible for logging these service transaction records, which is required for retrieval of the details of a service process.
- *Billing process:* Related to the preparation of a bill for a subscriber over a period of time from the service transaction records.

18.2.3 Managed object classes for accounting management

As shown in Figure 16.3, usageMeteringControlObject and usageMeteringDataObject are derived from the superclass top, while usageRecord (Figure 18.1) is a subordinate class of eventLogRecord. Note that we have included the statistical-ReportRecord, bufferedScanReportRecord, and scanReportRecord managed object classes used in the Summarization Function (ISO 10164-13). The three accounting managed object classes are:

- *usageMeteringControlObject:* Controls the collection of usage data of one or more accountable objects and identifies the policies, which refer to the usage data to be collected and under what circumstances they are to be collected. A managed object on which usage data are collected is known as an *accountable object.* As shown in Figure 18.2, usageMeteringControlObject can be part of the

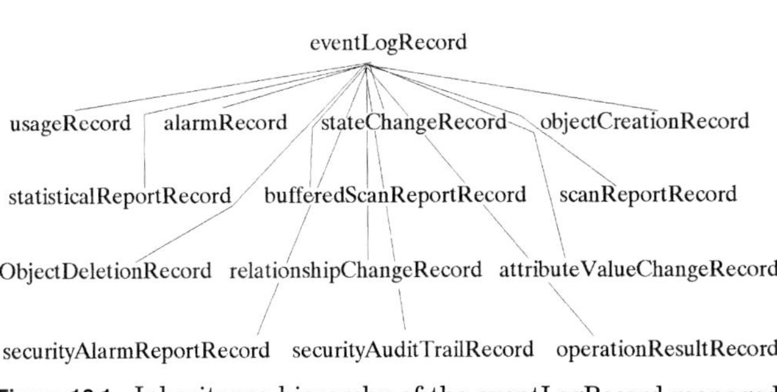

Figure 18.1 Inheritance hierarchy of the eventLogRecord managed object class.

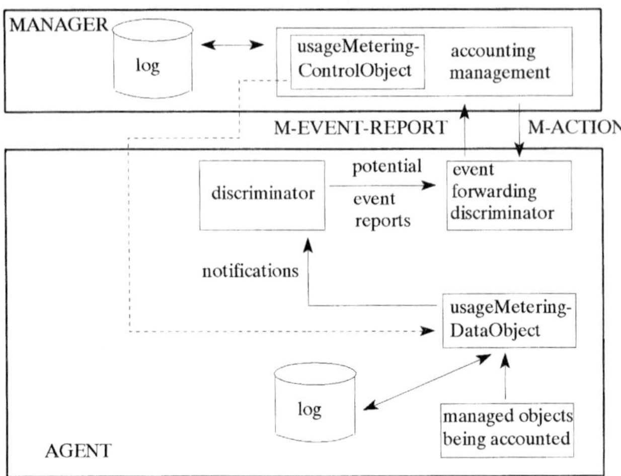

Figure 18.2 Accounting management overview.

managed system object (agent), and emits notifications when accounting is started, suspended, or resumed. Accounting management data are collected on the basis of triggering events, which are provided by incorporating attributes in usageMetering-ControlObject.

- *usageMeteringDataObject:* Associated with the usage of resources of a user. Usage data are retrieved either by doing a Get on the usageMeteringDataObject parameters or by using the data in the parameters of notifications triggered by accountable objects. The usageMeteringControlObject managed object class determines accounting record notification and when a notification has to be sent. Each instance of usageMeteringDataObject is responsible for the accounting associated with one accountable object. This managed object class can be part of an agent.
- *usageRecord:* Inherits attributes from eventLogRecord and also has attributes from usageMeteringDataObject provided through the usage report notifications. This class (see Figure 18.1) is primarily a log of the use of resources obtained through notifications triggered by instances of usageMeteringDataObject and the logging of the records. Accessing these records is controlled by the log control function, which was discussed in Section 16.4.

18.2.4 Procedures in accounting management

The data on the usage of resources are provided by the event reports generated as a result of notifications from usageMeteringDataObject.

The generation of M-EVENT REPORT is shown in Figure 18.2. Notification types generated are:

- meteringResumed
- meteringStarted
- meteringSuspended
- usageReport

When converted to M-EVENT-REPORTs using the discriminator and event forward discriminator, these notifications provide the necessary usage data. The parameters used in Event Information carry the details on the usage data. M-ACTION can also be used to control the monitoring of the usage of resources, if the meteringStart and meteringControl conditional packages are present in the usageMeteringControlObject. M-ACTION can be used for the following purposes:

- *Start Metering:* Used to start one or more instances of usageMeteringDataObject. M-ACTION information has details of the object instances to be started. However, if none of the instances are specified, then all instances are started.
- *Suspend Metering:* Suspends the collection of data by one or more instances of usageMeteringDataObject.
- *Resume Metering:* Resumes the collection of data by one or more usageMeteringDataObject instances.

Every M-ACTION has an action response or error response. For more details on the parameters of M-ACTION and M-EVENT-REPORT, consult ISO 1064-10.2 (Reference 18.1).

Like other systems management functions, accounting management may want the data to be stored in a log (Figure 18.1). This information may have to be retrieved later for analysis, reporting, or other purposes; therefore, there must be facilities to view the accounting data easily, to format the data in various ways, and, if necessary, to view and print these data. Here, security features may have to be incorporated to restrict the viewing and printing of the accounting data.

Some of the security features that may be provided in accounting management are authorization, identification, access control, and authentication, which are incorporated depending on the requirements. There may have to be restrictions on who can access accounting data. Extending this philosophy, only systems administrators who operate in the workstations configured as managers may be allowed to view and print the accounting data, in which case, these managers will require security features. Note that the accounting management security issues we discussed are independent of the security features which may be required in manager and agents to collect the accounting data. When collecting accounting data, the security features mentioned under security management may be incorporated.

18.3 Security Management

Security management is an important systems management function. When a considerable amount of problem, accounting, and usage data is stored, the data may be misused. In some cases, there are mala fide motives for accessing and manipulating the data, leading to the misuse and, sometimes, total disruption of the network services. Intruders may steal data important to a business. Data falling into the wrong hands may prove to be catastrophic for a business. Furthermore, the accounting data are usually very important in every setup, so this data should be safely guarded.

One of the common techniques adopted in security management is to ensure that the workstation engaged in systems management is in a safe physical location, where access by anybody but network administrators is not allowed. This is a very rudimentary form of security, which by itself will not be enough when networks expand and have workstations dispersed in different locations.

Another form of security used is identification. Here, the identity of the network or systems administrator is checked when logging on, which is analogous to checking the user identifier and password. This may be enough of a security check if the systems administrators are in one physical location; however, when they are dispersed in different locations and must communicate with one another, simple identification may not be adequate.

A problem arises when a manager and agents have to communicate. The agents must be sure that the management operations have come from a genuine manager instead of one masquerading as a manager. For this, authentication is required and may take the form of a secret key that ensures that the manager and agents are the ones that are really authorized to communicate. Here, a Kerberos authentication scheme can be used.

As we have seen earlier, a management domain may have more than one manager, so we must ensure that only managers of that domain communicate with the agents, rather than managers of some other domain communicating directly with agents in other domains. This can be done by having an identifier for the domain which may be checked before allowing access. In the case of communication with remote network administrators, digital signature authentication procedures can be used. This becomes necessary if two network administrators of a large corporation are in different physical locations such as counties, states, or nations.

When carrying CMIP PDUs between the manager and agent, some sort of checking of the identifiers in the data being transmitted may be required. This identifier may be checked in both the manager and agents.

18.3.1 Access control

Some of the managed objects in an agent may contain sensitive information, and access to these objects must be carefully controlled. For this reason, an access control mechanism can be included in the agent. Details on access control in the OSI environment are furnished in ISO 10164-9. Access control has the following objectives:

- *Restrict association,* which is the first prerequisite for controlling the access to management applications and management information.
- *Protect management information* by restricting the creation, deletion, modification, or disclosure of management information to only authorized users with appropriate access rights, which are read, write, and execute.
- *Control transmission of management information* to only authorized recipients, which must be done from data being transmitted in the form of M-EVENT REPORTs.
- *Prevent unauthorized users* from initiating management operations to collect management information. Necessary access rights are obtained at the time of the association itself.

Managed object classes for access control. For the purpose of access control, the concept of a *security domain* is introduced, which refers to a set of elements administered by one authority with certain specific security policies. The following managed object classes (Figure 18.3) have been defined for access control in security management:

- *accessControlPolicy:* This lays down access control rules for associations when initiating an association, for notifications which get converted to event reports, and for management operations. The access control policy for management operations on managed objects specifies restrictions: whether global object access rules apply or not, the granting or denial of certain management operations to access some of the managed objects and attributes, the default object access rules, and the precedence of access control rules in the case of a clash. In a managed system, there can be

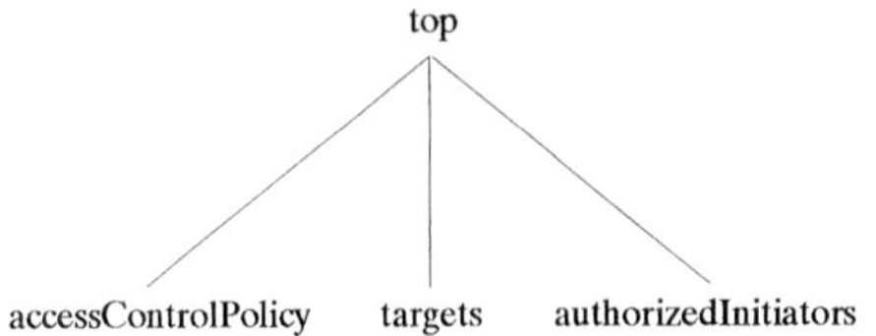

Figure 18.3 Inheritance hierarchy for access control objects.

only one accessControlPolicy managed object for a security domain.

The accessControlPolicy managed object can have the access rules for association, notifications, and management operations, name of the security domain, the identification of the security domain authority, the period during which access rules can be applied, and self-protection information such as whether this access control information itself has been protected and is valid.

- *targets:* This determines the managed objects that can be accessed, operations that can be performed on these managed objects, and who can access them. It enables control of the access to managed objects and the operations which can be done on them.
- *authorizedInitiators:* This specifies the authorized users, such as managers, that can access the managed objects in the managed system and the access rights of these users. Authorized initiators may be identified by capabilities, in which case access rights are governed by the capabilities of the initiators, by the possession of a security label, or by identity. For example, security classifications can take the form of A, B, C, D, and E, where A is the most secure data classification and E is the least secure data. If the management operation has a label of A, it will be allowed to access even the most secret data, while a label of E will only allow the access of managed objects which don't contain sensitive information. In case of an initiator being recognized by an identity, the access privileges of the initiator are based on the access rights of individual, anonymous, or group names.

The managed object classes for access control are a subclass of the managed object class top, as shown in Figure 18.3. These managed objects can be accessed only if they meet the rules framed for them. The definitions of these managed objects are furnished in ISO 10164-9 (X.741) (see Reference 18.2).

Access control for association, operations, and notifications. *Access control information* (ACI) is security-relevant information used for access control. ACI is represented by managed objects and attributes present in a managed system (agent). Figure 18.4 illustrates the procedures involved in access control for management association. The association process, which is responsible for starting an association, sends an association request (1) to the *access control enforcement function* (AEF). The AEF supplies the ACI to the *access control decision function* (ADF) (2), which checks whether the initiator has the rights to access the target and perform the operations. Then the ADF returns the decision (3) as to whether access to the requested target can be granted or not. If the decision is to grant access, then the ACI details are retained in the AEF, and the response from the AEF is sent to the association process (4).

In the ADF, decision making is governed by policy rules. Some of the policies determine what actions must be taken when an access control violation has occurred. Actions may be to generate a security alarm report, to log an event, to increment a counter on a security threshold, or to ignore the potential event report. There is no hard and fast rule here. Depending on the requirements and implementation considerations, a combination of actions may be taken.

As shown in Figure 18.5, management operations from managers are routed to the agent managed object processing component (1). From here, the management operation is routed to an AEF (2), which passes the management operation, along with who initiated it and the information needed from the requesting manager, to the ADF as an access request (3). In ADF, a check is made as to whether the

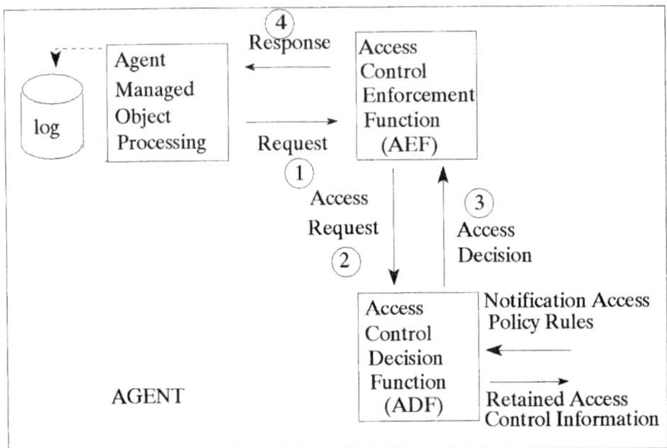

Figure 18.4 Access control for association. [*Adapted from* SNMP, SNMPv2, and CMIP: The Practical Guide to Network-Management Standards *(p. 508) by William Stallings. Copyright © 1993 by Addison-Wesley Publishing Company, Inc. Reprinted by permission of the publisher.*]

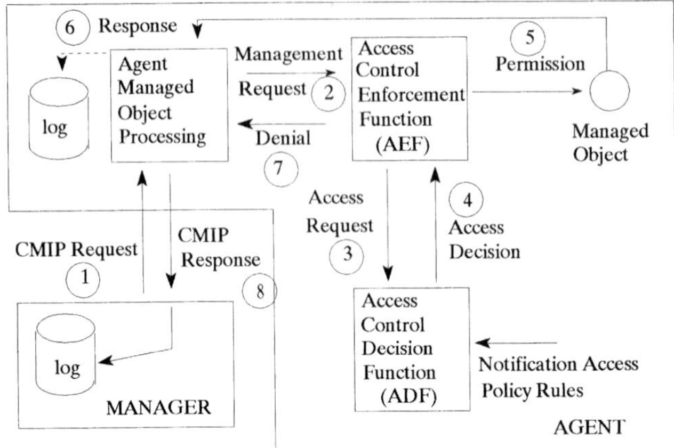

Figure 18.5 Access control for management operation. [*Adapted from* SNMP, SNMPv2, and CMIP: The Practical Guide to Network-Management Standards *(p. 508) by William Stallings. Copyright © 1993 by Addison-Wesley Publishing Company, Inc. Reprinted by permission of the publisher.*]

access request can be satisfied, and this decision is sent back to the AEF (4). If access permission is granted (5), then a managed object may be accessed and the response can be sent back to the agent managed object processing component (6). The response, in turn, can be forwarded to the manager which sent the request (8).

However, if the permission cannot be granted to access the managed object, then the denial is also sent to the agent managed object processing component (7). In this case, it may be required to log the denial of the service in a security alarm event log. This is an optional function depending on the amount of security required. In the manager also, depending on the security requirement, the denial may be logged in the event log.

Access control notifications are necessary to make sure that only authorized users receive the notifications emitted by the managed objects. This is shown in Figure 18.6. The notification emitted by a managed object passes through the filter in EFD. If the notification satisfies the discriminator filter, then the potential event report, which is generated by the EFD, is sent to the AEF. From this step on, the procedures are similar to the ones described in access control for management operations.

The two functions, AEF and ADF, can be made part of a single component, which can be termed the *access control component.* In fact, from the implementation point of view, it is better to tightly couple these two functions instead of making them separate.

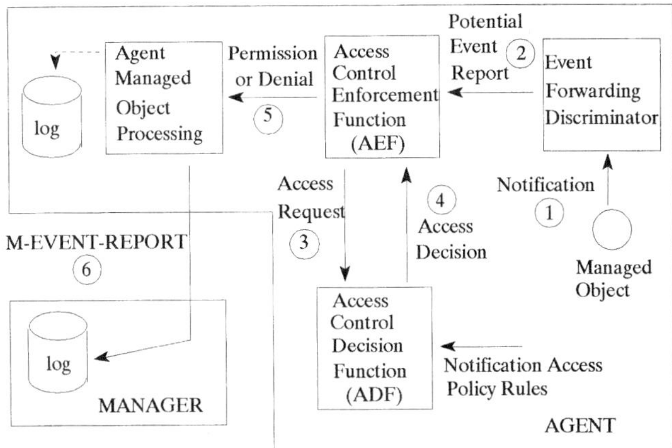

Figure 18.6 Access control for notifications. [*Adapted from* SNMP, SNMPv2, and CMIP: The Practical Guide to Network-Management Standards *(p. 508) by William Stallings. Copyright © 1993 by Addison-Wesley Publishing Company, Inc. Reprinted by permission of the publisher.*]

For details on access control attributes, refer to ISO 10164-7 (X.736) (see Reference 18.3).

18.3.2 Security alarm reporting

When there are security violations, security alarm reports are sent (refer to Figure 16.2). The mechanism for generating potential event reports is the same as that described for the alarm report function. When a security violation occurs, notifications are emitted by managed objects. These notifications are processed using discriminator filters and get converted to M-EVENT-REPORTs, which are sent from the agents to managers. A manager may or may not log the security alarm received. The parameters used in M-EVENT-REPORT are used here. Some parameters, such as event type and event information, are specific to security alarm reporting. Event types used are:

- *Integrity violation:* States whether the information on a managed object has been changed, including insertion and deletion.
- *Operational violation:* Refers to whether the requested service could not be performed for reasons associated with operations, such as unavailability, improper functioning, or wrong invocation of the operation.

- *Physical violation:* Used to report a security violation when some sort of physical security attack occurs.
- *Security service or mechanism violation:* Used for reporting security service such as access control violations.
- *Time domain violation:* If, for example, there is a restriction that a managed object should not be accessed after 10 P.M. and this managed object is accessed at 11 P.M. then the time domain violation is used to report the security alarm.

Event information has the following parameters:

- *Security alarm cause:* This is covered in the security alarm reporting function (ISO 10164-7). In addition, depending on the implementation requirements, alarm causes may be defined. The values in this field are registered as ASN.1 identifiers. The security alarm cause helps identify the event type to be chosen.
- *Security alarm severity:* This indicates the severity level of the security violation. The severity levels are indeterminate, critical, major, minor, and warning.
- *Security alarm detector:* This indicates who detected the security violation.
- *Service user:* This identifies the service user which requested the service leading to the security violation.
- *Service provider:* This identifies the service provider which is responsible for emitting the notification on the security violation.

We have already reviewed the parameters, such as Invoke Identifier, Correlated Notifications, Additional Text, and Additional Information in Section 16.2 under the alarm reporting function. The Event Reply parameter is not included. For purposes of logging the security alarm, securityAlarmReportRecord is defined. It is a subclass of eventLogRecord in the inheritance hierarchy shown in Figure 18.1. So, this record inherits the attributes, operations, and notifications of the superclasses eventLogRecord, logRecord, and top.

18.3.3 Security audit trail

Security-related events are maintained in security audit trail logs. These logs are available for analysis at a later date and can be maintained in the same system or in different systems. These security-related events are primarily due to notifications from managed objects. Security management users must be able to control how these logs are done. Some examples of security-related events which are logged are:

- Connections
- Disconnections
- Security mechanism utilization
- Management operations
- Usage accounting
- Security violations

The unique features in security audit trail logs are in event type and event information. The event types are:

- *Service report:* Refers to the provision, denial, or recovery of a service
- *Usage report:* Used for indicating a record with statistical information

Event information has the following unique security audit trail log parameters:

- *Service Report Cause:* Provides further details on the probable causes. The probable causes identified are request for service, denial of service, response from service, service failure, etc.
- *Security Audit Text:* Contains the description of the security audit trail.
- *Security Audit Data:* Provides information on the security audit trail, and consists of an identifier, significance indicator, and audit information. The identifier defines the data type of the audit information, the significance indicator indicates whether the receiving system needs to parse the audit information, and the audit information has the information relevant to the security audit.

For storing the information on the security audit trail in a log, securityAuditTrailRecord has been defined. It is derived from eventLogRecord (Figure 18.1). We examined the details of logs and how logging is done under log control in Section 16.4.

There are many security schemes that can be folded into security management, for which requirements should be determined. Remember that implementing a security function requires extra operations and memory and may affect performance. Some of the management data may not be important at all and do not need much security, so the tendency toward overkill when putting security functions into the systems management functions should be avoided.

18.4 Conformance Testing

Different vendors claim that they conform to the standards, and the implementations have various options. Checking whether an implementation really matches the specifications of OSI standards and ITU recommendations is done by conformance testing. One of the key aspects of conformance testing is to model the implementation as a set of states and transitions to these states; thus, protocol specifications and implementations are modeled as *finited state machines* (FSMs). An implementation of one or more OSI protocols is known as an *implementation under test* (IUT). For conformance testing, the OSI has developed a wide range of conformance-testing standards (see ISO 9646, References 18.5 through 18.11). In addition to these general standards, a specific standard has been developed for OSI management conformance (ISO 10165-6, see Reference 18.12). Conformance testing is a vast topic, so we will restrict the discussion to an overview. For more details, readers should consult the sources provided in the References (Section 18.9).

Conformance requirements have the following classifications:

- *Mandatory:* The requirement must be implemented.
- *Conditional:* The requirement must be implemented if the conditions specified in the requirement are satisfied.
- *Optional:* The requirement must be implemented only under certain conditions. Sometimes an optional requirement is implemented to provide extra functionality.

There are also the following types of conformance requirements:

- *Static conformance:* The requirements specify the minimum capabilities required for internetworking, indicating the capabilities to be included in a protocol and the requirements which are dependent on the underlying layers.
- *Dynamic conformance:* The requirements relate to the maximum capabilities an implementation can have. The major portion of OSI protocol specifications is devoted to dynamic conformance.

One comes across the following terms in conformance testing:

- *Protocol implementation conformance statement (PICS):* This is a document clearly stating the capabilities and options implemented such that they can be tested against the protocol specifications. The PICS must specify the mandatory, conditional, and optional static conformance requirements of the protocol and the other dependent layers. Notice that there are PICS specifications in most of the OSI protocols. For each protocol, one PICS is required.

- *Protocol implementation extra information for testing* (*PIXIT*): This provides the extra information in addition to that supplied by the PICS for actually performing the conformance testing. PIXIT is useful for test laboratories for performing conformance testing.

A conforming system must satisfy both the static and dynamic conformance requirements. There are four levels of conformance testing:

- *Basic interconnection test* (*BIT*): This is a preliminary test which can be used to determine whether an implementation is conformable and the IUT can be subjected to further conformance testing.
- *Capability test:* This helps to verify whether the claimed capabilities in the PICS are present, and provides for the testing of static conformance requirements in a protocol.
- *Behavior test:* This is useful for testing the dynamic conformance requirements of a protocol specification. This is a full-fledged test, which, along with the capability test, forms the basis for conformance testing.
- *Conformance resolution test:* This is a nonstandardized test to suit the specific implementations.

How these tests can be used to perform conformance testing is shown in Figure 18.7. The steps involved in conformance testing are:

- *Preparation for testing:* Involves preparing PICS and PIXIT, choice of appropriate test method, and preparation for test.
- *Test operations:* Related to the actual testing to check whether conformance requirements are met. This includes static confor-

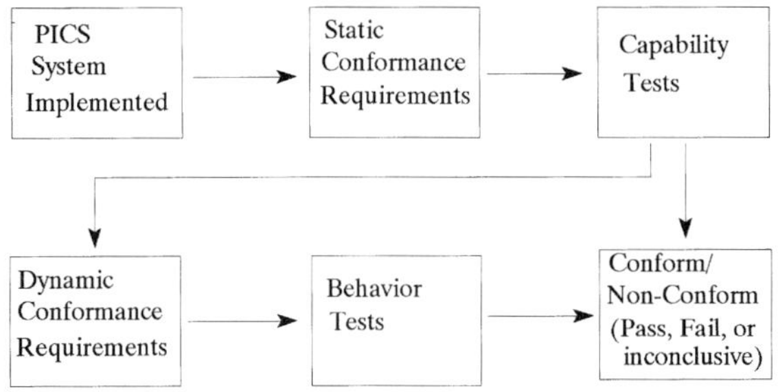

Figure 18.7 Relationship between conformance tests.

mance review, BIT, capabilities test, behavior test, and analysis of test results, which indicates verdicts of pass, fail, or inclusive.

- *Test report production:* Results in a summary report known as the System Conformance Test Report (SCTR), and a detailed report called the Protocol Conformance Test Report (PCTR).

A *test suite* is a collection of test cases. Proceeding from the bottom up in the hierarchy of a test structure, at the lowest level is a *test event*. This is the indivisible element of a test step in the test suite hierarchy. Moving up the hierarchy, a *test step* is a collection of test events or a collection of steps and test events. A *test case* has a single test objective and can again be a collection of one or more test steps. Grouping of test steps for convenience is known as a *test group*. Figure 18.8 depicts the hierarchical nature of the test suite components.

For testing OSI protocols, *Tree and Tabular Combined Notation* (TTCN) can be used. TTCN is a language for specifying test suites independent of the test methods, protocols, and layers. For more details on TTCN, refer to ISO 9646-3 (X.292) (Reference 18.7) and Stallings, *Network Management Standards* (Reference 18.20).

Having explained some of the terms used in conformance testing, let us examine conformance testing in relation to OSI management. OSI management uses the following documents for OSI management protocol conformance testing:

- *Management Conformance Summary* (*MCS*): This is a questionnaire to be filled up by a supplier on the conformance of an implementation to the OSI management standards.
- *Management Information Definition Statement* (*MIDS*): This is used to state the conformance of an implementation about management information. There are specific MIDS proforma specifications for attributes, attribute groups, actions, and notifications.
- *Managed Object Conformance Statement* (*MOCS*): This provides standard documentation for stating the conformance of an implementation to a managed object class.

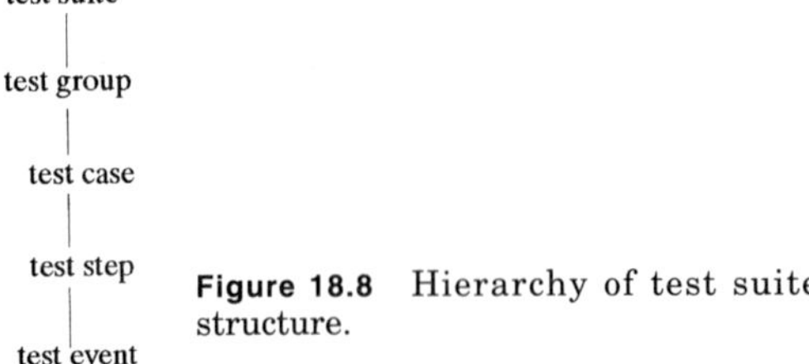

Figure 18.8 Hierarchy of test suite structure.

- *Managed Relationship Conformance Statement (MRCS)*: This is used for conformance statements of an implementation for name binding.

18.5 International Standard Profiles (ISP)

As previously indicated, one of the main drawbacks of standards is that there are so many of them. Each standards organization has its own set of standards. Furthermore, within each organization, there are many sets of standards. Even after complying to the standards, there is no guarantee that two products will interoperate. This is one of the main reasons that products implementing OSI were slow to appear. There must be guidelines for what set of implementations will make two products interoperate.

The systems management standards are at the application layers, and there are six layers below it, so for two systems management products to interoperate, there is a need for a uniform suite of standards in the layers below and the application layers. For this reason, a set of profiles, which is a combination of the standards from the lowest level to the highest level, has been developed. If there is conformance to the profiles, then products implementing the same profile should interoperate.

The framework for International Standard Profiles (ISP) and the relationships among different standards have been explained in Technical Report (TR) 10000. TR 10000 provides information on the concept of standard profiles, on how the standard profiles are to be framed, and classification schemes for ISPs. TR 10000 is not subject to the review and rigorous standard process as in other standards. TR 10000 has two parts, 10000-1: Framework and TR 10000-2: Taxonomy of Profiles. There are many documents on ISPs (Reference 18.14 through 18.18). Many ISPs are still in the *Draft International Standardized Profile* (DISP) stage. As with conformance testing, we will restrict our discussion to the basic concepts in ISPs. A full-blown discussion of the ISP topic is beyond the scope of this book, so for more details, readers should consult the documents listed in References (Section 18.9).

Some of the important terms in ISP are:

- *Base standard:* Covers an approved IS, TR, or ITU-T (previously CCITT) recommendation.
- *Profile:* Composed of subsets and/or a set of one or more base standards to accomplish a certain function.

- *ISP:* An internationally accepted document of one or more standards to accomplish one or more functions.
- *Group:* A set of compatible profiles. A group is of the form YXnnn, where Y refers to the class identifier, and X refers to the group identifier.
- *Taxonomy:* Refers to the structure and classification of profiles. It also mentions the relationship between profiles.
- *ISP Implementation Conformance Statement* (*ISPICS*): A slightly modified form of PICS, used by a supplier to mention the capabilities of the implementations.

OSI defined classes for profiles are:

- *F:* Refers to the interchange format and representation of profiles.
- *A:* Known as the application profile for connection-mode transport service and uses the T profile for transport service.
- *B:* Stands for the application profile using connectionless-mode transport service using the U profile for transport service.
- *T:* Refers to the connection-mode transport profile related to subnetwork type. A subnetwork spans layers one through three of the OSI seven layers, and layers one through three connect the distributed systems.
- *U:* Provides the profile for connectionless-mode transport service related to subnetwork type.
- *R:* Known as the relay profile, it provides for relay functions between T and U profiles.

T and U profiles are further divided into groups. Interworking within members of a group and between members of different groups is possible. TR 10000-2 explains groups in detail.

Figure 18.9 depicts the relationships between the different classes of profiles. Notice in the figure that there is only a limited combination of profiles possible between A and B and T and U profiles. Only the A profile can be combined with the T profile and, similarly, only the B profile can be combined with the U profile. However, at the level of the F profile, there is no such restriction between F and A and B profiles; any F profile can be combined with an A or B profile.

For management communication purposes, the following profiles have been defined:

- *AOM11:* Defined in DISP 11183-3, it provides the CMIS basic management communication services.

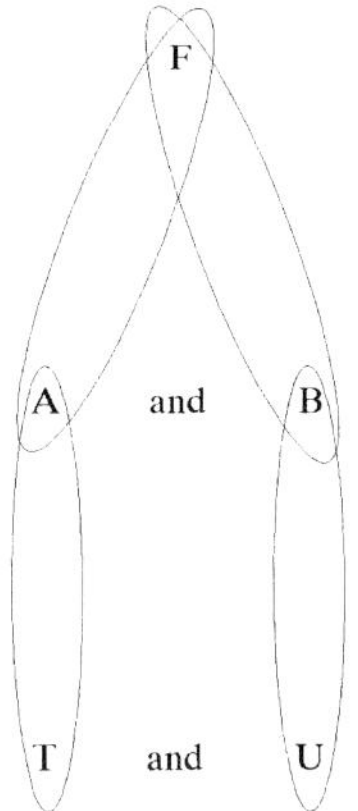

Figure 18.9 Relationship between profiles.

- *AOM12:* Defined in DISP 11183-2, it furnishes the enhanced management communication services, such as scoping and filtering in addition to the basic services defined in AOM11.

For management functions, the profiles defined in DISP 11183-1 are AOM211, AOM212, AOM213, AOM221, and AOM231. These functional profiles are applicable to a system in a manager or agent role and basically cover different management standards, varying from general management capabilities in AOM211 to general log control in AOM231. These management profiles have a relationship to parts of the AOM11 and AOM12 profiles and the managed objects defined in ISO 10165-2.

18.6 Systems Management Architecture

There are different ways in which systems management functions such as fault management, performance management, configuration management, security management, and accounting management can be arranged. One way is shown in Figure 18.10. By and large, these systems management functions are grouped into the network management framework (Section 1.7).

But all of the architectures have one thing in common. These systems management functions should be manipulated by users via panels or the command-line interface at the user workstations. These end-user interfaces can vary from very simple to the most sophisticated. They should have the flexibility to be tailored by users. In this context, "users" is a restricted term—these are not the average users of the networks. These users can be systems or network administra-

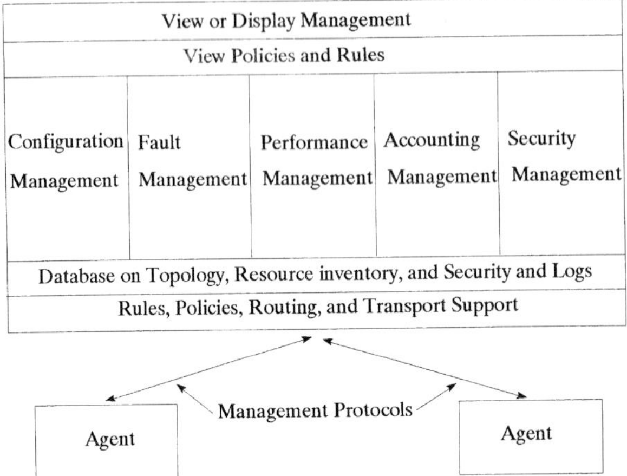

Figure 18.10 Network management platform.

tors. There should be security measures so that unauthorized users cannot access these systems management functions.

The view or display management must have the ability to be tailored by a set of rules or policies, which can range from simple to complicated. For average users, there should be default rules on the basis of which the views can be accessed. Because most of the systems management functions, such as configuration management, use topology management, these functions need to have access to topology management. Each systems management function can have its own set of rules, which adds flexibility to the model.

By and large, the systems management functions are placed in managers, which in turn can be located in workstations. These workstations must have enough processing power to be functional to the users. So performance by itself becomes a critical issue, and response times for the users is one of the performance factors. From implementation considerations, these workstations must have enough storage capacity and memory power to store massive amounts of data; hence, the capacities and speeds of the storage devices and processing power of the workstation processor are some of the factors to be taken into consideration when designing where these system management functions must be placed. The placement of managers into domains can be tailored such that too much work is not placed on one manager (see Section 3.3).

The basic common factor in all these functions is the design and definition of the managed object classes. If we need to monitor how a network behaves, we define the network as a managed object class, then we define the attributes which we would like to handle. In a similar manner, we have to define each and every aspect of the systems management functions in terms of managed object classes. We must be very careful in defining these managed object classes. There are various options available. We can make use of properties such as inheritance and polymorphism to make the definitions simpler. These managed object class definitions and details of the object instances must be stored in the database in agents, and their details relevant to management information must be transferred to the manager.

Information on some of the object instances will have to be stored in the manager itself. In some cases, it may be desirable to keep caches to improve performance. These databases and caches may impose their own restrictions on such factors as processing power and capacity and speed of memory and storage devices. It is best to take note of these issues during the design stage.

The flexibility needed in the definition of managed object classes cannot be overstressed. A user must be able to define his or her own set of managed object classes, attributes, operations, and notifications of these managed object classes. For complex functions, users must have the flexibility to write their own applications on top of the systems management functions provided.

It must be noted that the object instances are distributed all over the domain in the manager and its agents. Management information such as the details of the object instances must be transmitted from agents to managers, so the transport mechanism, the amount of management data, and the speed with which this management data are transmitted from the agents to the managers must also be considered.

If the managed object class definitions have too many unnecessary details, then the traffic carried in the network due to the systems management functions will be heavy. On the other hand, if there are not many details in a managed object class, it may not be of much use from the user's standpoint. Here, systems management function traffic is only a part of the network traffic. From the perspective of usefulness and performance, the frequency with which the management data is transferred from the agents to managers is also important.

It has been assumed here that each agent in the network will have the database of its object instances. But, what happens if the workstations do not have much storage or have no storage at all? In such cases, some agents will have to manage these workstations, and these agents are regarded as a sort of a manager with respect to the workstations. Here, the agent collects data and stores the data in its own storage, and it forwards the data to the systems management functions in the manager. From an implementation standpoint, some of these factors should also be considered.

18.7 Notes on the OSI Systems Management Implementation

The OSI systems management standardization effort is intensive and has covered all facets of systems management functions. However, because of the consensus approach, it takes time to come to decisions and for standards to stabilize. So, when implementing systems management standards, it is important to wait for documents to achieve the level of International Standards (IS). There have been many instances where even Draft International Standards (DIS) have changed substantially. So a note of caution is necessary here: Before implementing systems management, the latest document should be consulted. The standards documents can be procured from one of the sources mentioned in Appendix C.

Though OSI standard implementations have been quite slow to reach the market, they are gradually gaining acceptance. In the data communication area, the acceptance of standards has been slow because there are already many mature products that dominate the network management market. But with the gradual convergence of network management in the telecommunications and data communications areas, OSI systems management will eventually prevail. In the telecommunications area, OSI standards already have wide acceptability.

However, the pace of OSI implementations will be decided by the TCP/IP protocol suite as well. TCP/IP and applications based on SNMP are also gaining acceptance in many nations. For those who are looking for immediate solutions to their problems, TCP/IP has a wide appeal. However, many nations may resist switching to TCP/IP for various reasons. Taking all the factors into consideration, OSI implementations will take time before they are used worldwide. A final factor in the pace of OSI implementations is governmental backing and decisions.

18.8 Summary

Systems management functions such as accounting and security management have been discussed in detail in this chapter. Once the standards have been developed, it is important for the sake of interoperability to look into conformance and ISPs. Conformance is necessary to make sure that implementations meet the requirements laid out in the standards. ISPs are important to make sure that implementations that can interoperate can be achieved using a set of standards. We examined the issues of conformance and ISP, bearing these points in mind.

In Part 5, different systems management functions were discussed. With all the systems management functions, the basic question is: Can these functions be integrated into a network management platform such that management applications can be built on top of the platform? We discussed some of the important design issues involved in integrating different systems management functions. This chapter concluded with some of the author's own thoughts on OSI systems management implementation.

18.9 References

Accounting management

18.1 ISO DIS 10164-10.2, Information Technology, Open Systems Interconnection, Systems Management, Part 10: Usage Metering Function, 1993.

Security management

18.2 ISO DIS 10164-9 (X.741), Information Technology, Open Systems Interconnection, Systems Management, Part 9: Objects and Attributes for Access Control, 1993.

18.3 ISO 10164-7 (X.736), Information Technology, Open Systems Interconnection, Systems Management, Part 7: Security Alarm Reporting Function, 1992.

18.4 ISO 10164-8 (X.740), Information Technology, Open Systems Interconnection, Systems Management, Part 8: Security Audit Trail Function, 1993.

Conformance testing

Note: In addition to the following documents on conformance testing, DAMs have also been issued.

18.5 ISO 9646-1 (X.290), Information Technology, OSI Conformance Testing Methodology and Framework, Part 1: General Concepts, 1991.

18.6 ISO 9646-2 (X.291), Information Technology, OSI Conformance Testing Methodology and Framework, Part 2: Abstract Test Suite Specification, 1991.

18.7 ISO DIS 9646-3 (X.292), Information Technology, OSI Conformance Testing Methodology and Framework, Part 3: The Tree and Tabular Combined Notation (TTCN), 1990.

18.8 ISO 9646-4 (X.293), Information Technology, OSI Conformance Testing Methodology and Framework, Part 4: Test Realization, 1991.

18.9 ISO 9646-5 (X.294), Information Technology, OSI Conformance Testing Methodology and Framework, Part 5: Requirements on Test Laboratories and Clients for the Conformance Assessment Process, 1991.

18.10 ISO 9646-6 (X.295), Information Technology, OSI Conformance Testing Methodology and Framework, Part 6: Protocol Profile Test Specification, 1992.

18.11 ISO DIS 9646-7 (X.296), Information Technology, OSI Conformance Testing Methodology and Framework, Part 7: Implementation Conformance Statements, 1993.

18.12 ISO 10165-6 (X.724), Information Technology, Open Systems Interconnection, Structure of Management Information: Requirements and Guidelines for

Implementation Conformance Statement Proformas Associated with OSI Management, 1994.

18.13 Richard, Jr., J. Linn, and M. Umit Uyar, (eds.), *Conformance Testing Methodologies and Architectures for OSI Protocols,* Los Alamitos, Calif.: IEEE Computer Society Press, 1994.

International Standard Profiles (ISP)

18.14 ISO TR 10000-1, Information Technology, Framework and Taxonomy of International Standardized Profiles, Part 1: Framework, 1990.

18.15 ISO TR 10000-2, Information Technology, Framework and Taxonomy of International Standardized Profiles, Part 2: Taxonomy of Profiles, 1990.

18.16 ISP 10607-1, Information Technology, International Standard Profiles AFTnn-FTAM, Part 1: Specification of ACSE, Presentation, and Session Protocols for use by FTAM, 1991.

18.17 ISP 10607-2, Information Technology, International Standard Profiles AFTnn-FTAM, Part 2: Definition of Document Types, Constraint Sets, and Syntaxes, 1992.

18.18 ISP 10607-3, Information Technology, International Standard Profiles AFTnn, Part 3: AFT11, Simple File Transfer Service, 1991.

General

18.19 Held, Gilbert, *Network Management: Techniques, Tools and Systems,* New York: John Wiley, 1992.

18.20 Stallings, William, *Networking Standards: A Guide to OSI, ISDN, LAN, and MAN Standards,* Reading, Mass.: Addison-Wesley, 1993.

18.21 Terplan, K., *Communication Networks Management,* Englewood Cliffs, N.J.: Prentice Hall, 1991.

Chapter

19

Network Management Topics, Issues, and Trends

19.1 Introduction

As mentioned in earlier chapters, the management of large heterogeneous and multiprotocol networks is a major problem, which can be reduced to the incompatibility of different protocols below the application layer. Below this layer, there are standard protocols such as OSI, Internet, and proprietary protocols. There are major differences among the standard protocols and some have grown independently of the others.

These days, with the global reach of networks, the problems concern the integration of these networks based on various protocols so that the applications can interoperate with one another. To aggravate the problems, each network may have its own network management solution. To integrate these different network management solutions under one manageable solution, or umbrella, can be a huge task.

An important question that immediately comes to mind is: Should network management functions be distributed across different manageable areas, say by domains, or should centralized network management be opted for? In some cases, hybrid solutions are appropriate, in which some of the network management functions are distributed and some key functions are centralized.

Until recently, network management activities have mostly been centralized. Centralized network management (Figure 1.5) has the following advantages and disadvantages:

- There is one central manager, probably with a backup, where all management activities are centralized. This central manager coordinates and controls all the agents in a network and provides network management functions to all the resources, including the network.

- The user interface and manager are located in the network control center. Network administrators interface with the manager via consoles or workstation screens.
- Agents have very limited functions and send all the management information to the managers. This results in increased network traffic and may become a performance issue.
- Because all the management activities are centralized in one manager, the manager itself may become overloaded and may end up as a performance bottleneck.
- In the mainframe environment where the host is responsible for most of the computing activities, centralized network management is a natural extension to hostcentric computing.
- Mature and well-established network management products are available.
- Centralized network management is usually based on proprietary protocols, which are easier to manage because there is a tight coupling of protocol stacks below the network management.

To overcome some of the drawbacks of centralized network management, distributed network management is becoming popular. Some of the advantages and disadvantages of distributed network management are as follows:

- Distributed network management is a good match to the client-server environment, in which the resources in a network are more widely dispersed. There can be one or more servers to cater to the needs of a computing environment. When there is more than one server in a large network, centralized network management does not scale well.
- Network traffic is greatly reduced, because most of the network management functions are shared by more than one manager. Furthermore, the network traffic due to network management is more dispersed and localized because there is more than one management domain.
- Because there is more than one manager, it is easy to manage failures. A manager in another domain may take over from the manager which has failed.
- It is easy to accommodate extensions to the distributed network management. This characteristic is known as *scalability* in distributed computing. For extending network management to more man-

agement domains, replicas must be made of network management functions provided in one management domain.

- As agents acquire more functionality, it is easy to add new resources, which may mean making minor additions or modifications to the agents. In some cases, slight modifications to managers may also be needed.
- One major disadvantage of distributed network management is that of control. When managers get scattered all around in a large network, coordinating them becomes a major issue. Some of the network management actions need coordination.

19.2 Distributed Network Management

Distributed network management is required to cater to networks that are becoming decentralized and autonomous. There is a lot of interest in distributed network management in LAN-based environments. A model of this is provided in Figure 19.1. Some of the components of distributed network management are:

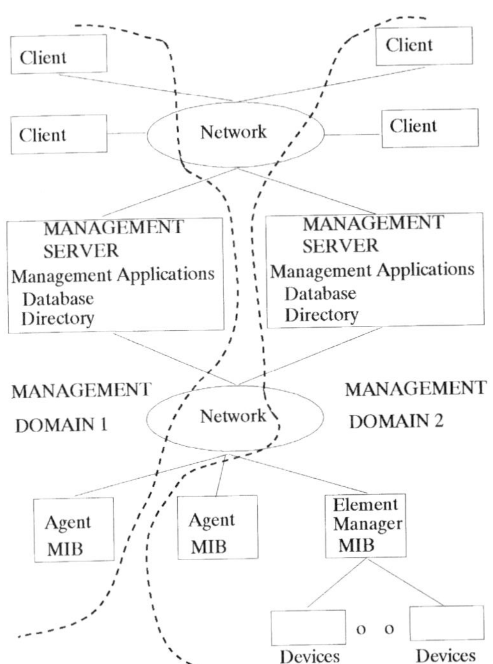

Figure 19.1 Distributed network management. (*Source: Modified from* Data Communications, *June 1992, copyright by McGraw-Hill, Inc., all rights reserved.*)

- *Management servers:* These need to include more functionality than just managers. They need to have directory services to locate where different databases are, where different managers and agents are, and, in some cases, even data on the locations of agents is required. Directory services is essential for distributed network management.
- *Agents and element managers:* These are required to manage the resources. Element managers manage vendor-specific resources. Agents and element managers interact with managers and databases on resources. These databases are usually MIBs and can be placed in managers if there are resource constraints in agents and element managers. But this involves unnecessary network traffic and it is better to make sure that only required data are stored in managers.
- *Management communication protocols:* These are essential for manager-to-agent and manager-to-manager communication. For communication between manager and agents, proprietary protocols, SNMPv2, or CMIP may be used. Also for manager-to-manager communication, we can use an RPC-like mechanism, proprietary protocols, SNMPv2, or CMIP.
- *Systems management functions:* These are the basic systems management functions such as configuration management, fault management, performance management, accounting management, and security management.
- *End-user interfaces:* These include graphical user interfaces and command-line interfaces.
- *Network management applications:* These add functionality and use systems management functions.

With so many variables, it is very difficult to provide a truly distributed network management. Herman (see Reference 19.1) discusses some of the distributed management products and strategies. Let us discuss some of the implementation issues in distributed network management. In large networks, the database required for configuration, fault, performance, accounting, and security management can become huge if it is centralized in one manager. This would require a lot of system resources and may affect the performance. In such cases, it may be better to distribute the database on the basis of the following:

Domains: Break up the whole network into domains, then the manager in each domain controls a particular section of the network. If these managers need to communicate with one another, there are two possible approaches: The managers can be purely peer-to-peer, or manager of managers (MOM) can be used to coordinate different managers. MOM is basically a centralized manager which is hierarchical in nature. MOM coordinates, controls, monitors, and manipulates the managers in each domain.

Subnetworks: It may be better to break up the large networks into subnetworks. As in the case of domains, each subnetwork can have a manager. The manager-to-manager communications can be done in a similar fashion to domains.

Segments: In the case of LANs, it is possible to break up the overall network on the basis of segments. The issues are the same as for domains and subnetworks.

The primary concern here is the distribution of workloads. Also, there are many issues such as the management protocol to be used between MOMs and the managers in respective domains or between peer managers. CMIP or SNMPv2 can be used for communication between MOM and managers. But there will again be a problem if some domains and their managers use CMIP and some other domains and managers use SNMPv2. This can be complicated further by adding the proprietary protocols to this mix. The proxy agent concept, where protocol conversions are done, can be a solution; however, this results in the loss of some functions. Another possibility is to use compensation methods, in which an extra set of functions is added to the functions provided by lower layers.

19.2.1 Some issues in distributed network management

It is quite complicated to provide truly distributed network management. *Location transparency* is one of the important characteristics of distributed systems, and it means that one user should be able to look at the entire network from wherever he or she chooses, regardless of whether it is at location A or location X.

However, the way network management functions are broken into manager and agents presents some problems. It is usually the agents which manage the managed objects; managers do not directly manipulate them. In addition, view management is provided in the workstation where the manager is located. So, without breaking some rules, it is difficult to provide true location transparency.

Besides, in network management, the availability of all the systems management functions may not be required in workstations where the manager software is located. For example, accounting information may not be required by all the users, being restricted to certain systems administrators. Also, there are issues such as processing power, memory, and storage capacity availability. So, in reality, location transparency need not be a rigid requirement.

The directory contains information on all the locations of different software and hardware such as manager and agents. Directories are used for name resolutions. For location transparency, the directories should be distributed, which adds its own set of problems, such as consistency. To provide for consistency of data, schemes such as two-phase commit can be used. In addition, concurrency control for sharing the directories is also required. All of these add complexity.

Copies of the directories in each of the managers can be maintained in different management domains. By carefully designing management domains and the agents that report to a manager, the size of these directories can be limited. Instead of having a directory and its replicas in different management domains, directories can be partitioned, as shown in Figure 19.2. If the details of another management domain are required, then the user can navigate to the manager which has the information and ask it for the details. CMIP or SNMPv2 can be used for manager-to-manager communication. Here, we are assuming that managers have sufficient security information and rights to access different managers.

Until now, we've discussed only the distribution of the directories. In addition to the directories, a database is required for storing information on topology and other systems management functions. This database is maintained in managers, just like the directories. The same strategy can be used for placing databases as was used for directories.

Maintaining multiple copies of the files, directories, or database is normally known as *replication* in distributed systems, and this is an

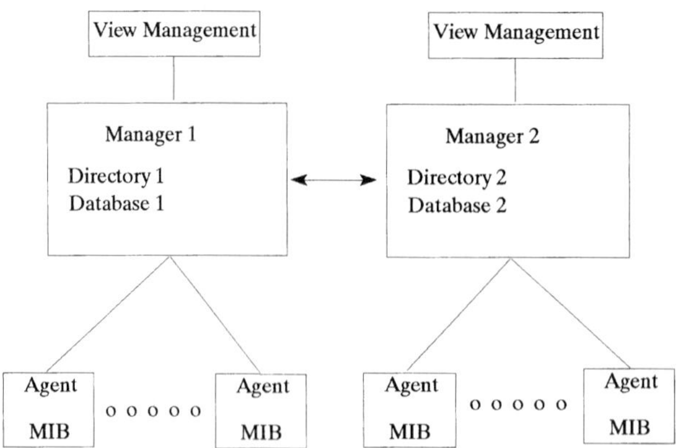

Figure 19.2 Strategies for distributed network management.

important characteristic. Replication of directories and databases improves reliability and performance, but there is a price to pay for this. Maintaining the consistency of the different copies of the database and directory can become a problem, especially if changes are frequent.

19.3 High-Availability Systems

It is possible that a manager will fail, and if so, none of the systems management functions will be available. To avoid this situation, there should be a backup manager which will take over when one system fails. In Figure 19.3, Manager B may be a backup for Manager A. Now, for managers A and B to know if the other one has failed, they will have to poll each other frequently or use an exchange of heartbeats. When the active manager fails, the backup takes over, but to take over, the backup manager must have access to all the data of the active manager, including the directory and databases of the active manager.

The designated backup manager can be a manager in another management domain. This backup manager will have roles similar to what we discussed earlier. But there is one disadvantage with this arrangement. The active manager of another domain, which acts as a backup manager, needs to have extra functionality. When a backup manager takes over the role of active manager in another domain in addition to its regular functions, it is possible that it will be overloaded, affecting its performance. The network traffic also will increase. But one advantage of this scheme is that it avoids redundancy. As we all know, reliability can be increased by providing redundancy, but redundancy can become an expensive proposition, too.

19.4 Some Ways to Reduce the Network Traffic for Systems Management

The basic philosophy when collecting data should be to collect only data that are needed. When a network is functioning normally, there is no need to collect unnecessary data. The data that is collected must

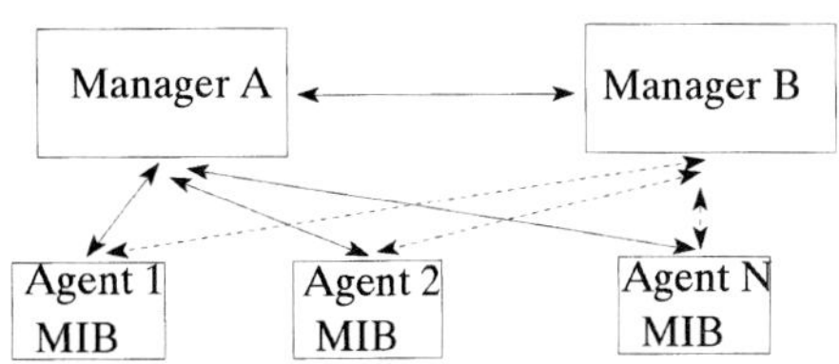

Figure 19.3 Backup manager.

be stored in agents. By *storing/collecting* data in agents instead of managers, unnecessary network traffic is avoided. When needed, managers normally have access to the data stored in agents.

One of the ways to reduce network traffic is to use filtering and scoping techniques when sending notifications to the managers from agents. Filtering is based on policies and rules. Policies are used to monitor a resource only if there are problems. Those notifications which are not functionally important and useful should be filtered. Another method is to reduce the frequency for sending notifications. When monitoring performance data, some of it may not be useful when the network is functioning normally. For example, consider the number of collisions in a CSMA/CD-based network. Only when they reach a critical stage such as crossing a threshold will a notification be useful. Under normal conditions, it may be better to filter out the data on the number of collisions. Also, sometimes when the network is functioning normally, changing the polling intervals saves a lot of resources.

Another method is to use exception reporting instead of polling, because polling requires a lot of network traffic and resources. To reduce this, one alternative is to send notifications to a manager when there are problems or impending problems. This can be monitored by watching whether or not critical threshold levels for a resource have been reached. Then the manager can use timeouts and polling to monitor the resource. This combination of polling and notifications is done in SNMPv2.

19.5 Object-Oriented Languages and Databases in Network Management

The concept of objects in object-oriented languages is slightly different from the concept of objects we have discussed in systems management. In object-oriented languages, an object consists of data and methods which surround the data (Figure 19.4). Methods are the operations that can be done on the data. This concept permits us to separate data from methods, unlike in traditional programming languages. This ability to hide data is known as *encapsulation.*

Many object-oriented languages such as Smalltalk have been in existence for a long time. But some of the problems have included the following:

- Performance was the main bottleneck. Till now in workstations and PCs, processing power, main memory, and hard disk capacities were not sufficient for object-oriented languages. These days, with powerful processors and memory having become cheaper, programming in object-oriented languages is becoming the trend.

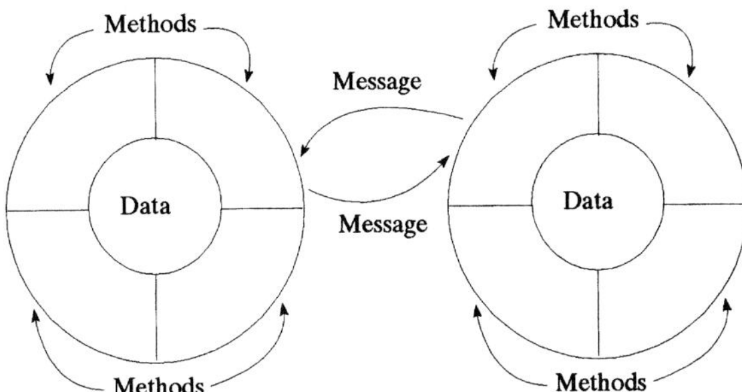

Figure 19.4 Concept of objects.

- It takes a lot of time in the design stages, and forming the object hierarchy requires thorough knowledge of the concepts of objects, hierarchy, and polymorphism. This is offset by the comparatively reduced time in the coding stage.
- Sometimes there were performance issues when user interfaces written in object-oriented languages had to interface to databases. Occasionally, this gave a negative impetus to the growth of practical implementations.
- There were not many case histories of successful large projects implemented with object-oriented design and languages.

A note of caution on the shift to an object-oriented programming environment may be in order. It is suggested that when changing from the traditional programming language environments such as C to an object-oriented programming environment, it is better to start with small projects so as to gain experience in the object-oriented concepts, design, and implementations. This will also provide an opportunity to overcome some of the paradigm shifts involved in changing from traditional programming languages to object-oriented design and programming. However, these comments are valid only if one is involved in programming in traditional programming languages. Those who are starting fresh may not notice some of the restrictions.

Object-oriented languages are particularly suited for user interfaces. They allow rapid prototyping and changes, and it is easy to add new features. With the stress on short product cycles, the transition to object-oriented programming, especially for desktop environments, can solve some of the problems. A major claim of object-oriented programming is the ability to reuse the existing code and extend the objects using the concepts of polymorphism and hierarchy.

For storing data, file systems were traditionally used. In file systems, the sharing of data between applications was difficult and required elaborate locking mechanisms. However, files provided *per-*

sistence, which means that data remained available for a long time on a reliable storage system—longer than the process that created the data. To provide persistence and data integrity even when there are failures, database systems such as hierarchical, network, and relational databases were developed. However, some of the drawbacks of these database systems are that they are primarily record-oriented and are good for record manipulations but have difficulty handling nonrecord format data, including three-dimensional graphics, voice, video, and images. Eliminating some of the shortcomings of the traditional database systems, object-oriented database systems are emerging and have the following advantages:

- It is easier to model the real world.
- They have better modularity and structuring because of characteristics such as inheritance.
- They have easier extensibility due to properties such as polymorphism, inheritance, and multiple inheritance. Note that Smalltalk does not have the provision of multiple inheritance, and if it is needed, it must be provided by other means.
- They have the ability to share objects, which makes groupware (team working) easier.
- They can have better integration with object-oriented programming languages, because they are designed on similar principles.
- They can handle and manage complex data such as images, video, voice, and three-dimensional graphics, which is especially important in multimedia systems.

In network management, we need to manipulate objects and store data about them. Storing the data about objects must be done on databases, which, in the future, will be object-oriented databases, though for some time in the real world, traditional databases will continue to exist. But the new implementations will increasingly tend to be object-oriented databases. To improve the performance, caching and combining of the objects into groups (clustering) can be done.

Object class libraries are commercially available, and they also provide a user application programming interface (API). These class libraries will need to have CMIP or SNMP function capabilities, including notifications, which can be provided by platforms on top of the object class libraries. These management functionalities that are provided on top of object class libraries, can be grouped under the *object-oriented management framework* (Figure 19.5). This object-oriented management framework must have the APIs "enabled" to write management applications.

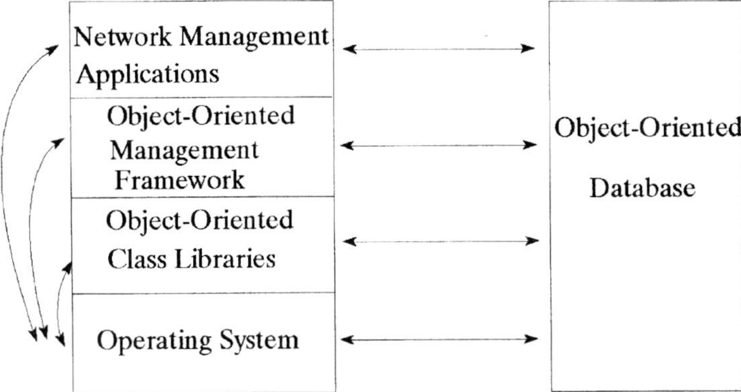

Figure 19.5 Object-oriented management framework.

19.6 Unresolved Issues in Network Management

SNMP is quite popular and is gaining ground in many nations. At the same time, there are many proprietary network management protocols such as IBM's SNA, DEC's DECnet, HP's Open Vision, and others, which have a wide user base. In addition to this, the OSI standards are bound to slowly gain acceptance in many nations. Given these circumstances, we must live with a multiprotocol situation for network management systems.

There is wide speculation regarding which approach will win out. This will not be decided for some time. In the long run, systems based on widely accepted and implemented standards are going to take over and the proprietary systems will adapt their protocols and products to the standard ones, providing the means to coexist with the standard protocols.

In addition, the coexistence of Internet network management protocols and products based on OSI will be a major issue. An important concern is whether SNMP will take a divergent path from OSI or provide for migration to OSI. The major strength and disadvantage of SNMP is that it is limited primarily to the United States and some European nations. There are also some far-reaching political and security issues. Because of these, Internet may not find favor all over the world. However, easy implementation and availability and access to implementations are strong points of SNMP. When the standards are released, the SNMP implementations are right there!

Object-oriented concepts and languages will also have their impact on implementations. Databases will slowly move toward an object-oriented approach. Also, in the client-server environment, some of the popular protocols, such as IPX/SPX of NetWare, are proprietary. There are not many standards in the network management area that are specific to the client-server environment. In this environment, there will be a need for network management standards.

19.6.1 Common protocol stacks below management protocols

The convergence of two protocols such as OSI and Internet can itself be a problem. As an example, to run the OSI applications on top of TCP/IP protocols, RFC 1006 takes an elaborate approach. RFC 1085 takes a different approach, proposing a skinnier stack and assuming that the mechanism provided in RFC 1006 is not required.

Similarly, there are different profiles to provide the presentation, session, and transport layers below the network management protocols in OSI and SNMP. Different RFCs provide different mechanisms such as IPX, NetBIOS, or Appletalk over TCP/IP. The approach taken is to provide different stacks with conversion mechanisms for a specific application. This may be suitable when there are two protocols.

However, there are cases where we may have more than two protocols below the application layer. For example, the systems management functions may have a mixture of TCP/IP, IPX, and OSI as underlying protocols. In such cases, some common conversion interfaces may be required. These common conversion interfaces may take the form of protocol conversion and protocol compensation methods (Figure 19.6).

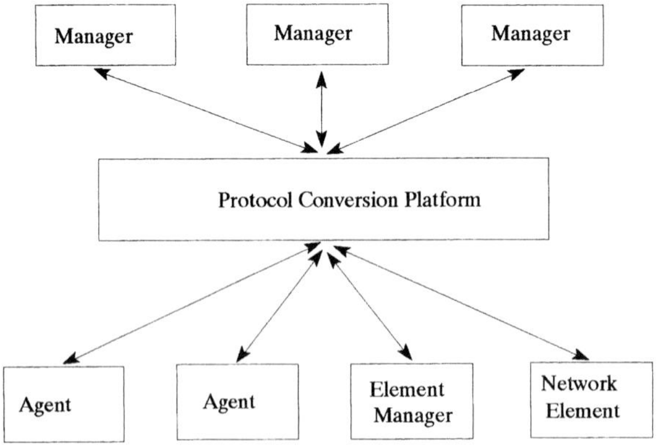

Figure 19.6 Protocol conversion platform.

To complicate the matter further, there are many forums such as OSI-NM, OSF, Object Management Group (OMG), Unix International, and X/Open trying to standardize the systems management functions and protocols. In addition, there are many applications using proprietary protocols, which are also popular in the user community. In light of this, the convergence to common systems management functions and protocols remains a question mark.

19.6.2 Common application programming interfaces

In network management, many management protocols are being used. Some of the popular protocols are CMIP, SNMP, SNA-MS, and others. To develop tools using these protocols involves major effort. Many applications use the protocols which are tightly coupled with the layers, such as transport, beneath them. Even the data representations are different in many cases.

To provide uniform systems management functions and APIs which can be used to build tools and applications on top of these protocols will require concerted effort. In addition, protocol conversions and data format conversions may sometimes be required, consuming a lot of resources. With networks spanning the globe, time synchronization, security aspects, the regulatory environments of different nations, and different languages and cultures all add their own problems.

19.6.3 Definition of managed objects

Resources are defined differently in the OSI MIB than in the Internet MIB. The OSI managed objects make extensive use of inheritance and polymorphism, unlike Internet objects. Also, the objects of the Internet MIB are like variables which can take different values. The definition of the Internet MIB is more amenable to tabular manipulations.

In addition, to meet the specific needs of applications, most of the forums are defining their own sets of managed object classes and MIB structures. There are some differences in semantics and syntax in the way managed object classes are defined. For example, an adapter of an Ethernet card may be defined in different manners in different cases. These managed object classes are sometimes defined with awareness of the individual applications. Because of these variations, there will be problems if they must be integrated in different protocols. Also, these differences in the definitions of managed object classes add their own problems if we are to have a common interface and a standardized way of handling the objects.

19.6.4 Network management function applications

Network management is a developing area. It has yet to mature fully. As new needs are felt, standardization efforts start, although the process takes much time. Meanwhile, there are cases where applications cannot wait for appropriate standards to come out.

LANs are popular, and as they deepen and grow into new areas, new requirements arise. Thus, many functions of systems management are yet to be very clearly defined. In addition, the area of distributed network management is still evolving and has not yet received full attention. Also, the issue of security, especially as it applies to important accounting data, needs to be fully explored.

When implementing some of the standards, the heterogeneous environments of computing can cause performance problems, so the implementors must encounter their own sets of limitations on performance, storage capacities, and processing powers. Added to that, changes in the hardware are occurring at a rapid rate, bringing different resources into the fold of network management, which also need to be accommodated.

Though automation will help reduce manual intervention in fault management, much more needs to be done. This is dependent on the ability of the hardware and software to provide redundancy and fault isolation mechanisms, which are areas that have not yet matured. In addition, there is a cost involved in providing these mechanisms. Such tradeoffs must be carefully considered.

Standardization covers a broad area, allowing implementors some flexibility. Though this usually helps, it can sometimes become problematic. The implementations can take different directions, making later integration of them difficult. A well-known example is that of network management protocols in the Internet that were developed purely as an interim measure; it was planned that Internet network management protocols would converge with OSI as time passed or as the OSI standards matured. But some of the directions taken were very different and, as a result, the convergence or integration of OSI and Internet are becoming major problems.

There are various interpretations of standards, as well as differences among many standards bodies about what systems management functions must include. For example, OSI's systems management consists of accounting management, security management, configuration management, performance management, and fault management. Internet does not deal with this problem at all. However, IBM's SystemView assigns the same set of functions to business management, change management, configuration management, operations management, performance management, and problem management.

19.7 Future Trends

19.7.1 Multiprotocol existence

Because different protocols, ranging from standards to proprietary ones, will be in existence for some time, efforts will be directed to making these differences transparent to users. Users and management applications need not bother about the underlying protocols, including the transport protocols, so the thrust will be to make these differences less visible by using techniques such as providing proxies and compensation methods.

19.7.2 Automation

Though there is much talk about automation, significant progress has not been made in this area. There are parts of network management, such as fault tracking, that have been automated. Automation is one area that would give an edge to products. What is urgently needed is the total automation of fault management and change management. Future focus will be on these areas.

19.7.3 Language independence

Management applications must be written in particular programming languages. There will be a move toward language independence so that an application can be written in any programming language or object-oriented language.

19.7.4 Operating system independence

Operating system independence is another area where much progress will be made in the future. When writing network management applications, programmers do not want to be tied to specific operating systems. Rather, they want network management applications to work in all operating systems in the same fashion.

19.7.5 Object-oriented databases

A database is very important for holding objects in storage, especially data on configuration, fault management, performance management, etc. Databases need good performance and large capacities. The direction for new data stores will be toward object-oriented databases, and performance will be an important issue. Though processors will be faster, the data storage and processing requirements will be growing equally fast. So performance will continue to be a critical issue in object-oriented data stores. To overcome some of the performance limitations, data caches may be used.

19.7.6 Integration of computing, telecommunications, and television

In the past, voice transmission was primarily analog, whereas computing is concerned with digital transmission. These days, in many nations, voice transmission uses digital signals. Computers have more demands, including such functions as graphics, images, voice, and data, and the integration of these. At the same time, the computing paradigm is slowly shifting from mainframe-based or hostcentric to client-server computing. This LAN-based client-server computing has also opened the transmission of data, voice, graphics, and images to the telecommunication industry. As a result of this development, the data communication and telecommunication areas are functionally converging, which will result in the integrated systems management of computing and telecommunication equipment.

In addition to this integration, there is an effort to integrate the cable industry into the mainstream of the computing and telecommunication industry. This overall integration with the cable industry will also have its impact on network management. The ideal is to integrate the network management and have an overall system instead of having network management in parts as it is today. This development will take time; however, the information superhighway concept may speed up the process, at least in the United States. A global information superhighway will require large investments, and some nations, because of financial and technological constraints, may need time to take their places along the integrated global information superhighway.

19.7.7 Security

Security will be a key factor when the networks are opened to the world, as it is in client-server computing. Even as new methods are devised to protect important data, further innovative ways to get into the networks, sometimes with mala fide intentions, will also be found. In addition, there is the issue of the security of sensitive data such as accounting records. So providing for the security of the network and the data in network management will be an ongoing struggle.

19.8 Summary

In this chapter, we examined distributed network management and the issues involved with it. Because object-oriented concepts will have a major impact on network management, we also discussed the issues involved in object-oriented languages and databases. We highlighted some of the problems presently encountered in network management, and, finally we examined future trends in network management.

19.9 Reference

19.1 Herman, J. June, "Distributed Network Management," *Data Communications,* 1992. Also reprinted in W. Stallings (ed.), *Network Management,* Los Alamitos, Calif.: IEEE Computer Society Press: 1993, pp. 64–71.

19.10 Further Reading

Alexander, Jim, *OS/2 Distributed Systems Management,* IBM Personal Systems, G325-5020-00, 1993, pp. 34–41.

Atwood, Tom, Joshua Duhl, Guy Ferran, Mary Loomis, and Drew Wade, *The Object Database Standard: ODMG—93,* R. G. G. Cattell (ed.), San Francisco: Morgan Kaufmann Publishers, 1994.

Booch, Grady, *Object-Oriented Analysis and Design with Applications,* 2d ed., Redwood City, Calif.: Benjamin/Cummings, 1994.

Brazier, F. M. T, and D. Johansen (eds.), *Distributed Open Systems,* Los Alamitos, Calif.: IEEE Computer Society Press, 1994.

Dean, G., T. Rodden, I. Sommerville, and D. Hutchison, "Distributed Systems Management as a Group Activity," *Proceedings of the IEEE First International Workshop on Systems Management,* April 14–16, 1993, Los Alamitos, Calif.: IEEE Computer Society Press, 1994, pp. 36–44.

Goldszmidt, G., "Distributed System Management via Elastic Servers," *Proceedings of the IEEE First International Workshop on Systems Management,* April 14–16, 1993. Los Alamitos, Calif.: IEEE Computer Society Press, 1994, pp. 31–35.

LaLonde, W., *Discovering Smalltalk,* Redwood City, Calif.: Benjamin/Cummings, 1994.

Nahouraii, Ez, and Frederick E. Petry (eds.), *Object-Oriented Databases,* Los Alamitos, Calif.: IEEE Computer Society Press, 1991.

Ozsu, Tamer M., Umeshwar Dayal, and Patrick Valduriez (eds.) *Distributed Object Management,* San Francisco: Morgan Kaufmann Publishers, 1994.

Appendix

ISO, ITU, and ISO Standardization Process

A.1 ISO

The United Nations comprises independent nations. The ISO is an agency of the UN, consisting of national bodies, and it is a voluntary organization. Under the ISO, there are many Technical Committees (TC), Sub-Committees (SC), and Working Groups (WG). TC97 was primarily responsible for the Information Processing Systems.

The International Electrotechnical Commission (IEC) is another voluntary international standards development organization. In the IEC, TC83 facilitated the standardization of Information Technology Equipment. In 1987, ISO TC97 and TC83 merged into the Joint Technical Committee known as JTC1 and comprising most of the original subcommittees of TC97. The relationship between these standards organizations is shown in Figure A.1. The subcommittees of interest to

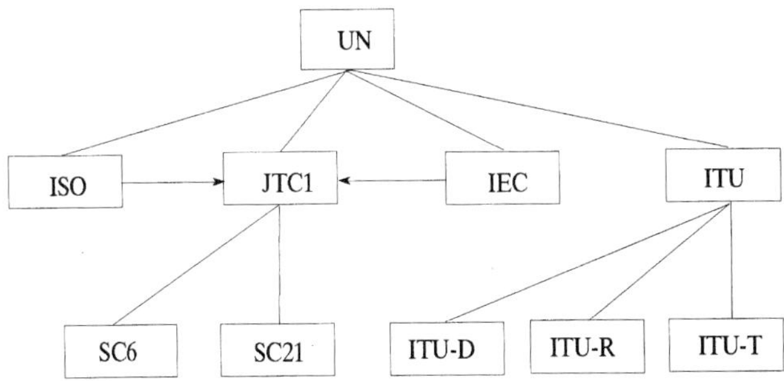

Figure A.1 Relationship of ISO with other international standards bodies.

us are SC6 and SC21. SC6 deals with telecommunications and information exchange between systems, and SC21 covers information retrieval, transfer, and management for OSI. The working of SC6 and the WGs related to it are shown in Figure A.2.

There are six Working Groups under SC21. Their activities are shown in Figure A.3. Though systems management involves standards of various WGs, the standards formed by WG4 are the most important and relevant to this book.

A.2 ITU

The ISO and IEC work in close association with other standards bodies such as the International Telecommunication Union (ITU). The ITU is a UN specialized agency and consists of post, telegraph, and telephone agencies of different nations. These agencies are usually government bodies. The ITU is organized into the following sectors:

- *ITU-T:* Concerned with telecommunication standardization. Until recently, the ITU-T was known as the Consultative Committee on International Telephone and Telegraph (CCITT). The ITU-T is also

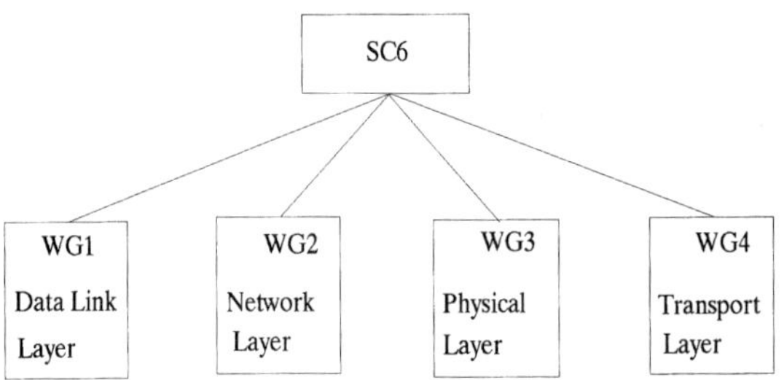

Figure A.2 Working Groups under SC6.

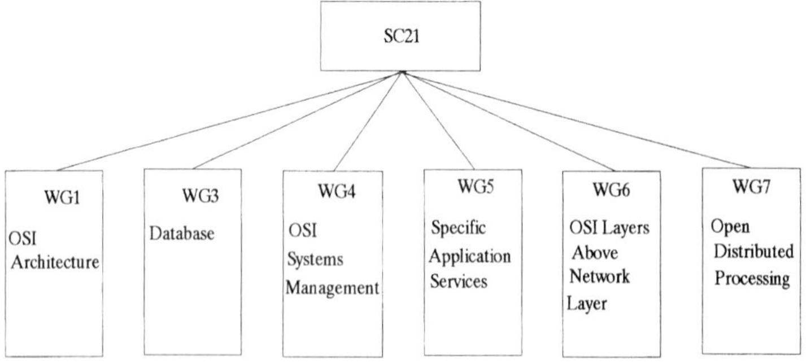

Figure A.3 Working Groups under SC21.

interested in data transmission aspects of telecommunication services. ITU-T standards are known as Recommendations. ITU-T encompasses the following areas:

Development of standards for architecture, planning, and operation of networks.

Development of standards for terminals, systems, and services. The ITU-T also develops guidelines regarding tariff and accounting rates.

- *ITU-R:* Primarily related to the standardization in the radiocommunication sector. The ITU-R deals with standardization and regulation on technical and operational issues in radiocommunication.
- *ITU-D:* Responsible for the telecommunication development sector.

The ITU-T has 15 Study Groups (SG) and a Tariff Group for Africa devoted to different specific areas. These SGs roll out recommendations. Each study group, in turn, is divided into Working Parties (WP) for focused responsibilities. Also, specific responsibilities or tasks are delegated to a Special Rapporteur. The WPs release draft documents.

The activities of the ITU-T start and end with Plenary Assemblies at four-year intervals, which are devoted to starting new working plans and approving the work completed. The ITU-T publishes the following series of Recommendations:

- *H Series:* Concerns digital sound and video encoding
- *I and Q Series:* Covers ISDN-related services
- *T Series:* Concerns text communication such as teletex, fax, and videotex
- *V Series:* Related to data transmission over telephone or telex networks, and mainly concerns the areas of analog data transmission
- *X Series:* Devoted to data transmission over public data networks, mainly in the realm of digital data transmission

Earlier, CCITT Recommendations came in the form of books with different colors coded to the year of publication—for example, 1988 documents were color-coded red. The ISO and CCITT worked in close cooperation. Many ISO standards were adapted by the CCITT, and these are known as paired standards. Also, some ISO standards were adopted by CCITT with minor modifications.

A.3 Cycle of ISO Standards

ISO standards are arrived at by consensus of the members. The requirements which are identified must be approved by JTC1 to be folded in as a *work item*. The working document has the title ISO/JTC1/SCsn/Nwnn. Here, "sn" stands for the Sub-Committee number, and "wnn" stands for the working document number. This work item is assigned an SC.

This Sub-Committee is responsible for arriving at a consensus on the work item, at which point it becomes a *Draft Proposal* (DP nnnn). Here, "nnnn" stands for a four-digit DP number. This is sent for ballot to ISO member bodies. If this is unresolved, it goes back to the development of a working draft. If a document is disapproved, it goes back one step for minor reworking.

If a DP is approved, it is registered as a *Draft International Standard* (DIS xxxx), where "xxxx" stands for a four-digits number. After a waiting period of six months, it is again sent for ballot. If it is approved, it becomes an *International Standard* (ISO/IS yyyy). "yyyy" represents a four-digit number. To become an IS, at least 75 percent of the voting members must approve it. Otherwise, depending on the level of disagreement, the DIS goes back through the standardization cycle. Once an IS is published, it can have revisions, which are brought out in the form of addenda.

A.4 Further Reading

ITU, *Document on Telecom Information Exchange Services (TIES)*, Public Services Guide, 1994.

Appendix

B

IAB and TCP/IP Standardization Process

B.1 Working of the Internet

The interests, activities, and development of standards for the Internet are controlled by the Internet Activities Board (IAB), which consists of a group of researchers and professionals with an interest in the Internet.

The structure of the IAB is shown in Figure B.1. It has two broad subgroups: the Internet Engineering Task Force (IETF) and the Internet Research Task Force (IRTF). Each group has its own steering groups. As shown in the figure, the steering group under IETF is known as the Internet Engineering Steering Group (IESG), and the steering group under IRTF is known as the Internet Research Steering Group (IRSG). Under these steering groups, there are many working groups entrusted

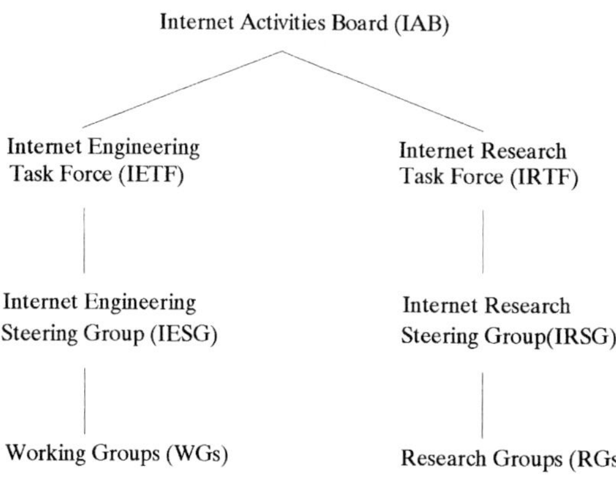

Figure B.1 Structure of the Internet Activities Board (IAB).

with solving specific issues. In addition to these, there is also an Internet Service Operators' forum known as the Internet Engineering and Planning Group (IEPG).

The IETF is involved in protocol development and standardization activities. The main objective of the IETF is to resolve any issues that may crop up and come up with solutions, standards, and architectures for short- and mid-term protocols. On the other hand, the main objective of the IRTF is to understand protocols, products, and the long-term issues of the Internet.

In the Internet community, topics of interest are written as *Requests for Comments* (RFCs), for which there are standardized formats. Internet standards are in the RFCs. Of course, not all RFCs are Internet standards; some RFCs are for informational purposes. There are two tracks for specifications: standard and nonstandard. These two tracks for specifications are shown in Figure B.2.

The IESG studies RFCs and recommends movements of standards to different maturity levels. These are examined and, on the basis of the recommendations of the IESG, an RFC may enter the *Proposed Standard* state. RFC 1602 defines a Proposed Standard (page 12) as follows: "A Proposed Standard specification is generally stable, has resolved known design choices, is believed to be well-understood, has received significant community review, and appears to enjoy enough community interest to be considered valuable." After reviews and a certain time limit, the Proposed Standard may enter the *Draft Standard* stage. Before reaching this stage, it must have at least two independent and interoperable implementations. Specification at a Draft Standard level is expected to be stable. In Draft Standards, changes are made only to resolve specific problems. A Draft Standard which has become

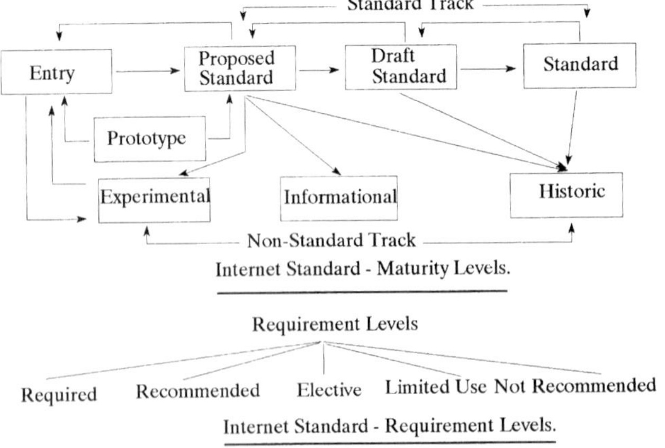

Figure B.2 Internet standardization process.

mature and stable with significant implementations and operational experience is moved to the next stage as an *Internet Standard.*

The specifications in the nonstandard track have levels of *Prototype, Experimental, Informational,* and *Historic.* When a specification is developed with the intent of moving it in the standard track, then it can be termed Prototype. Some RFCs in the first stage may be sent to the Experimental level. Experimental RFCs relate to research or developmental work. Informational RFCs cover topics of interest and provide general information. The specifications which become obsolete are relegated to the Historic level. Also, RFCs, while in standard track, can become obsolete. Under these circumstances, too, RFCs are assigned to the Historic level.

In addition to the maturity levels, there are requirement levels (status) of RFCs. The different requirement levels are shown in Figure B.2. *Required* is mandatory for any implementation for minimal conformance. *Recommended* states that a specification needs to be implemented unless there are enough justifications to exclude it. *Elective* protocols are for specific purposes such as routing protocols. *Limited Use* protocols are for special cases such as TCP/IP over IPX. In addition, there are certain protocols which are *Not Recommended* for use because they become outdated. One example of this is the Simple Gateway Monitoring Protocol (SGMP).

B.2 Philosophy Behind RFCs

New RFCs are brought out quite frequently. Some of them are taken out to reflect changes in the technology or to bring new technologies into the Internet fold. Sometimes new RFCs define new areas, such as defining new managed devices. Other RFCs correct errors, include new protocols, or provide for compatibility with other standards. Due to rapidly changing technologies, some RFCs become obsolete with time. However, care is taken to maintain compatibility with existing applications. Before any RFC becomes standard, there should be implementations related to the subject of the RFC. One good point about the Internet is that implementations are freely available. This is also one of the strong points responsible for the popularity and tremendous growth of TCP/IP. As mentioned in Section 10.15, start with RFCINDEX, which is a comprehensive list of all the RFCs and provides an indicator to the latest RFCs. The next important document before any implementation is to review the latest IAB Official Protocol Standards.

B.3 Further Reading

Cerf, V., The Internet Activities Board, RFC 1160, 1990.

Huitema, C., Charter of Internet Architecture Board (IAB), RFC 1601, 1994.

Huizer, E., and D. Crocker, IETF Working Group Guidelines and Procedures, RFC 1603, 1994.

Huston, G., Introducing the Internet Engineering and Planning Group (IEPG), RFC 1690, 1994.

Internet Architecture Board, Internet Engineering Steering Group, Internet Standards Process—Revision 2, RFC 1602, 1994.

Appendix

How to Procure Standards Publications

Standards publications can be acquired from the following sources. These addresses were furnished at the time of writing this book. It is possible that some of them have changed since then.

OSI

The OSI may be contacted through the following addresses:

OMNICOMPPI
1201 Seven Locks Road
Suite 300
Potomac, Maryland 20854
Telephone: 1-800-666-4266
Fax: 1-301-309-3847

Global Engineering Documents
2805 McGaw Avenue
Irvine, CA 92714
Telephone: 1-800-854-7179

ITU

For ITU documents, first contact Telecom Information Exchange Services (TIES). The e-mail address is as follows:

To: itudoc@itu.ch
From: (*Name*)
Subject: Ignored
START
GET ITU-2659
END

TIES explains how to procure ITU documents. ITU-1100, known as the *Road Map and Index for ITU Telecommunication Standardization Sector Group,* is a useful index of the various documents. Note that the documents may use ASCII, Microsoft RTF, Word for Windows, or Postscript.

RFCs

For RFC documents distribution, contact the following addresses:

DDN Network Information Center
SRI International
Room EJ291
333 Ravenswood Avenue
Menlo Park, CA 94025
Telephone:
1-800-235-3155
1-415-859-3695
Fax: 415-859-6028
e-mail: nisc@nisc.sri.com

DDN Network Information Center
14200 Park Meadow Drive
Suite 200
Chantilly, VA 22021
Telephone:
1-800-365-3642
1-703-802-4535
Fax: 1-703-802-8376

The Network Information Center provides many information services for the Internet community. RFCs can also be obtained electronically from this source. For details on this, please contact the above address or consult the IAB Official Protocol Standards.

IEEE

IEEE documents are published by the IEEE Computer Society Press, at the following address:

IEEE Computer Society Press
Customer Service Center
10662 Los Vaqueros Circle
P.O. Box 3014
Los Almitos, CA 90720-1264
Telephone: 1-800-CS-BOOKS
Fax: 1-714-821-4010

IEEE Draft Standards are available from Alpha Graphics (Phoenix, Ariz.) at 1-602-863-0999.

ANSI/ISO

ANSI and ISO standards documents can be ordered from the following address:

American National Standards Institute
11 West 42d Street
New York, NY 10036
Telephone:
1-212-642-4932
1-212-302-1286
Fax:1-212-398-0023

ANSI documents can also be procured from:

X3 Secretariat, CBEMA
1250 I Street NW, Suite 200
Washington, DC 20005-3922

OSF

OSF documents can be ordered from the following address:

Open Software Foundation
11 Cambridge Center
Cambridge, MA 02142
Telephone: 1-617-621-8700
Fax: 1-617-225-2782

OSI/NM

OSI/NM Forum documents can be ordered from:

Network Management Forum
40 Morristown Road
Bernardsville, NJ 07924
Telephone:
US 1-908-766-1544
UK 44-473-288595
Fax: 1-908-766-5741

Though the emphasis of the NMF is on OSI, it is also interested in SNMP.

X/Open

X/Open documents can be obtained from the following address:

USA:

X/Open Company Ltd.
3141 Fairview Park Drive
Falls Church, VA 22042-4501
Telephone: 1-703-876-0044
Fax: 1-703-876-0050

Europe:

X/Open Company Ltd.
Apex Plaza, Forbury Road
Reading, Berkshire RG1 1AX
United Kingdom
Telephone: 44-734-508311
Fax: 44-734-500110

Appendix D

Suggested Exercises

Chapter 1

1.1 Explain the rationale for breaking up data communication functions into the OSI seven layers.

1.2 What are the differences among network management, systems management, and enterprise management?

1.3 What are the main functions of network management? Mention one scenario where network management may be useful.

1.4 Take a specific case where you would like to use network management. List the resources you would like to manage. Also, list the instrumentation required to manage these resources.

1.5 List some of the potential network management applications in the network management applications area.

1.6 Choose one of the applications in Exercise 1.5, and design the application. Clearly spell out the requirements you have used in the design.

1.7 What are the pros and cons of standardization?

1.8 List the ISO standards used in each of the OSI seven layers.

Chapter 2

2.1 Explain the concepts of SAP.

2.2 Explain the terms manager, agent, managing systems, managed systems, and managed objects.

2.3 Compare the systems management functions of OSI with SNMP.

2.4 What specific changes are required for systems management for distributed systems?

2.5 If a system needs a cache to store information on managed objects, what design considerations will have to be taken into account?

2.6 We have discussed different systems management functions. Delineate areas of common ground between them.

2.7 Design a system which uses the systems management functional areas. Do not put all the functions in the initial release. Scale the system you have designed into a full-blown system after a few releases.

Chapter 3

3.1 Compare polling and notification mechanisms to retrieve management information from objects. Also explain where each one may be needed.

3.2 Explain the rationale behind using three management information hierarchies.

3.3 Design a management domain schema to view topologies of a network spread across continents.

3.4 Provide a set of commands and responses for communication between management domains.

3.5 Design a scheme whereby the concept of management domains may be used for distributing management functions. Use the concept of administrative domain judiciously.

3.6 Create your own example of containment hierarchy.

3.7 In the example you created in Exercise 3.6, what modifications may you need for naming the managed object classes?

3.8 Why are scoping and filtering necessary? Examine the cases where they may be avoided.

3.9 What is the idea behind synchronization, and can we do without it?

3.10 Compare the concepts of polymorphism and allomorphism. Explain with examples.

3.11 We have examined different management states and attributes. Define your own managed object classes using management states and attributes.

3.12 Furnish definitions of managed objects, showing different types of relationships.

3.13 Furnish examples of different types of relationships which suit your implementation from Exercise 3.12.

Chapter 4

4.1 Explain how ACSE services can be used in a multithreaded environment. Make changes if required. Use presentation services for this.

4.2 Design ACSE services for your specific scenario. Carefully choose the functional units that may be required.

4.3 Design a manager and an agent using ROSE. Also use ACSE services to form associations.

4.4 List and explain each of the CMIS services.

4.5 Name the attribute-based and managed object class–based operations.

4.6 State the advantages and disadvantages of using CMIP.

4.7 Explain the reasons why CMIP implementations have been slow to be developed.

4.8 Explain where pass-through services are used.

Chapter 5

5.1 Select a token-ring segment and define the ASN.1 for it. Convert it to BER.

5.2 Design a generic encoder/decoder to encode and decode the ASN.1 syntax for use in SNMP.

5.3 Discuss areas where the use of ASN.1 and BER may not be required; discuss areas where they are absolutely required.

5.4 Determine the impact of ASN.1 and BER on performance in your own processing situation.

Chapter 6

6.1 What are the motivations for defining managed object classes? Use a managed object class definition template to define a managed object class.

6.2 What are the salient points to consider when defining a managed object class?

6.3 Where are attribute groups used?

6.4 Why should the name of a managed object be unique?

6.5 Choose your own managed object class needed for a specific implementation and define it using the explanations provided in this chapter.

6.6 Use the concept of inheritance to define the managed object class you have chosen in Exercise 6.5.

6.7 What are the similarities between definitions of managed object classes used in ISO documents and managed object classes defined in object-oriented languages? What are the differences?

Chapter 7

7.1 Explain the reasons why TCP/IP has become popular and widely used.

7.2 Use the options field in IP frames to do reassembly of fragments in routers. Spell out your assumptions.

7.3 State the technique used for flow control in TCP. What are the advantages and disadvantages of the flow control used in TCP?

7.4 For TCP, formulate an algorithm where the receiver acknowledges that the segments have been correctly received. Note that with this modification only segments which have not been received are retransmitted. Hint: May need use of reserved fields.

7.5 Incorporate the preceding algorithm into the existing acknowledgment and retransmission used in TCP to formulate the overall algorithm for acknowledgement and retransmission.

7.6 How do you determine maximum segment size in TCP for different types of networks. Start from a simple network to the most complicated configuration. Make your own assumptions.

7.7 Explain the differences between UDP and TCP. Under what circumstances would one choose UDP? TCP?

7.8 A timer is set by a sender in TCP based on round trip time (RTT). Explain different possible algorithms to compute RTT and choose the best one. State the advantages and disadvantages of each of the algorithms. Remember that this must also account for the dynamic nature of a network and variations due to time zones.

Chapter 8

8.1 State the important principles involved in the Internet Network Management.

8.2 Explain the rationale for using UDP for SNMPv1.

8.3 What is MIB-II? State the main object group classifications of MIB-II.

8.4 Break down different MIB-II objects into network management functional applications such as configuration management. State the assumptions you are making.

8.5 Describe the SNMPv1 protocol messages, including their shortcomings.

8.6 Compare SNMPs with the CMIP protocols. State the strengths and shortcomings of both the protocols.

8.7 Why is a proxy required? Design a proxy service which uses SNMP, from the managing station to the proxy, and between the proxy and managing devices using the proprietary protocol of your choice. For this design, choose your own set of devices.

8.8 Explain how network management functions are extended to include new resources. What changes to the network management framework standards for SNMPv1 will simplify this process? Compare this list with SNMPv2 and check whether they have been solved in SNMPv2.

Chapter 9

9.1 What are RMONs, and why are they required?

9.2 What are the common features between RFC 1757 and RFC 1513? What are the differences?

9.3 Define RMON objects for FDDI and ATM devices. Make your own assumptions. Use RFC 1757 and 1513 as the basis.

9.4 Break down the RMON objects into different systems management functional areas, such as configuration management. Use this breakdown to provide systems management functional areas in a heterogeneous internetworked network environment. (Refer to Chapter 2 for the explanation of different systems management functional areas.)

9.5 Identify some network management applications (Section 1.7) that can be used along with the systems management functional areas developed in Exercise 9.4.

Chapter 10

10.1 What are the differences between SNMPv1 and SNMPv2?

10.2 Describe SNMPv2 management protocol messages, and state the differences between SNMPv1 and SNMPv2 PDUs.

10.3 Describe the salient points of SNMPv2 security.

10.4 Explain why clock synchronization is necessary, and state how clock synchronization can be accomplished for SNMPv2.

10.5 Explain how a migration of applications based on SNMPv1 to SNMPv2 can be made. Using a specific example, explain how such a migration is done.

10.6 Design a fault management application function for SNMPv2. It should manage bridges, routers, and gateways. Use your own domain for management. Also, try to automate as much as possible the diagnostic functions provided.

10.7 Using SNMPv2 protocols, design distributed management applications for Internet. Extend this to multivendor environments. Clearly state the various design alternatives examined and explain the reasons for choosing your particular case.

10.8 Design one management application using SNMPv2, considering the factors that may be required to extend the management application to a distributed system management application.

10.9 Discuss the pros and cons of migrating SNMP protocols to OSI systems management.

Chapter 11

11.1 What are the major differences among CSMA, token ring, and token bus? What are the reasons for using each one of them?

11.2 Incorporate a priority scheme into CSMA/CD.

11.3 Explain the modifications that can be made to the frame to provide security functions at the MAC layer for CSMA, token ring, and token bus. Is this enough? Where may one need the security functions provided by IEEE standard 802.11?

11.4 Compare bridges, routers, and gateways, and state reasons for using each one of them.

11.5 There are different bridge products available on the market. Choose some of the important ones and compare the characteristics of these bridges. Add your own list of improvements that can be made to each of them.

11.6 Consider adapting different data compression schemes to remote bridges. Explain which one you would choose for your implementation and why.

11.7 Add a security scheme to the bridges. Discuss different possibilities, from the simplest to the most complicated.

11.8 Furnish a design for a gateway to connect two networks, using SNA peer protocols on one side and OSI protocols on the other side. State the assumptions you have made.

Chapter 12

12.1 Why is layer management required?

12.2 Explain layer management operations. In what way are they different from OSI CMIS operations?

12.3 Using the example of a resource attached to a LAN and a MAN, formulate the layer management that may be required.

12.4 What are the reasons for using IEEE 802.1B standards for LAN/MAN management instead of the OSI system management standards?

12.5 Design a network management application using both the IEEE 802.1B LMMP protocols and the CMIP protocols.

12.6 Furnish a scheme to extend the access class table for access control up to the attribute level.

12.7 List other security measures that may be provided in addition to access control and state the reasons for them.

12.8 What are the functions of a proxy? Design a proxy function for carrying CMIP as well CMOL.

12.9 Design a fault management application using the IEEE 802.1B standard. What are the recovery functions that can be incorporated into the fault management application? Assume that the fault management application is for networked LANs with bridges.

12.10 Design a performance management application using the IEEE 802.1B standard, including security functions for some of the performance attributes. Assume that the backbone network is a MAN with many bridged networks connected to it via routers.

12.11 Refer to model 1 and model 2 described in Section 12.13. Using a specific implementation, compare the performances for these models. Mention some possible alternate models.

Chapter 13

13.1 Explain what SNA is, including the different layers.

13.2 Explain the different layers of the Networking Blueprint. State the important departures from traditional SNA made in the Networking Blueprint.

13.3 Explain peer SNA and list its components.

13.4 What is APPN?

13.5 State the salient points of APPC.

13.6 Explain how APPC and APPN can be used in a client-server environment.

13.7 How can APPC and APPN be accommodated in a distributed environment?

13.8 What is CPI-C? Write your own application which uses CPI-C and state your assumptions clearly.

13.9 Explain what MQI is and why it is needed.

Chapter 14

14.1 Describe the salient points of SNA/MS and state the changes made to it to accommodate the peer-to-peer computing environment.

14.2 Explain the terms *focal point, entry point,* and *service point.* Why are they needed?

14.3 Explain the concepts of dimensions and levels in SystemView.

14.4 What are the main disciplines of SystemView? Explain each one.

14.5 Explain the SystemView data model. Using a specific implementation of the client-server environment, model each resource using the SystemView data model. State your assumptions.

14.6 Explain the rationale behind using modeling resources as objects in the SystemView object model. Using your own implementation, extend the object model such that it fits into the SystemView object model.

14.7 Compare the disciplines of SystemView with the systems management functional areas of OSI.

14.8 Compare the SystemView with the systems management architecture of OSI and network management of Internet, stating the strengths and weakness of each protocol.

Chapter 15

15.1 Explain the functions covered by configuration management.

15.2 Why do we need view management? Explain the salient features.

15.3 Examine the different end-user interface packages available. Design the view management using one of these packages, stating your assumptions clearly.

15.4 Why do we need planned configuration?

15.5 Explain how topology information can be dynamically updated.

15.6 Design an algorithm for the correlation of logical and physical resources.

15.7 Explain the discovery mechanisms used by different protocols.

15.8 Design a software distribution scheme for a client-server environment. Add a scheduling function to the software design.

15.9 Add license management to the design in Exercise 15.8.

15.10 Why do we need inventory management?

Chapter 16

16.1 Why do we need fault management?

16.2 State the requirements of a fault management function.

16.3 How do we combine alarm reporting, event report management, and log control into fault management?

16.4 Write a fault management algorithm to pinpoint a problem in a workstation. Extend this algorithm to cover other devices in a network such as bridges, routers, switches, and multiplexers.

16.5 Furnish a high-level design to automate fault management in a network. Make your own assumptions.

16.6 Design an algorithm using a cache for fault management data that are logged.

16.7 What is a trouble ticket? Design an application to link trouble ticket and automation in a client-server environment.

16.8 Design an algorithm to correlate alarms.

Chapter 17

17.1 What are the functions of performance management?

17.2 What are counters and gauges? Explain where each is used.

17.3 Explain the different workload monitoring managed object classes used in performance management.

17.4 Explain the different summarization managed object classes. Why do we need them?

17.5 How is performance management related to fault management?

17.6 Study the different performance management packages available and compare them. Come up with modifications and extra functions you would provide, if you were to redesign each of these packages.

Chapter 18

18.1 Develop an accounting management application, making your own assumptions.

18.2 Provide a security management function for the application in Exercise 18.1.

18.3 Why are conformance testing and ISPs needed?

18.4 Develop a profile for SNMP and CMIP to interoperate, and also develop the conformance testing that may be required to carry out the procedure.

18.5 Design a network management platform using different systems management functions. First, make a list of the requirements and then state the assumptions you are making.

18.6 Design your own network management application.

18.7 Implement the network management application of Exercise 18.6 using one of the object-oriented languages.

Chapter 19

19.1 Explain the differences between distributed and centralized network managements. Choose your own network and decide which management system you prefer and why.

19.2 What functions would you like to distribute between different managers? Present a model for manager-to-manager communication.

19.3 Design a security scheme for manager-to-manager communication.

19.4 What are the advantages of using object-oriented databases in network management instead of the traditional databases.

19.5 Compare different object-oriented database implementations that are available, and choose one for your network management purposes.

19.6 Choose an object-oriented system with its own set of class libraries and design the object-oriented management framework. Assume that the management framework will be for OSI systems management functions. State clearly any other assumptions you are making. Also, make a performance comparison with some of the existing object-oriented management frameworks.

19.7 Implement the object-oriented management framework of Exercise 19.6 using one of the object-oriented languages such as C++ or Smalltalk.

19.8 Work out a strategy for network management, assuming that you have a mix of TCP/IP and some other popular protocol of your own choice, and that you wish to migrate to OSI systems management when it becomes available. Take into consideration the transport protocol that may be used.

19.9 List some of the impacts of the entry of the cable industry on network management.

19.10 List some of the issues that must be considered in network management when integrating voice, video, and data in the impending global information superhighway. Assume that this information superhighway is an extension of the information superhighway that is being talked about in the United States.

Further Reading

The following sources are too generic to be classified under specific chapters. Included here are some references Telecommunications Network Management (TMN).

Aguilar, L., "Using RPC for Distributed Systems Management," *Proceedings, Second International Symposium on Integrated Network Management,* New York: North Holland, 1991.

Aidarous, Salah, and Thomas Plevyak (eds.), *Telecommunications Network Management into the 21st Century: Techniques, Standards, Technologies, and Applications,* Piscataway, N.J.: IEEE Press, The Institute of Electrical and Electronics Engineers, Inc., 1994.

Bapat, S., "OSI Management Information Base Implementation," *Proceedings, Second International Symposium on Integrated Network Management,* New York: North Holland, 1991.

CCITT Recommendation E.410, International Network Management, General Information, 1992.

CCITT Recommendation E.411, International Network Management, Operational Guidance, 1992.

CCITT Recommendation E.412, Network Management Controls, 1992.

CCITT Recommendation E.415, International Network Management Guidance for Common Channel Signalling No.7, 1992.

CCITT Recommendation M.3010, Principles for a Telecommunications Management Network, 1992.

CCITT Recommendation M.3020, TMN Interface Specification Methodology, 1992.

CCITT Recommendation M.3100, Generic Network Information Model, 1992.

CCITT Recommendation M.3200, TMN Management Services: Overview, 1992.

CCITT Recommendation M.3300, TMN Management Capabilities at the F Interface, 1992.

CCITT Recommendation M.3400, TMN Management Functions, 1992.

Dallas, I. N., E. B. Spratt, and J. P. Cabanel, *Issues in LAN Management II,* New York: North Holland, 1991.

Network Management Forum, *Discovering OMNIPoint,* Englewood Cliffs, N.J.: PTR Prentice Hall, 1993.

Terplan, K., *Communication Network Management,* 2d ed., Englewood Cliffs, N.J.: PTR Prentice Hall, 1992.

Stallings, W., *Computer Communications: Architectures, Protocols, and Standards,* 3d ed., Los Alamitos, Calif.: IEEE Computer Society Press, 1992.

Stallings, W., *Data and Computer Communications,* 3d ed., New York: Macmillan, 1991.

List of Acronyms

AA	Application Association
AARE	Application Association Response, ACSE PDU
AARQ	Application Association Request, ACSE PDU
ABRT	Abort, ACSE PDU
AC	Application Context
ACF	Access Control Function
ACI	Access Control Information
ACSE	Association Control Service Element
ACT	Access Control Table
ADDMD	Administration Directory Management Domain
ADF	Access Control Decision Function
AE	Application Entity
AEF	Access Control Enforcement Function
ANSI	American National Standards Institute
AP	Application Process
APDU	Application Protocol Data Unit
API	Application Programming Interface
APPC	Advanced Program-to-Program Communication
APPN	Advanced Peer-to-Peer Networking
ARP	Address Resolution Protocol
ASE	Application Service Element
ASN.1	Abstract Syntax Notation One
ATM	Asynchronous Transfer Mode
ATP	Application Transaction Program
BER	Basic Encoding Rules
BF	Boundary Function
BIU	Basic Information Unit
BISDN	B-Integrated Services Digital Networks

BIT	Basic Interconnection Test
BPDU	Bridge Protocol Data Unit
BTU	Basic Transmission Unit
CCITT	International Telegraph and Telephone Consultative Committee
CCR	Commitment, Concurrency, and Recovery
CD	Committee Draft
CF	Control Function
CIB	Control Information Base
CLTS	Connectionless-mode Transport Service
CMI	Common Management Interface
CMIP	Common Management Information Protocol
CMIPM	Common Management Information Protocol Machine
CMIS	Common Management Information Services
CMISE	Common Management Information Service Element
CMOL	CMIP over LLC
CNN	Composite Network Node
CNOS	Change Number of Sessions
CONS	Connection-mode network service
COS	Class of Service
CP	Control Point
CPDU	CMIP Protocol Data Units
CPE	Convergence Protocol Entity
CPI-C	Common Programming Interface-Communications
CPMS	Control Point Management Services
CRC	Cyclic Redundancy Check
CSMA/CD	Carrier Sense Multiple Access/Collision Detection
CTP	Control Operator Transaction Program
CTS	Common Transport Semantics
CUA	Common User Access Architecture
DAP	Directory Access Protocol
DCE	Data Communications Equipment; Distributed Computing Environment
DEFED	Discovery and Event Forwarding Enable/Disable
DER	Distinguished Encoding Rules
DES	Data Encryption Standard
DIB	Directory Information Base
DIS	Draft International Standard

DISP	Draft International Standardized Profile; Directory Information Shadowing Protocol
DIT	Directory Information Tree
DLC	Data Link Control
DMD	Directory Management Domain
DME	Distributed Management Environment
DMTF	Desktop Management Task Force
DN	Distinguished Name
DOD	Department of Defense
DOP	Directory Operational Binding Management Protocol
DQDB	Distributed Queue Dual Bus
DS	Directory Services
DSA	Directory System Agent
DSAP	Destination Service Access Point
DSISG	Distributed Support Information Standards Group
DSP	Directory System Protocol
DTE	Data Terminal Equipment
DTR	Delay Throughput Reliability
DUA	Directory User Agent
EFD	Event Forwarding Discriminator
EIB	Enterprise Information Base
EN	End Node
EP	EP Entry Point
EWMA	Exponentially Weighted Moving Average
FCS	Frame Check Sequence
FDDI	Fiber Distributed Data Interface
FDM	Frequency-Division Multiplexing
FSM	Finite State Machine
FTAM	File Transfer, Access, and Management
FTP	File Transfer Protocol
FU	Functional Units
GDMO	Guidelines for the Definition of Managed Objects
GDS	General Data Stream
GOSIP	Government Open System Interconnection Profile
GP	Granularity Period
GUI	Graphical User Interface
HDLC	High-Level Data Link Control

IAB	Internet Activities Board
ICMP	Internet Control Message Protocol
IEC	International Electrotechnical Commission
IEEE	Institute of Electrical and Electronics Engineers
IEPG	Internet Engineering and Planning Group
IESG	Internet Engineering Steering Group
IETF	Internet Engineering Task Force
ILC	Identifier, Length, and Contents
ILCE	Identifier, Length, Contents, and End-of-Contents
IP	Internet Protocol
IPC	Interprocess Communication
IPX	Internet Packet Exchange
IRSG	Internet Research Steering Group
IRTF	Internet Research Task Force
IS	International Standard
ISDN	Integrated Services Digital Network
ISN	Initial Sequence Number
ISPICS	ISP Implementation Conformance Statement
ISMA	Information Systems Management Architecture
ISO	International Organization for Standardization
ISP	International Standard Profile
ITU	International Telecommunication Union
IUT	Implementation Under Test
JTC	Joint Technical Committee
LAN	Local Area Network
LEN	Low Entry Networking
LLC	Logical Link Control
LME	Layer Management Entity
LMI	Layer Management Interface
LMMP	LAN/MAN Management Protocol
LMMPE	LAN/MAN Management Protocol Entity
LMMS	LAN/MAN Management Service
LMMU	LAN/MAN Management User
LMS	Local Management Services
LU	Logical Unit
MAC	Medium Access Control
MAN	Metropolitan Area Network
MAP	Manufacturing Automation Protocol

MAPDU	Management Application Protocol Data Unit
MCS	Management Conformance Summary
MDS	Multiple Domain Support
MHS	Message Handling Systems
MIB	Management Information Base
MIDS	Management Information Definition Statement
MIM	Management Information Model
MOCS	Management Object Conformance Statement
MOM	Manager of Managers
MQI	Message Queuing Interface
MRCS	Managed Relationship Conformance Statement
MS	Management Services
MSS	Maximum Segment Size
MSU	Management Service Unit
NAU	Network Addressable Unit
NAUN	Nearest Active Upstream Neighbor
NE	Network Element
NetBIOS	Network Basic Input/Output System
NETID	Network Identification
NI	Network Interface
NIC	Network Information Center
NIST	National Institute of Standards and Technology
NMDSI	Network Management Data Service Interface
NMF	Network Management Forum
NMP	Network Management Process
NMPE	Network Management Protocol Entity
NMS	Network Management Station
NMVT	Network Management Vector Transport
NN	Network Node
NOC	Network Operations Center
NOF	Network Operator Facility
NSF	National Science Foundation
OMG	Object Management Group
OOB	Out of Band
OSF	Open Software Foundation
OSI	Open Systems Interconnection
PC	Path Control (in SNA); Personal Computer
PCI	Presentation Context Identifier

PCTR	Protocol Conformance Test Report
PDU	Protocol Data Unit
PE	Protocol Entity
PER	Packed Encoding Rules
PICS	Protocol Implementation Conformance Statement
PING	Packet InterNet Groper
PIXIT	Protocol Implementation Extra Information for Testing
PKCS	Public Key Cryptographic System
PLU	Primary Logical Unit
PPDU	Presentation Protocol Data Unit
PRDMD	Private Directory Management Domain
PRID	Procedure-Related Identifier
PSAP	Presentation Service Access Point
PU	Physical Unit
PUMS	Physical Unit Management Services
QOS	Quality of Service
RARP	Reverse Address Resolution Protocol
RDN	Relative Distinguished Name
RFC	Request For Comments
RLRE	Release Response, ACSE PDU
RLRQ	Release Request, ACSE PDU
RM	Resource Manager
RMON	Remote Network Monitoring
RODM	Resource Object Data Manager
ROER	Remote Operation Error, ROSE APDU
ROIV	Remote Operation Invoke, ROSE APDU
RORJ	Remote Operation Reject, ROSE APDU
RORS	Remote Operation Result, ROSE APDU
ROS	Remote Operations
ROSE	Remote Operation Service Element
RP	Reporting Period
RPC	Remote Procedure Call
RTSE	Reliable Transfer Service Element
RTT	Round Trip Time
RU	Request Unit
SAA	Systems Application Architecture
SAP	Service Access Point
SCTR	System Conformance Test Report

SDLC	Synchronous Data Link Control
SFD	Start Frame Delimiter
SG	Study Group
SGMP	Simple Gateway Monitoring Protocol
SILS	Interoperable LAN/MAN Security
SLU	Secondary Logical Unit
SM	Session Manager
SMAE	Systems Management Application Entity
SMASE	Systems Management Application Service Element
SMDS	Switched Multi-megabit Data Service
SMFA	Systems Management Functional Area
SMI	Structure of Management Information
SMTP	Simple Mail Transfer Protocol
SNA	System Network Architecture
SNA/MS	System Network Architecture/Management Services
SNMP	Simple Network Management Protocol
SNMPv1	Simple Network Management Protocol Version 1
SNMPv2	Simple Network Management Protocol Version 2
SONET	Synchronous Optical Network
SPDU	Session Protocol Data Unit
SPX	Sequenced Packet Exchange
SQL	Standard Query Language
SSAP	Source Service Access Point
SSCP	System Services Control Point
STP	Service Transaction Program
TCP	Transmission Control Protocol
TDM	Time-Division Multiplexing
TFTP	Trivial File Transfer Protocol
TG	Transmission Group
TMN	Telecommunications Management Network
TOS	Type of Service
TP	Transaction Processing; Transaction Program (in SNA)
TPDU	Transport Protocol Data Unit
TR	Technical Report
TRS	Topology and Routing Services
TTCN	Tree and Tabular Combined Notation
TTL	Time to Live
UDP	User Datagram Protocol

UN	United Nations
UTC	Coordinated Universal Time
UWMA	Uniformly Weighted Moving Average
VRN	Virtual Routing Node
WAN	Wide Area Network
WG	Working Group
XNS	Xerox Network Systems

List of Trademarks

	Trademark or Registered Trademark of
APPC	International Business Machines Corp.
AppleTalk	Apple Computer, Inc.
APPN	International Business Machines Corp.
DECnet	Digital Equipment Corporation
Ethernet	Xerox Corporation
IBM	International Business Machines Corp.
IPX/SPX	Novell, Inc.
NetView	International Business Machines Corp.
Netware	Novell, Inc.
Open Vision	Hewlett-Packard Company
OS/2 Warp	International Business Machines Corp.
SNA	International Business Machines Corp.
SystemView	International Business Machines Corp.
Unix	UNIX System Laboratories, Inc.
Windows 95	Microsoft Corporation
Windows NT	Microsoft Corporation

Index

ABOUT THE AUTHOR

Divakara K. Udupa has been working with IBM for more than 11 years, the last 6 years in the network management area of IBM's Networking Software Division, Research Triangle Park, NC. He has a wide range of experience as a designer and developer with network management protocols and networking protocols related to TCP/IP, SDLC, X.21, X.25, and others. Mr. Udupa has an M.S. in computer science from Rensselaer Polytechnic Institute, an M.E. in mechanical engineering from Calcutta University, and a B.Sc. in mechanical engineering from Banaras Hindu University. He is a member of the Association for Computing Machinery (ACM) and a senior member of the American Institute of Industrial Engineers (AIIE).